MASS
COMMUNICATION

8e

To my father, Roger J. Hanson

Sara Miller McCune founded SAGE Publishing in 1965 to support the dissemination of usable knowledge and educate a global community. SAGE publishes more than 1000 journals and over 800 new books each year, spanning a wide range of subject areas. Our growing selection of library products includes archives, data, case studies and video. SAGE remains majority owned by our founder and after her lifetime will become owned by a charitable trust that secures the company's continued independence.

Los Angeles | London | New Delhi | Singapore | Washington DC | Melbourne

MASS COMMUNICATION

LIVING IN A MEDIA WORLD

8e

RALPH E. HANSON

UNIVERSITY OF NEBRASKA AT KEARNEY

$SAGE

Los Angeles | London | New Delhi
Singapore | Washington DC | Melbourne

FOR INFORMATION:

SAGE Publications, Inc.
2455 Teller Road
Thousand Oaks, California 91320
E-mail: order@sagepub.com

SAGE Publications Ltd.
1 Oliver's Yard
55 City Road
London EC1Y 1SP
United Kingdom

SAGE Publications India Pvt. Ltd.
B 1/I 1 Mohan Cooperative Industrial Area
Mathura Road, New Delhi 110 044
India

SAGE Publications Asia-Pacific Pte. Ltd.
18 Cross Street #10-10/11/12
China Square Central
Singapore 048423

Acquisitions Editor: Lily Norton
Editorial Assistant: Sarah Wilson
Content Development Editor: Jennifer Jovin-Bernstein
Production Editor: Andrew Olson
Copy Editor: Heather Kerrigan
Typesetter: C&M Digitals (P) Ltd.
Proofreader: Rae-Ann Goodwin
Indexer: Integra
Cover Designer: Janet Kiesel
Marketing Manager: Staci Wittek

Printed in Canada

ISBN 9781544382999 (paperback)
ISBN 9781544383033 (loose-leaf)

LCCN 2020915253

This book is printed on acid-free paper.

21 22 23 24 25 10 9 8 7 6 5 4 3 2

BRIEF CONTENTS

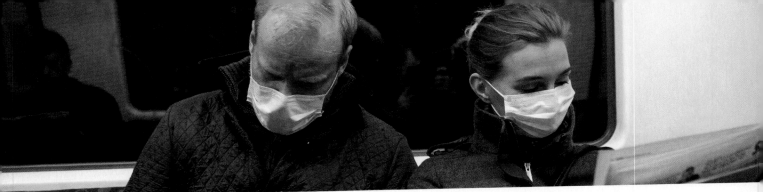

DETAILED CONTENTS

PART II. LEGACY MEDIA

WORLD THEATRE

THE WORLD IS TEMPORARILY CLOSED STAY SAFE KEARNEY!

Courtesy of Bryce Jensen

Matthew Hoist / Contributor / Getty Images

PART IV. STRATEGIC COMMUNICATION

Tide, "Gronk knows that Ride PODS® are for DOING LAUNDRY. Nothing else." January 12, 2018. Retrieved from YouTube at https://www.youtube.com/watch?v=-DrC_PF_3Lg.

PART V. REGULATION AND CONTROL OF THE MEDIA

Win McNamee/Getty Images News/Getty Images

PREFACE

Many of the defining moments of our lives come from our shared experiences with the media. It could be witnessing the Black Lives Matter protests across the country on both TV and through social media, following the scary news about the spread of the COVID-19 pandemic through the various news media, experiencing the thrill of the World Cup competition viewed streaming on the internet, going to the latest Marvel Cinematic Universe movie as the backdrop to a first date, or hearing "that" song from the summer you turned sixteen. For my generation, it was the moon walk. Parents across the United States let their nine-year-olds stay up way past their bedtimes to watch the biggest show of their lives on television—*Apollo 11* astronauts Neil Armstrong and Buzz Aldrin setting foot on the moon.

On September 11, 2001, my eldest son and his fellow fifth-grade classmates sat mesmerized by news coverage of the airplanes crashing into the World Trade Center Twin Towers, the Pentagon, and a field in southwestern Pennsylvania. Some parents questioned whether their children ought to have watched these events, but my son said, "We begged the teacher to keep the TV on. We had to know." As I write this, my former fifth-grader has his master's degree and has lived in Canada, Europe, and Asia with a global perspective brought in part by that fateful day in 2001. In the fall of 2021, I will have incoming freshman students for whom 9/11 is something that happened before they were born. It will simply be a thing that has always been. Now their top media memory might be watching the results come in as we elected our first black president, watching *Hannah Montana* (Miley Cyrus, was that really you?), Pixar's *WALL-E*, or listening and singing along to country music in their parents' cars.

Then there are the myriad trivial aspects of everyday life that come from our time with the media: finding the perfect little brunch café through restaurant review site Yelp, watching the band American Football play a music festival on the Minecraft game site during a COVID-19 online music festival, or arguing on social media as to who should be the top pick in your fantasy basketball league.

The media world we inhabit is constantly changing, as is our relationship with the media. In my first job as a college professor, I taught a course in media effects. On the first day of class, a student raised his hand and asked, "When do we get to the part where we talk about how television turns people into zombies?" His question has stayed with me through the years because it represents the view many people have about the media. The student's attitude had been fostered by media critics with an agenda—getting elected to office, getting a regulation approved, promoting a product, or even pushing a moral choice. I have long taken the view that the successful study of mass communication is also a journey of self-awareness. We are students of media and players in a media world.

Approach of the Book

Dr. James Potter, in his book *Media Literacy*, reports that people spend an average of twelve hours and one minute a day interacting with mass media of one form or another. Timewise, the biggest medium is television, but in terms of growth, it's online media—much of it mobile. Much of this time is also multitasking, interacting with your phone while watching TV, for example. That is how people squeeze in that much time with the media.

Mass Communication: Living in a Media World views the media in our world not as isolated institutions that somehow "do something" to us, but rather as forces that are central to how we live, work, and play. The media are not outside influences; they are part of who we are. From mobile media devices to streaming video, the pervasiveness of mass communication in our daily lives complicates our ability to understand the media's rich history of technical, cultural, sociological, political, economic, and artistic achievements. *Mass Communication* reveals the forces that drive the industry, while at the same time motivating readers to think critically about how they consume media. It uses compelling stories and examples drawn from everyday life. Readers are encouraged to consider the media industry from the inside out and, in so doing, to explore the many dimensions of mass communication that operate in our society.

My students over the years have told me that they remember information better if it is presented as a story, and so I strive to be a storyteller. Some of these stories are unpleasant and ugly. But that doesn't mean we don't need to tell them. The narrative style of this book will help motivate students to do the reading and facilitate their recall of the material. Many of the Test Your Media Literacy exercises are based on writing assignments I've used in classroom settings, as well as in more writing-intensive online sections. These exercises connect the material from the book to the media that students use every day, and students say that these assignments make them really think about how they experience the media.

Organization

Previous adopters will note that there have been substantial changes within the organization with this edition, including the retirement of the old magazine chapter and the addition of a stand-alone chapter on social media and video games. It was a difficult decision to remove the magazine chapter, but it is clear that much of the old magazine industry is dying. Former magazine giant Time Inc. has been sold by WarnerMedia, with some titles being eliminated and the flagship *Time* magazine sold off to an individual investor. It was becoming problematic trying to keep the chapter up-to-date with every month bringing news that another publication had gone digital-only or been discontinued completely. Much of the material about how magazines influence our culture has found its way into other chapters. This has made room for something users have been requesting for several years: a stand-alone chapter on video games and social media.

The book is organized into five parts, each examining critical dimensions that comprise the world of mass communication. *Part I: Introduction to the Media* presents the institutions, social effects, and business workings of the media in order to lay the foundation for understanding mass communication. *Part II: Legacy Media* explores the development of mass literacy and mass communication and what has traditionally been the paper-oriented print media, including newspapers and books, as well as legacy audiovisual media, such as audio, movies, and television. But these media are now increasingly delivered in digital form as well. *Part III: Digital and Global Media* covers the internet, social media, video games, and critiques of normative theories of the press in various countries; and it looks at how the media operate around the globe. *Part IV: Strategic Communication* delves into the advertising and public relations industries. *Part V: Regulation and Control of the Media* looks at the institutions, conventions, and rules that regulate and control the media in the United States and around the world.

Most of the chapters about the individual media (Parts II and III) are organized around the same basic structure. Following an opening vignette come four major sections:

1. How the medium developed along with major changes in society and culture. More than just a history of the medium, this section considers how societal, cultural, and technological elements came together to create the medium we have today.

2. How the medium operates within the business and social world. This section looks at why the medium behaves the way it does within our economy.

3. Current issues and controversies between the medium and society. These often include issues involving media effects, such as the concern about the importance of seeing people like yourself portrayed in the media.

4. The future of the medium, including the effects mobile technology and the long tail have had on it.

New to the Eighth Edition

The media world of 2021 is vastly different from that of 2015 or 2010, and it is unimaginably different from the year 2000 and the turn of the millennium. "Fake news" used to refer to late-night satirical comedy from *Saturday Night Live* or *The Daily Show*. Now that term is used as an attack on the news media or as a description of deceptive social media propaganda efforts. Powerful men showing up unexpectedly in the news used to mean they had completed some big business deal or died. Now, it often means they have been accused of sexual misconduct. Talk about hip-hop used to be talk about BET videos. Now it is a discussion of the Broadway hit show *Hamilton* or the Pulitzer Prize–winning album *DAMN.* from Kendrick Lamar.

In the seventh edition of *Mass Communication*, I focused on the importance of representation, inclusion, and diversity with an emphasis on whose voices get heard. Your author is a firm believer that everything can be explained by the hip-hop musical *Hamilton*. In this case, the line comes at the end from President George Washington, who asks the musical question, "Who lives, who dies, who tells your story?" In this eighth edition, we look at how media have covered the conflicts between police, journalists, and protesters marching for Black Lives Matter. It is almost exactly 216 years after the death of founding father and treasury secretary Alexander Hamilton as I write this preface. And the reason that no one questions why I would bring him up is that Ron Chernow wrote a brilliant biography of Hamilton that Lin-Manuel Miranda used as the basis for a musical. Hamilton, his nemesis Aaron Burr, his wife Eliza, and his sister-in-law Angelica live on for us because we tell their stories.

In 2020 we started hearing the story of the spread of a brutal emergent virus, COVID-19, that became a global pandemic, killing more than 200,000 Americans at the time of this writing. This virus forced many Americans out of their jobs with the more fortunate being able to work from home. College and university classes were almost universally moved online to slow the spread of the disease. The media industry also underwent massive effects, with virtually every movie theater in the United States closing for at least three months. Studios experimented with releasing first-run movies as premium video on demand, thus bypassing theaters entirely. Sports on all levels were cancelled, thus eliminating much of the most popular television programming. Local media lost devastating amounts of advertising leading to employee layoffs and furloughs, along with some having to just close their doors permanently.

We also continued to hear the stories of women who had suffered harassment and abuse by powerful men in Hollywood, politics, and business. The point here is that what we talk about in our media matters a lot. The stories we talk about are the stories that get told.

New Chapter-Opening Vignette. Seven of the chapters feature brand-new stories about key figures and issues in the media to provide a powerful narrative thread exemplifying the major themes of each chapter. These vignettes convey the excitement and relevance of media studies and critical inquiry by way of those whose lives have been profoundly affected by the media. New vignettes include how the story broke in early 2020 about the novel coronavirus as people slowly came to terms with a disease that would kill thousands of people and crash the American economy; how Amazon founder Jeff Bezos became the owner of the *Washington Post* and ended up transforming himself into a much more public figure; and how COVID-19 transformed the movie industry and forced televised sports to resort to covering reruns of old games, talking about sports returning, and broadcasting professional athletes playing video games of their sports.

Review Questions. The central concepts that were listed at the end of each chapter have been converted to review questions. These questions will encourage students to apply critical thinking skills to examples of mass communication from literature and popular culture.

Updated Chapters. Each chapter has been thoroughly updated to include new developments, new scholarship, and recent events in mass communication. Highlights of the revisions include the following:

- **Chapter 1**, *Living in a Media World*, starts the book with a look at how the news of the COVID-19 novel coronavirus spread and transformed the United States during the winter and spring of 2020. It would create new concepts of social distancing, create new norms about wearing masks in public, and lead to major changes in various media industries, along with killing more than 200,000 people in the United States as of this writing. There is also new material on how we develop our media literacy, drawing on the work of Dr. James Potter.

- **Chapter 2**, *Mass Communication Effects*, has been substantially reorganized, bringing in material on media effects that had previously been in other chapters. This includes critical theory examples on gender and race issues that had been previously covered in the magazine chapter. The materials on the Payne Fund Studies previously covered in the movie chapter have also been placed here. Finally, there is an expanded look at the history of the direct and indirect effects models.

- **Chapter 3**, *The Media Business*, has been updated to look at how Facebook handles the balance of targeting advertising and respecting user privacy. It looks at the big changes that have taken place at a number of media giants, including Disney acquiring much of Fox's properties, the launch of streaming service Disney+, the changes of what used to be Time Warner with its sale to AT&T to become WarnerMedia, the long anticipated re-merger of ViacomCBS, and investigations of both monopoly behavior and charges of bias at Google.

- **Chapter 4**, *Books*, continues its longstanding look at new words that have found their way into the dictionary. The chapter also looks at how independent booksellers are resurgent at a time when chain bookstores are having difficulties, the radical changes taking place in the textbook industry, and a look at how Japanese American actor George Takei has told his story of growing up in a World War II internment camp through a new graphic novel.

- **Chapter 5**, *The News Business*, looks at how buying the *Washington Post* was transformative for both the paper and its new owner, Amazon founder and world's richest man Jeff Bezos. There is a new section moved from elsewhere on the role magazines have played in the news industry. Finally, there is an in-depth look at the future of the local news industry.

- **Chapters 6 and** 7, *Audio* and *Movies*, both look at how the COVID-19 pandemic has transformed both the lives of musicians and the entire movie industry. With virtually every theater and concert venue in the country closed for months, both industries have been forced to reconsider how they reach their publics and make an income. The audio chapter also takes an updated look at the issue of smart speakers and privacy. The movie chapter has expanded its consideration of a wide range of diversity issues, including the role that black actor/director/producer Tyler Perry has had in making the state of Georgia a major location for movie production.

- **Chapter 8**, *Television and Video*, opens with a discussion of how live television, that depends on sports for viewers, has dealt with the complete shutdown of all sports globally during the spring of 2020 due to the COVID-19 pandemic. The chapter has also been updated with a continued look at how television has dealt with its lack of diversity, especially in terms of Asian characters, along with looking at the move of television from broadcasting to cable to streaming, and how streaming changes the economic model of television.

- **Chapters 9 and 10**, *Online and Mobile Media* and *Social Media and Video Games*, contain information that in previous editions was included in a single chapter on a range of interactive media. In this edition, online and mobile media continue to be in one chapter, while the more interactive social media and video games now have their own, expanded chapter. *Online and Mobile Media* looks at concerns about electronic tracking of individuals, both real and imagined, along with charges of bias in Google's search algorithms. *Social Media and Video Games* has a new opening vignette considering the costs of making unwise posts on social media and how these posts can change people's lives. The chapter continues with an examination of how conflict over recent political events have driven people on special interest and geographical community Facebook groups apart.

Finally, the new chapter includes a discussion of the controversy surrounding the Chinese video-sharing social media channel TikTok; an in-depth history of video games and how they have reshaped popular culture; an updated look at how the president has used social media to communicate directly with voters; and a consideration of how people have used online video game platforms for social interaction during times of social isolation.

- **Chapter 11**, *Global Media*, has been lightly restructured to match its movement from the end of the textbook to coming immediately following the individual media chapters, in part to highlight the importance of global media. There is an expanded analysis of press freedom around the world based on the World Press Freedom Index throughout the chapter, including an updated look at how press freedom has been rolled back in India, the world's largest democracy. Finally, material on international privacy laws has been moved from the law chapter to here and expanded to deal with recent changes in European Union privacy rules.

- **Chapter 12**, *Advertising*, opens with a new look at the role of YouTube influencers in the advertising market through the actions of kid-toy influencer Ryan Kaji and his parents. This is also an updated look at advertising to children. The chapter also has an expanded look at controversies companies can face for targeting ads at LGBTQ families and how they handle that criticism. The chapter closes with an expanded section on social marketing ranging from the role of online celebrities to the use of Twitter for marketing chicken sandwiches.

- **Chapter 13**, *Public Relations*, considers how aerospace giant Boeing mishandled its response to and communication surrounding its 737 MAX airplane safety crisis.

- **Chapter 14**, *Media Law*, has an updated look at media law, including a consideration of the writings of conservative United States Supreme Court Justice Clarence Thomas on *Times v. Sullivan*, along with a look at a high school student's libel suit against multiple national media.

- **Chapter 15**, *Media Ethics*, has an expanded section on how news outlets handle mistakes and misjudgments that includes how news media dealt with the rapidly breaking news of NBA star Kobe Bryant's death. Material on how the news media covered stories about the Flint, Michigan, water crisis was moved from the *News Business* chapter to here.

Returning Favorites

While some of the book's new features were described above, the eighth edition contains many returning features and coverage that have been updated to enhance and improve on the existing content.

In the sixth edition, it became clear that it was time to update the Seven Secrets to better match our changing media world. These updated secrets all deal with what the media are, who controls the media, how media content is selected, why the media behave the way they do, and how society and the media interact with each other. The Seven Secrets are as follows:

SECRET 1   The media are essential components of our lives.

SECRET 2   There are no mainstream media.

SECRET 3   Everything from the margin moves to the center.

SECRET 4   Nothing is new: Everything that happened in the past will happen again.

SECRET 5   All media are social.

SECRET 6   Online media are mobile media.

SECRET 7   There is no "they."

The secrets are presented in depth in the last section of Chapter 1, and they recur, when relevant, in the subsequent chapters to remind students of these concepts and also to serve as a springboard for discussions or writing assignments. These important principles of media literacy are highlighted to call attention to where the Seven Secrets appear throughout the chapters, reminding readers to be attentive and thoughtful.

Chapter Objectives. Learning objectives appear at the start of each chapter and call out key topics for close, focused reading. Students can refer to them for study guidance as well.

Test Your Media Literacy Boxes. There is no better way to cultivate critical media consumers than by modeling critical thinking. These boxes present students with current research, interviews, and issues relating to the practice of mass communication, and ask questions that challenge students to evaluate and analyze the story being told. The readings are engaging and fun, but more important, the questions get students to do more than summarize what they have read—they encourage them to think.

Test Your Visual Media Literacy Boxes. These boxes showcase images—sometimes controversial, sometimes disturbing—from various media to seek instinctive reactions from students before providing context and questions that encourage critical assessment of how we see and interpret images, and what more may be behind them. Both media literacy boxes are supplemented with up-to-the-minute additions and further related information through my blog at **https://www .ralphehanson.com/**.

Chapter Summary. Each chapter concludes with a brief recap of important points to assist students in reviewing key themes, events, and concepts.

Key Terms. A list of key terms—with page references—appears at the end of each chapter to make the terms easy to locate.

Living in a Media World's Social Media

Located at **https://www.ralphehanson.com/**, my blog *Living in a Media World* covers the entire mass media. One of the blog's biggest benefits to you is that it provides a single destination for up-to-date material on the topics covered in this book. It also occasionally features guest posts by national experts on a wide range of media issues. Think of it as a clearinghouse for current media news and features. You may find examples of new assignments or early versions of new book features, along with links associated with book material on the blog as well.

The *Living in a Media World* blog has been joined by several other social media feeds. You can follow me on Twitter **(https://twitter.com/ralphehanson)** for daily links to media news and whatever else I am reading. (Expect links to web comics, motorcycle news, and whatever I am reading to make an appearances as well.) I also have a Tumblr **(https://ralphehanson .tumblr.com)** that will feature a lot of great video clips that work well as a pre-class feature, along with photos and other images I have found online or created myself. Typical content includes music clips, viral videos, memes, and commentary on geek culture. The Tumblr tends to be a bit less focused than the blog and sometimes includes photos I have taken. Finally, this book has a Facebook page **(https://www.facebook.com/livinginamediaworld)** where you can share materials and find links to what I have been posting about on the blog and on Tumblr.

ACKNOWLEDGMENTS

As always, I want to thank my students at the University of Nebraska at Kearney for letting me test out materials from this book on them. I would also like to thank the many journalists, musicians, and media professionals who spoke with me about what they do, particularly Candice Roberts for her work on queer media; Doug and Telisha Williams, also known as the band Wild Ponies; Chip Stewart for his feedback on media law issues; Jeremy Littau for his work on local media economics; and Michael Socolow for his help with a whole range of journalistic issues. I would like to express a special thanks to the University of Nebraska at Kearney's Aaron Blackman for his research work on eSports and video game streams as well as sharing about his personal media use. I would also like to thank the many professors who use this book, have welcomed me into their classrooms electronically, and/or have provided me with invaluable feedback, particularly Chris Allen, Rosemarie Alexander-Isett, David Baird, Rick Bebout, Elaine Gale, Peter J. Gloviczki, Marty Sommerness, Jeff South, Brian Steffen, and Peggy Watt.

A panel of expert reviewers was instrumental in shaping the direction of this book, and I wish to thank them:

Glenda J. Alvarado, *University of South Carolina*

Herbert Amey, *Ohio University*

Tim J. Anderson, *Old Dominion University*

Karl Babij, *DeSales University*

Thomas Baggerman, *Point Park University*

Rick Bebout, *West Virginia University*

Frederick R. Blevens, *Florida International University*

Joan Blumberg, *Drexel University*

Mary A. Bock, *Kutztown University*

Jeff Boone, *Angelo State University*

Courtney C. Bosworth, *Radford University*

Michael Bowman, *Arkansas State University*

Scott Brown, *California State University–Northridge*

Larry L. Burriss, *Middle Tennessee State University*

Patricia Cambridge, *Ohio University*

Douglas J. Carr, *El Paso Community College*

Meta G. Carstarphen, *University of Oklahoma*

Aaron Chimbel, *Texas Christian University*

Tom Clanin, *California State University–Fullerton*

Lance Clark, *Huntington University*

Richard T. Craig, *George Mason University*

Barbara J. DeSanto, *Maryville University*

Roger Desmond, *University of Hartford*

Jules d'Hemecourt (late), *Louisiana State University*

Michael Eberts, *Glendale Community College*

Bobbie Eisenstock, *California State University–Northridge*

Anthony J. Ferri, *University of Nevada–Las Vegas*

Fred Fitch, *Eastern Kentucky University*

Jennifer Fleming, *California State University–Long Beach*

Dennis Owen Frohlich, *Bloomsburg University of Pennsylvania*

Donna Gough, *East Central University*

Kara Jolliff Gould, *University of Arkansas*

Christopher Gullen, *Westfield State University*

Meredith Guthrie, *University of Pittsburgh*

Louisa Ha, *Bowling Green State University*

Wendy J. Hajjar, *Tulane University*

Katharine J. Head, *University of Kentucky*

Aaron Heresco, *California Lutheran University*

Heloiza Herscovitz, *California State University–Long Beach*

Elizabeth Blanks Hindman, *Washington State University*

Sharon Hollenback, *Syracuse University*

Patricia Holmes, *University of Louisiana–Lafayette*

Brian Howard, *Brigham Young University–Idaho*

James L. Hoyt, *University of Wisconsin*

Hans Peter Ibold, *Indiana University*

Kim Mac Innis, *Bridgewater State University*

Marcia Ladendorff, *University of North Florida*

Kim Landon, *Utica College*

Phyllis Larsen, *University of Nebraska–Lincoln*

Christopher Leigh, *University of Charleston*

Charles W. Little Jr., *Santa Ana College*

Martin P. LoMonaco, *Neumann University*

Lori Kido Lopez, *University of Wisconsin–Madison*

Alfred L. Lorenz, *Loyola University*

Don Lowe, *University of Kentucky*

Jenn Burleson Mackay, *Virginia Polytechnic Institute and State University*

Stephanie Marchetti, *Mount Wachusett Community College*

Willie Terry Marsh, *Norfolk State University*

Denise Matthews, *Eastern Connecticut State University*

Karen Smith McGrath, *College of Saint Rose*

Carole McNall, *St. Bonaventure University*

Michael Meadows, *Griffith University*

Eileen R. Meehan, *Southern Illinois University–Carbondale*

Gary Metzker, *California State University–Long Beach*

Steve Miller, *Livingston College of Rutgers*

James C. Mitchell, *University of Arizona*

Andrew Moemeka, *Central Connecticut State University*

Timothy C. Molina, *Northwest Vista College*

Jennifer Mullen, *Colorado State University–Pueblo*

Mary Jo Nead, *Thomas More College*

Andrew T. Nelson, *Loyola University New Orleans School of Mass Communication*

Robin Newcomer, *Olympic College*

Sandy Nichols, *Towson University*

Dr. Shirley Oakley, *St. Petersburg College*

Kurt Odenwald, *Wentworth Institute of Technology*

Roy Overmann, *Webster University*

Douglas Pastel, *Bunker Hill Community College*

Martin J. Perry, *St. John's University*

Elizabeth L. Petrun, *University of Kentucky*

Mark Plenke, *Normandale Community College*

Terri F. Reilly, *Webster University*

Candice D. Roberts, *St. John's University*

Richelle Rogers, *Loyola University*

Felecia Ross, *The Ohio State University*

Marshel D. Rossow, *Minnesota State University*

Enid Sefcovic, *Broward College*

Mitchell E. Shapiro, *University of Miami*

Danny Shipka, *Louisiana State University*

Martin D. Sommerness, *Northern Arizona University*

Jeff South, *Virginia Commonwealth University*

Cathy Stablein, *College of DuPage*

Richard F. Taflinger, *Washington State University*

Christopher R. Terry, *University of Wisconsin–Milwaukee*

Phillip A. Thompson, *West Chester University*

Mike Trice, *Florida Southern College*

Venise Wagner, *San Francisco State University*

Yvette Walker, *University of Oklahoma*

Hazel Warlaumont, *California State University–Fullerton*

Patsy G. Watkins, *University of Arkansas*

Wendy Weinhold, *Coastal Carolina University*

Mark West, *University of North Carolina–Asheville*

Valerie Whitney, *Bethune-Cookman University*

Jan Whitt, *University of Colorado–Boulder*

Danielle E. Williams, *Georgia Gwinnett College*

Marvin Williams, *Kingsborough Community College*

David Wolfe, *Mountain View College*

Nerissa Young, *Ohio University*

Jonna Reule Ziniel, *Valley City State University*

I owe a great debt to the people at CQ Press and SAGE who took a chance on a different kind of introduction to mass communication textbook that had greater depth and a narrative story-telling style. I would like to thank Lily Norton, Acquisitions Editor; Jen Jovin-Bernstein, Senior Content Development Editor; and Sarah Wilson, Senior Editorial Assistant. I also thank Janet Kiesel, designer of the book's cover and interior; Heather Kerrigan, copy editor; and Andrew Olson, production editor, who have all been so patient with me over the past several months. I would like to give special thanks to development editor Kate Russillo for her great help and problem-solving skills!

This edition is dedicated to my father, Roger J. Hanson, who is ninety-two years old as I write this in the summer of 2020. Dad is a retired physics professor who instilled an intense sense of curiosity and wonder about the world in both me and my siblings. I would also like to thank the many teachers and students I am privileged to talk with about media literacy.

Finally, I would like to thank my wife, Pam; my sons, Erik and Andrew; my daughter-in-law, Jasmine; and my mother-in-law, Barbara Andrews. I will always be grateful to my late mother, Marilyn, for believing in me and pushing me as a writer.

REH, June 2020

ABOUT THE AUTHOR

Ralph E. Hanson is a professor in the communication department at the University of Nebraska at Kearney, where he teaches courses in writing, blogging, reporting, and mass communication. Previously, he was on the faculty at West Virginia University and Northern Arizona University. He has been teaching introduction to mass communication for more than twenty-five years, and he has worked extensively on developing online courses and degree programs. Hanson has a bachelor's degree in journalism and anthropology from Iowa State University, a master's degree in journalism from Iowa State, and a doctorate in sociology from Arizona State University. He recently completed a book chapter on the long-standing connections between the Martin Luther King Jr. holiday and the NFL's Super Bowl. When Ralph is not out on his motorcycle riding to places a long way from Nebraska, he is blogging on mass communication issues at **https://www.ralphehanson.com**. He tweets as @ralphehanson.

INTRODUCTION TO THE MEDIA

PART I

CHAPTER 1

LIVING IN A MEDIA WORLD

An Introduction to Mass Communication

I t is difficult now to think back to a time when most of us had not heard of words like coronavirus, COVID-19, pandemic, community spread, social distancing, and self-quarantining. A time before all classes were abruptly moved online.[1] A time before people started dying by the thousands from a newly emergent respiratory virus that forced people to stay isolated at home for weeks at a time and essentially shut down the world's economy. A time where we could go where we wanted, when we wanted without worry. A time when the story of the virus did not dominate our media for months at a time.

The *New York Times* ran its first story mentioning the coronavirus on January 8, 2020, announcing that researchers in China had identified a new virus that had infected "dozens of people across Asia."[2] (There actually was a mention of "a pneumonia-like illness, the cause of which is unclear" in the *Times* on January 6, but it was not yet labeled as a coronavirus.) On January 11, 2020, Chinese state media made the first reports about the new illness, "including seven severe cases and one dead case."[3] (Note that the English translation here is from Google Translate.) Less than two weeks after the *Times* story, the United States had its first documented case of the virus that would turn out to be one of the most contagious and deadly viruses since the massive flu epidemic of 1918.

As the disease moved from something to be concerned about to being considered a likely pandemic, events that we would normally consume through our media started to get canceled.

On March 11, 2020, Italian NBA star Danilo Gallinari was getting ready to start the evening's game between the Oklahoma Thunder and the Utah Jazz. But the game never started, given that Utah All-Star Rudy Robert had just disclosed that he had tested positive for the novel coronavirus that causes COVID-19. The cancellation was not a huge surprise to Gallinari, given the enormous toll that the disease had taken on his home country of Italy.[4] This cancellation would be the harbinger of the cancellation of most of the rest of the season. (And as of this writing, it appears likely that the whole season will be canceled.)

This was followed in short order with the cancellation of the NCAA basketball tournament, popularly known as March Madness, for the first time since it started in 1939. The College World Series also had to cancel, in large part

because none of the teams that might be in contention were able to play their regular season games.

Not long after this, essentially all competitive sports in the United States, from professional basketball to youth league soccer, have been shut down for the foreseeable future. And all of these sports cancellations have had an enormous effect on the television industry. The NCAA basketball tournament alone is worth an estimated $800 million a year to the television networks.[5] ESPN was making plans to have a H-O-R-S-E free throw contest for NBA players competing individually from their home gyms, given that globally there were no sports to broadcast.[6]

The pandemic has also had a massive effect on Hollywood. Summer blockbusters like the James Bond flick *No Time to Die* or the Marvel Cinematic Universe movie *Black Widow* have had their summer 2020 releases delayed, while Pixar's *Onward* went from being released in theaters on March 6 to having a digital release on March 20 and made it onto Disney's new streaming service on April 3. That is less than a month from initial release to showing up on a streaming service. Of course, most of the movie theater industry had shut down by March 17.[7]

New York's Broadway theaters went dark starting March 12, closing performances of hits like *Hamilton*, *Oklahoma*, and *Frozen*.[8] But the stars of these shows have turned to streaming and social media to keep the buzz going. For example, the Broadway Cares charity put together a crowd-sourced version of the song "Non-Stop" from *Hamilton*. The show's official Twitter account posted a request in late March 2020—after Broadway had been closed for several weeks—asking fans to submit videos of themselves performing all or part of the song. An editor then assembled the clips into a video featuring dozens of separate performances from singers of all ages as a charity fundraiser.[9]

As this is being written in April 2020, almost all college classes in the United States are being taught using distance education technology as students were sent home from their schools. Many students were home for spring break when they were told not to come back. This created a bit of a crisis for those students who had left their books back on campus, not having planned to study during vacation. In response, SAGE and other textbook publishers made e-book copies of their materials available for free for the rest of the semester.

The COVID-19 epidemic that started in the winter of 2020 will have a long-lasting impact with many thousands of deaths, people forced to stay home and away from public places, and massive changes to our media industry.

It's not just massive social disruptions like the COVID-19 pandemic that acquire significance and meaning from the media use that surround them—our whole world is shaped by the way we take in messages, share them with each other, and attach significance to them. In this chapter we are going to look at how we experience the world and define what it means though **legacy media** like newspapers, television, podcasts, streaming video and audio, and interactive social media.

The Four Levels of Communication

As the director of forensics and a communication instructor at the University of Nebraska at Kearney, Aaron Blackman communicates a lot, for both work and hobbies. His communication often flows through social media platforms, such as Twitter, Discord, Instagram, and occasionally Facebook. Using these outlets to stay in touch with friends and family, attend meetings, and form new connections with gamers around the world Aaron says that,

> Communicating with others through social media weaves in and out of my daily routine. I check numerous forms of social media throughout the day for a variety of reasons. I use Twitter the most to keep up on video game news, politics, and the weather. I'm a freelance esports journalist on top of being an instructor, so Twitter serves as my first point of contact when it comes to interviewing pro players and gauging fan reactions to pro games. Twitter is also useful for promoting my articles as well as when I go live with my Twitch stream. I've been streaming video games on Twitch every Monday night (my latest game was *Borderlands 3*), which, in addition to reaching my general audience, allows me to chat about gaming and life with my friends and family, including cousins from Minnesota that I don't get to see very often.
>
> I also use Instagram, but mostly for sharing pictures of our adorable 16-year-old Jack Russell terrier named Bailey. Additionally, I cross-stitch video game art as a hobby and have started to paint miniatures, so I tend to share my progress pictures via Instagram. Another major service I use every day is Discord, which is a voice/text chat app that lets me connect with various gaming groups and provides a fantastic option for voice communication for meetings or while playing video games. Finally, as a Facebook member since 2005, I don't update it very often anymore, but I find myself scrolling through from time to time to catch up on life updates from family members, friends, and the forensics community.[10]

When Aaron is on social media, he is engaging in almost every possible level of communication, but before we try to analyze these, we need to define what communication is. Media scholar George Gerbner provides a simple definition: **Communication** is "social interaction through messages."[11] More plainly put, communication is how we interact with our entire world, whether through spoken words, written words, gestures, music, paintings, photographs, or dance. In the classical theory of communication there are four distinct levels of communication:

1. Intrapersonal—One to Self

2. Interpersonal—One to One

3. Public Speaking—One to a Group

4. Mass Communication—One to Many

The important point is that communication is a process, not a static thing. Communication is an interaction that allows individuals, groups, and institutions to share ideas. Several of us engage hourly every day in a range of general levels of communication, often switching between them from moment to moment. Because of this, it is worth understanding what the four distinct levels of communication are and how we interact with them.

Intrapersonal Communication

Communication at its most basic level is **intrapersonal communication**, which is really communication within the self. This is how we think and how we assign meaning to all the messages and events that surround our lives. It ranges from the simple act of smiling in response to the smell of a favorite food coming from the kitchen to thinking about whether we really want to share that photo on Snapchat. Feedback, or the response from the receiver of the message, is constant because we are always (or should be always) reflecting on what we have done and how we will react. When Aaron is thinking over in his own mind whether to share a cute dog photo of Baily on Instagram, he is engaging in intrapersonal communication. Our own thoughts on what we want to communicate directly or indirectly with others are parts of important decisions that we may not pay enough attention to. People who have been drinking alcohol or using recreational drugs may suffer impaired intrapersonal communication, which may lead them to engage in more public communication they will later regret.

Interpersonal Communication

Interpersonal communication, or one-on-one communication, is "the intentional or accidental transmission of information through verbal or nonverbal message systems to another human being."[12] Interpersonal communication can be a conversation with a friend or a hug that tells your mother you love her. Like communication with the self, interpersonal communication is continual when others are around because we constantly send out messages, even if those messages consist of nothing more than body language indicating that we want to be left alone.

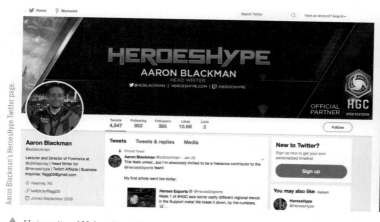

Aaron Blackman's HeroesHype Twitter page.

Courtesy of Michelle Blackman

▲ University of Nebraska at Kearney Director of Forensics Aaron Blackman handles his own communication with his friends, colleagues, and even fans of his video game streams through his Twitter account.

Interpersonal communication provides many opportunities for feedback. Your friend nods, raises an eyebrow, touches you on the arm, or simply answers your question. Not all interpersonal communication is done face-to-face, however. A telephone conversation, an SMS text message, an email, or even a greeting card can be interpersonal communication, though at a somewhat greater emotional distance than in a face-to-face conversation. When Aaron carries out a personal conversation over Discord, sends an email to an editor about a possible esports story, or talks to his wife over dinner, he's engaging in interpersonal communication.

Group Communication

Group communication is when a network of people are communicating with each other. There might be a leader who is dominating the communication in the group, such as with a teacher in the classroom. Students in the class will also have many opportunities to communicate—asking questions, demonstrating their boredom by playing games on their phone, or even by falling asleep and snoring in the back row of the room. But sometimes the group communication is more evenly interactive, such as when a group of friends are arguing about the merits of the latest movie they just watched.

Other situations test the boundaries of group communication, such as a Kendrick Lamar concert at an amphitheater or concert hall. With the amplifiers and multiple video screens, there is a high level of communication technology but limited possibilities for audience members to provide direct feedback to the performers. However, there is still interaction between the rapper and his audience through cheers, applause, and answering back. A key characteristic here is that our roles as senders and receivers are constantly changing. At one moment we are sending out messages and in the next instant we are receiving them. Aaron engages in group communication when he meets with his forensics team, cheers while attending an esports event in person, or shares a photo on Instagram.[13]

Mass Communication

Mass communication is a society-wide communication process in which an individual or institution uses technology to send messages to a large, mixed audience, most of whose members are not known to the sender. Nationally broadcast speeches by politicians, stories about crime in the newspapers, and popular new novels are all forms of mass communication. These communications are fundamentally different from the forms described previously because the sender is separated in space, and possibly in time, from the receiver. Also, the audience is not really known to the communicator. When a communicator appears on television or writes an article for a newspaper, he or she doesn't know who will be listening or reading. What is more, the audience consists of many types of people. It might contain a young man in prison, an old woman in a nursing home, a child eating Cheerios for breakfast, or Aaron as he's getting ready to go to the office to meet with his speech students. The message is communicated to all these people and to thousands or millions of others.[14]

Traditionally, mass communication has allowed only limited opportunities for feedback because the channels of communication are largely one way, but with the rise of interactive communication networks, the opportunities for feedback are growing rapidly. Aaron consumes a wide range of mass communication types during his day, including binge-watching shows on Netflix, Hulu, and Disney+; watching video game streamers and *Overwatch* tournaments on Twitch; playing video games on Blizzard, Steam, and the PlayStation Network; and listening to music through YouTube or Spotify. "My wife and I haven't paid for cable or satellite for years," Aaron says. "Aside from *Watchmen*, *Westworld* and *This is Us*, we are perfectly content to catch up on TV shows months or years after their initial run. Entertainment fits into our busy schedules, not the other way around."[15]

Always a Mix of Levels. The distinctions among the various levels of communication are useful, but don't assume that every instance of communication can automatically be placed in one category or another. There are frequent crossovers in the levels of communication. Consider online communication. You can share a photo with a friend via Snapchat. Through a Tumblr blog, you can share your favorite images and videos. With an intranet, an employer can communicate with employees throughout the world. And through websites and podcasts, messages can go out to the entire world. The same is true of a newspaper, in which a classified ad can carry a proposal of marriage, a notice of a group meeting, or a political manifesto. When Aaron goes out to dinner with friends, they cheer when the *Overwatch* esports tournament being shown on ESPN gets exciting and talk about the competitors with each other, thus engaging in mass and group communication at the same time. When Aaron thinks about what he is going to say to the friends he is with or share on social media, he's engaging is intrapersonal communication.

The purpose of this book is to help you better understand mass communication and the mass media. In the fifteen chapters of this book, we look at a variety of topics:

- The institutions that make up the media and how they function in and affect our society

- The owners and controllers of the media business

- The media themselves, including books, newspapers, audio, movies, television, online media and social media

- The roles the media play in countries and cultures around the world

- The industries that support the media, including advertising and public relations

- The laws and ethics that regulate and control the media

By the time you are finished, you will better understand what the media are, how we interact with them, and what roles they play in our lives.

Mike Marsland/WireImage/Getty Images

▲ Dan Middleton, better known as YouTube video game streamer DanTDM, has managed to become enough of a media star to be invited to attend the BAFTA Children's Awards in London.

Understanding Our Media World

Most people have ambivalent feelings about their high levels of media use. Dr. James Potter, in his book *Media Literacy*, writes that our society is overwhelmed with media content spraying out through a virtual firehose. These messages include the following:

- More than 700 hours of feature films per year. (Just think of how many hours of Marvel Cinematic Universe movies get released per year.)

- More than 300 hours of video are added to YouTube per minute.

- More than 48 million hours of video every year globally from commercial television.

- More than 1,500 book titles published globally per day.

With the pervasiveness of our mobile devices that seem to be physically attached to our bodies, we are rarely out of range of this content and our ability to share it with others. It is liberating to be connected to the entire industrialized world online, but the risk of invasion of privacy is troubling.

Research shows that this mix of growing amounts of content and easier access has resulted in us spending more and more time with our media, which by 2017 had reached an average of twelve hours and one minute—literally more than half our day.[16] The provocative question Potter raises is how do we deal with this high-pressure flow of content? How do we select what to consume? How do we process it? How do we integrate it or dismiss it from our lives? And, perhaps most importantly, what do we know about the choices we make? This section discusses the concept of media literacy and examines some common misconceptions about the mass media.

The term **media literacy** refers to people's understanding of what the media are, how they operate, what messages they are delivering, what roles they play in society, and how audience members respond to media messages. Potter defines media literacy this way: "Media literacy is a set of perspectives that we actively use to expose ourselves to the mass media to process and interpret the meaning of the messages we encounter."

Potter argues that media literacy is not something that we either have or lack; instead, it is something we each have in varying levels. Potter writes that people with high levels of media literacy have a great deal of control over the vision of the world they see through the media and can decide for themselves what the messages mean. In contrast, those with low levels of media literacy can develop exaggerated impressions of problems in society, even when those impressions conflict with their own experience. For example, media consumers who spend large amounts of time watching television often perceive society as far more dangerous and crime-ridden that it is because that's the image they see on television.[17] Potter says that too often consumers with low levels of media literacy assume that the media have large, obvious, and mostly negative effects on other people but little or no effect on themselves. Finally, those with low levels of media literacy are often unwilling to use the media literacy skills they have and thus those skills remain underdeveloped.

Potter has identified four basic perspectives or dimensions of media literacy:

1. Cognitive
2. Emotional
3. Aesthetic
4. Moral[18]

The Cognitive Dimension

The cognitive dimension of media literacy deals with the ability to intellectually process the information being communicated by the media. This can involve interpreting the meaning of words on a printed page, appreciating the implications of ominous music in a movie, or understanding that a well-dressed character in a television show is wealthy. For example, the *Wonder Woman* mythos has changed multiple times through its incarnations in comic books, as a TV series, and now as big-budget movies. The 2017 version directed by Patty Jenkins and portrayed by Israeli actress Gal Gadot makes extensive use of Greek and Roman mythology, giving a depth of meaning to those who know the stories.[19]

The cognitive dimension also includes the skills necessary to access the media: using a tablet, accessing 4K ultra high-definition (UHD) programming on your UHD television, or finding a book in the library. All of these are learned skills. We learn to read in school, learn the meaning of musical cues from movies we have seen, and learn how to navigate online through repeated practice.

The Emotional Dimension

The emotional dimension of media literacy covers the feelings created by media messages. Sometimes the emotions can be overwhelming; examples include the fear of a young child watching a scary movie or the joy of a parent watching a news story about a child in danger being rescued. People often spend time with songs, movies, books, and other media specifically to feel the emotions they generate.[20] *Wonder Woman* became a box office champion in part because groups of women went together to see the movie, sometimes attending special women-only screenings to experience a sense of empowerment from a story that focused on a powerful female superhero.[21] And it is unlikely that many of the truly fake news stories out there would spread so quickly if they didn't resonate so emotionally with audiences.

The Aesthetic Dimension

The aesthetic dimension of media literacy involves interpreting media content from an artistic or critical point of view. How well is the media artifact produced? What skills were used in producing it? How does it compare in quality to other, similar works? Understanding more than the surface dimensions of media content can require extensive learning. *Wonder Woman* was unquestionably a commercial success, and it was largely a critical success as well. The movie was praised for excellent performances by the leads Gadot and Chris Pine, but also for the casting of Robin Wright, who played Princess Buttercup in 1987's *The Princess Bride*, as the fierce and powerful General Antiope.[22] This didn't stop critics, though, from almost universally panning the movie's ending with an all-too-conventional boss fight.

iStockphoto.com/Paolo Cipriani

▲ One of the many reasons we go to the movies is to experience strong emotions, such as fear, horror, surprise, or romance, in a safe environment.

The Moral Dimension

The moral dimension of media literacy consists of examining the values of the medium or the message. In a television situation comedy, for example, an underlying message might be that a quick wit is an important tool for dealing with problems or that a problem can be solved in a short time. In an action movie, the moral lessons may be that violence and authority are needed if one is to succeed and that the world is a mean and dangerous place. The moral message of most advertisements is that problems can be solved by purchasing something.[23] According to *New Yorker* movie critic Richard Brody, one of the most powerful issues raised by *Wonder Woman* is that evil doesn't come from "overtly monstrous villains but arises within humankind itself."[24]

Developing Our Media Literacy. Like any skill, developing media literacy demands hard work and practice. It is also not something we develop all at once, Potter writes.[25] Instead we have a wide range of skills that are developed slowly across our lifetime. At the most basic level are the skills we learn as a baby or a toddler—acquiring the fundamentals of communication. As babies we learn there are people other than ourselves and that they can communicate with us through sounds and actions. This is the discovery that communication with other people exists.

The second step is acquiring language. Young children learn that sounds and expressions not only convey feelings through smiles, frowns, loving sounds, and angry shouts, but that sounds can have specific meanings. They learn they can communicate with others using those sounds. Beyond the language of words, young children can also start developing the vocabulary of music and other sounds; they start to understand happy and sad music along with the meanings of other non-verbal sounds.

The third step in developing media literacy is developing an understanding of narrative. Once we learn to use language, we can start to understand the meaning of stories, including the differences between fiction and non-fiction, as well as how stories are told in terms of the basics of plot and time sequence. Understanding the difference between stories that are true versus those that are made up is a basic level. At a higher level comes the ability to understand that stories that are made up can still tell us things that are real about our lives. At a different level, learning how to make sense out of flashbacks and varying points of view in a story that are not immediately obvious to the novice media consumer. A first-time moviegoer would likely have difficulty with complex narrative timelines used by movie director Christopher Nolan in his films like *Dunkirk* and *Inception*.

The fourth step is developing skepticism. As we learn to examine who is sending us messages, we use that knowledge to analyze how people sending out messages are trying to persuade us. As we learn the differences between advertisements and programming, we learn to discount the claims made in ads. As we learn more about the media outlets, we are consuming information from, we get a better idea of what kind of skepticism we need to be applying. Is this someone who is presenting us with unbiased information or is it someone who is making an active effort to persuade us?

The fifth step is intensive development. We start to have specific interests that we want to learn about in more depth. We will develop complex thought structures about the topics we are most interested in. These allow us to think about these topics in more intricate ways. For example, if you are interested in politics, you will likely seek out stories about the issues you are passionate about. You will also be much better at decoding the news about politics than people who don't care. The more you learn about current politics, the more you will be able to remember and the better you will be at analyzing the information you consume. The more you learn about your favored topic, the better you will be at learning more.

The sixth step is experiential exploring. We consume different types of media and content because we are looking for different types of experiences. You might watch a new horror movie because you are seeking the excitement and adrenaline rush that being frightened in a safe environment provides. Our reactions and sensations are not a negative part of media consumption, they are often the point of it.

The seventh step is critical appreciation. This is when we start being able to analyze media content apart from your own feelings about it. For example, you might not be a big fan of hip-hop, but you can still analyze and appreciate the complex rhymes and sampling that goes into producing the commentary and sonic mix. You don't have to like something to be able to appreciate it. Similarly, you realize that the fact that you like a particular book doesn't necessarily make it a brilliant bit of writing.

The eighth and final step is social responsibility. As we grow in media literacy, we learn to take a moral stand about the value of certain content over that of other content. We realize that some media content and our use of it can have moral and ethical consequences for society as a whole and that through our media decisions we have the ability to make the world a better place. As an example, you might decide to always check the accuracy of provocative social media posts that might be from a bot account or an online troll before passing it on. Even if a meme says something you absolutely agree with, you still try to figure out where it came from before you share it.

Models of Mass Communication

Although people often use the terms *mass communication* and *mass media* interchangeably, they are significantly different concepts. Mass communication is a process, whereas the **mass media** are simply the technological tools used to transmit the messages of mass communication.[26] Earlier in this chapter, we defined mass communication as a society-wide communication process in which an individual or institution uses technology to send messages to a large mixed audience, most of whose members are not known to the sender. There are many ways to approach looking at mass communication. Media scholar Denis McQuail lays out four models that help us answer different questions about the nature of mass communication:

1. Transmission Model

2. Ritual Model

3. Publicity Model

4. Reception Model[27]

Transmission Model

There is an old way of describing mass communication known as the **Sender Message Channel Receiver (SMCR) or transmission model**. The transmission model does not do justice to the complexity of the mass communication process because it tends to portray mass communication as a largely one-directional flow of messages from the sender to the receiver, rather than as a complex interaction where senders and receivers are constantly changing places. What it does is lay out the key elements in mass communication.

The **sender** is the source of messages that go out through mass communication. When critics talk about "the media" as a potent force, they are often talking about the few large corporations that control the flow of messages from our major commercial channels. But as you have already figured out, there are many other senders than just the major media corporations. For example, when the *New York Times* started reporting on the COVID-19 virus in January 2020, they were the sender.

The **message** is the content being transmitted by the sender and reacted to by the receiver. Before the message can be transmitted, it must be encoded. **Encoding** requires at least two steps. First the sender's ideas must be turned into a message—a script for the video is drafted, a graphic is created, or a tweet is written. Second, the message must be prepared for transmission—the script is recorded, the tweet is sent out, or the graphic is placed on an online page. When the various professional and collegiate sports leagues started cancelling their seasons and the broadcasts of their games, that started sending out a message of how serious the COVID-19 pandemic was likely to be. But did the message mean what the sender intended? That is a question we will address later in this chapter.

The **channel** is the medium used to transmit the message. Recall that a mass medium is a technological tool. Think about a newspaper. It consists of black and colored ink printed on relatively low-quality paper. It is portable, readily available, and cheap. Channels can include books, newspapers, social media, streaming audio and video, or movies in a theater. What about faxes, text messages, letters, and email? Do they fit in as channels for mass communication? It depends. If you receive sports scores sent out as mass SMS text messages by your favorite sports news service, then it certainly is a mass communication channel. When you send a text to your sweetie, it is much more like interpersonal communication. When the Broadway Cares charity created the crowd-sourced version of the song "Non-Stop" from the musical *Hamilton*, their channels were the YouTube video service and a variety of social media outlets.

The **receiver** is the audience for the mass communication message—that is, the people who are receiving and decoding the message. **Decoding** is the process of translating a signal from a mass medium into a form the receiver can understand. Receivers do not always get a clear message from the sender, however. Several types of **noise** can interfere with the delivery of the message. For example, there is semantic noise, which occurs when the receiver does not understand the meaning of the message, such as when you can't understand the lyrics on a Latin music channel because you don't speak Spanish; mechanical noise, which occurs when the channel has trouble transmitting the message, such as when you are a long way from a cell tower so you can't get a web page to load on your mobile device; and environmental noise, which occurs when the action and sounds surrounding the receiver interfere with the reception of the message, such as when your roommate's loud video game keeps you from concentrating on your *Media Literacy* textbook. It is also the receiver who ultimately assigns the meaning to the message they are receiving.

The sender may have intended a message as a sarcastic joke while the receiver might interpret the joke as an offensive serious statement. Which meaning matters? The one assigned to it by the receiver.

Though the transmission model (SMCR) is useful for laying out the various elements of the mass communication process, it does not explain how mass communication works in our lives. It focuses primarily on the process of transmitting messages largely from the point of view of a sender trying to influence the receiver. However, in the real world we are constantly switching between being a sender and receiver, translating messages from one channel to another. And as the messages bounce back and forth; their meanings transform depending on who is receiving them and who is sending them out.

▼ TABLE 1.1

Mass Communication Models

Model	Orientation of Sender	Orientation of Receiver
Transmission Model	Transfer of meaning	Cognitive processing
Ritual Model	Performance	Shared experience
Publicity Model	Competitive display	Attention-giving spectatorship
Reception Model	Preferential encoding	Differential decoding/construction of meaning

Source: Denis McQuail, *McQuail's Mass Communication Theory*, 6th ed. (Thousand Oaks, CA: SAGE, 2010). Reproduced by permission of SAGE. Copyright © Denis McQuail, 2005.

Ritual Model

Whereas the transmission model looks at how a message is sent, the **ritual model** puts audience members at the center of the equation. The ritual model looks at how and why audience members (receivers) consume media messages. This model suggests that we watch a program such as *The Voice* not so much to learn about aspiring singers or to receive advertising messages, but rather to interact with family and friends. Lots of people who are not football fans will attend Super Bowl watch parties to participate in the mid-winter celebration of sports, commercials, and chicken wings. Media consumption thus goes beyond simply delivering messages and becomes a shared experience that brings us together as a people.

Carter Wilkerson, a then sixteen-year-old from Reno, Nevada, holds the record for Twitter engagement with 3.6 million retweets and 1 million likes for his tweet trying to get a year's worth of free chicken nuggets from Wendy's. The fast-food chain told him he would need to get 18 million shares to gets his free chicken, but in the end, they gave him his nuggets anyway. For what it's worth, Wilkerson told the *New York Times* that he might use his experience as a launching ground for a career in marketing. "It'd be pretty cool to put on my college applications that I'm the No. 1 retweeted tweet of all time," he said.[28]

Publicity Model

Sometimes media messages are not trying to convey specific information as much as they are trying to draw attention to a particular person, group, or concept. According to the **publicity model**, the mere fact that a topic is covered by the media can make the topic important, regardless of what is said about it. For example, when Justin Timberlake exposed Janet Jackson's right nipple for nine-sixteenths of a second during the 2004 Super Bowl, there were all sorts of charges that broadcast network CBS was lowering the moral standards of America's young people. The major effect of Jackson's stunt was that the Federal Communications Commission adopted increasingly strict rules on broadcast decency. As a result, at least twenty Sinclair-owned ABC affiliates refused to air the World War II movie *Saving Private Ryan* the following November for fear that they would be fined for all the bad language contained in the movie. Concerns about changing television standards had existed for several years prior to Jackson flashing Super Bowl viewers, but the attention Jackson brought to the issue put broadcast decency in the limelight.[29] By 2018, however, Timberlake's role in the affair seemed to have been forgotten with the singer giving the Super Bowl halftime show. Miss Jackson, on the other hand, was not invited back.

Reception Model

The **reception model** moves us out of the realm of social science analysis and into the world of critical theory (something we will spend time on in Chapter 2). Instead of looking at how messages affect audiences or are used by the senders or receivers, the reception model looks at how audience members derive and create meaning out of media content. Rather than seeing content as having an intended, fixed meaning, the reception model says that each receiver decodes the message based on his or her own unique experiences, feelings, and beliefs. You can take a single news story and show it to liberal and conservative observers, and both will claim that it is biased against their point of view. In fact, a 1982 study showed that the more journalists tried to present multiple sides of an issue, the more partisans on either side of the issue viewed the story as biased.[30]

Evolution of the Media World

Where did our media world come from? Is it just a product of the late twentieth century with its constant flow of print and electronic messages? Not really. The world of interconnected and overlapping communication networks that surrounds us has been evolving for hundreds of years. Before the advent of the mass media, people interacted primarily face-to-face. Most of the time, they interacted only with people like themselves and had little contact with the outside world. But people gradually created communication networks that used first interpersonal channels, then print media, electronic media, and, most recently, interactive media. This section examines how various communication networks have grown over the centuries to form the media world in which we now live.

Before print, the first major communication network in the Western world predates the mass media and was developed by the Roman Catholic Church in the twelfth, thirteenth, and fourteenth centuries. During that period, messages flowed from the Vatican in Italy through the cardinals and bishops to priests in cathedrals and villages throughout Europe and finally to congregations through sermons from the pulpit.[31]

The first major expansion in communication beyond the Church was the development of the printing press—in particular, the development of practical movable type in the 1450s—and the subsequent mass production of printed materials. Mass printing made it possible for major social changes, such as the Protestant Reformation, to spread from their country of origin to the rest of Europe and the world beyond.

Although the printing press allowed for the mass production of information, printing was still relatively slow, and publications remained expensive. The addition of steam power to the printing press in 1814 dramatically increased the rate at which printed material could be reproduced.

The advent of electronic communication made the media world much more complex. This type of communication began in 1844 with the opening of the first telegraph line from Baltimore, Maryland, to Washington, DC. In 1866, telegraph cables spanned the Atlantic

AP Images/Associated Press

▲ By the 1880s, telegraph wires crisscrossed the New York City skyline, sending messages rapidly through the city, across the country, and around the world.

CAN TELEVISION TAKE ANYTHING SERIOUSLY?

Back in 1985, New York University communication professor Neil Postman published his book, *Amusing Ourselves to Death*. In it, Postman argues that the primary effect of television is that it changes how people see the world; that is, with television, people start viewing everything as entertainment. Young people get their news in a comedy format, watching *The Late Show With Stephen Colbert* the same way they watch the newsmagazine *60 Minutes* on CBS. They learn about politics on the same channel that shows a professional football game.[32]

In an interview with Robert Nelson for the *Civic Arts Review*, Postman described the major point of *Amusing Ourselves to Death*:

> Television always recreates the world to some extent in its own image by selecting parts of that world and editing those parts. So, a television news show is a kind of symbolic creation and construction made by news directors and camera crews. . . .
>
> Americans turn to television not only for their light entertainment but for their news, their weather, their politics, their religion, their history, all of which may be said to be their furious entertainment. What I am talking about is television's preemption of our culture's most serious business. It is one thing to say that TV presents us with entertaining subject matter. It is quite another to say that on TV all subject matter is presented as entertaining and it is in that sense that TV can bring ruin to any intelligent understanding of public affairs. . . .
>
> And stranger still is the fact that commercials may appear anywhere in a news story, before, after, or in the middle, so that all events are rendered essentially trivial, that is to say, all events are treated as a source of public entertainment. How serious can an earthquake in Mexico be or a hijacking in Beirut, if it is shown to us prefaced by a happy United Airlines commercial and summarized by a Calvin Klein jeans commercial? Indeed, TV newscasters have added to our grammar a new part of speech altogether. What may be called the "now this" conjunction. "Now this" is a conjunction that does not connect two things but does the opposite. It disconnects. When newscasters say, "Now this," they mean to indicate that what you have just heard or seen has no relevance to what you are about to hear or see. There is no murder so brutal, no political blunder so costly, no bombing so devastating that it cannot be erased from our minds by a newscaster saying, "Now this." The newscaster means

that you have thought long enough on the matter, let's say 45 seconds, that you must not be morbidly preoccupied with it, let us say for 90 seconds, and that you must now give your attention to a commercial. Such a situation in my view is not news. And in my opinion it accounts for the fact that Americans are among the most ill informed people in the Western world.[33]

....

WHO is the source?

Neil Postman (1931–2003), a prominent American educator, media theorist, and cultural critic, founded the media ecology program at New York University (NYU) and chaired the NYU Department of Culture and Communication. Postman wrote eighteen books and more than two hundred magazine and newspaper articles for such periodicals as the *New York Times Magazine*, *Atlantic Monthly*, *Harper's*, and the *Washington Post*. He also edited the journal *ETC: A Review of General Semantics* and was on the editorial board of the *Nation*.

WHAT is he saying?

Postman argues that the primary effect of television is that it changes how people see the world; that is, with television, people start viewing everything as entertainment. In comparison, think about your own viewing habits. Do you watch the news the same way you watch *Big Bang Theory*? Or learn about politics on the same channel that shows *Big Brother*? Or see news about the war in Syria, followed by a commercial for Domino's Pizza?

WHAT kind of evidence does the book provide?

What kind of data does Postman provide to support his arguments? What kind of evidence is needed to bolster these claims? Is there evidence that disputes his claims? How do you think Postman's background is likely to have shaped his view of television?

HOW do you or your classmates react to Postman's arguments?

What does the title *Amusing Ourselves to Death* mean to you? Do you feel that television trivializes important issues or makes them more palatable? Have you noticed similar effects in yourself as described by Postman? Do you notice differences in how news anchors make the transition from news to commercials and back again? Are the stories before and after the break any different from stories during the rest of the newscast?

Ocean, overcoming a seemingly insurmountable barrier that had long hindered transoceanic communication. Instead of sending a message on a two-week journey by boat across the ocean and waiting for a reply to come back the same way, two people on opposite sides of the ocean could carry on a dialogue via telegraph.

In the 1880s, Emile Berliner invented the gramophone, or phonograph, which played mass-produced discs containing about three minutes of music. Just as printed books made possible the storage and spread of ideas, the gramophone allowed musical performances to be captured and reproduced.

The invention of radio in the late nineteenth century freed electronic communication from the limits imposed on it by telegraph wires. Messages could come into the home at any time and at almost no cost to the receiver. All that was needed was a radio set to receive an endless variety of cultural content, news, and other programming.

Movies were first shown at nickelodeon theaters in the late 1890s and early 1900s and were produced by an entertainment industry that distributed films worldwide. Young couples on a date in London, Ohio, and in London, England, could see the same movie, copy the same styles of dress, and perhaps even practice the same kisses they saw in the movie. Due to radio and the movies, the media world became a shared entertainment culture produced for profit by major media corporations.

In 1939, patrons in New York's neighborhood taverns no longer had to settle for radio broadcasts of Yankees games being played at the Polo Grounds. Instead, a small black-and-white television set located on a pedestal behind the bar showed a faint, flickering image of the game. After a series of delays caused by World War II, television surpassed radio in popularity. It also became a lightning rod for controversy as people stayed home to watch whatever images it would deliver.

After several decades of television, people had gotten used to the idea that news, information, and entertainment could be delivered almost magically into their homes, although they could do little to control the content of this medium other than change channels. Then a new medium emerged, one that made senders and receivers readily interchangeable. The internet became a full-fledged mass communication network in the 1990s (though many people were unaware that the first nodes of this new medium were being linked together as far back as 1969). Rather than simply making it easier for individuals and organizations to send messages to a mass audience, the new computer networks were designed for two-way communication. Audience members were becoming message providers themselves.

AP Photo/Carlos Giusti

▲ After Hurricane Maria, power lines came down all over Puerto Rico. Facebook pledged to send a "connectivity team" to help restore communications to the island, in a move by one of several tech companies—among them Tesla, Google, Cisco, Microsoft, and a range of startups—who came with disaster response proposals, most aimed at getting phone and internet service up and running.

Online and Mobile Media: Interactive Communication

Online media's interactivity was the culmination of a trend toward giving audience members new control over their communication world. The growth of cable and satellite television, along with the VCR, had already given viewers more choices and more control, and the remote control allowed them to choose among dozens of channels without leaving their chairs.

In 2000, when the Pew Research Center first started tracking Americans' use of the internet, slightly more than 50 percent of us were online. That number has increased steadily during the ensuing two decades; in 2018, approximately 90 percent of American adults are online.[35] The implications of interactivity are significant. Whereas the commercial media have come to be controlled by a smaller and smaller number of large corporations (see Chapter 3), an important channel of mass communication is open to ordinary people in ways that were never before possible. With a trivial investment in a mobile device or computer, individuals can grab the spotlight with news and entertainment through social media and the World Wide Web.

Consider the example of artist Danielle Corsetto, creator of the popular web comic *Girls With Slingshots*. Her comic started under the name *Hazelnuts* when she was in high school, but she took it online in October 2004 when fans of her sketches asked her when she was going to start publishing her comic. Corsetto explained to the *Frederick News-Post* that *Girls With Slingshots* (or *GWS*) is a slice-of-life comic that tells the story of "sour, grumpy girl" Hazel and her best friend, Jamie, a "bubbly girl who is very comfortable with herself."[36] One of the fascinating things about the comic is the level of diversity within its cast. There is Melody, who is deaf; Soo Lin, who is blind; Darren, who is gay; Erin, who is asexual; and McPedro, a cactus who talks when Hazel's been drinking. Anna Pearce, writing for *Bitch Media*, says that her favorite thing about the comic is that it looks at disability from the point of view of a disabled person. "What I like about the jokes in this strip are that they are all over the place. Some are about how clueless people can be about blindness. Some are disability-related humour as told by people with disabilities."[37]

Although her comic is online, she still does her drawing by hand. Corsetto explains, "It's more realistic and less stereotypical. All the characters have these unusual relations, both romantic and platonic . . . that are not what you would find in, say, a sitcom, but it's written like a sitcom. I'm kind of trying to normalize these things that are taboo."

Since 2007, she has made her living exclusively through drawing and writing comics. In addition to *Girls With Slingshots*, Corsetto works on a variety of side projects, including writing three volumes of the *Adventure Time* graphic novel series. Although *GWS* started out small, Corsetto's website drew about one hundred thousand readers a day at its peak. In March 2015, Corsetto brought *GWS* to a close, with her heroine Hazel coming to terms with her long-absent father. Given the subject matter, alcohol use, and language in *GWS*, Corsetto would not have been able to publish her work in a legacy newspaper or magazine.[38]

Following the completion of the comic, Corsetto has taken what she called a "sabbatical," working on advancing her art skills, teaching art classes, editing a two-volume hardcover book edition of *GWS*, writing the text for a sex education comic for high school and college aged

Courtesy of Danielle Corsetto

▲ Self portrait of Danielle Corsetto with her cat.

students, and developing a graphic novel she has started publishing pages for on her Patreon page.[39] Corsetto says she has been depending on donations from the crowdfunding platform Patreon for most of her current income.

While Corsetto is "making a living" from her artwork, she wrote in a recent post to her Patreon supporters that this can mean different things to different people:

> I net more than the average schoolteacher, but less than the average accountant. My income fluctuates year to year. I live comfortably and I feel wealthy. . . . But I guarantee if I showed my bookkeeping to an old-school cartoonist who hit it big in newspaper syndication in the 90s, they'd think I was insane to say that I "feel wealthy."[40]

Some critics would argue that the growth of cable television stations, websites, and magazines creates only an illusion of choice because a majority of the channels are still controlled by the same five or six companies.[41] Even so, it is a new media world, one in which audience members are choosing what media content they will consume and when they will consume it. It's a world that even media giants are being forced to adjust to.

The Seven Secrets About the Media "They" Don't Want You to Know 2.0

Media literacy is a tricky subject to talk about because few people admit that they really don't understand how the media operate and how messages, audiences, channels, and senders interact. After all, since we spend so much time with the media, we must know all about them, right? As an example, most students in an Introduction to Mass Communication class will claim that the media and media messages tend to affect other people far more than themselves. The question of media literacy can also become a political question, for which the answer depends on whether you are a liberal or a conservative, rich or poor, young or old. But the biggest problem in the public discussion of media literacy is that certain routine issues get discussed repeatedly, while many big questions are left unasked.

- Secret 1—The media are essential components of our lives.

- Secret 2—There are no mainstream media (MSM).

- Secret 3—Everything from the margin moves to the center.

- Secret 4—Nothing is new: Everything that happened in the past will happen again.

- Secret 5—All media are social.

- Secret 6—Online media are mobile media.

- Secret 7—There is no "they."

Six editions of this book ago, I first came out with the Seven Secrets About the Media "They" Don't Want You to Know. These were things we do not typically hear about in the media. Secret things. Perhaps it is because there is no one out there who can attract an audience by saying these things. Or maybe it is because the ideas are complicated, and we do not like complexity from our media. Or maybe it is because "they" (whoever "they" may be) do not want us to know them.

But the media world has changed considerably since the secrets were first developed in 2006:

- Netflix had no streaming service—it was only a DVD-by-mail service.

- There was no iPhone—the BlackBerry with its little Chiclet keyboard was the height of smartphone technology.

- There were no tablet computers.

- Cell phone service was typically sold by the minute, and most mobile plans had a limit to the number of text messages that were included in the basic plan.

- Google was in the process of buying a cell phone video sharing service called YouTube created by three former PayPal employees.

- Facebook was only two years old, and use of it was limited to college students.

- Instagram had not yet gone online—that wouldn't happen until 2010. By 2018, it had eight hundred million active users.[42]

Today, my students tell me they watch most of their video using Netflix streaming, virtually all of them have a smartphone and several social media accounts, and their most frequent way of going online is with a mobile device. So in the sixth edition, it became clear that it was time to update the Seven Secrets to better match the current media world—we were releasing the Seven Secrets About the Media "They" Don't Want You to Know 2.0. These key issues of media literacy—which do not get the discussion they deserve—provide a foundation for the rest of the chapters in this book. (And just who are "they"? Wait for Secret 7.)

SECRET 1: The Media Are Essential Components of Our Lives

Critics often talk about the effects the media have on us as though the media were something separate and distinct from our everyday lives. But conversations with my students have convinced me otherwise. Every semester I poll my students as to what media they have used so far that day, with the day starting at midnight. I run through the list: checking Twitter, Snapchat, or Instagram; listening to the radio; checking the weather on a mobile device; binge-watching on Netflix; reading the latest Margaret Atwood novel; listening to Spotify on an iPhone; and so it goes. In fact, media use is likely to be the most universal experience my students will share. Surveys of my students find that more of my morning class students have consumed media content than have eaten breakfast or showered since the day began at midnight. Are the media an important force in our lives? Absolutely! But the media are more than an outside influence on us. They are a part of our everyday lives.

Think about how we assign meanings to objects that otherwise would have no meaning at all. Take a simple yellow ribbon twisted in a stylized bow. You've seen thousands of these, and most likely you know exactly what they stand for—"Support Our Troops." But that hasn't always been the meaning of the symbol.

The yellow ribbon has a long history in American popular culture. It played a role in the rather rude World War II–era marching song "She Wore a Yellow Ribbon." The ribbon was a symbol of a young woman's love for a soldier "far, far away," and the lyrics mention that her father kept a shotgun handy to keep the soldier "far, far away." The yellow ribbon was also a symbol of love and faithfulness in the John Ford film *She Wore a Yellow Ribbon*. In the 1970s, the ribbon became a symbol of remembering the U.S. staff in the Iranian embassy who had been taken hostage. This meaning came from the song "Tie a Yellow Ribbon 'Round the Old Oak Tree," made popular by the group Tony Orlando and Dawn. The song tells about a prisoner coming home from jail hoping that his girlfriend will remember him. She can prove her love by displaying the yellow ribbon.

iStockphoto.com/HildeAnna

▲ The meaning of yellow ribbons tied into a bow has transformed many times over the past several decades.

The prisoner arrives home to find not one, but one hundred yellow ribbons tied to the tree. The display of yellow ribbons tied to trees became commonplace in newspaper articles and television news stories about the ongoing hostage crisis after the wife of a hostage started displaying one in her yard.

Later, during the 1990–1991 Persian Gulf War, Americans were eager to show their support for the troops fighting overseas, even if they did not necessarily support the war itself, and the stylized ribbon started to become institutionalized as a symbol of support. The yellow "Support Our Troops" ribbon was followed by the red ribbon of AIDS awareness, the pink ribbon of breast cancer awareness, and ribbons of virtually every color for other issues. And how do we know the meanings of these ribbons? We hear or see them being discussed through our media. The meaning is assigned by the creators of a ribbon, but the success of the ribbon depends on its meaning being shared through the media. So, do the media create the meanings? Not really. But could the meanings be shared nationwide without the media? Absolutely not. The media may not define our lives, but they do help transmit and disseminate shared meanings from one side of the country to the other.[43]

SECRET 2: There Are No Mainstream Media (MSM)

We often hear charges related to perceived sins of the so-called mainstream media. But who exactly are these mainstream media? For some, the MSM are the heavyweights of journalism, especially the television broadcast networks and the major newspapers, such as the *New York Times*. For others, the MSM are the giant corporations that run many of our media outlets. New York University journalism professor and blogger Jay Rosen says that the term MSM is often used to refer to media we just don't like—a "them."[44] It isn't always clear who constitutes the MSM, but in general we can consider them to be the old-line legacy media—the big-business newspapers, magazines, and television.

But are these old media more in the mainstream than our alternative media? Look at talk radio. Afternoon talk radio is dominated by conservative political talk show hosts, such as Rush Limbaugh and Sean Hannity. Limbaugh is fond of complaining about how the MSM don't "get it." But how mainstream are the MSM? For 2019, Fox News averaged 2.49 million viewers in prime time, making it the number 1 basic cable network; MSNBC averaged 1.73 million viewers in prime time and was the second most watched basic cable network, and CNN averaged 971,000 viewers, making it the seventh most watched basic cable network.[45]

With all the talk of cable news, it's easy to forget that the legacy broadcast networks have significant audiences as well: ABC with 8.6 million viewers, NBC with 7.8 million, and CBS with 5.5 million, as of the final three months of 2019. (The Fox broadcast network does not have a network evening news broadcast.)[46] *The Sean Hannity Show*, on the other hand, averages 14 million radio listeners a week, followed closely by *The Rush Limbaugh Show*.[47] (Note that television audiences and radio audiences are measured differently.) So, which is more mainstream? A popular afternoon radio show with a large daily audience or a television news program with a somewhat smaller audience?

And then there is video game streamer Daniel Middleton, a.k.a. DanTDM, who has more than twenty-two million followers and more than sixteen billion (that is *billion* with a *b*) views on YouTube, streaming *Minecraft* and other video games. What could possibly be more mainstream than twenty-two million viewers and 16 billion views?[48] Again, these numbers are not directly comparable with television ratings—they are much, much bigger. Overall, YouTube claims to have more than two billion monthly users. Most videos do not get a particularly large viewership, but the combined total is massive.[49]

So, it is largely meaningless to describe one medium as mainstream and another as nonmainstream. They are all significant presences in our world. Can we distinguish between old and new media? Perhaps. Can we argue that our alternative sources of news and entertainment are any less significant than the traditional ones? Absolutely not.

SECRET 3: Everything From the Margin Moves to the Center

The mass media, both news and entertainment, are frequently accused of trying to put forward an extremist agenda of violence, permissiveness, homosexuality, drug use, edgy fashion, and nonmainstream values.

People in the media business, be they entertainers or journalists, respond with the argument that they are just "keeping it real," portraying the world as it is by showing aspects of society that some people want to pretend don't exist. They have no agenda, the argument goes; they just want to portray reality.

Now it is true that much of what the media portray that upsets people is real. On the other hand, it is a bit disingenuous to argue that movie directors and musicians are not trying for shock value when they use offensive language or portray stylized violence combined with graphic sexuality. Think back to any of a few recent horror movies. We all know that teenagers routinely get slashed to ribbons by a psycho killer just after having sex, right? Clearly, movie producers are trying to attract an audience by providing content that is outside of the mainstream.

The problem with the argument between "keeping it real" and "extremist agenda" is that it misses what is happening. There can be no question that audiences go after media content that is outside of the mainstream. Similarly, the more nonmainstream content is presented, the more ordinary it seems to become. This is what is meant by Secret 3—one of the mass media's biggest effects on everyday life is to take culture from the margins of society and make it into part of the mainstream, or center. This process can move people, ideas, and even individual words from small communities into mass society.

We can see this happening in several ways. Take the 1975 cult movie *The Rocky Horror Picture Show* that tells the story of a gay male transvestite (Dr. Frank-N-Furter) who is building a muscle-bound boyfriend (Rocky) for himself when a newly engaged straight couple show up at his castle's doorstep seeking shelter from a storm. While the movie found success as a midnight movie in the counterculture community, it took years to move from being considered a flop to a cult classic.

Dan MacMedan/Getty Images

▲ Laverne Cox starred in Fox's TV remake of *The Rocky Horror Picture Show* as the mad scientist/alien/transvestite Dr. Frank-N-Furter, replacing Tim Curry. The film is easily the most beloved camp cult movie of all time.

Rocky Horror Picture Show

▲ Tim Curry as Dr. Frank-N-Furter.

But in recent years *Rocky Horror* has moved from simply a midnight movie to a core element of popular culture. The Fox Broadcasting show *Glee* did a Halloween episode in 2010 where the kids in the show's glee club produced *The Rocky Horror Picture Show* as a high school musical. But the *Glee* version had actress Amber Riley playing the part of Dr. Frank-N-Furter, while the part of Rocky was still played by a male actor, Chord Overstreet. Thus, the central plotline went from gay to straight. The *Glee* version also had Frank-N-Furter singing about being from "Sensational, Transylvania" instead of "Transsexual, Transylvania." With these changes, *The Rocky Horror Glee Show* became a perfect example of Secret 3. *Rocky Horror* started out as a camp musical in the 1970s that found enormous success in the counterculture community. But *Glee* sanitized it from a celebration of cross-dressing gay culture into a mass-market story of straight people playing with gay themes. In 2016, Fox Broadcasting showed a full remake of *Rocky Horror* that aired in October featuring trans actress Laverne Cox (of *Orange Is the New Black* fame) as Dr. Frank-N-Furter. *Hollywood Reporter* reviewer Daniel Finberg noted in 2016 that the show is no longer shocking in that "one of the most unorthodox characters in the history of musicals has become oddly conventional."[50]

An alternative approach is to look at how the media accelerate the adoption of activist language into the mainstream. Take the medical term *intact dilation and extraction*, which describes a controversial type of late-term abortion. A search of the LexisNexis news database shows that newspapers used the medical term only five times over a six-month period. On the other hand, *partial-birth abortion*, the term for the procedure used by abortion opponents, was used in more than 125 stories during the same time. Opponents even got the term used in the title of a bill passed by Congress that outlawed the procedure, thus moving the phrase into the mainstream through repeated publication of the bill's name.

This process is not a product of a liberal or conservative bias by the news media. It's simply a consequence of the repeated use of the term in the press.

SECRET 4: Nothing Is New: Everything That Happened in the Past Will Happen Again

Secret 4 is a little different from the oft-repeated slogan, "Those who ignore the past are doomed to repeat it." Instead, it says that media face the same issues repeatedly as technologies change and new people come into the business.

The fight between today's recording companies and file sharers has its roots in the battle between music publishers and the distributors of player piano rolls in the early 1900s. The player piano was one of the first technologies for reproducing musical performances. Piano roll publishers would buy a single copy of a piece of sheet music and hire a skilled pianist to have his or her performance recorded as a series of holes punched in a paper roll. That roll (and the performance) could then be reproduced and sold to anyone who owned a player piano without further payment to the music's original publisher.[51]

Then, in 1984, Sony successfully defended itself against a lawsuit from Universal Studios by arguing that it had a right to sell VCRs to the public because there were legitimate, legal uses for the technology. Universal had protested the sales because the video recorders could be used to duplicate its movies. Before long, the studios quit trying to ban the VCR and started selling videocassettes of movies directly to consumers at reasonable prices. Suddenly, the studios had a major new source of revenue.[52]

This can also be seen with the repeated fears of new media technologies emerging over the years. In the 1930s, there was fear that watching movies, especially gangster pictures, would lead to precocious sexual behavior, delinquency, lower standards and ideals, and poor physical and emotional health. The 1940s brought concern about how people would react to radio programs, particularly soap operas.[53] Comic books came under attack in the 1950s. The notion that comic books were dangerous was popularized by a book titled *Seduction of the Innocent* by Dr. Fredric Wertham. Wertham also testified before Congress that violent and explicit comic books were a cause of teenage delinquency and sexual behavior. The industry responded to the criticism by forming the Comics Code Authority and ceasing publication of popular crime and horror comics, such as *Tales From the Crypt* and *Weird Science*.

The 1980s and 1990s saw controversies over offensive rap and rock lyrics.[54] These controversies reflected widespread concern about bad language and hidden messages in songs. In 2009, pop star Britney Spears had a not-so-hidden allusion to the "*F* word" in her song "If U Seek Amy." If you speak the title aloud, it sounds like you are spelling out *F, U, . . .* well, you get the picture. Critics were, of course, shocked and dismayed at this example of a pop star lowering public taste. Of course, Spears did not really create her naughty little lyric on her own. Aside from a host of rock and blues singers who have used similar lines, *Slate* writer Jesse Sheidlower notes that James Joyce used the same basic line in *Ulysses*, when he has a group of women sing:

▲ Congressional hearings in the 1950s about horror comics, such as those pictured here, show how adults are always concerned about the possible effects of new media on children.

©Bettmann/Getty Images

If you see kay

Tell him he may

See you in tea

Tell him from me.

A careful reading of the third line will let you find a second hidden obscenity as well.[55]

Numerous media critics and scholars have argued that television and movies present a distorted view of the world, making it look like a much more violent and dangerous place than it is. More recently, mobile devices have been blamed for a range of social ills, from car accidents caused by distracted drivers to promiscuity caused by sexually explicit mobile phone text and photo messages.

Why has there been such long-running, repeated concern about the possible effects of the media? Media sociologist Charles R. Wright says that people want to be able to solve social ills, and it is easier to believe that poverty, crime, and drug abuse are caused by media coverage than to acknowledge that their causes are complex and not fully understood.[56]

Writing in 1948, sociologists Robert Merton and Paul Lazarsfeld identified four major aspects of public concern about the media:

- Concern that because the media are everywhere, they might be able to control and manipulate people. This is a large part of the legacy of fear.

- Fear that those in power will use the media to reinforce the existing social structure and discourage social criticism. When critics express concern about who owns and runs the media, this is what they are worried about.

- Fear that mass entertainment will lower the tastes and standards for popular culture by trying to attract the largest-possible audience. Criticism of action movies, soap operas, and wrestling as replacements for healthier entertainment, such as Shakespeare's plays, is at the heart of this concern.

- The belief that mass entertainment is a waste of time that detracts from more useful activities. When your mother told you to turn off the television set and go outside, this was her concern![57]

SECRET 5: All Media Are Social

No matter what media you are using—whether it be a legacy newspaper or television station or a social media channel like Facebook—you are always interacting with it at a social level—whether it be face-to-face, with friends on Facebook, or with the entire world via Twitter.

Take, as an example, when your author went to hear President Barack Obama speak at the University of Nebraska at Omaha (UNO) campus. I got the expected reactions from friends to the selfie of my wife and me standing in line to enter the arena. I also shared news on Twitter about the president's visit from social media guru Dr. Jeremy Lipschultz. And while I was on Lipschultz's Twitter page, *Omaha World-Herald* weather reporter Nancy Gaarder tweeted out a photo of me at work. Now, in this case, Gaarder and I were interacting because she was sitting behind me and we got to talking face-to-face. But this was only the first of many social interactions for the day based on news being shared socially.

As everyone in the arena waited for the president to appear, I tweeted out a photo of the press corps area on the floor of the arena, along with the hashtag #POTUSatUNO, one of several in use at the event. Before long I picked up a response from Marjorie Sturgeon, a multimedia journalist for Omaha's Action 3 News, who noted she could see herself in my photo. Meanwhile, I was sharing news from the *Omaha World-Herald*, UNO student journalists, and other observers. Media recall research tells us that one of the best predictors of the news we will remember is the news we talk about. Thus, the news we share socially will become the news that matters most to us.

When important news breaks, it is likely we'll hear about it first through social media. When a mass shooter killed at least fifty-eight people and left more than five hundred people injured in Las Vegas in October 2017, there were a lot of contradictory stories circulating on Twitter and other social media. But with all the reports circulating, it could be hard to tell which stories should be believed. New Hampshire Public Radio reporter Casey McDermott noted that NPR included the following statement at the bottom of its web stories about the shooting:

> This is a developing story. Some things that get reported by the media will later turn out to be wrong. We will focus on reports from police officials and other authorities, credible news outlets and reporters who are at the scene. We will update as the situation develops.[58]

SECRET 6: Online Media Are Mobile Media

When the internet first started to gain a following, going online used to mean a person would need to physically go to a location where there was a computer that was plugged into an Ethernet cable. At the turn of the millennium, going online typically involved a slow, loud, dial-up line. However, as of 2019, approximately 75 percent of adults had access to high-speed broadband Internet at home, most likely using either a cable modem or a landline-based DSL service.[59] Increasingly, going online now means a person needs only to access a smartphone; in many parts of the world, the mobile Internet is the only Internet.

In January 2007, Apple announced the first version of its iconic iPhone, and the world of mobile internet would never be the same. It is not that the iPhone was the first phone to access the internet. The BlackBerry had been around for eight years at that point with its little chiclet keyboard. But the BlackBerry was always primarily an email and messaging device.[60] If the BlackBerry looked like

Casey McDermott
@caseymcdermott

A small thing right now, but I really appreciate this disclaimer at the bottom of @NPR's report from Las Vegas. n.pr/2yiNzZY

This is a developing story. Some things that get reported by the media will later turn out to be wrong. We will focus on reports from police officials and other authorities, credible news outlets and reporters who are at the scene. We will update as the situation develops.

Twitter/@caseymcdermott

▲ New Hampshire Public Radio reporter Casey McDermott noted that NPR included the following statement at the bottom of its web stories about the Las Vegas shooting.

a glorified pager, Apple's iPhone looked like something out of Steven Spielberg's futuristic movie *Minority Report* with its touch screen interface and full internet access.[61] Android phones featuring Google's mobile operating system were launched in the United States in October 2008, bridging the gap between the iPhone and the BlackBerry with both a touch screen and a slide-out keyboard.[62]

In 2013, the *Washington Post* reported that mobile internet use was expected to grow at a rate of 66 percent a year globally as an increased number of people connect more devices online. In fact, the number of online devices in the world was expected to exceed the number of people on earth. (You wondering when the computers are going to take over? They already outnumber us.)[63] In addition to outnumbering people, mobile devices have outnumbered traditional personal computers since 2012.[64]

With the prevalence of mobile media, going online is not something we do; it's something we are. In the days of AOL and dial-up internet, going online involved planning for internet use at a specific time and space. With the coming of broadband access, you could go online as much as you wanted, but you were still tethered to a space. But with mobile internet, the online world is where we live. It goes with us everywhere. We have moved to a world where, instead of deliberately going online, we need to deliberately go offline.

Another way to get a feel for the growing impact of mobile media is to look at the size of the audience for various channels. Those that allow people to express themselves publicly through their mobile devices have much bigger audiences than those that call for passive consumption. So, Facebook has 2.5 billion active monthly users, YouTube has 2 billion, and the 2019 Super Bowl (on television) had an audience of 98.2 million. Think about it—the Super Bowl has less than 4 percent of the audience size of Facebook.[65]

If you look outside the United States, the use of mobile media becomes even more significant. Among refugees from Syria and elsewhere in the Middle East, mobile media are the only media people have access to. During the Arab Spring movement in Egypt in 2011, much of the news coming out of the country was by way of mobile phones.[66]

Computers and laptops are still important tools for going online, but with the growing power, size, and availability of mobile devices, we can now think of online being everywhere/all the time.

SECRET 7: There Is No "They"

If you listen to media criticism for long, you will hear a pair of words used over and over again: *they* and *them*. It is easy to take potshots at some anonymous bogeymen—they—who embody all evil. I even engaged in it at the beginning of this section with the title "The Seven Secrets About the Media 'They' Don't Want You to Know 2.0."

So, who are they? No one. Everyone. A nonspecific other we want to blame. Anytime I used *they* in a news story, my high school journalism teacher would ask who "they" were. And that's what you need to ask whenever you hear criticism of the media. It is not that the criticism is not accurate. It very well may be. But it probably applies to a specific media outlet, a specific journalist, a certain song, or a particular movie. But *we* can make few generalizations about an industry so diverse that it includes everything from a giant corporation spending a reported $1 billion to produce *Avengers: Infinity War* and *Avengers: Endgame* to young people posting photos and messages on Snapchat.[67] There are a lot of media out there, but no unified *them*.

CHAPTER REVIEW

CHAPTER SUMMARY ▶▶

Communication takes place at several levels, including intrapersonal (within the self), interpersonal (between individuals), group (between three or more individuals), and mass (between a single sender and a large audience). Mass communication is a process that covers an entire society, in which an individual or institution uses technology to send messages to large, mixed audiences, most of whose members are not known to the sender. Communication is an interactive process and rarely takes place at just a single level.

The rapid growth of the mass media has led the public and critics to raise questions about the effects various media might have on both society and individuals. Researchers have suggested that the best way to control the impact of the media in our lives is to develop high levels of media literacy—an understanding of what the media are, how they operate, what messages they are delivering, what roles they play in society, and how audience members respond to these messages. Media literacy includes cognitive, emotional, aesthetic, and moral dimensions. Developing media literacy requires active work on a range of skills over a person's lifetime. These include acquiring the fundamentals of communication, acquiring language, acquiring an understanding of narrative, developing skepticism, intensive development, experiential exploring, critical appreciation, and social responsibility.

Mass communication can be examined in terms of the process of transmission; the rituals surrounding its consumption; the attention its messages draw to persons, groups, or concepts; or how audience members create meaning out of media content.

The first communication network was developed by the Roman Catholic Church, which could send messages reliably throughout Europe as early as the twelfth century. In the mid-fifteenth century, the development of printing made it possible for books and other publications to be mass produced for the first time, leading to numerous cultural changes. Books, magazines, newspapers, and other printed media forms became readily available, although they were expensive before steam-driven printing presses became common in the nineteenth century.

The electronic media emerged in the mid-nineteenth century with the invention of the telegraph, followed by recorded music, radio, movies, and television. These media allowed popular culture to be produced commercially and to be delivered easily and inexpensively into people's homes. The first interactive digital communication network, the internet, was developed starting in the late 1960s but wasn't available to the general public until the 1990s. Online media added a return channel to the mass communication process, initiating a much higher level of audience feedback. Online media also allowed individuals to disseminate their own ideas and information without the costs of a traditional mass medium.

Your text suggests that the following seven principles can guide your understanding of how the media operate: (1) The media are essential components of our lives, (2) there are no mainstream media, (3) everything from the margin moves to the center, (4) nothing is new—everything that happened in the past will happen again, (5) all media are social, (6) online media are mobile media, and (7) there is no "they."

KEY TERMS ▶▶

legacy media   4

communication   4

intrapersonal communication   5

interpersonal communication   5

group communication   6

mass communication   6

media literacy   8

mass media   10

Sender Message Channel Receiver (SMCR) or transmission model   11

sender   11

message   11

encoding   11

channel   11

receiver   11

decoding   11

noise   11

ritual model   12

publicity model   12

reception model   13

REVIEW QUESTIONS ▶▶

1. How did the spread of the COVID-19 pandemic affect how and where we consume mass media?

2. What are the four different levels of communication? Explain how many of our interactions with mass communication involve several levels of communication.

3. What are the elements that make mass communication mass? Would you consider social media like Facebook to be mass communication? Why or why not?

4. Some people compare the development of the internet to the invention of moveable type and the printing press. Do you think they are of comparable importance? Why or why not?

5. List two of the Seven Secrets and provide a current example of each from the news.

CHAPTER 2

MASS COMMUNICATION EFFECTS

How Society and Media Interact

During 2017, attention to the issue of sexual harassment and abuse, both sensational and serious, became the major cultural story for our media. As Secret 3 points out, the stories moved this issue from the margins of society to the center. While there are many points on the timeline we could highlight as the start of the media's focus on sexual harassment and abuse, there is no doubt that it exploded when multitudes of women started coming forward and telling their stories of mistreatment at the hands of Hollywood producer Harvey Weinstein.

On October 8, 2017, following the news that he had paid financial settlements to eight women to drop their claims, The Weinstein Company fired Weinstein from the movie production company he helped found. And while this may have been the point where most people started paying attention to the story, it certainly was not the beginning. According to the *New York Times*, the accusations and rumors about Weinstein dated back for three decades. It was not as though these stories weren't known about by reporters; they simply weren't reported.[1]

In November 2017, the *New York Times* started keeping track of the number of men who have been fired or forced to resign over accusations of sexual misconduct since Weinstein was fired.[2] As of February 8, 2018, the *Times* count had reached seventy-one. The paper also had a second list of twenty-eight men who had faced charges of sexual misconduct but who had only been suspended or received similar lesser punishment. The list was a who's who of the powerful behind and in front of the scenes in the entertainment business, industry, and politics. Among them were former *Today Show* host Matt Lauer and CBS CEO Les Moonves.[3,4]

So, this leaves us with a question:

Why, after years of neglect, did the press, in all its varied forms, suddenly start paying attention to these accusations and the women making them?

While the story of women being sexually harassed and abused by powerful men had been slowly breaking further into the media for several years, the real explosion came when actress Ashley Judd went public with her story from two decades earlier.

Judd told the *New York Times* in early October 2017 that she went to what she thought was a breakfast meeting at a hotel. She was instead sent up to Weinstein's room where he greeted her wearing a bathrobe and suggested either he give her a massage or she "watch him shower."[5]

It is at this point that we see the basic elements of the narrative coming through. Judd had to figure out how to get out of the room without alienating one of the most powerful producers in Hollywood.

The *Times* goes on to report that Weinstein reached "at least eight settlements with women," paying them to drop their claims and keep their silence. When all of these stories started surfacing, Weinstein said in a statement to the *Times*,

I appreciate the way I've behaved with colleagues in the past has caused a lot of pain, and I sincerely apologize for it. Though I'm trying to do better, I know I have a long way to go.[6]

Judd had previously talked about what had happened with Weinstein back in 2015 with *Variety* magazine, but she didn't name him.

Judd told *Variety* she felt bad because she didn't do anything about it at the time:

I beat myself up for a while. This is another part of the process. We internalize the shame. It really belongs to the person who is the aggressor. And so later, when I was able to see what happened, I thought: Oh god, that's wrong. That's sexual harassment. That's illegal. I was really hard on myself because I didn't get out of it by saying, "OK motherf—er, I'm calling the police."[7]

After studying this chapter, you will be able to

1. Discuss the history and development of our understanding of media effects

2. Identify and describe four types of effects the mass media can have on people

3. List and describe Lasswell's three major social functions the media perform

4. Explain the three steps Alfred Bandura created to engage in social learning

5. Describe how the critical/cultural approach takes a more qualitative examination of who controls media systems

The common theme between Judd and the other women who say Weinstein abused or harassed them was that women did not speak out because they didn't know each other; they didn't live in the same cities. But while they did not talk about it publicly, they did talk about it among themselves.

So, what kept these women's stories from getting published?

Many of the women were embarrassed that this had happened to them and sometimes wondered whether they were responsible for it.

They still wanted to work where they worked. They wanted the access the abuser gave them.

They were afraid they would get blacklisted in some form if they spoke out (something that happened with several of Weinstein's victims).

They were afraid they would not be believed.

As of this writing, Harvey Weinstein has been found guilty in New York City of two felony sex crimes but acquitted of charges that he is a sexual predator.[8] He is also facing charges in Los Angeles for rape and assault.[9]

In this chapter, we will look at various explanations of how the mass media interact with and affect audience members. We will return to the story of Harvey Weinstein and the explosion of stories about abuse by powerful men to look for explanations. It will not so much be a question of which of these explanations is correct as it will be one of what kind of understanding the theories give us. In this chapter, we look at how our understanding of media and their effects has evolved over the past century and consider several approaches to studying these effects.

The Evolution of Media Effects Research

As we discussed in Chapter 1 in the section on media literacy, media consumers often assume that the media have large, obvious, and generally negative effects on people, and they look to blame the media for complex social problems.[10] In this section, we look at media effects research and how this research has evolved over the past two hundred years.

Prior to the 1800s, most people in Europe and North America lived in rural communities where their neighbors were likely to be similar in ethnic, racial, and religious background. People knew their neighbors, and their neighbors knew them. There were only limited opportunities for people to change their station in life or to learn much about the outside world. But with the rise of the Industrial Revolution in the nineteenth century, we started to see massive migration from the rural areas into the cities and from various countries to the United States. As people moved into the cities, they started working for wages in factories with people who were quite different from them. With industrialization, people went from small, close-knit communities where they knew everyone to a mass society where they learned about the world from mass media sources, such as the new inexpensive newspapers, magazines, and paperback novels.[11]

At the end of the nineteenth century, people came to believe that the traditional ties of church, community, and family were breaking down and losing their power to influence people. The comfortable local community was being replaced by something impersonal, complex, and removed from the traditions that had previously held people together; people felt that their community was being replaced by a mysterious "they" or "them." Concerned observers noted that people seemed to be alienated, isolated, and interchangeable members of a faceless mass audience, separated by the decline of the family and the growth of technology. So, what held this new mass society together?[12] The increasingly frequent answer was that the mass media were replacing the church, family, and community in shaping public opinion.[13] This is an example of Secret 7—There is no "they." (For additional discussion of the growth of the mass media from its origins in the 1400s to the present day, see Chapter 1.)

Fears that media messages would have strong, direct effects on audience members grew out of propaganda efforts by all combatants during World War I and by Nazi Germany and Fascist Italy in the 1930s. Critics worried that mass media messages would overwhelm people in the absence of the influences of family and community. With traditional social forces in decline, it was inevitable, critics feared, that the media would become the most powerful force within society.

This argument viewed audience members as passive targets who would be hit or injected with the message, which, like a vaccine, would affect most people in similar ways. But research looking for powerful, direct effects leading to opinion and behavioral changes generally came up short. In fact, in the 1940s and 1950s, researchers sometimes doubted whether media messages had any effect on individuals at all.[14] Although most scholars now focus on the media's indirect effects on society rather than their direct effects on individuals, they remain concerned about how the media influence individuals.

The big problem is that the direct effects approach viewed media messages as a stimulus that would lead to a predictable attitudinal or behavioral response with nothing intervening between sender and audience. But although people have a shared biological heritage, they have different backgrounds, needs, attitudes, and values. In short, everyone has been socialized differently.

Beat back the HUN with LIBERTY BONDS

Library of Congress

▲ Allied propaganda posters designed to build support for World War I weren't afraid to make use of strong negative stereotypes of the Germans.

The Limited Effects Model

The research conducted on the effects of media, up to and during World War II, showed that there were not dramatic, predictable, or consistent effects of media messages on the public, and research began to focus on more limited and indirect effects of these messages. The indirect effects approach reviews the effects that messages have on individuals, but it accounts for how audience members perceive and interpret these messages selectively according to personal differences. Because people's perceptions are selective, their responses to the messages vary as well. For example, a person who is preparing to buy a car, a person who just bought a car, and a person who does not drive will each react differently to an automobile commercial.

The Payne Fund Studies. Researchers soon found an excellent source for studying the effects of media on the population in the form of a major new cultural institution—the movies. As movies grew in popularity in the 1920s, people became concerned about their effects on viewers, especially young people. The film industry claimed that movies do not shape society; they just reflect it. But that argument ignored the fact that movies were a central part of society; even mirrors have effects. Movie historian Gerald Mast notes that "movies have . . . been an immensely powerful social and cultural force. . . . They have produced social changes—in ways of dress, patterns of speech, methods of courting. And they have mirrored social changes—in fashion, sexual mores, political principles."[15]

Researchers often use examples from the movies to demonstrate the purported effects that movies have on society. An example of how a movie can have a significant effect on society is the 2004 science fiction disaster feature *The Day After Tomorrow*. The movie's plot centers around two climate scientists who discover that earth is experiencing accelerating climate change and are trying to warn the public about the potential devastating effects of global warming. As the movie progresses, several (scientifically implausible) storms arise around the globe causing catastrophic floods, hail, and snowstorms proving the scientists' warnings. After several adventure and disaster sequences, the movie ends with a view from space showing the earth covered in icecaps.

Percent of watchers and nonwatchers who found each item *somewhat* or *very likely*.

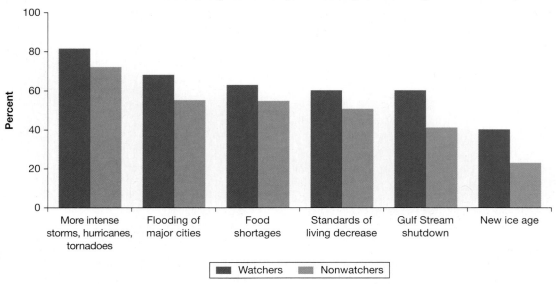

"In the United States, how likely do you think it is that each of the following will occur during the next 50 years due to global warming?"

Source: Anthony A. Leiserowitz (2004) Day After Tomorrow: Study of Climate Change Risk Perception, Environment: Science and Policy for Sustainable Development, 46:9, 22–39, DOI: 10.1080/00139150409603663

Note: Nonwatchers weighted (*n* = 390), watchers weighted (*n* = 139).

Even though the movie exaggerates the size of the storms and their devastation, the message it portrays is familiar to many of us; that increased awareness of climate change is essential to saving the planet. And those who watched it were apparently moved to act on that message. For example, researchers at Yale showed that after participants saw the movie, they appeared to be more thoughtful about the environment and began to consider how their own actions could help prevent a catastrophe, such as the one depicted. The researchers consistently found that the movie had a strong influence on all the participants they studied, and that after watching the movie, these participants better understood the risks of global warming.[16]

The Payne Fund, a private foundation studying the effects of media on the public, sponsored a series of thirteen studies, several of which analyzed the content of movies, who was going to the movies, and what, if any, effects the movies were having on the audiences. The researchers found that a small number of basic themes continuously appeared in movies: crime, sex, love, mystery, war, children, history, travel, comedy, and social propaganda. Of these themes, more than three-fourths of all movies dealt with crime, sex, or love.

A second major finding by the Payne Fund was that people could remember a surprising amount of what they had seen in movies, even six months after seeing them. Why such a high level of recall? Perhaps it was because movies were novel at the time, but another explanation was that movies gave people something to talk about, thus stimulating recall.

Some critics had suggested that movies might be responsible for moral decay, and one of the studies looked at whether the morals portrayed in movies were at odds with those of the viewing public. Not surprisingly, the moral standards of characters in movies tended to be lower than those of viewers. After all, people who behave differently from us are the most interesting to watch.

Herbert Blumer, a noted social psychologist, conducted a major study that examined the diaries of young people who recorded how they thought they had been influenced by movies. He found that participants reported imitating the behaviors they saw in movies and copying the actions of their favorite stars in their games and play. Young people reported that they saw movies as a source of ideas about action, romance, and standards of beauty. They were using the movies to learn how to behave as an adult.[17] In short, Blumer was looking at how social interaction shaped young people's reaction to the movies, thus demonstrating Secret 5—All media are social.

The People's Choice. In addition to worrying about how movies were affecting young people, critics also feared that political media campaigns would "inject" people with ideas that would lead to the message creator's desired actions, such as supporting a particular candidate, ideology, or point of view. This model of powerful direct campaign effects was largely discredited by voter studies in the 1940s and 1950s, but it remains important because many people still believe that it is accurate.[18]

One of the first large-scale social-scientific studies of campaign influences was *The People's Choice*, a study of the 1940 U.S. presidential election contest between Democrat Franklin D. Roosevelt and Republican Wendell Willkie. A team of researchers led by Paul Lazarsfeld looked at how voters in Erie County, Ohio, decided which candidate to vote for. Lazarsfeld's team found that people who were highly interested in the campaign and paid the most attention to media coverage of it were the least likely to be influenced by the campaign. Why? Because they had decided whom they supported before the campaign had even begun.[19]

In contrast, voters who decided at the last minute usually turned to friends or neighbors, rather than the media, for information about the campaign. In general, they turned to people who followed the campaign closely, the ones whom Lazarsfeld called opinion leaders. **Opinion leaders** are influential community members—friends, family members, and coworkers—who spend significant time with the media. Lazarsfeld suggested that information flows from the media to opinion leaders, and then from opinion leaders to the rest of the public. Keep in mind that the opinion leaders are ordinary people who are simply interested and involved in a topic. Although this finding was not expected, it should not be surprising that interpersonal influence is more important than the media. The idea here is simple: People in groups tend to share opinions with one another, and when they want reliable information, they go to the people they know. This serves to illustrate Secret 5—All media are social. Even decades before so-called social media (like Facebook and Twitter) existed, people were still drawn to talk about the news at length.

With the lengthy campaigns today, people find it easier to turn to interpersonal sources than the wealth of media information. Yet this trend is nothing new. Although many people believe that our election campaigns are starting earlier and earlier every election cycle, presidential candidate William Jennings Bryan started his campaign for the 1900 election one month after the election of 1896![20] Even as early as the 1830s, when the penny press was just getting started, presidential campaigns could run as long as two years.

The People's Choice, as well as other early voter studies, found that campaigns typically reinforced existing political predispositions and that few people changed their minds about whom they were going to support. There are several reasons for this:

- The voters who start off with strong opinions are unlikely to change them.

- The voters who pay the most attention to a campaign are those with the strongest political views; thus, they are the least likely to change their opinions.

- The most persuadable voters (those who are least informed) are not likely to pay attention to political communication and therefore are not strongly influenced by media coverage of the campaign.[21]

The Two-Step Flow Today. The two-step flow of information process described by Lazarsfeld and his colleagues back in the 1940s continues to be relevant in the age of twenty-first century social media influencers. A study of opinion leaders on the Chinese microblogging site Weibo (essentially an equivalent of Twitter) found no evidence of massive persuasive effects of the messages from opinion leaders, but that these messages did reinforce people's subjective attitudes and opinions.[22] A study out of South Korea found that messages from opinion leaders were more likely to get shared than those of non-opinion leaders.[23]

The Importance of Meaning. The approaches to studying mass communication that we have looked at fall under the transmission model discussed back in Chapter 1. As media scholar James Carey wrote, the transmission model "is defined by terms such as 'imparting,' 'sending,' 'transmitting,' or 'giving information to others.'"[24] These explanations view mass communication as an extension of transportation; and indeed, before electronic media, the fastest form of transportation was also the fastest form of communication.

The transmission model focuses on the sending of messages with fixed meanings rather than on how we interact with them. Explanations that focus on the importance of meaning, on the other hand, look at who gets to decide what the messages will be, how we interact with these messages, and how we negotiate meanings for these messages. When we look at the ritual model of communication (again, looking back to Chapter 1) we think about how we use messages to interact with those around us, where the interaction is the key concept rather than the message itself.

The reception model, for example, looks at how meaning is derived and created from the message rather than treating the message within a fixed content that everyone accepts as being correct.[25]

Effects of Media in Our Lives

Media scholars throughout the twentieth century who studied the effects of the mass media on individuals and society questioned several aspects of the media, including the messages being sent, the media sending them, the owners of the media, and the audience members themselves.[26] Some of the major effects studied were as follows:

- Message Effects—How media messages might change behaviors, attitudes, or beliefs

- Attitudinal Effects—Changes in feelings about a product, an individual, or an idea based on media content

- Behavioral Effects—Media content can influence buying a product, making a phone call, and voting for a candidate

- Psychological Effects—Media content can inspire fear, joy, revulsion, happiness, or amusement, among other feelings

- Medium Effects—The particular medium being used to transmit messages

- Ownership Effects—The influence of those who own and control the media

- Active Audience Effects—Unique members who respond as individuals, not as undifferentiated members of a mass

Message Effects

Not surprisingly, the earliest concerns about the effects of mass communication focused on how messages might change people's behaviors, attitudes, or beliefs. These message effects can take a variety of forms. The types of these effects have been broken down into categories such as cognitive, attitudinal, behavioral, and psychological.

The most common and observable message effect is on the short-term learning of information. This can be as significant as learning about a new medical treatment or as trivial as remembering the lyrics to a popular song. The amount of learning that takes place from media content depends largely on the motivation level of the person consuming the media.

Political scientist Doris Graber found that people who want to be able to talk intelligently with others about media content (whether it be the news, a sporting event, or an entertainment program) learn much more from the media than people who are simply seeking entertainment. This is one more example of Secret 5—All media are social. Remember, you do not need to be using Facebook or Twitter to make media social. Research also shows that people learn more from people they identify with and pay more attention to political commentators they agree with than ones they dislike.[27] Hence the most popular political radio talk shows, such as those hosted by conservatives Rush Limbaugh and Sean Hannity, argue a single and consistent point of view rather than providing a range of views.[28]

Attitudinal Effects

People can develop attitudinal effects—feelings about a product, an individual, or an idea—based on media content. Viewers might decide that they like a new product, political candidate, or hairstyle because of what they have seen in a television commercial, a news broadcast, or a sitcom. Typically, it is much easier to get people to form new opinions than to get them to change existing ones.[29] For example, political advertising generally tries to change the opinions of uncommitted voters rather than those of voters who already have strong political loyalties. In the 2016 presidential election cycle, the Bernie Sanders campaign found substantial success by targeting young, uncommitted voters who value being asked directly for their support.[30]

▲ The youth vote's biggest beneficiary has been Bernie Sanders, who won 80 percent of the youth vote in Iowa and Nevada. The candidate was the internet's darling, dominating the competition on Facebook, Tumblr, Instagram, and Twitter.

Behavioral Effects

Behavioral effects include actions such as clipping a coupon from a newspaper, buying a product, making a phone call, and voting for a candidate. They might also include imitating attractive behaviors (for example, dressing a certain way). Behavioral effects are in many ways the most difficult to achieve because people are reluctant to change their behavior. Sometimes, however, people go to the media deliberately looking for behavior to copy, as when a child watches an episode of *Batman* and then imitates it in play, or when a teenager watches a movie to learn how to behave on a date.[31]

Psychological Effects

Media content can inspire fear, joy, revulsion, happiness, or amusement, among other feelings.[32] A major psychological effect of media content, especially violent or erotic material, is arousal. Symptoms of arousal can include a rise in heart rate, adrenaline levels, or sexual response. Seeking a psychological response is a common reason for spending time with the media, whether the response sought is relaxation, excitement, or emotional release. Arousal can come from content (action, violence, sexuality, loud music or sound) and from style (motion, use of color, the rate and speed at which new images appear). Notice that music videos, which often offer little in terms of learning, provide many of these elements.[33]

▲ Canadian media scholar Marshall McLuhan, right, is best remembered for his statement "The medium is the message." He became such a pop-culture figure in the 1970s that he had a cameo playing himself in the film Annie Hall.

Legendary film composer John Williams is known for his sweeping, emotionally memorable scores for movies like the Indiana Jones series, the Jurassic Park series, and even Kobe Bryant's Academy Award–winning animated short *Dear Basketball*. But he is undoubtedly best known for his scores for the nine core Star Wars films. From the opening fanfare played over the crawling text, to the menacing "The Imperial March (Darth Vader's Theme)," to the love theme for Han Solo and Princess Leia, these melodies are instantly recognized cultural icons. They also are a key part of how the Star Wars movies are capable of so blatantly manipulating our feelings.

Alex Ross, music critic for the *New Yorker*, writes that Williams manipulated the audience in *Episode VII: The Force Awakens* by composing vaguely menacing music for Luke Skywalker to make the audience question whether the Jedi hero has gone over to the dark side. "The new film tells us otherwise," Ross says, "but shadowy chords surround the exiled hero for much of the film, leaving us in suspense as to his intentions."[34]

Medium Effects

As mass media consumption grew in the 1950s, scholars also started paying more attention to the particular medium being used to transmit messages. Until the 1950s, most media effects research focused on the interactions among the sender, the message, and the receiver, ignoring the influence of the medium itself. But the medium used to communicate is crucial. Canadian communication researcher Marshall McLuhan argued that the medium used for transmission can be as important as the message itself, if not more so. McLuhan is best known for his statement "The medium is the message," by which he meant that the method of message transmittal is a central part of the message. For example, television does an excellent job of transmitting emotional messages because it includes both visual (explosions, luxury interiors) and audio (laugh tracks, scary music) cues along with words. And consider technology that enhances the sound of movies: Surround sound systems are designed to create a realistic experience by surrounding viewers with five distinct sound channels, as well as shaking them with a deep bass channel. The goal is not to transmit the message better, but to create a more overwhelming experience. (Think of how the impact of a summer blockbuster film would be diminished if the sound were turned down.) The same is true of large-screen high-definition television sets. Books and newspapers, in contrast, are much better at transmitting complex rational information because these media allow us to review the information and consider its meaning at our own pace.[35] The web excels at providing obscure materials that appeal to a limited, widely dispersed audience, and it makes it easy for receivers to respond to what they've seen or heard. Media scholars now recognize that communication technology is a fundamental element of society and that new technologies can lead to social change.[36] As Secret 1 points out, the media are essential components of our lives.

Media sociologist Joshua Meyrowitz, for example, argues that the existence and development of various media can lead to radical changes in society. He writes that the development of publishing and books in the sixteenth century made it easy for new ideas to spread beyond the person who originated them and that this tended to undermine the control of ideas by both the monarchy and the Roman Catholic Church.[37]

As can be seen by the Edward Snowden story discussed in this chapter's "Media Transformation," the existence of digital documents, encrypted email, and high-capacity thumb drives now allows a small group of technically skilled individuals to spread news and documents around the world, with governments powerless to stop them. Meyrowitz also identifies some social effects of particular media. In *No Sense of Place*, he argues that the major effect of print as a medium is to segregate audiences according to education, age, class, and gender. For example, a teenager needs to be able to read at a certain level to understand the content of a magazine targeted at young women or young men—content that a young child would be unable to comprehend. In contrast, electronic media such as television tend to cross the demographic boundaries. A child too young to read a magazine or book can still understand at least some of the information in a television program targeted at adults.[38] This is why parent groups and childhood educators push to have early-evening programming on television contain more "family-friendly" programs and why parents seek to restrict certain sites and apps on a child's smartphone or tablet.

Ownership Effects

Instead of looking at the effects of media and their messages, some scholars examine the influence of those who own and control the media.[39] These critical scholars are concerned because owners of media determine which ideas will be produced and distributed by those media.

In the United States, media outlets are mostly owned by a few multinational conglomerates and newly formed media companies, such as Disney, News Corporation/Fox Corporation, WarnerMedia, ViacomCBS, Bertelsmann, Comcast/NBCUniversal, Google, and Apple. Some observers, such as German academic and sociologist Jürgen Habermas, fear that these corporations are becoming a sort of ruling class, controlling which books are published, which programs are aired, which movies are produced, and which news stories are written.[40] As we discuss in Chapters 3 and 11, Disney, News Corporation, Google, and Apple have all had to compromise at times with the Chinese government in order to keep doing business in China. For example, Google had to agree to censor its search results about sensitive topics in China for the company to be allowed to operate there.[41]

Media critic and former newspaper editor Ben Bagdikian suggests that the influence of media owners can be seen in how the news media select stories to be covered. He argues that large media organizations will kill news stories and entertainment programs that don't reflect well on the corporation. The roots of this tendency go back to when captains of industry such as J. P. Morgan and the Rockefellers bought out magazines that criticized them to silence that criticism. What we end up with, Bagdikian says, is not the feared bogeyman of government censorship, but rather "a new Private Ministry of Information and Culture" that gives corporations control over what we will see, hear, or read.[42] Increasingly, however, the new alternative media are providing channels that allow consumers to bypass Big Media controls.[43] (See the section on long-tail media in Chapter 3 for more on how these new channels are enabling anyone who wants to distribute content to do so on a large scale.) Websites such as Brietbart or Daily Kos give voice to issues from a partisan point of view with no controls at all other than those the authors choose to employ. There are also data-driven, online news sources like Nate Silver's FiveThirtyEight that have an underlying political point of view but nevertheless are committed to honest reporting backed up by hard, supporting data.

Active Audience Effects

Some of the early fears about the effects of the media on audience members arose from the belief that the audience truly was a faceless, undifferentiated mass—that the characteristics of the audience en masse also applied to the audience's individual members. Early critics viewed modern people as alienated and isolated individuals who, separated by the decline of the family and the growth of a technological society, did not communicate with one another. After World War II, the concept of the mass audience began to change as scholars came to realize that the audience was made up of unique members who responded as individuals, not as undifferentiated members of a mass.[44]

Today, communicators, marketers, and scholars realize that individuals seek and respond to different messages at different times and for different reasons. Therefore, they divide audiences on the basis of **geographics**, or where people live; **demographics**, or their gender, race, ethnic background, income, education, age, educational attainment, and the like; or **psychographics**, a combination of demographics, lifestyle characteristics, and product usage. Hence, a young woman buying a small SUV to take her mountain bike out into the mountains will respond to a very different kind of advertising message than a mother seeking a small SUV so that she can safely drive her child to school during rush hour in the winter.

Audiences can also be classified by the amount of time they spend using media or by the purposes for which they use media. Each segment of the media audience will behave differently.

Take television viewing as an example. Some people tune in daily to watch their favorite soap opera or talk show and will not change the channel for the entire hour. This is known as appointment viewing. Others surf through several channels using the remote control, looking for something that will capture their interest. Still others switch back and forth between two channels.

With regard to television, the concept of a mass audience consuming the same content at the same time existed to some extent from the 1950s to the 1970s when the vast majority of viewers had access to only three broadcast networks, but that concept broke down completely with the advent of cable, satellite, multiple broadcast networks, TiVo, DVDs, and VCRs. This is an example of Secret 7—There is no "they."

In addition to recognizing that different people use the media in different ways, scholars have realized that mass communication messages are generally mediated through other levels of communication. One reason this book discusses intrapersonal, interpersonal, and group communication in addition to mass communication is that these levels all come into play in how mass communication operates. People discuss political news with one another, cheer together for their favorite teams while watching a hockey game on television, and think about how stock market information is going to affect their investment plans. A young man's reaction to a love scene in a movie will differ depending on if he watches it with a group of friends, with his sweetie, or with his parents.[45]

Media and Society

Much like most scientific research, mass communication research depends, in large part, on theory and the questions posed by these theories. It is helpful to understand these theoretical approaches and how the effects of the media are not limited to those on individuals or groups.

Researchers know that some of the media's most significant messages can have an effect on our major social functions. According to media scholar Harold Lasswell, the mass media are simply "an extension of basic functions that society has always needed. Earlier societies had priests, town criers, storytellers, bards who sang ballads, and travelers who brought news from distant lands."[46]

Researchers also know that communication can be functional or dysfunctional but, in either case, it operates within the social system.[47] For example, some people respond inappropriately to the news of approaching danger. Instead of going to the basement during a tornado warning, a functional response, they go outside with their video cameras to get footage of the storm, a dysfunctional response. In both cases, they are responding to the news of the storm.

Lasswell wrote that the media perform three major social functions:

1. Surveillance of the environment, looking for both threats and opportunities

2. Correlation of different elements of society, allowing segments of society to work together

3. Transmission of culture from one generation to the next[48]

Media sociologist Charles Wright adds a fourth—the function of entertainment—to the above list.[49]

Surveillance of the Environment

Much of what we know about the world we learn from the media through the process of **surveillance**. The media show us what is happening not only within our own culture, but in other societies as well. Our only other sources of knowledge about the world are our own direct experiences and the direct experiences that others share with us. For example, people who live in the Middle East learn much of what they know about the outside world through their use of social media and direct messaging software like WhatsApp, which allow them to bypass much of the local censorship that limits legacy media.[50]

The constant flow of information from the media allows us to survey our surroundings. It can give us warnings of approaching danger—everything from changes in the weather to earthquakes to violence in the streets. This flow of information is essential for the everyday operation of society. The stock markets depend on the business news, travelers depend on weather forecasts, and grocery shoppers depend on knowing what is on special this week.

Surveillance can also serve to undermine society. For example, when people in poor nations see media images of what life is like in the United States and other industrialized Western nations, they may become dissatisfied with the conditions of their own lives, and this may lead to social unrest and violence. News about violence may also make people more fearful for their own safety.

Surveillance is not just for the masses. Government and industry leaders worldwide watch CNN or C-SPAN or read the *New York Times* or *Financial Times* to know what other government leaders are saying and thinking.

News can also give status to individuals. Because media coverage exposes them to large audiences, they seem important. This process is known as **status conferral**. In a rather extreme example, Omarosa Manigault Newman initially became famous after being a villainous character/competitor on the first season of Donald Trump's *The Apprentice* reality TV series back in 2004. After becoming a celebrity through being on the show, she went on to be featured on a range of television shows primarily designed to feature people who had become prominent on reality TV. Then, in a strange twist of fate, Manigualt Newman became President Trump's director of communications for the White House Office of Public Liaison. After getting fired from the White House, she went on to star on the CBS series *Celebrity Big Brother*.[51] Thus Manigualt Newman became a television celebrity and a national political figure, and then used that status to return to reality TV.

CBS Photo Archive/Getty Images

▲ A striking example of status conferral, Omarosa Manigault Newman came into the public eye in 2004 as a contestant on Donald Trump's reality TV show *The Apprentice*. She later became a director of communications in Trump's White House, serving there for several months until she left and returned to reality television as a contestant on *Celebrity Big Brother* in 2018.

Correlation of Different Elements of Society

Correlation is the selection, evaluation, and interpretation of events to impose structure on the news. Correlation is accomplished by persuasive communication through editorials, commentary, advertising, and propaganda. Through media-supplied correlation, we make sense out of what we learn through surveillance. It puts news into categories and provides cues that indicate the importance of each news item. Does it appear on the front page of the newspaper? Is it the first item on the broadcast? Is there a teaser on the magazine cover promoting the story?

Although many people say that they would prefer just the facts, virtually the only news outlet that provides no interpretation of events is the public affairs network C-SPAN, which has rigid rules governing how every event is covered. Far more viewers choose to go to the broadcast networks or cable news channels, which provide some interpretation, rather than watch the relatively dry, "just the facts" C-SPAN.[52]

It is often difficult to distinguish between communication that is informative and communication that is persuasive. Editorial judgments are always being made as to which stories should be covered and which should be omitted, which picture of a politician should be published, or what kind of headline should be written. Thus, it is useful to view surveillance and correlation as two functions that can be shared by a message.

Socialization and Transmission of Culture

Socialization is the process of integrating people within society through the transmission of values, social norms, and knowledge to new members of the group.

It is through the media, as well as through our friends, family, school, and church, that we learn the values of our society. Socialization is important not only to young people as they are growing up but also to immigrants learning about and assimilating into their new country, high school students heading off to college, and new graduates going to work.[53] Here is another example of Secret 1—The media are essential components of our lives.

The media provide socialization in a variety of ways:

- Through role models in entertainment programming

- Through goals and desires as presented in media content

- Through the citizenship values portrayed in the news

- Through advertisements for products that may be useful to us in different stages of our lives

Entertainment. **Entertainment** is communication designed primarily to amuse, even if it serves other functions as well, which it almost always does. A television medical drama would be considered entertainment, even though it might educate a person about life in a hospital or the symptoms of a major illness. In fact, a major characteristic of all television programming, including entertainment programming, is to let people know what life outside their own world is like.[54]

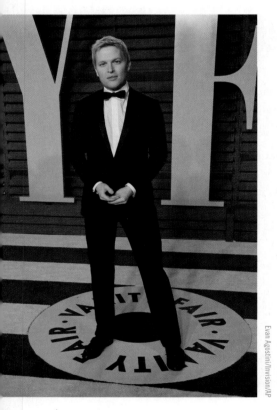

▲ Journalist Ronan Farrow shared a Pulitzer Prize for Public Service in 2018 for his reporting on the allegations of sexual assault brought against Harvey Weinstein. The attention that his and others' reporting brought to the issue helped put the #MeToo movement on the national agenda.

Evan Agostini/Invision/AP

Agenda Setting. Although explanations of powerful direct effects did not hold up under research scrutiny, people still had a hard time accepting that the news media and political campaigns had little or no effect on the public. **Agenda-setting theory** provides an alternative explanation that does not minimize the influence of the media on society.[55] This theory holds that issues that are portrayed as important in the news media become important to the public—that is, the media set the agenda for public debate. If the media are not able to tell people what to think, as the direct effects model proposed, perhaps they can tell people what to think about. Agenda-setting theorists seek to determine whether the issues that are important to the media are also important to the public.[56]

The initial study of agenda setting was conducted in Chapel Hill, North Carolina, by Donald Shaw and Maxwell McCombs. The researchers found, among uncommitted voters in the 1968 presidential election, a strong relationship between the issues the press considered important and the issues the voters considered important. Since these voters had not already made up their minds about the upcoming election, their most likely source of cues, the researchers concluded, was the mass media. The study compared the content of the press and the attitudes of voters and found a strong correlation. Even though the researchers did not find evidence that the press persuaded people to change their opinions, they did find that the issues featured in the campaign and in the press were also the issues that voters felt were important.[57]

There are, however, some limits on the usefulness of the agenda-setting concept. If a story does not resonate with the public, neither the media nor the candidates will be able to make people care. For example, reports that Ronald and Nancy Reagan had conceived a child before they were married did not seem to do any damage to Reagan's image; nor was the Rev. Pat Robertson's campaign damaged by reports that the candidate and his wife had lied about the date of their wedding anniversary to hide the fact that their first child was conceived premaritally.

Our Interactions With Media

The media, by widening the information about the world that we are exposed to, play an important role in social learning. Students and young professionals have all been warned on numerous occasions to be careful what they post on social media. But media coverage of a public relations practitioner named Justine's social media self-destruction has likely helped a lot of folks avoid her mistake. Just before her twelve-hour flight took off from London for Cape Town, South Africa, Justine sent out a tweet that read, "Going to Africa. Hope I don't get AIDS. Just kidding. I'm white!"

Her tweet spawned an extended online firestorm under the hashtag #HasJustineLandedYet. Tweets ranged from mocking her insensitivity, to parody accounts, to expressions of offense and hurt. Once Justine did land, she learned she had been fired while she was in the air. Despite having only about five hundred followers at the time she took off, her tweet rapidly spread around the world. With a case like #HasJustineLandedYet, social media users can learn from the example of one woman without having to suffer all the consequences she did.[58]

At some point in your life, you have likely been told that experience is the best teacher. While experience may be a good teacher, it is also a harsh one, forcing us to suffer from our mistakes. Fortunately, we do not have to make all these mistakes ourselves, according to social psychologist Albert Bandura's **social learning theory**. Bandura is best known for conducting an experiment that had children observing an adult beating an inflatable (life-size) "Bobo" doll. In the experiment, only some of the children saw the adult being reprimanded for behaving so aggressively, while others saw the adult suffer no consequences for their behavior.

Bandura found that children who saw the adult "get away with" the aggressive behavior, were more likely to behave aggressively when they were left in a room alone with the Bobo doll than were those who saw the adult get reprimanded. In short, what Bandura found was that children based their behavior on what they had learned from observing adult behavior. Bandura writes, "If knowledge and skills could be acquired only by direct experience, the process of human development would be greatly retarded, not to mention exceedingly tedious and hazardous."[59] Instead, he says that we are able to learn by observing what others do and the consequences they face.

Bandura says humans go through three steps to engage in social learning:

1. We extract key information from situations we observe.

2. We integrate these observations to create rules about how the world operates.

3. We put these rules into practice to regulate our own behavior and predict the behaviors of others.

▲ In Albert Bandura's famous "Bobo" doll experiment, the social psychologist found that children who see adults "get away" with aggressive behavior were more likely to behave aggressively toward an inflatable life-size doll.

Uses and Gratifications Theory

Uses and gratifications theory turns the traditional way of looking at media effects on its head. Instead of looking at the audience as a sheep-like mass of receivers of messages, uses and gratifications theory views audience members as active receivers of information of their own choosing. Uses and gratifications theory is based on the following assumptions:

- Audience members are active receivers who have wants and needs. They then make decisions about media use based on those wants and needs. For example, in this approach, video games do not do things to children; children make use of video games.

- Media compete with many sources of gratification. I might watch television in the evening to relax. Television would be competing with reading a magazine, going for a walk, and playing with my son as alternative ways of relaxing.

- Audience members are aware of these choices and make them consciously.

- Our judgments about the value of various media uses must come from the audience's perspective.[60]

The idea behind uses and gratifications theory is that individuals are constantly seeking gratifications, and the media compete to provide them. Media scholar Arthur Asa Berger says that among the gratifications that audience members might seek are to be amused, to experience the beautiful, to have shared experiences with others, to find models to imitate, and to believe in romantic love.[61] So someone who doesn't care about football might still watch a game on television and enjoy it because he wants to spend time with friends. Although he is consuming media, that is not the real point of his interaction with the television set.

Symbolic Interactionism

George Herbert Mead wrote back in 1934 that what holds us together as a culture is our common creation of society through our interactions based on language, or **symbolic interactionism**. We engage in symbolic interactions in which we continually attempt to arouse in others the feeling we have in ourselves by telling others how we feel.

▲ The panic many people think was inspired by Orson Welles made *War of the Worlds* perhaps the most notorious event in American broadcast history.

Ullstein Bild/Getty Images

If our language is understood, we are able to communicate; if, on the other hand, we do not share common meanings, we will not be understood.[62] The mass media are by far the biggest source of shared meanings in our world. This is an example of Secret 1—The media are essential components of our lives.

If you think back to our discussion of the meaning of the yellow ribbon in Chapter 1, you can see how this works. We start with an arbitrary symbol: the yellow ribbon. We assign it meaning and then propagate that meaning through portrayal through the media. Eventually, nearly everyone comes to have the same shared meaning of the looped ribbon, and the ribbon becomes a universal symbol of support—support for the troops, for disease sufferers, and for all kinds of social causes.

Sociologist W. I. Thomas provides us with one of the most quoted and understandable statements of symbolic interactionism: "If men define situations as real, they are real in their consequences."[63] If we ignore the outdated gender bias of the quote, there's a lot to analyze there. What Thomas is saying is that if people view a problem as being real, and behave as though a problem is real, it will have real consequences, even if the problem does not truly exist. Back in 1938, Orson Welles narrated a famous radio adaptation of H. G. Welles's *War of the Worlds*. The radio play was misinterpreted by some to be an actual news story, and there were many accounts at the time of people panicking and even committing suicide out of fear of the Martians invading New Jersey. Ever since then, broadcasters have been very careful to run extensive disclaimers on the air every time they run a *War of the Worlds*–style story, to make sure they don't panic their audience. There is also a widespread fear of powerful effects that the mass media can have on susceptible audience members. The only problem is that the research conducted at the time on the *War of the Worlds* panic was seriously flawed, and criticism of the research, which dates back to the 1940s, has largely been ignored, in part because the belief in the *War of the Worlds* effect is so strong. The truth is that there was far more perception of panic than actual panic at the time. In summary, it doesn't matter much now whether the panic took place. What matters is that people believe that it did.[64]

Cultivation Analysis

George Gerbner (1919–2005), the best-known researcher of television violence, did not believe televised violence has direct effects on people's behavior, but he was deeply concerned about its effect on society as a whole.[65] Gerbner developed an alternative to traditional message effects research called **cultivation analysis**. His argument was that watching large amounts of television cultivates a distinct view of the world that is sharply at odds with reality.[66]

Over the years, Gerbner and his colleagues analyzed thousands of network television programs for the themes they presented and the level of violence they included. In a series of studies beginning in 1967, Gerbner's team found high levels of violence on television. They defined violence as "the overt expression of force intended to hurt or kill."[67]

Network officials have been openly critical of Gerbner, saying that his studies weren't representative of television as a whole and that his definition of violence is not useful because it does not discriminate between the fantasy violence of a *Road Runner* cartoon and the more graphic gore of a *Saw* or *Hostel* movie.

Gerbner compared the rate of violence on television to the rate of it occurring in the real world. He concluded that television cultivates a view of the world that is much more violent than the world we live in. The nature of the violence is different as well, with most television violence occurring between strangers rather than between family members, as does real-life violence. Gerbner said that, because of this, people who watch a great deal of television perceive the world differently than do light viewers. Heavy television viewing cultivates a response that Gerbner calls the **mean world syndrome**.

Gerbner explained what he considered to be major misconceptions about the effects of televised violence and what his research suggested the real effects were. He argued that watching large amounts of television cultivates a distinct view of the world that is at odds with reality.

Gerbner argued that, because of televised violence, heavy television viewers are more likely to

- overestimate their chances of experiencing violence.

- believe that their neighborhoods are unsafe.

- state that fear of crime is a very serious personal problem.

- assume that the crime rate is rising, regardless of the actual crime rate.[68]

In an appearance before Congress, Gerbner testified,

The most general and prevalent association with television viewing is a heightened sense of living in a "mean world" of violence and danger. Fearful people are more dependent, more easily manipulated and controlled, more susceptible to deceptively simple, strong, tough measures and hard-line postures. . . . They may accept and even welcome repression if it promises to relieve their insecurities. That is the deeper problem of violence-laden television.[69]

The effect of violent television, Gerbner argued, is not that it will program children to be violent; instead, the real harm is more complex. Violent programming

- pushes aside other ways of portraying conflict.

- deprives viewers of other choices.

- facilitates the victim mentality.

- discourages production of alternative programming.[70]

Gerbner's point was that the most obvious-to-imagine effects might not be the most important actual effects.

The Critical/Cultural Approach

In the decades between World War I and World War II came the rise of a revolution in social science thinking known as **critical theory**. Originated by a group of German scholars known as the Frankfurt School, these cultural critics were trying to make sense of a changing world that was leaving people alienated, exploited, and repressed with no good way of making sense of what was happening. Many of these scholars were Marxist in their political and social views, and deeply concerned by the upheavals brought about by the end of World War I. These upheavals led to the rise of fascism in some parts of Europe and communism divorced from Karl Marx's ideas in others. There are several key principles to this approach:

- There are serious problems that people suffer that come from exploitation and the division of labor.

- People are treated as "things" to be used rather than individuals who have value.

- You can't make sense out of ideas and events if you take them out of their historical context.

- Society is coming to be dominated by a culture industry (what we might call the mass media) that takes cultural ideas, turns them into commodities, and sells them in a way to make the maximum amount of money. This separates ideas from the people who produce them.

- You cannot separate facts from the values attached to them and the circumstances from which these facts emerged.

Political science scholar Stephen Bronner writes that it is out of critical theory that people saw the rise of environmentalism, racial equality, sexual equality, and the examination of privilege. While critical theory cannot always help us understand ideas themselves, it can, Bronner writes, help us understand where they come from: "To put it crudely, critical theory can offer fruitful perspectives on the historical genesis and social uses of, say, the theory of relativity introduced by Albert Einstein. But it should not attempt to make philosophical judgments about its truth character."[71]

C. Wright Mills, who was heavily influenced by critical theorists, argued that media coverage of private problems helped turn them into major public issues. Bronner writes, "Women have already turned incest and spousal abuse from private into public concerns; gay and lesbian citizens have advocated the need for legislation against 'hate crimes'; people of color are challenging institutional racism; and countless other attempts have been made . . . to render the myriad institutions of the powerful accountable to the disempowered."[72] In other words, this is Secret 3—Everything from the margin moves to the center.

Up through the 1940s, most of the research on the mass media focused on direct and indirect effects of media messages on the behaviors of groups and individuals. But another school of thought looks at how people use media to construct their view of the world rather than looking at how media change people's behaviors. Instead of using the quantitative data analysis of the voter studies, the **critical/cultural approach** takes a more qualitative examination of the social

AGENDA SETTING VERSUS CRITICAL/CULTURAL THEORY

So far in this chapter, you have seen the application of several of the Seven Secrets, and you might be thinking, which of these is most important? As you work your way through this text, you will likely suspect that the author would put forward Secret 3—Everything from the margin moves to the center.

Note the introduction to this secret:

One of the mass media's biggest effects on everyday life is to take culture from the margins of society and make it into part of the mainstream, or center. This process can move people, ideas, and even individual words from small communities into mass society.

So, if we apply this to the case study that opens this chapter, we are left with this question:

Why, after years of neglect, did the press, in all its varied forms, suddenly start paying attention to these accusations and the women making them? (Want to read more on this subject? You can find that here: www.ralphehanson.com/tag/me-too/.) Why did these stories move to the center?

Two of the theories you have read about so far could be used to answer this question. Here is a simplified summary of each:

Agenda Setting	Critical/Cultural Theory
Issues that are portrayed as important in the news media become important to the public.	There are serious problems that people suffer that come from exploitation and the division of labor.
While the media don't tell people what to think, they can tell people what to think about.	People are treated as "things" to be used rather than individuals who have value.
This theory asks whether people take their cues from the media as to what the most important stories are that they should attend to.	You can't make sense out of ideas and events if you take them out of their historical context.
	Society is coming to be dominated by a culture industry (the mass media) that takes cultural ideas, turns them into commodities, and sells them in a way to make the maximum amount of money.

WHO are the sources?

Who were the sources for the sexual harassment and abuse stories? Who was publishing the stories? Where did the information come from?

WHAT are they saying?

Read either the opening vignette or the series of blog posts linked to above. What reasons do the sources give for the sexual harassment/abuse story breaking out when it did? Whom do they say was responsible for this happening?

WHAT evidence exists?

What evidence is there for the story spreading because news organizations were interested in making the story spread? What evidence is there for the story spreading because women (and men) who had been abused were willing to speak out?

WHAT do you think explains what happened?

How would you explain the spread of the story using agenda setting? Critical/cultural theory? Which do you think does a better job of explaining what happened? Why?

structure in which communication takes place. It considers how meaning is created within society, who controls the media systems, and the roles the media play in our lives. Instead of looking at how messages affect people, it looks at how people use and construct messages.[73]

Media and Body Image

Eating disorders in girls and women are typically a result of many factors, one of which is a desire to be thin. It is no secret that in the United States, being thin is equal to being beautiful, leading a significant number of girls and young women to suffer from eating disorders to achieve thinness.

Unfortunately, this trend toward excessive thinness as a standard of beauty has become more prominent in recent decades. In 1972, 23 percent of U.S. women said that they were dissatisfied with their overall appearance. By 1996, that figure had grown to 48 percent. Critics frequently charge that the thin models in fashion magazines (both in ads and in editorial content) are at least partially responsible for promoting extreme thinness as attractive. In 1953, when Marilyn Monroe was featured in the debut issue of *Playboy*, she was a size twelve with measurements close to the then-ideal of 36-22-35, which by today's standard would make her a **plus-sized model**. Today, the much-photographed Jennifer Aniston is an impossible (for most women) size zero.[74]

Diversity and Size. Danish model Nina Agdal is not a plus-sized model; but, as she points out, she does not have a conventional model's gaunt figure. After she was dropped from a magazine cover story because, as she tells it, she wasn't able to fit into the sample sizes during the photo shoot, resulting in the magazine telling her agent it "did not reflect well on my talent" and "did not fit their market," she decided to take her anger to social media. She posted an Instagram of herself from the shoot to show how she looked and wrote, "If anyone has any interest in me, they know I am not an average model body—I have an athletic build and healthy curves. . . . Some days I'm a sample size, some days I'm a size 4, some a 6. I am not built as a runway model and have never been stick thin. Now, more than ever, I embrace my curves and work diligently in the gym to stay strong and most of all, sane."[75]

By using this negative event to promote body positivity through her photo shoots, she told *Glamour* magazine, "I feel a responsibility, since I'm one of the girls in the ads, in the magazines, in the commercial." In response to this, the former Victoria's Secret model has signed to be part of the unretouched #AerieReal campaign for American Eagle's underwear and swimwear brand.[76]

Several European countries have put regulations in place that control industry use of underweight models. France, for example, has weight minimums for fashion models while the United Kingdom requires that fashion advertisements use "a sense of responsibility to consumers." While laws have been introduced at a variety of levels to regulate the weight and health of fashion models, it appears likely that the proposed regulations could violate both the Americans with Disabilities Act and the First Amendment.[77]

Remember Secret 3—Everything from the margin moves to the center? It's possible that the willingness of women's magazines to use models of differing sizes is becoming more commonplace than it was several years ago.

It all started back in 2005 with the Dove Campaign for Real Beauty and its so-called "Lumpy Ladies." That ad campaign, featuring attractive women of a variety of sizes posing in their underwear for photographer Annie Leibovitz, helped open a dialogue about size, beauty, and magazine content. Were we going to see more images of realistic-looking women in magazine features and advertisements?[78] (That, of course, begs the question as to what constitutes "real women." Are size-two women not real? Or is it more that average-sized women are ignored by the media?)

Nina Agdal took to social media to promote body positivity after having been rejected for modeling jobs due to her body size.

The Dove campaign paved the way for differently sized models. The contrast between plus-sized models and more conventionally sized magazine models was highlighted with a story in the online publication *PLUS Model Magazine* that had relatively tame naked photos of plus-sized model Katya Zharkova next to an unnamed "straight-sized" model. *PLUS Model* editor in chief Madeline Jones explained the magazine's photo spread thusly:

> The answer to the question is this, there is nothing wrong with our bodies. We are bombarded with weight-loss ads every single day, multiple times a day because it's a multi-billion-dollar industry that preys on the fear of being fat. Not everyone is meant to be skinny, our bodies are beautiful, and we are not talking about health here because not every skinny person is healthy.
>
> What we desire is equality to shop and have fashion options just like smaller women. Small women cannot be marketed to with pictures of plus-size women, why are we expected to respond to pictures of small size 6 and 8 women? We don't! When the plus size modeling industry began, the models ranged in size from 14 to 18/20, and as customers we long for those days when we identify with the models and feel happy about shopping.[79]

The Importance of Representation. Standards of beauty are emphatically not a static thing. Journalist Nicole Spector writes that when she was a girl in the 1990s, *People* magazine's list of "The World's Most Beautiful People" was predominantly white (76 percent). An analysis using a medical scale of skin tones found that only 12 percent of the people on the list had moderate brown to dark brown skin. By 2017, that list had nearly 30 percent of the people ranked most beautiful in the darker categories. Gabriela Garcia, a Latina writer who founded the online publication *Modern Brown Girl*, told Spector that media attention to Hispanic women role models like Jennifer Lopez, who headlined the 2020 Super Bowl halftime show, has been vital for young Latina women:

For the first time, a brown girl with curves was popular and mainstream. She didn't shy away from her Latina-ness. I think she paved the way for other types of beauty. It wasn't until the media started to show women of different colors, sizes, and cultures that I began to realize that I was beautiful. And as silly as it sounds, women like J-Lo and Kim Kardashian have really helped promote body confidence for women who are not tall, blonde, and white."[80]

Instagram/@thesunk

But while Spector, whose mother is Latina, was impressed by the greater diversity in *People*'s list, she was bothered by the fact that in 2017 only 12 percent of the list were male, while back in 1990, nearly half the individuals on People's list were male; hence, beauty and appearance are characteristics that we continue to use to judge women but not men. History and women's studies professor Dr. Catherine Kerrison tells Spector that no matter what accomplishments women have, they will still be judged on how they look. "As any woman in the public eye knows, it's crucial to her acceptance, her success that she present herself in ways that are acceptable to this standard. . . . Women will be evaluated by the standards of beauty and though those standards are expanding they are still critical to our success."[81]

Range of Beauty. As a young person, Anok Yai did not see herself reflected in the lighter-skinned models shown in most magazines, but since the image (above) taken of her by photographer Steve

▲ As a young person, Anok Yai did not see herself reflected in the lighter-skinned models shown in most magazines, but since the image (above) taken of her by photographer Steve Hall went viral in 2017, Yai has since worked steadily in the industry, becoming the first Black model in over twenty years to open for the famous fashion house Prada.

Hall went viral in 2017, Yai has since worked steadily in the industry, becoming the first Black model in over twenty years to open for the famous fashion house Prada.

As was mentioned earlier, diversity is not limited to race. Even among African Americans in media, light-skinned models are more likely to be featured in fashion than those with darker skin.

Anok Yai did not set out to be a model. She thought it might be an interesting thing to try, but that was about it. As a child, she and her sister would watch *America's Next Top Model*, hosted by Tyra Banks, but she did not think that kind of life was in her future. Yai is of Sudanese heritage, was born in Egypt, and moved to the United States with her family when she was two years old.

As she grew up, people told her she was beautiful, that she could be a model, that she could be on the cover of magazines. But the models Yai saw were always white or light-skinned Black women.[82]

"When I was younger, I was insecure about my skin because I looked up to people in the media and, though I looked up to the black women, I never saw black women that were as dark as me," Yai said.[83]

So Yai headed off to college at Plymouth State University in New Hampshire to study biochemistry with the goal of becoming a doctor. But then a friend suggested that they go to Howard University's homecoming. It would be a chance for Yai to immerse herself in the ultimate African American student experience. Yai dressed sharp for the weekend—her friend told her she had to. "My friend was like 'If I see you in a t-shirt and jeans, you're not walking with me,'" Yai said.[84]

But then Steve Hall, a Howard University graduate and a photographer for the fashion/Black culture website TheSUNK, took a picture of her. It is not the photo you would think would change a woman's life. Yai is looking straight at the camera; she says she thinks the photo makes her look like a "deer in the headlights."[85]

The next morning, Hall posted the photo to Instagram, and Yai's life was transformed. Hall's photo quickly amassed more than nineteen thousand likes, and Yai soon went from having three hundred Instagram followers to more than fifty thousand. Soon after that, the calls and emails from modeling agencies started coming in. Her childhood dream of being *America's Next Top Model* was starting to get real.

Yai eventually signed with Next Management, and in February 2018, she became the first Black model to open a runway show for the fashion house Prada since Naomi Campbell did so in 1997, more than twenty years before. "It was an honor and I'm proud that I was the one chosen to open, but this is bigger than me," she told *Vogue* about modeling at Milan Fashion Week. "Me opening for one of the top fashion houses is a statement to the world—especially for black women—that their beauty is something that deserves to be celebrated."[86]

Photo Manipulation. The level of photo manipulation going on in both magazines and social media has been an ongoing controversy, with performers such as Adele, Kelly Clarkson, and Kate Winslet being made almost unrecognizable as photographers and photo editors try to make the curvy stars' bodies comply with fashion magazine standards of beauty.

When Lena Dunham, the unconventional star of the HBO series *Girls*, posed for famed photographer Annie Leibovitz for the cover of *Vogue* magazine, questions were raised as to how authentic her images were. Dunham, in case you have missed the story, is famous for being naked in *Girls*—a lot—and her tattooed, untoned body is both celebrated and criticized for being an alternative to conventional standards of Hollywood beauty.

Dunham told *Slate* she had no problem with how Leibovitz had digitally altered her, and that she understands and appreciates the difference between reality and what is published in a fashion magazine:

A fashion magazine is like a beautiful fantasy. *Vogue* isn't the place that we go to look at realistic women, *Vogue* is the place that we go to look at beautiful clothes and fancy places and escapism and so I feel like if the story reflects me and I happen to be wearing a beautiful Prada dress and surrounded by beautiful men and dogs, what's the problem? If they want to see what I really look like go watch the show that I make every single week.[87]

Oscar-winning actress Kate Winslet specified in her contract with cosmetic company Lancôme that the company could not make digital changes to her appearance. Speaking at a Women in Hollywood event, Winslet said, "It does feel important to me, because I do think we have a responsibility to the younger generation of women . . . I would always want to be telling the truth about who I am to that generation because they've got to have strong leaders."[88]

While people have long wanted to look like their favorite celebrity, more recently there has been controversy over how young people are wanting to make themselves look in real life the way they look in their filtered social media photos. There has even been a term coined to describe this—"Snapchat dysmorphia."[89] Body dysmorphia is when a person becomes obsessed with a perceived flaw in their own appearance. Both cosmetic surgeons and psychologists are becoming concerned about people who have an obsessive interest in trying to look like either social media celebrities or their filtered self.

While Snapchat dysmorphia has gotten a fair amount of attention in popular media, the dissatisfaction people have at not looking like their filtered photos has even merited an article in the respected *Journal of the American Medical Association* (*JAMA*).[90] Along with the built-in filters on social media apps, there is also an inexpensive app called Facetune that will let users give themselves whiter teeth or a smaller forehead, nose or waist. Neelam Vashi, a dermatologist who is one of the authors of the *JAMA* article, told the *Washington Post*, "Sometimes I have patients who say, 'I want every single spot gone, and I want it gone by this week or I want it gone tomorrow,' because that's what this filtered photograph gave them. . . . That's not realistic. I can't do that."[91]

CHAPTER REVIEW

CHAPTER SUMMARY ▶▶

With the rise of mass society and the rapid growth of the mass media starting in the nineteenth century, the public, media critics, and scholars have raised questions about the effects various media might have on society and individuals. These effects were viewed initially as being strong, direct, and relatively uniform on the population as a whole. After World War I, critics were concerned that media-oriented political campaigns could have powerful direct effects on voters. This view, though still widespread, was largely discredited by voter studies conducted in the 1940s and 1950s. These studies found that the voters with the strongest political opinions were those most likely to pay attention to a campaign and hence least likely to be affected by it. Other studies from the same period looked at what effects going to the movies had on young people. More recently, research has expanded to move beyond looking just at the effects that media and media content have on individuals and society to examinations of how living in a world with all-pervasive media changes the nature of our interactions and culture.

Understanding the effects of media on individuals and society requires that we examine the messages being sent, the medium transmitting these messages, the owners of the media, and the audience members themselves. The effects can be cognitive, attitudinal, behavioral, or psychological.

Media effects can also be examined in terms of several theoretical approaches, including functional analysis, agenda setting, uses and gratifications, social learning, symbolic interactionism, and cultivation analysis.

In addition to looking at how media and their messages affect people and their interactions, there has been a rise of media scholarship in the area known as critical theory. This approach looks at how meaning is created within society, who controls the media systems, and the roles that media play in our lives. Critical theory has been used to consider topics such as how media can establish acceptable standards of beauty, size, and skin color.

KEY TERMS ▶▶

opinion leaders   31

geographics   35

demographics   35

psychographics   35

surveillance   36

status conferral   37

correlation   37

socialization   37

entertainment   38

agenda-setting theory   38

social learning theory   39

uses and gratifications theory   39

symbolic interactionism   40

cultivation analysis   41

mean world syndrome   41

critical theory   42

critical/cultural approach   42

plus-sized model   44

REVIEW QUESTIONS ▶▶

1. Why did the number of stories of sexual harassment and abuse explode in October 2017? What are at least two theoretical explanations of what happened then?

2. What were the major problems with the direct effects model—the original theory of media effects?

3. What are the four major types of media effects? Give an example of each.

4. Compare and contrast how the direct effects model, versus the cultivation theory, would explain the effects of media violence.

5. What kind of questions can you best answer using critical theory? What kind of questions is it weakest at answering?

Theo Wargo/Staff/Getty Images

CHAPTER 3

THE MEDIA BUSINESS

Consolidation, Globalization, and the Long Tail

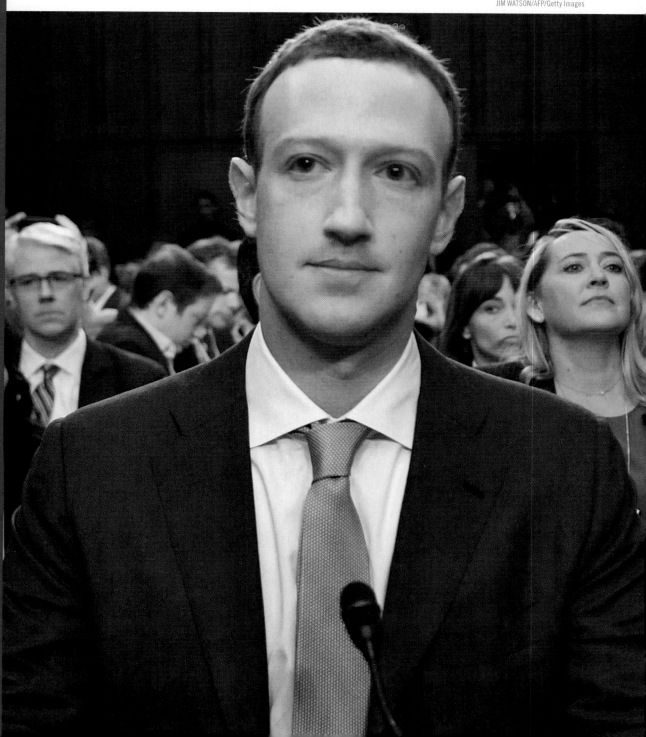

JIM WATSON/AFP/Getty Images

M ark Zuckerberg legendarily invented Facebook in his dorm room at Harvard in 2004. Depending on whom you believe, it was either a re-creation of the paper face books printed to help students get to know the other people in the dorm or a way to rate girls according to how attractive they were.

Journalist Jose Antonio Vargas (whom we will talk about more in Chapter 15 on media ethics) summed up Facebook this way:

> The site is a directory of the world's people, and a place for private citizens to create public identities. You sign up and start posting information about yourself: photographs, employment history, why you are peeved right now with the gummy-bear selection at Rite Aid or bullish about prospects for peace in the Middle East.[1]

Of course, you really do not need this explained. Chances are fairly good you used to have a Facebook account that you used to share family-friendly photos and stories with your friends, your siblings, your parents, and perhaps even your grandparents. (In fact, your grandma is why you have largely abandoned your Facebook account these days.)

Zuckerberg's fascination with computers and programming started at an early age, with Vargas reporting that Zuckerberg at age twelve wrote an early instant messaging program used to communicate in his dad's dental office.

The business model of Facebook is dependent on us being willing to share, well, just about everything. Depending on your privacy settings, your photos, where you ate lunch, where you shop, your opinions on movies, and your latest political rant are all used to serve up advertising targeted specifically at people like you.

Talk with friends on Facebook about your interest in a specific new little SUV, and suddenly, your social media are full of information about that cute little vehicle. Look at a trailer for the latest Marvel Cinematic Universe movie, and suddenly ads for streaming the rest of the Marvel movies are popping up in your feed.

While Facebook's use of your data to target you with advertising has brought the social network a certain level of criticism, more has come from Zuckerberg's decision to open Facebook to work with corporate partners.

That means that when you choose to play a game on Facebook, take a quiz to tell you which house at Hogwarts in the world of Harry Potter you belong in, or fill out a survey on where you stand politically, those data do not stay with Facebook. Instead, they get shared with Facebook's corporate partners, who use those data, and perhaps data on your friends, to sell a profile of you to other companies and organizations—perhaps even political candidates you oppose.

Critiques of Facebook kicked into high gear back in 2016 when political research company Cambridge Analytica started using Facebook for data collection purposes. Cambridge collected data on tens of millions of Americans through a Facebook quiz app and used those data to help political candidates and movements, often ones that might be at odds with the values of the people who took the quizzes. When Cambridge's use of the data was revealed, Facebook suspended the company's access to it, and the scandal surrounding the incident eventually resulted in Cambridge being shut down.[2]

Roger McNamee, who had been an early investor in Facebook and a mentor to Zuckerberg, points out that Facebook's business model is built on finding as much information as possible about its subscribers and then using that information to either micro-target advertising at them or sell the information outright to companies.[3]

Wall Street Journal reporter Katherine Bindley tried to see if there was a way to use Facebook without turning over too much knowledge about her life to the company; she was not able to. Despite turning off location services (allowing her phone to "tell" Facebook where she was) and expressly asking Facebook, and its subsidiary Instagram, not to use her web browsing history to target her, she kept getting what she called "eerily relevant ads." For example, she downloaded a pregnancy app to her phone, but provided no personal information, not even her e-mail address. Nevertheless, within twelve hours she was seeing ads for maternity ware in her Instagram feed. Keep in mind, Bindley was not actually pregnant or showing any interest in it. She just downloaded an app related to the topic of pregnancy. Bindley reports she was never able to get anyone at Facebook/Instagram or the app provider to explain how she was being targeted after engaging the maximum privacy settings.[4]

In the summer of 2019, Facebook entered a settlement with the Federal Trade Commission in which they promised to improve their record of protecting consumer privacy in addition to paying a $5 billion fine. Whether this will be enough to get the tech giant to change its behavior is a matter of some debate, given its history and the fact that the fine was less than 10 percent of Facebook's annual revenue.[5]

As of November 2019, Facebook had 2.5 billion active monthly subscribers worldwide, making it by far the largest social network. Beyond that, Facebook reports that it has 2.8 billion monthly users of at least one of its products, including Facebook, WhatsApp, and Facebook Messenger and Instagram.[6]

The only non-Facebook social media networks that come close are Google's YouTube with 1.5 billion registered users and WeChat (a China-based social network) with 1.13 billion users.[7] Twitter, by comparison, has a wee 330 million subscribers, and the upstart Snapchat has an estimated 314 million.[8]

While Facebook has one of the largest audiences of any media company, it's not the largest financially. For 2018, it had revenue of $55.8 billion with a net income of $22.1 billion. That gave the company an impressive 39.6 percent profit.[9] Comcast, owner of NBCUniversal and a major supplier of cable television services, in comparison had revenue of $94.5 billion but a more modest 12.3 percent profit; pop culture giant Walt Disney Company had a profit of 24 percent; Apple (in 2019) had a whopping revenue of $260 billion and a 21.2 percent profit;.[10]

What Zuckerberg's Facebook has taught us is that a media outlet's importance and influence can be measured in many ways—how much money it brings in, how big a profit it makes, how many audience members it serves, and how engaged its audience is. Those are just a few of the questions we are going to attempt to answer in this chapter as we look at the companies that own and run our media.

In recent years, ownership of newspapers, book and magazine publishers, recording labels, movie companies, and internet companies has become increasingly concentrated, moving from the hands of the families that started them into the hands of a small number of very large corporations. However, entrepreneurs can use digital technologies to create new media that can turn upside-down Big Media's focus on delivering media via the same tools and techniques they have used for years. Instead of looking at "the media" as a unified whole, we look at who owns and controls the varied mass media and how new channels are emerging rapidly.

The U.S. Media Industry

Stay up to date on the latest in media by visiting the author's blog at ralphehanson.com

The U.S. media industry is unique in the world in that it is almost entirely privately owned and operated for profit. Even the broadcasting industry, which in most countries is tightly controlled by the government, is run by private businesses.[11]

The media industry in the United States and the companies that make it up have a long history of private ownership that dates to the 1640s. In fact, the media industry was among the first in the American colonies: the first printing press came to the Massachusetts Bay Colony in 1638. It was used to establish the Cambridge press, publisher of *The Whole Booke of Psalmes*, better known as the Bay Psalm Book. This became the colonies' first best seller and was even exported back to Great Britain and Europe. Traditionally, most of the early published works consisted of religious tracts, such as sermons, and were printed under license of the colonial government.[12]

Newspapers were published throughout the colonial and revolutionary period, but they were not the large, general-appeal publications we are familiar with today. Instead, they provided commentary and gossip that would appeal to members of a particular political group. Benjamin

Harris, who published the first newspaper in the colonies in 1690, also ran a coffeehouse, and the content of his paper, *Publick Occurrences Both Forreign and Domestick*, resembled the talk in his coffeehouse. Only one issue of the paper appeared, in part because Harris had failed to obtain a license to publish.

Although the newspapers of the colonial period were much smaller than those to come during the 1800s, they could nevertheless be quite profitable. Publisher and statesman Benjamin Franklin became relatively wealthy publishing his *Pennsylvania Gazette*—although his success was due at least in part to his ability, as postmaster general, to prevent competing newspapers from being distributed through the mail.[13] Franklin, along with several other successful publishers, was able to use his paper's profitability to improve his publications and thus increase his success. He was an intense competitor, vying with other publishers for the top writers and editors in the book, newspaper, and magazine businesses.[14] In many ways, he established the pattern that media moguls would follow for the next two and a half centuries.

Even though print media were widespread in America in the 1700s, subscription prices were high, and publications were subsidized by political parties. It was not until the development of **penny press** newspapers in the 1830s that the news industry really got started. These inexpensive, widely circulated papers were published in large numbers and were the first American newspapers to be supported primarily through advertising revenue and read by large numbers of people.[15] The same model of advertising-supported media guided the development of the magazine industry in the 1800s.

In the United States, unlike in most other countries, the electronic media have always been privately owned, beginning with the telegraph line between Washington, DC, and Baltimore, Maryland, in 1844. By 1849, the telegraph was being used to transmit news on a regular basis. Although it was replaced by newer technology in the twentieth century, the telegraph set the stage for private ownership of electronic media.[16] Today the broadcasting industry is primarily a private business in the United States, although it is regulated by the government. In contrast, while Britain has a thriving commercial broadcasting industry, the publicly funded British Broadcasting Corporation (BBC) has a much bigger presence than the U.S. Public Broadcasting Service (PBS). And while the internet, the most recent of the electronic media, began as a partnership between the military and universities in the 1960s and 1970s, it was fully opened to business and the public in the 1990s.

The Growth of National News

Nationally circulated magazines provided news and entertainment in the nineteenth and early twentieth centuries, and radio networks carried national news from the 1930s on, but it was the growing popularity of television networks in the 1950s that gave the United States a true national media culture. For the first time, people routinely depended on nationally available media for their news. The CBS and NBC television networks started carrying a half-hour nightly news broadcast in 1963; ABC followed suit in 1967, and CBS added its weekly newsmagazine *60 Minutes* in 1968. In 1979, ABC started running a late-night news update called *America Held Hostage* when U.S. embassy employees in Iran were taken hostage. As the hostage crisis dragged on for 444 days, the update evolved into the program now known as *Nightline*.

In 1971, National Public Radio (NPR) went on the air with its first program, the evening newsmagazine *All Things Considered* followed in 1979 with *Morning Edition*, which has become the most-listened-to morning news program in the country.[17] Public affairs network C-SPAN began broadcasting on cable in 1979. Funded by the cable and satellite television industry, it carries full coverage of the U.S. House of Representatives live and unedited; C-SPAN2 coverage of the Senate was added in 1986; and C-SPAN3 coverage of congressional hearings and other public affairs events went on air in 2001. CNN went on cable in 1980, promising not to go off the air until "the end of the world." CNN subsequently went worldwide with CNN International and CNN en Español.

All this means that, even though a relatively limited number of companies own the media outlets, Americans have access to a wide range of competing news sources. The absolute number of independent sources has declined, but their availability is vastly improved.[18] In addition to these giants, several slightly smaller companies are extraordinarily influential on how our media operate. While the focus in this chapter is on the media in the United States, we take a much broader look at global media in Chapter 11.

Big Media: The Legacy Conglomerates

Media journalist Ken Auletta notes that massive changes have taken place in the media industry during the past forty years. In 1980, the VCR was a scarce luxury, cable television was just starting to become popular, the personal computer was for hobbyists, the internet was available only to academics and the military, *USA Today* had yet to be published, MTV and CNN were not yet on cable, there were only three broadcast television networks, you couldn't buy a CD, and mobile phones were connected to large boxes and used only by the wealthy and people with mobile offices.

As the 2010s decade ended, more than 60 million households subscribed to Netflix's streaming video service and 28 million subscribed to competitor Hulu.[19] (Note that these subscriber groups may overlap to a certain degree.) Approximately two-thirds of households had either cable or satellite television; radio was universally available; 68 percent of American adults had access to broadband internet at home, and another 10 percent had smartphone-only internet; the *Wall Street Journal* had 2.5 million paper and digital readers per day; there were at least six national broadcast networks; and more than 90 percent of Americans between the ages of eighteen and twenty-nine had smartphones (which means they had always-on online access as well).[20]

Since corporations control so much of what is available to the public, it is worth examining who they are and what they control, as well as how they have had to change to react to the new media environment of the twenty-first century. Companies that had counted on consolidation to bring in profits from synergy were likely to be disappointed as often as they were pleased. In general, the word **synergy** refers to a combination of effects that is greater than the sum of the individual effects. For example, two medications given together may do more than twice as much good as the two medications given separately. In the media business, synergy means that a combined company can offer more value, cost savings, or strength than two companies could separately.

The Legacy Conglomerates:

- Disney
- NewsCorporation/Fox
- WarnerMedia
- ViacomCBS
- Bertelsmann

Disney: The Mouse That Grew and Grew

Disney, also referred to as "The Mouse," may be the world's most famous media company due to its wealth of recognizable characters, such as Mickey Mouse and Donald Duck. It is also the largest of the legacy media conglomerates, and it's been getting even bigger with its acquisition of LucasFilm, Marvel, and, most recently, 21st Century Fox's entertainment properties. As of fiscal year 2018, Disney had sales of $52.47 billion and profits of $12.6 billion.[21]

The company got its start in 1928 when Walt Disney started producing Mickey Mouse cartoons. The first two silent Mickey cartoons came and went with little fanfare, but the third, which

▲ A still from the 2017 movie *Coco* captures the changing face of Disney with characters Miguel (right, voiced by Anthony Gonzalez) and his *abuela* Mamá Coco (voiced by Ana Ofelia Murguía).

featured synchronized music and sound effects, was a huge hit. Walt Disney produced more than one hundred short animated cartoons featuring Mickey and his friends. In 1937, he took animation to the next level by releasing the first feature-length cartoon, *Snow White and the Seven Dwarfs*. A major success for the studio, the film held the box-office record of $8 million until *Gone With the Wind* was released in 1939.

In the 1950s, Disney started producing live-action feature films and continued production of the wildlife documentaries it started in the late 1940s.[22] It was also in the 1950s that Disney opened its first theme park, in California.

Walt Disney was among the first Hollywood movie producers to see the potential of television, for which he produced and hosted a weekly program for more than a decade.[23] He understood the concept of synergy very early and used his television show to promote his movies and theme park. Disney has also been licensing merchandise longer than almost any other media company. In 1930, the company signed its first international licensing contract for Mickey Mouse products, and the famous Mickey Mouse watch went on sale in 1933. By 1954, the company was selling more than three thousand Disney items, ranging from pajamas to school supplies.[24]

From Mickey Mouse to Media Giant. After Walt Disney's death in 1966, the company lost much of its direction.[25] But in 1984, Michael Eisner, formerly of ABC Television and Paramount Pictures, took over as head of the studio, a job he held until 2005. Under Eisner's leadership, Disney produced a series of popular animated films; formed new movie companies, including Touchstone Pictures (which has produced films for adults, such as *Pretty Woman*); and moved into television.[26]

In addition to being a significant force in American media, Disney has been developing a presence throughout Europe and Asia. As of 2016, approximately 23 percent of Disney's earnings came from outside North America, but the quest for an international audience has not always gone smoothly.[27] For example, Disneyland Paris, which opened in 1992, went through four name changes and numerous cultural changes before it became profitable. Tokyo Disneyland, which opened in 1983, started off slowly but was soon busier than the California Disneyland.[28]

The Twenty-First Century at Disney. Disney has immensely transformed over the past twenty years. In the late twentieth century, the company was best known for children's programming, theme parks, and cruise ships as well as owning the ABC television broadcast network and ESPN family of cable networks. But in the twenty-first century, it has been working hard at becoming the dominant force in the movie industry, buying up the Pixar animation studio from Apple founder Steve Jobs, Marvel Entertainment with the massive Marvel Cinematic Universe, LucasFilm and its family of Star Wars properties from George Lucas, and, most recently, the 21st Century Fox family of entertainment properties. With the acquisition of 21st Century Fox, Disney gained control of the rest of the Marvel Universe by bringing the X-Men into the fold. It also gave Disney notable TV properties including *The Simpsons*, the FX cable channel, and National Geographic. Finally, the purchase gave Disney Fox Searchlight, which is known for small-budget, critically acclaimed films.[29]

As a part of this acquisition, Disney is in the process of removing the "Fox" name from many of these properties by renaming 21st Century Fox movie studio as 21st Century Studios, and Fox Searchlight as Searchlight Pictures.[30] With its newly expanded portfolio, Disney produced or co-produced eight of the top ten grossing movies of 2019.[31] (For the record, these included three Marvel movies, two animated sequels, two remakes of classic Disney animated films, and one Star Wars sequel—notice any kind of trend here?) The purchase of Fox also gave Disney majority ownership of the streaming service Hulu, offering consumers online access to its large library of cable programming.

Just as Eisner handled Disney's transition into the 1980s and 1990s media world with its revitalized animation studio, former ABC producer Bob Iger has been the CEO of The Mouse through its transition into a company for the new century. Iger has been the driving force behind the acquisitions of Pixar, Marvel, LucasFilm, and Fox, as well as having continued Disney's tradition of being a pioneer in new media. Walt Disney himself brought the company into the television industry; Iger has led the company into the online era.[32] This was initially by making Disney-owned studios the first to offer their movies for purchase and download through the iTunes store.[33] This has now been followed up with the launch of Disney+ in 2019 to compete with Netflix, HBO, and Amazon, featuring a massive back catalog of its now enormous collection of content. As of the end of 2019, entertainment news source *Variety* had estimated that Disney+ had 24 million U.S. subscribers.[34] A majority of these are paying $6.99 a month for the service, while as many as 8 million of them are on one-year free subscriptions provided to Verizon customers with high-end mobile phone plans.[35] As of February 2020, Iger announced abruptly that he was stepping down as CEO of Disney while remaining the company's executive chairman (whatever that means) and director of creative endeavors. Bob Chapek, who has been the chair of Disney's parks and experience programs, is the new CEO. While Disney watchers expected Iger to retire at some point in the next couple of years, no one saw this sudden retirement coming.[36]

With its launch of Disney+, production of $7 billion global box office films, and its fingers in almost every part of American media, there can be no question that Disney is the dominant media company in the United States and quite likely the world.

News Corporation and Fox: A Worldwide Giant Downsizes

Throughout all previous edition of this book, Rupert Murdoch's global news and entertainment empire of 21st Century Fox and News Corporation has remained a giant in the media business. But in 2019, Murdoch sold off about half of Fox's movie and television business to Disney for an estimated $71 billion.[37] The new Fox Corporation still owns the Fox Broadcasting Network, Fox News, and a group of twenty-eight local Fox affiliate television stations, along with other

▲ Baby Yoda merchandise for Disney's "The Mandalorian."

properties.[38] The Murdoch family are also the principal stockholders of newspaper, publishing, and information services such as News Corporation, which is best known for publishing the *Wall Street Journal* and the *New York Post* in the United States, along with the *Times* and the *Sun* in London. (Its biggest paper, the *News of the World*, was shut down following a phone hacking scandal in 2011. You can learn more about this and sexual harassment problems at Fox News in Chapter 15, Media Ethics.)

For fiscal year 2019, the new Fox Corporation had sales of $11.4 billion, making it less than a third of its former size in terms of revenue.[39] News Corporation, for the 2018 fiscal year, had revenue of approximately $9 billion, giving the two companies together sales of just over $20 billion. That makes Fox Corporation and News Corporation combined less than 40 percent of the size of Disney.

From Australia to the World. Rupert Murdoch's father owned two Australian newspapers, but when the elder Murdoch died in 1952, the younger Murdoch had to sell one of the papers to cover inheritance taxes. So, Murdoch's News Corporation empire grew out of a single newspaper, the *Adelaide News*, which had a circulation under one hundred thousand.[40]

By 1964, Murdoch had put together a major newspaper chain and had begun publishing the *Australian*, a national newspaper. In 1969, he moved to Britain, taking over the Sunday tabloid *News of the World* and eventually acquiring four more tabloids. In 1977, he moved to the United States, where he acquired the *New York Post* and transformed it into a lively, politically conservative paper.

In the 1980s, Murdoch bought the 20th Century Fox movie studio and several U.S. television stations and used them to create the Fox television network. He also became a U.S. citizen at this time because the United States does not permit foreign ownership of a television network. The Fox News cable network was launched in 1996 and has for years been the most popular of the cable news operations. In 2018, Fox News was not only the top-rated cable news channel; it was the top rated of all basic cable networks for prime-time audiences.[41] In 2019, the Murdoch's completed the sale of much of 21st Century Fox to the Disney Corporation, as detailed earlier in this chapter.

The Murdoch family owns a controlling interest in voting stock in both News Corporation and the new, smaller Fox Corporation, and Murdoch runs his business using the same hands-on style he employed when it was a small family-owned company. The sale of 21st Century Fox to Disney has made the Murdoch family the second-largest Disney shareholder.[42]

The Twenty-First Century at News Corporation and Fox. Rupert Murdoch has long demonstrated that he is willing to change with the times. Originally, all of Murdoch's media empire was a part of his giant company News Corporation, but in 2013 it split into News Corporation and 21st Century Fox. Then, in 2019, Murdoch sold off most of the movie and television production arms of Fox to Disney. Along with the resizing of the companies has come a change in leadership, with son Lachlan Murdoch taking over as chairman and CEO of Fox Corporation.[43] Why did this happen? According to a multi-part series published by *New York Times Magazine*, there were multiple reasons for the sale, including the family struggle for control of the company and that the Fox entertainment empire was not really big enough on its own to compete with the giants like Disney and Comcast. The solution that Rupert Murdoch settled on was to create a "leaner, scrappier company" focused on the parts that could be "main tools of influence."[44]

Both News Corporation and Fox are in the business of giving consumers what they want. Although Murdoch is known for his politically conservative newspapers and cable news channel, his companies are generally pragmatic about delivering what audiences want. For example, juxtapose the *Wall Street Journal* against News Corporation's racy British tabloids such as the London *Sun*, which long included a photo of a topless woman as a daily feature. And Fox Broadcasting carries shows such as *The Simpsons*, *Family Guy*, and *American Dad*, which frequently make the lists of the most objectionable shows on television; definitely not considered conservative TV.

HBO/Photofest

▲ Time Warner's pioneering pay-TV network HBO is home to many popular series, including *Game of Thrones*, one of its all-time most watched. Here Tyrion Lannister (played by Peter Dinklage, left) and Daenerys Targaryen (Emilia Clarke, right) plot to take over the fictional realm of Westeros near the end of season seven.

WarnerMedia: Back to Basics

In June 2018, telecommunications giant AT&T completed its purchase of media conglomerate Time Warner in an $85 million deal.[45] AT&T is planning to use its mobile and satellite distribution network to deliver programming ranging from Home Box Office's (HBO) *Game of Thrones* to basketball on TNT. This is not Time Warner's first go at the merger merry-go-round. Time Warner was owned by AOL back at the start of the millennium, but since then it has split off into several divisions and is now a much smaller company than it was in 2008. Among those sold-off divisions are the Time Inc. magazine division that gave the company the *Time* part of its name. Under AT&T's ownership, it is now called WarnerMedia.[46]

Time, Warner Bros., and Turner Broadcasting.

Time Warner started out as the publisher of *Time* magazine, founded in 1922 by Henry Luce and his prep-school friend Briton Hadden. Time quickly prospered, and by 1930, Luce had started the business magazine *Fortune*, which was followed in 1936 by the photo magazine *Life*. By the 1980s, Time Inc. had added multiple magazines, book publishers, local cable companies, and the HBO cable movie channel to its holdings. In 1989, Time merged with Warner Communications, which had grown out of the Warner Bros. movie studio. This merger combined a major movie studio with the nation's largest magazine publisher.

Among Time Warner's businesses were a large number of **local cable television systems**, which delivered programming to individual homes (these have since been spun off as the separate company Time Warner Cable, which has been acquired by Charter Communications), and HBO, one of the first premium cable networks. In 1996, Time Warner vastly expanded its stable by purchasing cable pioneer Ted Turner's group of channels, which included the CNN networks, WTBS, TNT, Turner Classic Movies, and Cartoon Network. Along with his cable properties, Turner also sold his internet operations and movie studio. When Time Warner took over Turner Broadcasting System (TBS), Turner became a vice president of the new company and its largest stockholder. More significantly, the Turner networks had passed from the control of a single individual to that of a publicly owned company, in much the same way that Robert Johnson's Black Entertainment Television (BET) would later be bought by Viacom.[47]

The Twenty-First Century at Time Warner.

Although Time Warner had been among the biggest of the Big Media, that bigness proved to be a mixed blessing for the company since 2000. In 2001, the big news was that AOL, then known as America Online, was merging with (some said buying) Time Warner. At the time of the merger, AOL was valued at $124 billion; when the companies separated in 2009, AOL's value was below $3 billion. The goal of the merger was to have greater synergy between AOL's online offerings and Time Warner's older legacy media. The only problem? The AOL–Time Warner synergy never really worked. The new company soon cut more than four thousand jobs and sold off numerous properties, including its sports teams, its book division, and the Warner Music Group.[48] In 2014, Time Warner took its magazine publishing arm, Time Inc., and made it into its own, independent company. This means that the part of the media giant that gave Time Warner half of its name was no longer a part of the company. In November 2017, the Time Inc. family of magazines was purchased by Iowa magazine publisher Meredith Corp.[49]

Under AT&T ownership, WarnerMedia's focus has been building a new streaming service that brings together the three elements of the old Time Warner: Warner Bros. movie and television, Turner cable television properties, and the HBO pay-cable network. John Stankey, who is

CEO of WarnerMedia, will be launching HBO Max, a streaming subscription service expected to cost $15 a month, that will provide consumers with access to HBO, Cinemax, Warner Bros. content such as the DC comic book films and TV shows, and popular 1990s shows like *Friends* and *ER*.[50] Later on, it might also offer livestreams of CNN and sporting events. In other words, this new service could be seen as something approaching a cable package offered through streaming—coincidentally, that's exactly what Disney is trying to do with its new streaming service as well.[51]

ViacomCBS: Together Again

You know how there is always a story on TMZ about the celebrity couple of the week? First they're frolicking on a beach in the Caribbean, then they're breaking up after a drunken fight in a trendy vegan restaurant, and then . . . they are having a baby! That could also describe the relationship between media conglomerate Viacom and established broadcast network CBS. After years of having an on-again, off-again relationship, the two companies merged to become ViacomCBS in late 2019. The combined company has revenue of more than $28 billion and more than four billion cumulative global TV subscribers. ViacomCBS owns a wide range of properties including the broadcast network CBS, the Paramount movie studio, and a host of basic and premium cable networks including the MTV family of channels and Showtime, several streaming services, and book publisher Simon & Schuster.[52]

The Child Buys/Sells the Parent. The 2019 merger of Viacom and CBS has been an epic struggle spread out over literally decades. CBS became a force in broadcasting when William S. Paley and his father bought United Independent Broadcasters in 1928 and turned it into the Columbia Broadcasting System (CBS). In the mid-1980s, when all three of the original broadcast networks changed ownership, investor Laurence Tisch (and Loews Corporation) bought CBS. Westinghouse bought Tisch's company in 1995, and by 1997, it had sold all its nonmedia businesses and was simply CBS Inc.

Then, in one of the strangest twists in media history, Viacom bought CBS in 1999. What made this transaction so unusual was that Viacom had begun as a small film production unit within CBS. Later, in 1971, the federal government became concerned that the broadcast networks were becoming too powerful, so it forced them to sell their content production units. As an independent company, Viacom grew into a major producer of cable television programming; its products included MTV and Nickelodeon.

In 1987, theater owner Sumner Redstone bought Viacom. Under Redstone's leadership, the company became a dominant media corporation in the 1990s. It acquired the Paramount movie studio and the start-up television network United Paramount Network (UPN). (In 2006, UPN was merged with the WB network to become the CW.) Finally, Viacom bought CBS, the television network that had given birth to it decades before.[53] But then, in 2005, Viacom and CBS split back into two separate corporations with separate stocks being traded. So, they are no longer a single Big Media company, right? Well, sort of. The two companies were still both headed up by either Sumner Redstone or his daughter Shari. And the Redstone family was still the top investor.

Sumner died in August of 2020 at the age of 97, leaving Shari firmly in control. The story over the re-merger of the two companies has been nearly as much a family soap opera as a business

Bloomberg / Contributor / Getty Images

▲ Shari Redstone (above) and her father, Sumner, engaged in a long battle over control of CBS and Viacom before the two companies were reunited in 2019.

narrative. Since 2018, the companies have been dancing back and forth, considering becoming one company again, with the issues seemingly focused on how much one company would be willing to pay for the other.[54] Complicating matters were the problems of CBS's former chairman Les Moonves, who was forced out of the company by multiple charges of sexual harassment.

The Twenty-First Century at ViacomCBS. What does the merger of Viacom and CBS mean going forward?

- One of the major objectives of the merger was to get the two companies into better position to compete in the cord-cutting, streaming world of the Fox-enhanced Disney, Comcast, AT&T/WarnerMedia and Netflix.[55] As television moves away from being a product delivered by cable or satellite, the legacy media companies all have to figure out how they can preserve their place in this new media world—just as they did back in the 1980s when television moved from being something delivered for free over the air to something viewers paid for that arrived via cable. This is an example of Secret 4–Nothing is new: Everything that happens in the past will happen again.

- Even with the merger, ViacomCBS will still be relatively small compared with AT&Ts $85 billion acquisition of WarnerMedia and Disney's more than $50 billion acquisition of 21st Century Fox. And that says nothing about the size of the newer players like Comcast, Apple, and Alphabet/Google.[56]

- But as *Variety* magazine points out, the new company will not be that much different from the two that merged to create it. There will still be a member of the Redstone family near the top of the company and a fair amount of existing management still in place.[57]

Bertelsmann: The World's Largest Publisher

Although the German media corporation Bertelsmann has historically been known for its book and music publishing and management business, it also has a major presence in magazines, newspapers, and internet and broadcast properties. Bertelsmann is both the world's largest publisher and the largest publisher of English-language books. In 2018, it had sales of $19.6 billion.[58]

Books Still Matter. Bertelsmann started out in 1835 as a publisher of Christian music and prayers. It was also the original publisher of the fairy tales of the Brothers Grimm in the nineteenth century. After World War II, the company was run by Reinhard Mohn, a former German Luftwaffe officer who learned to speak English while in a prisoner-of-war camp in Kansas.[59]

Unlike most of the other media giants, Bertelsmann is a privately held company—it is owned by a German foundation that mandates that the company not only earn a profit but also operate for the benefit of its employees and various social causes.[60] Bertelsmann sees book publishing as one of the key media of the twenty-first century and, having purchased major American publishers Random House in 1998 and Penguin in 2013, has a much stronger presence in this area than the other media giants. It also owns the RTL Group, Europe's largest television broadcaster, and a large number of magazines through its Gruner + Jahr division.[61]

The Twenty-First Century at Bertelsmann. As a publisher and European broadcaster, Bertelsmann is not in the public eye the way Time Warner, Viacom, and Disney are. It does not have Scooby-Doo, SpongeBob, or Mickey Mouse as a mascot, but it has quietly made its presence felt by utilizing the following methods:[62]

- Returning to core strengths—Up until 2002, under the leadership of CEO Thomas Middelhoff, Bertelsmann looked like it was preparing to become a generalized media giant on the scale of Time Warner or Disney. But members of the Mohn family forced Middelhoff out and returned the company to its core business of book and magazine publishing. Ever since, the company has been gradually selling off peripheral businesses and buying back its stock. In October 2017, Bertelsmann bought more stock in Penguin Random House, bringing its ownership up to approximately 75 percent and it committed to buying the rest of the publisher in 2019.[63]

- Broadcasting in Europe—Bertelsmann is big in European television, owning 90 percent of the RTL Group, Europe's largest broadcaster. In addition to operating more than forty-five television channels in a dozen countries, it also produced the long-running *American Idol* and a wide range of other *Idol* versions around the world.[64]

▲ Bertelsmann merged Random House and Penguin into a single company in 2013.

Big Media: The New Players

The conglomerates have long been the unquestioned rulers of the American media. But trying to rank the biggest media companies has gotten to be harder and harder with the rise of new media companies. Look at Disney, generally considered to be the largest of the media conglomerates with annual income of approximately $52 billion. Then compare it to cable giant Comcast, which now owns NBCUniversal. For 2018, Comcast had annual revenue of $94.5 billion, up $9 billion from 2017. Or consider search giant Google and its parent company Alphabet. In 2018, Alphabet had annual sales of $136.8 billion, most of which came from advertising. That makes it even bigger than Comcast.[65] So, let us now look at the other contenders in the Big Media business. This applies to Secret 2—There are no mainstream media. These newer companies, Comcast, Google, and Apple are becoming a huge part of our media landscape. Then there are the companies that are more limited in the scope of their media ownership, such as iHeartMedia, which has more than 850 radio stations. A wide range of media exists, all of which are significant.

Comcast/NBCUniversal: Cable Buys Broadcaster

NBCUniversal (NBCU) is one of the oldest broadcasters in the United States. It was founded in 1926 by the Radio Corporation of America (RCA), the original monopoly in the broadcast business. Initially, the federal government established RCA to consolidate all the patents required to start the radio business. RCA formed the National Broadcasting Company (NBC) to provide radio programming across the country. As is described in more detail in Chapter 6, NBC had two networks, the "Red" and the "Blue." In the 1940s, it sold the Blue network, which became ABC, now owned by Disney.[66] In the 1930s, RCA began developing television technology and was the first network with regularly scheduled television broadcasts.

In 1985, General Electric (GE) bought both NBC and RCA. The purchase was controversial from the very beginning because GE's primary business is not media but manufacturing and financial services. GE makes consumer electronics, electric generating plants, and aircraft engines. Critics questioned whether a major defense contractor ought to be allowed to own a broadcast network.[67]

Up until the fall of 2009, cable, internet, and phone service provider Comcast was not on anyone's list of American media giants. Sure, it was the largest single supplier of cable television and internet services in the United States, but it was not talked about in the same breath as Disney, ViacomCBS, or WarnerMedia. But then the news started breaking that the cable giant was in negotiations to purchase 51 percent of NBCU from GE, which would give the Philadelphia-based company controlling ownership of the network/movie studio.[68] In February 2013, Comcast announced it would be completing its purchase of NBCU.[69] Purchasing NBCU made Comcast the nation's most valuable pure-media company. (Apple is often considered the world's most valuable company, depending on its stock price, but it is only partially a media company.)[70] For 2015, Comcast had revenue of $94.5 billion, making it more than 40 percent bigger than Disney.[71]

Comcast makes most of its revenue by selling cable television, internet, and phone services to its nearly twenty-eight million subscribers. Along with its media-related properties, Comcast owns an interest in professional sports teams and arenas in Philadelphia. The purchase of NBCU gave it the NBC broadcast network, the number-two Spanish-language broadcast network Telemundo, ten NBC affiliate stations, and more than twenty cable networks. These cable networks include the top-rated USA Network, along with Bravo, Syfy, and MSNBC. On the film side, the deal gave Comcast control of the major film studio Universal Studios and small-picture/indie studio Focus Features. And, finally, the deal included the Universal Studios theme parks in Florida and California.[72] In the spring of 2016, NBCU purchased DreamWorks Animation, the home of the *Minions* and *Despicable Me* series, for $3.8 billion. The purchase was seen as doing more than just strengthening Comcast's animation presence. "DreamWorks will help us grow our film, television, theme parks and consumer products business for years to come," said Steve Burke, CEO of NBCU.[73]

Although Comcast is a publicly owned corporation, one-third of the company's voting stock is controlled by CEO Brian Roberts, son of the company's founder. Comcast got its start in the cable business in Mississippi in 1963 and got its name in 1969. After acquiring cable systems in Pennsylvania, it moved to Philadelphia. Throughout the 1980s, Comcast grew by buying up local cable service throughout the United States. In the late 1980s and early 1990s, Comcast started buying up mobile phone companies as well. In 2004, Comcast made its first bid at buying a Big Media company with an offer for Disney. While that deal was not successful, it did set the stage for the cable giant making the play for NBCU.

Like most of the other major players in the media marketplace, Comcast is preparing to launch a streaming service for customers wanting to get away from traditional cable television.[74] This is an important move for Comcast because while its overall revenue is climbing, the company's revenue from providing home cable service is declining. On the other hand, revenue for providing broadband internet services is climbing.[75]

Alphabet: Google and Company

In previous editions of this book, I raised the question "Are search engines a new part of mass communication?" Certainly, the internet and the World Wide Web are a part of our mass media, and search engines, such as Google and Bing, are the tools we use to find information on the web. They might even be considered news media. Think about Google News. It's a search tool that decides what the major news stories of the day are, collects links to them on a single page, and presents them to the reader. According to Google, Google News draws stories from more than 4,500 English-language news sources from around the world. The articles are evaluated by Google's computers as to how often and on what sites the stories appear. Google claims this leads to an unbiased presentation of the news.[76]

Google has become so much a part of our lives that the search engine's name has become a synonym for searching on the internet—I will just go Google the answer. But Google is more than just a search engine. Therefore, in the summer of 2015 cofounder Larry Page announced on his blog that the company would restructure into a new parent company called Alphabet. Alphabet is the home for a range of products, including the following:

- Google—Advertising, search engine, email, YouTube, Android mobile operating system, maps, and apps

- Android—The most used smartphone operating system

- Chrome—A laptop operating system and web browser

- Nest—Connected Internet of Things devices

- Calico—Antiaging research
- Loon—Delivering internet services to remote areas using high-altitude balloons
- Verily—Health care and disease prevention research
- Waymo—Self-driving car development[77]

In 2018, Alphabet/Google had worldwide sales of $136.8 billion, with more than 45 percent of its income coming from the United States, 30 percent from the Europe, Middle East and Africa region, and 15 percent from the Asia/Pacific region. This places Google, like Comcast, ahead of all the legacy media conglomerates in terms of revenue. Of this income, the vast majority came from advertising sales. Not only is Google bringing in a lot of income; it is among the most profitable of the media companies as well. Given all this, Google must be considered one of the major new players in the media business.[78]

TEST YOUR VISUAL MEDIA LITERACY

GOOGLE DOODLES

Back in 1999, before Google was even incorporated as a company, back before its name was a verb meaning "to search online," Google founders Larry Page and Sergey Brin wanted to use their search engine's home page to advertise that they were "out of the office" to attend the Burning Man celebration of technology and counterculture in the Nevada desert. A couple of years later, the second doodle was created in honor of Bastille Day by webmaster and intern Dennis Hwang; and with the doodle's success, Hwang was in charge of producing the playful illustrations, animations, and interactions honoring events or anniversaries.[79]

The Google doodles have come a long way from those early static illustrations. Some of these doodles are essentially short films in tribute to their subject, oftentimes honoring an underappreciated individual in an area's

history. For example, in June 2016, there was a doodle honoring animated film pioneer Lotte Reiniger, who did creative films featuring paper cuts and shadow puppets. She was born in Berlin, Germany, in 1899 and was known best for her fairy tale films.[80]

Others, in addition to having cool animation and music, have a big interactive component. The one from August 11, 2017, honored the forty-fourth anniversary of the birth of hip-hop at a back-to-school party in the Bronx, New York. The doodle gives you a history lesson followed by a chance to practice your DJing skills by picking records, scratching, and matching beats. (You can read more about this in Chapter 6.)[81]

A significant amount of work goes into each of these doodles. For the hip-hop project, there is a front logo created by graffiti artist Cey Adams; the history part is narrated and hosted by an animated Fab 5 Freddy, former host of *Yo! MTV Raps*. The final project includes credits for the more than forty people who worked on it.

Because the Google doodles are free on the internet, there are, of course, people who inevitably find them offensive. The controversies over the doodles seem to be as much over what they are not about as what they are. Conservative news and conspiracy website *WorldNetDaily* complained in 2006 that Google was not honoring U.S. veterans or war dead.

Google Doodles Archive

(Continued)

(Continued)

Then, in 2007, Google took heat for honoring the fiftieth anniversary of human spaceflight—something that was accomplished first by the communist Soviet Union.[82] Additional criticism of Google's choices of topics have come from Fox News and the website *Infowars*. What sometimes gets missed amidst the criticism is that Google is a global company that brings in more than 50 percent of its income from outside the United States.[83] (This is also a long-running example of Secret 5—All media are social; even cartoon illustrations on a search engine page.)

The ideas for the doodles that do get created come from a range of sources, including the staff at Google, who look for "interesting events and anniversaries that reflect Google's personality and love for innovation."[84] Ideas also come from Google users. Following criticism for not honoring Christmas and Easter with doodles, Google has adopted a formal policy of not recognizing any religious holidays.

You can see the doodles discussed here:

www.ralphehanson.com/2018/05/11/ch-3-visual-media-literacy-google-doodles/

WHO is the source?

Who is creating the Google doodles? Who comes up with the ideas for the doodles? Who is being critical of the doodles?

WHAT are they saying?

What kinds of doodles get made? What kind of messages do they have? What kinds of messages are not getting made?

WHAT is the lasting impact?

What does it mean for a website with millions of visitors daily to offer short films and interactions to its users? Do the doodles bring in more traffic?

HOW do you and your classmates react to the Google doodles?

Do you or your friends enjoy the Google doodles? Do you ever deliberately go to see them? Have you ever been upset or offended by one of them?

▲ In 2016, Google announced its reconfiguration into a conglomerate called Alphabet. Eric Schmidt (above), the executive chair of Alphabet, has traveled the world to speak about how technology will revolutionize our day-to-day lives.

Bloomberg/Getty Images

Google was founded in 1998 by two engineers who did not even suspect they were going into the advertising business. Brin, the child of Jewish-Russian immigrants, learned to program at age nine when his parents gave him a Commodore 64 computer. He partnered with Page, whose father was a professor of computer science at Michigan State and whose mother was a database consultant. Brin and Page met each other while in graduate school at Stanford. One night, Page explains, he had a dream: "I was thinking: What if we could download the whole Web, and just keep the links?"[85]

The two classmates created a search system based on that idea that worked by analyzing the quality of links to a topic and then scored them according to a system known as PageRank, which stood for both Page's name and the rank of the web page itself. Google was initially launched not in a garage (though it would later move into a garage) but in graduate housing at Stanford. Google was founded without a business plan or a strategy for making money. But what the founders did have was a strategy for creating the most simple, clean search system.

While Brin and Page were quite happy to burn through investors' money without worrying about generating any, the venture capitalists who were bankrolling the company did want a return on their investments. It was in 2002 that Google finally figured out that to make money for its investors, it had to be in the advertising business. What Google's engineers came up with was the AdWords system, where advertisers bid on the rights to advertise next to search results. The advertisers buy certain keywords that they want their ads to appear next to. But Google requires that the ads that appear be relevant to the people doing the search. So, for example, advertisers can't buy the word *chocolate* and use it to put up links selling cars. But the words *helicopter parts* would be perfect for someone wanting to sell tools for repairing helicopters. Advertisers are only charged when audience members click on their ads.

Google's second big advertising product was AdSense, which places ads on blogs and websites that match the ads with the content of the site. Then Google splits the revenue, with about two-thirds of the money going to the owner of the website. This put Google in the position of collaborating with a lot of smaller, independent sites and being seen as a benefactor. This not only made Google quite profitable; it allowed lots of small sites to make money as well.

All this brings us back to Secret 2—There are no mainstream media. We have lots of different media out there, ranging from the legacy corporations, to new media giants, to individuals sharing their work through services like YouTube. And they are all our media. It also reminds us of Secret 6—Online media are mobile media—given that Google makes the mobile operating system Android that powers huge numbers of phones, and that Apple has defined the mobile market with its iPhones and iPads.

While in retrospect using search as an advertising medium seems obvious, Google was founded on the idea of making the best possible search engine, not making money. The founders figured that if they built a great product, they would eventually come up with a good source of revenue.

Unlike so many of our legacy media, Google has been unafraid of the massive changes taking place in the media business. At a time when the music and movie industries are terrified of their fans/users/customers and are taking them to court for being "pirates," Google is trying to figure out how to better serve them. Google cofounder Page told media journalist Ken Auletta, "[Thinking that] your customer or users are always right, and your goal is to build systems that work for them in a natural way is a good attitude to have. You can replace the system. You can't replace the user."[86]

Given Google's dominance in the search (and streaming video, and online advertising, etc. . . .) industry, it's not surprising that it's facing criticism and investigation on a range of fronts:

- The Federal Trade Commission negotiated a settlement for a multimillion dollar fine for Alphabet over YouTube's violation of children's privacy for "tracking and targeting of users younger than 13."[87]

- Republicans have charged that Google uses its size and power to suppress conservative speech online. The company denies that it does anything to promote progressive over conservative websites. The *Wall Street Journal* reports that it would be difficult to go after Google, however, given that the search service is popular with consumers and that it has funded a wide-ranging "support network" in Washington, DC, to help oppose regulation and control of the company.[88]

- The federal government is giving news publishers a four-year exemption from anti-trust laws so they can better negotiate for fairer payments for how their content is used by Google.[89]

Apple: Reinventing the Media

Although Apple is best known as a technology company, it has done as much as any corporation to change the media business in the twenty-first century. Apple has gone through incredible levels of growth. The tech company had $66 billion in revenue for 2010, which grew to $260 billion in 2019. That's close to quadrupling its income in less than a decade.[90]

Justin Sullivan/Getty Images

▲ Apple CEO Tim Cook introduces the Apple Watch at one of the company's highly anticipated media events. While Apple is primarily in the hardware business, it's transformed how people consume media in the twenty-first century.

A quick check of Apple's balance sheet shows that in 2019 the California company made 55 percent of its revenue from iPhone products, with the rest coming from sales of its iPad tablets; conventional computers; wearable devices like the Apple Watch or the AirPod wireless ear buds; the Apple TV streaming box; software and media; and a range of services like the Apple Music and Apple TV streaming services. Looking at the numbers, it becomes obvious that laptop and desktop computers are only a small part of the company's business. That is why these days the company's name is Apple, not Apple Computer.

Steve Jobs cofounded Apple back in 1976 with his friend Steve Wozniak. "Woz" was the inventor, and Jobs was the businessman and visionary. Wozniak left the company in 1983, and Jobs was forced out by Apple's board of directors in 1985.[91] After leaving Apple, Jobs founded NeXT Inc., which built an innovative UNIX-based computer that was used by Tim Berners-Lee to create the World Wide Web.[92] (You can read more about Berners-Lee in Chapter 9.)

Then, in 1997, Apple reconsidered, bought out NeXT Inc., and brought Jobs back as its interim CEO. The NeXTSTEP software morphed into OS X, Apple's radical and successful remake of its computer operating system. By 2001, Jobs had dropped *interim* from his title and started Apple on the path to its current success. It was also in 2001 that Apple introduced its iconic media player, the iPod.[93]

With the iPod, and its accompanying iTunes software, Jobs solidified his company as a player in the new media business. Jobs did numerous things people told him he could not do. He persuaded the major recording labels to offer their music through Apple's iTunes Store. He persuaded the major broadcast and cable networks to sell their television shows through the iTunes Store. He persuaded major movie studios to sell and rent their movies through . . . oh, you get the picture.[94]

In addition to running Apple, Jobs took Pixar, a computer graphics company he bought for $10 million from Star Wars director George Lucas, and turned it into America's leading animation studio, valued in excess of $7 billion when he sold it to Disney in 2006.[95] Upon the sale of Pixar, Jobs became Disney's biggest stockholder and a member of the company's board of directors, thus cementing an already strong relationship between Apple and Disney.[96] Disney CEO Iger depended on Jobs for guidance on how his company could avoid the problems the music industry faced in dealing with the internet. Iger's response was to license his studio's content to Apple's iTunes Store so that customers could legally buy and watch Disney entertainment on their computers and mobile devices.[97]

When Jobs lost his long battle with pancreatic cancer in 2011, the response from fans and the news media—from Facebook to cable news—was at a level you might have expected from the death of Prince or David Bowie, not from the head of one of the world's most valuable corporations. But then few companies inspire the level of intense loyalty that Apple does, and few companies have been more associated with the personality and identity of its founder.[98] Tim Cook took over as Apple's CEO in 2011 after Jobs stepped down due to his illness, and Apple initially continued its rapid growth under Cook's leadership.[99] In the spring of 2018, Apple reached a market value of $1 trillion after being in business for 42 years. Just two years later, in the summer of 2020, it had doubled that valuation to $2 trillion with the world in the midst of a pandemic-driven recession.[100]

Media Economics and the Long Tail

Lists of major media companies generally include the cable television provider Comcast, the streaming service Netflix, or the movie and music available from Sony. What do not show up as often are the independent artists, writers, and videographers whose works appeal to a relatively small group of consumers. But, when those many small groups are added together, they become an audience big enough to rival those being attracted by Big Media.

The world of Big Media is the world of blockbusters—selling a lot of copies of a limited number of products. Blockbusters include the big summer movies that cost more than $250 million to produce and require the sale of millions of tickets to be a financial success. They are books by Ta-Nehisi Coates and Margaret Atwood. They are albums by Beyoncé, Chris Stapleton, and Drake. They are the common media products, the common culture we all share.

Despite the consolidation of the media business and the ever-growing emphasis on the importance of blockbusters to Big Media, a strange phenomenon has been taking place. The annual ticket sales have been falling for movies, broadcast television has lost one-third of its audience, and sales of CDs are plummeting, yet people seem to be consuming more media content than ever.

Chris Anderson, in his book *The Long Tail*, argues that we are leaving the era of mass culture and entering one that is vastly more individualistic and much less mass oriented. He writes that, when he was growing up, the only alternatives to Big Media were the library and the comic book store. But today there are vastly more choices at both the commercial and noncommercial levels. Take Apple's iTunes music and video store. Through it, you can buy current blockbuster songs, movies, and television shows, but you can also find rather obscure materials, such as the songs of indie music duo Pomplamoose (*pamplemousse* means "grapefruit" in French), who have built a following through videos on YouTube. Or an EP by the Arizona-based band Calexico. Or the crowd funded *Veronica Mars* movie that rebooted the popular TV series using $5.7 million raised from fans. Or you could look at the comedy-horror film *Tucker & Dale vs. Evil* from mail-order DVD rental/streaming video company Netflix.

This is how Anderson describes the shift that has taken place as consumers turn from the mass content produced by broadcasters and publishers to the more focused content provided by broadband connections to the internet:

> The great thing about broadcast is that it can bring one show to millions of people with unmatchable efficiency. But it can't do the opposite—bring a million shows to one person each. Yet that is exactly what the Internet does so well. The economics of the broadcast era required hit shows—big buckets—to catch huge audiences. The economics of the broadband era are reversed. Serving the same stream to millions of people at the same time is hugely expensive and wasteful for a distribution network optimized for point-to-point communication.[101]

In short, our mass communication is becoming less mass, and we have new media companies that specialize in providing narrowly focused content. Anderson uses the statistical term the **long tail** to refer to this phenomenon.

Figure 3.1 depicts this phenomenon as a distribution curve showing that a relatively limited number of media products—books, songs, DVDs—sell the most copies. This area of a limited number of products and high sales on the left—the **short head**—is where Big Media companies like to live. When a movie comes to a local theater, it needs to attract about 1,500 people over a two-week period for the run to be a success. That means that you won't see a lot of the more obscure movies in your local theater. A CD must sell at least four copies a year to justify the shelf space it takes up—that is, to pay the rent on its shelf space. Even if it sells five thousand copies nationwide, if it can't sell four copies in your local store, your local store can't pay the rent on the half-inch of shelf space the CD takes up. So Big Media are all about finding the limited number of hits that will appeal to the most people. As Anderson observes, that's what they must do to survive.[102]

To see the short-head portion of the demand curve, look at Walmart, the United States's biggest music retailer. As recently as 2013, the discount giant carried about 3,500 different CDs in its stores. Of those, 200 CDs accounted for more than 90 percent of its sales. But in 2014, Walmart cut its selection of discs by 40 percent, offering only about 2,100 titles.[103] And now big-box

The New Media Marketplace

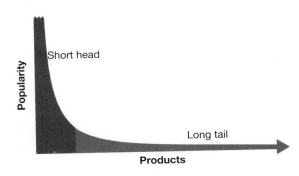

retailers like Target and Best Buy have largely eliminated their CD offerings.[104] But what about the remaining thousands and thousands of songs that a limited number of people are interested in buying? They constitute the long-tail portion of the graph that extends off to the right. This is where a limited number of people are interested in buying a lot of different products (as opposed to the short head, where a lot of people are interested in buying a limited number of products).

In contrast to Walmart, Anderson used online music seller Rhapsody (which is now operating as Napster[105]) as an illustration of the long-tail portion of the demand curve. But now much of the download market, along with CDs, has been replaced by streaming services. Streaming is a great place to explore the long tail of music because you have no marginal cost of trying out new music other than the time it takes you to listen. One of the biggest challenges for streaming services like Spotify, Pandora, or Apple Music is to keep you as a paying customer. Supplying new music that you might not have known about but still like is a great way to keep you on the hook. Stefan Blom, then Spotify's chief content and strategy officer, told *Billboard* magazine in 2016, "I think we are really onto something in terms of democratizing the overall discovery process."[106] Spotify uses its Discover Weekly tool to connect millions of listeners with literally billions of new songs.

How can Spotify do this? Two factors come into play: (1) Its cost of inventory is minimal—it just has to store the songs on a big array of hard drives; it doesn't have to physically stock the music, and (2) it does business over the entire country with a single store, so it doesn't need a lot of consumers in a single location who want to listen to something. If they live anywhere in the United States, that's good enough.[107]

Characteristics of the Long Tail

The biggest players in the long tail include Apple, the largest seller of legal music downloads; Netflix, which offers hundreds of thousands of different movies through online streaming and by DVDs sent through the mail; and Amazon, with its Amazon Prime streaming service and sales of books, movies, and CDs.[108] These companies can offer selection far beyond the current hits. Anderson argues that there are six principles that drive the success of the long-tail portion of the media marketplace:

NurPhoto/Getty Images

▲ In January 2019, Amazon revealed that Amazon Prime has more than one hundred fifty million members globally.

- High number of goods—There are far more niche goods than hits. This means that if you can sell enough different niche goods, you can get as many sales as if you were selling a limited number of hits.

- Low cost of reaching markets—The cost of reaching niche markets is falling dramatically, thanks to the ease of access provided by the internet and the ability to—in many cases—sell a digital download rather than a physical product.

- Ease of finding niche products—Consumers need to be able to find these niche products. This means there need to be tools—Anderson calls them filters—that allow consumers to search through a huge selection of media content to find the particular material they are looking for. This is something at which internet movie rental store Netflix excels. Netflix has consumers rate a series of movies and then provides recommendations based on those ratings.

- Flattening of the demand curve for mainstream hits—Once consumers can find their niche products, the demand curve tends to flatten. Now that consumers can find the full range of products available, there will be relatively less demand for the hits and more demand for the niche products. This will make the long tail longer and lower the demand for the hits.

- Size of collective market—There are so many niche products that they collectively can have as big a market as the hits do. In other words, you can sell as much focusing on the long tail as on the short head if you can offer enough choices.

- Tailoring to personal tastes—Once niche products become available, findable, and affordable, consumers will choose to go with media content that fits their personal wants and needs rather than consuming the hits that hold a mild appeal to so many. Media hits will become less important because consumers can get what they want rather than what happens to be available locally.[109]

Consequences of the Long Tail

Anderson says that several consequences arise out of a shift to the long tail from traditional mass media:

- Democratization of the means of production—It used to be that to record a CD you needed a big, expensive recording studio. Now anyone with a laptop computer and some inexpensive software can put together a multitrack recording or edit a short video. You can publish a professional-looking book without the benefit of a major publisher using a laser printer and a local copy shop. The development of the powerful home computer has made it possible for anyone to be a media producer.

- Democratization of the means of distribution—Through the internet and sites such as eBay and Amazon, anyone can open a national, or even international, sales channel. YouTube gives ordinary people a place to distribute their home-produced videos. I even run a tiny media-oriented bookstore using an Amazon partnership. As Anderson puts it, "The PC made everyone a producer or publisher, but it was the Internet that made everyone a distributor."[110]

- Greatly reduced cost of connecting suppliers and consumers—Sellers and consumers can now find each other through tools such as Google Search, iTunes, YouTube, and blogs.

Big Players in the Long Tail

Our twenty-first-century media world has room for a wide range of distribution channels. For the hits, there is nothing like Big Media for distribution. Movie theaters, bookstores, big-box retailers (such as Walmart), broadcast network television, and magazines do a great job of selling or distributing media content that appeals to a large group of people. Second are the hybrid retailers—companies such as Amazon and Netflix that have no brick-and-mortar retail stores but have to send out a physical product, such as books, CDs, or DVDs. The hybrid retailers can have national distribution and serve niches, but they still deliver a physical product. Finally, the digital retailers, such as Apple iTunes and Napster, sell downloads with no physical product. Any store that sells a virtual rather than a physical product handles the farthest end of the long tail.[111]

One of the most successful providers of long-tail content has been Google's video service YouTube. While YouTube started as a way to make video easy to share, it quickly grew into a major alternative source of video entertainment. "We are providing a stage where everyone can be seen. We see ourselves as a combination of America's Funniest Home Videos and Entertainment Tonight," cofounder Chad Hurley told Associated Press reporter Michael Liedtke.[112]

AP Photo/Noah Berger

▲ Steven Chen (left) and Chad Hurley launched the video-sharing website YouTube in 2004. It has since become one of the top locations on the internet for user-generated video.

Unlike the infamous site Napster, which used to share music files, YouTube has not been confrontational with Big Media. It has always promptly removed any content at the request of corporate copyright owners, but it has also pursued extensive revenue-sharing projects with those same companies. It also limits clips by users to ten minutes, which helps prevent large-scale copyright infringement from users posting entire movies or television shows.[113] (YouTube has entered into contracts with Big Media companies to stream longer videos of professionally produced content.)[114]

As of the spring of 2019, YouTube reported having two billion monthly visitors and the *New York Times* estimated that the video service generates somewhere between $16 billion to $24 billion per year in revenue.[115] With approximately two hundred million viewers in the United States per month, YouTube has a bigger audience than most cable channels.[116] But YouTube differs significantly from cable television. A television channel decides to put up a limited amount of programming each day and hopes that an audience will look at it, whereas YouTube puts up lots of content produced by both professionals and amateurs and then sees what the audience decides to look at. Unlike traditional television, YouTube is capable of delivering programming that reaches audiences that range in size from dozens to millions. "We accept everyone that uploads video to our site, and it's the community that decides what's entertaining," Hurley says.[117] YouTube's expansive approach is a prime example of Secret 1—The media are essential components of our lives. YouTube combines the roles of creator, program manager, and viewer into a single person. YouTube is an expression of the audience's interests with almost unlimited levels of choice. Given that half of all YouTube views are done on mobile devices, this is also a prime example of Secret 6—Online media are mobile media.

Diane Mermigas of the *Hollywood Reporter* sees the merger of Google and YouTube as "the first viable new-media successor to broadcast and cable television."[118] She says the combination provides the tools needed to post, view, find, and place advertising on both amateur and professional video programming over broadband channels. She sees the pair leading the charge to have the "eyeballs, ad dollars and creative content that have sustained traditional television" move over to online video.[119] This is also why Steve Jobs succeeded in making Apple a success in the online media world. Apple understood that consumers needed an easy way to find and then use digital content, providing both the online iTunes Store and the various iPads and iPhones to play back the downloads. Using Apple's products, a consumer can download, transport, and access content anywhere and at any time.[120] The new media companies that are becoming significant and growing players understand the nature of the long tail and will deliver what consumers want.

CHAPTER REVIEW

CHAPTER SUMMARY ▶▶

The American media industry, the largest in the world, is run by private business with only minor government control. Having gotten its start in the 1640s, it was among the first industries in the American colonies. However, media business did not become big until the 1830s, when high levels of literacy and the development of the steam-powered printing press allowed for the mass production of newspapers, books, and magazines. The growth of the electronic media in the second half of the twentieth century helped create a national media culture, as the same content became available simultaneously throughout the country.

The American media industry can be divided up between the legacy media conglomerates and newer, more tech-oriented companies that own both traditional and newer forms of media. The legacy conglomerates grew out of media companies that have existed for decades or even centuries. They own the major television networks, broadcast stations, cable channels and providers, newspapers, magazines, record labels, movie studios, and internet services. But there are new players in the media business who provide cable television and internet services, online search and content, and integrated media content and hardware. Among the legacy media conglomerates in the United States are Disney, Fox, News Corporation, WarnerMedia, ViacomCBS, and Bertelsmann. The new players include Facebook, Comcast/NBCUniversal, Google, and Apple.

Recent years have seen both legacy and newer media companies struggle over what is the right size to be the most competitive they can be in the marketplace. This has resulted in a rapid series of sales, mergers, and transformations of these companies.

Widespread access to the internet has brought about the rise of smaller-scale new-media companies that specialize in providing a wide range of media content that appeals to relatively small numbers of consumers. When combined, these niche markets, known as the long tail of media, can rival the size of the markets for blockbuster media content.

KEY TERMS ▶▶

penny press 53	local cable television systems 58	short head 67
synergy 54	long tail 67	

REVIEW QUESTIONS ▶▶

1. How does Facebook use and profit from user data? How has this created problems for the company?

2. How is media ownership different in the United States than in much of the rest of the world?

3. What do the "legacy conglomerates" have in common as media companies?

4. How do the new Big Media companies differ from the older legacy companies?

5. Why are large media companies constantly merging and breaking up with each other?

6. How do long-tail media differ from short-head media?

LEGACY MEDIA

BOOKS

The Birth of the Mass Media

When John Green first started publishing, the young adult best sellers were science fiction and fantasy dystopias with the fate of the world on the line. Green's novels are different. They are more personal; typically involve a "bright, troubled teenager"; and feature a lead female character who could be described as a "manic pixie dream girl."[1]

The author was not an immediate success. Green's first book, 2005's *Looking for Alaska*, was a somewhat autobiographical novel that was not a best seller, but it did win the Printz Award, a major prize for young adult fiction. This was followed by several more titles that helped grow a group of committed fans.

But in January 2012, Green became a literary star, with the publication of his story of a romance between two teen cancer patients called *The Fault in Our Stars*. The book was a huge success, spending 124 weeks on the *New York Times* best-seller list and 43 weeks as the number-one young adult book. (To be fair, children's and young adult best-seller lists tend to be more stable than those featuring books for adults.) The book was also at the top of the Amazon best-seller list, based on preorders, six months before it was released, though Green helped make that happen by promising in advance to personally autograph all 150,000 copies of the title's first printing.[2] The book ultimately sold more than 23 million copies and was the basis for a hit movie that made more than $307 million on a production budget of only $12 million.[3] Since then, a high school drama teacher and four of his students adapted the book into a stage play with Green's permission that was produced in 2019.[4] If that's not enough, Elon Musk's SpaceX reusable rocket company has named its satellite-based broadband internet project "Starlink" in honor of *The Fault in Our Stars*.[5]

In addition to having best-selling novels and hit movies, Green is well known for the YouTube videos he makes with his brother Hank. Starting in 2006, he and his brother decided to spend a year communicating with each other exclusively through public videos on YouTube at a point where the video-sharing service was only entering its second year. Their videos posted as Vlogbrothers have been tremendously popular.[6] Fourteen years after starting the project, the Green brothers are doing live recordings of their podcasts to raise money to help reduce child and maternal mortality in Sierra Leone.[7]

Despite all his success, Green says he still gets nervous working on each new book. "I remember thinking when I was writing my first book, 'The great thing if I get the opportunity to do this again will be that I will then know how to write a book.' Then when it came time to write my second book, I was like, 'I have no idea how to write a book,' and each time that was the case."[8]

While he had previously turned out books on a roughly annual schedule, it took nearly six years for him to complete *Turtles All the Way Down*, his follow-up to *Fault*. Aza Holmes, the heroine of *Turtles*, is a typical Green heroine, the "bright, troubled" teen, who also suffers from obsessive compulsive disorder (OCD), a characteristic she shares with her creator. "Having OCD is something that is an ongoing part of my life and I assume will probably be part of my life for the rest of it."[9]

Green has suffered from anxiety disorder and OCD for as long as he can remember. Following the success of *The Fault in Our Stars*, he had a particularly tough time with his illness. "I couldn't escape the spiral of my thoughts, and I felt like they were coming from the outside," Green told the *New York Times*.[10] During his bout of serious mental illness, Green started and abandoned several writing projects, but following his recovery in 2015, he dug into writing and revising *Turtles* as a way of dealing with what he had experienced. "Coming out of that, it was difficult to write about anything else. The topic demanded itself."[11]

"I want to talk about it, and not feel any embarrassment or shame because I think it's important for people to hear from adults who have good fulfilling lives and manage chronic mental illness as part of those good fulfilling lives." But Green also wants to make sure he doesn't romanticize his illness or claim it as a source of his creativity. "For me, it's a way out of myself, to not feel stuck inside myself. I want to be super careful not to claim there's some huge benefit to this brain problem that I have."[12]

Green is best known for the insight that he brings of the teenage mind. He told *New Yorker* writer Margaret Talbot, "I love the intensity teen-agers bring not just to first love but also to the first time you're grappling with grief . . . , the first time you're taking on why people suffer and whether there's meaning in life. . . . Teen-agers feel that what you conclude about those questions is going to *matter.* And they're dead right."[13]

Green is not without criticism for how he relates to teens and for relying too heavily on his well-known catchphrases, such as "don't forget to be awesome," frequently abbreviated to "DFTBA." In 2015, a teenage girl accused him online of being a "creep who panders to teenage girls so he can amass some weird cult-like following."[14]

Despite Green's occasional setbacks from criticism and his mental illness, Green has managed to create a wildly successful career in publishing (and on social media, which we will talk about later on). "[OCD] is not a mountain that you climb or a hurdle that you jump, it's something that you live with in an ongoing way," Green said. "People want that narrative of illness being in the past tense. But a lot of the time it isn't."[15]

Books are a source of entertainment, culture, and ideas for society and have given rise to more lasting controversies than almost any other medium. Book publishing is also a major business that is supported by the people who buy books. In this chapter, we look at how books developed from a hand-copied medium for elites into a popular medium consumed by millions, how society was revolutionized by the development of printing, how the publishing business operates, the conflict between literary and popular writing, and efforts to censor writers.

Books and Mass Communication

Books, consisting of words printed on paper, were the original medium of mass communication (although the Roman Catholic Church had previously achieved a degree of mass communication through sermons, as discussed in Chapter 1). Books allowed ideas to spread, encouraged the standardization of language and spelling, and created mass culture. Books and other printed materials also helped bring about such major social changes as the Protestant Reformation. However, before there could be books, there had to be writing.

Writing is thought to have originated around 3500 BC in the Middle East, in either Egypt or Mesopotamia. This means that written language is around 5,500 years old; spoken language, in comparison, is thought to be at least 40,000 years old. The great advantage offered by writing was that information could be stored. No longer did people have to memorize enormous amounts of information to maintain it. Stories could be written down and preserved for generations. However, early writing was not yet a form of mass communication. Reading and writing were elite skills held by people called scribes; their rare abilities gave them power within religious institutions and governments (which were often the same).[16]

The earliest form of writing was the **pictograph**, which consisted of pictures of objects painted on rock walls. The next major development was the **ideograph**—an abstract symbol that stands for an object or an idea. An ideograph is more formalized than a pictograph, with one symbol for each object or idea. Languages such as Chinese, Korean, and Japanese still make use of ideographs. The major challenge created by having one symbol for each word is that people must learn thousands of individual symbols. For example, literary Chinese has fifty thousand or more symbols, and everyday written Chinese has between five thousand and eight thousand symbols.

▲ This Proto-Elamite tablet is one of the earliest forms of writing.

▲ These Newspaper Rock petroglyphs are among the earliest forms of writing.

Ideographs are often used as international symbols, for example street signs use ideographs that are recognizable throughout the world, think of the red hexagon—it means STOP. Ideographs are useful in areas where many languages are spoken and helpful to travelers looking for bathrooms, hospitals, and train stations. Imagine a traveler in Europe looking for a place to take a bath. With an ideograph, a single symbol can stand for *bain* in French, *bad* in Danish, or *baño* in Spanish.

▲ The Egyptians developed papyrus, an early form of paper made from the papyrus reed, around 3100 BC. These hieroglyphics are from a papyrus scroll of the Egyptian Book of the Dead.

Most Americans typically have seen or heard of Egyptian hieroglyphics, the millennia old style of writing with symbols, but outside of that probably have never read a book written with ideographs. Chinese writing uses ideographs, but those symbols are relatively abstract and a long way from being recognizable drawings of something more than a symbol for an idea.

Surprisingly though, it's likely that you've used ideographs lately to send a text message, add content to an uploaded photo, or even in an email message. By using the emoji keyboard on your computer or mobile device, a smiling face, a smiling pile of poop, a smiling devil, a smiling cat, an Edvard Munch screaming face—you get the idea—are all available (plus hundreds more) for your messaging needs. It is tempting to think that these **emojis**, or small icons that stand for emotions or ideas, carry universal social meanings; however the truth is that people often do not agree on what they mean. For example, consider this one: While officially this is praying hands (available in any number of skin colors), some people see it portraying a reciprocal high five. A study by researchers at the University of Minnesota's GroupLens lab found that people looking at the same emoji can come up with dramatically different interpretations of it. Further complicating things is that each social media platform has its own versions of emojis. Consider the "grinning face with smiling eyes" icon. The icon is quite different depending on whether you are looking at it on an Apple, Google, Microsoft, Samsung, or LG platform.[17]

In 2018, the Unicode Consortium (which establishes the standards for the character sets on computers and mobile devices) published a list of new emojis to include in upcoming smartphone software updates, including redheads in the assortment of skin tone and hair color smiley emojis. There is also a wide range of skin tones to go with natural African American hair—not to mention a lacrosse stick, a strand of DNA, and a skateboard.[18]

At some point after 2000 BC people began using **phonography**, a system of writing in which symbols stand for spoken *sounds* rather than for objects or ideas in their writing. The use of phonographs pre-dates the more familiar concept of an **alphabet**, developed between 1700 BC and 1500 BC, in which letters represent individual sounds. Sound-based alphabet writing, with only a few dozen symbols, was relatively easy to learn compared to the earlier systems of ideographs. Being a scribe thus became less of an elite position. Among the earliest surviving written works are the Greek poet Homer's *Iliad* and *Odyssey*.[19]

Chesnot / Contributor / Getty Images

▲ These stylized smiley faces and images are examples of emojis, small digital icons used in electronic communication to express feelings. Every year, the Unicode Consortium proposes new emojis.

Once people had a way to record ideas in writing, they needed something to write on. The earliest documents were written on cave walls, rocks, and clay tablets, but these media had limited usefulness. Imagine taking notes on slabs of wet clay that had to be taken back to your dorm room to dry. Something light, portable, and relatively inexpensive was needed. **Papyrus**, a primitive form of paper made from the papyrus reed, was developed by the Egyptians around 3100 BC. Papyrus was placed on twenty- to thirty-foot-long rolls known as scrolls. Although it was more useful and portable than stone or clay tablets, papyrus tended to crumble or be eaten by bugs. **Parchment**, which was made from the skin of goats or sheep, eventually replaced papyrus because it was much less fragile.

Paper, made from cotton rags or wood pulp, was invented by the Chinese between 240 BC and 105 BC.[20] Knowledge of papermaking was brought from China to Baghdad by the Muslims in the late 700s, and then to Europe by way of Spain in the mid-eleventh century. Papermaking spread throughout Europe during the 1300s, but it did not replace parchment until printing became common in the 1500s.

A Demand for Books

Throughout the early medieval period (AD 400–800), most books in Europe were religious texts hand-copied by monks in the **scriptoria**, or copying rooms, of monasteries. Because of the difficulty of preparing parchment, monks sometimes scraped the writing off old parchments to create new books. This led to the loss of many Greek and Latin texts. Books that had lasted hundreds of years and survived the fall of Rome were lost simply because they were erased!

With the rise of literacy in the thirteenth century, the demand for books increased. It soon exceeded the output of the monks, and the production of books shifted to licensed publishers, or stationers. Books were still copied by hand one at a time from a supposedly perfect original (or exemplar). One title from this era was Geoffrey Chaucer's *Canterbury Tales*, which is still in print today.

By the fourteenth century, books were becoming relatively common. Religious texts known as illuminated manuscripts were embellished with pictures and elaborately decorated calligraphy, in part to help transmit the message to nonliterate audiences.[21]

The Development of the Printing Press. Printing was invented in China toward the end of the second century. Images were carved into blocks of wood, which were inked and placed on sheets of paper, thereby reproducing the image. However, woodcuts saw limited usage because materials could not be reproduced rapidly. Between 1050 and 1200, both the Chinese and the Koreans developed the idea of movable type, but with thousands of separate ideographs, printing was not practical.

Johannes Gutenberg (1394–1468), a metalworker living in Mainz, Germany, in the mid-1400s, became the first European to develop movable type. Although he developed the first practical printing press (using a modified winepress), Gutenberg's most significant invention was the **type mold**, which enabled printers to make multiple, identical copies of a single letter without hand-carving each.

The most famous of Gutenberg's printed books was his edition of the Bible published in 1455. Approximately 120 copies of this Bible were printed, of which 46 are known to survive. In the

1980s, one of Gutenberg's Bibles sold for $5.39 million at Christie's auction house.[22]

Typesetting was a difficult task in Gutenberg's day. The printer selected a type case containing all the characters of a typeface in a particular size and style known as a **font**—from a font or fountain of type. (Today the word *font* has become largely synonymous with *typeface* and is no longer restricted to mean a size and style—for example, bold or italic.) The printer then took from the case the letters needed to spell the words in a line of type and placed them on a type stick, which looked something like the rack used to hold letters in a Scrabble game. Once an entire line had been set, the printer placed it in a printer's frame, which held the type down.

German metalworker Johannes Gutenberg (right), depicted here, developed the type mold and printing press that led to the first mass-produced books.

Italics were invented in 1501 by the Italian printer Aldus Manutius (c. 1450–1515), from whom the early desktop publishing firm Aldus took its name. By the 1600s, printers could purchase mass-produced type rather than making their own type molds. Many popular typefaces originated in the seventeenth and eighteenth centuries and are named after the printers who devised them: Claude Garamond, William Caslon, John Baskerville, and Giambattista Bodoni. A quick check of a computer's font menu will show how many of them are still in use.[23]

Books and Mass Culture

Gutenberg's development of the type mold and printing press signaled the invention of mass communication and some major cultural changes. During this time, culture was rapidly changing from the concept of beliefs, traditions, and ways of life in small communities to a phenomenon that, by reaching a mass audience, had a regional, national, or even international effect on large populations. The invention of movable type brought a major cultural change: the printing of standardized books.

With the invention of the printing press, text could be stored in multiple "perfect" copies. No longer could copyists insert mistakes when they reproduced a book. Printing allowed students to have identical copies of books to study. The printing press also made books available in greater numbers and at lower cost. Although printing did not make books inexpensive, it did make them affordable to people besides priests and the wealthy, especially due to the growth of libraries. The printing press also made new types of books available, particularly those written in a country's common language, such as German, instead of Latin, which was spoken only by the highly educated.

The second major cultural change happened when English printer William Caxton (c. 1422–1491) helped to establish the rules for English: standardizing word usage, grammar, punctuation, and spelling. He accomplished much of this simply by publishing books in English rather than in the more scholarly Latin.[24] The standardization of the English language came about gradually, though. For example, in his journals written in the early 1800s, explorer William Clark notes that he and Meriwether Lewis set out "under a jentle brease."[25] It's not so much that Clark didn't know how to spell these words; at the time, there was still no single "correct" spelling.

What was necessary for standardizing of language was putting together a definitive English dictionary. Work on the first edition of the *Oxford English Dictionary* (OED) began in 1857 with the goal of finding the origin of every word in the English language. When the authors started the project, they thought it might take ten years. Instead, the first edition, all ten volumes of it, was not completed until April 1928.

Today the OED has been through two editions and several supplements. In the 1990s, work began on an electronic version of the dictionary. In June 2018, the editors completed their most recent updating of the dictionary and started over again with the letter A.[26] Each month, contributors to the OED submit more than eighteen thousand new words to be considered for inclusion.

The January 2020 update included several words and new definitions from a range of cultures within the American melting pot:[27]

- *Bodega*—"*U.S. regional (New York City)* A small local shop, usually with extended opening hours, where customers can buy a limited range of household goods and groceries; a convenience store." The word's current usage comes from Puerto-Rican owned shops in New York. Many Americans may get their first exposure to the term through the movie version of Lin-Manuel Miranda's hit Broadway show *In The Heights* that tells the story of a Dominican Republic immigrant in Brooklyn Heights, New York, who owns a bodega.

- *Jewish penicillin*—"*n. colloquial* (a humorous name for) chicken soup, strongly associated with Jewish culture, and popularly considered as a remedy for all ailments or valued for its supposed restorative properties."

- *Taxi wallah*—"*n.* originally and chiefly *Indian* English a taxi driver." While the use of the term to describe a taxi driver dates back to the 1920s, using the term "wallah" to describe someone who carries things or does a job dates back to 1776.

Spreading Ideas Through Publishing

By far the most important effect of the printing press was that it allowed ideas—such as those of the Protestant Reformation—to spread easily beyond the communities where they originated. Although the printing press did not cause the Protestant Reformation, it certainly helped it take root.

▲ Many Americans may get their first exposure to the term bodega through the movie version of Lin-Manuel Miranda's hit Broadway show *In The Heights* that tells the story of a Dominican Republic immigrant in Brooklyn Heights, New York, who owns a bodega.

Don Arnold / Contributor / Getty Images

Martin Luther, the German monk who founded the Lutheran Church, clearly understood how the printing press could be used to spread his ideas throughout Europe. In 1522, Luther translated the New Testament of the Bible into German so that ordinary people might be able to read it.

The first printing press in the New World was set up by the Spanish in Mexico City in 1539; by 1560, the press had issued more than thirty-seven titles. This was a full century before the British in the Massachusetts Bay Colony would start printing. Unfortunately, none of the books from the Spanish press survive today.[28]

Printing in North America began in 1640 with the publication of *The Whole Booke of Psalmes*, known familiarly as the **Bay Psalm Book**. Put together by Puritans who were unhappy with existing translations of the psalms, the first edition sold 1,700 copies, a spectacular accomplishment when one considers that only 3,500 families lived in New England at the time. (Book historian James D. Hart suggests that some of these copies were exported back to England.[29]) During the next 125 years, the Bay Psalm Book went through at least fifty-one editions in the colonies and Europe. (You can read more about how the Bay Psalm Book played a role in the establishment of the media business in the New World in Chapter 3.)

The advent of the printing press and the publication of books in the language of everyday life helped doom Latin as a spoken language and put literacy—and the ability to interpret religious texts—within the reach of common people for the first time in history. The creation of a literate mass society also helped spread scientific ideas, such as Copernicus's claim that Earth was not the center of the universe. Books made it possible for people to learn individually, thus allowing new ideas to break into an otherwise closed community. This is also why every government since Gutenberg's time has wanted at least some control over the mass media.[30] So, with the advent of mass media barely begun, we see the first examples of Secret 1—The media are essential components of our lives, and Secret 4—Nothing is new: Everything that happened in the past will happen again.

What did people in the American colonies read? Among the best-known authors was Benjamin Franklin, whose *Poor Richard's Almanack* sold nearly ten thousand copies per year, far more to date than any other books at the time in North America.[31] Nonreligious books that sold well in New England included those on agriculture and animal husbandry, science, surveying, and the military.

But not everything was of serious interest. In the 1680s, Boston's leading bookseller attempted to order two copies of the book *The London Jilt, or, the Politick Whore; shewing all the artifices and stratagems which the Ladies of Pleasure make use of, for the intriguing and decoying of men; interwoven with several pleasant stories of the Misses' ingenious performances*, a title not that different from what might be ordered today.[32]

Samuel Richardson's *Pamela*, published in 1740, was the first English novel. It was a book for the middle class, with characters and situations that ordinary people could identify with. Franklin published a colonial edition of the novel in 1744, but it would be forty-five years until the first American novel was published.

The Development of Large-Scale, Mass-Produced Books

The industrial prosperity of the mid-1800s spurred the growth of cities and the emergence of the middle class. During this time, the number of people who attended public schools grew as well. Education up to the high school level, although still not universal, was becoming common.[33] Mass culture in the United States expanded throughout the nineteenth century, disseminating widely through penny press newspapers, magazines, Sunday School tracts, and inexpensively produced books.

Serial novels, which were published in installments, were popular in the 1830s and 1840s. Charles Dickens published *The Pickwick Papers* as a serial novel. Serial publication made each section of the book less expensive than a whole book, which appealed to readers, and brought in a steady flow of income, which appealed to publishers.[34] (Serial novels got a boost again in the 1990s when Stephen King published his novel *The Green Mile* in paperback serial form.) The first paperbacks, the so-called **dime novels** (which, despite their name, often sold for as little as a nickel), were heroic action stories, popularized by authors such as Bret Harte, and they generally celebrated democratic ideals. The Civil War was a big time for sales of dime novels, with copies being shipped to Union soldiers as a morale booster.

The 1800s saw massive changes on the business side of publishing, too. Hand-powered flat-bed presses could print no more than 350 pages a day, but the new steam-powered **rotary press** (invented in 1814) could print as many as sixteen thousand sections (not just pages) in the same amount of time. Through all this, type still had to be set by hand, much as it was in Gutenberg's day. But 1885 saw the introduction of the Mergenthaler Linotype typesetting machine, which let a compositor type at a keyboard rather than pick each letter out by hand, thus speeding up the printing process once again. The **Linotype** was the standard for typesetting until the age of computer composition.

The nineteenth century thus brought the first real mass media that could be recognized today, with books, newspapers, and magazines being printed and distributed in forms that anyone could afford. With the growth of democracy and mass-produced reading materials came the growth of mass literacy.

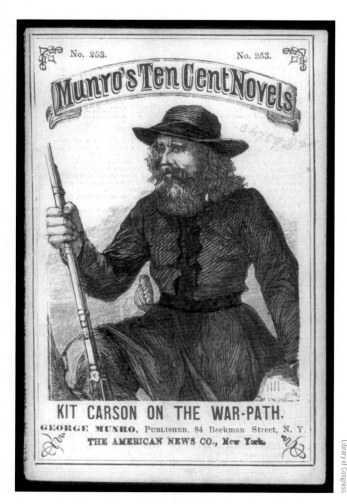

▲ *Kit Carson on the War-Path*, published by Munro's Ten Cent Novels, was one of the many dime novels read by the newly literate public in the nineteenth century.

Buying and Selling Books

In the twentieth century, the writing and selling of books became big business, with a huge variety of books being published. The numbers have continued to grow in the early twenty-first century. In 1995, 1.2 million separate books were available, and by 2005, Amazon.com claimed to have more than 3.7 million titles available.[35] But getting a reliable number from Amazon is problematic at best. The company almost never discusses the specific number of items sold. Derek Haines, writing for the *Just Publishing Advice* blog in April 2018, tried to do a search on Amazon to come up with a number and estimated that there were 3.4 million Kindle e-books on the market and 48.5 million paper titles.[36] (We'll talk more about Amazon's competitors in just a minute.)

Getting all those books from the authors' computers or typewriters into the hands of readers is what the publishing business is all about. It involves three major players:

1. Publishers—Companies that buy manuscripts and develop them into books

2. Writers—People (authors) who write the books

3. Booksellers—Companies that take the book from the publisher to the book-buying public

Publishers

Publishers are the companies that buy manuscripts from authors and turn them into books. Although there are thousands of publishers worldwide, a small number of companies publish most of all books sold today. This proportion has grown substantially since the 1920s, when the twenty largest publishers were responsible for only 50 percent of all books published.[37] This transformation has taken place because regional publishers are buying up small independent publishing houses, and international conglomerates are buying up major national publishing companies. As a result, the range of ownership of the publishing business is increasingly limited, and fewer people are making more of the decisions that determine what people will be able to read.[38]

You can get a visual representation of this consolidation with a chart that shows what the five biggest U.S. trade book publishers own: https://almossawi.com/big-five-publishers/.

The process of consolidation in the publishing industry can be seen in the story of American publisher Random House. Random House was founded in 1925. After years of growth, in 1960 the company acquired another major American publishing house, Alfred A. Knopf. In 1965, media conglomerate RCA bought Random House, and throughout the 1970s and 1980s, Random House continued to grow, buying up a host of publishers. In 1998, German media giant Bertelsmann bought Random House and combined it with its existing publishing holdings, and in 2013, the group added trade publisher Penguin to the mix.[39]

Penguin Random House has continued to grow by acquiring smaller publishers. In 2009, it acquired Ten Speed Press, an independent alternative publisher of titles such as *What Color Is Your Parachute?* and the *Moosewood Cookbook*. This acquisition brings to mind another, when News Corporation, through its HarperCollins division, bought out literary publisher Ecco Press. Daniel Halpern, founder of the press, told the *Washington Post*,

People will say, "There goes another independent press, isn't it too bad." The short answer is, "Yes, it's too bad." But that's the reality. Let's not be sentimental about this stuff. This is not a time when the small press can survive.[40]

The World's Top Publishers. The publishing business is a global industry, with owners in the United States, Germany, the United Kingdom, Canada, China, and the Netherlands. These companies publish a variety of books, ranging from best-selling fiction to textbooks to technical references. Table 4.1 reports the world's top publishers of **trade books**—the commercial, mass market fiction and non-fiction books targeted at general audiences.

▼ TABLE 4.1

Big Five Trade Publishers

	Top Five Trade Publishers	Revenue	Ownership
1.	Penguin Random House Sells 800 million copies of print, audio, and e-books annually	$4.4 billion	Co-owned by publishing giants Pearson PLC and Bertelsmann
2.	Hachette Livre Publishes more separate titles than Penguin Random House	$2.7 billion	Lagardère Group, a media conglomerate headquartered in France
3.	HarperCollins Has more than 120 separate imprints	$1.5 billion	News Corp.
4.	Macmillan Publishers Original publisher for Lewis Carroll, Rudyard Kipling, and W.B. Yeats	$1.4 billion	Holtzbrinck Publishing Group, a family owned German publisher
5.	Simon & Schuster Original publisher for Ernest Hemingway and F. Scott Fitzgerald	$830 million	ViacomCBS

Source: Adapted from "The Largest Book Publishers in 2020," Reedsy Blog, https://blog.reedsy.com/largest-book-publishers/

University and Small Presses. Not all publishing is done by large corporations; a substantial number of **university and small presses** issue a limited number of books and may not be in the business for profit. Among their titles are books that serve a limited geographic or subject area or an academic discipline—mostly scholarly books or textbooks. An example of a small press is Interweave, which publishes books about knitting, weaving, and crafting. But academic presses occasionally print breakout books. The late Norman Maclean, an English professor at the University of Chicago, had his memoir about growing up in Montana and fly-fishing published by the University of Chicago Press. The book, *A River Runs Through It*, was an enormous success (and was made into a movie directed by Robert Redford and starring Brad Pitt).[41]

Small Publishers. Not all successful books come from big publishers, and not all big books are conventional novels or biographies. Newcomer independent publisher Cottage Door Press has had big success since it was founded in 2014 by publishing a wide range of books targeted at children. In 2014, the company had nine employees and had published no books. By 2018, Cottage Door Press had reached twenty-four employees and was releasing 158 titles that year. Those books also might not match your stereotypes of what a book should look like. These include padded board books, lift-a-flap books, touch-and-feel books, and books that make sounds. Marketing manager Melissa Tigges told *Publishers Weekly*, "We believe in educating and entertaining both children and their grown-ups. We choose artwork and language that interests, informs, and stretches their growing minds."[42] Similar to the bigger publishers, Cottage Door has started acquiring titles from other struggling publishers that are going out of business.[43]

The Government Publishing Office. Surprisingly, the federal government is one of the nation's biggest publishers. The U.S. Government Publishing Office (GPO) has been producing government documents and books in a variety of forms since it was founded back in 1861.

BSIP/Universal Images Group Editorial/Getty Images

▲ Small press publisher Cottage Door Press has found a market niche publishing a range of books for small children, including board books for infants.

While most of its titles are dry government reports, the GPO has published occasional best sellers, including the *9/11 Commission Report*, the Warren Commission's report on the Kennedy assassination, and the so-called Pentagon Papers (discussed in Chapters 2 and 13). To mark the fiftieth anniversary of the Warren Commission report, the GPO published a digital edition, including the 888-page report along with the twenty-six volumes covering the hearings.[44]

Writers

The next group of players in the publishing business is composed of the people who write the books—the authors. Most media attention goes to blockbuster writers and authors, such as Margaret Atwood and, as mentioned at the beginning of the chapter, John Green, or literary authors, such as Richard Russo and Alice Munro; less is written about the vast majority of authors who write without multimillion-dollar contracts, book tours, or television commercials during *The View*. But what is the publishing experience like for an ordinary author?

Consider the story of a typical book, a science fiction romance titled *Moon of Desire*. Pam Hanson (a first-time author and the wife of this book's author) and her mother, Barbara Andrews (who authored several romance novels in the 1980s), wrote a proposal for the novel and a sample chapter and submitted them to a publisher in March (see Figure 4.1).

Then they waited. In June, the publisher agreed to acquire the manuscript. The authors received a contract for the book, which called for the manuscript to be delivered by December 1. With the contract signed, the authors were paid the first half of their advance. This did not mean, however, that they got rich. Advances for first novels at the time were typically between $1,000 and $5,000, and this advance was typical.

Then came the work of writing the book—ninety thousand words, or about 360 typed, double-spaced pages. The mother and daughter traded drafts back and forth between their computers. A week before the deadline, they sent the finished book to their editor at the publishing company. If the authors had missed their deadline, the publisher would have had the right to reject the book and cancel the contract.

A few weeks later, in early January, the editor sent revisions to the authors. Manuscript revisions may consist of anything from trivial changes in punctuation or grammar to major changes in characterization or plot. In this case, the only major change was that the mutant cannibals menacing the heroine in one chapter had to be toned down a bit. Once the manuscript was accepted, the authors received the second half of the advance. But keep in mind that advances are against royalties (a percentage of the selling price of each book paid to the author), meaning that the advance payments will be deducted from the author's royalty payments.

After a manuscript has been accepted and revised, the book goes into production. An artist creates a cover illustration based on information from an "art fact sheet" that suggests possible scenes for the cover and describes what the hero and heroine look like. The *Moon of Desire* cover featured the hero and heroine on a raft floating on a flaming sea. A book designer lays out the rest of the book, deciding what the pages will look like, what typeface will be used, and how big the book will be. (These can be serious considerations. Stephen King was required to cut 150,000 words, nearly half its length, from the original edition of *The Stand* to make it more marketable.[45])

Once the book is set in type, a copy of the ready-to-print pages—known as **proofs**—is sent to the authors. Authors are supposed to correct only blatant errors in proofs, although

Ten Steps in the Book Publishing Process

1 Authors write proposal and sample chapters. Submit to publisher.

2 Publisher signs book. Authors paid first half of advance.

3 Authors write book.

4 Book delivered to publisher.

5 Authors revise manuscript. Book is accepted; authors paid second half of advance.

6 Book enters production. Cover is designed.

7 Authors read and correct proofs.

8 Book is printed and distributed to bookstores.

9 Book can be purchased in bookstores.

10 Authors get first royalties.

Time from proposal to bookstore: twenty months

Source: iStockphoto.com/penfold, iStockphoto.com/julichka, iStockphoto.com/5455586, iStockphoto.com/frender, iStockphoto.com/LonelySnailDesign, iStockphoto.com/milosluz, iStockphoto.com, iStockphoto.com/Warchi, iStockphoto.com/4x6, iStockphoto.com/tashka2000

some have been known to start rewriting the book at this point. As is usual in popular fiction, Hanson and Andrews had about a week to read the proofs of their book and send them back to the publisher; after the corrections were made, the proofs were sent to a printer to produce the finished book.

At this point, it is time to start marketing the book. This may include placing advertisements in newspapers, in fan magazines, or even on television and scheduling a book tour and media appearances. But Andrews and Hanson, like most first-time novelists, had to make do with virtually no marketing support. Twenty months after the original proposal was submitted, the book was available in bookstores.

Book publishing can be lucrative for some, but most writers make very little money. Nicholas Sparks's multimillion-dollar advances are exciting but not typical. The median annual wage for writers and authors was $62,170 in May 2018.[46] Hanson and Andrews, who wrote their book under a single pseudonym, Pam Rock, saw their first royalties beyond the initial advance more than two and a half years after the initial proposal was sent in.

The Photo Works / Alamy Stock Photo

▲ *Hamilton* creator Lin-Manuel Miranda, along with three of his collaborators, purchased the Drama Book Shop to save it when rents in its Times Square location became to expensive for the store to stay open. The new owners plan to find it a more affordable Midtown location. Miranda wrote much of his first musical *In The Heights* in the basement of the store.

Booksellers

The last major players in the book business are the book wholesalers and retailers—the companies that take the book from the publisher to the book-buying public. The Ingram Book Company, the nation's largest book wholesaler, distributes more than fourteen million book titles to more than thirty-nine thousand retail, library, and educational outlets. Essentially, Ingram and its smaller competitors are the sources from which bookstores buy their books.[47] The buyers at Ingram are among the most important in the book business; they determine how many copies of a book will be stocked in the company's warehouses. This can, in turn, determine the size of a book's press run. Ingram's buyers are respected not only by bookstore owners but also by scholarly presses.[48]

Among booksellers, Barnes & Noble has been the one legacy chain still standing, but it was bought in 2019 by Elliott Advisors private equity fund for $683 million. What that will mean for the remaining brick-and-mortar bookstore chain is unclear.[49] As of 2018, the company's revenue totaled $3.7 billion for the year, and it operated 630 superstores. Through its education division, it operated 724 college bookstores throughout the United States with an annual revenue of $1.9 billion.[50] In 2020 during Black History Month the company stepped into a big controversy when it issued a line of classic British novels, such as *Frankenstein* and *Moby Dick*, with covers featuring black or brown characters. Only one of the books, *The Count of Monte Cristo* by Alexandre Dumas, was written by a person of color. Critics accused Barnes & Noble of engaging in "literary blackface." Writing in an editorial, the *Guardian* newspaper pointed out, "[I]f Barnes & Noble really wanted to honor black history, the company could *promote books by black authors*."

While there can be little question that online bookseller Amazon has killed off the chain book superstores, recent years have seen independent bookstores resurging in popularity. The American Booksellers Association reports that between the mid-1990s and 2009, the number of independent bookstores dropped by about 40 percent. But between 2009 and 2015, something amazing happened—the number of indie bookstores grew by 35 percent, going from 1,651 to 2,227. That growth has continued. Dane Neller, owner of New York's Shakespeare & Co., has opened his third successful bookstore. "Bookstores are back and they're back in a big way," he told CBS News. "I'm not giving into hyperbole—it was record-breaking for us."[51]

Organizational behavior professor Ryan Raffaelli found three major reasons for the resurgence of independent booksellers:

- The sense of community they provide. Just as people love their local coffee shops, they like the community connection of a local bookstore.

- Successful independent bookstores have a good sense of what their customers are interested in and can make recommendations that go beyond the national best-seller lists.

- Local bookstores provide an intellectual hub for their communities with lectures, book signings, and reading groups, to name just a few.[52] As an example, when Stephen King did a book tour to promote his novel *End of Watch*, he was hosted by independent bookstores in twelve cities of varying size across the country.[53]

If you're paying attention as you read through the reasons why independent bookstores are finding new life in the past decade, you'll notice that it's all about the interaction of customers with the store, with authors, and with each other. In other words, it's because of Secret 5—All media are social.

Books and the Long Tail. The internet launched the long-tail segment of the media by allowing a company to produce a catalog that is available to everyone with little marginal cost for each additional viewer. Amazon.com founder Jeff Bezos started selling books on the internet because the web was the only practical way to offer the variety that he sought:

> It . . . turns out that you can't have a big book catalog on paper; it's totally impractical. There are more than 100,000 new books published every year, and even a superstore can't carry them all. The biggest superstores have 175,000 titles and there are only about three that big. So that became the idea: let Amazon.com be the first place where you can easily find and buy a million different books.[54]

And this was the radical notion—instead of offering a selection of books, why not offer every book, all 7.5 million or so English-language books in print? Amazon can keep the most popular books in stock in its warehouses and seamlessly order books from publishers if they are in smaller demand. It can even offer out-of-print books from private stores that partner with Amazon or custom-publish them through arrangements it's made with publishers. (This is a prime example of Secret 2—There are no mainstream media. Due to long-tail retailers like Amazon, consumers are no longer limited to just the biggest books from the biggest publishers.)

The online bookstore began operations in July 1995, and by December 1998, it had served more than 4.5 million customers. Why is it called Amazon? Because it begins with an *A* and therefore will appear first on alphabetical lists. In 1998, Amazon started selling videos and CDs, and since 1999, it has added toys, clothing, kitchen equipment, and other merchandise.

A key feature of Amazon is that it tracks customers' interests by recording what they've already bought on Amazon.com. Each time a buyer enters the site, a personalized home page shows related books that the customer might not have known about otherwise. A shopper looking at the description of the thriller *Red Sparrow* by Jason Matthews gets a recommendation for Brad Meltzer's *The Escape Artist*. Or at a more prosaic level, checking out *Personal Finance for Dummies* by Eric Tyson will get you a recommendation for *How to be a Real Estate Investor* by Phil Pustejovsky.

Online bookstores are among the most successful businesses in electronic commerce. One reason for their initial success was that in the early days of the commercialized internet, people who owned computers were also likely to read books. Also, well-educated people, who tend to read for pleasure and entertainment, are likely to work in offices where they have internet connections and thus can buy books online. Finding books online can be easier than finding them in a bookstore, especially if the title is obscure. A former Penguin Random House executive notes that online bookstores provide instant gratification.[55]

Marketing partnerships are an important element of online bookstores. Anyone who wants to can set up an online bookstore on his or her website in partnership with Amazon and receive a small commission for every book sold. In the past, barnesandnoble.com had partnerships with the *New York Times* and *USA Today* websites that let readers purchase the books being written about in the papers. Of course, such partnerships raise questions about objectivity: Can a book review be objective when the newspaper that's reviewing the book is also selling the book?[56]

The Textbook Business. Textbooks are different from other books in one major respect—the people who select the books are not the same as the end users, the people who must buy and pay for them. Students charge that, because of this disconnect, faculty members do not take price sufficiently into account when picking books for their courses.

Estimates on how much students spend per year on textbooks vary widely. The United States Bureau of Labor Statistics suggests that students spend an average of $1,250 a year on books and supplies.[57] On the other hand, figures from the National Association of College Stores reports that student spending on course materials has dropped on average from $701 per year in 2007–2008 to $415 in 2018–2019.[58] Among the reasons for these possible price drops are the growth of book rentals, inclusive access plans, and electronic books.[59]

The textbook industry is currently going through a big period of change, says John Fallon, CEO of education publishing giant Pearson. In an interview with tech journalist Kara Swisher, Fallon said that the era of the "$300 textbook" is over. Instead, students will be buying access to a host of electronic resources ranging from e-books, to study sites, to mobile phone apps.[60] Fallon told Swisher that revenues for the big publishers have been falling steadily, with Pearson's dropping from $2 billion in 2013 to $1.3 billion for 2019. This change is being driven in large part by the fact that students can rent books from companies like Amazon or Chegg.

Under a rental plan, students pay a fee that is between two-thirds and one-half the cost of either a new or used book, then they turn the book back into the bookstore at the end of the semester. In essence, it's a guaranteed buyback plan.[61] A report from Orbis Research suggests that students are also saving money by renting e-textbooks rather than paper books at substantially lower costs.[62] The disadvantage of rentals, of course, is that after the semester is over, students no longer have the books to use as a reference.

While students like e-textbooks in principle, when forced to choose between a printed book and an e-book, most choose a printed textbook.[63] An informal survey of your author's students showed that while students liked e-books for recreational reading, they much preferred paper editions for the textbooks. They do, however, like the lower prices of e-books.

One of the students' major complaints about textbook costs is having to use one-time purchase access codes. These codes are sold by publishers and can be used for review and other study materials, but they can also be for homework systems required to complete the class. In addition to objecting to the costs, students complain that unlike paper and electronic textbooks, homework accounts cannot be shared.[64]

A radically different approach a few universities are taking is so-called **inclusive access** programs where schools license all the assigned books electronically from a major publisher and make them available to students at either a discounted rate or no additional charge. In some cases, the e-books are integrated into the school's course management system that delivers other class materials. Students are typically signed up for the rental automatically and then have a short period of time when they can opt out from using the book. The advantage for faculty is that all students will have access to their books on the first day of class rather than waiting until sometimes weeks into the semester to get their books.[65] McGraw-Hill, Cengage, and Pearson have all found success with these programs.

There are also downsides to these inclusive access programs. In many cases, students only have access when they are online. If they want a downloadable version, there is often an extra fee. Another issue is that these contracts strongly push faculty to order their texts from a preferred company rather than from the publisher that has what they consider to be the best book. Nicole Allen, an advocate for research libraries and open access materials, told *Inside Higher Ed* these programs are "the opposite of inclusive, because it is premised on publishers controlling when, where and for how long students have access to their materials."[66]

As this period of transition in textbook publishing progresses, it is possible that the already concentrated ownership of textbook publishers will get even more concentrated. Currently four publishers control more than 80 percent of the higher education marketplace: Pearson, Cengage, Wiley, and McGraw-Hill.[67] As of this writing in the spring of 2020, McGraw-Hill Education and Cengage had announced plans to merge but were facing strong opposition from consumer groups, students, and college bookstores. Critics worry that combining two of the top four educational publishers into an even larger company would continue to reduce competition in the marketplace and give the new company more control over prices. The two companies claim the merger will let them be more efficient and lower costs.[68]

Books and Culture

For all the attention that movies, television, CDs, and video games get from social critics, books continue to be a major source of excitement, controversy, money, and even violence. A continual tension exists between blockbuster books that make large amounts of money for publishers and so-called important books that have lasting literary value. But this tension is nothing new—it dates back at least to the middle of the nineteenth century. As noted earlier in this chapter, the mid-1800s were a period of strong growth for the publishing business, with the number of serious novels and popular fiction titles increasing rapidly. Americans wrote almost one thousand novels from 1840 to 1850, up from the 109 books of American fiction published between 1820 and 1830.[69]

The 1850s saw the publication of Nathaniel Hawthorne's *Scarlet Letter*, Herman Melville's *Moby-Dick*, and Walt Whitman's *Leaves of Grass*, but none of these "great books" sold nearly as well as popular novels written by and for women. Hawthorne resented losing sales to popular women authors. He once became so frustrated that he commented, "America is now wholly given over to a d——d mob of scribbling women, and I should have no chance of success while the public taste is occupied with their trash—and should be ashamed of myself if I did succeed."[70]

The **domestic novels** that Hawthorne was complaining about told of women who overcame tremendous problems through their Christian strength, virtue, and faith, ending up in prosperous middle-class homes. One of the best known of Hawthorne's "scribblers," at least today, is Sarah Josepha Hale. She was well known not only as a novelist but also as a writer of children's books (she was the author of "Mary Had a Little Lamb") and the editor of *Godey's Lady's Book*, a popular women's magazine of the day (see Chapter 5).[71]

Women authors of popular fiction continue to sell well today. According to the Romance Writers of America, romantic fiction had annual sales of $1.08 billion in 2013, the majority of which was written and read by women. Nearly 40 percent of the sales of romances were as e-books, and the rest were spread among mass-market paperbacks, trade paperbacks, and hardbacks.[72]

Hawthorne's complaints about popular fiction outselling serious writing are often echoed today. Major publishers work hard to promote a limited number of blockbuster books—in part because only a small percentage of books make a profit. For example, in 2000, romance publisher Harlequin recorded a dramatic increase in profits primarily because of two best-selling titles.[73] Typical among the best-selling authors whom publishers love is mystery writer Janet Evanovich. She started writing romance novels for Bantam, then branched out into the wildly successful Stephanie Plum bounty hunter novels. Evanovich's novels mix humor, adventure, mystery, and romance. "I wanted to write the book that made people feel good. If you are having a bad day, you could read my book and I might make you smile," she said.[74] Why did Evanovich choose to write about a somewhat inept female bounty hunter? According to her, she saw a space for it in the marketplace: "So I took what I loved about the romance genre and squashed it into a mystery format."[75] The first printing of her 2009 novel *Finger Lickin' Fifteen* was two million copies, and thirty million copies of her books are in print. In contrast, Marilynne Robinson's Pulitzer Prize–winning novel *Gilead* sold only 345,000 copies. Good sales, to be sure, but nowhere near the levels of popular fiction.[76]

Library of Congress

▲ Famed photographer Mathew Brady took this portrait of celebrated American author Nathaniel Hawthorne in the mid-nineteenth century. Brady's role in the development of photojournalism is discussed in Chapter 5.

Not every best-selling book is popular fiction, however. Harper Lee's classic *To Kill a Mockingbird*, which has stayed in print for more than sixty years, continues to sell nearly one million copies a year.[77]

These blockbuster authors illustrate the main thrust of the publishing business today—finding writers who can turn out one big hit after another. Harry Hoffman, a former bookstore chain CEO, points out that books must compete with Nintendo and television. In Hoffman's view, publishing no longer views itself as being in the literature business; instead, it considers itself to be in the entertainment business.[78]

Of course, popular fiction and literature can sometimes intersect. Among the most influential best sellers of the past fifty years is John Ronald Reuel (J. R. R.) Tolkien's epic-length fantasy trilogy, *The Lord of the Rings*. Initially published in England in 1954 and 1955, the story has remained continuously in print and has now sold more than hundreds of millions of copies—eleven million during 2002 alone. (The sales boost in 2001 and following years can be attributed in part to the popularity of the movie series based on the books.)

Tolkien, an English professor at Oxford, was a colleague of Clive Staples (C. S.) Lewis, author of the popular *Chronicles of Narnia*, which also formed the basis for a popular movie series. A veteran of World War I, Tolkien specialized in the history of language and literature, and his passion was European myths and sagas. He started work on *The Hobbit*, his first book set in the fictional Middle Earth, in 1930, telling the story of Bilbo Baggins and his adventures. *The Hobbit* was written initially to entertain Tolkien's four children, but the book was published in 1937 after the ten-year-old son of an editor read the manuscript and liked it. The book was a success, and the publisher asked for a sequel. Seventeen years later, the first part of *The Lord of the Rings* was published.

Tolkien wrote the story as a single book, but the publisher divided it into three volumes to make it more practical to print and sell. In fact, the story was so long that even Tolkien didn't know what to do with it. In a letter to his publisher, Tolkien wrote, "My work has escaped from my control, and I have produced a monster: an immensely long, complex, rather bitter, and rather terrifying romance, quite unfit for children (if fit for anybody)."[79]

Although Tolkien died in 1973, his books have had a lasting influence on American popular culture. *The Lord of the Rings* strongly influenced rock groups such as Yes and Led Zeppelin, and it inspired Gary Gygax to quit his job as an insurance salesperson and devote himself to developing his role-playing game Dungeons & Dragons. There is even an academic journal devoted to Tolkien's Middle Earth and its linguistics. Most important, the entire genre of contemporary fantasy literature owes its existence to Tolkien. The fantasy sections in bookstores and the whole genre of swords-and-sorcery movies would not exist but for the inspired writings of a British professor.[80]

The Role of Libraries in Culture

For as long as people have been reading books, there have been libraries. For example, the earliest known libraries date from the 2nd millennium BC with collections of clay tablets. More than thirty thousand tablets were found in the ancient city of Lagash, located at the confluence of the Euphrates and Tigris rivers in what is now modern-day Iraq. Scribes used reeds to inscribe wedge-shaped cuneiform letters on wet clay; if you are interested, the Library of Congress has a small collection of these dating from between 2144 BC and 2124 BC. (We will talk more about this at the end of the chapter.)[81]

The ancient library that gets the most recognition is the great Alexandrian Library, which although located in Egypt was primarily a Greek repository. It was founded by Alexander the

CM Dixon/Print Collector/Getty Images

▲ This ancient Sumerian cuneiform tablet records the distribution of barley rations to about two hundred workmen and their children within the city-state of Lagash.

Great in 332 BC and is described as a "combination university, think tank, foundation and library [that] contained most of the world's books."[82] The library was gradually destroyed over an extended period of time, with blame being handed out to a fire in 48 BC, destruction of offensive books by early Christians in 391 AD, and the burning of the remaining books for fuel in 641 AD by Caliph Omar.[83]

What is likely the oldest currently existing library is located at St. Catherine's Monastery in Sinai, Egypt, which claims to have been housing religious manuscripts since at least 383–384 AD. Among the items in the collection are texts that are some of the only existing manuscripts written in the almost lost language of Caucasian Albanian.[84]

In 1731, Benjamin Franklin established one of the American colonies' earliest circulating (or subscription) libraries in Philadelphia. Patrons had to pay forty shillings initially, then ten shillings a year to continue borrowing volumes. Franklin's patrons were businessmen and tradesmen. Franklin's name occurs repeatedly in discussions of the media of the colonial era. He was an important book, magazine, and newspaper publisher—the Rupert Murdoch of his day.[85]

The nineteenth century was a period of growth for libraries; the number of subscription libraries tripled between 1825 and 1850. American industrialist Andrew Carnegie financed the construction of nearly 1,700 public libraries from 1900 to 1917; since then, the number of public libraries has continued to grow and was estimated at nearly 17,000 separate facilities in 2015.[86]

Libraries today are much, much more than just collections of books, though that continues to be an important function:

- They are places where people without computers can find one to go online.

- Those with a laptop or mobile device, but no access to the internet, can use a library as a Wi-Fi hot spot.

- They often have massive collections of electronic documents patrons can access.

- Many now "check out" books to Kindles, allowing the borrower to keep the book on his or her e-book device for a limited checkout time.

- Some have "book club bags" with eight to fifteen copies of a book that would be of interest to a book club, along with discussion questions, author information, and even a large-print copy of the book.[87]

New York Public Library president Anthony Marx said in an interview that "[libraries] are a foundational part of the First Amendment. All libraries are. . . . And in this day and age, when accusations of false news are flying every day, the citizens need to be able to check facts and gather facts and argue about facts."[88]

Books and Censorship

Books are capable of inciting great passion in readers who love them and those who hate them. Wherever there are books, there are people who will want to ban or control them for one reason or another. Attempts at control can range from removing the book from a school library to threatening to kill the author. Most book censorship efforts in the United States are local rather than national in scope. Book banning is generally limited to removing specific titles from school libraries or reading lists. Typically, such efforts involve books thought to contain sexually explicit material, offensive language, violence, or offensive treatment of religion. Other reasons given are for being "unsuited" for a given age group or for being "anti-family."[89] Occasionally, though, a book's publisher will instigate the censorship. Ray Bradbury's novel *Fahrenheit 451* tells the story of a "fireman" whose job is to burn books rather than put out fires. (Fahrenheit 451° is the temperature at which book paper starts to burn.) The book was originally published in 1953, but in 1967, Ballantine Books brought out an edition for high schools that modified seventy-five passages in the text to eliminate such words as hell, damn, and abortion. This was done without Bradbury's knowledge or consent. When he found out about it thirteen years later, he demanded that the edited version be withdrawn.[90]

Different titles show up on various lists of banned or challenged books, but a few appear repeatedly. Maya Angelou's *I Know Why the Caged Bird Sings* has had its position on many school reading lists challenged because of its description of the rape of the author as a child. Other frequently challenged books include the *Goosebumps* series by R. L. Stine, J. D. Salinger's coming-of-age novel *The Catcher in the Rye*, and Kurt Vonnegut's account of the firebombing of Dresden, *Slaughterhouse-Five*.[91]

The American Library Association has been tracking the most-challenged books for several years. Challenged books are those that some individual or group has attempted to remove or restrict. The challenger does not need to have been successful in getting the title banned for it to appear on the list. See Box 4.1 for the most-challenged books of 2019. It is worth noting, however, that most of these "challenged" books are not banned. Instead, they are subject to complaints from a few concerned parents, for whom they might get removed from a required reading list. Or perhaps a school district will send a consent note home with students. But that is the extent of most of the attempts to "ban" books in the United States.[92] As an example, in 2019, Harper Lee's *To Kill a Mockingbird* was removed from a Mississippi junior high reading list because of complaints that the book's language "makes people uncomfortable." The book was not removed from the school district's libraries, however.[93] Not all challenged books are contemporary. Several classics have received complaints as well. According to the American Library Association, the following books are frequently challenged:

- *The Scarlet Letter* by Nathaniel Hawthorne, because a book about adultery conflicts with a community's values

- *Of Mice and Men* by John Steinbeck, because it contains profanity

- *Twelfth Night* by William Shakespeare, because the comedy is perceived as promoting homosexuality[94]

Adventures of Huckleberry Finn, Mark Twain's classic, has, for a range of reasons, been in trouble ever since its publication in 1885. *Little Women* author Louisa May Alcott said of *Huck Finn*, "If Mr. Clemens cannot think of something better to tell our pure-minded lads and lasses, he had best stop writing for them." Twain was not bothered by Alcott's comments in the least, responding, "That will sell 25,000 copies for us, sure."[97] The town library of Concord, Massachusetts, banned the book as unfit, while others described it as "rough, coarse, and inelegant."[98] The basic complaint was that the novel was disrespectful and contained profanity. More recently, *Huck Finn* has been criticized as being racist. While Pulitzer Prize–winning novelist Jane Smiley does not want to see *Huck Finn* banned, she suggests that it does not deserve its position in the canon of great American literature.[99] This is, of course, an example of Secret 4—Nothing is new: Everything that happened in the past will happen again.

While most attempts at censoring books in the United States result in at most a book's being removed from a school library, that is not always the case in the rest of the world. Few cases of censorship have been quite as spectacular as the efforts to suppress Indian-born novelist Salman Rushdie's intensely controversial novel *The Satanic Verses*, a religious satire/allegory that is extremely offensive to Muslims. Rushdie's book was first banned in India in the fall of 1988 and caused rioting in Pakistan in 1989. At that time, Iran's Ayatollah Khomeini placed a religious ruling, or *fatwa*, on Rushdie for the book's blasphemous content and called for the author's death.

GRAPHIC NOVELS

George Takei is best known for playing the part of helmsman (and later captain) Hikaru Sulu in the science fiction television and movie series Star Trek starting back in the 1960s. More recently, the Japanese American actor has been known to a new generation of social media fans as the gay rights advocate "Uncle George." But in 2019 he co-authored the graphic novel *They Called Us Enemy* that tells the story of his family's imprisonment in an internment camp during World War II. The Takeis were among 120,000 Japanese American civilians who were ripped out of their homes by soldiers and sent to one of ten different detention camps in remote areas.[95]

Takei says he co-wrote the graphic novel to help people today understand what the U.S. government did to innocent people during times of war because the government was scared of its own citizens. Takei also connects the experiences he went through starting as a six-year-old boy to those happening today to immigrants and asylum seekers attempting to enter the United States.

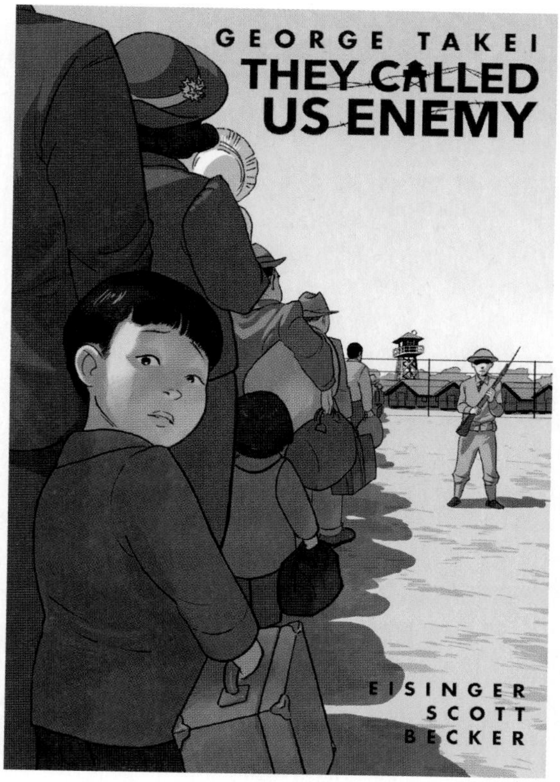

Civil rights history has been a popular topic recently for graphic novels. U.S. Representative John Lewis, who was the youngest speaker at Martin Luther King Jr.'s March on Washington, co-wrote the graphic novel series *March* that tells his personal story about the civil rights movement, including being nearly killed during a beating by a state trooper in Selma, Alabama, in 1965. There have also been graphic novels depicting the life of boxer Muhammad Ali, holocaust victim Anne Frank, and the federal government's official 9/11 report.[96]

HOW does a graphic novel differ from a novel that just has text?

For decades, high school students have been reading about the Japanese detention camps created during World War II. How does telling the story with drawings that convey the story through the eyes of a six-year-old transform the experience?

WHY are they sending this message?

What is the publisher trying to accomplish with the graphic novel? Is it appropriate to tell a serious story like that of the Japanese internment camps or the 9/11 attacks in comic book format?

WHAT is the publisher trying to accomplish with the graphic novel?

Is it appropriate to tell a serious story like that of George Takei's experience or that of U.S. Representative John Lewis in comic book format? Have you ever read the graphic novel *Maus* by Art Spiegelman that tells the story of the Holocaust with the Jews as mice and the Germans as cats? If so, what was your reaction?

HOW do you and your classmates interpret graphic novels?

Do you or your classmates read graphic novels/comic books? Would you be more likely to read a graphic novel than a text novel on a serious subject? What can you do with a graphic presentation that you can't do with text?

GEORGE TAKEI
THEY CALLED US ENEMY

EISINGER
SCOTT
BECKER

Most-Challenged Books of 2019

1. *George* by Alex Gino
   Reasons: challenged, banned, restricted, and hidden to avoid controversy; for LGBTQIA+ content and a transgender character; because schools and libraries should not "put books in a child's hand that require discussion"; for sexual references; and for conflicting with a religious viewpoint and "traditional family structure"

2. *Beyond Magenta: Transgender Teens Speak Out* by Susan Kuklin
   Reasons: challenged for LGBTQIA+ content, for "it's effect on any young people who read it," and for concerns that it was sexually explicit and biased

3. *A Day in the Life of Marlon Bundo* by Jill Twiss, illustrated by EG Keller
   Reasons: challenged and vandalized for LGBTQIA+ content and political viewpoints, for concerns that it is "designed to pollute the morals of its readers," and for not including a content warning

4. *Sex Is a Funny Word* by Cory Silverberg, illustrated by Fiona Smyth
   Reasons: challenged, banned, and relocated for LGBTQIA+ content; for discussing gender identity and sex education; and for concerns that the title and illustrations were "inappropriate"

5. *Prince & Knight* by Daniel Haack, illustrated by Stevie Lewis
   Reasons: challenged and restricted for featuring a gay marriage and LGBTQIA+ content; for being "a deliberate attempt to indoctrinate young children" with the potential to cause confusion, curiosity, and gender dysphoria; and for conflicting with a religious viewpoint

6. *I Am Jazz* by Jessica Herthel and Jazz Jennings, illustrated by Shelagh McNicholas
   Reasons: challenged and relocated for LGBTQIA+ content, for a transgender character, and for confronting a topic that is "sensitive, controversial, and politically charged"

7. *The Handmaid's Tale* by Margaret Atwood
   Reasons: banned and challenged for profanity and for "vulgarity and sexual overtones"

8. *Drama* written and illustrated by Raina Telgemeier
   Reasons: challenged for LGBTQIA+ content and for concerns that it goes against "family values/morals"

9. Harry Potter series by J. K. Rowling
   Reasons: banned and forbidden from discussion for referring to magic and witchcraft, for containing actual curses and spells, and for characters that use "nefarious means" to attain goals

10. *And Tango Makes Three* by Peter Parnell and Justin Richardson, illustrated by Henry Cole
    Reasons: challenged and relocated for LGBTQIA+ content

Source: Adapted from American Library Association, "Top 10 Most Challenged Books of 2019," http://www.ala.org/advocacy/bbooks/frequentlychallengedbooks/top10.

In the early days of the *fatwa*, Rushdie went into hiding and moved from house to house daily. According to some sources, the *fatwa* played a role in eventually breaking up his marriage.[100] Khomeini died several months after issuing the *fatwa*, making it difficult to remove the death sentence and leaving Rushdie in a kind of life-long limbo. One of the reasons why the book offends Muslims is that it contains a dream sequence in which prostitutes pretend to be wives of the Prophet Muhammad to increase their business. Additionally, it refers to Muhammad as Mahound, a Christian demon.[101] The text also contains trilingual puns that require an understanding of Hindu, Muslim, and British culture.

After the death threat, several major chain bookstores did not carry *The Satanic Verses*, but most independent booksellers continued to sell it. The chain stores eventually relented, and *The Satanic Verses* ended up at the top of the *New York Times* best-seller list.

In the fall of 1998, the Iranian government, through its foreign minister, Kamal Kharrazi, said that it would give no reward or assistance for killing Rushdie. However, as of this writing, militant Islamic organizations are still allegedly offering bounties of as much as $3 million on the author's life.[102] Despite the lifting of the official government death threat, Rushdie is not allowed to fly on British Airways planes.[103] Rushdie was fifty-one when the nine-year-old *fatwa* was lifted, and although he still sees a continued need for caution, he views the threat as ended. Rushdie had this to say to the *New York Times* about what it was like living under the *fatwa*:

It's an extraordinary thing to see people walking down the streets of foreign cities, carrying your picture with the eyes poked out and calling for your death. It's as if somebody were to break your picture of the world, and everything you think about somehow ceases to be true.[104]

Although Rushdie himself was never attacked, several other individuals with connections to his book were killed or injured. Hitoshi Igarashi, the Japanese translator of *The Satanic Verses*, was stabbed to death in Tokyo in July 1991; Italian translator Ettore Capriolo was beaten and stabbed by a man demanding Rushdie's address; and William Nygaard, Rushdie's Norwegian publisher, was shot and wounded in October 1993. As recently as January 2012, Rushdie had to cancel an appearance at a major literary festival in India because of death threats against him. He was rescheduled to speak via television, but threats of violence against the festival organizers led to even that being canceled.[105]

Rushdie is not the only author to face threats. In 2008, Britain's Scotland Yard stopped an attempt to firebomb the publisher of *The Jewel of Medina*, a controversial book about the Prophet Muhammad and his child bride by American author Sherry Jones. The attack targeted Jones's Dutch publisher, Martin Rynja. The American publisher of *Jewel*, Random House, canceled its publication because the company feared it might incite violence. (Random House is the largest English-language publisher and is owned by German publishing giant Bertelsmann.) Random House has been accused of canceling publication of the book after having the manuscript criticized by an associate professor of Islamic history at the University of Texas. Jones was able to replace Random House with Beaufort Books as her American publisher.[106]

Other authors who have received death threats include Bangladeshi doctor, poet, and novelist Taslima Nasrin; Nigerian poet Ken Saro-Wiwa; and Nobel Prize–winning Nigerian author Wole Soyinka.[107]

The Future of Books

As we discussed in Chapter 3, digital media and the internet are bringing big changes to the media business, providing consumers with alternatives to blockbuster books. Instead, a limited number of consumers spread out across the country can access far more specialized content than they could find in even the biggest **brick-and-mortar** bookstore. This phenomenon is known as the long tail. The long tail recognizes that we are no longer limited by geography

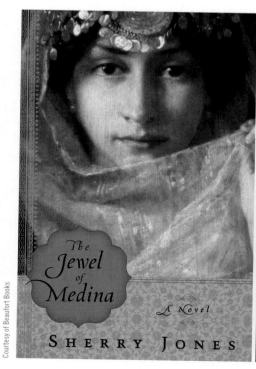

Courtesy of Beaufort Books

Zoe Boysen

▲ *The Jewel of Medina*, written by Sherry Jones, generated international controversy when extremists attempted to firebomb the offices of its British publisher.

▲ Author Sherry Jones.

as to what media we will buy and whom we will talk to. As Chris Anderson, the author of *The Long Tail*, explains, "We are turning from a mass market back into a niche nation, defined now not by our geography but by our interests."[108]

After several years of being the perpetual "next big thing," electronic books have finally hit the mainstream. Classic books, such as *Treasure Island*, are being posted online, best-selling crime novels and romances are being released in electronic form, and so-called indie books, such as those by best-selling fantasy author Amanda Hocking, are being sold directly to readers by the authors.

Consumers have been justifiably nervous about jumping into e-books for technical and logistical reasons. And then there is the whole question of "Why?" What do you get out of an e-book that you can't get from a traditional paper book?

Slate writer Jacob Weisberg is typical among fans of Amazon's Kindle, which has become the dominant **e-book reader** on the market for a variety of reasons, not the least of which is that you can buy the books from Amazon.com and have them downloaded directly to your e-book reader without any connection to a computer.[109] In the fall of 2017, Amazon offered its first waterproof e-reader at the admittedly premium $249 price tag.[110]

Superstar author Jonathan Franzen, famous for his novels *The Corrections* and *Freedom*, came out in 2012 solidly opposed to e-books. Why? Franzen's main objection to e-books is their lack of permanence. Commenting at the Hay cultural festival in Colombia, he said,

> The technology I like is the American paperback edition of *Freedom*. I can spill water on it and it would still work! So it's pretty good technology. And what's more, it will work great 10 years from now. So no wonder the capitalists hate it. It's a bad business model. . . . I think for serious readers, a sense of permanence has always been part of the experience. Everything else in your life is fluid, but here is the text that doesn't change.[111]

Central to Franzen's critique is that books ought to be in a fixed format that doesn't need to be updated; therefore, they don't need to be delivered on a platform that lets them be changed.

Author and commentator Jonathan Segura admits that there are limitations to e-books. As he writes at the blog *Monkey See*. "I am a scribbler, and you cannot scribble in the margins of an ebook. Not all books are available in digital editions. . . . E-books do not allow you to advertise your literary affectedness on the subway."[112] But Segura does not buy the argument that there is a conflict between traditional paper books and e-books:

> You can choose to have your text delivered on paper with a pretty cover, or you can choose to have it delivered over the air to your sleek little device. You can even play it way loose and read in both formats![113]

Aside from the reasons discussed in these debates, why would you want an e-book reader, other than to have the latest gadget?

We think of ourselves as being tech-savvy and modern these days, especially when we're reading the latest best seller on a Kindle or iPad. Have you ever considered what was state-of-the-art for e-readers back in the 1930s? Did e-readers even exist? Well, Matt Novak, a curator for the Smithsonian Institution, found this illustration in the April 1935 issue of *Everyday Science and Mechanics* for a microfilm-based book reader that could be mounted next to your favorite chair. It's a wonder why it never caught on.

Journalist Ezra Klein sums up the conflict book lovers feel when they start using e-books instead of paper books:

> I like books. And I feel guilty every time I look up from my iPad and see the hundreds of books lining my walls, looking at me like Woody and Buzz watching Andy discover video games. But it's getting easier and easier for me to see how they get replaced by eBooks, and harder and harder for me to come up with arguments about why that's a bad thing.[114]

At least one alternative e-book format has been successful for many years, and that's the audiobook. For an audiobook, a voice actor, famous or not, reads books (or even magazine articles) aloud so that they can be listened to on a smartphone or one of the new voice-activated smart speakers. Major publishers are reporting that although they have had a slight decline in the number of e-books sold, they have made up for some of that by the increased popularity of audiobooks. According to the Audio Publishers Association, sales grew to $2.5 billion in 2017, up from $2.1 billion in 2016. They provide a distinct value to consumers in that they allow readers to consume books and similar material in environments where they can't easily read. Audiobooks also have the advantage of being readily understandable—everyone knows what "audiobooks" are. Finally, though you can use special equipment like an Amazon Kindle to listen to them, you likely already own a smartphone that is more than capable of playing audiobooks. This means there's very little risk in adopting this new technology.[115]

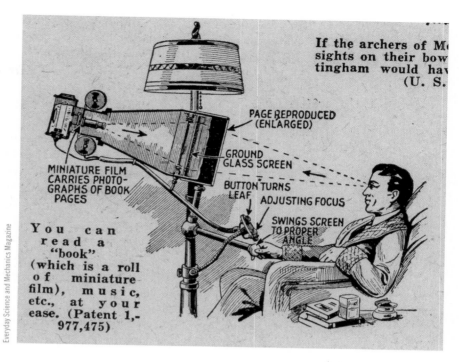

▲ We think we're pretty modern these days if we're reading the latest best seller on a Kindle or iPad. But what was state of the art for e-readers back in the 1930s? Matt Novak, a curator for the Smithsonian Institution, found this illustration in the April 1935 issue of *Everyday Science and Mechanics* for a microfilm-based book reader that could be mounted next to your favorite chair. Wonder why it never caught on . . .

From Clay, to Paper, to Electronic

The medium we use to consume books and other written materials has gone through multiple transitions over the decades, centuries and even millennia. Back in 1971, Pentagon official Daniel Ellsberg leaked copies of many of the volumes of the so-called **Pentagon Papers** to reporters first at the *New York Times*, and later at the *Washington Post*. The Pentagon Papers were a top-secret forty-seven-volume report commissioned by the secretary of defense to explain how the United States got involved and fought in the Vietnam War. The story of Ellsberg and the Pentagon Papers was recently told in the Steven Spielberg movie *The Post*. You can read more about the Pentagon Papers case and Ellsberg in Chapter 13. Leaking the documents was physically a big job. To do so, Ellsberg had to photocopy pages at a time when copy machines were uncommon and typically locked down after hours. Smuggling the thousands of copied pages out of a secure building was also a major undertaking.[116]

Forty-one years later, former National Security Agency contract worker Edward Snowden decided he wanted to leak a massive collection of meticulously categorized top-secret documents that he believed would show the overreach of the National Security Agency (NSA) without endangering lives.[117] Snowden delivered the thousands of pages of documents to journalist Glenn Greenwald in electronic form on a flash drive that fit in his pocket. Snowden had to know how to bypass computer security, but beyond that, all he had to do was a few keystrokes and mouse clicks.

Just as Ellsberg's leaked documents helped Americans better understand what had happened during the Vietnam War, so did Snowden's documents help us understand what the NSA was doing with all the information it was secretly collecting about the American people following the 9/11 terrorist attacks.

A blogger writing for the newsweekly the *Economist* says that whether you view people who leak top-secret electronic documents as heroes or traitors really doesn't matter. The writer argues that we are undergoing a major shift from a world with paper documents that are heavy and tied to a place to electronic documents that can be moved around the globe with the click of a mouse, and no amount of prosecuting cyberleakers will change that. The writer is not defending those who release electronic documents; rather, he's explaining the long-term impact that this change of media means.

The blogger is essentially bringing to the forefront the ideas of Canadian economist Harold Innis, who believed that any given medium has a bias of lasting a long time or of being easy to distribute. Paper documents, which we are more used to, are heavy and hard to move. Electronic documents, on the other hand, don't have a physical form and thus can be moved about with incredible ease.[118] To be fair to Innis, he considered parchment, clay, and stone to be durable media biased toward the concept of time, while paper and electronic media were easy to distribute and thus biased toward space. But we should keep in mind that Innis wrote his original book on the subject, *Empire and Communications*, in 1950 when it was published as a hardback paper book. Your author downloaded his copy electronically from Amazon's Kindle store.[119]

Innis was the scholar who inspired media theorist Marshall McLuhan's popular concept of "the medium is the message" and the importance of the inherent characteristics of different media. But while Innis was a much more serious and meticulous scholar than McLuhan, McLuhan's writing was much more popular and accessible. And Innis biographer Alexander Watson credits McLuhan with popularizing Innis's often dense writing.[120]

As you think about the transformations that electronic documents have brought to our society, remember that it is a key example of Secret 5—All media are social. Because electronic documents are so portable, they can always be shared. Although both Innis and McLuhan predated computers and the internet, their work on the influence of the changing nature of our media continues to be relevant today.

Print on Demand

The other side of electronic publishing is **print on demand**, in which the physical book is not printed until it is ordered or until the distributor of the book prints additional copies in small batches. This is how Amazon supplies some of its smallest-selling titles. The company has banks of large-capacity laser printers that can turn out fresh copies of books from digital copies stored on a computer. This allows the company to stock books at a cost that approaches zero until the book is ordered.[121] Book wholesaler Ingram also does print on demand through its subsidiary Lightning Source, which can print and deliver books within forty-eight hours.[122]

But don't write off traditional books printed on actual paper just yet. The NPD BookScan service reports that 687 million printed books were sold in 2017—an increase of 1.9 percent over the year before.[123]

CHAPTER REVIEW

CHAPTER SUMMARY ▶▶

Early forms of writing first appeared in the Middle East about 3500 BC. Over the next two thousand years, writing evolved from simple pictographs to highly developed ideograms and the sound-based alphabet system. Picture writing has seen a revival in twenty-first century culture with the growth of emoji keyboards on mobile devices. Modern rag-based paper was developed in China between 240 BC and 105 BC. In medieval Western Europe, early hand-copied books were created primarily by monks and other religious figures. Because they were difficult to produce, these books were expensive and rare.

In the mid-fifteenth century, Johannes Gutenberg developed the type mold. Printing presses using Gutenberg's movable type allowed books and other publications to be mass produced for the first time, leading to numerous cultural events, including the

Protestant Reformation, the rise of literacy, and standardization of grammar and spelling.

In the New World, publishing began soon after European settlement, first in Mexico City by Spanish settlers and later by British colonists in the Massachusetts Bay area. As literacy and education spread throughout the growing middle class during the nineteenth century, improvements in printing technology made inexpensive popular reading materials, such as dime novels and serials, readily available. The first comprehensive dictionary of the English language was also produced during the nineteenth century.

The modern book business has three major participants: publishers, authors, and booksellers. The book business, like the rest of the media industry, has been characterized by rapid consolidation, with a limited number of companies controlling a substantial portion of the publishing, distribution, and retail business.

Publishers produce a wide range of books, but most of the industry's profits come from a limited number of best-selling titles from authors such as Margaret Atwood and Stephen King. Among the types of publishers are trade publishers, university presses, small presses/publishers, and the government printing office. While Amazon is the dominant corporate bookseller in the United States, independent bookstores have been staging a comeback since 2009.

The textbook industry has come under increased scrutiny by both legislators and consumers for high costs. Responses have included textbook rental, electronic editions, and lowered costs of production. Ownership in the education publishing business, like the rest of publishing, is becoming increasingly concentrated in the hands of a small number of companies.

Libraries have existed as long as there have been books, dating back to as early as 2100 BC. They played an important role in the American colonies prior to the Revolutionary War and continue to be important institutions today providing a wide range intellectual and cultural resources to their communities.

Although books rarely attract the degree of controversy that movies, television, or video games do, they are occasionally challenged in the United States, typically by an individual library or school district. The most common reason for restricting books is that they contain offensive language, racial bias or stereotypes, sexual material, or offensive comments about religion. Outside of the United States, some controversial authors have faced threats of violence or even death, most notably Salman Rushdie, author of *The Satanic Verses*. Such bans and threats almost never prevent the books from being sold, however.

Books and other print documents have changed radically in form over the millennia, going from clay tablets to bound paper books to electronic documents. As the media for books have changed, so has their basic characteristics. Books that used to be very difficult to move from place to place can now be sent instantly halfway around the world digitally. The internet has become an important marketplace for books, especially those for which demand is limited. Online bookstores, such as Amazon.com, can keep books available by selling them as digital downloads or as print-on-demand titles. E-book readers are becoming increasingly popular as a means of distributing books, especially textbooks.

KEY TERMS ▶▶

pictograph 76	type mold 78	university and small presses 83
ideograph 76	font 79	proofs 84
emojis 77	Bay Psalm Book 80	inclusive access 88
phonography 77	serial novels 81	domestic novels 89
alphabets 77	dime novels 81	brick-and-mortar 95
papyrus 78	rotary press 81	e-book readers 96
parchment 78	Linotype 81	Pentagon Papers 97
paper 78	publishers 82	print on demand 98
scriptoria 78	trade books 83	

REVIEW QUESTIONS ▶▶

1. How and why does young adult author John Green deal with mental illness in his novels?

2. How do ideographs and phonetic alphabets differ from each other? What are advantages and disadvantages of phonetic alphabets?

3. How did the development of movable type transform the book publishing industry?

4. How does a publisher differ from a printer?

5. Are books often banned successfully in the United States? Why or why not? Defend your answer.

6. Aside from not involving paper, how do e-books differ from conventional books?

CHAPTER 5

THE NEWS BUSINESS

Reflection of a Democratic Society

Drew Angerer / Staff / Getty Images

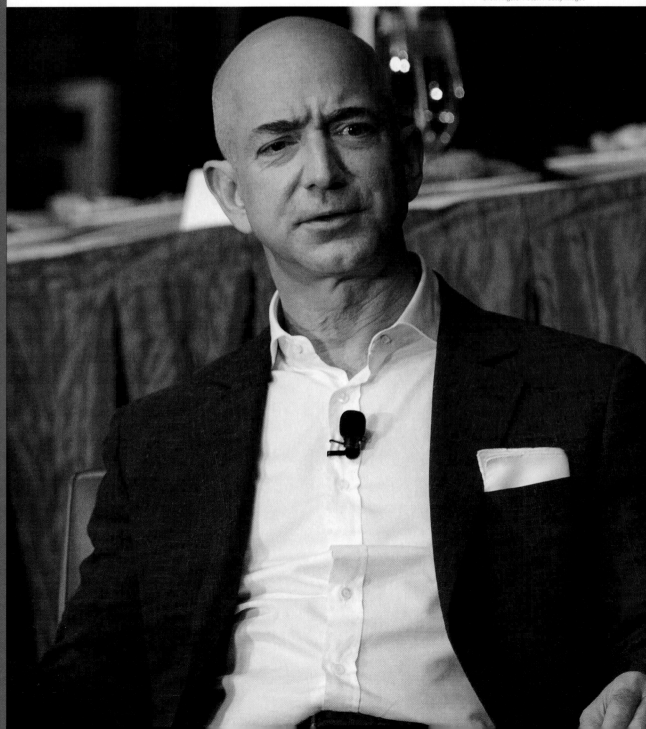

On the afternoon of August 6, 2013, news started breaking on Twitter about a big meeting scheduled to take place at the *Washington Post*. Not long after, word came that Amazon founder Jeff Bezos had purchased the paper for $250 million from the Graham family, who had run the paper for four generations. Bezos founded (and is the largest stockholder) the book sales and media giant Amazon.com and he bought the *Washington Post* out of his own personal fortune.[1] The fact that this was a personal purchase is important. *Washington Post* reporter Paul Farhi pointed out at the time of the purchase that under Bezos the paper will be privately owned, so he will not be accountable to shareholders or other investors. When the Graham family decided to sell the *Washington Post*, they were looking for an investor who could pay the $250 million asking price and not demand an immediate return on the investment. And that's when CEO Don Graham thought about his friend Bezos. Despite dealing with cutting-edge technology, Bezos has a reputation for taking the long-range view of business.[2]

One of Bezos's first innovations after buying the paper was to provide subscribers unlimited free access to the *Post*'s web site, as well as mobile apps for other metropolitan papers, eliminating the monthly subscription fee typically paid by people wanting to view more than a limited number of articles offered by the paper. The goal of Bezos's plan was to bring people to the site who were outside of the paper's print circulation area and unlikely candidates for paying customers, but who still had an interest in news. In short, he was taking a "digital point of view." By doing so, he was going to need knowledgeable customers who were invested in technology, as well as reporters, to improve his product.[3]

One of the big changes that came from Bezos was moving the *Post* from being a paper "for and about Washington" to having a national or even global presence.[4] No longer would the *Washington Post* limit itself to news within its print circulation area. By 2016, under Bezos's ownership, the *Post* had a growing audience, increasingly ambitious reporting, and was gaining recognition as a national newspaper. *Politico*'s Ken Doctor said that the *Post* was joining the ranks of the *New York Times*, the *Wall Street Journal*, and *USA Today* as a national paper.[5] The *Post* was drawing in this audience in part through more investigative journalism served up in a way that looked good online and on mobile devices.

After studying this chapter, you will be able to

1. Describe how the American press was developed during the colonial era

2. Identify the two types of broadcasting media that forever changed the news industry

3. Explain how in recent years the newspaper industry has gone from one of the most profitable businesses in the United States to an industry on the verge of collapse

4. Explain what media scholar Jay Rosen means when using the phrase "the view from nowhere"

5. Describe the economic challenges local and community news organizations are facing in the twenty-first century

Bezos had reportedly been more concerned with the "vision" side of the paper rather than the details of how to carry that out. Because of this, the details were left to executive editor Marty Barron, who became somewhat of a national celebrity after being played by actor Liv Schrieber in the Boston journalism movie *Spotlight*. As an example of Bezos's vision, he told the *Post* staff back in 2014 that they needed to "take advantage of the gifts the internet gives us." Very simply, this means "projects that are designed to draw a disproportionate amount of traffic per journalist."[6] Along with hiring journalists, Bezos has also brought in technology people who include "software development engineers, digital designers, product managers, mobile developers, and video engineers."

Despite the great things happening at the *Post*, all is not well with the staff there. *Vanity Fair* reports that while Bezos is seen as a savior for the paper and an effective owner providing great leadership, he is also the same Jeff Bezos who has faced criticism from labor at this other business—Amazon. It is worth noting here that Bezos is generally considered to be the world's richest man.[7] Money aside, owning the *Washington Post* isn't always a pleasant thing for Bezos.

President Donald Trump has not been fond of the renewed journalism from the *Washington Post*, and the president often takes out his anger on Bezos. President Trump has not generally separated Amazon from the *Post*, referring to the paper as Amazon's "chief lobbyist." But by all accounts, Bezos has exerted no influence over coverage of anything in the paper. Publisher Fred Ryan said, "Jeff has never proposed a story. Jeff has never intervened in a story. He's never critiqued a story. He's not directed or proposed editorials or endorsements."[8]

Perhaps the more serious problems created for Bezos has been the *National Enquirer*'s published stories about Bezos's extramarital affair and subsequent divorce. The tabloid reportedly obtained a collection of text messages between the lovers, along with several explicit photos they had shared. While the *Enquirer* published many of the text messages, they threatened to publish the "below-the-belt selfie" if Bezos (and presumably the *Post*) did stop its criticism of the *Enquirer* and its reporting methods.[9] Bezos, rather than backing down, published an extended essay on the Medium online platform, complete with images of the threatening letters. Bezos also applied his considerable resources to investigating how the *Enquirer* obtained his text messages and photos.[10]

Bezos has been largely successful with his purchase of the *Washington Post*. Since acquiring it in 2013, he has improved readership, revenue, and reporting at the paper. He has also worked at building it up as a national news source that is primarily delivered digitally. Like he did before with Amazon, Bezos is more concerned with investing in the future of the *Washington Post* than with short-term profits; more interested in reader engagement than revenue. Overall, the newsroom is happy to have a forward-thinking owner who has deep pockets investing in the long-term success of the paper, but the staff would like it better if Bezos were willing to share more of that revenue with them.

Some media observers have questioned whether the news business has any future, given the challenges involved in getting people to pay for media; an issue that has sharpened through the coronavirus pandemic–caused recession. There have also been serious concerns about how the news industry can function in an environment where some politicians are calling coverage they don't like "fake news." However, it is good to remember that the 2020s are *not* the first time the news industry has faced a crisis. In this chapter, we look at how journalism and the press developed in the United States, how newspapers and other news organizations operate today, and how the news business is being transformed in the digital age.

Inventing the Modern Press

Stay up to date on the latest in media by visiting the author's blog at **ralphehanson.com**

Newspapers first appeared soon after Gutenberg developed a usable movable type. The first English-language newspaper was *Curanto*, which was published in Amsterdam in June 1618. This was not a newspaper as we would recognize it today, but rather a single broadsheet filled with both British and foreign news. By 1622, similar papers (or newsbooks, as they were called) were being published in Britain. The government attempted to control these papers, which were empowering the new capitalist class at the expense of the aristocracy, but the papers were still distributed through places such as coffeehouses.[11]

If you look ahead to the United States during the 1960s and 1970s, the type of censorship and control of print media people experienced in the 1700s is not all that different from how the early gay and alternative newspapers were treated. This illustrates Secret 4—Nothing is new: Everything that happened in the past will happen again. Among those who were publishing broadsheets were major church reformers, such as Martin Luther and John Calvin; their religious writings also helped bring about some of the earliest attempts at censorship.[12]

Publick Occurrences, printer Benjamin Harris's newspaper, is frequently cited as the first newspaper in the American colonies; its first and only issue was published in Boston in 1690. As happened with many papers of the era, the government promptly shut it down. In this case, the government objected to the paper's disparaging remarks about the king of France, along with the fact that Harris had failed to obtain a license to publish. The first paper to publish multiple issues was the *Boston News-Letter*, which was founded in 1704.

Just as media dynasties exist today, they existed in the American colonies, with Benjamin and James Franklin having their hands in just about every medium available at the time. Starting in 1721, James, the elder of the two brothers, published the *New-England Courant*, the first newspaper to be published without the explicit approval of the British Crown. When James was sent to prison for irritating the authorities, sixteen-year-old Benjamin, who had been working as a printer's apprentice, took over the paper. By 1729, he had purchased the *Pennsylvania Gazette* and began turning it into the most influential paper in the colonies. Benjamin published the colonies' first political cartoon, the oft-reprinted "Join, or Die" cartoon, and he introduced the weather report as a regular feature.[13]

The newspapers of the American colonies had little in common with newspapers today. Before the 1830s, daily papers contained shipping news and political essays. Designed primarily for the wealthy elite, these papers were often underwritten by political parties, and their content was determined by the editors' opinions. Although we might consider this biased coverage, these early papers made no pretense of objectivity. Why should they? Each political party had its own paper, and the small number of subscribers (two thousand at most) tended to share similar viewpoints. Battles between rival newspapers could get quite heated, even extending to physical violence.

Library of Congress

▲ Newsboys sold newspapers on the streets of New York and other major cities for one or two cents a copy during the penny press era of the nineteenth century.

Colonial newspapers were quite expensive, costing as much as six cents a day at a time when a worker might make eighty-five cents a day. Papers were typically available only by annual subscription, which had to be paid in advance. These papers showed their business bias with names like the *Advertiser* or the *Commercial*. They typically consisted of four pages, with the front and back filled primarily with advertising and the inside pages with news and editorial content.[14]

The Penny Press: Newspapers for the People

In the 1830s, Benjamin Day conceived a new type of newspaper, one that would sell large numbers of copies to the emerging literate public. On September 3, 1833, he started publishing the *New York Sun*. The paper's motto was "It shines for all." It was the newly developed steam engine that made mass distribution of the *Sun* possible. Hand-powered presses, which hadn't changed much since Gutenberg's time, could print no more than 350 pages a day, but a steam-powered rotary press could print as many as sixteen thousand sections (not just pages) in the same amount of time (see Chapter 4).[15]

The *Sun* emphasized facts over opinion. Papers that followed in its wake had names like *Critic*, *Herald*, or *Star*. These inexpensive papers sold for a penny or two on the street, so they soon earned the name "penny press." Instead of being subsidized by political parties, the penny papers were supported by circulation and advertising revenues. They also didn't have to worry about subscribers who wouldn't pay their bills, since they were all sold on the street for cash.[16]

Now that publishers could economically print large numbers of papers, they could command a big enough circulation to attract advertising. As a result, their profits came primarily from advertising revenues, not from subscriptions or subsidies. The makers of patent medicines, which often consisted largely of alcohol or narcotics, were the biggest advertisers. Want ads (today's classifieds) also became a prominent feature of the papers.

A Different Kind of Journalism. Penny papers were typically independent rather than being the voice of a political party. In fact, they tended to ignore politics altogether because their readers weren't interested in political issues. The *Sun*'s editors knew their audience; as an example, their congressional news column once reported, "The proceedings of Congress thus far, would not interest our readers."[17]

The concept of "news" was invented by the penny press: These papers emphasized *news* or "new things," such as the newest police actions, court verdicts, and happenings on the streets. Traditional papers called the penny papers sensationalistic, not because they ran big headlines or photos—neither existed at the time—but because they were printing *news* instead of political arguments or debates. The penny press also moved toward egalitarianism, representing people as equals, in the press. The affairs of ordinary people were now as much news as accounts of the rich and famous.[18]

The British press went through a similar period of change, moving from the highly partisan press of the 1700s to a more "objective" focus on news by the end of the nineteenth century—again a change largely in response to the rise of a literate working class and the desire to reach a large audience for the paper's advertising.[19]

A Modern Democratic Society

The 1830s were a period of intense growth for the United States—in industry, in the economy, and in political participation. The penny newspaper was a vital part of this growth, providing the information the public needed to make democracy work. In 1830, there were 650 weeklies and 65 dailies in the United States, but in just ten years, those numbers had doubled to 1,241 weeklies and 138 dailies.[20] It was a period when more people were working for wages outside the home and were starting to use consumer goods purchased with cash. The penny press provided a means for advertising these goods, which in turn expanded the market for them.

The United States was being transformed from a rural community to an urban society, from an agricultural nation to an industrial one, from self-sufficient families to a market-based economy. Michael Schudson argues that the penny papers were a strong force in this change:

These papers, whatever their political preferences, were spokesmen for egalitarian ideals in politics, economic life, and social life through their organization of sales, their solicitation of advertising, their emphasis on news, their catering to large audiences, their decreasing concern with the editorial.

The penny papers expressed and built the culture of a democratic market society, a culture which had no place for social or intellectual deference.[21]

During the Civil War era, the press continued its move toward being independent from political parties. The press provided people with news about the war and whether the nation would continue to exist. Following the war, newspapers continued to grow and began to be an important part of people's everyday lives. This was the establishment of Secret 1—The media are essential components of our lives. Hazel Dicken-Garcia, in her history of the nineteenth-century press, wrote,

The press became a "habit" as Americans, perhaps for the first time, recognized a vital need for it and established it as [a] part of their lives in a way that was unprecedented. Families sought news of relatives fighting in the war, and national leaders needed information about events as a basis for making decisions and forming policies for conducting the war. . . . Since everyone had a stake in the war and thus a driving need to know about events, the newspaper became primary reading material as never before.[22]

Bill Gates, the founder of Microsoft and one of the world's richest men, said in an interview in 2017 that democracies still have a need for the press habit:

So if we define media very broadly to be the things that help voters assess what's being said, assess how those things have worked, and therefore played their role of picking, on balance, reasonable leaders who pursue reasonable policies—you can't have a democracy without a media function like that. If anybody says we don't need the media, that's a little scary. Yes, some parts of the media may have bias or they may be wrong, but to attack the phenomenon of the media, I'm not sure how many populists of the past have gone to that level.[23]

Pulitzer, Hearst, and the Battle for New York City

If the penny papers of the first half of the nineteenth century gave birth to modern journalism, the battles between New York publishers Joseph Pulitzer and William Randolph Hearst in the 1880s and 1890s provided journalism's turbulent adolescence.

Pulitzer and the *New York World*. Pulitzer came to the United States from Austria in 1864 at the age of seventeen to fight in the Civil War. He survived the war, studied law, and went on to become a reporter for a German-language newspaper. In 1878, he bought the *St. Louis Post and Dispatch* and became its publisher, editor, and business manager.

In 1883, Pulitzer bought the failing *New York World*, and in just three years, he boosted its circulation from 15,000 to more than 250,000. High circulation was critical because large readership numbers attracted advertisers who were willing to pay premium prices. Twelve years after Pulitzer bought the paper, it had a daily circulation of 540,000.[24]

Pulitzer changed the appearance of the paper's front page, replacing dense type with huge multicolumn pictures and big headlines. He brought to journalism a sense of drama and style that appealed immensely to his turn-of-the-century audience. Author and press critic Paul Weaver credits Pulitzer with the invention of the modern newspaper's front page. Before Pulitzer, the front page was no different from any other page in the paper. Pulitzer started the practice of giving the most important story the biggest and widest headline and running that story **above the fold** of the paper, where it would be immediately visible to anyone looking at the paper on a newsstand. Thus, *above the fold* came to refer to a prominent story.

Pulitzer made many other innovations. He changed headlines so that they said something more specific about the story. For example, a pre-Pulitzer New York paper ran the story about President Abraham Lincoln's assassination under the headline "Awful Event." Pulitzer required his editors to use headlines containing a subject and an active verb, so the Lincoln assassination might have run under the headline "Lincoln Shot." Pre-Pulitzer stories told readers what they needed to know in a formal, structured way. Pulitzer presented the news as a story that people wanted to read; journalists went from just being reporters to being storytellers as well.[25]

New Readers: Immigrants and Women. The New York City of the 1880s and 1890s was a city of immigrants—people who wanted to learn to speak and read English—and the city's newspapers were important teachers. Pulitzer's *New York World* used big headlines, easy words, and many illustrations, all of which helped the paper appeal to the immigrant community. This was also the period when the modern Sunday paper got its start. In 1889, half of all New Yorkers bought Sunday papers. To make his Sunday editions more appealing, Pulitzer started trying out illustrations, comic strips, and color comics.

Pulitzer also tailored his newspaper to female readers by publishing women's pages and romantic fiction. He had a difficult time balancing the interests of women against those of male readers. He didn't want to offend working-class male readers by making the paper too feminist in content, but he couldn't ignore the independent women who were now reading papers. Women were the primary purchasers of household items, and advertisers wanted to reach them. So, the newspaper needed to tailor its content to reach these "new women" while still appealing to its working-class male readers.

No one epitomized the journalism of Pulitzer's *New York World* better than "stunt journalist" Nellie Bly, who proved that women could go to the same extremes as men when trying to get a story. From her first act at the *World* (pretending to be insane in order to get an insider's report on a women's lunatic asylum) to her most famous stunt (traveling around the world in under eighty days), she always did things more extravagantly than anyone else.[26]

▲ Pioneering woman journalist Nellie Bly created a sensation in the late 1800s with her "stunt journalism" written for Joseph Pulitzer's *New York World.*

New York Public Library Archives

Bly, who lived from 1864 to 1922, authored hundreds of newspaper articles, which were generally long and written in the first person, for the *Pittsburg Dispatch*, the *New York World*, and the *New York Evening Journal*. She was born Elizabeth Jane Cochran but went by the nickname Pink (probably for the pink dresses she wore). It was at the *Dispatch* that she started using the pen name Nellie Bly. In addition to covering women's stories for the *Dispatch*, Bly wrote a travelogue of a journey to Mexico under the headline "NELLIE IN MEXICO." She also made a name for herself covering the plight of young women working in factories.

In 1887, Bly moved to New York in the hope of finding a job at one of the city's vibrant daily papers. First on her list was Pulitzer's *New York World*. She eventually was able to see John Cockerill, managing editor of the *World*. It was Cockerill who suggested that Bly go undercover to write a story about the women's lunatic asylum. If her story was good, he told her, she would get the job.

The asylum had been charged with abusing inmates, but none of the stories written about it had the power of Bly's insider account. To gain access, Bly moved into a rooming house and proceeded to act erratically so as to be committed to the asylum. Once inside, she wrote articles describing patients being fed rotten food and being choked and beaten by nurses. After ten days, an attorney for Pulitzer came to rescue her. The series of stories she produced was a masterpiece.

With this series, Bly proved that a woman could find success in sensationalistic journalism and that she could tell a great story under dangerous circumstances. Today many people would consider it unethical for reporters to pretend to be someone they aren't, and many major papers would reject their work. But in the New York of Hearst and Pulitzer, Bly's stunts were wildly successful and were imitated by other reporters.[27]

The Era of Yellow Journalism. Hearst came from a wealthy family and began his newspaper career as editor of the *San Francisco Examiner*, which was owned by his father. Having dominated the San Francisco newspaper market, Hearst followed Pulitzer into the New York market by purchasing the *New York Journal*. Soon he was using Pulitzer's own techniques to compete against him. Hearst and Pulitzer became fierce rivals, each trying to outdo the other with outlandish stories and stunts. This style of shocking, sensationalistic reporting came to be known as **yellow journalism**. Why yellow? At one point, the two papers fought over which one would publish the popular comic strip "The Yellow Kid," which featured a smart-aleck character and could be considered the "Doonesbury" of its day. Eventually, both papers featured their own "Yellow Kid" drawn by different artists.

Pulitzer eventually repented for his excesses during the era of yellow journalism by endowing a school of journalism at Columbia University. He also endowed the Pulitzer Prizes that every year honor the best reporting, photography, and commentary in journalism.

Magazines and the News

Along with newspapers, magazines are a big part of the American news industry from the later part of the nineteenth century up through the first ten to fifteen years of the twenty-first century. As the 2010s progressed, news magazines have had a hard time competing with the growing range of online news outlets, and many once-proud publications have become mere shadows of their old glory.

Photojournalism. In addition to providing the first national source of news and commentary, magazines were the first source of **photojournalism**— the use of photographs to portray the news in print. Initially, pictures were printed in periodicals by using hand-engraved plates copied from photographs. Then in the 1880s came the invention of the **halftone**, an image produced by a process in which photographs are broken down into a series of dots that appear in shades of gray on the printed page. The halftone allowed the photograph to be reproduced directly in the publication rather than being copied into a drawing.

Photographer Mathew Brady is often credited with inventing photojournalism in the mid-nineteenth century. In 1845, Brady rose to prominence for his portraits of noted Americans. He attempted to sell printed reproductions of his photographs, and though the effort failed because the costs were too high, he set the stage for later celebrity photographers, such as Annie Leibovitz. Brady also realized that much of the value of his photographic portraits came from their being reproduced as engravings, woodcuts, lithographs, and the like. The original was valuable, but so were the reproductions. Today, Brady is best remembered for his pictures of the American Civil War, the first war to be photographed from beginning to end.

During the war, Brady was as much a studio operator as a photographer. He supervised the work of several talented photographers, and he made sure that the photos found their way into magazines and newspapers. By 1863, *Harper's Weekly* was reproducing Brady's Civil War photos; these images horrified American audiences and brought the atrocities of the war into their homes. The brave photographers of these images followed the Union Army in wagons filled with their camera equipment and portable darkrooms. It's important to note that many of the photos credited to Brady, whose eyesight was failing, were likely

AP Photo/AP Images

▲ "The Yellow Kid" was such a popular early comic strip character that both the *New York Journal* and the *New York World* had separate versions of the feature drawn by two different artists.

Library of Congress

NurPhoto/Corbis via Getty Images

▲ War photography, in terms of the horror of the images, hasn't changed that much since its beginnings during the American Civil War. This image of the Battle of Gettysburg (left) was taken in 1863 by photographer Timothy H. O'Sullivan, who initially trained under Mathew Brady. The photo on the right, taken by an unnamed photographer working for the NurPhoto Agency and Erbin News, shows the bodies of those killed in a suspected chemical weapons attack on a suburb of Damascus, Syria, during the country's ongoing civil war.

shot by his assistants. To get the best image, photographers working for Brady often got extremely close to the line of fire. Photographer Thomas C. Roche, who often worked for Brady, got so close that he was seen shaking dirt off himself and his camera after shells hit nearby. Because of the extreme danger, some of Brady's best photographers left his employ to get the credit they deserved for taking such risky pictures. Brady's greatest contribution was not so much the individual war photographs that he may or may not have taken, but what evolved from the photographs: the idea that photographs are published documents preserving history.[28]

The Muckrakers. Investigative reporting, made famous by the 1970s Watergate political scandal, actually started in the late 1800s at several newspapers and magazines publishers. The most lasting examples of early investigative reporting came from the so-called muckraking magazines. The term *muckrakers*, coined by President Theodore Roosevelt, was used to describe socially activist investigative journalists who were publishing in progressive-minded magazines in the early years of the twentieth century. Although Roosevelt favored the social and political reforms that the exposés clearly indicated were necessary, he suggested that the investigative reporters who published such stories were "muckraking"—that is, they were digging up dirt without stopping to see the good things in the world.

The most famous of all the muckrakers was Samuel S. McClure. At the beginning of the twentieth century McClure led the fight for "business, social, and political reform."[29] Although McClure was a reformer, he also sought to make a profit through the investigative articles he published in his magazine, *McClure's*. The writing in *McClure's* was sensationalistic, but it was based on fact. Circulation skyrocketed, and it was hard to find copies of the magazine on newsstands. Advertisers liked the magazine for the attention it attracted and its high readership.

McClure's took on the important topics of the time, such as the insurance industry, the railroads, and the plight of urban communities. Two of the most prominent writers at *McClure's* were Lincoln Steffens and Ida Tarbell. Steffens started work at *McClure's* in 1902 and was quickly sent out into the field to report on municipal government corruption. During the next two years, his reporting on the misdeeds of officials in St. Louis, Minneapolis, Pittsburgh, Philadelphia, Chicago, and New York led to indictments and reform. The resulting six articles were eventually collected in the classic book *The Shame of the Cities*.[30] But the magazine's most famous target was Standard Oil. Tarbell had been assigned to write a series of stories that would highlight the oil giant's achievements. Working with the full cooperation of company officials, she spent five years writing the fifteen-article series, which revealed that the company had achieved its incredible success through the use of bribes, fraud, and violence.[31] By 1908, the muckraking movement had played itself out. The original talented and committed muckrakers had moved on to other pursuits, and they were replaced by people who were more concerned with sensationalism than with accuracy.

Time Life. Henry Luce, through his now split-up Time Warner media empire, probably did more to shape the American media environment than virtually anyone else. Luce was born in China, the son of Christian missionaries, and he graduated from Yale in 1920. He conceived the idea of *Time* magazine while in prep school with his friend Briton Hadden.

The two founded the magazine in 1923 as a reaction against the journalism of the time. They wanted a single weekly magazine that would keep readers up-to-date on current events. Organized around news departments, *Time* was written in a style that put the news in context and told the reader how to think about the issues—a style that the magazine maintains to this day. While *Time* presents multiple sides of a story, it also indicates which side the magazine thinks is correct, rejecting the notion of objectivity as impossible.

Luce later took on the world of business with *Fortune*, a glossy magazine featuring the photography of Margaret Bourke-White. The magazine's purpose was to "reflect industrial life as faithfully in ink and paper and word as the finest skyscraper reflects it in stone, steel, and

architecture."[32] Luce also was convinced that Americans wanted to get their news through pictures, so in 1936 he started *Life* magazine. A success from the start, *Life* had 230,000 subscribers for its first issue and a print order for 466,000 copies. Within four months, the print order was for more than 1 million copies.[33] When *Life* was launched, the big star at the magazine was neither the editor nor a writer; it was photographer Bourke-White. Bourke-White was more than just a photographer—she became a cultural icon. Bourke-White's greatest love was industrial photography. Smokestacks, trains, steam pipes, bursts of flame—these were the subjects she most wanted to shoot. In 1929, Luce, the cofounder of *Time*, saw Bourke-White's photos of the Otis Steel mill and foundry and decided that she was the photographer he wanted to take pictures for his new magazine called *Fortune*. Bourke-White shot photos using such daring methods as hanging off the steel gargoyles at the tops of skyscrapers. She also photographed in Russia at a time when most foreigners were not allowed to take pictures of Soviet industry.[34]

▲ Margaret Bourke-White rests her camera on a steel gargoyle at the top of New York's Chrysler Building in 1934.

Following Bourke-White's work at *Fortune*, Luce put her to work on *Life* two months before it started publication. Her first assignment for the new magazine was photographing the dams of the Columbia River basin. But she also shot pictures of people living in Montana—the taxi drivers, dancers in the bars, the prostitutes, the customers bowling.[35] During World War II, Bourke-White became the first female photographer accredited by the U.S. Army. The army even designed a uniform for her that became the model for those worn by all women correspondents. During the war, she was on an American ship in the Mediterranean Sea that was torpedoed by a German U-boat. As she left the ship on a lifeboat in the middle of the night, Bourke-White's biggest frustration was that the darkness prevented her from taking photographs:

> I could think of nothing but the magnificent pictures unfolding before me, which I longed to take and could not. I suppose for all photographers their greatest pictures are their untaken ones, and I am no exception. For me the indelible untaken photograph is the picture of our sinking ship viewed from our dangling lifeboat.[36]

In 2014, Time Inc. was spun off by its parent company Time Warner as a separately traded company that includes more than twenty magazines in the United States and fifty websites. Properties include *Time*, *Sports Illustrated*, and *People*.[37] Then, in November 2017, the Time Inc. family of magazines was purchased by Iowa magazine publisher Meredith Corp., bringing to a close the Time Warner era as one of America's premier magazine publishers.[38]

Broadcast News

Starting in the 1920s and carrying into the 1940s and 1950s, newspapers were facing competition from two newly created outlets: radio and television broadcasts. Broadcast media was providing up-to-the-minute news delivered with a speed and immediacy that newspapers could not match.

News on the Radio

News was a natural part of radio programming from the very start. KDKA demonstrated the power of radio news with its 1920 nighttime broadcast of the Harding–Cox presidential election results—before the newspaper stories appeared the next morning. The newspapers, understandably, were upset by radio's apparent poaching of their territory. In fact, in the 1930s, they threatened to cut off radio stations' access to AP news and even threatened to stop running radio program listings. The newspapers insisted that unless the news was of "transcendent importance," radio should not broadcast it until the newspapers were available. Not surprisingly, the radio networks did not think much of this idea. Although various restrictions were tested for a short while, in the end, radio news could not be stopped. As we will see repeatedly, old media usually try unsuccessfully to hold back the development of new media, providing yet another example of Secret 4—Nothing is new: Everything that happened in the past will happen again. Yet the old media do not go away. Instead, after a period of resistance, they change and adapt to the new environment.[39] Radio eliminated the extra editions of newspapers that used to be published whenever dramatic news occurred, but newspapers as a whole suffered only a slight decline in circulation.[40]

One place where radio held clear superiority over newspapers was in the realm of live news. Radio could, for the first time, bring news from around the world to people "as it happened." At no time was this more apparent than during World War II. When Adolf Hitler's army marched into Austria in 1938, CBS was on the air from Europe with immediate news and up-to-the-minute commentary. No radio correspondent of the era stood out more than CBS's European director, Edward R. Murrow. When Germany declared war on England in 1939, Murrow reported it from London in a voice that became familiar to all Americans. During the bombing of London, Americans listened to his live reports, which contained not just the news but also the sounds of everyday life: the air raid sirens, the antiaircraft guns, and the explosions of bombs. Murrow spoke directly to listeners from London rooftops and made them feel as if they were there with him.[41]

Television News Goes 24/7

Television news started with brief coverage of the 1940 Republican National Convention on an experimental NBC television station in New York City. By 1948, both the Democratic and Republican conventions were covered extensively for the still-tiny television audience. Documentary programs, such as *See It Now*, which was hosted by former CBS radio newsman Murrow, took on lightweight topics, as well as intensely controversial issues, such as Wisconsin senator Joseph McCarthy, who had accused numerous people of being communists. The program also aired notable segments on the Korean War. In 1947, NBC started TV's longest-running news and commentary program, *Meet the Press*, which is still on today.

In August 1948, the CBS-TV News started airing for fifteen minutes every weeknight, setting the standard length for network news until the 1960s. When the ocean liner *Andrea Doria* sank in 1956, a CBS camera crew on a seaplane got footage of the ship going down, which was broadcast promptly. Journalist and broadcast professor Edward Bliss Jr. noted that with the film of the *Andrea Doria*, "television had demonstrated that it could take the public to the scene of a major story more effectively than any other news medium."[42]

In 1963, CBS expanded its nightly news show to half an hour, with Walter Cronkite at the anchor desk. Along with the news, the program featured commentary from veteran newsman Eric Sevareid. NBC soon followed the new format, joined four years later by ABC. During this time, videotape, satellite communication, and color started coming into common use, giving television news more immediacy and impact than ever before. With correspondents bringing into American homes graphic news from the war in Vietnam, as well as spectacular coverage of the moon landing in 1969, television news rose in importance as the way to see what was happening in the world.

Francis Miller/The LIFE Picture Collection/Getty Images

▲ Television started playing a major role in presidential elections starting in 1960 with the famous Kennedy–Nixon debates.

On November 3, 1979, the staff of the U.S. Embassy in Tehran was taken hostage by Iranian militants, and ABC started a nightly news update at 11:30 p.m. Eastern time. That news update eventually turned into *Nightline* with anchor Ted Koppel, and it became one of the most respected news shows on television. The following year, Ted Turner's CNN went on the air with news twenty-four hours a day and the promise that the station would not sign off until the end of the world.[43] By the time the Gulf War began in January 1991, viewers were turning to CNN, not the networks, for news.[44] But CNN's dominance was not to last. By 2003 and the war in Iraq, CNN was facing competition in the twenty-four-hour news business from Fox News and, to a lesser extent, MSNBC. As early as 2002, the year after the September 11 terrorist attacks, Fox News was getting consistently higher ratings than the more established CNN. Fox did several things to distinguish itself from its rival. Most significantly, it was willing to take a point of view. While CNN and the broadcast networks followed the traditional objective, or neutral, style of reporting, Fox took an opinionated view in the manner of the major newsmagazines and European newspapers.[45] According to the Nielsen ratings, all three of the major cable news networks rank in the top ten of all cable channels, Fox News having the largest audience, followed by MSNBC and CNN.[46]

According to the Pew Research Center, a nonpartisan think tank that informs the public "about the issues, attitudes, and trends shaping America and the world," currently only about 50 percent of Americans get news regularly from television in any of its varied forms—cable news, national network news, and local news. Some of this decline is a generational effect, with young people being less likely than older people to use TV in any of its forms for news.[47]

The News Business

The newspapers during the era of yellow journalism were the primary source of news at the time. They faced competition from magazines, but heavyweights such as *Time* and *Newsweek* had yet to weigh in. Radio news was a decade or two away, television news would have to wait half a century, and CNN was nearly a hundred years in the future. Although newspapers today owe a huge debt to the great papers of the past, they are operating in a substantially different media environment, one that is saturated with fast, up-to-the-minute competition.

Unlike those of Hearst and Pulitzer, today's newspapers typically face little competition from other newspapers. Most newspapers today are owned by large **chains**, corporations that control a significant number of newspapers or other media outlets. Former journalist Ben Bagdikian notes in his book *The Media Monopoly* that before World War II more than 80 percent of all newspapers published in America were independently owned. Today that picture has reversed, with chains owning more than 80 percent of all papers. The British press has had a longer tradition of concentration of ownership, with three lords owning 67 percent of the daily circulation as early as 1910.[48]

Until recently, newspaper publishing was one of the most profitable businesses in the United States. The Gannett newspaper chain had earnings as high as 30 to 40 percent profits from its papers.[49] The average profit for publicly owned newspaper chains in 2005 was nearly 20 percent, noticeably higher than that for companies in the Fortune 500.[50]

But newspapers have been facing rough times for the past three decades. Newspaper circulation had been declining since the 1990s. But it is difficult to measure now with papers having a mix of print and digital audiences. Advertising revenues have also fallen by nearly two-thirds over the past ten years, dropping from $49 billion in 2006 to $14.3 billion in 2018.[51] That's not to say, however, that there have not been pockets of good news as well. Several major national and metropolitan papers have had substantial growth recently. In 2018, the *New York Times* had a 27 percent increase in digital circulation while the *Wall Street Journal* was up by 23 percent. This was on top of large digital gains during the previous several years.[52]

In late 2019, Gannett newspapers merged with GateHouse to form the nation's largest newspaper chain. Critics questioned whether this would lead to layoffs, even though the companies claimed the merger would lead to a stronger newsroom.[53] As of February of 2020, Gannett proved the critics right with layoffs taking place at multiple newsrooms.[54]

National and Metropolitan Newspapers

Until 2009, the United States had three national newspapers: *USA Today*, the *Wall Street Journal*, and the much smaller *Christian Science Monitor*. But in April 2009, the *Monitor* suspended its daily publication as a newspaper and became an all-electronic, web-based news channel.[55] Both *USA Today* and the *Journal* rely on satellite distribution of newspaper pages to printing plants across the country. In other respects, the two papers could not be more different: The *Journal* has the look of an old-fashioned nineteenth-century paper, and *USA Today* originated the multicolored format. The *New York Times*, although it is a major metropolitan newspaper, is also generally considered to be a national newspaper.

The *Wall Street Journal*. The nation's premier newspaper for business and financial news has been doing well recently and experiencing increases in both its print circulation and digital revenues. At a time when other papers have been cutting newsroom staff size and budgets, the *Journal* has been hiring staff and producing new features. The *Journal* stands out in contrast with its major competition, *USA Today*. The *Journal* was the last major paper to start using color, and it has still not fully embraced photography. Instead, it uses pen-and-ink drawings for the "mug shots" that accompany its stories. The *Journal* has cultivated a traditional look that deliberately evokes the newspaper layouts of the pre-Pulitzer era.[56] It did undergo a substantial redesign in 2006, primarily to make the paper narrower so that it didn't use as much newsprint, and it has continued a slow movement toward a more modern look. The *Journal*'s circulation is the second largest of any American newspaper, with a combined print/digital circulation of 2.27 million.[57] It is the definitive source of financial news, it is highly regarded for its national and international news, and its editorial page is one of the nation's leading conservative voices. It should be noted that unlike *USA Today*, almost every view of a major article from the *Journal* is by a paid subscriber. There are virtually no free views.

AP/Associated Press

▲ The *Wall Street Journal* is the United States's biggest paid circulation newspaper with a mix of business, national, and international news, along with a conservative editorial focus.

USA Today; News McNuggets. When the Gannett newspaper chain founded *USA Today*, journalists made fun of the new national paper, calling it McPaper. They claimed that the brightly colored paper full of short stories was serving up "news McNuggets" to an audience raised on television news. John Quinn, a former editor of the paper, once joked that *USA Today* was "the newspaper that brought new depth to the meaning of the word shallow."[58] Critics of the paper warned that starting a national newspaper was a good way for Gannett to lose a lot of money in a hurry, and the critics were right. In its first decade, *USA Today* reportedly lost more than $800 million, but by 1993, the paper started turning a profit. Coming out of the recession, *USA Today* had declining circulation, and it had fewer "sponsored" copies being bought in bulk by hotels; in 2017, it had an average daily combined print/digital circulation of 4.14 million.[59] It can be difficult comparing *USA Today*'s circulation with that of other major newspapers because much of its circulation comes from being inserted into Gannett's other newspapers. It also gets extensive unpaid readership through its major online presence.[60]

The *New York Times*. While there has long been debate over what is the nation's biggest paper, there is no question about which paper is most influential. When people in the United States refer to the *Times* without naming a city, they are almost certainly referring to the *New York Times*. According to at least one definition, news is what is "printed on the front page of the *New York Times*." News stories in the United States often don't become significant until they have been covered in the *New York Times*. The front page of the *New York Times* has as much news on it as is contained in an entire half-hour network newscast.[61]

▲ The *New York Times* is an American daily newspaper that was founded and has continuously published since 1851. It has won 125 Pulitzer Prizes, more than any other news organization.

While the company's longtime motto is "All the News That's Fit to Print," the Hoovers business report suggests that a better choice would be "All the News That's Fit to Print and Post Online."[62] While the *New York Times* has traditionally been considered a New York City newspaper, with the massive growth of its digital circulation, it (along with the *Washington Post*) is really now a national paper.

The *New York Times* has been a respected newspaper ever since Adolph Ochs bought the failing penny press paper in 1896 and gave it an emphasis on serious national and international news. Its stodgy look, with long columns of type, earned it the nickname "Gray Lady." However, on October 16, 1997, the *Times* started running color photos on its front page, joining virtually every other paper in the country in this practice.[63]

The *Washington Post*. The *New York Times* set the standard for newspaper journalism in the twentieth century and continues to do so today, but in the 1970s, the *Washington Post* inspired a generation of young journalists with its coverage of the **Watergate scandal**, the subsequent cover-up, and the downfall of President Richard Nixon. Watergate was a story that shook the nation and transformed the *Post* from a big-city paper to one with a national reputation.

The scandal started with a "third-rate burglary" of the Democratic National Committee headquarters in the Watergate office and apartment complex on June 16, 1972. When the five Spanish-speaking burglars were arrested, one was found carrying an address book that contained the number for a phone located in the White House.

Among those assigned to cover the story were two young reporters, Bob Woodward and Carl Bernstein. They soon realized that this was no ordinary burglary. As weeks and then months went by, their painstaking reporting connected the burglars to the White House and eventually to the president himself. They further discovered that the White House had been systematically sabotaging the Democratic presidential candidates and attempting to cover up these actions. During the summer of 1973, Americans were spellbound by the Senate hearings into the Watergate scandal. Finally, with impeachment seeming a certainty, Nixon resigned as president on August 8, 1974.[64]

In more recent years, the *Washington Post* has become known for its national importance through its online presence and for the fact that it was purchased by Amazon founder Bezos, as we discussed in the chapter opening.

Like the *New York Times*, the *Washington Post* has had a growing paid online presence, on both desktop and mobile screens.[65]

The *Los Angeles Times*. When people talk about the press in general, they are usually speaking of the major East Coast papers, such as the *Washington Post* and the *New York Times*. In the early 2000s, the *Los Angeles Times* established a national presence as well. While it may not have "push[ed] the *New York Times* off its perch,"[66] it has been one of the most respected papers on the West Coast, winning a Pulitzer Prize in 2016 for its coverage of the San Bernardino terrorist attack, two in 2015, two in 2011, one each in 2009 and 2007, two in 2005, and five in 2004.[67]

▲ Bob Woodward (left) and Carl Bernstein helped bring the *Washington Post* to national prominence in the 1970s with their coverage of the Watergate break-in and the subsequent cover-up.

Ken Feil/Washington Post/Getty Images

In 2017, the Disney corporation entered a battle with the *Los Angeles Times* because the media conglomerate didn't like how the newspaper was covering the company's business relationships with the city of Anaheim, California. Disney retaliated against the paper by banning *Los Angeles Times*' critics from attending the studio's movie press screenings. (These screenings are so critics can publish reviews on the day that movies are released.)[68]

But Disney quickly had to back off from that ban after movie critics and pop culture writers across the country responded by standing with the *Los Angeles Times*, refusing to attend early screenings or consider Disney movies for end-of-the-year awards until the ban was lifted. All this controversy only served to promote the story about Disney's sweetheart relationship with Anaheim that the media conglomerate so desperately wanted suppressed.[69]

Local and Community News

While people who talk about "the media" mostly talk about the national and metropolitan newspapers and broadcasters, community media are at least numerically the biggest number of them. Jock Lauterer, in his book *Community Journalism: Relentlessly Local*, points out that of the more than nine thousand newspapers in the United States, 97 percent are small or community papers. The **community press** consists of weekly and daily newspapers serving individual communities or suburbs instead of an entire metropolitan area.[70] Lauterer points out that these communities are "not just 'communities of place' but also communities of ethnicity, faith, ideas or interests." He goes on to list that in addition to the stereotypical small-town paper there are alternative, African American, ethnic, gay and lesbian, Hispanic, Jewish, military, religious, and senior community papers. (This is an example of Secret 2—There are no mainstream media.)

One of the reasons community papers are important is that they publish news that readers can't get anywhere else. Journalism professor Eric K. Meyer points out that community newspapers "have the most loyal audiences and the news that you can't get elsewhere. A local newspaper won't get scooped by CNN."[71] A study by the Pew Research Center found that people who valued and used local news were also more likely to feel connected to their community and vote in local elections.[72]

The fact that a paper serves a small town does not necessarily mean that it lacks hard-hitting, significant reporting. Consider Art Cullen, editor of the *Storm Lake Times* in rural Iowa, who won the 2017 Pulitzer Prize for best editorial writing for a series of editorials about nitrate water pollution coming from fertilizer runoff from farm fields. Cullen investigated how the counties that were being sued for allowing the pollution to take place had their legal defense being paid for by the chemical companies that manufactured the fertilizer that was causing the pollution.

The paper, with a circulation of 3,330, is a family effort. In addition to Art working as editor, his brother, John, is the publisher, and his son, Tom, is a reporter. The paper has a total staff of about eight people. "Everybody here does everything," Art says. "If you want to buy an ad, I'll sell it to you."[73] Just to be clear, though, the paper isn't all hard-hitting reporting. Art told the *Washington Post*'s Eric Wemple, "We strive to have a baby, a dog, a fire and a crash on every front page."

There will be much more about the challenges facing local news near the end of this chapter.

News Media, Identity, and Political Bias

One of the main reasons the direct effects model still has some support is that many critics believe the media affect the public's political opinions by presenting reports that are biased toward a candidate or political party. But, as we discussed earlier in this chapter, by holding up detached, factual, objective journalism as an ideal for reporting, the press was making a commercial decision, not a moral one. During the penny press era of the 1830s to the 1860s, newspapers tried to appeal to the broadest possible audience. The best way to attract many people, publishers felt, was not to take an identifiable political point of view, as had newspapers of the colonial era. The alternative to this supposedly objective style is a more opinionated form of reporting that takes on an explicit point of view, such as that found in *Time*, *Newsweek*, and many British or European newspapers, such as London's liberal *Guardian* or conservative (Tory) *Telegraph*. These publications have a clearly understood political viewpoint that is designed to appeal to a specific audience.[74]

Erik Sorenson, former president of the MSNBC cable news channel, suggested that there is nothing wrong with taking a particular point of view: "I think a lot of people are beginning to ask, 'Is there something phony about pretending to be objective and reading off a teleprompter in the twenty-first century?'"[75]

Gans's Basic Journalistic Values

There is more to the bias argument than the liberal-versus-conservative issue. For example, some observers charge that the media have a bias toward attractiveness or charisma. There can also be a bias toward making money or attracting an audience. Political scientist and media scholar Doris Graber argued that when it comes to selecting stories for coverage, the strongest bias is for those that will have the greatest appeal to the publication's or program's audience.[76]

Rather than looking for examples of bias in the news, media sociologist Herbert Gans set out to find the actual values exhibited within the stories themselves. He asked what the values—the biases—of journalism were. To find the answer, he studied the content of the CBS and NBC news programs, *Time* magazine, and *Newsweek*.

Gans found eight enduring values in the stories he studied: ethnocentrism, altruistic democracy, responsible capitalism, small-town pastoralism, individualism, moderatism, social order, and leadership. These values were not stated explicitly; rather, they emerged from what was presented as good and normal and what was presented as bad.[77] Let's look briefly at each of Gans's values:

1. *Ethnocentrism* is the idea that your own country and culture are better than all others. This shows up in the U.S. media in stories that compare other countries' values to American values. To the degree that other countries live up to American ideals, they are good; if they are different, they are bad. Therefore, enemies of the United States are presented as evil because they don't conform to our values. Stories can be critical of the United States, but they are criticizing deviance from basic American values, not those values themselves.

2. *Altruistic democracy* is the idea that politicians should serve the public good, not their own interests. This leads to stories that are critical of corrupt politicians. Similarly, citizens, as voters, have the same obligation to work for the public good and not for selfish interests. Special interest groups and lobbyists are suspect because they are not working for the common good. This was perhaps best illustrated by the Watergate hearings in the 1970s, which revealed the corrupt behavior that occurred in the White House so that President Nixon could stay in power. President Bill Clinton was criticized for his affair with Monica Lewinsky in part because he was serving his own interests rather than working for the good of the American public. President Trump has been criticized for maintaining a controlling interest in his global business empire while overseeing American foreign policy that could affect the value of that business.

3. *Responsible capitalism* is the idea that open competition among businesses will create a better, more prosperous world for everyone. But similarly, businesses must be responsible

and not seek excess profits. The same is true of labor unions. Hence the news media tend to be harsh in their coverage of greed and deception by big businesses, yet they still tend to praise people who develop and grow companies. Therefore there has been so much negative coverage of banking and investment companies following the stock market crash and recession in the late 2000s.

4. *Small-town pastoralism* is nostalgia for the old-fashioned, rural community. The agricultural community is where all goodness is rooted, while big cities are dangerous places that suffer from numerous social problems. Suburbs, where many people live, tend to be overlooked entirely.

5. *Individualism* is the constant quest to identify the one person who makes a difference. People like the notion that one person can make a difference, that we are not all cogs in a giant machine. Reporters like to use a single person as a symbol. That explains in part why journalists focused on the actions of Emma González following the Parkland school shooting. Instead of trying to talk about the gun control movement, the press used González as a symbol to represent all the protesters.[78]

6. *Moderatism* is the value of moderation in all things. Extremists on both the left and the right are criticized. Although the media attempt to present a balance of opinions, they tend to report on views that are mildly to the left and right of center. One of the strongest criticisms the media can make is referring to an individual as an extremist.

7. The value of *social order* is seen primarily in the coverage of disorder. When journalists cover stories that involve disorder, such as protests, floods, disasters, or riots, the focus of the story tends to be on the restoration of order. Once media coverage of the Flint water crisis got started, social order was a big issue, and the press focused heavily on how that order, in the form of clean, running tap water, might be restored.

8. Finally, the media value *leadership*. The media tend to look at the actions of leaders, whereas the actions of lower-level bureaucrats—which may well be more important—are ignored. This is in some ways an extension of the bias toward individualism, the difference one person can make.

Overall, Gans argues that there is reformist bias to the media, which tend to advocate "honest, meritocratic, and anti-bureaucratic government."[79] Journalists like to argue that since both sides criticize the press, they must be doing a good, balanced job.[80] Perhaps a better explanation for why both conservatives and liberals charge the media with bias is that the eight values Gans found within the media reflect a combination of both liberal and conservative values—again illustrating why people holding a particular viewpoint will see bias in the media's attempt to be neutral and balanced.

There has been a lot of talk about the role of objectivity in journalism without much agreement on what that means. Objectivity in journalism could mean the kind of coverage that C-SPAN does where journalists set up cameras at fixed locations and provide (typically live) gavel-to-gavel coverage of events with no interpretation. That is probably as close as you can get to a "just-the-facts" type of objective coverage that many people claim they want. But while C-SPAN certainly serves an important role, most people are not going to choose to watch an entire congressional hearing from gavel to gavel rather than reading or watching a summary report of it.

Objectivity in journalism is a problematic concept. People oftentimes see it as happening when a journalist presents a report featuring "both sides" of the issue without providing personal opinions or making commentary on which side has the better argument, whether either or both sides are lying, or whether there are more than *two* sides. This is sometimes referred to as "he said, she said" journalism.

Objectivity in journalism could also mean reporting what evidence suggests is the truth without presenting a contrasting point of view. Journalists, of course, always want to be reporting "the truth;" but knowing what is true, what is false, and what is opinion can be challenging. And a substantial portion of the audience might disagree with what the journalist considers to be the truth and accuse the journalist of being biased.

Too often, to news sources and consumers, objectivity means "something I agree with."

New York University journalism professor Jay Rosen, who has been an outspoken critic of the approach mainstream journalists take to objectivity, says that journalists often seem more concerned about appearing "unbiased" than presenting an accurate, unbiased picture of the world. He wrote on his blog *PressThink*,

> Something happened in our press over the last 40 years or so that never got acknowledged and to this day would be denied by many newsroom professionals. Somewhere along the way, truthtelling was surpassed by other priorities the mainstream press felt a stronger duty to. These include such things as "maintaining objectivity," "not imposing a judgment," or "refusing to take sides." . . . Journalists felt better, safer, on firmer professional ground—more like pros—when they stopped short of reporting substantially untrue statements as false.[81]

Instead of trying to report what is objectively true, Rosen writes that journalists use a reporting convention based on philosopher Thomas Nagel's "view from nowhere." Back in 2010, Rosen wrote that the view from nowhere exists for three reasons:

1. Because it places journalists between the extremes of the left and the right, the reporters can call this "neither–nor" position balanced.

2. Since they are being balanced in their coverage, they are not being biased.

3. And so because they are not biased, they have a claim at being legitimate reporters.[82]

Rosen suggests that journalists might do better working with "transparency" rather than the view from nowhere:

> In the old way, one says: "I don't have a horse in this race. I don't have a view of the world that I'm defending. I'm just telling you the way it is, and you should accept it because I've done the work and I don't have a stake in the outcome. . . .
>
> In the newer way, the logic is different. "Look I'm not going to pretend I have no view. Instead, I am going to level with you about where I'm coming from on this. So factor that in when you evaluate my report. Because I've done the work and this is what I've concluded."[83]

Rosen also suggests that reporters can gain credibility by making sure readers understand where the story is coming from, by making sure that audience members can see that this is reporting, not just opinion writing: "Don't believe me, look for yourself. Don't accept it, here's the data. You think we're biased, check it out."[84]

He gives the example of *Washington Post* reporter David Fahrenthold, who won a Pulitzer Prize for his reporting on President Trump's charitable giving. In addition to the stories he wrote, Fahrenthold listed the people he talked to and the documents he examined. Fahrenthold asked the public for help and made it clear the entire time he was working on the story what he was doing. The materials Fahrenthold provided not only showed his evidence, but also showed how hard he worked on the story.[85]

From Where Do People Get Their News?

Given the divisiveness of the 2016 election, it is not surprising that Trump and Hillary Clinton voters got their news from different places. A survey by the Pew Research Center found that Trump supporters were relatively uniform, with 40 percent saying their main source was Fox News. Coming in at a distant second was CNN with 8 percent. Third place was Facebook at 7 percent. Clinton supporters listed CNN as their top choice with 18 percent, the liberal-leaning MSNBC was at 9 percent, and Facebook was third at 8 percent.[86] Pew is one of the best sources of information about media habits of people in the United States, and its reports are used consistently throughout this book.

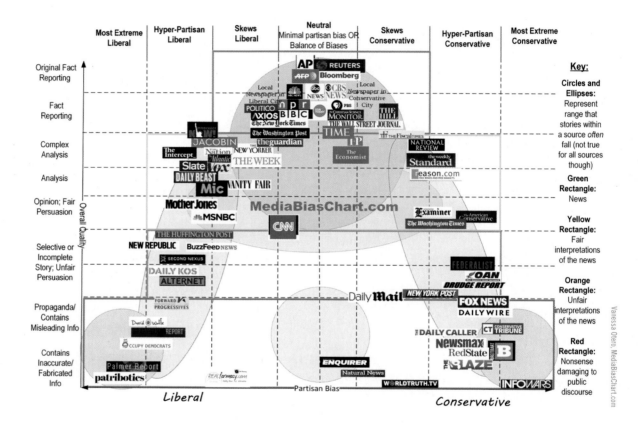

It is worth noting that Facebook itself does not produce any news; it simply allows its users to post links to news. So, although similar percentages of Trump and Clinton supporters listed Facebook as their news source, as the Pew report suggests, it is likely they are getting news from vastly different sources and sometimes from illegitimate or erroneous sources.

Given the wide range of news sources available, it can be hard to know which provide reliable, balanced, and objective news; which provide good sources of opinion and analysis; and which are the fringe news organizations full of actual fake news and false reporting.

Patent attorney Vanessa Otero created the chart printed on this page and has taken it through multiple revisions. She distributed it by posting it on Facebook. The chart rates news organizations on two axes:

1. Overall Quality—Ranging from Original Fact Reporting to Contains Inaccurate/ Fabricated Info

2. Partisan Bias—Ranging from Liberal to Conservative

"We are living in a time where we have more information available to each of us than ever before in history," Otero wrote. "However, we are not all proficient at distinguishing between good information and bad information. This is true for liberal, moderate, and conservative people. I submit that these two circumstances are highly related to why our country is so politically polarized at the moment."[87]

Unsurprisingly, Otero got lots of criticism of her chart. Infowars (which she categorized as "Utter Garbage/Conspiracy Theories" in an early version of her chart) completely rejected her work and suggested instead a chart that listed liberal-leaning sites as promoting "tyranny" and the conservative sites as promoting "liberty and freedom."

Otero has continued to revise her chart, doing away with the "Utter Garbage/Conspiracy Theories" and going instead with "Most Extreme Liberal" and "Most Extreme Conservative" on the horizontal axis. The chart is now up to version 3.1.

Otero does not demand that readers accept her analysis, offering a blank version of the template where people can create their own chart, but she does offer some advice:

I respectfully submit that if you make your own, you should be able to place at least one source in each of the vertical columns, because they exist, and at least one in each of the horizontal rows, because they also exist. If you have just a couple sources that you think are in the middle but none exist either to the right or left of them, or up or down from them, you may be on the wrong track."[88]

You can access the full chart and the template here: www.ralphehanson.com/2018/05/21/ch-6-categorizing-news-sources/.

Fake News

Since Trump started his successful 2016 campaign for president, the term **fake news** has become a popular way to describe a wide range of stories ranging from outright fabrications to news a person simply doesn't like. By 2020, the term fake news was so commonly used to refer to so many things that it became hard to know what it means. But there were least five common usages:

1. Satire—*Fake news* as an ironic term refers to stories that stretch the facts in order to make a joke or cultural criticism.

2. Mistakes and fabrication—Sometimes news stories have errors in them that eventually get corrected. Sometimes stories are fabricated by unethical reporters (you can read more about this topic in Chapter 15—Media Ethics).

3. Partisan clickbait—Sometimes websites make up sensational stories designed specifically to attract readers to their pages so that the readers will see the ads that appear with the fake articles. Oftentimes, if you dig deeply enough into these pages, you will see a mention that the stories are "fictional and presumably satirical news."

4. Foreign political manipulation—The Russian intelligence agencies have planted and amplified stories throughout the United States and Europe in order to try to manipulate elections. Some of these stories are made up, similar to partisan clickbait, while others are simply manipulated to appear more important and popular than they really are.

5. Media criticism—Politicians and others often use the term *fake news* to refer to news outlets they don't like as a general-purpose media criticism.

We will take much deeper look at the issue of fake news in Chapter 15—Media Ethics.

حول العالم

▲ Jamal Khashoggi

Patriotism and the Press

The job of being a journalist around the world can be a dangerous one; reporters literally risk their lives to report the news. The Committee to Protect Journalists reports that worldwide in 2019 twenty-five journalists were killed "in direct connection" to their work; most of them in Syria (seven) and Mexico (five).[89] Almost all of the journalists killed in Syria died in the crossfire of fighting going on during the country's civil war, while all of the journalists killed in Mexico had been murdered.

In 2018, Saudi Arabian journalist and *Washington Post* columnist Jamal Khashoggi went into the Saudi embassy in Turkey to get documents he needed to get married. While there he was captured by a Saudi death squad, tortured, killed, and then had his body cut up into pieces so it could be smuggled out of the embassy. Khashoggi was a legal resident of the United States at the time he was murdered, reportedly by the order of the thirty-four-year-old Saudi crown prince Mohammed bin Salman, or MBS as he is often referred to. Khashoggi had been highly critical of the Saudi government for its "oppression and brutality toward its people."[90]

War zones are always dangerous places for journalists, especially photographers who need to be out on the front lines to capture combat images. Photojournalist James Foley was beheaded by Islamic State militants in August 2014 after having been held hostage since November 2012.[91] British photographer Tim Hetherington and U.S. photographer Chris Hondros were killed by a rocket-propelled grenade while covering fighting near the Libyan city of Misrata in 2011. Two others were injured in the attack. Hetherington was best known for codirecting the Oscar-nominated war documentary *Restrepo*.[92] He was in Libya covering the anti–Moammar Gadhafi rebellion at the time he was killed. This was far from the first time Hetherington had been under attack. Photojournalist Lynsey Addario told the *New York Times* blog *Lens* about a time when she and Hetherington were pinned down by fire in Afghanistan: "We were ambushed from both sides," she said.

> It was a terrifying situation. I was trying to find a place to hide, to shield myself. And I remember looking over and there was Tim—just calmly sitting up, filming the whole ambush on a video camera. And I thought to myself, "Oh my God, I want to be a photographer like him."[93]

Journalists can also be soldiers. In 2013, Spec. Hilda Clayton, a U.S. Army combat photographer, was killed while photographing a live-fire exercise in Afghanistan when a mortar tube accidentally exploded in front of her. The blast also killed an Afghan military photographer she was training, along with three others. In 2017, the journal *Military Review* published (with her family's consent) the last photo Clayton took an instant before the explosion that took her life. Combat photographers like Clayton face all the same dangers the soldiers they cover face in their efforts to document the troops' operations.[94]

Death or injuries are not the only risks reporters face. BBC journalist Alan Johnston was held hostage for 114 days in the Gaza Strip, Fox News's Steve Centanni and Olaf Wiig were held hostage in Gaza for 13 days, and the *Christian Science Monitor*'s Jill Carroll was held hostage for three months in Iraq.[95] Fox News cameraman Wiig says that the most serious consequence of attacks on journalists is that the stories from war zones won't get told:

> My biggest concern, really, is that as a result of what happened to us, foreign journalists will be discouraged from coming here to tell the story. And that would be a great tragedy for the people of Palestine, and especially for the people of Gaza.[96]

Spc. Hilda I. Clayton, US Army combat photographer. May 3, 2017 from Wikimedia Commons.

Mortar explosion that killed Hilda Clayton and 4 Afghan soldiers. July 2, 2013 from Wikimedia Commons.

▲ U.S. Army photographer Spec. Hilda Clayton was killed while taking pictures during a training exercise in Laghman province, Afghanistan, when a mortar tube accidentally exploded, claiming five lives, including hers.

▲ This is the last frame Spec. Clayton shot. Combat journalists face the same risks as the soldiers that they cover.

The Ethnic Press

Along with the small-town and suburban papers, there is also a wide range of **ethnic papers** that serve specialized communities, such as racial and ethnic minorities.

The African American Press.

The African American press has had a significant presence in the United States since at least 1827. Nearly four thousand Black newspapers have been published in the United States at one time or another.[97]

Freedom's Journal was among the first Black newspapers; it was founded in 1827 to show all readers, white and Black, that "black citizens were humans who were being treated unjustly."[98] Many Black editors of the era faced great danger when they printed articles that contained fact-based accusations against whites. Mobs would destroy the newspaper's offices, and editors who had not left town might be murdered.

Editors of Black papers faced further difficulties because much of the intended audience for the papers was illiterate. Moreover, because most of the audience was poor, relatively little advertising was available. These editors put their lives and livelihoods at risk publishing a paper that few might read and that probably would lose money.

A variety of emancipation papers followed in the footsteps of *Freedom's Journal*, but none had as great an impact as the *North Star*, which published its first issue in Rochester, New York, on December 3, 1847. Its editor, Frederick Douglass, was known as a gifted writer, and his new paper let readers know that it would be fighting for an end to slavery and the recognition of the rights of Blacks. The *North Star* was read and noticed, but it faced the same problems as earlier Black papers, including anti-Black violence, a shortage of qualified staff, and a chronic lack of money. What it did have was a clear mission and a distinctive journalistic style. The *North Star* was published from 1847 until 1860.[99]

Another important African American paper is the *Chicago Defender*. Founded in 1905, the *Defender* was considerably less serious than the *North Star*, modeling its style on the yellow journalism of Hearst. It was designed to be a Black paper with a mass following rather than a publication for Black intellectuals and white elites. It was also designed to appeal to advertisers and even make money for its publisher.

Clearly, the *Defender*'s goals included profit as well as advocacy. The paper was sensational, with large red headlines trumpeting stories of crime. By 1920, the *Defender* had a circulation of more than

▲ John H. Sengstacke, part owner and manager of the *Chicago Defender*, a leading African American newspaper with a national circulation in the middle of the twentieth century, reviews layouts with an assistant.

280,000, a spectacular number at the time. It reached far beyond Chicago, with two-thirds of its readers located outside the city.[100] The *Defender* encouraged southern Blacks to move north to find jobs in Chicago and, not coincidentally, become loyal subscribers to the paper. In retaliation, it was banned throughout the South, and at least two of the paper's distributors were murdered. *Defender* editor Robert Abbott fought for civil rights and an end to lynching. Abbott, born in 1868, has been credited with founding "the modern Negro press."[101] He demonstrated that Black papers could be profit-making institutions, as well as activist publications.

In the 1950s, the *Defender* became a daily tabloid. For a while it provided extensive, day-by-day coverage of the civil rights movement. In 2003, following the death of longtime publisher and editor John H. Sengstacke in 1997, the *Defender* and three other papers owned by relatives of Abbott were sold to Real Times Media. In 2011, the *Defender* laid off its executive editor, news editor, and several staffers in an attempt to cut costs.[102] In the summer of 2019, the *Defender* ended its 114-year print run and become a digital-only publication. At the time it went digital-only the paper's circulation had dropped only about sixteen thousand. At the time of the transition, the publisher would not say how big the newsroom staff was.[103]

The Spanish-Language Press. Spanish-language newspapers are seeing some of the same declines in circulation that have been affecting the rest of the newspaper industry. According to the Pew Research Center, the average circulation for the top twenty Hispanic weekly or semi-weekly newspapers in 2018 was approximately ninety-one thousand down from about ninety-three thousand in 2016.[104] *El Nuevo Herald*, published as a companion to the *Miami Herald*, had a circulation of eighty thousand at its peak, but that declined to approximately forty thousand in 2016.[105] But the two papers differ in many more ways than just the language. Journalist Dan Grech, speaking on the NPR radio show *On the Media*, said, "The *Miami Herald*, like most U.S. newspapers, prizes objectivity. *El Nuevo Herald* is more like papers in Latin America and Europe that push for social change."[106] (You can read about Spanish-language television networks Univision and Telemundo in Chapter 8.)

The Future of News

Trying to make sense of what is happening to the newspaper business is difficult, in part because of Secret 2—There are no mainstream media. Some of the most visible segments of the newspaper business are facing major challenges, which critics are fond of pointing out. And the rural community newspapers are facing an existential threat both from structural changes in the news business and the crashing of the economy during the 2020 pandemic. So, to understand the changing newspaper market we must look at it as several media, not just one.

Newspapers may not be selling as many sheets of newsprint as they did in the past, but they are certainly not going away as a place that people turn to for news. Consider the *New York Times*. Over the past several years, *New York Times* owner and former publisher Arthur Sulzberger has been talking about how the paper will be changing. He set off a storm of controversy in spring 2007 with a comment at the World Economic Forum in Switzerland: "I really don't know whether we'll be printing the *Times* in five years, and you know what? I don't care either. . . . The Internet is a wonderful place to be, and we're leading there."[107]

This statement generated comments on almost every major press blog, but what few people noticed was that Sulzberger had been saying the same thing for at least eight years. When he was part of an *Ad Age* roundtable in 1999, Sulzberger was asked about the future of the *Times*. He answered,

> I don't care how they get it 100 years from now. And the key is not caring. It goes back to knowing the audience, and being, not ambivalent, but agnostic, rather. Agnostic about the methods of distribution. Because we can't afford to be tied to any production process. . . . There will still be communities of interest. There will still be a need, both socially and politically, for common and shared experiences.[108]

Now there is a big difference between "I don't care how they get it 100 years from now" and "I really don't know if we'll be printing the *Times* five years from now." But the basic thought, the real point of his comments, is the same—the *New York Times* is no longer in the business of putting black ink on white paper. Instead, the *Times* is in the news business and the ad sales business, and it is going to be delivering news and advertising in whatever forms will turn a profit. It is worth noting that the Reuters news agency published a story in July 2017 that suggested the *New York Times* was rapidly approaching the time when it would be profitable for the company to quit printing the news on paper and go 100 percent digital.[109]

Under its latest ownership by Amazon founder Jeff Bezos, the *Washington Post* is now moving from a strategy of being "for and about Washington" to building a national and international readership, where its targeted audience is the English-speaking world. As *Columbia Journalism Review*'s Michael Meyer wrote in June 2014, Bezos's main objective for the *Washington Post* is "reaching the maximum number of customers by putting the *Post*'s journalism in a package (a tablet, a mobile site) that will draw the greatest number of readers. As it has been with Amazon, his obsession at the *Post* is finding a way to integrate product into millions of people's lives in a way they haven't yet experienced."[110]

Marty Baron, the *Post*'s executive editor, argued in a speech back in 2015 that the future of the paper was as an online mobile product: "It's wrong to say we're becoming a digital society. We already are a digital society. And even that statement is behind the times. We're a mobile society."[111] (Yes, even in 2015 Baron was arguing for Secret 6—Online media are mobile media.)

But even with all the changes taking place, Baron said some things need to remain stable in the journalism business. "The press is routinely disparaged and demonized. That leaves many news organizations fearful—fearful that we will be accused of bias, or that we will lose customers, or that we will offend someone," he said.

"Today our profession feels shaken. But fear cannot be our guide. If there is one thing that must remain unshakeable, this is it: That we will publish the truth when we find it and when the public deserves to know."[112]

The newspaper industry has been facing major changes during the past several decades. Between the 1970s and 2016, approximately five hundred daily newspapers went out of business. In 2017, the American Society of News Editors quit counting.[113] One of the oddest things about this decline is that until very recently, Americans had no idea how much trouble their local papers were in financially. A Pew survey on United States adults found that 71 percent of the respondents believed that "their local news outlets are doing very or somewhat well financially."[114] Yet at the same time, only 14 percent of respondents said they had paid or given money for any kind of local news. This includes paying for print or digital news or making a pledge for public radio in the past year. Among those who don't pay for local news, nearly 50 percent say that they can find enough free local news, so they don't have to pay for it.

The decline of local news is a profoundly serious issue. Local news strengthens small towns and communities by providing information on civil and administrative issues, such as what their city council, school board, or zoning board is up to or what candidates to vote for in an upcoming election. Local papers provide communities with news about high school sports, events, business

COMIC STRIP TELLS STORY OF SYRIAN REFUGEE FAMILY

© Jake Halpern and Michael Sloan. "Welcome to the New World."

To call "Welcome to the New World" an editorial cartoon is vastly underselling the storytelling of writer Jake Halpern and artist Michael Sloan. In what is essentially a serialized graphic novel, they tell the story of a real-life refugee family from Syria who left for the United States on Election Day 2016.

Halpern, in an interview with *Buffalo Spree* magazine, said that he had always been interested in graphic narratives, especially the classic *Maus* that retells the story of the Holocaust using cats and mice to represent the Nazis and the Jews. Halpern started talking with refugee resettlement agencies looking for a family to feature in his story. The head of the agency asked him, "What would you think about the prospect of following a family from the moment they arrive? We've got two brothers with their families arriving on election day."[123]

The story for the family is particularly difficult because shortly after President Trump took office, he implemented a travel ban against people from Syria, which leaves the family in doubt about their status.

Halpern met with the family regularly during the twenty-episode run of the story.

The family includes Ammar, his brother Jamil, their wives Raghida and Oulah, and their children. Halpern did change the family members' names in order to help protect them. Although the family has not been identified, they still worry about having a journalist tell their story. "One of the things Jamil said to me early on was, 'Am I safe talking to you? Will it cause me trouble?' Because, where he came from in Syria, he was at risk for talking to the press. . . . I was in the process of saying, 'No, you're fine. This is America.' But, I paused for a good, long minute to just think it through. It's crazy that I had to stop and think about it. In the back of my mind, I worried about him."

Halpern says the response to the comic has been positive: "A lot of people have said that there was something about the graphic form of it that they found really touching."

Halpern said he was really excited to partner with Sloan because he liked the warm style of his work. "I thought that would work great, because there's a temptation to turn this into a really moody, brooding, edgy, darker type of story," he said. "But, my goal was to humanize these people, and the warmth that was so evident and alive in Michael's drawings would get it."

Sloan actually lives near Halpern in New York, and has done art for a variety of outlets, including the *New York Times*, the *Washington Post*, and the *New Yorker*.

Their work won the 2018 Pulitzer Prize for editorial cartooning, the first time it had been awarded to a reporter and an artist working together.[124] Bruce Headlam, the pair's editor, said the story could have been a conventional *New York Times* feature series, but instead it became "the first fully reported, regularly published comic strip to appear in the *Times*."[125]

While the *Times* has had editorial cartoons, it has not run comic strips, so when Headlam came up with the idea of telling a refugee family's story with a comic strip, he wasn't sure how the paper's management would react. To his surprise, the editors and art directors thought it was a great idea.

Perhaps the biggest challenge was having to tell the story so tightly. Headlam points out that a typical opinion piece in the *Times* runs about one thousand words. Each episode of "Welcome" ran on average two hundred words.

Halpern said he felt the length restriction keenly as he and Sloan worked on the series. There was a story he wanted to include about Jamil and Ammar seeing each other in taxis at an intersection in New York after arriving in the country on separate flights from separate countries that he just couldn't include. "The one thing that's frustrating about this strip is there's such little space," Halpern said.

"There's so much on the cutting room floor. If I were writing this story in any other form, there's no way I'd omit that story."[126]

WHO is the source?

Who are the artist and writer of this story? What makes their partnership unusual?

WHOSE story are they telling?

Whom are they writing about? How did they select them for this story? What makes their story significant?

WHY did the *Times* choose to use a comic strip to tell this story?

Does the *New York Times* use comic strips to report stories very often? What made the paper think this would be a good story to tell that way? Could it have been told with a conventional newspaper feature story? What did the *Times* gain from using a comic strip form?

HOW do you and your classmates react to this story as a comic strip?

Have you ever read a serious journalistic story as a comic strip or as a graphic novel before? If so, what was it? What did you think of it? Do you think "Welcome to the New World" was successful? Why or why not?

openings and closures, retirements, moves, as well as obituaries and stories from "around town." And as we all realize, in the wake of the COVID-19 pandemic, local news is how we find out about public health issues.[115]

Long before it became a national story, the Flint, Michigan, water contamination crisis was an important local media story. Flint is an old industrial city with a population of about one hundred thousand people. It is poor, and the auto industry jobs that have left the city aren't coming back. The city is predominantly Black.[116]

As early as May 2014, the *Flint Journal* local newspaper was running stories about "murky or foamy" water. By September, the paper was running stories about the boil advisories because of bacterial contamination. And by October, the *Journal* was reporting about the GM plant switching water suppliers because of the corrosion.

Michigan Radio, a public radio news service, started covering the story in June 2014 with news about complaints about the smell and taste of the city's water. In January 2015, a full year before the national media really started to pay attention to the story, Michigan Radio had a story about the fact that the city's water violated the Safe Drinking Water Act because the high level of chlorides was creating other problems with the water.[117] It wasn't until December 2015 that Flint's water crisis started to get national attention.

Exactly why local newspapers are failing has not always been well understood, with a lot of misconceptions being thrown about as explanations. On January 24, 2019, Dr. Jeremy Littau from Lehigh University sent out a series of more than thirty tweets trying to explain why newspapers are closing or laying off employees. The initial tweet in the series on the rather dry topic of media economics got more than 17,000 shares and 37,000 likes. (Remember Secret 5—All media are social.) He has since written extensively on the subject.[118]

Littau argues that popular sentiment is that the newspaper business began failing when newspapers stated giving away their content online for free back in the mid-1990s. But Littau sees the issue as a bit more nuanced. For decades, publishing a newspaper was essentially a way to print money with conglomerates buying up family-owned papers, taking on enormous amounts of debt to do so, and then making 30 percent or higher profits on the papers they've bought up.[119] Unfortunately, these newspaper chains used these profits to give shareholders large returns rather than investing in the quality of their product.

In the 1990s, however, things started to change. Anyone who wanted to put content up online through a blog or website could. And newspapers big and small, across the country started to post their stories online. Suddenly, people did not have to just rely on a single local source for print news. They could get news from aggregators, such as Google News or the *Huffington Post*, which profited off repacking content from newspapers without compensating the people who created the stories. The fact that people suddenly had many choices of places to get news where they were not paying for it put local newspapers in a difficult position.

The loss of classified advertising revenue has been another big blow to local papers. This has not just been the frequently villainized Craigslist, but any of a number of local online swap groups, eBay, and Amazon Seller. One final issue has been that people are no longer loyal to their local newspaper. People have long read their local newspaper not only for the so-called hard news of politics, crime, and local events, but also for news about births, deaths, engagements, anniversaries, and the like. And now people can get the same kind of information from social media sources, such as Instagram, Snapchat, Twitter, LinkedIn and Facebook. These social media channels get the revenue for this news we are self-sharing rather than our local papers.

As this is being written in the spring of 2020, the United States, along with the rest of the world, is immersed in the global COVID-19 pandemic and the associated cratering of the economy. With businesses closed and millions of people newly out of work, newspapers that were already hurting have lost a catastrophic amount of advertising. Papers have furloughed substantial portions of their staffs, put remaining workers on short hours, and suspended paper publication to go exclusively digital. Penny Abernathy, the Knight chair in journalism and digital media economics at the University of North Carolina told the *Guardian* newspaper that hundreds of newspapers may close because of the pandemic. "An extinction-level event will probably hit the smaller ones really hard, as well as the ones that are part of the huge chains."[120]

In Abernathy's study "The Expanding News Desert," published in 2018, well before the pandemic, she found that half of the counties in the United States have only one newspaper, usually a small weekly, and nearly two hundred counties have no newspaper at all. Most of the places where alternative news sources have arisen are in metro areas and not the poorer rural areas.[121]

There are multiple alternatives newspapers are investigating as ways of adapting to this new economic reality. One was the approach the Graham family took with the *Washington Post*—sell the paper to an incredibly rich billionaire (Bezos, who we discussed at the beginning of the chapter) who has deep enough pockets to take the paper into the future. Another approach is the one the *Salt Lake Tribune* took—becoming a nonprofit corporation. That means that members of the public can make tax-deductible contributions to the paper, in much the same way as they would pledge to public radio or television. When the paper announced the change in status in November 2019, the editor committed to maintaining its reputation for investigative reporting, sports coverage, and even restaurant reviews. The one thing that had to go, however, were political endorsements, which are forbidden for nonprofit corporations.[122]

CHAPTER REVIEW

CHAPTER SUMMARY ▶▶

Newspapers were first published in Britain and Europe in the seventeenth century. Numerous papers were later published in the American colonies, but faced extensive censorship from the British government. Newspapers printed before the nineteenth century tended to be partisan publications that were supported through high subscription fees and political subsidies. This changed with the rise of the penny press in the 1830s. The penny papers were mass produced on steam-powered printing presses and contained news of interest to ordinary people. The papers cost one or two cents and were supported by advertisers who wanted to reach the papers' large numbers of readers.

The late nineteenth and early twentieth centuries were characterized by the yellow journalism of the New York newspapers published by Joseph Pulitzer and William Randolph Hearst. The two publishers tried to attract circulation and attention by running comic strips, advice columns, and sensational stories about sex, crime, and scandal. This was the time when female reporters, such as *The World*'s Nellie Bly, started coming to prominence with exciting sensationalistic stories. This was also the time when newspapers started running extensive headlines and illustrations.

Magazines were another big part of the development of the American news industry. Magazines were where the work of early photojournalists, including Mathew Brady and his cohort of Civil War photographers, appeared. The early twentieth century saw a trend in investigative magazine reporting known as muckraking. The work of the muckrakers set the stage for much of the investigative reporting done today by newspapers and television news.

Henry Luce founded *Time* magazine in 1923, creating what would become one of the nation's largest media companies—Time Warner. Luce's publishing empire grew to include not just the news in *Time*, but also photojournalism in *Life*, sports journalism in *Sports Illustrated*, and personality and celebrity journalism in *People*.

Evolving technology has brought changes to the news business. Radio stations started broadcasting news in the 1920s, bringing live reports into people's living rooms

The rise of television news began in the late 1940s, bringing strong images of current events home and making national figures out of news anchors like Walter Cronkite. Cable television grew in popularity. Cable television news first came to prominence in 1991 with CNN's live 24/7 coverage of the first Gulf War. They were soon joined by competitors MSNBC and the now-dominant Fox News.

Newspapers today face a range of challenges, including declining advertising revenue and print circulation. Major national papers like the *Wall Street Journal*, the *New York Times*, and the *Washington Post* have successfully transitioned into being major online publications with steadily growing digital circulation.

Community newspapers continue to be a vital source of local news but are facing severe financial problems. These problems grew out of decades of concentrated ownership focusing on profits over investing in newsrooms, changing advertising markets, and ways of sharing personal news. Newspapers that serve specific ethnic communities still exist but are facing the same problems that mainstream papers do, with declining print circulation and ad revenue. Newspapers are considering a range of strategies for going forward, including finding wealthy owners willing to support local news or becoming nonprofits.

Many people claim that the media are biased toward one political view or another. Conservative critics argue that there is a liberal bias arising from the tendency of reporters to be more liberal than the public at large. The liberals' counterargument is that the press has a conservative bias because most media outlets are owned by giant corporations that hold pro-business views. Finally, some critics argue that the media hold a combination of values that straddle the boundary between slightly left and slightly right of center. The press in the United States began as partisan during the colonial period but adopted a detached, factual, objective style in the 1830s to appeal to a broader audience. In the twenty-first century, audience members are likely to choose media outlets that conform to their own social and political views. Despite these concerns about bias, journalists continue to risk their lives to report important and accurate news. During the 2016 presidential campaign, the term fake news became popular as a way of describing stories ranging from news the person didn't like to outright fabrications.

KEY TERMS ▶▶

REVIEW QUESTIONS ▶▶

1. What have been the good and problematic aspects of Amazon.com founder Jeff Bezos becoming owner of the *Washington Post*.

2. How was the penny press responsible for creating our modern version of the newspaper?

3. What are the challenges facing local newspapers? How are they dealing with them?

4. How does the news media experience differ between people who are politically liberal and politically conservative?

5. What did *Washington Post* executive editor Marty Baron mean when he said, "It's wrong to say we're becoming a digital society. We already are a digital society. And even that statement is behind the times. We're a mobile society."

Drew Angerer / Staff / Getty Images

CHAPTER 6

AUDIO

....

Music and Talk Across Media

The news that rapper Kendrick Lamar won the 2018 Pulitzer Prize for Music for his album *DAMN.* was seen as somewhat of a shock. The music award had never been given to anyone who is not a classical or jazz musician before, let alone a hip-hop artist. But Lamar's album was the unanimous choice of the Pulitzer jury. *New York Times* culture reporter Joe Coscarelli wrote that Lamar tackled "thorny issues both personal and political, including race, faith and the burdens of commercial success."[1]

In the pool of compositions being considered in 2018 for the Pulitzer, some were more traditional classical compositions that made use of hip-hop. David Hajdu, one of the jurors and a critic for the *Nation*, told the *Times*, "That led us to put on the table the fact that this sphere of work has value on its own terms and not just as a resource for use in a field that is more broadly recognized by the institutional establishment as serious or legitimate."

Lamar's work is not the first time that hip-hop has been recognized by the Pulitzers, however. That honor belongs to Lin-Manuel Miranda's musical *Hamilton*, which won the award for drama in 2016.

The extraordinarily popular production of *Hamilton*, which nearly everyone in the United States must know by now, tells the story of America's first treasury secretary using a multiethnic cast to play the Founding Fathers with a musical mix that includes lots of rapping, R&B, Brit pop, and good old-fashioned show tunes.

Miranda grew up in a Hispanic neighborhood in Manhattan, the son of Puerto Rican parents who had literally hundreds of Broadway cast albums. But while he was listening to *Camelot* and *The Unsinkable Molly Brown* at home, on the school bus his driver was introducing him to rappers Geto Boys and the Sugarhill Gang. So, it seemed to Miranda while he was growing up that bringing together show tunes and rapping was the most natural thing in the world.[2]

"There's been lots of theater that uses hip-hop in it, but more often than not, it's used as a joke—isn't it hilarious that these characters are rapping," Miranda said. "I treat it as a musical form, and a musical form that allows you to pack in a ton of lyric."[3]

Miranda was inspired to write the show when he read Ron Chernow's biography of Alexander Hamilton while he

was on vacation following the success of his first musical, *In the Heights*. He said he thought that hip-hop matched the American Revolution because it is "the language of youth and energy and rebellion."

New York Times classical music reviewer Anthony Tommasini writes, "On a basic level, the American Revolution was driven by words: fiery statements of principle; charges of imperialist oppression; accusations of betrayal; fine points of governance; even wordy obfuscations to gloss over disagreements that could have sabotaged the country at its start. What better musical genre to tell this tale?"[4]

Jon Caramanica, Tommasini's pop music colleague, says that at its core, the American Revolution was hip-hop. "[Miranda's] writing about a moment of total political upheaval, when upstart thinkers were building a nation on principles vastly different from the ones they fled . . . It's a position statement about the nation's founding ideals, the revolution that was hip-hop, and also the unrelenting whiteness of Broadway."[5]

One of the most distinctive characteristics of the show is the multiracial cast. Leslie Odom Jr., the African American actor who played the show's villain Aaron Burr on Broadway, said seeing the song "The Story of Tonight" during a workshop production had a big effect on him.

"That's the one that made me a puddle, because it was four men of color onstage singing a song about friendship and brotherhood and love, and I had never seen that in a musical. I had seen white guys do it, in *Jersey Boys*, in *Les Miz*. Never seen a black guy. So I was a mess, and from that point, I was along for the ride."[6]

Daveed Diggs, the rapper who debuted the part of Thomas Jefferson on Broadway, noticed how Miranda could give each character his or her own distinct rap style. "When you're developing your voice as a rapper, you figure out your cadence—your swag—and that's how you write," Diggs told *Rolling Stone*. "Lin managed to figure that out for *all* of those different characters—everyone has their own swag, and it feels germane to them."[7]

When Miranda first started writing *Hamilton*, he envisioned it as more a concept album or song cycle than a stage show. With the musical selling out nightly in multiple productions across the country, he has gone back to that idea with an album of outtakes and remixes of songs from the show published in the album *The Hamilton Mixtape*. Throughout 2018, he continued to put out show-related music monthly as what he referred to as "Hamildrops"—essentially the second volume of *The Hamilton Mixtape* released serially online. It includes an *F*-bomb-filled "Benjamin Franklin's Song" performed by The Decemberists, a complete-show polka medley from (who else?) Weird Al Yankovic, and a mashup of "The Story of Tonight" from *Hamilton* and "You Will Be Found" from the musical *Dear Evan Hansen*.[8] There's even a version of "One Last Time," based on George Washington's farewell address with the excerpts from the speech being given by former President Barack Obama.

By 2017 hip-hop was the most popular musical genre in the United States, according to the Nielsen media measurement company.[9] Eight of the top ten artists were also from hip-hop, including Drake and Lamar as the top two. So, this is an example of Secret 3—Everything from the margin moves to the center. Hip-hop has gone from being a subgenre of R&B music to the dominant sounds of the day. (We will talk more about the birth and growth of hip-hop later.) This has continued into 2018, when a quarter of all streaming tracks listened to were hip hop.[10]

In this chapter, we look at how the recording industry and audio developed together as our first electronic media. We then examine how society has changed, how cultures have grown and merged, and how audience members have responded to the production of shared music and talk. Finally, we look at where the industries are headed in the twenty-first century.

Stay up to date on the latest in media by visiting the author's blog at **ralphehanson.com**

The History of Audio Recording and Transmission

Before there could be mass consumption of popular music, there had to be a means of recording and distributing it. Those means evolved via inventors, such as Thomas Edison, who's early efforts with the phonograph and his development of the gramophone paved the way for the creation of the **long-playing record (LP)** and the **compact disc (CD)**.

The creation of the recording industry completely changed the way people bought and listened to music. For example, before the inventions of the phonograph and gramophone, the only way for people to experience music was to perform it themselves or go to a concert. The invention of the record meant that recordings of professional musicians could be heard in the home and soon became the standard way to listen to music.

A variety of stories have been told about Edison and his invention of an early sound-recording machine, the **phonograph**, in 1877. One version has him giving a sketch of the phonograph to employee John Kruesi with the instruction, "the machine must talk."[11] Another has him sketching the phonograph, with a note at the bottom telling his assistant to "build this."[12] These stories do not do justice to Edison's true genius or to the difficulties of creating a machine that could record and play back the voice. Running through these myths is the mistaken notion that Edison came up with an idea for sound recording that worked perfectly the first time it was tried. However, in reality, Edison and his assistants probably worked as long as ten months on the problem of the phonograph before they finally succeeded in recording Sarah Josepha Hale's children's rhyme, "Mary Had a Little Lamb." This famous first recording lasted no more than ten seconds.[13] As with so many media inventions, no one was quite sure what to do with Edison's phonograph. Edison envisioned it as a dictation machine. Reproducing music was only the fourth on his list of possible uses.[14] The biggest flaw with his invention was that Edison's foil cylinders did not hold up to repeated playing and could not be reproduced. It took the work of a young German immigrant to make the phonograph a truly practical device.

Emile Berliner arrived in the United States in 1870 at the age of nineteen. By 1888, he had developed a method for recording sound on flat discs rather than on cylinders. Berliner's disc recordings (or records) were louder and more lifelike than the cylinder recordings of Edison or Alexander Graham Bell. Berliner called his device the **gramophone**. Eventually, however, all record players were called phonographs.

Berliner also helped develop the idea of the recording industry. With Edison's phonograph, every recording was an original. Berliner viewed his invention not as a business dictating machine, but as an entertainment device. His discs could be reproduced from the original etched-zinc master, allowing publishers to mass produce high-quality—at least for the time—musical recordings almost as easily as printers could reproduce books. Because of this, Berliner saw that "prominent singers, speakers, or performers may derive an income from royalties on the sale of their phonautograms."[15]

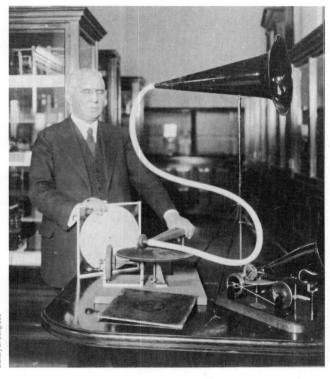

Library of Congress

▲ Emile Berliner was able to turn Thomas Edison's idea for a phonograph into a commercially viable product that lasted in one form or another for more than one hundred years.

A New Way of Publishing Music

By 1935, the term **high fidelity (hi-fi)** was being used to refer to a combination of technologies that allowed recordings that reproduced music more accurately, with higher high notes and deeper bass, than previous forms of recording had allowed. One of the developments that helped pave the way for hi-fi was the electric phonograph (along with the amplifier and loudspeakers), which began replacing the all-mechanical gramophone. By 1949, magnetic tape recorders were commonplace in recording studios. Musicians no longer had to record directly onto discs.

The phonograph changed the face of music. Previously, there were only two ways to store music. The first, and oldest, was for parents to teach their children the traditional songs of their culture. The alternative was written music, or musical scores, that contained symbols for the musical notes to be played. The phonograph provided a revolutionary way of storing the actual music, not just the symbols written down by the composer. It also made possible the storage of **non-notated music**, such as folk songs or jazz solos, which did not necessarily exist in written form. Music scholar Charles Hamm has compared the phonograph to a musical time machine that allows listeners to go back and hear the actual sounds.[16]

Evolving Formats for Recorded Music. For as long as there have been methods for recording and playing back sounds, there have been debates over how to make money selling music. Berliner's 78-rpm discs were fragile, held only three-and-a-half minutes of music, and had only marginal sound quality by today's standards. So, while there was no question that 78s needed to be replaced, there was no consensus on what the new format should be.

The popular "LP" record was developed by Columbia Records and introduced in 1948. The LP discs were labeled *unbreakable*; this was not quite true, but the vinyl LPs were much less delicate than the 78-rpm discs. More importantly, an LP could reproduce twenty-three minutes of high-quality music on each side. Columbia Broadcasting System (CBS) demonstrated the system to RCA president David Sarnoff and offered to let RCA, its competitor, use the system. But RCA declined the offer and put out its own format, the **45-rpm disc**. It had high-quality sound, but the 45 could play only about four minutes of music at a time.[17] Eventually, record players were sold that could play both 45s and LPs, and both formats existed side by side, with the LP (long playing) used for longer compositions and the 45 for single popular songs.

Work on the CD was started by Philips Electronics physicist Klaas Compaan as early as 1969. Compaan had the idea of photographically recording music or video on discs that could be read with a laser. Not wanting to get into the kind of format war that raged between the 45 and the LP in the 1940s, Philips joined with Sony to create a standard for the compact disc. The CD was launched in Europe in 1982 and in the United States in 1983.

While we have generally talked about new media being scary to consumers, **digital recording** (a method of recording sound that involves storing it as a series of numbers) has been the scariest of the new media to people in the music industry. With **analog recording** (the original method of recording that involved cutting a groove on a record or placing a magnetic signal on a tape that was an image of the sound wave being recorded), copies were not as good as the originals, and copies of copies showed further degradation in quality. Thus, the prospect of home digital recordings, which are the same as the originals without loss of quality, upset companies whose livelihood depended on the sales of original recordings.

For several years, home digital copying was held up by the recording industry, which wanted CD players to include security chips that would stop people from making copies. Of course, as soon as the industry came up with a way to stop people from copying digital music, hackers responded with ways of breaking the system. Ultimately, home CD copying emerged from the computer industry rather than the music industry. People wanted to be able to "burn" CDs with their own data, programs, and music.[18] With the coming of the more compact **MP3** music format and higher speed internet, it became easy for music fans to "share" online the music they had scanned from CDs.

The Birth of Radio: Transmitting Music and Talk

Around the time the recording industry was getting started, radio was under development as one of the first media to break through the barrier of space. With print media, such as books, magazines, and newspapers, the message being transmitted was always on a piece of paper that had to be carried from one place to another. Thus, the fastest form of transportation at the time was also the fastest channel of communication. This meant that it could take weeks for a message to cross the Atlantic or Pacific Ocean, or even to get from New York to California or from London to Moscow. But in the nineteenth century, several inventions separated communication and transportation, starting with the wired media of the telegraph and telephone and moving on to the wireless technology of radio.

Samuel Morse's invention of the **telegraph** in 1844 allowed messages to be sent electrically, so they did not have to be carried from place to place. No longer did transportation set limits on communication. Messages could travel at the same speed as electrons traveling along a wire.[19] By 1866, a telegraph cable extended across the Atlantic Ocean, so even that giant barrier had been conquered.

But the wire itself was a serious limitation. Telegraph wires could break (or be cut, as they frequently were during the U.S. Civil War). To communicate with ships at sea, a wireless telegraph was necessary.

In 1888, German physicist Heinrich Hertz found that he could detect the signal created by an electrical spark on one side of a room with a small loop antenna on the other side. What he had created was essentially the simplest possible radio transmitter and receiver. In 1894, Guglielmo Marconi read about Hertz's work and concluded that he could create a **wireless telegraph**, a

▲ Beyoncé's *Lemonade* was released on April 23, 2016, through Tidal's streaming service, and amassed 485,000 album sales and 115 million streams within its first week.

Larry Busacca/PW/Getty Images

point-to-point communication tool that used radio waves to transmit messages. Over a period of several years, he developed a system to send and receive radio signals, with the distance traveled by his signals expanding from the length of his attic to the width of the Atlantic Ocean.[20]

Radio as Mass Communication.

In 1901, physicist Reginald Fessenden started sending voice signals over a radio in his laboratory. On Christmas Eve in 1905, he broadcast poetry and Christmas carols. Since his continuously modulated voice signals could be received by the same equipment that received Morse code, wireless operators up and down the Atlantic coast heard Fessenden's amazing broadcast. Though it would be years before regularly scheduled commercial broadcasts would begin, Fessenden had set the stage for broadcasting something more than just Morse code.

Up until 1905, it was the scientists who were driving the radio business with their new technologies, but a young American Marconi employee saw that radio could be much more than just a way to send messages from one person to another. David Sarnoff, born in 1891, was a good student, but the need to help support his Russian-immigrant family led him to leave school after eighth grade to work full time. In a story that seems almost too good to be true, the fifteen-year-old Sarnoff went to the *New York Herald* to try to get a job as a journalist. As luck would have it, the first person he met at the *Herald* building worked for a telegraph company. Sarnoff went to work for the Commercial Cable Company, and from that point on, he never left electronic media.[21]

The Radio Music Box Memo.

In 1915, Sarnoff addressed to the director of American Marconi a document that he considered the most important of his career. The so-called **Radio Music Box memo** outlined radio's potential as a popular mass medium. While Sarnoff did not invent the technology of radio and was not the first person to send out entertainment over the radio, he did summarize what radio could, and indeed did, become. Sarnoff's insight was that radio could be more than a point-to-point medium, a one-on-one form of communication. As Sarnoff saw it, what was then perceived as the great disadvantage of radio as a telegraph tool—that everyone who listened could hear the message—could be turned into an enormous advantage if one wanted to send out messages that everyone was supposed to listen to. In his memo, Sarnoff wrote,

> I have in mind a plan of development which would make radio a household utility in the same sense as the piano or phonograph. The idea is to bring music into the houses by wireless.
>
> While this has been tried in the past by wires, it has been a failure because wires do not lend themselves to this scheme. With radio, however, it would be entirely feasible. For example, a radio telephone transmitter having a range of, say, 25 to 50 miles can be installed at a fixed point where instrumental or vocal music or both are produced. . . . The receiver can be designed in the form of a simple "Radio Music Box" and arranged for several different wave lengths, which should be changeable with the throwing of a single switch or pressing of a single button.[22]

With this memo, Sarnoff essentially invented radio as a social institution. But this new medium would have to wait, because on the eve of U.S. involvement in World War I, the navy was buying all of Marconi's transmitters. Although American Marconi did not act on Sarnoff's memo, the young immigrant did not forget the ideas for radio's potential that he had laid out so clearly.

More Receivers Than Transmitters.

One of the biggest surprises of the radio business was that so many more receivers were sold than transmitters. Manufacturers had assumed at the start that there would be almost as many people sending as receiving messages.[23] In reality, however, electronic communication was following in the footsteps of print. The earliest books had been copied by hand and passed from one person to another. But just as the printing press provided books, magazines, and newspapers to the masses, radio was now becoming a mass medium.

▲ Listening to music over headphones is nothing new, but in the 1920s, this farmer needed a wheelbarrow to move the radio set (left) from place to place.

The RCA Radio Monopoly. During World War I, the navy took control of all radio technology, including the patents, and tried to maintain control after the war. But civilian government officials in the United States, in keeping with the U.S. tradition of independent media, rejected the idea of all-government control. To avoid anarchy in the new medium, the navy advocated creating a private monopoly to control radio development.

The Radio Corporation of America (RCA) was formed as a consortium of four major U.S. companies: General Electric, AT&T, Westinghouse, and United Fruit Company. General Electric was included because it made radio transmitters and owned what had formerly been American Marconi. AT&T was the world leader in wired communication, and Westinghouse owned many critical patents. But why was United Fruit Company a part of RCA? United Fruit had used radios to connect its boats to banana plantations in South America and while doing so had developed improved technology that the monopoly needed.

These four companies brought together the two thousand or so patents that were needed to make the radio business work. RCA not only became a major producer of radio equipment, but it also founded the National Broadcasting Company (NBC), the first of the major broadcasting networks.[24] Frank Conrad, a Westinghouse employee and self-educated engineer, was the first to start making Sarnoff's dream of the Radio Music Box come true. In 1920, with Westinghouse's support, Conrad started broadcasting music on Sunday afternoons. Westinghouse then built Conrad a more powerful transmitter and put together a broadcast schedule. Pittsburgh's radio station KDKA was licensed for broadcast on October 27, 1920, and others soon followed. In 1922, the British Broadcasting Company (BBC) was created, initially, as a privately run company owned by the manufacturers of broadcasting equipment. The BBC's first station was licensed in 1923. In 1927, the company changed to a corporation and became the British Broadcasting Corporation, a public, noncommercial monopoly for broadcasting in the United Kingdom.[25]

Radio Advertising. Although Pittsburgh's KDKA was the first commercial radio station, it was not the first station to broadcast a commercial. The KDKA station existed to provide programming with the goal of getting people to buy radio sets. But WEAF, a broadcasting station in New York City, was the first to sell airtime to advertisers. The modest success of these commercials soon led to radio advertising by oil companies, department stores, and American Express.

During this time, the radio industry considered several possibilities for making money. One possibility was to support radio broadcasting with a "tithe" (a specified percentage) of revenues from sales of radios by all manufacturers. Another possibility was to support it with a substantial public endowment. The problem was that neither of these schemes would provide enough money to pay for the high-priced entertainers that listeners wanted to hear. This meant that radio stations were going to need advertising revenue. Ultimately, the rest of the media industry would accept advertising as the main source of income for broadcasting. In Britain, by contrast, the original BBC was supported by revenue from selling radio receivers and radio-receiving licenses, and it was prohibited from selling commercials.[26]

Radio Networks. By 1923, more than six hundred radio transmitters were broadcasting in the United States. These stations were limited to the programming they could produce locally. How did these stations fill their broadcast day? In big cities, this was no problem because there were plenty of concerts, lectures, and sporting events to put on the air, but rural areas or small towns were limited in their selection of locally produced culture and entertainment. In another of his

The Early Red and Blue NBC Radio Networks

NBC networks as of January 1, 1937

——— Red network
– – – Blue network
·········· Supplemental cities

Source: "Bob Hope and American Variety," July 24, 2002, http://www.loc.gov/exhibits/bobhope/images/vc85.jpg.

famous memos, Sarnoff suggested that RCA form a new company, a **network**, to provide programming to a large group of broadcast stations, thus making a wider selection of programming available to smaller stations.

Sarnoff's suggestion took root and on July 22, 1926 RCA established NBC. It was the United States's first major broadcasting network, and it survives today in the form of the NBC television network. NBC was originally two networks, the "Red" and the "Blue." (See Figure 6.1.) (Due to an antitrust ruling, RCA was eventually forced to sell the Blue network, which then became ABC.)

William Paley and the Power of Radio Advertising. With the growing demand for radio programming, the two NBC networks soon faced new competition, none more significant than William Paley's CBS. Although Paley was born in the United States, his parents were Russian immigrants. He grew up in a wealthy household, and his family owned a successful cigar company. William's father, Sam, had been approached about advertising his cigars on the fledgling United Independent Broadcasters (UIB) network. Sam was not interested, but William was.

William bought his first radio ads while his father was away on business, and although Sam initially chastised his son for wasting money, he soon heard people talking about the wonderful show his company sponsored. That was enough to convince him. William then developed a program called *La Palina Smoker* that featured an orchestra, a singer, and a comedian. It also resulted in increased cigar sales. Before long William, who was not quite twenty-seven years old, had the opportunity to buy UIB, which he did with help from his father. Once he became president of the network, he promptly renamed it the Columbia Broadcasting System.[27]

Paley understood better than anyone else that broadcasting was a business that had to make a profit on its own. NBC believed that its mission was to develop programs for the benefit of its listeners, but CBS realized that its real clients were the advertisers who sponsored the programs. Its programs were designed and produced specifically to attract the kind of audience a particular advertiser was looking for. For CBS, the "product" was the audience its programs attracted.

From Radio's Golden Age to the Television Age

The 1920s, 1930s, and 1940s came to be known as the **golden age of radio**, an era in which radio played the same role that television does today. Radio was the mass medium that served as the primary form of entertainment in the household. This was a big change. It meant that people were getting most of their entertainment from outside the home rather than from within. Instead of being entertained by Aunt Martha and Cousin Sue's piano duets, they were listening to Bing Crosby's crooning or Bob Hope's comedy on the radio.

Golden Age Radio Programming. A wide range of programming was available on the radio during the golden age. Live music, both popular and classical, was a staple. NBC even had its own orchestra that performed on a regular basis. There were also dramas and action programs, including *Little Orphan Annie*, *The Lone Ranger*, and *The Shadow*.

Some radio programs from the golden age survive today as television programs, most notably **soap operas**. The soaps, as they are called for short, are daytime dramas targeted primarily at women; they got their name from the commercials for soap and other cleaning products that ran during the shows. For better or worse, soaps were the first programs targeted specifically at women, a key audience for advertisers. It wasn't until the advent of television in the 1950s that soaps ceased to be a major part of radio programming.[28]

CBS's soap opera *Guiding Light* started on the radio in 1937, moved over to television in 1952, and finished its seventy-two-year run on September 18, 2009. In February 2014, ABC's *General Hospital* officially became the longest-running soap opera still in production, having had its thirteen-thousandth-episode spread over fifty years of both radio and television.[29]

Amos 'n' Andy. Despite the popularity of soap operas, no radio show attracted a bigger audience than *Amos 'n' Andy*, the first nationally broadcast daily drama.[30] *Amos 'n' Andy* began in January 1926 on Chicago radio station WGN as *Sam 'n' Henry*. The show was a fixture on the radio, in one form or another, for nearly thirty-five years. Starring on the show were two white actors—Charles Correll and Freeman Gosden—who played the roles of two African Americans, Sam and Henry, who owned the Fresh Air Taxi Company. Correll and Gosden wrote all the scripts themselves and furnished the voices for the title characters and the members of their fraternal lodge, the Mystic Knights of the Sea. Their names were later changed to Amos and Andy when Correll and Gosden syndicated the show nationally, since the WGN station owned the characters of Sam and Henry. At the peak of its popularity, *Amos 'n' Andy* was played in restaurants and in movie theaters between shows so that people would not have to stay home to listen.

The show was condemned as racist by many groups, including the National Association for the Advancement of Colored People (NAACP), accusing the humor in the show as being demeaning to the characters who were portrayed as uneducated and ignorant of city life. The most lasting criticism of the show, however, was that whites produced the program for the entertainment of a white audience. One of my African American students summed up the issue clearly: "So what you are telling me is that the most popular show in the country was about white people making fun of black people?"

Becoming a Companion Medium

As television began claiming more of the broadcast audience, radio was forced to change. No longer were people sitting down in their living rooms to listen to programs on the radio.

Instead, they turned on the radio while they did other things: working, washing dishes, driving. Yet radio did not fade away; instead, it reinvented itself as companion radio, a medium that would always be there to keep listeners company. Radio host Julius Lester put it this way:

> Radio is so integral a part of us now that we do not consciously notice its presence; it is a member of the family, a companion, and the voices issuing through its speakers are those not of strangers but of friends.[31]

Radio Consolidates and Goes High-Tech. Prior to 1985, broadcast owners were restricted nationally to seven AM radio, seven FM radio, and seven television stations.[32] During the 1980s, with the growth of cable and satellite television, the **Federal Communications Commission** (FCC) relaxed some ownership rules, which resulted in greater consolidation of ownership through media mergers. The trend toward broadcast deregulation was accelerated with the Telecommunications Act of 1996. Most of the 1996 law dealt with cable television and telephone industries, however it also lifted the restrictions on overall broadcast ownership, meaning a single company could now own unlimited numbers of radio stations, with up to eight stations in a single market.[33]

The impact of the Telecommunications Act on radio was almost immediate. Within a year and a half, radio ownership had become far more concentrated and far *less* diverse. By 2003, the number of radio stations on the air had grown by 5.9 percent, but the number of station owners had fallen by 35 percent.[34] Clear Channel used the rule change to buy up $30 billion worth of radio stations nationwide, going from owning 42 stations in 1995 to more than 1,200 stations by 2003.[35] As of 2014, when Clear Channel changed its name to iHeartMedia to highlight its streaming audio business along with its legacy radio stations,[36] the company was still the largest station owner in the United States, with approximately 850 stations reaching more than 245 million listeners.[37] In May 2019, iHeartMedia emerged from bankruptcy. It was briefly owned by a group of hedge funds before going public in July 2019.

The act's impact has been detrimental to independent and progressive stations. One example is the lack of female voices on country radio broadcasts. By 2002, the radio industry was essentially an oligopoly—just ten parent companies controlled two-thirds of the listeners and revenue.[38] "If local radio stations are getting their content fed in from some distant studio in another state, you have less information about your home," said Dennis Deninger, a communications professor at Syracuse University's Newhouse School. "Having less information about where you live and the people you live with I can't think that's a good thing."

Many stations now operate with virtually no staff other than a few people to sell and produce advertising. The music, news, weather, and talk all come from either a satellite service or a computer hard drive, with automation software serving up the local commercials, announcements, and programming. If it sounds like programming on the radio is the same from one side of the country to the other, it could be because the stations you are listening to all get their programs from the same centralized source.[39]

Radio's New Look: HD and Satellite

Among the digital technologies closest to **terrestrial radio** are HD radio and satellite radio.

Terrestrial radio is not just sitting still as digital technology takes over the sound business. In many markets, **HD radio** provides listeners with CD-quality sound and the choice of multiple channels of programming. But HD radio has not really taken off as a new medium. As of 2017, no more than 8 percent of Americans ever expressed an interest in HD radio, and beyond that, a high percentage of people do not even know what HD radio is, confusing it with satellite radio. While increasing numbers of cars are offering HD radios either as options or as standard equipment, buyers now have the option of adding streaming internet audio, such as Pandora or Spotify, to their vehicles. And even without dedicated streaming players in cars, as of 2020, 45 percent of cell phone–owning adults report using their mobile devices to stream music in their vehicles.[40] As a worrying sign, HD radio has not even been mentioned in the *New York Times* since 2017.

In 2008, the two competing **satellite radio** services, Sirius and XM, merged to become SiriusXM. The two services still offer separate programming but have overlap between them. They have also united their efforts to promote the idea of subscription radio. As of 2017, SiriusXM had nearly thirty-three million subscribers.[41] Neither of the two companies turned a profit as independents, and the newly merged company came close to filing for bankruptcy in February 2009, saved only by an infusion of cash provided by Liberty Media, the owner of major pay TV services.[42] However as of 2017, the service was making close to $650 million of income on $5.4 billion of revenue.

The biggest name on satellite radio is former broadcast **shock jock** Howard Stern, who moved over to Sirius after his protracted and very public battle with Viacom, which syndicated him, and the FCC, which fined his stations more than $2.5 million over a ten-year period.[43] Stern seems to be thriving on satellite radio with no corporate or FCC censors to put limits on him. Stern is now in his sixties and has been moving from being primarily a shock jock into being a respected interviewer. "When you go on 'Stern,' you get the best insight into who the person is of any medium other than maybe the New Yorker," writes music industry critic Bob Lefsetz.[44]

Of course, not everyone is happy about this transformation from making jokes about the Columbine High School shooting or AIDS to becoming a serious talk show host. "Howard has become a lot of the things that he always told people not to become," comedian Jackie Martling (formerly of the Stern show) told the *Washington Post*. Stern has essentially become one more example of Secret 3—Everything from the margin moves to the center.

Satellite radio also provides news and public affairs channels, such as CNN, Fox News, BBC World Service, and NPR. One advantage of satellite over regular radio is that travelers can tune in to a channel in New York and listen to it all the way to California. The disadvantage, other than the cost, is that these services cannot provide the depth of local content, such as traffic reports, local news, or weather forecasts—the staples of car radio.[45]

Streaming Audio

The original online alternative to radio was **streaming audio**, which can take a wide range of forms. Some content played on streaming radio platforms is tied to a terrestrial station; others are internet only, such as Pandora, Spotify, and Apple Music. Pandora, for example, was started in 2005, and according to a survey conducted in early 2018, 31 percent of Americans age twelve or older listened to Pandora in the last month, and 20 percent listened to Spotify.[46] In essence, smartphones and other mobile devices are becoming the new portable radio, as well as being players for your personal collection of recorded music or listening to the latest podcast.

Cars are also increasingly having internet streaming built into their audio systems, but how much they are getting used is still up in the air. Edison Research and Triton Digital's "Infinite Dial 2020" report found that 50 percent of survey respondents still used AM/FM radio the most in their car. Despite the attention being given to in-dash car infotainment systems, only 18 percent of Americans age eighteen or older have access to this new way of consuming mobile media.[47]

Streaming audio also greatly extends the reach of stations, especially small ones with low-powered transmitters. A 3,800-watt student station that can barely cover fifteen miles over the air can reach an entire city, not to mention the world, through streaming. Streaming can do for a small radio station what cable did for Ted Turner's local Atlanta television station, WTBS—turn it into a radio superstation that anyone in the world can receive.

The "Infinite Dial 2020" study found that an estimated 192 million Americans listen to an online radio station or other streaming audio service monthly. That is 68 percent of American adults.[48] (We'll talk more about streaming and digital audio at the end of this chapter.)

SMART SPEAKERS

One new way that people are listening to a wide range of audio programs are the new smart speakers. These include Amazon's Echo devices, Google Home speakers, and Apple's HomePods. Although they each offer somewhat different services, they are all about delivering online services (including audio programing) by voice command. You can use them to answer a question, order a product, turn lights on or off, arm your alarm system, or play audio programming.[49] While it might seem great to be able to just ask your speaker to start playing your favorite music or podcast, there are also some creepy aspects to these devices. To be able to respond to your commands, your smart speaker has to be always listening to you. And these speakers don't have the capability built in to respond to your commands. Instead, their software, be it Alexa, Google Assistant, or Siri, have to talk to a central server to process your request. That means that Amazon, Google, or Apple is literally listening to everything that happens in your home. Now maybe you trust these companies with all your most private moments. But think about the implication of someone hacking these speakers and installing malware on them. Your smart speaker could then be used as a wiretap in your house. There would also be the possibility of a government security agency listening in. These may all sound like conspiracy theories, but they are all technically possible when you deliberately install an always-on listening device in your house.[50]

In fact, the companies that produce these devices do record and potentially listen to you to improve the quality of their speech recognition. Amazon, for example, employs thousands of people to listen to these recordings so they can transcribe them to improve the accuracy of Alexa's speech recognition. While most of what these transcribers hear is rather routine—clarifying that the words "Taylor Swift" refer to a pop singer—they do occasionally hear children screaming or a sexual assault.[51] *Washington Post* technology columnist Geoffrey Fowler took on the task of listening to four years of what Alexa had recorded from his home. During his listening, Fowler heard,

> "Spaghetti-timer requests, joking houseguests and random snippets of 'Downton Abbey.' There were even sensitive conversations that somehow triggered Alexa's "wake word" to start recording, including my family discussing medication and a friend conducting a business deal."

Fowler notes that consumers can go back to erase Alexa's recordings, but they cannot stop the recordings from being made in the first place. Apple's Siri records everything that it hears, but Apple says that the company attaches an anonymizing identifier to each recording. Only Google, with its Google Assistant, does not record everything by default.

. . . .

WHO is the source?

What are the smart speakers out on the market? Who makes them?

WHAT are they saying?

What are the criticisms of smart speakers? Why do some people consider them an invasion of privacy?

WHAT kind of evidence is provided?

What did the *Washington Post* reporter find when he listened to what Alexa had recorded? How do the tech companies deal with the information they collect?

HOW do you and your classmates feel about smart speakers?

Do you have a smart speaker? Do you worry about them invading your privacy? Are they worth the convenience of having a voice command computer ready all the time?

Podcasting

A long-tail alternative to terrestrial radio and prerecorded music is the **podcast**. Podcasts are audio programs distributed over the internet as compressed MP3 sound files that can be listened to online or downloaded to a computer or phone. They open distribution of audio programming to anyone with a basic computer and an online connection. An example of a popular podcast would be NPR's morning news program *Up First*, which is available for downloading about the time you get up. It has a couple of popular NPR hosts presenting a ten- to twelve-minute newscast with a bit of depth and analysis.[52]

It is difficult to say exactly when podcasting got started, but the summer of 2004 is the commonly held period because that's when RSS 2.0, which could handle enclosures (essentially attachments) along with straight text, was released. It is also when former MTV VJ Adam Curry and software developer Dave Winer wrote the program iPodder. It was one of the first programs available that could download a podcast off the internet and transfer it to an iPod. It's much easier to say when podcasting became widely known—February 9, 2005, when *USA Today* ran two articles about the new medium and phenomenon in the paper.[53] In May 2005, podcasting became easier when Apple's iTunes software started supporting subscriptions to podcasts. As of 2018, Apple has essentially stopped making iPods, and most people listen to podcasts by downloading them directly onto their phones.[54]

Podcasting and the Long Tail. Rob Cesternino became reasonably well known as a two-time cast member of the hit CBS reality game show *Survivor*. But since competing on the show, he has gone from being a star of the short head, to a force in the long tail. He has created the popular site "Rob Has a Website" and a series of podcasts about reality TV under the brand "Rob Has a Podcast."

He has a crowdfunding Patreon account that brings in more than $8,000 a month and even beat out *Serial* for a People's Choice Podcast Award in 2015. Cesternino started Rob Has a Website several years ago when he was unemployed and wanted to do something reasonably secure to earn a living for his family. "For me, it came down to a conscience shift: I wanted to do what was safest for me and my family," he told the news site *24 Hours Toronto*. "But then it hit me that working for some random company without any security wasn't any safer, either. So, I invested all my time into Rob Has a Website. I thought, 'Hey, it may not work, but I'm not going to be in any risker position if I were employed in a media company because those people are let go all the time.'"[55]

After starting with just a single, *Survivor*-oriented podcast, he now has several shows put out by his company covering a range of reality programing. He also does shows in person with live audiences. Before the fortieth season of *Survivor*, for example, he had a live show that included the premier episode followed by a conversation with *Survivor* alums.[56] Cesternino says that one of the essential parts of working in the long tail is being involved with his fans. He told *24 Hours Toronto*, "I want the people listening to me to know they're in this thing with me. That's why I'm very responsive on social media and integrate their questions into the show."[57]

Terrestrial broadcast radio is still the dominant medium for listening to audio programming, with 89 percent of Americans age twelve or older listening each week. This is a percentage that has not changed significantly in the past decade. Listening to broadcast stations online is a growing behavior, with "The Infinite Dial" report finding that 68 percent of Americans had listened to online audio in the past month. This includes the 45 percent who have ever listened to online audio in a car using a mobile phone.[58]

That is not to say that podcasting is anywhere nearly as popular as radio. As of 2020, a "The Infinite Dial" report found that 55 percent of Americans had ever listened to a podcast and that 37 percent had listened to a podcast in the past month. So, despite their growing popularity, podcasts have a long way to go to come even close to terrestrial broadcasting in popularity.

Music, Youth Culture, and Society

Though recorded music was on the market long before there was **rock 'n' roll**, rock 'n' roll was born alongside modern recording technology and flourished on the radio. It was amplified from the start, featured new instruments such as the solid-body electric guitar, and brought together a host of traditions from white hillbilly music to Black rhythm and blues. World War II spurred the development of rock 'n' roll as a cross-cultural phenomenon because young Blacks and whites mixed socially during the war more often than they had before and because the Armed Forces Radio played a range of musical styles.

Before 1948, recordings by popular Black musicians were referred to as **race records** and included everything from blues to gospel to jazz. But in 1949, the editors of *Billboard* magazine, which ranks sales of all types of records, started calling the genre rhythm and blues (R&B).[59] It was at the same time that "folk" records began to be called "country and western."[60]

Why did R&B emerge when it did? There are several reasons. One is that the big bands that played jazz and swing (popular in the 1930s and 1940s) were expensive because there were so many musicians. An amplified blues band with a singer, an electric guitar, an electric bass, and a drummer could make a lot of sound, and great dance music could be built around the strong bass beat.[61] Also, African American musicians gained respect when white artists recorded cover versions of Black songs.[62] On December 28, 1947, a Black R&B singer named Wynonie Harris recorded "Good Rockin' Tonight" in a studio in Cincinnati, Ohio. The song would become a big hit on Black jukeboxes and radio stations. Was this the first rock 'n' roll song? Entire books have been devoted to answering that question, but "Good Rockin'" is as likely a candidate as any. It was a jukebox hit for Harris, and later became a radio hit when **covered** by young Elvis Presley. It certainly helped give this new kind of music its name. The following year brought a series of songs with the word *rock* in the title, including "We're Gonna Rock, We're Gonna Roll," "Rockin' at Midnight," "Rock the Joint," and "Rock and Roll."

By and large, these songs were not played on white radio stations. The problem was not the color of the musicians; it was the meaning of the word *rock*. As record promoter Henry Glover put it,

We were restricted with our possibilities of promoting this song because it was considered filth. . . . They had a definition in those days of the word "rock," meaning the sex act, rather than having it known as "a good time," as they did later.[63]

Library of Congress

▲ Rhythm and blues records produced by African American artists (then known as "race records") were more likely to be played on jukeboxes in clubs than on the radio in the 1940s.

Blending Black and White Musical Traditions

While Harris and numerous other R&B singers were performing rock 'n' roll in the late 1940s and early 1950s, two stars—one white, the other Black—would put rock 'n' roll on the national and international map. Presley and Chuck Berry demonstrated what could be done with the blending of hillbilly (or country) and R&B.[64]

Presley made his first recording in 1953, although no one knows the exact date. Marion Keisker, the woman behind the desk at Memphis Recording Service, remembered a young man who recorded a couple of songs on a ten-inch acetate disc for his mother. When she asked Presley whom he sounded like, his response was "I don't sound like nobody."[65] Keisker had the good sense to make an extra copy of Presley's recording and file it under the heading "good ballad singer." "The reason I taped Elvis," she explained, "was this: Over and over I remember Sam [Phillips, Keisker's boss] saying, 'If I could find a white man who had the Negro sound and the Negro feel, I could make a billion dollars,' [and] this is what I heard in Elvis."[66]

The man who would become known as "the king" soon started performing hillbilly music in Memphis and recording for Phillips, starting with "Good Rockin' Tonight." To Presley, performing was almost a religious experience: "It's like your whole body gets goose bumps," Presley said. "It's like a surge of electricity going through you. It's almost like making love, but it's even stronger than that."[67]

Ronald Wittek/picture-alliance/dpa/AP Images

▲ Rock 'n' roll legend Chuck Berry performs in Germany in November 2008. Berry (and others like Elvis Presley) combined elements of hillbilly and R&B into their music, which ultimately led to the creation of a brand new genre.

Just as hillbilly singer Presley borrowed from R&B, blues guitarist Berry borrowed from the white hillbilly singers. The song "Maybellene" was based on an old fiddle tune called "Ida Red" and supposedly got its name from a mascara box. Others claim that Maybellene was the name of a cow in a third-grade reading book. Either way, the song combined a hot guitar, a hot car, and a hot woman.

Berry wanted to break out of some of the restrictions of traditional blues. While his audience at the clubs would not stand for any change in the basic blues style, they had no problem with Berry's original rendition of an old white fiddle tune. Berry's unconventional style made people sit up and take notice. Berry recalls people talking about his music at an African American club:

> Some of the clubgoers started whispering, "Who is that black hillbilly at the Cosmo?" After they laughed at me a few times, they began requesting the hillbilly stuff and enjoyed trying to dance to it. If you ever want to see something that is far out, watch a crowd of colored folk, half high, wholeheartedly doing the hoedown barefooted.[68]

Presley started playing "Maybellene" in Louisiana while Berry was playing it in New York. This illustrates a key feature of the birth of rock 'n' roll: Two previously segregated types of music were coming together and becoming a new musical form—one that teens could not get enough of.

Rock Radio. Another reason for rock 'n' roll's growing popularity was that DJs such as Alan Freed and Dewey Phillips were playing rock 'n' roll and R&B records on their radio shows. On October 29, 1949, Phillips started a show on WHBQ in Memphis called Red, Hot & Blue that played R&B records. The show became an instant hit and quickly went from forty-five minutes in length to three hours. WHBQ's program director remembered it this way: "He got something like seven requests his first night. Well, the next night, I don't know the exact amount, but it was more like seventy requests. Then, even more incredible, the next night, it was closer to seven hundred."[69] Although Phillips was white, he played music by Black artists and had a substantial audience of Black radio listeners in Memphis. This was unusual at a time when most stations appealed to either the white or the Black community, but not to both.

The Changing Face of Popular Music

The 1950s were a period of transition for popular music, with tastes shifting from the Tin Pan Alley songs of an Irving Berlin or Cole Porter to the songs of a Chuck Berry or Buddy Holly that were rooted in R&B. Already firmly established through concerts and radio airplay, rock 'n' roll now took center stage with records produced by artists ranging from **girl groups** to the Rolling Stones.

Motown: The Sound of Young America. No record label was more important in bringing R&B to the masses than Detroit's Motown Records. Motown, founded by Berry Gordy Jr., was the most successful of the independent record labels and one of the most successful Black-owned businesses.

Popular culture scholar Gerald Early says that the real importance of Motown was that it took Black music and sensibilities and made them important for the public at large. He also credits Motown with establishing a Black popular culture at a time when jazz—especially the improvisational work of Miles Davis and John Coltrane—was becoming highbrow culture. One of the big accomplishments of Motown was that it no longer published songs by Black artists for white artists to cover, as was common practice in the 1950s and early 1960s. Instead, the African American Motown artists themselves turned out the hits. Motown moved Black music into the mainstream and out of the world of race records, thus illustrating Secret 3—Everything from the margin moves to the center.[70]

The move of soul music and artists out of just the African American community and into more predominantly white areas mirrored larger changes in society. In May 1961, African American

Freedom Riders staged sit-ins in bus stations in the South to desegregate restrooms and lunch counters. In October 1962, the Motown Revue was doing its part to promote desegregation with such established acts as the Marvelettes, Marvin Gaye, and the Supremes. While the Motown artists were not Freedom Riders, they broke some of the same ground on their tour. Mary Wilson of the Supremes put it this way:

> Our tours made breakthroughs and helped weaken racial barriers. When it came to music, segregation didn't mean a thing in some of those towns, and if it did, black and white fans would ignore the local customs to attend the shows. To see crowds that were integrated—sometimes for the first time in a community—made me realize that Motown truly was the sound of young America.[71]

Diana Ross and Cindy Birdsong. GAC–General Artists Corporation–IMTI–International Talent Management Inc. Retrieved from Wikimedia Commons.

▲ Motown Records put together several African American girl groups, including the Supremes (pictured) and Martha and the Vandellas.

Motown's years as an independent company ended in 1988 when Gordy sold the label to Boston Ventures for $61 million. Motown was subsequently sold to PolyGram in 1993 for $301 million. It still exists, but it is now a small unit within media giant Universal Music Group.

The lasting effect of Motown artists can be seen with the huge outpouring of affection for Michael Jackson following his death in 2009.

The British Invasion: A Rougher Rock. In the 1960s, rock underwent a few changes. The most significant of these were brought about by groups that came to the United States from England. The so-called **British invasion** began in 1964 and brought a rougher edge to white rock 'n' roll with the music of the Beatles, Dusty Springfield, the Hollies, the Who, and, of course, the Rolling Stones. To appreciate the influence of these British bands, one need only look at the charts. In 1963, only one British band made it onto Billboard's charts; in 1964, thirty-four did so.[72]

Traditionally, recorded music by popular groups was a means of promoting their live shows. But by 1966, it had become almost impossible for the Beatles to perform live because their screaming fans drowned them out. In fact, Beatles scholar Allan Moore notes that by 1966 the band had ceased touring because they could not hear themselves play. Instead, they became a studio band whose music was heard primarily on records and the radio.[73] In 1967, the Beatles recorded an album, *Sgt. Pepper's Lonely Hearts Club Band*, that transformed rock in a number of ways: It was one of rock's first **concept albums**—an album that brought together a group of related songs on common themes. It was also one of the first rock albums that was more than a collection of hit singles and their flip sides.[74]

What exactly is the concept of this album? Many of the songs have autobiographical themes derived from John Lennon's and Paul McCartney's childhood memories of Liverpool, England. Also, the songs are supposedly being played by the fictional band of the title.[75]

Sgt. Pepper gave rise to albums that were designed to be played from beginning to end, though these two-sided vinyl records had to be turned over at the twenty-three-minute mark. The seamless presentation of seventy minutes of music would have to wait for the 1980s and the advent of the CD.

Sgt. Pepper highlights a change that was starting to take place in the music business: The LP was replacing the single as rock music's main format. Moore notes that in 1967 bands still relied

Michael Ochs Archive/Getty Images

▲ The Beatles' album *Sgt. Pepper's Lonely Hearts Club Band*, along with the Beach Boys' *Pet Sounds* and Frank Zappa's *Freak Out!*, was among the first rock concept albums that brought together a set of songs on a common theme.

primarily on singles to promote themselves and albums were of secondary importance. But that was changing with groups such as Cream and Led Zeppelin focusing on albums. Led Zeppelin's greatest hit, "Stairway to Heaven," was never released as a single, probably because it would not fit the short format of the 45.[76]

The Growing Importance of Producers.

As popular music increasingly became a studio creation, the albums' **producers** became as important as the artists themselves. The main job of a producer is to put together the right songs, songwriters, technicians, and performers in the creation of an album.

Rock historian Charlie Gillett argued that the producer is the person who is responsible for making hit records. Producer Rick Rubin revitalized Johnny Cash's career near the end of his life with a series of albums that included songs by U2, Nine Inch Nails, and Tom Petty, among others. He also produced albums for other artists including Kanye West, Jay-Z, Adele, Lady Gaga, Lana Del Rey, Ed Sheeran, the Avett Brothers, and most recently the Strokes. Producer Kenneth "Babyface" Edmonds has created or revived the careers of such artists as Aretha Franklin, Toni Braxton, Whitney Houston, Beyoncé, Zendaya, and Ariana Grande.[77] With rock, the producer shapes the sound and becomes an integral part of the musical process. Few albums demonstrate this as clearly as Pink Floyd's *Dark Side of the Moon*. Starting in 1973, *Dark Side of the Moon* spent 741 weeks on the Billboard Top 200 album chart, far longer than any competitor (though other albums have sold more copies). Alan Parsons produced the album, released in 1973, which paints a bleak picture of "alienation, paranoia, schizophrenia." But more than any message of the songs, *Dark Side of the Moon* presents an incredible sonic picture. It uses stereo to its fullest extent, sending sounds swirling around the listener's head. Parsons recorded a wide variety of voices talking, laughing, and screaming, which were mixed in at various times and speeds.[78] Pink Floyd continued the direction of the Beatles's *Sgt. Pepper* album, in which rock was music made to be recorded and constructed as much as performed.

The role of the producer continued to grow throughout the 1970s with the advent of **disco** and a range of heavily produced club music, including rap, house, and techno. Disco was primarily a means of getting people to dance. It came out of the gay male subculture in New York City and was popularized in the 1977 hit movie *Saturday Night Fever*. Disco was in many ways the ultimate producer music, in which the beat and the overall sound created by the producer mattered more than the vocals or talents of the instrumentalists.

Why does disco matter today? Primarily, it was an entire genre of music that depended on technology and the producer, building on trends started by bands such

Frazer Harrison / Staff

▲ Rick Rubin

as Pink Floyd and the Beatles. It also made Black and Latino music more important commercially and led the movement toward the splintering of pop music into a range of genres.[79]

Hip-Hop Brings Together DJing, Dancing, Rapping, and Art. While the terms **hip-hop** and *rap* are often used interchangeably, rapping is just a single facet of the larger world of hip-hop. According to English professor Mickey Hess, the hip-hop sound got started in the 1970s, when DJs began name-checking where they were from, including their cities, streets, or even neighborhoods. Although the music went national, it was still local in its orientation and was a statement of pride about the rapper's home. As Mr. Cheeks from the Lost Boyz put it, "It's only right to represent where I'm from."[80]

Where did hip-hop begin? Many sources point to a block party in the Bronx, New York, on August 11, 1973, at which DJ Kool Herc is credited with inventing the breakbeat, "using two turntables and two copies of the same record to loop the same instrumental break over and over."[81] But Hess argues that it wasn't so neat and clear-cut of a start. He claims instead that credit goes to a series of DJs working in Harlem nightclubs using similar techniques along with doing "call-and-response" from the audience. Hess lists four main elements of hip-hop culture:

1. MCing—The spoken word or rapping over recorded music

2. DJing—Playing recorded music from multiple sources, oftentimes overlapping

3. B-boying—Physical movement, a style of hip-hop dancing, often referred to as breakdancing

4. Graffiti art—The visual images of the culture

These separate elements show how hip-hop evolved from a variety of areas of the country, with DJing coming out of New York, graffiti art growing out of styles popularized in Philadelphia, and the dancing coming from both New York and Los Angeles. The MCing, or rhyming, is credited as coming from the work of a variety of rhyming radio hosts in cities such as Detroit, Philadelphia, New Orleans, and Austin.

Rap music started to spread out of the Bronx via cassettes that were passed from person to person. Remember, however, that these were analog recordings that could not be copied repeatedly like digital recordings can today. There was also a high level of borrowing/stealing/remixing going on even at the very beginning. Sugarhill Gang's "Rapper's Delight," which introduced rap and hip-hop into the mainstream, used lyrics from a Bronx MC who had not released a record. Blondie's rap hit "Rapture," which came out in 1980, was among the first rap songs to receive radio airplay on stations that appealed to white audiences[82] (thus showing us another example of Secret 3—Everything from the margin moves to the center). Sugarhill Gang were also among the rappers who brought *Hamilton* composer Miranda into the world of hip-hop as a junior high student.

Understanding the importance of a rapper's roots and locale is key to understanding how hip-hop has spread around the world. Global rappers give shout-outs to homes as varied as Norway, Japan, Egypt, and Korea. Linguistics professor Marina Terkourafi talks about how hip-hop has followed in the footsteps of rock and jazz in moving out of the United States and then blending with traditional and regional musical styles from around the world.[83] She writes that while the central themes of hip-hop in the United States have typically centered on race and gender, globally it has been used to protest against the status quo and raise awareness of local issues.

Syrian exile Mohammad Abu Hajar tells *Huck* magazine about how he came to use hip-hop as a way of expressing his rebellion against the political problems in his native country along with the issues of honor crimes and interfaith marriages. His path to hip-hop was a bit rocky given that

Amy Harris/Invision/AP

▲ Kendrick Lamar performs at the Coachella Festival, April 2017, in Indio, California. Lamar's album *DAMN.* won the Pulitzer Prize for Music in 2018 and was one of the most successful albums commercially that year.

he did not even like rap to begin with. "I thought it was just [crappy] American music only concerned with promoting drug use," he said.[84] But he soon learned that hip-hop could be a tool for social awareness.

Mohammad's music eventually got him in trouble with the Syrian government, and he fled to Lebanon. "When the cops showed up at my door to arrest me over a song I had written I knew this wouldn't end well," he said. "I jumped the fence in the backyard and managed to lose them." He now makes his home in Berlin where he works as a project coordinator for a nongovernmental organization and continues to rap about refugee issues. "I've got nothing left to lose at this point. . . . And I will not be intimidated into silence."[85]

Country: Pop Music for Adults. **Country music** was born in the late nineteenth century, evolving out of a range of musical forms that included Irish and Scottish folk music, Mississippi blues, and Christian gospel music.[86] It was originally called "old-timey" or hillbilly music. Country grew in the 1950s and 1960s with the so-called Nashville sound that was popularized by musicians such as Jim Reeves, Eddy Arnold, and Patsy Cline. It was at about this time that Elvis Presley took the hillbilly sound in another direction with early rock 'n' roll, but country never disappeared.

In 1980, many Americans rediscovered country music due to the hit film *Urban Cowboy*, starring John Travolta, and the 1990s and 2000s saw the further growth of country music thanks to songs from artists such as Rascal Flatts, the late Johnny Cash, and Carrie Underwood, as well as the soundtracks of movies such as *O Brother, Where Art Thou?* and *Walk the Line*.[87] In 2017, *Rolling Stone* magazine published a list of the top hundred country artists of the modern era. The top five were these:

▲ Country legend Merle Haggard helped bridge the gap between electric country and country rock.

Stephen Lovekin/Getty Images for Big Barrel

5. The Carter Family of A. P. Carter, his wife Sara, and his sister-in-law Maybelle created modern country music in the late 1920s with their folk vocals over guitar, autoharp, and banjo.

4. Loretta Lynn, who was proud to be a coal miner's daughter, brought a whole new world of scorned wives and "women who weren't in the mood for lovin'."

3. Johnny Cash, the man in black, really had multiple careers in music, being rediscovered by many young people with his Rick Rubin–produced American Recordings series. Cash was also connected to the Carter family by way of his second wife, June Carter Cash.

2. Hank Williams died at age twenty-nine from alcohol and pills, but he left behind a legacy of songs and musical style that lives on today.

1. Merle Haggard's electric-tinged music that represented the rougher-edged Bakersfield Sound brought country to generations of rock bands from the Beatles to the Eagles.[88]

Why does country music continue to be so popular? "Country music is about lyric-oriented songs with adult themes," according to Lon Helton, a music journalist. "You've probably got to be 24 or 25 to even understand a country song. Life has to slap you around a little bit, and then you go, 'Now I get what they're singing about.'"[89] Unlike the sex and drugs of rock 'n' roll, country deals with suburban issues like "love, heartache, family ties, and middle-aged renewal."[90]

Finding a Niche: Popular Radio Formats

With the coming of television, radio was forced to change and no longer tried to be all things to all people. Instead, each station now appeals to a particular audience. Teenagers don't have to listen to the same programs as store clerks; stockbrokers don't have to listen to the same programs as college students. Want rock 'n' roll? There is a station for it. Oldies? Another choice or two. News? Talk? Classical music? Soul? If you live in an urban area, chances are you can find stations providing all these different radio formats. During the past decade, radio has continued to evolve, undergoing a massive change of ownership, and seeing the growth of numerous new competitors.

The most popular radio format in 2019 in the United States was news/talk with 9.5 percent of stations carrying it (see Table 6.1), followed by adult contemporary (AC) with 8.1 percent and country with 6.7 percent. Adult contemporary (AC) and soft AC consist of light and soft rock and are designed to appeal to listeners aged twenty-five to forty. Pop contemporary hits **format radio** is what used to be known as Top 40 and is made up of a range of current hits; while it would seem to be primarily a teen format, more than half of its audience is older than twenty-five. While audience members might call a lot of what they listen to oldies, the radio business breaks it down into a variety of categories, including classic hits, classic rock, and oldies. Rhythmic contemporary hits radio was a format developed to appeal to the United States's changing ethnic makeup, with listeners spread fairly evenly among Black, Hispanic, and "other."[91]

▼ TABLE 6.1

Top Ten Popular Radio Formats

Format	Audience Portion
News/Talk (Commercial and Noncommercial)	9.5%
Adult Contemporary (AC)	8.1%
Country	6.7%
Pop Contemporary Hit Radio (CHR)	6.5%
Classic Hits	5.8%
Classic Rock	5.1%
Hot Adult Contemporary	5.0%
Urban Adult Contemporary	4.7%
All Sports	4.3%
Urban Contemporary	3.6%

Source: "Tops of 2019: Radio," *Nielsen*, December 18, 2019, https://www.nielsen.com/us/en/insights/article/2019/tops-of-2019-radio/.

Talk Radio: Politics, News, Shock Jocks, and Sports. As mentioned earlier, news and talk are among the top radio formats. Talk radio has exploded during the past three decades. In 1985, only 200 stations carried the format; in 1995, that number had grown to approximately 1,900. By 2020, news/talk was available on 1,315 stations, compared with 1,882 stations carrying country music.[92] (Note that Table 6.1 is about audience size, not number of stations.) Marvin Kalb, formerly with CBS News, credits talk radio with providing a sense of community that people don't find anywhere else: "If we still gathered at town meetings, if our churches were still community centers, we wouldn't need talk radio. People feel increasingly disconnected, and talk radio gives them a sense of connection."[93]

Political Talk. Talk radio is a major source of political information, and the political information they are getting from talk radio is largely conservative.[94] Although journalism generally values balanced coverage, New York radio host Brian Lehrer notes that such coverage doesn't mesh well with the nature of talk radio:

> Some people's views don't fit neatly into traditional conservative or liberal labels. But that's not what's wanted in the media these days, especially in talk radio. They want you to be 100 percent confident that you have the truth and 100 percent predictable in your views.[95]

Carl Anderson, then market president at iHeartMedia, said in 2008 that radio stations are looking for entertaining hosts who have a strong point of view and the ability to "connect with an audience."[96] Overall, talk radio leans strongly conservative, with Sean Hannity and Rush Limbaugh being the two most important hosts, according to industry magazine *Talkers*.[97] If you look at the publication's list of the top ten hosts, six are clearly conservative, one covers financial issues, two lean progressive, and one is Howard Stern.[98]

Stern, the most controversial of the shock jocks, left terrestrial radio in 2006 for satellite broadcasting, where he had a multiyear contract worth $500 million. As mentioned earlier in

 The image shown has the credit text:

Icon Sportswire Via AP/AP Images

▲ English-speaking soccer fans have turned to Spanish broadcasts because of the energy in the commentary. Throughout his successful career, Enrique Bermúdez has coined a series of phrases that are well known by soccer fans including *como jefe* ("like a boss") and *tenla, te la presto* ("here, you can borrow it").

this chapter, while Stern can still be outrageous on SiriusXM satellite radio, he has focused more in recent years on high-quality in-depth interviews. In 2015, Stern signed a new five-year contract with SiriusXM reportedly worth $80 million a year for him and his staff.[99]

Spanish-Language Broadcasting. As the Hispanic population in the United States, especially in the Southwest and Florida, continues its rapid growth, Spanish-language stations have been an important part of the broadcasting market. Audience data are not available for Spanish-language news radio, but revenue has remained steady, according to a report from the Pew Research Center.[100] Spanish-language formats include multiple styles of music, news/talk/information, and religious programming.[101] The Los Angeles Dodgers baseball team has two sets of play-by-play announcers, one for English broadcasts, and the other for the team's Spanish-language network. And ESPN has a Spanish-language, all-sports radio network based out of Miami that focuses heavily on soccer games and news.[102]

While Spanish-language stations have traditionally maintained substantial listenership from the immigrant community, the fact that an increasing proportion of the American Hispanic population was born in the United States means that larger proportions of the population are either English speakers or bilingual.[103]

All-Sports Radio. All-sports is similar in popularity with all-talk, with 844 stations commanding 4.3 percent of the national audience.[104] The cable television network ESPN provides sports radio programming and simulcasts on the ESPNews cable/satellite television channel. (And, yes, this is exactly what you think it is—a couple of hosts and their guests sitting in a radio studio in front of microphones talking.)[105]

Although it is a narrow segment of the radio-listening public, the dedicated, loyal, and fanatic fans are very attractive to advertisers. "What separates sports radio from other radio is the passion of its listeners, and that makes it fertile hunting ground for us," says one major advertiser. "These are men who scream at their radios instead of punching the dial looking for the next cool song."[106]

Public Radio. With approximately eleven thousand commercial stations, radio is a big business in the United States. But for all the power and reach of the commercial radio business, public radio provides a significant alternative.

Public radio was authorized by the 1967 Public Broadcasting Act, which was designed primarily to create educational television. The act allocated stations at the lower end of the FM dial for noncommercial broadcasting, and most of the station licenses went to colleges and universities. In 1971, National Public Radio (NPR) went on the air with its first program, the evening newsmagazine *All Things Considered*.[107] One thing *All Things Considered* can do that other news shows cannot is present the news in depth. Eight-minute-long stories are not unusual, and twenty-minute stories are broadcast when the topic merits the length. This occurs in a medium in which thirty seconds is considered a long story.

The public radio network remained relatively small until two major developments occurred. The first was the growth of the satellite delivery of network programming. Satellite allows good signals to go out to all stations no matter how remote they are. The second development was the installation of FM radios in most private cars. Since public radio was almost exclusively on the FM band, the advent of FM car radios made it possible to reach interested people with enough time to pay attention.

Not surprisingly, NPR's biggest audiences are in cities whose workers have long commutes.[108] By 2018, there were 996 NPR member stations reaching a monthly audience of 37.7 million.[109] NPR launched the two-hour news program *Morning Edition* in 1979, and since then it has become the most-listened-to morning news show in the country, with 14.9 million listeners tuning in every week.[110] This is more than the *Today* show and *Good Morning America* audiences combined.[111] Of course, it isn't a completely fair comparison because *Morning Edition* is on radio and the other two shows are on television.

One of the major challenges facing public radio is funding. For fiscal year 2018, NPR had revenue of $221 million, and of that money, approximately 26 percent came from sponsorship, which allows corporations, organizations, and individuals to run short messages during programs. While most of these underwriting announcements promote the companies themselves as institutions, there are also announcements promoting books or television programs. The largest sources of revenue for NPR are programming fees paid by local member stations (38 percent of the budget) and the above-mentioned sponsorship fees (26 percent). While NPR gets relatively little money directly from the federal government, it does get government funds indirectly through the programming fees paid to its member stations, which do get federal funds.[112]

You may have noticed that in this section of the chapter I refer to "NPR" and not "National Public Radio." That is because in 2010 the network changed its name from National Public Radio to just NPR to reflect the fact that much of its programming is delivered over the web or via apps for mobile devices and tablets. So to understand the full reach of NPR, it should be noted that in addition to its 37.7 million radio listeners, it has 41 million average monthly unique visitors to its website, and 7.1 million weekly unique downloaders of NPR podcasts, the majority of which are being listened to using mobile devices.[113] It has also launched the NPR One app for phones—which simply goes to show Secret 6—Online media are mobile media.[114]

NPR's Giles Snyder working in a makeshift studio in his basement in May 2020. Many NPR newscasters, show hosts, reporters, and producers worked from home to bring the network's popular news programs to Americans during the coronavirus pandemic.

Courtesy of Giles Snyder

Concerns About Effects of Music on Young People

Some of the biggest controversies surrounding rock have involved not the music but the words—from 1950s lyrics dealing with "rocking and rolling" to references to drugs in the 1970s to derogatory comments about women in contemporary rap.

It is difficult to know what the influence of a song's words will be. Adults often read metaphorical meanings into a song while young people see only the literal meaning of the lyrics. Understanding music also goes beyond the content of the lyrics. Listeners pay as much attention to the melody, rhythm, and style of music as they do to the lyrics. Finally, songs are often as much about feelings as they are about rational thought. They set a mood rather than transmit a specific message.[115]

Since rock's inception, parents and other concerned adults have wondered about the effects of its lyrics on impressionable listeners. This questioning has led to product liability trials, congressional hearings, and movements to label and/or ban certain albums for objectionable content.

Controversy and Hip Hop. Few music formats have engendered as much controversy as rap and hip-hop. Rap can be partially understood as an outgrowth of several trends, dating back to the Beatles's *Sgt. Pepper* and Pink Floyd's *Dark Side of the Moon*. With the advent of multitrack recording, producers were adding layers of talk and ambient sound to the music created by band members. Rap simply extended this process, making the DJ part of the music and sampling from a range of already completed musical recordings. There was no longer a single "correct" mix of the various tracks; instead, the final version was constructed by whoever wanted to work with it.

Among the controversies surrounding rap is the complaint that it is misogynistic and violent. Rappers defend the violence in their recordings by noting that we live in a violent world; the violence in the recordings is simply "keeping it real." Michael Fuchs, a former executive of media giant Time Warner, says that he sees some of the criticism of rap as racist:

> It's a fact that white kids are buying black music and are being influenced by it, and that frightens their parents. It's not very different than the feeling my parents had thirty years ago when rock and roll came out—about the influence of black music.[116]

The Importance of Pop Music. Popular music today goes well beyond just the composition; it is an entire social statement. Besides the music, there are the photos on the cover of the album, the text within the electronic booklet that comes with the download, the music video, the gossip on *TMZ*, the posters, the mobile app, and the fashion. It is through popular music that young people often have their first contact with much of our culture. It provides young people not just with music, but with an entire identity.[117] Our identification with the music of our youth is something that sticks with us throughout adulthood. Alternative rocker Liz Phair points out,

> There's something that happens to people as they reach adulthood. They spend a lot of time trying to figure out what first hit them about rock 'n' roll. It's like the first time you took a drug. You want that first time back.[118]

Changing the Musical Experience: From Social Music to Personal Soundtracks

Being able to store and transmit musical performances was extremely important, but that may not have been the biggest change brought about by the invention of the phonograph and radio. Rock historian James Miller writes that the phonograph (and eventually radio) represented a vast expansion of people's access to music: "Symphonies that a person living in the nineteenth century would have been lucky to hear once were available for repeated listening on home phonographs."[119]

The Death of "Social Music." The phonograph and radio brought a wider range of music into the household, but this led to the loss of so-called **social music**, or music that people play and sing for one another in the home or in other social settings. As you have read, prior to the new technology, people had to play an instrument or sing to have music in the home. Sheet music was a common and popular feature in nineteenth century magazines like *Godey's Lady's Book*, along with recipes and sewing patterns. For most people, there was little social distance between the performer and the audience, and musical instruction played a greater role in the education of the upper and middle classes.

With advances in technology over the years, however, the social connections available through a shared musical experience changed profoundly. This could be viewed as an early example (and a sadly lost one) of Secret 5—All media are social.

Akio Morita's "Personal Soundtrack." Akio Morita is not a household name, but the Japanese engineer who invented the Sony Walkman has influenced how people listen to music as much as anyone since Thomas Edison and Emile Berliner.

When the Walkman was introduced in 1979, it was available in two versions—either as a tiny tape player or as a stereo FM radio. They were relatively expensive, with the tape player version costing upward of $200 (or a little over $700 in 2020 dollars), but they allowed each person to live in his or her own "personal musical cocoon."[120] Until 1979, the only way to take music away from home was with either a poor-quality pocket AM radio or a giant boom box. Writer RiShawn Biddle points out that the Walkman was more than just a way to protect your fellow bus passengers from your choice of music: "It's also been a coach, concert hall, and personal reader for millions of workout warriors, housewives, and retirees. For travelers, it is a trusty companion, something to ward off talkative salesmen and grandmothers loaded with wallet-size photos."[121]

Media scholar Michael Marsden notes that the Walkman gave people privacy in public areas: "It's your personal space that you've created, in a world in which we don't have a lot of personal space. It's a totally private world."[122] Not everyone was so enthralled with the effects of the Walkman, however. Critic John Zerzan argues that the Walkman is one of a number of technologies that lead to a "sort of withdrawal from social connections."[123] One thing the Walkman has clearly done, however, is contribute greatly to the trend of personalized media use characterized by downloads, podcasts, and streaming audio from our smartphones.

Music and the Long Tail: The Future of Sound

The entire audio industry is going through a massive change and the question is: what will emerge? Before the internet, people used to listen to radio predominantly in their cars and at home. Now, people are also listening in the office using web streams provided through a radio station's internet site, allowing people to listen to broadcasts from all over the world. Options for downloading audio podcasts or paid-subscription satellite services have also become extremely popular and have led to the technological changes happening in the audio industry. (See Figure 6.2.)

An example of this shift taking place happened when Project for Excellence in Journalism (now known as the Pew Research Center Journalism Project), which has been discussing the state of American media since 2005, replaced its chapter on "radio" with one on "audio" in 2009, noting "audio has done better as a medium of holding its audience than some other sectors."[124]

It would be a mistake, though, to just look at the Big Media alternatives such as HD radio and satellite radio that play the biggest stars in the music industry. Individual audience members as well can now become message providers by setting up their own webcasts or podcasts with nothing more than a computer, a microphone, and a connection to the internet.

With these technologies, even programming that extends deep into the long tail of media content can be distributed easily. These new technologies have also created a faction of musical artists, from big names to relative unknowns, finding success with alternative audio distribution formats.

There is a popular trope out there these days that with streaming music and file sharing, there is just no way for musicians to make a living as musicians. Game over. Done. Unless you are already big and famous. But do not tell that to Doug and Telisha Williams, a.k.a. the band Wild Ponies. In 2017, the Williamses released an album they recorded in a family member's shed in rural Virginia called *Galax*. The album featured several of their favorite musicians from Nashville along with several local players from Galax, Virginia.

▼ FIGURE 6.2

Digital Audio Audiences, 2020

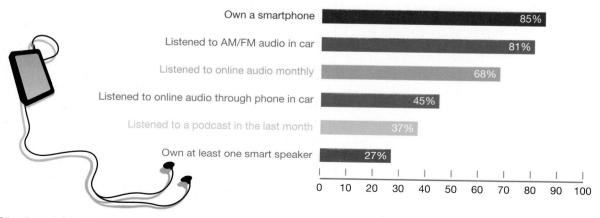

Source: Edison Research, "The Infinite Dial 2020," http://www.edisonresearch.com/wp-content/uploads/2020/03/The-Infinite-Dial-2020-from-Edison-Research-and-Triton-Digital.pdf.

After touring throughout the United States and Europe, they even completed a two-week tour of the Yukon. Yes, in northwestern Canada, where they traveled from the airport on a trailer attached to a snow machine (that's north country speak for a snowmobile).

Doug and Telisha met in high school, he was drum major and she was a majorette in the school's marching band. Later they played together in a rock 'n' roll cover band. "We eventually got married and tried day jobs, and that didn't work, so we went to being musicians," Doug said in an interview.[125] They have now been married more than twenty years. Playing roots and Americana music—sort of a mix of country, bluegrass, blues, folk, and rock—when they got started, everything was acoustic, but their latest album has shifted to all-electric and features Doug's guitar and Telisha on the upright bass.

"We've never been with a traditional record label," Doug said. "We've never courted any of the major labels. And while we've flirted with the small indie labels, we've now formed our own small label. When you have your own label, it means you spend more time on the business side than you want to. But it also gives you the responsibility. You have to do your own work with radio promoters and the promotion person.

"It also means you have to raise your own capital, which is tough. It means you have to have a closer relationship between you and your fans."

Doug says that principles for success he and Telisha count on come from the work of *Wired* magazine founder Kevin Kelly and his theory of the "1,000 True Fans." This is the idea that artists can be successful apart from a large company or media organization if they can find a thousand true fans. Kelly writes,

A True Fan is defined as someone who will purchase anything and everything you produce. They will drive 200 miles to see you sing. They will buy the super deluxe re-issued hi-res box set of your stuff even though they have the low-res-version. They have a Google Alert set for your name. They bookmark the eBay page where your out-of-print editions show up. They come to your openings. They have you sign their copies. They buy the t-shirt, and the mug, and the hat. They can't wait till you issue your next work. They are true fans.[126]

Doug says that artists who have a thousand or so true fans can have "a pretty good middle-class life. We don't survive without fan engagement. We don't play a show anywhere where we don't know someone in the audience on a first-name basis. Anywhere in the world. Amsterdam, London, southern Germany—little towns in southern Germany." (Full disclosure: Your author and his wife are true fans of Wild Ponies.)

Wild Ponies inhabit a part of the music business (media business, really) located somewhere between the megastars who bring in enormous numbers of fans and the garage bands who hope to get a hundred plays on YouTube. They inhabit a spot between the long tail and the short head on the media distribution curve. (We will talk about this at the end of the chapter.)

For their album *Galax*, the Ponies raised more than $24,000 from 344 backers through the crowdfunding website Kickstarter. To get funding through Kickstarter, musicians (like everyone else seeking Kickstarter funding) put together a video pitch along with written details about their qualifications and the album they intend to make. Potential contributors pledge to fund projects they find interesting on the site, but creators only get charged if the project reaches its originally set financial goal. If the project doesn't reach its funding goal, no money is exchanged.[127] Assuming the project does reach its goal and gets funded, the people who pledge do not get an investment in the album; instead, they get the satisfaction of supporting the project and very often some kind of reward, such as a copy of the album, a T-shirt, or even a weekend-long creativity workshop with the band. Contributions to fund the *Galax* album ranged from $1 to $1,000.[128]

The COVID-19 pandemic in the spring of 2020 presented a stark problem to touring musicians like Doug and Telisha with as much as 85 percent of their income coming from touring. But all touring came to a screeching halt when their venues were closed to protect both musicians and audiences from catching the deadly virus. "We immediately had to cancel 38 U.S. dates. . . . And we've lost an entire U.K. and European tour," Doug told the Associated Press. "For us, that's pretty much all of our income."[129] The only option for Wild Ponies during this difficult time has been to do live streaming concerts from their home. One they did in April 2020 drew about 300 people and raised $800 in donations, about what they might make on a single night of a tour.

▲ Musicians Doug and Telisha Willams, along with their dog Hazel Dickens, do a live streaming concert from their Nashville home while they were unable to tour during the cornoavirus pandemic. They tour as the band Wild Ponies.

New Economic Models for the Music Industry

There can be no question that the many sectors of the sound industry are currently facing a massively changing media world and not just because of the pandemic. The issues of file sharing, user-generated content, and music videos (topics also covered in Chapters 9 and 10) are forcing changes in how audio and the recording industries can make money.

The debate has now shifted from how to make people *pay for music* to how to make people *want to pay for music*. Young people are listening to music streaming over their computers or phones rather than buying discs or downloads. And yet, according to a 2019 Recording Industry Association of America (RIAA) report, revenue from recorded music has continued its recent increases.[130]

Streaming revenue grew 26 percent in first half of 2019 with the biggest source of revenue being paid subscriptions. It is clear people are moving away from buying music and moving into subscribing to it instead. According to the RIAA, paid subscriptions made up 62 percent of recorded music revenue and 77 percent of U.S. streaming revenue. Advertising revenue for streaming grew during the same time, but it only accounted for 10 percent of streaming revenue. And there is the big difference between streaming and broadcast radio, which gets almost all its revenue from advertising.

Music is moving from a purchase to a subscription model. Sales of digital downloads fell by 18 percent in the first half of 2019. Physical media sales went up slightly, with vinyl growing much faster than CD sales, and actually set to surpass CD sales soon. But be advised, this is more because CD sales are so low, not because vinyl sales are so high.[131] Vinyl LPs have staged a resurgence in recent years, as both artists and consumers have latched onto the twelve-inch discs containing analog music. Vinyl LPs made up 14 percent of all physical recording sales in 2017. But since then sales of CDs have been falling and sales of LPs have been growing. In fact, sometime in 2019 or 2020, sales of LPs were predicted to surpass sales of CDs.[132]

Why are LPs regaining their popularity? Part of it is their size. The discs come with big covers that have plenty of room for dramatic art and liner notes. Recording artists, from big names like Justin Timberlake and Pink to obscure indie acts, like the prestige and "specialness" that a vinyl release brings. And consumers often get a code for a free digital download with the premium-priced analog recording so they can still listen to the music on their computer or phone.[133] Doug Williams of Wild Ponies said in an interview, "Vinyl is great for us. We can't skip it. We have fans who specifically want it. It's good to us." He noted that there can be as much as a year-and-a-half wait for "normal" people to get their albums pressed at Nashville's biggest vinyl pressing factory.[134]

CHAPTER REVIEW

CHAPTER SUMMARY ▶▶

The ability to record sounds began in 1877 with Thomas Edison's invention of the phonograph. Though Edison's machine could record and play back sound, it was relatively fragile, and the foil-covered cylinders could not be reproduced and did not stand up to repeated playing. Emile Berliner's gramophone, however, played music on flat discs that were stronger than Edison's cylinders and could be mass produced. This technology allowed musical performances to be stored and replayed. As prerecorded music became widely available, the nature of music consumption changed. People's major contact with music became recordings by professional musicians rather than live performances by amateurs.

A wide range of recording formats has been used over the years, including the 78-rpm disc, the 45-rpm single, the LP, the CD, and the MP3 computer file. Each has given rise to concerns about changes in the purchasing and use of music.

Radio was an outgrowth of work done on the telegraph by Samuel Morse. Physicists such as Heinrich Hertz conducted early experiments on the detection of radio waves, but it was Guglielmo Marconi who developed the commercially viable wireless telegraph.

Radio was used initially as a tool for sending messages from one person to another. David Sarnoff was among the first to see radio's potential as a tool for mass communication; CBS founder William Paley saw its potential as an advertising medium that incidentally provided entertainment. KDKA, the first commercial radio station, went on the air in 1920, ushering in the golden age of radio, in which radio was the dominant medium for home entertainment. Radio was also a major source of news, offering an intimacy and immediacy that newspapers could not match.

As television displaced radio as the dominant broadcast medium, radio was transformed into a companion medium with a wide range of formats designed to appeal to narrow, specific audiences. These formats include many types of music, Spanish-language broadcasting, talk, news, and sports. FM has gradually replaced AM as the dominant radio band. Although FM has a shorter broadcast range, it has much higher-quality sound (higher fidelity). Radio has continued to evolve with new technologies, such as HD and satellite broadcasting.

In the 2000s, streaming and digital downloads of music and other audio programing became popular through services such as Pandora and Spotify. Downloadable audio programs known as podcasts are popular among listeners and are produced by both legacy media providers and long-tail artists.

Rock 'n' roll is a hybrid style of music that grew out of rhythm and blues and country music in the late 1940s and early 1950s. Because rock 'n' roll crossed racial lines between Blacks and whites, it became part of the integration of American society in the 1950s and 1960s. Rock 'n' roll became popular largely through recordings sold in record stores and played on the radio rather than through live performances. It evolved into an art form that existed primarily for recorded playback rather than live performance. Motown Records, out of Detroit, brought Black music and sensibilities to the public at large as well as being a major force in the civil rights movement.

In the 1960s and 1970s, rock music became more heavily produced, and there was a shift from hit singles to albums. Music by groups such as the Beatles and Pink Floyd brought the role of the producer to the forefront, a move that accelerated with the development of musical styles disco and rap. Hip-hop music and culture brought together playing music, talking over the songs, dancing, and a distinctive graffiti art style.

These varied musical styles have led to the creation of a wide range of radio formats featuring music, talk, news and sports. Although most radio stations are commercial, public radio—a staple of FM radio programming—provides an important alternative.

Parents and other adults have expressed concern about lyrics that include profanity, references to suicide and violence, and sentiments that are derogatory toward women. However, musical styles such as hip-hop, which paint a realistic portrait of the racial discrepancies in this country, has been considered controversial to some and to others it has highlighted our social inequalities.

As consumers have more choices with the digital expansion of audio programming, musicians can break away from traditional record labels and have more direct control over their professional lives. Musicians can make a living by interacting directly with their fans.

KEY TERMS ▶▶

long-playing record (LP)   132

compact disc (CD)   132

phonograph   132

gramophone   133

high fidelity (hi-fi)   133

non-notated music   133

telegraph   134

digital recording   134

analog recording   134

wireless telegraph   134

Radio Music Box memo   135

network   137

golden age of radio   138

soap operas   138

Federal Communications Commission (FCC)   139

terrestrial radio   139

HD radio   139

REVIEW QUESTIONS ▶▶

1. How has the musical *Hamilton* helped bring hip-hop music to a new audience?

2. Is radio still a distinct, separate medium, or is it just part of a larger world of audio programming? Why or why not?

3. What is the role of a producer in music like rock, R&B, and hip-hop? Why do producers seem to have such a big influence on the music industry?

4. Can musicians still make a living in the music industry today? Why or why not? How has this changed during the past twenty years?

5. How are musicians using long-tail tools to create new ways of sharing their music while still making money?

MOVIES

Mass Producing Entertainment

In March 2020, it was becoming clear to the movie industry that it was going to be a significant amount of time before audiences would be gathering in large numbers anywhere, let alone close-packed movie theaters. The final Daniel Craig James Bond movie *No Time to Die* was the first of the blockbusters to be delayed because of COVID-19, with MGM announcing the postponement on March 4, 2020. At the time, the biggest concern was about the closure of theaters in the international marketplace, given that the United States was still largely open. Among the other early movies announcing their delays were Disney's live-action version of its animated hit *Mulan*, Marvel's *Black Widow*, and DC's *Wonder Woman 1984*.[1]

Pixar's animated feature *Onward* was already in release when the novel coronavirus started driving down audience sizes and closing theaters. For *Onward*, Pixar's parent company Disney decided to offer it earlier than expected to the home market, and much earlier than expected to Disney's new streaming service Disney+. "While we're looking forward to audiences enjoying our films on the big screen again soon, given the circumstances, we are pleased to release this fun, adventurous film to digital platforms early for audiences to enjoy from the comfort of their homes," said director Dan Scanlon and producer Kori Rae in a statement.[2]

While Disney managed to maintain a good relationship with theaters throughout this difficult time and taking some of their films to early digital release, not all the studios managed to do things quite so smoothly. Rather than postponing its kids film *Trolls World Tour*, Universal decided to send the animated sequel straight to premium video on demand (PVOD). This was not a particularly surprising move for a kids film that was not going to be released on schedule.[3]

Universal already had a high-end marketing campaign going for *Trolls World Tour* at the time, so they went ahead with making the film available for rental at $19.99 through various digital platforms. In three weeks, *Trolls World Tour* brought in $100 million in rentals, more than the original *Trolls* made during its five-month theatrical release. Now, this was not a typical digital release. It had a massive marketing campaign behind it, it had a higher quality production than most straight-to-video animated films have, and there was a pent-up demand for something, anything, to entertain kids with while everyone is confined to home.

But nevertheless, it was a revelation to the studio that a high-end digital release could be as or more important than

a theatrical release, even after the pandemic is over. "The results for *Trolls World Tour* have exceeded our expectations and demonstrated the viability of PVOD," Jeff Shell, head of NBCUniversal, told the *Wall Street Journal*. "As soon as theaters reopen, we expect to release movies on both formats."[4]

That quote is what set off the AMC theater chain—America's largest. Under normal circumstances, a movie will play in theaters at least two months before going into some level of home release. But when Shell said that after the pandemic Universal expected to do some home releases simultaneously with theatrical releases, well, that was too much. In an open letter to the industry, AMC Chief Executive Adam Aron said his theaters would refuse to book any of the studio's movies under a policy of dual release.

While movie producers had streaming options to help rescue their businesses, times have been harder for the movie theaters themselves. Theaters have received some rescue funding from the federal government, and independent art house theaters have gotten some small grants from foundations. But for the most part, the COVID-19 shutdown meant a complete stop of revenue. Even when the theaters do reopen (something that has yet to happen as this was being written) the plan was that they would have to bring in much smaller crowds to allow for social distancing. John Fithian, of the National Association of Theatre Owners, said the speed at which they can reopen depends on how successful the country and world are at "tamping down the virus."[5]

If theaters are only able to open in a limited number of areas, studios will be reluctant to release their big "tentpole" movies and may stick with re-releasing older titles.

The shutdown has also hit independent community theaters quite hard, like Kearney, Nebraska's, The World Theatre. Bryce Jensen, the theater's executive director and only full-time paid employee, said, "It's hit us pretty hard because we were just finishing up a fund-raising campaign to help renovate the theater, But all of our fundraising has been done over the last year to get this renovation done."[6]

The World has gotten some of the COVID-19 government relief funds, and it also got a small grant from the Criterion Collection's foundation. "We're a non-profit," Jensen said. "All the folks there are volunteers. We explore motion pictures and get people talking about them. We show one movie per weekend at the same prices since we opened. We'd love to always keep it at $5."[7]

For the summer of 2020, The World drew socially distant crowds to a pop-up drive-in theater at the local county fairgrounds, using stacked-up shipping containers to hold the screen. This was something the theater had been contemplating experimenting with even before the pandemic hit.

One big reason people want to get back to the movies is to escape from the world around us. We spend a couple of hours in a darkened room with a group of people and share a created experience—a bit of excitement, sentiment, or romance. In this chapter, we look at how the movie industry developed from peep show kinetoscopes to today's IMAX theaters. We examine the roles of movies in society, public concerns about movies, and efforts by government and industry to regulate the content of films.

Stay up to date on the latest in media by visiting the author's blog at **ralphehanson.com**

The Development of Movies

The movie industry has its roots in the 1880s, but it was not until the early twentieth century that movies became a major source of public entertainment. In the late 1920s and early 1930s, movies gradually grew from ten-minute silent films into talking films up to two hours long. Although movie attendance peaked in the 1940s, viewing movies in theaters remains popular today, despite competition from television and home video.

Thomas Edison is generally credited with developing the American motion picture industry, but like other media, movies came into being because of the work of many people; Edison was just one of several scientists and engineers who created the new medium of film.

In the 1870s and 1880s, at least two people were working on the problem of capturing and portraying motion. The first was Étienne-Jules Marey. Trained in medicine, Marey sought to measure and transcribe motion, starting with blood and the heart and then progressing on to how animals move. While Marey was never able to project moving pictures, he did help develop systems for taking repeated photos of people and animals in motion.[8]

British photographer Eadweard Muybridge was the second major influence on Edison. Muybridge, like Marey, wanted to capture the motion of animals on film. To settle a bet, the governor of California hired him to establish whether all four hooves of a horse leave the ground when it is galloping.[9] Muybridge set up twenty-four cameras at evenly spaced locations around a racetrack. Tripwires allowed the passing horse to trigger the cameras. Muybridge then projected the images using a type of zoetrope, a child's toy that put a series of images on a spinning cylinder. He was thus able to establish that all four hooves do leave the ground during a gallop.

Muybridge eventually photographed both animals and humans moving against a black-and-white grid; his photos were published in 1887 in a book titled *Animal Locomotion*. He became a celebrity, touring the country to lecture and display his photographs.

At about the same time, Edison assigned an employee to work on the motion picture project. The first movies were not projected on a screen; instead, they were viewed by an individual viewer on a peep show–like device that Edison called the **kinetoscope**. The moving picture was first demonstrated to the public on May 9, 1893, at the Brooklyn Institute of Arts and Sciences in the form of a thirty-second film called *Blacksmith Scene*. Other early films showed a man sneezing, "Sandow the Strong Man" displaying his muscles, and Annie Oakley riding her horse.

The kinetoscope was soon replaced by a system in which films were projected on a screen, and the viewing of movies was transformed from a solitary activity to a group experience. The first American theaters grew out of the penny arcades where kinetoscopes had been located. These early theaters came to be known as "nickelodeons"

The photos of a woman in motion in this collection are typical of the images Eadweard Muybridge created for his book *Animal Locomotion*. With these repeated photographs, Muybridge demonstrated that you could create an illusion of motion by displaying a series of still images.

because tickets cost five cents. By 1900, the nickelodeon theaters were a popular form of entertainment throughout American cities. (Another example of Secret 3—Everything from the margin moves to the center.)

The Earliest Filmmakers

In France, brothers Auguste-Marie and Louis-Jean Lumière started working with Edison's motion picture ideas in 1894. They created what they called a cinématographe, a portable movie camera that could also be used as a projector. The brothers also set the standards for the speed at which film would be shot and for the format of the film, details that Edison would eventually adopt. On December 28, 1895, they opened their first theater, where they showed short movies portraying everyday life in families, at factories, and on the street.

One of the earliest films to tell a story, rather than record everyday life, was created by another Frenchman, Georges Méliès. His most famous film was 1902's *A Trip to the Moon*, which featured special effects, such as a spaceship hitting the man in the moon in the eye. But although it told a story, it was essentially a stage show captured on film.[10]

Edwin S. Porter Telling a Story With Film. Edwin S. Porter expanded on Méliès's ideas to create one of the first hit movies in the United States. While working as a projectionist for Edison, Porter saw Méliès's *Trip to the Moon* many times. He soon started making movies for Edison, most notably the 1903 film *The Great Train Robbery*. Porter laid out almost every element of the action in the film, which tells the story of a group of outlaws who get on a train, rob the strongbox and the passengers, kill everyone who gets in their way, and are eventually shot and killed by the posse hunting them down. The movie, containing twelve separate scenes shot in a variety of locations, tells a realistic story. *The Great Train Robbery* helped establish how stories could be told through film.[11]

D. W. Griffith: The Birth of the Blockbuster. Director D. W. Griffith was the George Lucas or Steven Spielberg of the silent movie era, creating epic films that captured the entire nation's imagination. At a time when most directors were making movies that ran for twenty-five minutes at most, Griffith produced films that ran for an hour or more. Griffith created the first modern **feature-length film**. Griffith's most significant film—*The Birth of a Nation*, released in 1915—tells the story of the rise of the Ku Klux Klan in the years following the Civil War. The film runs for over three hours and, at a cost of more than $110,000, was the most expensive movie to date. It also cost audiences more to see it; tickets were $2 in the big cities at a time when admission to most pictures was less than $1.

Based on Thomas Dixon's book *The Clansman*, Griffith's film is blatantly racist. At the time of its release, the film was criticized for a range of reasons, including its portrayal of African Americans as "nothing but beasts" and its attack on the North. One critic, referring to the three

Library of Congress

▲ Young people in the 1940s dressed a little more formally when they went to the movies than do today's movie audiences, but these Chicago moviegoers were still looking to have fun away from parental supervision for an afternoon or evening.

miles of film used in making the movie, called it "three miles of filth."[12] Griffith soon outdid himself with another movie, *Intolerance*, which ran even longer than *The Birth of a Nation*. It cost nearly $500,000 to make and tells four separate stories spread out over a period of 2,500 years. It is a bold, dramatic film, but it was a financial failure, costing Griffith the fortune he had made with *The Birth of a Nation*.

Intolerance marked the point at which outside financial backing became necessary for a movie to get produced. Today the only exceptions to this are low-budget movies, such as *The Blair Witch Project*, and movies made by very wealthy directors, such as George Lucas. (Lucas financed the *Star Wars* prequel series, Episodes I, II, and III, in part with profits from *Star Wars* merchandise and his special-effects house, Industrial Light & Magic. He eventually sold his company Lucasfilm to Disney in 2012.)

Outside financing means that directors are accountable to the people who control the purse strings. Few directors today have the right to a "final cut," or final version, of the movie. That right is generally reserved by the people who control the money.[13]

Movie Stars. In the early days of the movie industry, studios were reluctant to give actors screen credit for fear that this would encourage them to ask for more money. But the studios soon discovered that the public liked some actors and actresses better than others and were more likely to go to a movie featuring one of their favorites.

Directors such as Griffith employed a group of regular players in all their films. Florence Lawrence was one of the first to break out of this anonymous group; Griffith's studio, Biograph, paid her a stunning (for the time) $25 a week. Linda Griffith, D. W.'s wife, wrote in a memoir, "[Florence's] pictures became tremendously popular, and soon all over the country Miss Lawrence was known as 'The Biograph Girl.'"[14] After Lawrence left Biograph for a rival studio, Independent Moving Pictures, she became one of the first actresses to receive a screen credit.[15]

The Studio System

Why are so many movies made in Hollywood? Although the earliest movies were filmed in New Jersey and New York, the appeal of southern California soon became apparent. One argument for going west was to get away from Edison's "patent police," who tried to control the use of movie technology. But California also offered almost constant sunlight, as well as the varied settings of ocean, desert, and mountains. In addition, the new movie studios needed a great deal of space, and at the beginning of the twentieth century, land in California was still relatively cheap.

At about the same time, the movie studios figured out that the most effective way to produce movies was with a factory-like process known as the **studio system**, in which all of the talent worked directly for the movie studios. Paramount Pictures, MGM, Warner Bros., and other major studios controlled every aspect of the production process, from writing to editing. They employed a few writers, directors, and actors ("stars") who were under contract to work for a weekly salary.

The movies were put together in assembly-line fashion. The studios also had almost absolute control of the distribution system.

Distribution was carried out in two ways. The first way was **block bookings**, in which theater owners were required to book a whole series of movies to get a few desirable films. The studio package might offer four headliner movies with big-name stars, ten mid-range pictures, ten more low-level films, and twelve no-star, bottom-of-the-line pictures. Sometimes salespeople insisted that theaters take the studio's entire package of fifty-two films, one for each week of the year. The second, and even more effective, way for studios to guarantee that their movies would be shown was to buy up theaters.[16]

Actors and directors soon rebelled against the controls placed on them by the studio system. Despite being pampered and well paid, they had to make the movies the studios told them to make. By 1919, several of the most popular performers and directors, including Griffith, Charlie Chaplin, Mary Pickford, and Douglas Fairbanks, joined forces to create their own company, United Artists.

Instead of producing movies as the other major studios did, United Artists acquired and distributed movies after independent film producers had completed them. United Artists was essentially a model for the modern film studio—not a maker of films but a distributor and a source of financing.

United Artists remained a significant independent force in the movies until 1981, when one of its movies, Michael Cimino's *Heaven's Gate*, managed to lose almost its entire cost of production—$44 million—forcing the nearly bankrupt studio to merge with MGM. (*Heaven's Gate* is a dusty, confusing, and depressing western that was relatively expensive for the time it came out.)[17]

Library of Congress

▲ Silent movie stars "sweet" Mary Pickford and "swashbuckling" Douglas Fairbanks were one of the first Hollywood power couples and were two of the founders of the United Artists movie studio.

Talking Pictures

In terms of technological developments in the movies, color and black-and-white movies coexisted for many years, but movies with sound replaced silent films almost immediately. Once people had both seen and heard their favorite stars, there was no turning back.[18]

Although many people point to *The Jazz Singer*, released in 1927, as the first talking film, it was actually a silent film with two talking (and singing) segments. The first successful demonstration of the talking picture was a series of short films that accompanied the feature *Don Juan* in 1926. *Don Juan* was a silent film, but it had a **synchronized soundtrack** (wherein sounds are synchronized with the pictures in a movie) with musical accompaniment, and the accompanying films demonstrated the equipment that would make talking films possible. This set of short films included performances by opera singers and a talk by Will H. Hays, president of the Motion Picture Producers and Distributors of America.

The Jazz Singer was called a **talkie**—a movie with synchronized sound—but it was the singing as much as the talking that impressed most people. In the movie, Al Jolson, talking to his mother, delivered one of the cinema's most prophetic lines, "Come on, Ma. Listen to this."[19] The public loved it. It was talking (and singing) pictures such as *The Jazz Singer* that helped build Warner Bros. into one of the nation's premier movie studios. Until then, Warner Bros. had been a relatively small player. The studio's breakthrough came with the realization that talkies were about more than talk. As Harry Warner put it, "If it can talk, it can sing."[20] The movie industry was leery of talking pictures for a couple of reasons. On the simplest level, talking pictures in the early days required stars to speak well while acting, something that was not necessarily easy to do. (In the contemporary movie industry, much of the dialogue is rerecorded after the photography is finished.) A bigger problem was that talking pictures were expensive. Not only did theaters have to upgrade their equipment, but the noisy movie projectors had to be muffled in soundproof booths. Sound issues existed during the filming process as well, as noisy equipment that allowed cameras to swoop around the actors could not be used. This problem restricted the camera's mobility in the early talkies and kept them from being as visually interesting as the best of the silent films, such as *Metropolis* or *Nosferatu*. There was also the problem of noise in the vicinity of the studios (such as the roar of passing trains). Even the bright arc lights used to light the sets made a sizzling sound that had to be eliminated. As one industry observer noted, "It was easy to make pictures, easy to make records; but another matter to make them together."[21]

The influence of talking films soon gave rise to concerns like those familiar to us today. One newspaper columnist complained,

> The talkies will make Hollywood the slang center of the United States. . . . A wisecrack recorded in Hollywood will be heard in all corners of the country months before the same quip could travel from town to town across the continent with a road show or a vaudeville troupe.[22]

It took awhile for the talking movies to find their way. As one critic pointed out in *Harper's* in 1929, the talkies were neither plays nor silent movies. They were something new, and Hollywood had to determine what that was. Writers, directors, and actors had to figure out what could be done with the new medium. Animation pioneer Walt Disney, for example, saw sound more as a way to add music and sound effects to his cartoons than as a way to make them talk.[23] In recent years, the quality of sound has become increasingly important, both in theaters and at home. Lucas's *Star Wars*, released in 1977, broke new ground not only with its visual effects, but also with its sound effects. It was among the first movies to fully exploit the Dolby sound system, and the Lucas-developed THX theater sound system has become a standard for high-quality movie sound.

The End of the Studio System. By 1938, the U.S. Department of Justice was starting to view the movie studio system as a monopoly that needed to be brought under control. It decided to make a test case of Paramount Pictures. Paramount and the other major studios were charged with conspiring to set the terms for theaters renting their films—requiring them to charge certain minimum prices and to accept block booking—and discriminating in favor of certain theaters. The studios also worked to keep independent films out of theaters they owned.

An early portion of the settlement of what became known as the "Hollywood Antitrust Case"[24] required studios to show theater owners films before booking them, limit block bookings to five movies at a time, and no longer force theaters to book short films. But the power of the studios was not truly dismantled until 1948 when the U.S. Supreme Court ruled that the studios must sell their theaters. This final portion of the case's settlement led to the system in use today, in which the studios primarily finance and distribute films produced by independent companies rather than make movies themselves with their own staff.[25]

The Blacklist

The years following World War II were a dark time for the movie industry. The studios' power was diminished by the Supreme Court's rulings in the antitrust case, and some politicians had an overwhelming fear that Hollywood and its movies might be playing a role in spreading communism. In 1947, a congressional committee known as the **House Un-American Activities Committee**, under the leadership of J. Parnell Thomas, held hearings on possible communist influences in Hollywood.

In his introductory remarks, Thomas laid out the fears quite clearly:

> We all recognize, certainly, the tremendous effect which moving pictures have on their mass audiences, far removed from the Hollywood sets. We all recognize that what the citizen sees and hears in his neighborhood movie house carries a powerful impact on his thoughts and behavior.
>
> With such vast influence over the lives of American citizens as the motion-picture industry exerts, it is not unnatural—in fact, it is very logical—that subversive and undemocratic forces should attempt to use this medium for un-American purposes.[26]

▲ The congressional hearings on communists in Hollywood extended over a several-year period. This photo shows actor Lionel Stander testifying before the House Un-American Activities Committee in 1953.

It is this legacy of fear—fear that the movies and other media could have undesirable effects on unsuspecting audience members—that led to the research and controls on the movie industry. (This topic is discussed in depth later in this chapter.)

Two weeks of committee hearings were held, the most divisive of which involved ten "unfriendly witnesses" who questioned the right of the committee to ask them about their associations and beliefs. The committee repeatedly asked the question, "Are you now, or have you ever been, a communist?" Instead of answering, the witnesses, known as the **Hollywood Ten**, challenged the constitutionality of the hearings. They were jailed for contempt of Congress, and the movie industry instituted a **blacklist** that banned anyone from working in Hollywood who was a known communist, a suspected communist, or a communist sympathizer.[27] In December 1949, Thomas was convicted of padding his payroll and went to jail himself. But hearings continued under new leadership in the early 1950s, and by 1953, the blacklist contained the names of as many as 324 suspected communists. The contracts of those who were blacklisted could be canceled; if they were freelancers, the studios simply wouldn't buy their work.[28] The hearings tore Hollywood apart. Some of the unfriendly witnesses had to move. The uncooperative witnesses lost their jobs and were ostracized, and those who had provided names were viewed as informers.

While the blacklist was in place, several writers continued to sell screenplays under assumed names or wrote screenplays without receiving any credit at all. In 1956, Dalton Trumbo, writing under the name Robert Rich, won an unclaimed Academy Award for his screenplay *The Brave One*. In 1957, David Lean's epic movie *The Bridge on the River Kwai* won an Oscar for best screenplay. The script, written by Carl Foreman and Michael Wilson, was based on a novel by the French author Pierre Boulle. But since the scriptwriters were blacklisted, the credit went to Boulle, who could not write or speak English.[29] (And in case you were wondering, Boulle also wrote the novel that inspired the *Planet of the Apes* movie series.) The blacklist was finally broken in 1960, when Trumbo received screenwriting credits for the films *Spartacus* and *Exodus*.

Television and the Movies

In the 1950s, people began turning to television rather than movies for routine entertainment. The exodus of families to the suburbs also contributed to a decline in movie audiences, especially in the old urban Art Deco movie palaces. Sports, both professional and collegiate, started drawing audiences away from the movies as well.[30] In 1946, movie audiences reached their peak, and eighty million tickets were sold every week. But by 1953, ticket sales had dropped by almost half, to forty-six million a week. It was clear that Hollywood would have to do something to reverse this trend.

One thing Hollywood did to entice viewers away from television was to make the movies shown in theaters bigger and better than before. Hollywood tried 3-D movies, but they required special projection equipment and 3-D glasses. The gimmick started out successfully, but people soon became bored with the novelty, which ultimately added little to the movie experience. Almost the only serious movie to be released in the 3-D format in its first incarnation was Alfred Hitchcock's *Dial M for Murder*. The 3-D format experienced a revival in the 2000s, especially with movies targeted at children, such as Pixar's *Up* and Brendan Fraser's *Journey to the Center of the Earth*.[31] But now many big-budget action movies get a 3-D release as well, whether they were designed for 3-D or not, with a goal of drawing in the higher ticket prices that 3-D movies command. And, of course, there are the rare films envisioned as 3-D movies from the start, such as James Cameron's *Avatar*, Ridley Scott's *Prometheus*, Alfonso Cuarón's *Gravity*, and Steven Spielberg's *Ready Player One*.

After the first effort to popularize 3-D films fizzled out, more successful were attempts to project a larger picture on the screen. The most extreme of these was the Cinerama process, in which each scene was filmed from three slightly different angles and projected on a huge curved screen using three projectors. The purpose was to create the feeling of realism using peripheral vision. The Cinerama theaters could also handle smaller wide-screen systems such as CinemaScope.

Along with the larger screens came larger movies, including epics such as *The Ten Commandments* and the gladiator movie *Spartacus*. Today, widescreen HDTV is passé with 55- to 70-inch Ultra HD 4K screens being the go-to standard with streaming in 4K resolution from the major sources as well as 4K Blu-ray discs. What is Ultra HD or 4K? It's a television set that displays 3,840 pixels by 2,160, as opposed to the HD standard of 1,920 by 1,080. In a more meaningful comparison, 4K televisions have four times the resolution of a standard HD TV.[32]

Warner Bros./Photofest

The Advent of Color.

Television also helped bring about the conversion to color movies. During the 1950s, television was almost exclusively black-and-white. Color was first used in Hollywood in the 1920s at about the same time that sound came in, but it was expensive, the studios were focusing on the conversion to sound, and black-and-white film was easier to work with. Still, there are some important color movies from this era. Both *Gone With the Wind* and *The Wizard of Oz* made effective use of color: Think of the vivid images of Dorothy's ruby red slippers—silver in the original L. Frank Baum books—and Scarlett O'Hara's green velvet dress made from the parlor drapes.

▲ Steven Spielberg's *Ready Player One* was a 3-D IMAX celebration of all that could be done technically with an immersive summer action film. Though it does not quite have the same level of virtual reality its protagonists (Parzival/Wade, left, and Art3mis/Samantha, right) experience in the movie, it did provide a step in that direction for viewers.

One factor that delayed the conversion to color movies was that they initially required a complex camera that shot simultaneously on three separate reels of film (one for each of the three additive colors—cyan, magenta, and yellow). After World War II, American studios adopted a process used in Germany to shoot in color using a single reel of film, which made color filming much easier. Competition from television forced Hollywood to start using color in virtually every film from the 1950s on.[33] Occasionally, prestige movies are released in black-and-white for effect—think of 2011's multiple-Oscar-winning *The Artist* (which was also largely a silent film with a musical soundtrack); the 2005 Oscar-nominated *Good Night, and Good Luck*; or *Schindler's List*, which won the Oscar for Best Picture in 1993. Mexican director Cuarón was nominated for the Oscar for Best Picture for his black-and-white Spanish language film *Roma*, which went on to win Best Foreign Language Film. *Roma* was also the first movie to be primarily distributed by a streaming company to be nominated for Best Picture. (We will talk more about that in a bit.) More recently, there have been movies reissued in black-and-white at the time they are being released for home video. *Mad Max: Fury Road* got what director George Miller called a "Black & Chrome" edition. Miller says he had wanted to film the postapocalyptic story in black-and-white to begin with, but the studio was never going to agree with that. But with movies always having their color digitally manipulated, it was not difficult to create a black-and-white version for the home video version and for a short theatrical release. (The fact that most movies are delivered to theaters digitally means there isn't a high cost of making film prints to stand in the way.[34]) *Logan*, featuring the final appearance of Hugh Jackman as Wolverine in the *X-Men* franchise, also got a black-and-white version for home video, along with a single-night theatrical run, under the title *Logan: Noir*.[35]

ASSOCIATED PRESS

▲ Projectionist Joe Columbo works at splicing together an IMAX print of Christopher Nolan's Batman film *The Dark Knight Rises* for showing at the Liberty Science Center in Jersey City, New Jersey. Nolan was among the first directors to shoot substantial portions of his commercial films on large-format IMAX film.

The Growth of Multiplex Theaters. In recent decades, movie theaters themselves have been changing to meet the needs of a changing audience. As large numbers of people moved from cities to suburbs, the vast Art Deco movie palaces that seated as many as two thousand people were no longer being filled. Gradually, these megatheaters have been replaced by smaller theaters grouped together in what is known as a **multiplex**. These have a single box office and concession stand, but contain anywhere from three to twenty screens. Each of the auditoriums is relatively small, but when a major movie is released, it can be shown in several of the theaters.[36] The number of theater screens declined in 2001 to approximately thirty-five thousand but has grown in recent years to over forty thousand. Many of these new theaters feature stadium seating, improved sound systems, and premium refreshments, such as real butter on the gourmet popcorn.[37]

Ricardo DeAratanha/Getty Images

The Blockbuster Movie Era

If the early 1900s were the silent-film era and the 1930s and 1940s were the studio era, then the period from the late 1970s to the present day is the **blockbuster era**, in which studios try to make relatively expensive movies with a large, predefined audience. These movies are packaged with cable deals and marketing tie-ins, such as McDonald's Happy Meal toys.

Spielberg is generally credited with creating the blockbuster era with the release of his 1975 summer hit *Jaws*. It was the first movie to gross more than $200 million, and it set the stage for

▲ Theaters have started attracting audiences by offering a wide variety of food and drink options while promoting high-end experiences. Here, a bartender serves beer to two customers seated on plush leather recliners.

▲ The overwhelming success of the Marvel Universe feature films, with complex, interwoven, character-driven plots as well as all the usual merchandising extensions, may mark a shift from the blockbuster era to that of the franchise. *Avengers: Endgame* was the 23rd film in the series over a thirteen-year period.

the big summer movies. Prior to *Jaws*, it was believed that a movie had to be released during the Christmas season to be a major success. *Jaws* had a number of things going for it: It was directed by one of the most popular directors of the late twentieth century, it featured a compelling musical score by John Williams, and it was based on a best-selling novel by Peter Benchley.

Jaws was accompanied by a giant television advertising campaign that began three days before the movie's release. But the marketing of the movie had started two years earlier with an announcement that the movie rights had been acquired and speculation about the stars. Journalists were taken to the production site in record numbers to keep the stories flowing. The movie's release was scheduled to occur within six months of the publication of the paperback book, and the book's cover included a tie-in to the movie. As the release date for the movie approached, copies of the paperback were sent out to waiters, cab drivers, and other ordinary people to build word of mouth. Finally, the movie was given a summer release date to capitalize on the beach and swimming season.

The *Jaws* campaign was designed to get people to the movie and talk about it. If the talk had been negative, all the advertising in the world could not have saved the movie. But with everyone talking up the movie, *Jaws* took off.[38] The success of *Jaws* started a tradition of larger-than-life summer movies that continued with the *Star Wars* trilogies, the *Indiana Jones* series, Christopher Nolan's *Dark Knight* trilogy, and the *Pirates of the Caribbean* series.[39] There is an argument to be made that we have moved out of the blockbuster era and into the franchise era. That is, it's not enough for an individual movie to stand out in its own right—it needs to be part of a complex, consistent universe containing multiple movies, such as the eleven (so far) *Star Wars* movies, the twenty-three Marvel Cinematic Universe movies (with at least six more in production), and the eight DC Extended Universe films (with at least seven more in development). These movies come with a built-in market of fans waiting to see them. Paul Bettany, the British actor who plays Vision in the *Avengers* movies, says the series is so successful because the films are made by and for fans. "[The people at Marvel] really love those characters," he said. "Their love for these stories is really infectious and you become really invested, and there's a lot of invested people beyond the financials of it all. . . . This movie is made by geeks. They love them, they feel it when they're talking about it."[40]

Star Wars Episode VII: The Force Awakens is currently the most commercially successful movie in U.S. history (see Table 7.1) with a domestic box office of $936 million, but it didn't have the biggest audience.[41] That honor belongs to the Civil War epic *Gone With the Wind*, which sold more than one hundred million tickets in 1939 and countless more for multiple rere-leases over a decades-long period (see Table 7.2).[42] One reason the 2015 *The Force Awakens* is at the top of the box office charts is that tickets to see it cost much more than the Depression-era tickets for *Gone with the Wind*. Adjusted for inflation, *Gone With the Wind* ticket prices would have brought in a total of $1.89 billion, considerably more than the domestic box office receipts of *The Force Awakens*. (*Avengers: Endgame* has the largest worldwide lifetime gross as of this writing, with a total of $2.80 billion.)

Movie Viewership in the Digital Era

Prior to COVID-19, the movie industry had been doing well, especially with blockbusters. For 2018, movie box office revenues were up 8 percent over the year before. But not all is well. More than a third of that revenue came from ten movies (virtually all either superhero or animated) out the seven hundred that were released during the year.[43] Even with all the alternative ways of viewing entertainment, going to the movies is something special. People go for a variety of reasons—to learn things, to escape from everyday life, to enjoy a pleasant activity, to pass the time, to avoid feeling lonely, to fit in with others, or to learn about themselves.[44] Young people who are dating may go to the movies for no other reason than to be alone in the dark away from parental supervision.

But there are other things that make going to the movies unique. Movies are typically "edgier" than what is shown on television, although cable and home video have changed this substantially. There is also the larger-than-life aspect of movies such as the Marvel, DC Expanded Universe, and *Star Wars* series, which bring people into theaters for an overwhelming visual and sonic experience.

Large Format Films. While the giant-screen Cinerama and 70mm systems have largely died out, large-format IMAX theaters that were traditionally used for science and nature films at museums are now showing popular releases on their screens that can be several stories tall. Numerous movies are being filmed now with segments or even the entire film being shot natively in IMAX format. Action and science fiction movies can bring in more than $100 million globally from IMAX showings, in part because IMAX theaters can charge $15 a person (or more!) for tickets.[45] (Your author has a history of driving up to 180 miles each way to see movies at large-format theaters.)

Movies can also be a group experience. People watching the *Annabelle* horror movies at home may not have the overwhelming sense of dread that comes from being in a theater full of terrified people.

According to movie scholar Garth Jowett,

Teenagers and young adults will probably always want to escape the confines of the home, and others will more than likely continue to be motivated to seek out an experience which allows intense individual involvement with little risk within an appealing social context.[46]

IMAX CEO Richard Gelfond, speaking with Deadline, said he and his business partner have worked hard since 1994 to grow IMAX from being a source of nature and science documentaries into a spectacular format for blockbuster "fanboy" movies. They have been so successful with their large-format cameras and theaters that top directors like Nolan (*Dunkirk*, the *Dark Knight* trilogy), the Russo brothers (*Captain America: Civil War*, *Avengers: Infinity War* and *Endgame*), and J. J. Abrams (*Star Wars Episode VII: The Force Awakens*) shoot substantial portions of their films in the IMAX format.

When directors shoot their film in IMAX, they get exclusive access to premium theaters. "So one of IMAX's powers is because we can help deliver a large number of screens for a particular filmmaker, that encourages the filmmaker to make the film with special DNA—IMAX DNA. So whether it's Christopher Nolan using the camera or Sam Mendes shooting to our aspect ratio, the fact that they know they're going to get close to 1,000 theaters in the world enables them to do special things," said Gelfond.[47]

Nolan shot his World War II story *Dunkirk* almost entirely in the IMAX format. (The only parts not shot in IMAX were some boat interiors where the large IMAX cameras wouldn't fit.) *Avengers: Endgame* was also shot entirely in IMAX format.[48]

Gelfond told *USA Today* that the blockbuster movies will tend to draw audiences in to see movies in theaters, while smaller movies will appeal to people viewing at home or on the go: "When you have blockbuster movies, people are still going to want to go to a theatre and see them. When you have more independent movies, or more movies that rely [more] on plot than on special effects, I think people will see them on devices."[49]

Home Video. VCRs started becoming an important source of movies in the 1980s, and by 1994, more than 85 percent of all U.S. homes had one. However, by about 2005, DVDs and high-definition Blu-ray discs had largely displaced the VCR. In 2006, nearly 81 percent of all households had a DVD player, whereas 79 percent had VCRs. This was a big change from 1999, when 89 percent of households had VCRs, and fewer than 7 percent had DVD players.[50] DVDs provide a higher-quality image and dramatically better sound than videocassettes, and they have popularized the letterbox (or wide-screen) format. Pixar's *Incredibles* brought in $261 million in theaters, making it one of the most successful films of 2004. When it was released on DVD, it made an additional $368 million.[51] At their peak in 2005, DVDs made up 65 percent of the sales of home video, but by 2019, that had fallen to just 10 percent of the market.[52]

Previously, movie lovers could see a film only when it first came out or was rereleased, when it was shown in 16mm format on a college campus or in a revival house, or when it finally appeared on late-night television. With the wide range of home video options now available, people can watch movies repeatedly, whenever they want.

Digital Production and Projection

The revolution that started with desktop publishing—which enabled people to produce books, newspapers, and magazines on their computers and laser printers—has begun transforming the production of movies.

Computers first came to Hollywood in a big way with *Star Wars* (*Episode IV: A New Hope* for those of you geeky enough to care). Director Lucas used a computer-controlled camera to shoot the space battle scenes. He was able to create multiple layers of images more easily because he could make the camera move exactly the same way on each shot. Lucas's *Star Wars Episode II: Attack of the Clones* was the first big-budget feature to be shot entirely using high-definition video.

Computer Generated Images. *Sky Captain and the World of Tomorrow*, released in 2004, was the first mainstream American movie in which all the backgrounds and sets were computer animated in an otherwise live-action movie.[53] Director Kerry Conran wrote his own software to create backgrounds using **computer-generated imagery (CGI)** that would meld with the live-action footage of the actors shot before a blue screen, in much the same way that computer special effects are added into movies. In this case, though, without the computer-generated backdrops, there would be nothing other than the actors. There were no "sets" to speak of. The only "real" things in the film were the actors, their costumes, and the props they were holding.

While the technology might have allowed Conran to make a movie he could not have otherwise, the film did not come cheap, costing a reported $70 million. But Conran saw that $70 million price tag as a bargain compared to the much more expensive action thrillers.

At the time the film came out, no one had seen anything quite like it, and veteran movie producer Jon Avnet proclaimed the process "a version of the virtual studio" and "unquestionably the wave of the future."[54] Unfortunately for the film's creators, audiences neither in the United States nor anywhere else in the world were particularly interested in the film. With a domestic gross of only about $38 million and a worldwide gross of $58 million, the film did not make back its production costs through ticket sales.[55]

The surprise hit *300*, based on a graphic novel, would likely never have been made if not for the budget economies of digital production. The movie, which features an over-the-top re-creation of the Battle of Thermopylae with all-digital sets and backgrounds, cost only $65 million to produce, cheap compared to the sword-and-sandal epic *Troy*, which cost $175 million, and *Gladiator*, which cost $103 million. With that low cost of production, *300* was able to earn back its basic budget the first weekend of release, and it eventually earned more than $210 million domestically and $456 million worldwide.[56] What made the film so cheap? First, it was shot in Canada, where production and labor costs are lower. Second, it was shot completely on high-definition video on a blank soundstage using the technology pioneered in *Sky Captain*. With the success of *300*, we see avant-garde techniques becoming mainstream, providing yet another instance of Secret 3—Everything from the margin moves to the center.[57]

Digital Projection. *Star Wars* creator Lucas wrote in 1999 that he believed that film and projectors would soon be replaced by digital computer projection. Aside from questions about the quality of the images, digital projectors give a better 3-D image than do conventional projectors, and they drastically lower the cost of distributing prints to theaters.[58] The initial conversion over to digital projection was seen as risky and expensive, costing between $20,000 and $100,000 per screen, but by 2017, virtually every theater in the United States was projecting digitally.[59]

Despite the efforts of the studios to kill off film, some directors still want to work with it. Cult director Quentin Tarantino shot his neo-western *The Hateful Eight* in the old film format Ultra Panavision 70mm, a format that saw limited use in the 1950s and 1960s. The film has a much wider aspect ratio than conventional film or digital projection, and it creates a dramatic image when projected on a big screen.[60] Although *Hateful Eight* showed in most theaters using standard digital projection, it was shown in 70mm on ninety-six screens in the United States and four in Canada at a cost of about $80,000 per theater. Nolan's *Interstellar* showed at eleven theaters in the same format, which is not to be confused with the somewhat different 70mm IMAX film format.[61] Aside from the issue of projecting movies using film, many more movies are shot using film. The video game movie *Ready Player One*, directed by Spielberg, had the "real world" portions of the movie shot on film and the virtual reality portions shot on video to make the two separate worlds stand out from each other. It also played in twenty-two theaters in the 70mm film format.[62]

What Makes a Movie Profitable?

Although a blockbuster movie can be enormously profitable, a relatively low percentage (20–30 percent) of movies actually make money. Movies can be financial failures even if they make $200 million and can be successful even if they make only $2 million—it all depends on how much the movie cost to produce and promote.[63] The best-known way to make money in the movies is to produce a big-budget blockbuster with big stars and a big-name director, have a giant domestic and international box office, sell lots of licensed products, sell millions of DVDs, and generally turn the movie into a Fortune 500 corporation. Sometimes this process even produces a fairly good film.

Let's look back at the Marvel Cinematic Universe blockbuster *Black Panther*. It had a reported production budget of $200 million.[64] It had been given a larger-than-usual budget for a Marvel nonsequel film, such as *Doctor Strange* or *Ant-Man*, despite there being concerns about the sale of *Black Panther* toys.[65] But it brought in more than $700 million domestically and $1.34 billion globally. When you spend that much money making a movie, it must be a success. Of course, with talent such as up-and-coming writer/director Ryan Coogler and some of the top Black actors in the world, it was bound to be a success. Sometimes the international box office can help redeem a domestic stinker. That was the case with actor Tom Cruise's remake of *The Mummy*. Cruise has a reputation for reliable box office, but *Mummy* did not live up to it. The movie cost an estimated $195 million to produce and had a disastrous $31 million opening weekend. Over the course of its theatrical run, it brought in only $80 million domestically. But the additional $329 million internationally kept the movie from being a total disaster.[66]

▼ TABLE 7.1

Box Office Receipts of Top Movies (Actual Domestic Revenue)

Film	Year Released	Revenue
1. *Star Wars Episode VII: The Force Awakens*	2015	$936,662,225
2. *Avengers: Endgame*	2019	$858,373,333
3. *Avatar*	2009	$760,507,625
4. *Black Panther*	2018	$700,059,566
5. *Avengers: Infinity War*	2018	$678,815,482
6. *Titanic*	1997	$659,363,944
7. *Jurassic World*	2015	$652,270,625
8. *Marvel's The Avengers*	2012	$623,357,910
9. *Star Wars Episode VIII: The Last Jedi*	2017	$620,181,382
10. *Incredibles 2*	2018	$557,335,440

Source: "Top Lifetime Grosses: Domestic," *Box Office Mojo,* May 2020, https://www.boxofficemojo.com/chart/top_lifetime_gross/. Used with permission.

▼ TABLE 7.2

Box Office Receipts of Top Movies (Adjusted for Inflation—2020)

Film	Year Released	Revenue
1. *Gone With the Wind*	1939	$1.90 billion
2. *Star Wars Episode IV: A New Hope*	1977	$1.67 billion
3. *The Sound of Music*	1965	$1.34 billion
4. *E.T.: The Extra-Terrestrial*	1982	$1.33 billion
5. *Titanic*	1977	$1.27 billion
6. *The Ten Commandments*	1956	$1.23 billion
7. *Jaws*	1975	$1.20 billion
8. *Doctor Zhivago*	1965	$1.16 billion
9. *The Exorcist*	1973	$1.04 billion
10. *Snow White and the Seven Dwarfs*	1937	$1.02 billion

Source: "Top Lifetime Adjusted Grosses – 2020 Ticket Price," *Box Office Mojo,* May 2020, https://www.boxofficemojo.com/chart/top_lifetime_gross_adjusted/?adjust_gross_to=2020. Used with permission.

Note: Star Wars Episode VII: The Force Awakens was ranked eleventh on the inflation-adjusted list as of May 2020, coming in just behind *Snow White* (1937). At the time it was initially released, *Snow White* was the most expensive and biggest box office movie ever. But it was replaced the following year by *Gone with the Wind*.

The alternative approach is to make a movie with a tiny-to-small budget that has a clear target audience, have a modest box office, and make a great return on investment. A good example of this is 2014's *The Fault in Our Stars*. The movie started with a built-in audience of fans of the best-selling young adult novel that tells the story of two teens who fall in love while suffering from cancer. The movie was filmed for $12 million and had huge social media buzz from its target audience of teen and twentysomething women. The film had a spectacular opening, earning $48.2 million over its first weekend, and it went on to earn more than $124 million in the United States and $182 million internationally. The movie was not one of the top-ten grossing movies of 2014, but it was one of the most profitable, earning more than ten times its cost of production.[67]

On a smaller scale was the faith-based *I Can Only Imagine*, which tells the true story of successful Christian singer Bart Millard, the lead singer of MercyMe, who writes a hit song about his reconciliation with his abusive father. Produced for a budget of only $7 million, it had a $17 million opening weekend. While that would be disastrous for a bigger-budget movie, this was fantastic for such a low-budget film. But even more impressively, *I Can Only Imagine* held onto that audience with minimal fall-off for several weeks, likely indicating that it was drawing a general movie audience interested in a compelling biopic, not just those looking for a Christian-themed film. It finished its run with a total domestic box office of $82 million, more than ten times its production budget.[68] (For lists of top movies, by revenue, refer to Tables 7.1 and 7.2.)

The problem for studio executives, of course, is figuring out in advance which movies can support a large budget and which ones cannot. It is easy to figure out the big-budget movies that are likely to be blockbusters (well, maybe, at least those that ought to be blockbusters, if they are done right). But why do the little movies, like Jordan Peele's *Get Out* or M. Night Shyamalan's *Split*, break out to become hits?

According to *USA Today* movie critic Susan Wloszczyna, these movies, and others like them, are ones that "grab the people who actually part with money to see movies."[69] The basics are pretty straightforward: Make an interesting film that doesn't fit a big-budget mold, keep its costs under control, and be savvy about how you promote it. If it does well, the upside is almost unlimited. If you miss, the movie is still likely to make back its cost through video, cable, and broadcast rights.

Take, for example, two movies from legendary director Spielberg—both were profitable, but quite different from each other. *The Post*, which tells the story of the *Washington Post*'s involvement in the Pentagon Papers case, took a prominent story from journalism history, had a pair of top stars with Meryl Streep and Tom Hanks, and had a modest budget of $50 million. It brought in $81 million domestically and another $92 million internationally. The serious, historical movie was never going to be a big hit, but with an A-list director, a good story and cast, and a modest budget, it was clearly a success. In the spring of 2018, Spielberg released another movie, *Ready Player One*. The virtual reality–themed movie was based on a popular novel, had a flashy and exciting look, and had a respectable, but not excessive, budget of an estimated $150 million. While it was not a huge hit domestically, bringing in $137 million, its international box office topped $445 million. Not a hit for the record books, but still a solid success with a total global box office of $583 million. Two movies from one director over a four-month period—both were successful, at very different levels.[70]

Where Are Movies Made?

When we talk about movies, we often speak as though they are all made in Hollywood and the traditional movie studios. But the truth is now that movies are produced across the United States and around the world. And that diversity of sourcing brings us a range of styles and voices to our movies.

If you watch the credits following a Marvel Cinematic Universe movie for more than just the ubiquitous post-credit scenes, you'll often notice near the end the Georgia Film Commission peach-shaped logo indicating that the film was shot at least in part and supported by the state of Georgia. In fact, more movies have lately been produced in Georgia than any other state, including California.[71]

Why is Georgia so popular with moviemakers? The state has a good movie production infrastructure and has massive tax incentives for companies shooting movies in the state. Georgia has more than a million square feet of sound stage space, lots of skilled local crews, and excellent transportation in and out of the area.[72]

Tyler Perry's Georgia. The root of Georgia's growth as a movie production space is that fact that African-American actor, director, producer, and studio owner Tyler Perry—routinely one of the wealthiest Black stars in the movie industry—set up his own company's studio in Atlanta. Perry's efforts to promote the Georgia movie industry has not only led to making the state a good place to film, it has also become known as a home for diverse crews producing stories by people of color. While Perry has his hand in a wide range of creative projects, he is best known for directing and starring in the Madea movies. In these films, Perry tells stories about families of faith headed up by the grandmother-figure Madea, played by Perry in drag.

"Tyler Perry has inspired creatives that were here to know that it is possible to become a filmmaker and do it in your own backyard," said Phillana Williams of the Atlanta Mayor's Office of Film and Entertainment. "You can thrive and tell stories about your culture in your own city."[73]

Hooray for Bollywood: India's Movie Industry. The biggest source of movies in the world is not California or even the United States as a whole. That honor belongs to Bollywood—the filmmakers of India, especially the city of Mumbai (formerly Bombay). Although Bollywood films are popular worldwide, they were not seen frequently in the United States. But 2009's Oscar winner for best picture helped change that. *Slumdog Millionaire*, a British movie set in India that makes use of a lot of the stylistic conventions of Bollywood, won eight Oscars and made more than $140 million in the United States.[74]

Each year, Bollywood produces more than one thousand films that are distributed throughout Africa, China, and the rest of Asia. A 2002 *BBC News* online poll found that the world's most popular movie star at that time was not Harrison Ford or Julia Roberts; it was Indian actor Amitabh Bachchan, who had starred in more than one hundred Bollywood movies.[75] More recently, Bachchan has been replaced as the world's biggest movie star by another Bollywood actor—Shah Rukh Khan, who in 2014 was making more than Tom Cruise. He has made more than eighty films, owns his own production company, and—because he's a movie star from India—owns his own cricket team, the Kolkata Knight Riders.[76]

Typical of India's films are the masala, or spice, movies. They feature several musical numbers, a strong male hero, a coy heroine, and an obvious villain.[77] The movies have as many as ten separate story lines—a contrast to American movies, which typically tell one or two stories.

One reason for the musical numbers in Indian films is that they help break through language barriers. India alone has more than twenty-five languages. Anupam Sharma, who works in the Indian movie industry, says that Bollywood movies touch people throughout the world: "Because of the distances and different dialects in India, music is the universal language."[78] When it comes to romance and sex, Bollywood films tend to be far more conservative than American films. "India is still clinging on to its social values, which explains Bollywood's success everywhere but in America," said Priya Joshi, an Indian cinema scholar. "Bollywood films don't have any kissing in them or tend not to. Warner Bros. used to make movies like this in the past. . . . If it's ready to return to its roots, then it's ready for Bollywood."[79] Movie critic Roger Ebert wrote that American audiences could enjoy these films:

It is like nothing [Americans] have seen before, with its startling landscapes, architecture and locations, its exuberant colors, its sudden and joyous musical numbers right in the middle of dramatic scenes, and its melodramatic acting (teeth gnash, tears well, lips tremble, bosoms heave, fists clench).[80]

Bollywood is increasingly coming into competition in India with American imports that are being dubbed into multiple Indian languages, including Hindi, Tamil, and Telugu. Indians, like Americans, are also increasingly doing their movie watching on Netflix, Amazon Prime, and Hotstar—an Indian streaming service.

Movies and Society

During the 2016 Oscars, there was a hashtag campaign #OscarsSoWhite to highlight that none of the acting nominees in any of the four categories were nonwhite. Since then, things have obviously improved. The Oscar-winning Pixar-animated film *Coco* told a Hispanic story with a largely Hispanic cast. The Oscar-nominated horror/comedy film *Get Out* has a Black writer/director and a Black leading actor. It was also a big commercial and critical success. *Moonlight*, telling a Black coming-of-age story, won best picture in 2017.[81]

The problem is turning these individual successes into a long-term trend. Darnell Hunt, who works on the annual UCLA movie diversity study, said the number of women and people of color in front of and behind the camera does not change much. "Every year we see a series of exceptional films like 'Moonlight' that tells a different story and features women or POC [people of color], but they have always prove[d] to be exceptions to the rule. We see a bump here and there, but nothing that points to a sustained trend."[82]

The 2016 Academy Awards ceremony was as notable for who was not there as for who was. Pull out a photo of all the nominees for an acting award, and you will immediately notice something. All the nominees are white. Not just all the winners, but all the nominees. And 2016 was not a fluke. That was also the case in 2015. It is not as though there were not any great performances by nonwhite actors. Idris Elba got rave reviews for starring in *Beasts of No Nation*, Michael B. Jordan was well regarded for playing the lead in the boxing movie *Creed*, and the entire cast of the NWA rap biopic *Straight Outta Compton* got good reviews—not to mention a really good box office.[83]

Of course, both *Creed* and *Straight Outta Compton* did get Oscar nominations—to white actor Sylvester Stallone for *Creed* and to the white screenwriters of *Straight Outta Compton*.[84]

The lack of recognition for nonwhite actors led attorney April Reign to establish the social media hashtag #OscarsSoWhite to point out the lack of diversity, and several movie figures stayed away from the ceremony, including filmmakers Spike Lee and Michael Moore, along with actors Jada Pinkett Smith and Will Smith.[85]

Has Hollywood gotten better since the 2016 Oscars?

On Oscar night for 2019, for the first time ever, actors of color won three of the four acting awards—Rami Malek for playing Freddie Mercury in *Bohemian Rhapsody*, Regina King for *If Beale Street Could Talk*, and Mahershala Ali for *Green Book*.

One bright spot for diversity at the 2020 Oscars was *Hair Love*'s win as best animated short. The cartoon tells the story of an African-American father learning how to style his daughter's natural hair. Former NFL player Michael Cherry wrote the film that was produced in part with $284,000 from a 2017 Kickstarter crowdfunding campaign.[86] Going to thousands of backers from outside Hollywood let Cherry make a film that studio executives might not have been willing to finance. Cherry said that while he was not a father himself, he was concerned about the lack of representation in animated films: "I wanted to see a young Black family in the animated world." Cherry collaborated on the film with two established African-American animators.[87]

In February 2018, when the Marvel movie *Black Panther* opened as the first big-budget superhero film to have a Black director and star a Black hero, people had high expectations. Experts thought the movie might bring in as much as $165 million domestically its opening weekend. But that turned out to be a serious underestimate—it brought in *$218 million*. And by the end of its run, *Black Panther* would bring in more than $700 million in the domestic market, putting it at the sixth spot on the top money makers. (See Table 7.1.) *Black Panther* had a largely Black cast hailing from the United

DOES IT LOOK AS IF WOMEN HAVE MAJOR FILM ROLES?

There are lots of movies that feature great relationships between men. There are several movies with interesting roles for women. But how many movies out there feature multiple major female characters who interact with each other? That is the question the Bechdel Test for Women in Film tries to answer.

The Bechdel Test, named after cartoonist and graphic novel artist Alison Bechdel, attempts to test whether women have a meaningful presence in a movie.[97] It does so by asking three questions:

1. Are there two or more women who have names in the movie?
2. Do they talk to each other?
3. Do they talk to each other about something other than a man?

Not surprisingly, male-centric movies, such as *1917*, *Ford v Ferrari*, and *Ad Astra*, do not pass. Movies focusing on the activities of multiple women, such as *Hidden Figures*, *The Farewell*, and the Harley Quinn comic book–based *Birds of Prey*, clearly do pass. But as media critic Anita Sarkeesian points out, some not-so-obvious fails include

- The original *Shrek*
- *The Big Lebowski*
- *Slumdog Millionaire*
- And even *The Princess Bride*

Remember, the Bechdel Test does not judge the quality of the movie or whether it treats women with respect. It only requires that the movie have two or more women who talk to each other about something other than a man.

Oddly enough, even in the most female-centric movies—the Disney princess films—most of the dialog goes to male characters. While female characters dominate the dialog in classic Disney princess films like the original animated *Cinderella* and *Sleeping Beauty*, the princess movies from the 1980s and 1990s are a different story. Male characters have 68 percent of the dialog in *The Little Mermaid*, 71 percent in *Beauty and the Beast*, and 76 percent in *Pocahontas*. (Do not even think about *Aladdin*, where 90 percent of the lines go to male characters.)[98]

WHO is the source?

What is the Bechdel Test? By whom was it developed?

WHAT are they saying?

What is the goal of the Bechdel Test? What does it tell us? What doesn't it tell us?

WHAT evidence is there?

Watch a recently released movie and take notes on the Bechdel questions. Which of the questions does your movie pass? What are some examples of why the movie does or does not pass the Bechdel Test?

WHAT do you and your classmates think?

Were you surprised by how your analysis turned out? Does thinking about the Bechdel Test change how you view movies? Does the Bechdel Test address an issue we should be concerned about? Why or why not? Does the lack of female dialog in the Disney princess movies surprise you?

BFA / Alamy Stock Photo

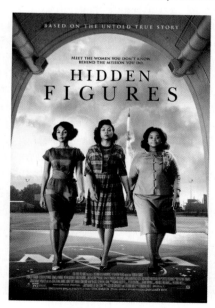

AF archive / Alamy Stock Photo

States, Britain, and across Africa. It also had a particularly diverse crew, having far more women and people of color working on it than most movies. Actor Chadwick Boseman, who portrayed King T'Challa in *Black Panther*, died of colon cancer in August of 2020. Boseman had been fighting the disease for four years, including while *Black Panther* had been in production. While it was filming, Boseman pushed for characters to have African rather than British accents. Boseman learned the South African Xhosa accent, while others in the cast had Kenyan, Nigerian and Ugandan accents. The key issue was not trying to make the African characters all sound the same but rather to sound like Africa.[88] (For more on the importance of diversity in movies like *Black Panther*, see Chapter 15)

The problem is clearly not an unwillingness of audiences to go to movies starring people other than white males. *New York Times* critic-at-large Wesley Morris notes that audience members are more than happy to pay "to see women, films with mostly Black actors and racially diverse casts."[89] He points to the success of *Star Wars Episode VII: The Force Awakens* (young woman and Black man as leads), *Furious 7* (featuring a multiethnic cast), the *Pitch Perfect* series, the *Hunger Games* movies, and *Straight Outta Compton*.

Emily VanDerWerff, writing for *Vox*, notes that the problem isn't just casting people other than white men: "It's about acknowledging that white men don't have a lock on good stories, and letting others' stories be told as well as possible."[90]

There has been an active effort by the Academy to be more inclusive in its membership since 2015 and 2016 when all of the acting nominees were white, leading to the #OscarsSoWhite social media controversy. "Women and people of color don't have the same blind spots as the minority of white straight men that currently dominate American storytelling," *Dear White People* director Justin Simien told *Entertainment Weekly* in 2019, shortly after his invitation to join the group was announced. "The more diverse the Academy is, the greater variety of stories and storytellers that will get seen and promoted."[91]

The challenge facing the Academy is keeping up the idea of representation. For the 2020 Oscars, all the nominees for best director were males. And this was a year when one of the most acclaimed movies was director Greta Gerwood's version of *Little Women*.

Problematic Depictions of Race

When Disney launched its new streaming service Disney+ in the fall of 2019, the channel offered a lot of classic films from The Mouse that contained what could charitably be called "problematic depictions of race."[92] There were questions about whether Disney was going to cut these scenes. But instead Disney put disclaimers before them. For example, the disclaimer before the 1941 animated version of *Dumbo* says, "This program is presented as originally created. It may contain outdated cultural depictions." For *Dumbo*, the disclaimer referred to the crows who were based on blackface minstrel characters.

Warner Brothers has presented a stronger disclaimer to go with its *Tom and Jerry* cartoons that were originally created to show in theaters before Warner Bros. feature films. The disclaimer that appears on the iTunes copies of the shorts states,

> "These animated shorts are the products of their time. Some of them may depict some of the ethnic and racial prejudices that were commonplace in American society. These depictions were wrong then and are wrong today. While the following does not represent the Warner Bros. view of today's society, these animated shorts are being presented as they were originally created, because to do otherwise would be the same as claiming these prejudices never existed."[93]

Whitewashing. The problem is not just with Hollywood not creating parts for nonwhite performers; it extends to casting white actors in parts intended for people of color—a process known as **whitewashing**. A prime example of whitewashing was the remake of the Japanese anime cyberpunk classic *Ghost in the Shell* as a live-action movie, staring the white actress Scarlett Johansson as Major Motoko Kusanagi. Johansson's character is a cybernetic organism holding the brain of a dead female Japanese agent. Fans of the manga and the original animated film argued that the film should have had a Japanese actress. Whether it was backlash or just because the movie was not particularly good, *Ghost in the Shell* only brought in $43.8 million domestically with a $110 million production budget.[94] In the Marvel Studios film *Doctor Strange*, a character who was a Tibetan monk in the comic was remade into a Celtic mystic played by Tilda Swinton. While Marvel points out that there are a variety of race and gender swaps in its movies, Asian American actor George Takei was not impressed. "It's all too plainly outlandish," he told the *New York Times*. "It's getting to the point where it's almost laughable. . . . Hollywood has been casting white actors in Asian roles for decades now, and we can't keep pretending there isn't something deeper at work here."[95]

In the past couple of years, the movie industry has started to realize that audiences are open to movies with Asian actors and stories. In 2018, the rom-com *Crazy Rich Asians* became the first contemporary film in the United States in twenty-five years to feature a predominantly Asian cast. This was followed in 2019 by the Chinese family comedy/drama *The Farewell*, starring actress and rapper Awkwafina. But the biggest breakout was when the Korean-language thriller *Parasite* won the Oscar for Best Picture, the first for a non-English-language film.[96]

The Production Code: Protecting the Movies From Censorship

Movies are somewhat different from other media in that their producers have always been conscious of the need for limits on what they can portray. In 1909, theater owners formed the New York Board of Censorship (now the National Board of Review of Motion Pictures) to establish a national standard for movies. The idea was that the board would ban offensive

▲ The movie *Ghost in the Shell*, based on a popular Japanese manga (or comic book) featuring the Japanese character Major Motoko Kusanagi, was criticized for whitewashing for hiring Scarlett Johansson, a white American actress, for the part.

▲ The web comic *Dumbing of Age* tells the story of a group of students at a Midwest college. In this strip, the characters are discussing movies in a women's studies class.

films, with the implication that approved films were suitable to be shown. Ironically, the board was formed primarily to protect the theater owners from trouble rather than to protect their audiences from offensive films.[99] What was considered objectionable content in movies of this era? Prostitution, childbirth, and masturbation were all decried in the 1920s, as was drug use.[100] One critic argued that there was no question that censorship was necessary. The only question was whether the censors should be controlled by the industry or by the government.[101]

One of the factors prompting censorship efforts was that the behavior of stars off screen was considered as immoral as some of the movies themselves. When Pickford, a silent-movie star who made a specialty of heroines with ringlets, such as Rebecca of Sunnybrook Farm, quietly divorced her husband to marry her costar Fairbanks, her behavior became the talk of the nation. Actor Fatty Arbuckle became entangled in scandal after it appeared that he had bribed a district attorney to cover up the presence of a dozen "party girls" at one of his parties. He was later accused of murdering one of his guests—a young aspiring actress—at another party. Although he was eventually acquitted after three trials, the public never fully forgave him, and he didn't appear on screen for more than a decade.[102] A 1922 pamphlet charged that Hollywood was a mass of "wild orgies," "dope parties," "kept men," and "kept women."[103]

The Birth of the Production Code. The motion picture industry began formalizing its morality rules with "The Don'ts and Be Carefuls," a set of guidelines passed in 1927. The impetus for this action was a series of hearings by the Federal Trade Commission and the threat of government regulation.[104] As has generally been the case with the movie industry, censorship of the movies came from within the industry for economic reasons. Movie historian Gerald Mast described the moral dilemma in which the moviemakers found themselves:

> Because the movies have sold sex and violence from the beginning (what extremely popular and public art ever sold anything else?), and because they were created within and supported by a society that condoned neither the doing nor the display of sex and violence, the motion picture industry has been in the paradoxical position of trying to set limits on how much it would let itself sell.[105]

Facing a range of accusations of immorality, the studios looked for someone who could improve the industry's image. They found that person in Will H. Hays, who had been U.S. postmaster general from 1921 to 1922. Hays was named president of the Motion Picture Producers and Distributors of America and became famous for his development of the **Production Code**, which controlled the content of movies from the 1930s until movie ratings came into use in 1968. The purpose of the code, in its early days, was primarily to convince people that Hollywood was doing something about morality in the movies. But by 1933, Hollywood was forced to start living up to the standards it professed to support.[106]

Among other things, the code required that evil not be made to look alluring and that villains and lawbreakers not go unpunished: "Crime shall never be presented in a way that might inspire others with a desire for imitation. Brutal killings are not to be presented in detail." Also, there could be no profanity or blasphemy in the movies. The code was also strict about sex, noting that scenes of passion needed to be handled carefully: "Excessive and lustful kissing, lustful embraces, suggestive postures and gestures, are not to be shown." Interracial romance was also forbidden.[107] Only occasionally could anything "immoral" get past the code, and big-budget movies from major studios were more likely to get away with pushing the edge of acceptability. Rhett Butler's closing line in *Gone with the Wind*, "Frankly, my dear, I don't give a damn," was shocking to audiences in 1939 because nothing so raw had previously been allowed by the censors.[108]

The Ratings System

By the 1960s, many movies were violating provisions of the Production Code, and some were even released without the code's approval. This forced a reevaluation of how movies were judged. Otto Preminger's 1953 movie *The Moon Is Blue* was the first major American movie to be released without code approval. Although it was controversial at the time, it would be considered mild today—imagine a movie causing a stir for including the words *virgin* and *mistress*.

In 1968, under the direction of its new president, Jack Valenti, the Motion Picture Association of American (MPAA) scrapped the increasingly outdated Production Code. The code was replaced with a system of voluntary ratings indicating the audience for which the movie was most appropriate.

Movie ratings are assigned by a panel of ten to thirteen parents who live in the Los Angeles area. In 1999, the panel consisted of seven women and five men ranging in age from twenty-eight to fifty-four. It included homemakers, carpenters, a teacher, a food and beverage manager, and a manicurist. On a typical workday, the raters screen and discuss three movies. They then assign each movie one of the following ratings:

- G: General audiences. All ages admitted.

- PG: Parental guidance suggested. Some material may not be suitable for children.

- PG-13: Parents strongly cautioned. Some material may be inappropriate for children under age 13.

- R: Restricted. Persons under age 17 will not be admitted unless accompanied by a parent or adult guardian.

- NC-17: No one under age 17 will be admitted.

This system evolved from the original system of four ratings: G, M, R, and X. The rating of M (mature audiences) was soon changed to GP (general audiences, parental guidance suggested) and then to PG (parental guidance).

Certain kinds of content usually prompt particular ratings. Drug use generally requires at least a PG-13 rating. Sexually oriented nudity results in an R rating. (*Titanic* got by with a PG-13 rating because its nudity occurred when an artist sketched his model, and not in a later love scene.) Violence that is rough and persistent requires an R. A single use of the "*F* word" requires a PG-13. If that word is used more than once, or used in a sexual sense, the movie is supposed to be rated R, though the board may override that rule by a two-thirds vote. (As an example, the Julia Roberts movie *My Best Friend's Wedding* used the *F* word in a sexual sense and still received a rating of PG-13.)

Some critics charge that gay sex is more likely than heterosexual sex to receive a severe rating. It appears likely that the 1969 Oscar-winning movie *Midnight Cowboy* was given an X rating primarily because actor Jon Voight portrayed a male prostitute who serviced male clients. Others have charged that female sexuality is more likely to receive restrictive ratings than is male sexuality; interracial sex is also considered inflammatory.

In the mid-1980s, it became clear that the rating system had a weakness. Movies were being released with a PG rating that did not merit an R but nevertheless included content that went beyond a PG rating. A new rating was proposed, PG-13, which would inform parents of the content of the film but not set limits on who could be admitted. The rating change was supported strongly by director Spielberg, who forced the issue with *Indiana Jones and the Temple of Doom* and *Gremlins*. Both movies were attacked for being too violent and intense for preteens, although they did not include content that would require an R rating. Spielberg observed ironically, "I've never made an R movie and hope never to make one, so I've been one of the first to appeal for a ratings change that would take the onus off the filmmaker as parent to America. That's not our role."[109] (This was back when Spielberg was making youth-oriented summer blockbuster action films rather than his more serious films dealing with World War II, the Holocaust, and terrorism.)

Traditionally, PG-13 is seen as the most desirable rating because teenagers see these movies as more sophisticated than those rated G or PG.[110] In the spring of 2018, all ten of the all-time top ten box office movies had a PG-13 rating. You had to go all the way down to number thirty-eight—*The Passion of the Christ*—to find an R-rated movie, followed closely by Marvel's wisecracking and rude *Deadpool* at forty-two. All of the top ten box office G-rated movies were either Disney or Pixar.[111]

Writer and director James Mangold broke with conventional wisdom of PG-13-rated movies with his brooding finale to the Wolverine story with the R-rated *Logan*. He said, "It wasn't because of the violence and it wasn't because of the language, but because I didn't have to write a movie, and neither did my compatriots, for 11-year-olds. If we had a rated-R movie there were gonna be no Happy Meals. There can be no action figures . . . so that suddenly you're not making a movie written for someone under 14, 15. And that changes the length of the scenes. It changes what they're talking about."[112] Mangold says the R rating gave Wolverine and Professor X time to talk about mortality in an extended scene that would never be tolerated in a PG-13 film.

The X Problem. A second major problem with the rating system had to do with the X rating. The trouble began when the MPAA did not trademark the X rating and therefore could not control its use. The pornography industry began labeling its unrated films XXX on the theory that if X was adult, XXX would be really adult. Because the X rating became associated with pornography, many newspapers and television stations refused to carry advertisements for X-rated movies, and many theaters pledged not to show such movies, despite the artistic merit that some movies receiving the rating might have.

In 1990, the MPAA threatened to assign an X rating to *Henry & June*, which portrayed the relationship between writer Henry Miller, his wife, and writer Anaïs Nin. The producers protested, and the MPAA responded by creating a new rating, NC-17, which supposedly was less prejudicial than X. In reality, little changed; theaters and media outlets treat the new rating as equivalent to X.

Movies that receive the dreaded NC-17 rating often must be reedited to qualify for the more commercially viable R rating. But the producers of *Midnight Cowboy*, the first and only X- or NC-17-rated movie to win an Oscar for best picture, decided against reediting the film. Producer Jerome Hellman notes that after the movie won the Oscar, the film board offered to give the film an R rating if the producers would cut one frame from the movie so that it could be advertised as a "re-cut" version. The producers refused, but the board relented and changed the movie's rating to R.[113] Some people in the movie industry have speculated that Spielberg's World War II film *Saving Private Ryan* should have received an NC-17 rating for the violence in the opening scene, which depicts the D-Day invasion of France, but avoided it because of Spielberg's reputation. Filmmaker Lee, speaking at the Cannes Film Festival, said,

▲ *Deadpool*, part of the Marvel Cinematic Universe, proved that a superhero movie could find success with an R rating if it brought a clever script that matched the comic book's edgy style.

Deadpool/Photofest

> The MPAA has two different standards: one for violence, one for sex. I mean, I like Saving Private Ryan very much, especially the first hour. But if that's not an NC-17 film, I don't know what is. That's the way war should be depicted. But when people walk around picking up their severed arms and stuff like that, that's an R?[114]

Former MPAA president Valenti defended *Saving Private Ryan*'s R rating:

Saving Private Ryan was a reenactment of one of the most crucial days in American history. I think every 13-year-old in the country ought to see it, even though it was rated R, to understand that the freedom you take for granted was paid for in blood.[115]

In 2007, the MPAA made some slight revisions to the rating scheme. These include a new warning to discourage parents from bringing young children to more intense R-rated movies. The ratings board now reveals the demographics of the people who do the ratings. There have also been calls to expand the acceptability of the NC-17 rating so that the R rating is not applied to movies that children should not be allowed to see. But the updates to the rating system did not go so far as to create an official "hard R" rating that would ban all viewers under the age of seventeen from attending the movies.[116]

Regardless of the criticisms, parents appreciate the rating system. A 2015 survey showed that 93 percent of U.S. parents find the ratings useful in deciding what their children should be allowed to see.[117]

The Long Tail and the Future of Movies

The long tail is going to have a bigger and bigger effect on the movie industry in the years to come, but 2007 marked the point at which it jumped to the forefront. Before then, unless you lived in New York or Los Angeles, you were not likely to have seen the Oscar winners for best animated short film and best live-action short. But in 2007, the films were available as digital downloads from Apple's iTunes Store for $1.99 each. This means that for less than the price of a movie ticket in an urban market, you could download and view all five nominated films in either category, even if you live in Kearney, Nebraska. What you are seeing here is nothing less than the full impact of the long tail hitting the mainstream movie industry.

When *Long Tail* author Chris Anderson tries to explain the central concepts of his book, he often points to the online DVD rental store Netflix as a prime example. In 2012, Netflix carried one hundred thousand different DVD and Blu-ray titles. It also had more than twelve thousand titles available for immediate viewing over either a computer or a streaming video box that connects the subscriber's television set to the internet. Today, Netflix is primarily a streaming service that also rents discs. Anderson found that audiences are not just interested in a few big hits; they are interested in a deep pool of choices. The problem has always been distribution. Movie theaters are great for showing a limited number of movies to a lot of people. That is why theater owners love the summer blockbusters. But when you can draw from audiences nationwide, even movies with a limited appeal can be successful.

The popularity of Netflix has led to more competition in the streaming market, with Amazon Prime Video, Disney+, and Hulu being the digital natives, and Showtime and HBO jumping in to offering streaming services along with their cable products. (We will talk more about these streaming services in Chapter 9 on television.)

To retain subscribers, Netflix works hard to figure out, based on your viewership and movies you have reviewed, what kind of movies and TV shows you've enjoyed. It then uses that information to recommend other movies you would probably like. Anderson says that if Netflix can use consumer data to recommend films, the cost of marketing small movies to consumers is lowered to almost zero:

Advertising and other marketing can represent more than half of the costs of the average Hollywood blockbuster, and smaller films can't play in that game. Netflix recommendations level the playing field, offering free marketing for films that can't otherwise afford it, and thus spreading demand more evenly between hits and niches.[118]

Famed film critic Ebert found that on his website, www.rogerebert.com, no single posted review accounts for more than 1 percent of the page views. Instead of the blockbusters dominating the traffic, almost all the ten-thousand-plus reviews on the site are attracting some level of attention.[119]

When Daniel Myrick and Eduardo Sánchez headed out into the Maryland woods in October 1997 to film *The Blair Witch Project*, they had no idea they were creating what would become one of the big hits of 1999 or that they would change how movies are promoted.

Blair Witch purports to be a documentary filmed by three students investigating the legend of a murderous witch who lived in the woods near Burkittsville, Maryland. The movie did not even have a script; instead, the actors started with only a thirty-five-page plot outline. The actors were also the film crew, using an old 16mm film camera and a $500 Hi8 video camera. The total cost of filming the movie was between $35,000 and $60,000, although some critics wonder how it could have cost even that much.[120] The movie eventually grossed more than $248 million worldwide.

The performers shot twenty hours of film and tape over an eight-day period while wandering about in the woods. The directors left notes for the actors each day, but the performers were given a lot of latitude. "We let [them] do what they wanted to do," Myrick said. "We gave them little clues as to where we wanted the scenes to go, but most of it was improvised."[121] Myrick and Sánchez, along with production company Artisan, promoted *Blair Witch* in the same low-budget way in which it had been filmed, making use of cable television and the internet rather than mainstream media. The pair created a mock documentary about the making of the movie, *The Curse of the Blair Witch*, which aired on the Syfy channel, and many viewers took this as evidence that the events recorded in the film had actually occurred. The promotional campaign capitalized on the confusion over whether the movie was fact or fiction, and many people who saw the film during the first week or two after its release thought that it might be real.[122]

Ten years after the movie scared movie fans and producers alike, *Los Angeles Times* blogger Glenn Whipp argued that the biggest impact of *The Blair Witch Project* was the effectiveness of the web-based viral marketing campaign put together for the movie. The movie had good buzz coming out of showings at the Sundance and Cannes film festivals, and marketing materials made it sound like the footage for the film was real footage that had been found. Horror film director Scott Derrickson told Whipp, "The blurb on the poster said this was 'found footage,' and there was nothing in the marketing to lead you to believe it was anything but that."[123] Websites are now being used to court fans months or even years before a movie comes out. In many cases, the site is designed to maintain awareness of the movie even after the advertising is done and to build awareness once again when the movie is released on video. Independent film producer Mark Duplass (*The Puffy Chair*) says that in addition to changing how movies are promoted, *Blair Witch* changed how movies look, with "the semi-improvised nature, the hand-held digital camera work, the naturalistic acting inside a genre piece, the idea of 'We don't have a [lot] of money, so let's build a budget that's appropriate, so we can execute it correctly.'"[124]

▲ *The Blair Witch Project* is considered the first widely released movie marketed primarily through the internet.

Declining Ticket Sales

A large part of why the long tail will be the future of movies is that the business itself is facing an uncertain future. For the week of February 14–20, 2020, the overall U.S. box office brought in more than $215 million, with *Sonic the Hedgehog* leading the pack. A month later, March 13–19, and the weekly take dropped sharply to $59 million. Then the next week, virtually every theater in the country closed and the weekly box office fell off a cliff to just over $5,000.[125] By the time you are reading this, movie theaters will likely be open, but under what conditions? Until a vaccine or cure is found for COVID-19, will people be willing to go to theaters? What level of capacity will theaters be allowed to sell? Will they be required to block off half of their seats to preserve social distancing?

But worries about theatrical box office did not start in 2020 with the global pandemic. In 2005, the U.S. box office was down by 6 percent from the year before.[126] There were a lot of explanations for what caused the downturn. Conservative critics claimed that Hollywood was too liberal and was making movies that did not appeal to the American public.[127] Others claimed that the problems were too many sequels and remakes. While sequels, remakes, and raunchy movies have continued to draw big audiences, the total size of the movie audience has stayed below the 1.58 billion ticket level it hit in 2002. (Keep in mind that audience size peaked back in the 1940s, with sales of just more than 4 billion tickets a year.[128]) Since 2005, movie ticket sales have hovered in the area of 1.24–1.4 billion tickets per year.[129] Although the Hollywood box office has continued its climb in dollars earned, that has been driven more by increased ticket prices than by an increase in audience size.

Why are movie audiences declining, or staying the same? The sharp decline in movie audiences back in the 1940s and 1950s was clearly a function of the rise of television as a new medium.[130] As *Long Tail* author Anderson points out, currently, movie audiences have many more alternatives than they did in the 1950s, due to cable/satellite television, home video, pay-per-view, and streaming sources. In its latest report on the state of the industry, the MPAA is reporting on movies' combined income from theatrical box office, physical disc sales, and digital sales.[131]

Movie studios and theaters have been facing the question as to whether the multitude of streaming movie and video services have been stealing their lunch money. But the answer to this question is not immediately obvious. Fithian, head of the National Association of Theatre Owners, notes that people who watch a lot of streaming movies also go to movies in theaters a lot, too. And, unsurprisingly, those who watch few movies on streaming rarely go to the theater. In short, people who like to watch movies watch them everywhere they can.[132] But there are more metrics we can use in this comparison. According to data from MPAA, globally consumers spent $42.6 billion on in-home digital entertainment, compared with $41.1 billion for movie tickets in 2018.[133] There are, of course, non-electronic forms of entertainment people engage in. The most popular cultural activity for 2019 was vising the library, something the average American did 10.5 times a year. This is about twice as often as people go to movie theaters and three times more often than attending a concert or live theater.[134]

Movies as a Brand. In the 1980s, domestic box office receipts accounted for more than 50 percent of movie income for studios; by 1995, this figure had fallen below 15 percent. Today, studios earn as much or more from **ancillary, or secondary, markets** as they do from domestic ticket sales. These are movie revenue sources other than the domestic box office. For example, home video rights may be worth twice the theatrical box office total.[135] Ancillary markets include the following:

- International distribution rights
- Pay-per-view rights
- Premium cable channel rights

- Network television
- Home video
- Book rights
- Toys and clothes
- Product placement

Summer and holiday blockbuster movies have evolved into more than just films. They have become entire cottage industries—brands, if you will—in and of themselves. Take the 2009 hit movie *Transformers: Revenge of the Fallen*. It was one of the highest-grossing movies for the year, producing $402 million in domestic box office; it also did $434 million in international ticket sales for a total of $836 million.[136] Electronics company LG created a limited-edition *Transformers* phone. *Transformers* director Michael Bay then directed a thirty-second television commercial for the phone, using the talents of Digital Domain, the same special-effects company that brought the robots to life in the movie. Digital Domain also did the effects for *Transformers*-themed commercials for fast-food company Burger King.[137] Prior to the movie's release, Kmart had a promotional tie-in giving away free tickets to the movie to people who bought at least $50 in menswear, as well as a promotion of *Transformers* toys, video games, and clothing. The 7-Eleven convenience store chain offered *Transformers* Slurpee cups, character straws, and movie-themed flavors.[138] On a much larger scale, the 2010 Chevy Camaro was featured in the movie as the Transformer called Bumblebee. Bumblebee served as a major character in video games developed for the Sony PlayStation 3, Microsoft Xbox 360, and Nintendo Wii. And if the toy version was not enough, Chevrolet built a special-edition Camaro with Bumblebee paint and a *Transformers* badge.[139]

The *Transformers: Revenge of the Fallen* brand example illustrates how important marketing tie-ins can be for a big-name movie and how the brand can become as important—and lucrative—as the movie itself.

CHAPTER REVIEW

CHAPTER SUMMARY ▶▶

Ways of recording motion on to film were first developed by photographers Étienne-Jules Marey and Eadweard Muybridge in the 1880s. Inventor and entrepreneur Thomas Edison applied their ideas in building the first practical motion picture display system, the kinetoscope. In France, the Lumière brothers invented the first portable movie camera and the first projector that could be used to display movies to a crowd.

Early directors such as Edwin S. Porter developed movie storytelling techniques that were expanded eventually into the feature-length film by D. W. Griffith. Griffith demonstrated that the public was interested in and willing to pay for larger-than-life films with longer running times. Griffith was also one of the first directors to seek outside financing for his movies.

From the 1920s through the 1940s, the studio system dominated moviemaking in the United States. Under the studio system, all the talent—from writers to directors to actors—was under contract to the studios. The major studios, such as Paramount and Warner Bros., ran the movie industry like a factory assembly line, controlling which movies were made and how they were distributed. The studio system ended when the U.S. Supreme Court broke up the studios' monopoly in 1948.

A troubled time followed for the movie industry. The 1950s brought new competition from television and a controversial blacklist of writers, directors, and actors who were suspected of being communists. Hollywood responded by producing bigger, more spectacular movies; making almost all movies in color; and breaking up giant theaters into smaller, multitheater complexes known as multiplexes.

The movie industry is currently dominated by high-budget blockbuster movies with a large, predefined audience and marketing tie-ins. The top ten movies for the year, generally either superhero stories or animated films, can account for more than a third of the annual box office. Although the initial domestic box office receipts are still important, movies often make more income from ancillary, or secondary, markets, such as foreign rights, video rights, and cable television rights. Blockbuster movies are now seen as a brand of interrelated products rather than just a movie. Yet smaller, low-budget movies often carry less risk of failure because they do not have to make nearly as much money to be profitable. Movies targeted at niche audiences can also be profitable if they have a controlled budget.

Moviemakers are increasingly relying on digital technology to make and promote movies. In addition to being used for special effects, digital technology makes it possible to shoot and edit low-budget movies using digital video rather than more expensive film, though several prominent directors still prefer to shoot using film. Directors can even shoot the movie on a blank soundstage and insert the sets and backgrounds digitally. Digital technology in the form of the internet is also being used to promote movies directly to consumers. While we still refer to the movie industry as coming out of Hollywood, states like Georgia and countries such as India produce more films than California does.

The movie industry has had a long history of dealing badly with race, with the Oscars generally giving most of its attention to films produced by men and starring white actors, though there have been bright spots in recent years with actors of color receiving honors. The industry has also had issues with how they have portrayed nonwhite characters and used white actors to portray characters of color.

Since the 1920s, there have been concerns about the effects that movies may have on young viewers. Hollywood has attempted to protect itself from criticism, initially by limiting the content of movies through its Production Code and more recently with age-based ratings.

In the late winter and spring of 2020, the entire movie industry closed globally in response to the COVID-19 pandemic, and it is unclear how movie audiences will respond to theaters opening back up. Movie studios have responded by experimenting with alternative ways of releasing new movies. Theatrical movies are also facing increased competition from home video. While the total box office has risen in recent years, the number of people attending the movies has declined. Moviemakers are responding with innovative new ways of promotion and by finding audiences for movies of more limited interest.

KEY TERMS ▶▶

kinetoscope   160

feature-length film   161

studio system   162

block bookings   163

synchronized soundtrack   163

talkie   163

House Un-American Activities Committee   164

Hollywood Ten   165

blacklist   165

multiplex   167

blockbuster era   167

computer-generated imagery (CGI)   170

whitewashing   176

Production Code   178

ancillary, or secondary, markets   183

REVIEW QUESTIONS ▶▶

1. How did the COVID-19 pandemic change the movie industry? What might be the long-term implications of those changes?

2. Why is Georgia considered to be such a friendly state for making movies?

3. How did the coming of television change the nature of the movies? How has the rise of online media transformed this process?

4. Explain how blockbuster movies become more than just movies for the companies releasing them. What products are developed to go with them?

5. What are the consequences of having a movie industry that is mostly controlled by white men? How would the movie industry be different if the people running the industry looked more like the people in the audience?

6. How does having access to a wide range of both popular and obscure movies change our movie-viewing habits? Is this level of choice a good thing or a bad thing? Why?

CHAPTER 8

TELEVISION AND VIDEO

Broadcast and Beyond

Watching live sports is the activity around the world that draws people age 18-49 to conventional TV and is a cornerstone of social gatherings in homes, restaurants, and bars. So, what happens when live sports abruptly stop? With all the live sports choices globally, that is an almost impossible thing to imagine. Think about it, there are the major U.S. professional leagues in football, basketball, baseball, and hockey; endless collegiate sports featuring both women and men; soccer from around the world; Japanese and Korean baseball leagues; there is even curling out of Canada.

So, what if it all those sports mysteriously disappeared, all at once, across the globe?

Broadcasters got a chance to discover what this would be like on March 11, 2020, when Rudy Gobert, center for the NBA's Utah Jazz, tested positive for the COVID-19 virus and the NBA suspended its season. Using the assumption that the NBA had to cancel the remainder of its 2020 season and the all-important playoffs, it would cost The Walt Disney Company's ESPN and ABC $481 million and WarnerMedia's TNT $211 million.[1]

Soon after the NBA's announcement, the Tokyo Summer Olympics got postponed until 2021. In addition to affecting thousands of athletes, this was also a big deal to broadcast partner NBC because the Olympics are one of the biggest live TV events of the year. NBCUniversal had already sold 90 percent of its commercial time worth $1.25 billion. In addition to making ad revenue for NBCU, the games were also designed to be part of the launch of their ad-supported streaming service Peacock and an opportunity to promote their fall shows.[2] In an era where people watch a wide range of programming, each with relatively small audiences, the Olympics are important because they are part of a very small group of programs that can still draw big audiences over an extended period of time.

No sporting event, professional or collegiate, is more important to broadcasters than the NCAA's annual March Madness collegiate basketball tournament. When the 2020 March Madness got canceled, the NCAA cut its annual payment to member schools from $600 million to $225 million. The biggest portion of the NCAA's annual income comes from the tournament. Yes, ticket sales and marketing partnerships matter, but most of the money comes from a fourteen-year, $10.8 billion television deal with CBS Sports and Turner Sports.[3]

SportsCenter has been ESPN's flagship show since 1979, but in the spring of 2020, for the first time there were no live sports. The host of ESPN's SportsCenter, Scott Van Pelt, describes what happened once all the sports were canceled. "Well, the analogy that I've landed on is that it's much like being a waiter in a restaurant where there are no chefs and there is not food," he told CNN. "[I] just don't know how long we can continue to trot out, 'Hey, baseball said they might play July' . . . I mean we basically call people and talk to them. It just turns into kind of this, 'How are things, how are you, what are you doing?'"[4] At a deeper level, Van Pelt says the show helps people continue on. "SportsCenter for the longest time has been that, this comfortable place to go."

The one thing Van Pelt says he cannot get let go of is missing the NCAA basketball tournament. "That was the one I'll never get over. For the young men and women, there were these remarkable stories that didn't get to end."

The other side of the shutdown is the fact that cable and satellite subscribers are spending an average of about $20 a month for sports programming, but these viewers likely have not received a refund for any of the games they did not get to see because they were not being played. But that does not mean that subscribers are happy with that outcome. Subscribers, especially those who got laid off during the pandemic recession, may be dropping their pay-TV packages and going to cheaper bundles of streaming content. "For some people, the decision may come down to economics," said Michael Huyghue, a sports lawyer and professor at Cornell Law School. "If someone loses their job or pay is cut, and they are paying for something they can't watch, they are more likely to cut the cord."

While subscribers were still paying for their sports channels during the pandemic shutdown, they were not watching them. Viewership of sports channels fell sharply from mid-March to mid-April 2020, compared to a similar period the year before. The *Wall Street Journal* found that ESPN had a 54 percent drop and the NBC Sports Network had a 58 percent drop.

The networks would have had to either lower the cost advertisers paid for their spots during this downturn or else give them "make good" spots later. But they still get their subscription money from every cable/satellite subscriber whether viewers ever actually watch the channel.

So, what did the sports networks program during the sports shutdown? In addition to running "classic" games (i.e., rerunning previously aired old games), they also showed an eSports basketball tournament with real-life NBA players at the video game controls, a H-O-R-S-E playground free-throw tournament with NBA stars playing from their homes, as well as sports-related programming, such as the NFL's player draft and a multipart documentary on the Chicago Bulls of the Michael Jordan era.[5]

Given that most sports revenue comes from television money, sports like baseball, basketball, and football could potentially play without fans present, but to athletes, that just did not feel right. NBA star LeBron James said in a podcast, "I just don't know how we can imagine a sporting event without fans. There is no excitement. There is no crying. There's no joy."

Dallas Mavericks team owner (and reality TV star) Mark Cuban said that once athletes start playing again there will be an enormous, pent-up demand for sports. "People will literally be doing anything to watch us," he told the *Wall Street Journal*. "They won't even necessarily be basketball fans. They will just be starving for new content, and we will be there to feed them."[6]

The television environment the sports networks are coping with has radically changed since ESPN launched back in 1979 on the relatively unknown medium of cable television with an episode of SportsCenter and a slow-pitch softball game from Wisconsin.[7]

Television has morphed from three nationwide broadcast networks to at least six; from no cable-only stations to hundreds; it's gained multiple formats for viewing prerecorded movies and shows at home. In this chapter, we look at how this new television world came about and how it has influenced society. We start with the development of broadcast television and then cable/satellite television. We then consider who controls the television industry, how the world portrayed on television compares to the "real" world, and how television is reinventing itself in an era where people are binge-watching shows on Netflix, Disney+, and Amazon Prime.

Broadcast Television

Television has progressed through massive changes since its birth in the 1930s. Initially, it provided a limited number of options that were broadcast at no cost to viewers. Viewers could watch only the programs offered by the major networks, and only at the times when those programs were being broadcast. But in the 1980s, the balance of power between audience and broadcasters began to change. Not only did VCRs allow viewers to choose when they would watch programs, but a range of broadcast, cable, and satellite channels allowed viewers a wider choice of what programs to watch.

Broadcast television in the United States is based on the idea that programming should be available to all viewers and should be paid for through advertising. Although today broadcast television is just one part of our TV diet, for many years it was the only item on the menu.

The story of Philo T. Farnsworth, the man who invented electronic television, is almost too good to be true. He was born in a log cabin, he rode a horse to school, and he developed the central concepts of television at the age of fourteen. Unlike Thomas Edison or even Samuel Morse, Farnsworth did not become a household name, yet he invented one of the most significant devices of the twentieth century.

Farnsworth was born in Utah in 1906. When he was twelve, his family settled in Idaho, and in their new house were magazines about radio and science, which fueled Farnsworth's creativity and imagination.[8] Farnsworth's heroes were Edison and Alexander Graham Bell, but he wanted to do them one better. He wanted to send out moving pictures as well as sound, and he wanted to do it all electronically, without any moving parts.

Farnsworth came up with the idea of breaking a picture into lines of light and dark that would scan across a phosphor-coated screen like words on a page. The electrons that would paint the picture on the screen would be manipulated by an electromagnetic field. According to television scholar Neil Postman, legend has it that Farnsworth's great idea came to him "while he was tilling a potato field back and forth with a horse-drawn harrow and realized that an electron beam could scan images the same way, line by line, just as you read a book."[9] By age twenty-one, Farnsworth had developed an all-electronic system for transmitting an image using radio waves. On September 7, 1927, he successfully transmitted an image of a straight line. "There you are, electronic television," he commented.[10]

Farnsworth, however, was not the only person working on the concept of television. Vladimir Zworykin, a Russian immigrant with a doctorate in engineering, was trying to develop television for David Sarnoff at RCA. Although he had made progress on electronic television and had filed for a patent on it in 1923, the U.S. Patent Office eventually ruled that Farnsworth had been the first to make a working television transmitter. The ruling was based in part on testimony from Farnsworth's high school chemistry teacher, who presented drawings that Farnsworth had made when he was sixteen showing almost exactly how to build a television transmitter. RCA kept fighting Farnsworth and promoting Zworykin and Sarnoff as the inventors of television, but Farnsworth eventually prevailed. For the first time, RCA had to pay royalties to an outside inventor.[11] Just when all looked rosy for Farnsworth, World War II broke out, and for four years, nothing was done with commercial television. Farnsworth's patents expired in 1947, right before television took off. Yet it was not missing out on the chance to cash in on his invention that Farnsworth came to regret. Farnsworth's son Kent later noted that his father was rather bitter about his invention in general:

I suppose you could say that he felt he had created kind of a monster, a way for people to waste a lot of their lives. Throughout my childhood his reaction to television was "There's nothing on it worthwhile, and we're not going to watch it in this household, and I don't want it in your intellectual diet."[12]

Library of Congress

▲ Philo T. Farnsworth developed the central principles of television broadcasting at age fourteen, and by the age of twenty-one, he had produced a working television transmission system.

The Beginning of Broadcasting

The first significant television broadcasts using all-electronic systems occurred in 1939, when NBC started sending out television broadcasts from the New York World's Fair. But U.S. involvement in World War II halted the manufacture of television sets in 1942, and most stations went off the air. Peace came in 1945, and by 1946, RCA had television sets back on the market.

From 1948 to 1952, the licensing of new television stations was frozen to give the Federal Communications Commission (FCC) and television producers time to figure out how the technology should be used and controlled. Because of the freeze, only some cities had television. The television cities saw drastic drops in attendance at movies and sporting events. Restaurant owners hated the popular variety program *Your Show of Shows*, which aired on Saturday nights, because customers rushed home to watch television instead of staying out to eat and drink.[13] During the same period, the Supreme Court issued its ruling in *United States v. Paramount Pictures* that broke the studios' control over the movie industry (see Chapter 7). Television was ready to take over the entertainment industry.

A number of shows characterized this early period of television. Milton Berle, host of the *Texaco Star Theatre*, came to be called "Mr. Television" and was known for his funny costumes and physical humor. *The Ed Sullivan Show* (originally called *Toast of the Town*) became the place to see new and innovative talent. In later years, Sullivan would feature the Beatles and Elvis Presley. The 1950s also saw a number of anthology dramas, essentially short plays or movies, with a new cast and story each week. One show that made a successful leap from radio to television was Edward R. Murrow's CBS news documentary series *Hear It Now*, which became *See It Now* on the new visual medium.

Lucy, Desi, and the End of Live Television. No other entertainment program of the 1950s would have a longer, more lasting impact than one produced by a brash redheaded actress and her Cuban American husband.

When Lucille Ball and Desi Arnaz created their groundbreaking sitcom *I Love Lucy* in 1951, they had to overcome two major obstacles. The first was persuading CBS to let Arnaz play Lucy's television husband. At that time, this was controversial because Ball was white and Arnaz Hispanic. The second challenge was that most television shows at the time were being broadcast live from New York City studios, but Lucy and Desi wanted to continue to live in California. Their solution was to film the show before a studio audience, edit the program like a movie, and ship it to New York to be broadcast. Within a year, *I Love Lucy* was the most popular show on television.

Being filmed rather than performed live meant that there were high-quality copies of *I Love Lucy* that could be shown repeatedly. Arnaz held the rerun rights to the show, which gave the couple the money to build their own television production company, Desilu Studios. More than fifty years after *Lucy* first went on the air, audiences are still laughing at the show.

The format Ball and Arnaz helped pioneer, a half-hour comedy filmed with three cameras before a live studio audience, became a mainstay of television programming. Today, the situation comedy remains one of the most popular program formats.[14]

The Arrival of Color Television. The networks started experimenting with color television as early as 1954, but by 1959, only three shows were regularly being shown in color. (The familiar NBC peacock logo was initially created to show black-and-white viewers that they were missing programs in color.) It was not until 1965 that all three of the original television networks were broadcasting in color. One reason for the slow acceptance of color was the price of the television sets. The *Boston Globe* notes that in 1965 color televisions cost the equivalent of what a midline HDTV set cost in 2000 (between $2,500 and $5,000).[15] The switch to color was not completed until the early 1970s.[16]

Cable and Satellite Television

Television has in effect become two media: broadcast and cable/satellite. Today, cable and satellite television constitutes almost a separate medium from broadcast television, but initially cable was designed as nothing more than a delivery system for broadcast channels.

▲ Lucille Ball and her husband, Desi Arnaz, helped create the modern situation comedy in 1951 with their show *I Love Lucy*, which was filmed rather than performed live.

In the 1940s, the early days of television, people in remote areas or in communities sheltered by mountains frequently could not receive the new signals. Among these was L. E. Parsons of Astoria, Oregon. Parsons wanted to have television, but the nearest station was 125 miles away. Her husband Ed solved the problem by placing an antenna on top of a local hotel and running a cable into their apartment. Once word got out that the Parsons family had television, the hotel, local bars, and even the neighbors started asking for connections to their antenna. This early form of cable television, which simply retransmitted broadcast channels, came to be known as **community antenna television (CATV)**.[17] Connecting to these early cable systems was expensive; the cost ranged from $100 to $200. Although there were isolated experiments with subscription channels, for the most part cable remained a way to serve areas with poor reception, and the FCC devised restrictive rules to keep it that way. Until the 1970s, cable was primarily a way to get a good TV signal, not additional programming.[18] By 1975, the face of cable television was beginning to change. The FCC began loosening the rules on cable companies, and new channels were being distributed via satellite.[19]

Home Box Office (HBO) was the first service to make the leap from merely providing access to providing programming. In 1975, it requested permission from the FCC to start sending out its programming nationwide via satellite. Surprisingly, not one of the **Big Three networks** (NBC, CBS, and ABC) objected to the upstart service as it gained access to their viewers across the country. After all, HBO was just an office, some videotape machines, and a satellite uplink. It had no affiliates, had no stations, and could reach only people who were on cable, a small fraction of the viewing market. But the satellite system had a key advantage. Five hundred cable systems could obtain the programming as cheaply as one. They just had to put up a dish to bring in the signal.

Ted Turner's Cable TV Empire

Although HBO was the first to go nationwide, no one has done more than Ted Turner to create modern cable television. After his father's suicide in 1963, the twenty-four-year-old Turner inherited a billboard company that was in financial trouble.[20] Turner was not content with running one of the nation's largest billboard companies, so in 1970, he bought Channel 17 in Atlanta. The ultrahigh-frequency (UHF) station was in serious financial trouble, largely because it was located on a part of the broadcast band that many television sets couldn't receive and many people didn't bother to look at. Turner promptly renamed the station WTCG, which stood for Turner Communications Group.

Turner's next big step was buying the last-place Atlanta Braves baseball team and the Atlanta Hawks basketball franchise, thus guaranteeing him exclusive rights to a pair of shows (the teams' games) that would run more than two hundred episodes a year. It was also programming that would motivate Atlantans to make the effort to find Channel 17.

When RCA launched a television satellite in 1976, Turner saw his next big opportunity. He realized that he could use the satellite to send his station nationwide and provide programming to the growing number of cable systems. On December 27, 1976, WTCG became Superstation WTBS (Turner Broadcasting System). With that step, Turner became one of the first of a new breed of television entrepreneurs who were turning local stations into national powerhouses.

At this point, Turner made the riskiest move of his career: He created Cable News Network (CNN), the first twenty-four-hour news channel. In its early years, CNN had many technical problems and no reputation to speak of. Critics, in fact, referred to CNN as the "Chicken Noodle Network" because it paid its employees poorly and was run amateurishly.[21] Despite the network's problems, however, viewers soon discovered that if they wanted breaking news, they could find it immediately on CNN. Unlike ABC, NBC, and CBS, CNN did not have to interrupt soap operas or sitcoms to put news on the air.

When ABC and Westinghouse tried to start a competing cable news service in 1982, Turner launched his second news network, CNN Headline News, which featured round-the-clock, half-hour newscasts. Since then, CNN has expanded to provide CNN Radio, CNN International, CNN Airport Network, and CNN en Español.

Jude Domski/Wire Image/Getty Images

▲ Cable television pioneer and CNN founder Ted Turner created a media empire with global reach that attempts to fulfill the ideal of the global village.

Turner took his idea of repackaging material a step further by buying up the MGM movie library and the Hanna-Barbera cartoon library, which gave him control of the *Flintstones*, the *Jetsons*, and *Scooby-Doo*. He used these pop-culture figures, along with additional sports broadcasting rights he acquired, to program WTBS, along with Turner Network Television (TNT), the Cartoon Network (CN), and Turner Classic Movies (TCM).

In 1996, Turner Broadcasting was acquired by media giant Time Warner, and although Turner lost direct control of his networks, he did get access to the Warner Bros. library of movies and classic cartoons. When *Time* magazine's editors declared Turner their "Man of the Year" in 1991, they wrote that he had fulfilled Marshall McLuhan's ideal of the global village. CNN has not made all people brothers and sisters, but *Time* said that the network has given people a window on the world:

> In 1991, one of the most eventful years of this century, the world witnessed the dramatic and transforming impact of those events of live television by satellite. The very definition of news was rewritten—from something that has happened to something that is happening at the very moment you are hearing of it. A war involving the fiercest air bombardment in history unfolded in real time—before the cameras.[22]

Before long, numerous channels were available to cable companies via satellite, including Black Entertainment Television (BET) and the children's network Nickelodeon. In 1978, amid much ridicule, the Entertainment and Sports Programming Network (ESPN) was launched as a twenty-four-hour-a-day sports channel carrying such little-known sports as Australian-rules football and curling. But ESPN quickly grew into one of the most popular channels on cable.[23] During this period, nine out of ten viewers were watching prime-time programs on the networks, which were still controlled by the people who had started the first radio networks: William Paley at CBS, David Sarnoff at NBC, and Leonard Goldenson at ABC.[24] However, the 1980s saw the growth of a new kind of cable—a service that brought new channels into the household along with the original networks. Cable television viewers now have access to a wide range of programming, most of which can be grouped into a few major categories:

- Affiliates of the Big Four broadcast networks (ABC, NBC, CBS, and Fox)

- Independent stations and smaller network affiliates

- Superstations—Local independent stations that broadcast nationwide via satellite (WTBS, WGN, etc.)

- Local-access channels—Channels offering local government programming and community-produced shows

- Cable networks—Advertiser-supported networks that may also receive small fees for each subscriber on a particular cable system (MTV, CNN, BET, etc.)

- Premium channels—Extra-cost channels that don't carry advertising (HBO, Showtime, etc.)

- Pay-per-view channels—Channels showing special events, concerts, and movies that subscribers pay for on an individual basis

- Audio services—High-quality music services[25]

Cable services offered massive competition to the broadcasters and created a new television landscape (though their importance as a television provider has fallen in recent years.) Approximately fifty-one million American households (less than 45 percent of all U.S. households) subscribe to cable service.[26] By way of comparison, streaming service Netflix has sixty-one million U.S. subscriptions (or about 76 percent of households), and Amazon Prime has sixty million. (See Figure 8.1.)

Top Ten Video Subscription Services

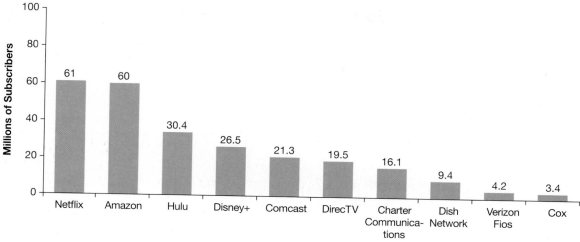

Source: Q4 2019 - S&P Global Intelligence, Company filings; data aggregated by NCTA.

Hollywood and the VCR. Although videotape has been used in television studios since the 1950s, it was not until the late 1970s that the **videocassette recorder (VCR)** became a household appliance that allowed viewers to make permanent copies of television shows. VCRs took time to catch on. Initially, there were two incompatible formats (VHS and Beta), and the machines themselves were expensive, costing $800 or more. In 1985, only two out of ten U.S. homes had VCRs, but by 1991, they could be found in seven out of ten homes.

Consumers loved the fact that they could record programs and watch them later, but movie and television producers were upset that people were recording—and keeping—programs without paying for them. They were also concerned that movies and programs would be duplicated and resold around the world. Universal and Disney sued Sony over its promotion of the VCR for recording movies, but in 1984, the U.S. Supreme Court ruled that television viewers had the right to record copyrighted programs for their own personal use. Piracy of the programming was clearly illegal, but this was not the fault of the equipment manufacturers.[27]

VCR ownership peaked in 1999, with nearly 89 percent of households owning a VCR. By the end of 2013, a survey by Gallup found that 58 percent of households still had a VCR. These were likely there to play old tapes in people's collections rather than to record new programming.

Direct-Broadcast Satellites. Satellite programming providers have been competing with cable since the 1980s, but their success was limited initially because of the rapid growth of cable, the large dish antennas required, and the limited number of channels consumers could receive. All this changed in the 1990s with the advent of the low-earth-orbit **direct-broadcast satellite (DBS)**. Several DBSs were launched to deliver programming through a new kind of antenna about the size of a pizza.

While it is difficult to find accurate current estimates of the number of DBS subscribers, approximately thirty-eight million U.S. households get satellite programming from either Dish Network or DirecTV.[28] Satellite service in the United States grew rapidly from the mid-1990s until about 2007, when adoption of the new delivery system stabilized. With the rise of online-based video sources, the use of both cable and satellite programming is expected to drop.[29] In Europe, which has less of a tradition of cable television than the United States, DBS services are very popular.

DBS is now competing head-to-head with cable. A problem the satellite services face in this competition is that their subscribers still must put up an old-fashioned antenna to get local broadcast stations. To address this drawback, in major markets DBS companies provide local stations via satellite as well.[30] Satellite providers are also starting to offer their programming as an online streaming service.[31]

Digital Television: HDTV and DVRs

Just as sound recording has moved to digital formats with CDs and MP3 files (see Chapter 6), so is television shifting from the analog technology of Farnsworth and Zworykin to computerized digital technology. All television broadcasting in the United States was scheduled to be digital by February 17, 2009, but in January 2009, the federal government decided that people weren't ready for the transition, despite several years of warnings that the change would be taking place. Critics of the move to digital broadcasting pointed out that many of the households that rely on broadcast signals for television have incomes under $30,000 and may have trouble affording the set-top box that converts digital broadcast signals into analog signals that old-fashioned television sets can display. To help solve this problem, the government issued coupons to help poor families buy the converters. In fact, a shortage of the coupons was among the reasons that the conversion was delayed.

VCRs were replaced predominantly by DVD or Blu-ray players, which were reported in 80 percent of all homes. While still very popular, disc players are down from 83 percent in 2005, likely because of the increased popularity of streaming content provided by companies like Netflix, Amazon, Disney+, and Hulu.[32] VCRs also faced replacement from digital video recorders (DVRs), such as TiVo or boxes provided by the cable/satellite company, that record television programs on a hard drive. The DVR lets a viewer jump in to start watching a recorded show fifteen minutes after it comes on the air. The viewer can then fast-forward through the commercials, and by the time the show is over, the viewer has caught up with the "live" broadcast. As of 2017, DVRs were in 53 percent of U.S. households, up from 40 percent in 2010 and 23 percent in 2007.[33] (This gives us another example of Secret 4—Nothing is new: Everything that happened in the past will happen again.)

As you may have noticed from those figures, the rate of growth of DVR adoption has slowed dramatically in the past few years. Why? It is probably not that people don't want to be able to watch shows on their own schedule. Instead, people have many more options now than just pre-recording shows to watch. For example, a 2015 study showed that 76 percent of U.S. households had access to a DVR or some form of **video on demand (VOD)**, including streaming services like Netflix, smart TV apps from the channel, or an on-demand system from their cable or satellite provider.[34]

On June 12, 2009, the last of the analog television broadcast stations was shut off. That does not mean that everyone started using new digital sets, however. Instead, many people continued to get their television from a digital cable or satellite box or get a converter box. On the two days following the shutdown of analog broadcasting, the FCC received approximately four hundred thousand calls to its hotline, considerably below the six hundred thousand to three million calls it was expecting.[35]

There are two distinct digital formats. **High-definition television (HDTV)** is in a wide-screen format (like a theater movie) and features an ultra-clear high-resolution picture with superior sound. The other digital format is **standard digital television**, which makes it possible to broadcast up to six channels on the same frequency space that now carries one channel.

▲ Although cable television remains the largest alternative to broadcast programming in the United States, satellite delivery is much more common throughout much of the world, as is illustrated by these rooftops in Fez, Morocco.

iStockphoto.com/Necip Yanmaz

(However, the picture is no better than that produced by existing signals.[36]) Using standard digital, a **Public Broadcasting Service (PBS)** station can choose to put out a single HDTV program or four digital programs at the current resolution, giving children a choice at any given time between *Arthur*, *Splash and Bubbles*, *Daniel Tiger's Neighborhood*, and *Dinosaur Train*.

The development of HDTV began in the 1980s, and on November 1, 1998, the launch of the space shuttle *Discovery* was the first event to be covered in a nationwide broadcast using a digital television signal. The broadcast was viewed by a tiny audience of just a few hundred people in twenty cities, with forty-two stations carrying digital signals.[37] As of March 2015, approximately 81 percent of U.S. homes had at least one HDTV set, and 52 percent of U.S. homes had more than one HDTV. Overall, 79 percent of the televisions in use in the United States in 2017 were HDTVs, up from 59 percent in 2014 and just 11 percent in 2007.[38]

Scott Olson/Getty Images

▲ Since all television broadcasting went digital in 2009, HDTVs have become increasingly popular. Viewers need either a cable/satellite connection or a converter box if they want to keep using old-school analog sets.

The Changing Business of Television

Television got its start with the three networks that dominated the radio industry in the 1940s: NBC, CBS, and ABC. There were some independent stations as well, such as WGN in Chicago and WOR in New York, which had grown out of major independent radio stations, but for the most part, everyone in the country was watching NBC, CBS, or ABC. This would remain the status quo until cable and VCRs exploded in popularity in the 1980s.

The Big Three **television networks** are the companies that have provided programs to local stations around the country since the start of the television industry. These affiliate stations require a license from the FCC, equipment, and a local staff. The choice of what shows to carry is up to the local station. If a station carries a particular program, the station receives a fee from the network, along with the revenue from selling local commercials during the show. The network makes its money from the national commercials that run during the program. If an individual station decides that it could make more money running a locally produced program, such as a college basketball game, or a program from an independent producer, it can do so. In that case, the station pays for the program but keeps all the advertising revenue. The only exceptions are the dozen or so stations that each network owns and operates; although they have a certain amount of independence, these stations must please their network owners.[39]

Noncommercial broadcasting in the United States was conceived as a way of delivering educational programming. Then Congress passed the Public Broadcasting Act of 1967, which established the Corporation for Public Broadcasting to provide funds for a wide range of noncommercial programs, including public service and educational programs. The noncommercial, or public, stations came to share programming through a new network, PBS. This nonprofit broadcast network is funded by government appropriations, private industry underwriting, and support from viewers.[40]

While PBS stations eventually became widely available, they tended to have small audiences except for their daytime children's programming, which included the groundbreaking

▲ *Sesame Street* features guests from a wide range of backgrounds, including James Earl Jones with regular cast members Big Bird, Mr. Hooper, and Maria.

Sesame Street.[41] *Sesame Street*'s creator, Joan Ganz Cooney, says that the goal of the show was to give disadvantaged inner-city children a head start on school: "We argued that it would make all the psychological difference in their success in school if [disadvantaged children] came in with the same kind of skills as a middle-class child."[42] *Sesame Street* was also designed to have a slick, fast-paced, commercial look. It even had "sponsors," such as the number 5 and the letters *Q* and *U*.

When the show premiered on November 8, 1969, it immediately grabbed a significant audience, and even now it is among the most watched of all children's shows. But was it a success at helping disadvantaged children develop reading and math skills? That question is difficult to answer. At least one major study found that *Sesame Street* was successful in preparing children for school, but that "advantaged" children gained fully as much from it as disadvantaged students; thus, the show was not closing the gap between the haves and the have-nots.

In the summer of 2015, Sesame Workshop, the nonprofit group that produces the show, announced that it was signing a five-year agreement with premium cable network HBO to air thirty-five new episodes a year, up from the eighteen new episodes per year it had made for PBS. After a nine-month period of being exclusively on HBO, the new episodes would appear for free on PBS. Officials from Sesame Workshop said they signed the contract to give the production company a more stable financial footing and to make the show available on mobile devices. Critics charged that airing the new episodes first on HBO would undermine the educational goals of helping low-income children with the show.[43]

In the 1990s, PBS started attracting a significant audience with programming such as the Ken Burns documentaries *The Civil War* and *Baseball*. Those larger audiences, in turn, led to support from a number of large corporations that hoped their brief underwriting announcements would reach the upscale audiences who watch PBS. These announcements are not quite commercials, but they do allow corporations to present a short message to viewers. Among recent PBS underwriters are oil giant BP, GMC Trucks, AT&T, and State Farm Insurance. More recently, PBS has been attracting big audiences with British imports such as *The Great British Baking Show*, *Victoria*, and *Poldark*.

The 1980s brought numerous changes to the broadcasting market. Not only were VCRs and cable becoming popular, but there was also a new broadcast network. Australian newspaper publisher Rupert Murdoch started the Fox broadcast network after buying 20th Century Fox and incorporating it into his mammoth global media empire (see Chapter 3). He put the new network on the air in 1986 by buying stations in six of the top ten television markets. Although companies had tried to set up alternative broadcast networks before, none had really succeeded. Murdoch had an advantage in that during the 1980s people were becoming accustomed to watching cable channels, which meant they were no longer wed to regular network programming.

Fox was able to attract independent stations because it was offering them free programming rather than making them rely on syndicated material, most of which consisted of network reruns. The offerings were initially limited, with a late-night talk show starring Joan Rivers followed by Sunday evening programming beginning in 1987.

While Fox managed to attract viewers with shows such as *The Simpsons* and *Married . . . With Children*, what put it on the map was stealing NFL football away from the Big Three.

NFL football was a show that people were accustomed to watching; now they just had to watch it on a new network. Fox also brought in the under-thirty viewers coveted by advertisers with hit programs such as *The X-Files* and *Melrose Place*.[44] The Big Three broadcast networks were becoming the **Big Four networks**.

More recently, Fox has been attracting large audiences with hit shows such as *The OT*, *The Masked Singer*, *Bob's Burgers*, and *The Simpsons* (which as of this writing has been on the air more than thirty years!).

Defining Ratings

One of the biggest concerns for television networks, whether broadcast or cable, is the size of their audiences. Rates for commercials, which provide all the income for broadcast networks and a substantial portion of the income for cable services, are determined by how many people are viewing a show at a given time.

Measuring television audiences used to be pretty simple, at least in principle. You found out how many people watched a given show at a given time on one of three major networks, and you had your answer. The fact that you depended on a limited sample of people who had to fill out complex diaries or use a set-top "people meter" may have complicated things a bit, but basically it was simple. But now we have four major English-language broadcast networks, the Univision Spanish-language broadcast network, PBS, several minor broadcast networks, dozens of major cable networks, and hundreds of specialized cable networks. There is also the issue of measuring the alternative methods for viewing these programs, the most important of which is delayed viewing on DVR.

Due to the expansion of viewing choices, the ratings required for a show to be a success have gotten smaller. In 2019, the top-rated show on broadcast television was NBC's *Sunday Night Football* which could have as many as 24 million viewers. The top scripted show was the long-running *Big Bang Theory*, which drew 24.8 million viewers for its series finale.[45]

Now that DVRs are in more than 53 percent of all homes, the number of people watching shows on a delayed basis has become more important. Nielsen, which measures television audiences, now considers the following:

- Live only—People who are watching the program live as it happens.

- Live + SD—People who watch the program the same day as it airs. If you record a program on your DVR and start watching it fifteen minutes after it starts, this is you.

- Live + 3—People who watch the program live or within three days of airing.

- Live + 7—People who watch the program within seven days of its airing. This is the most complete measure of a show's popularity. (It does not, however, account for the episode of the Food Network's competition show *Chopped* that I recorded three months ago but finally watched last night.[46])

The major provider of viewership data, known as ratings, is Nielsen Media Research. The company keeps track of the shows watched in nine thousand homes located across the United States. Although the Nielsen families receive a token payment for their participation, they are essentially volunteering to keep track of all their television viewing. Nielsen uses a combination of methods to measure audience size. In the largest urban markets, the company uses a **people meter**. Viewers push buttons on the machine to record who is watching programs at specific times. In smaller markets, viewers fill out daily diaries, listing what they watched.

While Nielsen tracks overall network viewership throughout the year, the company looks at the audience size of individual stations four times a year (November, February, May, and July) during periods known as **sweeps**. Networks and individual stations often schedule their best—or at least most popular—programming during sweeps periods to attract the highest possible ratings. These higher ratings allow them to charge more for commercials. Nielsen also tracks the ages and sex of audience members, and advertisers are oftentimes as concerned about the demographics of their audience as they are about the absolute size of it.

Nielsen provides networks and stations with several different measurements. The most important of these is the **rating point**, the percentage of the total potential television audience actually watching the show. For example, Nielsen estimated that there were 119.6 million households with televisions in use in 2017. If 1,196,000 homes viewed a particular program, that would produce a rating of 1 (1,196,000 / 119,600,000 = .01, or 1 percent of the total potential audience). A program viewed in 15 million households would have a rating of 12.5.[47]

The second major measurement Nielsen provides is the **share**, the percentage of television sets in use that are tuned to a particular show. Instead of telling producers how many households are watching the show, the share measures how popular a particular show is compared to everything else that is broadcast at the time. Although a show that airs at 1:00 a.m. might have a relatively low rating (say, 3 or 4), it could have a high share (15 or 20) because a large portion of a small audience is watching it.[48]

An Earthquake in Slow Motion

Fox, cable, and the VCR changed everything for the television industry—a set of changes that media writer Ken Auletta has called "an earthquake in slow motion." In 1976, the prime-time viewing audience belonged to the Big Three, with nine out of ten viewers watching network programming. By 1991, the Big Three had lost a third of their viewers. These viewers hadn't stopped watching television; they had just moved to other channels. In 1976, the typical home had a choice of seven broadcast channels; by 1991, it had a choice of thirty-three cable channels.[49] Today, homes with digital cable programming can have access to hundreds of channels along with a host of streaming services.

Another part of the earthquake was that the original Big Three networks were sold to new owners in 1985. NBC was taken over by General Electric, CBS was purchased by investor Larry Tisch, and ABC was purchased by Capital Cities Communications. Since that time, ABC has been acquired by Disney, CBS has been purchased and spun off by Viacom, and Comcast has bought NBC. The networks are no longer controlled by the people who started them.[50] The earthquake also affected profits. Revenues for the broadcast networks plummeted in the 1990s, whereas cable network revenues grew. Cable channels typically make more profit than the broadcast networks. Cable channels are the most profitable part of The Walt Disney Company, NBCUniversal, Fox Corporation, and WarnerMedia.

As one of the main homes of live sports, the ESPN group of sports networks has long been one of the most profitable parts of the Disney empire, but it may be facing challenges in the changing television environment that go far beyond the lost viewers from the spring of 2020 when the COVID-19 virus shut down virtually all sports programming. ESPN spent nearly $8 billion on sports broadcast rights in 2018, but the network declined from 100 million subscribers in 2012 to just under 90 million in 2017.[51] Given that each subscriber pays an average of about $8 per month, that's a loss of $80 million a year of income. Despite their lower profitability, the broadcast networks generally have much bigger audiences than cable services. The most popular basic cable show of 2018–2019 was AMC's zombie drama *The Walking Dead*, which attracted an average of 7.9 million viewers per week, while more typical shows attract audiences of 4 million or so. Top-rated network shows such as *NCIS* typically attract 17 to 18 million viewers.[52]

Why, then, are cable channels making more money than the broadcast networks? Traditionally, cable programs have cost less to produce than network programs, but spending on cable shows has been growing rapidly over the past several years. But the biggest difference is that broadcasters have a single source of revenue—advertising—whereas most cable channels have both a subscription fee and advertising revenue. The cable channels collect their subscription fees whether a given subscriber actually watches the channel. Those fees range from $7.69 a month for ESPN, to $2.09 for TNT, to approximately $2.00 for Fox News, down to 22 cents for the Food Network.[53]

While Auletta initially wrote about the earthquake in slow motion in the 1990s, the changes that got started then have not gone away. In the past decade-and-a-half, we have seen the rise of a whole new form of television—streaming services like Netflix, Hulu, and Amazon Prime. Netflix is the most popular of these services with approximately 158 million subscribers globally and 61 million in the United States.[54] Each of those U.S. subscribers pays approximately $12.99 per month for the most popular plan to access a host of movies, old TV shows, and original programming. Sound a lot like cable? Except that Netflix doesn't require a cable contract to watch— only access to a high-speed online connection—and viewers can choose what they want to watch and when they want to watch it.[55]

(We will talk more about streaming and how it's transforming television later on in this chapter, including how Disney and WarnerMedia are putting forward their new streaming services.)

Diversity on Television

Broadcast television and the major cable networks have been roundly criticized for presenting a distorted view of reality. Aside from the issue that people on television comedies and dramas not only are attractive and funny but also resolve problems in less than an hour, there are complaints that television presents a world that is overwhelmingly white, male, and middle class.

Portrayals of Asian Americans. Scott Sassa, a Japanese American network television executive, recalls being upset as a child when he saw an Anglo playing an Asian character. "I've got to tell you, growing up, seeing David Carradine as a Chinese guy [ticked] you off," Sassa said, referring to the martial arts series *Kung Fu*. (For more on the practice of having white actors play characters of color, see the section of Chapter 7 on whitewashing.) Sassa says that the networks will have to reach out to nonwhites in a meaningful way if they want to hold on to their audiences:

> You not only want to see someone that looks like you on TV—you want to see someone that is a role model, someone that you want to aspire to be. That's what we need to do— create role models that are diverse, that make people in these minority groups feel good.[56]

Improvements in portrayal of Asian characters has been a mixed bag since Sassa's childhood. For decades, white actor Hank Azaria played a range of characters on Fox's long-running animated show *The Simpsons*. But for all the characters he played—Moe the bartender, Police Chief Wiggum and Professor Fink—the one he was best known for was Apu, the Indian immigrant proprietor of the Kwik-E-Mart convenience store. Azaria, who had voiced Apu since the show's start back in 1990, says he based Apu in part on British actor Peter Sellers's performance of a bumbling Indian actor in brownface. Azaria gradually became uncomfortable with performing the character after hearing a range of criticism, most notably that from comic Hari Kondabolu, who produced the documentary *The Problem With Apu*. Kondabolu said in a 2012 performance, "There's now enough Indian people where I don't need to like you just because you're Indian," he said. "Because growing up, I had no choice but to like this: Apu, a cartoon character voiced by Hank Azaria, a white guy. A white guy doing an impression of a white guy making fun of my father."[57]

"Once I realized the way this character was through of, I just didn't want to participate in it anymore," Azaria told the *New York Times*. "It just didn't feel right." So in 2019, Azaria dropped Apu from his set of *Simpsons* characters.

Contrast this with ABC's show *Fresh Off the Boat* that featured a predominantly Asian cast portraying the life of a Taiwanese-American immigrant family. Randall Park, a Korean-American actor, plays the part of Louis Huang, the husband/father on the show. Park had resisted playing accented parts in the past to avoid parts that "were either stereotypical or offensive in some way," he said. "The problem is when a character represents nothing but being foreign, and that accent is symbolic of the only thing that character represents. . . . I felt like with [*Fresh Off the Boat*'s] Louis and other characters that I've played, the accents were more a part organic to who the person was."[58]

Fresh Off the Boat ran six seasons from 2015 to 2020. Comedian Jenny Yang, who played the matriarch of the series, said she created the term "rep sweats" to describe the pressure of having to be one of the few Asian-American characters on TV who was responsible for how Asians would be represented. "[Asians] are so invisible, every time you have an opportunity to see yourself on TV, you hold your breath," she said.[59]

Huffington Post pop culture blogger Meron Mogos noted in 2013 that most recent shows on television had at least one supporting ethnic character, but few had nonwhites in starring roles. This started to change in 2012 when the hit ABC show *Scandal* went on the air, the first show in four decades to have an African American woman as the lead.[60] The show, starring Kerry Washington, was created by Shonda Rhimes, who also did *Grey's Anatomy*. Washington's character is based on real-life African American woman Judy Smith, who was a communication director for the George W. Bush White House and then went to work as a crisis management expert.

(It has been accurately pointed out by some media literacy students in California that the popular kids series *That's So Raven* was fronted by Raven-Symoné Pearman, who played an African American girl with psychic powers that let her see briefly into the future.[61] The show ran on the Disney Channel from 2003 to 2007.)

Washington told CNN in an interview that her character Olivia "is someone who happened to be born female and black and those elements add to who she is as a human being. Do I think another person of another race could play her? Yes. Do I think it would change the story a little bit? Do I think it would change the character a little bit? Yes."[62] Washington told *BlackAmericaWeb*,

> It's really exciting that the business of storytelling is beginning to understand that people respond to inclusivity. You don't make a success of yourself by leaving people out. You don't make a success of yourself by leaving people off the table. We are starting to see more diversity and it's really great. It's great for everybody. It's great for Black people, it's great for white people, it's great for everybody.[63]

Scandal has been followed with several more shows featuring Black female leads (or as leading characters), including Viola Davis of ABC's *How to Get Away With Murder*, Tracee Ellis Ross in the ABC series *Black-ish*, and HBO's *Insecure*, which is based on Issa Rae's web series *The Misadventures of an Awkward Black Girl*. Madeline Berg, writing for *Forbes*, notes that these shows all draw substantial non-Black audiences. *Black-ish* has a 79 percent non-Black viewership, and *Insecure*'s audience is 61.5 percent non-Black. Marketing professor Miro Copic told Berg, "The notion that consumers and viewers would be resistant to seeing a show with main characters that are African American or another ethnicity is finally starting to decline."[64]

LGBTQ programming may not be particularly common on broadcast television, but it is finding more of a home at streaming services like Netflix. In April 2018, the LGBTQ arts and culture website *Autostraddle* ran a list of "53 Queer TV Shows to Stream on Netflix." Dr. Candice Roberts, who teaches and researches media studies along with queer theory, wrote, "A few years ago 53 different queer-themed television shows on any single media platform would have seemed implausible if not impossible." Not all the movement of LGBTQ content into the mainstream (Secret 3) has been seen as positive, however. There are certainly critics and consumers who would prefer not to see such material and wish that they could block it from showing up in their search. But there has been pushback from the gay community as well. Roberts wrote, "Eve Ng, a media researcher at Ohio University, often discusses what she calls 'media gaystreaming,' the process by which queer narratives are appropriated in mainstream media." The move of *RuPaul's*

Drag Race from the gay-themed LOGO network to VH1 is an example of this.[65]

On the management side of things, in February 2016, Disney announced that Channing Dungey, an African American woman, was named president of ABC Entertainment. Dungey is the network's first African American president and has been involved with the development of hit shows such as *Scandal*, *Criminal Minds*, *How to Get Away With Murder*, and *Once Upon a Time*.[66] If you want to make some comparisons on your own, 2019 U.S. Census Bureau estimates break down the current population of the United States by race and origin as follows:

- White, not Hispanic—76.5 percent
- Hispanic—18.3 percent
- African American—13.4 percent
- Asian—5.9 percent
- More Than One Race—2.7 percent
- American Indian—1.3 percent
- Pacific Islander—0.2 percent

(These values add up to more than 100 percent because some people overlap in categories.[67])

▲ Peppermint (aka Agnes Moore) was the runner-up in season nine of the VH1 show, *RuPaul's Drag Race*. The show moved to the more mainstream channel VH1 from the gay-themed LOGO network that season.

Univision and Spanish-Language Broadcasting. Although Latinos are seriously underrepresented on the Big Four English-language networks, there has been substantial growth in Spanish-language television. The network's popular telenovelas helped take the network to the number-four spot in the ratings for a week in August 2015 in the eighteen-to-thirty-four demographic; and in 2013, Univision got the critical fourth place in the Nielsen February sweeps period among the prized audience demographic of adults aged eighteen to forty-nine. For 2017, Univision was tied for fifth place with The CW among all broadcast networks, but was suffering the downturn that much of Spanish-language media has as larger portions of the Hispanic community are native born rather than immigrant, and are either bilingual or speak English exclusively.[68] More recently, Univision has been facing increased competition from a range of streaming services as well as the growing presence of NBCUniversal-owned Telemundo.[69]

News on Univision tends to take a clear point of view that has more in common with Latin American and European journalism than that of the more detached, objective American broadcast network reporting. Anchor Jorge Ramos says his journalistic role model is really Italian journalist Oriana Fallaci, who was famous for her confrontational interviews with Yasir Arafat, Moammar Gadhafi, and Ayatollah Khomeini. During the 2016 presidential campaign, Ramos battled with Republican candidate Donald Trump, even getting thrown out of one of Trump's press conferences in Dubuque, Iowa, during the primary season. But confronting difficult sources is nothing new for Ramos. He and his cameraman once tried to do an ambush

▲ Univision news anchor Jorge Ramos has said that his work involves drawing attention to issues that are important to Latinos and immigrants, people he says don't ordinarily have a voice.

interview with Cuban leader Fidel Castro outside of a summit meeting in Mexico, which led to Ramos being knocked to the ground by Castro's bodyguard. On another occasion, Ramos got death threats after questioning Colombian president Ernesto Samper about taking campaign contributions from the Cali drug cartel.[70]

The most popular programs on Univision have been the **telenovelas**, or soap operas, which make up fifteen of the top twenty Spanish programs and are popular in both Latin America and the United States. Produced primarily in Mexico and Brazil, the telenovelas are exceedingly detailed and involved miniseries, with each story lasting six months to a year.[71] But Telemundo is doing a good job of attracting a younger audience with its so-called *narconovelas* about Mexican drug lords that target bilingual American-born Latinos. As the *Wall Street Journal* noted in 2018, Latino immigration has slowed significantly during the past ten years, the direction of flow being more from the United States to Mexico than the other way around. *Journal* television reporter Keach Hagey writes that Telemundo is dealing with the fact that the American Hispanic population has become increasingly dominated by Hispanics born in the United States. "Telemundo has developed a more dynamic content that is more attuned with U.S.-based Latinos than is the case with Univision content, which has been more traditional, with an emphasis on the values of traditional Mexico," said Latino media consultant Federico Subervi.[72]

Black Entertainment Television. Cable television also has networks that attempt to appeal to non-white audiences. The most significant is Black Entertainment Television (BET). The twenty-four-hour network reaches nearly 85 million households. For 2017, the network was ranked forty-ninth among basic cable networks, averaging a viewership of 475,000, up 7 percent from the year before.[73]

Started in 1980 as a local Washington, DC, channel, BET was the nation's first Black-owned cable network.[74] BET initially carried primarily talk shows and music videos; more recently, the network found considerable success in 2017 with the hip-hop reality wedding series *Gucci Mane & Keyshia Ka'Oir: The Mane Event* along with a range of dramas, comedies, competition shows, awards shows, and reruns of programs from other networks.[75]

Aside from the network's success in attracting viewers, BET became profitable because major advertisers such as General Motors were looking for media to reach nonwhite consumers. The *New York Times* says that this is part of an ongoing trend of multicultural marketing aimed at African American, Hispanic, and Asian American consumers, which account for increasing segments of the U.S. population. BET's Louis Carr says that nonwhite consumers have to be taken much more seriously, not as a secondary target but as a primary target. In places like New York, Chicago, Los Angeles, Detroit, and Philadelphia, if you add up the African American population, the Hispanic population, and the Asian population, they are not minorities anymore. They are majorities (another example of Secret 3—Everything from the margin moves to the center).[76]

Television and Society

Few new social institutions have become an integral part of society faster than television did in the late 1940s and early 1950s. In 1948, there were fewer than one hundred thousand televisions in use; a year later, that number was more than one million, and by 1959, there were fifty million sets in use. In less than ten years, television had become a part of everyday life in the United States. Television viewership tended to grow more slowly in the highly regulated European market, something we talk about in depth in Chapter 15.

As television became commonplace, people started to worry about its effects on viewers: How much time were people spending viewing television? What activities would it replace? Why were people watching television? Most important, what effect, if any, would the content of television programs have on viewers? Would it lead to violence and juvenile delinquency? Would it take children into the world of adults too early? Would it transform society?

In *Tube of Plenty*, Erik Barnouw argues that television had a revolutionary impact on society:

The advent of television was widely compared, in its impact, with that of the Gutenberg printing press centuries earlier. Television was beginning to be seen as the more revolutionary innovation. The reasons were so obvious that they had seldom been discussed. Television viewing required no skill beyond normal human functions. Reading, on the other hand, was a skill acquired over years via effort and drilling—and not acquired by everyone. It generally involved the mediation of father, mother, grandfather, grandmother, teacher, priest, and others, a factor favoring social continuity, a transmittal of values. Television short-circuited all this. It could begin in cradle or playpen, and often did. It could bypass father, mother, grandfather, grandmother. It reached the child long before teacher and priest. Their role in the acculturation process had been sharply reduced. They had sporadically, fitfully, sought to recapture a more decisive role by seeking to control the images on the tube—but that control had slipped elsewhere, to the world of business. In a development of historical significance, the television's messages had become dominant social doctrine.[77]

Barnouw is arguing that although television audiences have fragmented with the growth of cable, satellite, and home video, television is still the dominant shared experience in the modern world, reaching more people than schools, families, and churches.

One reason social critics have been so concerned about the influence of television is that Americans spend a lot of time watching it. The *Recode* blog reported that in 2017, Americans multitasked themselves to a little more than 12 hours of media use per day. Conventional television (broadcast, cable, and satellite) makes up about 4 hours a day, 3 hours and 17 minutes on mobile devices, 2 hours on a desktop computer, and 36 minutes a day on other connected devices. Keep in mind that binge-watching a program on your computer, tablet, or phone would not be considered watching television by this study, even though you might see it that way.[78] The U.S. Bureau of Labor Statistics estimates that people age fifteen and older spent an average of 2.7 hours a day watching television. This study did not account for time on mobile devices or other streaming sources.[79]

Television viewing can also be looked at in terms of how it dominates our free time. A study of the functions of television in everyday life notes that on average Americans spend half of their leisure time watching television. The same study showed that at any given moment in the evening more than one-third of the U.S. population is watching television; in the winter, that proportion rises to more than 50 percent.[80] A study by the Kaiser Family Foundation found that children spend an average of four and a half hours a day watching television content. This is despite the fact that they are spending less time in front of a television set. How is this possible? While television sets are still the most popular media device among young people, the TV set is gradually losing ground to video they can watch on their computer screens, tablets, or phones.[81] (For more on these figures, turn back to Chapter 1.)

Although television viewing is often reported in terms of average amounts of time spent viewing, such figures do not always give a complete picture. The differences between heavy and light television viewers can be significant. A 1990 study found that people who watch a lot of television tend to spend more time home alone than light viewers. The study also showed that light viewers spend more time walking than heavy viewers.

Unfortunately, these studies usually cannot determine why people behave in these ways. Do heavy viewers stay home specifically to watch television, or are they unable to get out of the house for one reason or another? Perhaps busy people who like to walk do not have time to watch television. One finding that is not difficult to interpret was that people who watch sports on television also tend to participate in sports. The study also found that the amount of time people spend reading does not seem to be affected by how much television they watch.[82]

How Do Viewers Use Television?

In addition to examining how much television people are watching, researchers have studied how and why people watch television. These studies seek to determine what uses people make of television

CBS Photo Archive/Getty Images

▲ Actress Mary Tyler Moore raised havoc with network censors in 1961 when she danced on *The Dick Van Dyke Show* wearing capri pants. Moore defended her outfit, saying, "I'll dress on the show the way I dress in real life."

viewing and what gratifications (or benefits) they gain from it. The central premise of these studies is that television (like other media) is not an actor that does things to viewers. Instead, audience members are active participants who select programming to meet particular needs.

What might these needs be? The study *Television in the Lives of Our Children* found that children watch television for many of the same reasons that adults do:

- To be entertained.

- To learn things or gain information. In many cases, this information relates to socialization: how to act like an adult, how to be a better athlete, how other people live.

- For social reasons. The content of TV doesn't matter so much as the fact that they watch it with friends or talk about it at school the next day.

The researchers also found that different children watched the same program for different reasons. One child might watch a cartoon show because he was lonely and the show provided company, another might watch it because it made her laugh, and a third might watch it because his friends were watching it.[83]

Standards for Television

In the 1950s and 1960s, networks and advertisers imposed strict controls on what could be shown on television. For example, Mary Tyler Moore and Dick Van Dyke played the married couple Laura and Rob Petrie on *The Dick Van Dyke Show*, which aired from 1961 to 1966. Although married, the Petries had to sleep in separate twin beds. Sponsors also raised their eyebrows when Moore wore jeans and capri pants on the show because these garments might be considered suggestive. Moore fought the sponsors and won, saying, "I'll dress on the show the way I dress in real life."[84] This was the era when comedian Ball had to use the word *expecting* rather than *pregnant* on her show when she was obviously carrying a child.[85] What could be shown was determined by each network's own standards and practices department. The goal of these departments, which at one time had as many as sixty people working in them, was to make sure the network did not lose viewers or sponsors because of offensive content. Since the 1980s, they have decreased in size by 50 percent or more. This change is due partly to a loosening of societal standards throughout the 1970s, but it is also a response to the more explicit content of cable television programming.[86] Alfred Schneider, who served as a censor for ABC television for more than thirty years, observes that the networks feel freer to deal with difficult topics today than in earlier decades:

> Sometimes the quality of a particular program allows you to do things that you would not permit in other programs. I once said that in my lifetime there would never be full frontal nudity on network television. I was wrong. I lived to see *War and Remembrance*, where I permitted full frontal nudity in the concentration camp scenes. I finally justified it by saying that this was not nudity, this was death.
>
> As we see the growth of more distribution systems, the growth of independents, my position will have to change. As the populace becomes more educated, more inquisitive, more concerned about issues, I will be more comfortable taking greater risks knowing that people will seek out their choices.[87]

In 1997, broadcasters fundamentally changed their programming controls; instead of placing an occasional warning before programs considered inappropriate for children, they implemented a two-part rating system modeled after the one used for movies. There is an age-appropriateness rating that closely matches the movie system, with ratings of G, PG, TV-14 (for fourteen-year-olds and older), and TV-MA (for mature audiences). Many networks also provide a content rating of S (sexual content), V (violence), L (crude language), and/or D (adult dialogue).[88] It was also in 1997 that the so-called V-chip, an electronic device allowing parents to block programs with certain content ratings, began to be included in television sets.

TEST YOUR MEDIA LITERACY

NO SENSE OF PLACE

Media scholar Joshua Meyrowitz, in his book *No Sense of Place*, argues that the very existence of television is an influence on society because it breaks down the physical barriers that separate people. In the past, he says, people were limited to interacting with those whom they could see and hear face-to-face. Meyrowitz describes how the coming of electronic media, and television in particular, changed this:

> The boundaries marked by walls, doors, and barbed wire, and enforced by laws, guards, and trained dogs, continue to define situations by including and excluding participants. But today such boundaries function to define social situations only to the extent that information can still be restricted by restricting physical access.[89]

These boundaries can be broken at many levels. A child watching television can see people talking about adult topics such as infidelity, pregnancy, or cross-dressing. A teenager in New York City can see the impact of drought on people in Iowa. Young men can listen in on what women say on a "girls' night out." In each of these cases, in the pretelevision era, the viewer would have been isolated because of his or her "place," whether it was geographic location, age, sex, or socioeconomic status. But television gives everyone an equal view into these formerly separate worlds.

This breakdown of place has occurred not just within the United States, but throughout the industrialized world. As we discussed in Chapter 3, the United States is the world's largest supplier of entertainment programming; it is also the largest supplier of imagery to the world. The most important effect of CNN and other satellite-based television news services is that they give people everywhere in the world access to the same information at the same time, whether those people are heads of state,

diplomats, soldiers, or citizens. The late Don Hewitt, longtime producer of the CBS newsmagazine *60 Minutes*, has said that this global sharing of information is changing the world:

> When there was a disaster, it used to be that people went to church and all held hands. Then television came along, and there was this wonderful feeling that while you were watching Walter Cronkite, millions of other Americans were sharing the emotional experience with you. Now the minute anything happens they all run to CNN and think, "The whole world is sharing this experience with me."[90]

WHO is the source?

Who is Joshua Meyrowitz? What book has he written?

WHAT is he saying?

According to Meyrowitz, how has television transformed society? What does Meyrowitz mean when he says television and other electronic media break down the barriers of place? What kind of barriers does Meyrowitz suggest are being broken by television?

WHAT evidence is there?

What examples of this process does Meyrowitz provide? When and where does this process take place?

WHAT do you and your classmates think about Meyrowitz's arguments?

List some examples of how television has let you see aspects of everyday life that would normally remain hidden from you. Does television take you "places" you couldn't go to otherwise? If so, list some examples. Do you ever use television to deliberately watch worlds you wouldn't be able to see otherwise?

Television producers were initially concerned that shows with ratings for violence or sexual content might be harder to market. But rather than restricting television content, broadcasters have used the ratings to warn viewers that material on a program will be explicit. As Robert Thompson, director of Syracuse University's Bleier Center for Television and Popular Culture, has noted,

> The people who wanted ratings to put the brakes on this new explosion of raunchy television saw just the opposite happen. Anybody should have seen this coming. If you give producers the opportunity to use a TV-MA rating, it's an invitation to make TV-MA programs.[91]

For the most part, the R-equivalent TV-MA rating has been confined to cable and streaming shows such as History's *Vikings*, HBO's *Westworld* and *Game of Thrones*, Netflix's *13 Reasons Why*, Hulu's *The Handmaid's Tale*, AMC's multiple *Walking Dead* series, and, of course, Comedy Central's raunchy cartoon *South Park*.[92] The Big Four broadcast networks have rarely aired programs with the TV-MA rating, the most notable exceptions being uncut broadcasts of serious R-rated movies such as *Schindler's List* and *Saving Private Ryan*.

The Problem of Decency

The line of what was acceptable on broadcast television was redrawn following the 2004 Super Bowl halftime show on CBS when Justin Timberlake exposed Janet Jackson's breast for nine-sixteenths of a second. The FCC received more than five hundred thousand complaints.[93] Immediately following the broadcast, the FCC started talking about the problem of indecency on television. References to sexual or bodily functions are considered to be indecent. FCC rules say that broadcast radio and television stations can't air indecent material between 6:00 a.m. and 10:00 p.m., when children are most likely to be listening or watching. This differs from obscene programming (discussed further in Chapter 14), which "describes or shows sexual conduct in a lewd and offensive way" and has no "literary, artistic, political, or scientific value."[94] Obscene material is not protected by the First Amendment. Rules about indecency apply to broadcast materials but not to cable or satellite material. On June 29, 2012, the case regarding CBS finally came to a conclusion with the U.S. Supreme Court declining to review a lower court decision throwing out the fine.[95] As a side note in this case, cable news host Nancy Grace also exposed her nipple on the reality show *Dancing with the Stars*, this time for almost an entire second. But so far the FCC has not acted on any complaints, and it appears unlikely to lead to any fines or other legal action.[96] There is no single standard for what constitutes broadcast indecency, and this standard clearly changes over time. During the 1990s and early 2000s, bare bottoms became common on shows such as *NYPD Blue*. But since the Janet Jackson fuss, even this minimal nudity has been digitally blurred when shown on broadcast television, and reality programs such as *Survivor* have become careful to digitally blur any hint of nudity that occurs during the programs' competitions as well.

There has been some serious fallout from the Jackson stunt. Several CBS affiliates hesitated to rebroadcast the documentary *9/11* because of the rough language used by firefighters in the film.[97] In 2004, sixty-six ABC affiliate stations refused to air the R-rated movie *Saving Private Ryan* for fear they would be fined for the movie's graphic violence and extensive profanity.[98]

Christopher Polk/Getty Images

▲ In 2012, during the halftime show for Super Bowl XLVI, rapper M.I.A. pointed up her middle finger during her performance. That incident drew comparisons with the brief exposure of Janet Jackson's breast in the Super Bowl halftime show eight years prior.

(Congress raised the fines from $32,500 to $325,000 per "incident" following the Jackson case, which is why smaller stations are cautious about any program that might trigger an FCC response.)

Broadcast standards in Europe are far more likely to regulate hate speech, advertising, and materials that are harmful to children than to control nudity.[99] Gene Policinski, executive director of the First Amendment Center, questions whether television can really tell the story of events such as the 9/11 attacks or the invasion of Normandy during World War II within the limits of decency rules:

> War is a bloody hell, and *Private Ryan* brought home the terror and anguish, as well as the heroics and sacrifices, of the heralds of the "greatest generation" who stormed ashore at Normandy in a manner no sanitized depiction had done previously. Who can view any veteran of that invasion in the same manner after seeing that film?[100]

Redefining Television in the Twenty-First Century

Whether it is delivered by broadcast, cable, or satellite, television is changing so quickly that it might be unrecognizable to Farnsworth. The cable industry, for example, has largely replaced copper wire with fiber-optic cable that uses light rather than electricity to send out video and other types of signals. Fiber-optic cable has the advantage of being able to carry much more information than copper wire can, but more importantly, it has the capacity to allow audience members to send signals back to the program providers.[101]

If I were to ask you what you mean when you say you are going to watch television, your answer would likely be quite different from what your parents might say. Every semester I ask my media literacy students a fairly simple question: What is television? The answers that come back are revealing, to say the least. One time the first word that came up was *box*. And by *box*, my student meant a big, old-school analog TV with a big ol' picture tube. Literally, a giant box. But I think that's informative—television is seen as a device for consuming video wherever it comes from.

After that comes some more use-based terms—*entertainment* and *reruns*. But then comes the description that really grabs my attention: "moving pictures that you stream."

I do not know that the student who said *stream* was really talking about online streaming; more likely, she was just talking about the unending flow of images that stream out of the television box. But the one term that did not come up much was *broadcasting*. And there is a good reason for that. The young people in my class do not really distinguish between broadcast and cable/satellite channels, or even from streaming channels. They are all just television.

One big step in our redefinition of television occurred in 2005 when Apple started selling an iPod that could play video, and it offered current television shows the day after they aired for $1.99 an episode through the iTunes Store. At first, it was primarily ABC programming, owned by Disney, that was available on iTunes.[102] (Remember, at the time of his death, Apple founder Steve Jobs was a member of the Disney board of directors and the company's biggest single stockholder.) But by 2007, the Big Four networks were selling episodes through iTunes, as were many cable powerhouses. So, Apple got broad acceptance of the idea that people would pay cash to download current television shows and that they could use portable devices to view those shows almost anywhere.

That was also the year that DVD rental service Netflix started streaming movies and TV shows over the internet. Initially, the streaming was just to computers, but it soon expanded to devices such as the Roku box, Blu-ray players, and video game consoles that could play Netflix programming instantly on a television set.

Now Netflix and other streaming services, such as Amazon Prime Video and Hulu, can be accessed on smartphones and tablets.[103] And premium cable giant HBO, home of the massive hit *Game of Thrones*, can be accessed from the HBO Max streaming service for $14.95 per month.[104]

Traditional television viewership peaked in 2010 and has been declining in the years since. Young people are increasingly watching streaming video on smartphones, tablets, streaming boxes, or game consoles. Over 2015, use of these devices increased by 25 percent while traditional TV viewing declined by 10 percent.

In 2016, *New York Times* media writer Farhad Manjoo poses the question that he thinks should be keeping Disney's or Comcast's CEOs up at night: "How worried are you about Netflix? And more to the point: Are you worried enough?"[105]

Disney answered that question in the fall of 2019 when it launched its Disney+ streaming service. Disney, with its library of Pixar, Marvel, Lucasfilm, and now 20th Century Studios films certainly had the depth to offer an impressive service. But is has also had popular original programs such as the *Star Wars*-based series *The Mandalorian* featuring a bounty hunter from the same tribe as Boba Fett and an adorable Baby Yoda. Then, during the peak of the COVID-19 pandemic, Disney announced that it would be debuting the movie version of Lin-Manuel Miranda's *Hamilton* on Disney+ more than a year before it was scheduled for a theatrical release.[106]

Disney introduced their streaming service for the relatively affordable price of $6.99 per month or $69 a year. What does Disney get out of this? The biggest thing is a lot of data about and relationship interaction with their customers. A columnist for the *Economist* points out, "Generating another $50 a year in [subscription revenue] is trivial compared to the ability to sell more $5,000 Disney family cruise vacations and $1,100 annual park passes.

This highlights the fact that different streaming services have differing economic models. Disney owns a huge portfolio of product, and so Disney+ gives them an outlet to distribute it and simultaneously collect marketing data on their customers. This might be compared with Amazon's Prime Video that comes with their subscription-based expedited delivery service. Apple is giving away its new video service to people who buy its devices. AT&T, which owns WarnerMedia, will be using its new HBO Max streamer to promote its cable and internet service. Seemingly Netflix is the only company exclusively interested in its streaming service.[107]

These developments raise the question as to whether people are ready to disconnect from a traditional pay video service such as cable or satellite and replace it with content streamed over the internet. Do you really need a cable or satellite subscription to watch a wide range of television programming anymore? Among those who have **cut the cord** is famed media blogger Jim Romenesko, who writes that he made the change when his cable bill hit $203 a month in February 2011. At that point, he says he sold his three flat-screen TVs and took to doing all of his television viewing on his iPad. He says he has no regrets about making the switch, though he might feel differently if he were a big sports fan.[108]

There has been talk for years about the eventual declining fortunes of traditional satellite/cable packages. The basic idea is that you pay a fee for a big group of cable channels, most of which you don't watch. But you get them all as part of a single package—or perhaps a basic package with a group of add-ons. There has been talk about "a la carte" pricing of cable, where subscribers would buy each channel individually. The problem is that cable economics depend on everyone buying the same group of channels, even if they never watch them. Les Moonves, former CEO of CBS, told an investor conference in March 2015, "Clearly the bundle is changing. The days of the 500-channel universe are over. The days of the 150-channel universe in the home are not necessarily over but they're changing rapidly. People are slicing it and dicing it in different ways."[109]

But even if cable companies are unwilling to change, with cord cutting, consumers are increasingly able to do their own a la carte packages. ESPN, HBO, Showtime, and many others are now available for purchase individually.

Big Media companies are responding to the threat from streaming by starting their own services. CBS has its All Access service that runs both on mobile devices and on streaming boxes hooked up to TV sets. All Access provides more than ten thousand episodes on demand, dating back as far as *I Love Lucy* and as current as the network's online-only *Star Trek: Discovery*.

The service also livestreams the network.[110] But the big player here is clearly Disney.

Some internet providers are responding to this change by putting a limit on how much data you get per month. This is something like the limits we've had on our mobile device accounts. Comcast is experimenting with charging customers between $30 and $35 more per month to have unlimited data, as compared to its normal cap of 300 GB. This is one way that multiplatform media companies like Comcast can profit from the cord cutters, who won't be buying cable services directly from them.[111]

Video on demand has followed Secret 3, moving from the margin to the center. As mentioned earlier, more than 76 percent of Americans have access to Netflix. Taking a look at the bigger pictures, the Leichtman Research Group, which does some of the most in-depth commercial research on television behavior, found that 82 percent of Americans have access to some kind of video on demand, including the DVR, Netflix or another streaming service, or video on demand from a cable/satellite provider.[112]

▲ Alden Ehrenreich (as Han Solo) and Joonas Suotamo (as Chewbacca) star in 2018's *Solo: A Star Wars Story.* Disney's launch of its new streaming service would include the *Star Wars* franchise as well as Marvel, Pixar, and other popular offerings.

The Earthquake in Slow Motion Continues

Earlier in this chapter, we discussed Auletta's "earthquake in slow motion"—how the cable and satellite revolution brought about massive changes to the television business in the 1980s and 1990s. This earthquake has continued to shake up television into the twenty-first century due to the growing importance of broadband video and alternative viewing devices. We can see this transformation with an event that took place on June 22, 2016.

The reason that C-SPAN exists is to provide live coverage of the U.S. House of Representatives when it is in session. At other times, C-SPAN carries a variety of speeches, campaign events, and original programming. The key words here, however, are "when they are in session." When the House is not in session, the majority party (the Democrats as of this writing) controls whether the cameras are on or off. So, it is no surprise that then Speaker of the House Paul Ryan, a Republican, shut off the House feed to C-SPAN while the Democrats held an out-of-session sit-in on the House floor on June 22, 2016, to call for votes on gun legislation.[113]

But just because the official cameras were turned off did not mean there wasn't video coming out of the House. Rep. Eric Swalwell (D-CA) used his Periscope streaming video account to livestream the sit-in from his smartphone, thus bypassing the Republican's efforts to limit the sit-in's exposure, as did Rep. Scott Peters (D-CA).[114] To be fair, the majority party always has control of the cameras in the House, and Democrats shut off the cameras, as well as the lights, in August 2008 to stop feeding attention to the Republicans who wanted votes on energy legislation.[115]

That Swalwell would stream the sit-in is not particularly surprising—he's also known as the House's king of Snapchat. He is a young, hip representative from tech-savvy California. What was amazing was when C-SPAN started carrying Periscope feeds on its cable, satellite, and streaming channels.[116]

▲ Georgia Rep. John Lewis, center, led a sit-in of more than two hundred Democrats that effectively shut down the House's legislative work on June 22, 2016. The sit-in was livestreamed by Rep. Eric Swalwell (D-CA) via Periscope.

C-SPAN spokesperson Howard Mortman told the *Washington Post*'s Erik Wemple (whose blog covers media issues), "This is the first time we've ever shown video from the House floor picked up by a Periscope account."[117] This is a big deal because now mobile social media is providing programming straight into a legacy media channel. We are seeing how members of Congress can use their mobile devices to feed video out to their followers, and how long-tail media can pick up a much broader audience through short-head media.

The flow can also go the other direction—with legacy media being retransmitted through social media like Periscope. While these apps are certainly used to create original content, they are also used to bypass Big Media contracts and rebroadcast sporting events that others are paying as much as $100 to receive. In 2015, there was a major boxing match between Floyd Mayweather Jr. and Manny Pacquiao. Pay-per-view audiences were charged $100 per screen to have access to the fight, but dozens of paying customers livestreamed the fight via Periscope, and anyone who wanted to could watch for free. While many of these illegal streams were shut down, the *Washington Post* reported it was not difficult to see the fight without paying. Individuals are also streaming MLB baseball games and NFL football games live over both YouTube and Facebook. Sometimes these are going out openly, and other times the streams are only available to private groups. In either case, the streamers are bypassing multibillion-dollar contracts between legacy media and the sports leagues.[118]

If you look carefully, you can see many the Seven Secrets coming into play here:

- Secret 2—There are no mainstream media: A social channel was getting the news out nationwide, and sports programs were going from Big Media to social streams.

- Secret 3—Everything from the margin moves to the center: A new social media channel was taking a stunt protest from inside the beltway to the entire country.

- Secret 4—Nothing is new: Everything that happened in the past will happen again: In November 2008, terrorists hit Mumbai, India, and there were not Western legacy media channels there to report the news. In that absence, news organizations like CNN, Fox News, and the *New York Times* relied on images and reports coming from social media. (Obviously, the similarity here is not because of terrorist attacks but because of reports coming from places where legacy media cameras cannot reach.)

- Secret 5—All media are social: The story about the protest going out on C-SPAN from Periscope spread through social media, word of mouth, and people talking about it on legacy media. The same happened when boxing matches or ballgames popped up on social media. It was a social interaction.

- Secret 6—Online media are mobile media: This one was perhaps the most obvious. Members of Congress took their always on/on everywhere mobile devices to send out a stream that could be seen on television, computers, and mobile devices. And sports fans used mobile devices to take closed-access sporting events and make them available to nonpaying audience members.

CHAPTER REVIEW

CHAPTER SUMMARY ▶▶

Television was developed in the 1920s and 1930s by independent inventor Philo T. Farnsworth and RCA engineer Vladimir Zworykin. Commercial broadcasting began in the United States in 1939, but its development was put on hold by the outbreak of World War II. By the early 1950s, television was established as the dominant broadcast medium. In the early days of television, virtually all programming was presented live. But Lucille Ball and Desi Arnaz shot their show on film, thus creating a product that would have long-term value. Color television broadcasts came into widespread use in the 1960s.

Although primitive forms of cable television existed in 1948, cable did not become a significant medium until the early 1980s when satellite distribution of channels became common. Among the early cable channels were a number of networks created by Ted Turner. Viewers gained access to additional choices in the form of VCRs and direct-broadcast satellite service. Television broadcasting has switched from analog signals to multiple digital formats, and VCRs have almost completely been replaced by DVRs, DVDs, video on demand, and streaming technology.

Television was initially dominated by the Big Three networks, but audience choices were gradually expanded with public broadcasting, the Fox Network, and cable channels.

Television networks have been criticized for failing to include women and minorities in their programming, but cable channels have delivered more programming that addresses diverse interests. Networks have also been criticized for carrying too much violent and sexually explicit programming. But television has been praised for breaking down geographic and social barriers. Broadcast television is currently going through a cycle in which "indecent" content is being suppressed by the government.

Television is changing rapidly, with audience members getting many new options to control how and when they receive programming. With VCRs, DVRs, interactive television, and streaming video, viewers can choose what they watch and when they watch it. They are also able to interact with the programming through online and mobile resources.

KEY TERMS ▶▶

community antenna television (CATV)   191

Big Three networks   191

videocassette recorder (VCR)   193

direct-broadcast satellite (DBS)   193

video on demand (VOD)   194

high-definition television (HDTV)   194

standard digital television   194

Public Broadcasting Service (PBS)   195

television networks   195

Big Four networks   197

people meter   197

sweeps   197

rating point   198

share   198

telenovelas   202

cut the cord   208

REVIEW QUESTIONS ▶▶

1. How did the absence of live sports affect television broadcasters in the spring of 2020?

2. How did Ted Turner transform cable television?

3. What does media journalist Ken Auletta mean by "an earthquake in slow motion"? How is that earthquake still going on today?

4. How did Janet Jackson's 2004 Super Bowl appearance transform our standards for decency on broadcast television?

5. How have technological changes transformed how we think of "watching television"?

DIGITAL AND GLOBAL MEDIA

PART III

CHAPTER 9

ONLINE AND MOBILE MEDIA

During the spring and summer of 2020, there was a pandemic sweeping the nation and the world. The virus called COVID-19 had people social distancing and self-isolating for months at a time. With some early misinformation being distributed through the White House and among other outlets, it was difficult to know exactly what was happening with respect to treatments, vaccines, quarantines, and face masks.[1] Needless to say, this created an information environment that was ideal for spreading a range of rumors, fake news, and conspiracy theories claiming that the COVID-19 illness was being caused by 5G mobile phone towers.[2]

But the biggest conspiracy theory of all during this time was that somehow Microsoft founder Bill Gates was using the pandemic (maybe even creating it) so that everyone would have to get vaccinated with a microchip that could track virtually everyone in the world. (Please note, there is absolutely no evidence that Gates has had anything to do with the creation of the illness or a desire to microchip people. He has long been a supporter of vaccinations.) It is ironic that 28 percent of American's expressed belief in this conspiracy theory while it is undeniable that 85 percent of all American adults are already carrying a device with them everywhere that tracks and reports their location, spending habits, search behavior, and even how often they are having sex.[3]

At the most basic level, our mobile devices need to know where we are to communicate with the network that lets us go online, send text messages, and, yes, even make phone calls. That location data from our mobile providers is probably not as private as we would like to think it is, with geolocation data being readily available for purchase by property managers, car salesmen, and even bounty hunters.[4] But that location data is just the tip of the iceberg about the data your phone is collecting about you.

A pair of reporters for the *Wall Street Journal* looked at eighty popular apps from Apple's app store and found that all but one of them used third-party tracking apps. Journalist Joanna Stern says the issue is not so much the tracking—because that is central to the economic model for apps—but that it is being done without people's knowledge or consent. One example she pointed out was a kid's iOS app with a Curious George theme that was collecting and reporting to Facebook the user's age, name, and every book on which the user clicked. When confronted about it,

LEARNING OBJECTIVES

After studying this chapter, you will be able to

1 Identify why the original technology behind the internet was developed

2 Identify and describe the three major components of the World Wide Web

3 Explain Tim Berners-Lee's original idea for how web browser content should be written and distributed

4 Describe the four elements of the "hacker ethic" and how they apply to the contemporary internet

5 Explain how the telegraph and subsequent technologies paved the way for the internet and the World Wide Web

6 Explain why people believe that the convergence of old and new media will replace "dead-tree" media (newspapers, magazines, and other formats) as the main source for news

the app's company claimed there was "some rogue code" in the app. In another case, a meditation app had sent out three location pings giving Stern's latitude and longitude in five minutes. The app company said it only used the data to "ensure user privacy and security."[5] To be fair, Sterns reported that the *Wall Street Journal*'s app has five separate trackers in it.

There are also apps that women use for tracking their menstrual cycles and fertility that have users enter their physical data along with when they have had sex. Some of these apps, provided as a "wellness benefit" by employers and insurance companies, are reporting data about users back to the company's human resources department or insurance provider. Sometimes even to Facebook. The apps do help couples with fertility issues, but they also serve up in-app ads for providers of life insurance, supplements, and cleaning products.[6]

Why do these apps do so much tracking and data collection? Several reasons. Stern says companies want to know what you are doing with the app, where you are when you use it, details about your phone, your IP address (the internet address for the Wi-Fi network you're using), and for advertising tracking. One way these apps do this is through your phone's unique **mobile advertising ID**, a code that identifies your phone and lets advertisers know all about your interests, even though they do not necessarily know your name. Even if your phone lets you set the advertising ID to all zeros (as iPhones do), apps can still do a lot to figure out who you are, using your location, IP address and browsing record. (For more on how companies can identify you, read ahead to Chapter 12 on advertising to see how the store Target can identify women who are pregnant.)

Aside from potentially violating your privacy, these apps are also eating up your phone's data allowance, especially if you do not have Wi-Fi at home. Geoffrey Fowler, a technology columnist for the *Washington Post*, worked with the privacy firm Disconnect to find out who his phone was talking to. He discovered that his phone had an active late-night social life with apps "phoning home" in the middle of the night, especially while he had "background app refresh" turned on.[7]

Not only are these companies collecting data on you, they are selling it as well. A study by the *New York Times* found that even though much of the information being collected is supposedly "anonymized," it can be surprisingly easy to connect it to an individual. The *Times* was able to

document that a forty-six-year-old math teacher had gone to a Weight Watchers meeting, to her dermatologist's office, out for a walk with her dog, and then stayed at her ex-boyfriend's home. "It's the thought of people finding out these intimate details that you don't want people to know," the teacher told the *Times*.[8]

As we will discuss in Chapter 14—Media Law, Apple has worked hard at making it difficult to hack into the phone itself, and that is important, but that security does little to stop apps on your phone from constantly streaming out data about you. (Most of the details in this section have been about the iPhone. Given that Google's Android phone operating system is advertising supported, its issues with data privacy are even bigger than Apple's.[9])

Mobile devices have transformed our understanding of what it means to be online and connected. They have also transformed how much others can know about us. In this chapter, we look at the origins of the internet, how it has changed from its original government roots, how it has evolved from a tool for computer sharing into a major new mass medium, and how it has caused social change everywhere from the corporate boardroom to the Middle East.

Stay up to date on the latest in media by visiting the author's blog at **ralphehanson.com**

The Development of the Internet

The internet is the most recent of the mass media. It is still rapidly evolving and changing, just as radio did in the 1920s and television did in the 1950s. (Remember Secret 4—Nothing is new: Everything that happened in the past will happen again.) Like radio, the internet was not conceived initially as a mass medium. Instead, the first wide-area computer networks were designed to enable academics and military researchers to share data. But these early users soon found that the most useful benefit of the network was being able to send electronic mail to one another instantly.

Although the earliest components of the internet were in use by 1969, the net was limited largely to interpersonal communication until 1991, when Tim Berners-Lee released the World Wide Web as an easy and uniform way to access material on the internet. Since then, the internet has become a medium unlike any other because it is the only one that incorporates elements of interpersonal, group, and mass communications.

So, what is the **internet**? A national panel on the future of the internet defines it this way: "The Internet is a diverse set of independent networks, interlinked to provide its users with the appearance of a single, uniform network."[10]

The net starts with the link from your computer to an internet service provider (ISP). For an ISP, you might choose AOL, a cable company, your telephone company, or possibly a small local company that sells internet service in one or two counties. The messages then flow from the smaller links into bigger and bigger digital pipelines (the internet's "backbone") that carry millions of messages across the country.

Packet switching is at the core of how wide-area computer networks operate. The sending computer breaks down the message into a few smaller pieces, or packets, that can be sent

Packet-Switching Networks

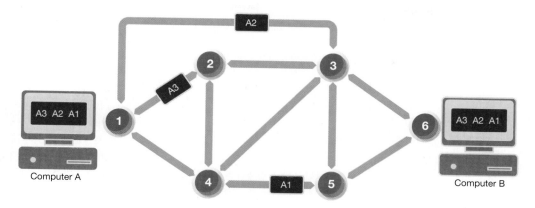

separately across the network. These packets each follow their own routes to the destination computer, where they are reassembled into the original message.

The backbone was initially a set of high-speed data lines controlled by the National Science Foundation as part of a replacement of its original network, but these lines have since been replaced by high-speed fiber-optic lines run by about a dozen major communication companies.

Today, people use the internet to communicate with other people, but the technology was originally developed to let computers talk to one another. In the early 1960s, researchers on both sides of the Atlantic Ocean were working on the problem of how to transfer information stored on one computer to another.

In 1964, engineer Paul Baran was designing a military communication network that could survive a nuclear strike. He sought to design a network in which every computer was connected to several other computers so that if one computer failed, an alternative route using different computers could be established. Baran's second insight was that computers could break large messages into a few smaller message blocks, or packets, which could be sent independently across the network. **Packet switching**, as Baran's scheme came to be known, cuts messages into little pieces and sends them along the easiest route to their final destination (see Figure 9.1). The receiving computer starts reassembling the messages and asks for any missing packets to be resent.[11]

The U.S. Air Force was initially willing to implement Baran's network, but the company AT&T, which had a monopoly on long-distance phone service at the time, refused to cooperate, so Baran put his idea on hold.[12] Meanwhile, in England, researcher Donald Davies was working on a proposed public communication network. Davies and Baran, working independently, came up with remarkably similar notions for packet switching.[13]

ARPAnet

Eventually the U.S. military built the first nationwide packet-switching network. However, the network that was built was intended to serve the needs of academic researchers, not to survive nuclear war.

The network was built by a farsighted division of the Pentagon called the Advanced Research Projects Agency (ARPA).[14] In 1968, the contract to build the network was given to a Boston-based consulting firm on the condition that it be built in less than one year. By the fall of 1969, ARPAnet connected four different institutions, and the first component of the internet was running. As the hand-drawn map of ARPAnet in Figure 9.2 shows, the initial nodes were University of California–Los Angeles, Stanford Research Institute, University of California–Santa Barbara, and University of Utah. **ARPAnet** came online at about the same time as the first moon landing. Whereas Neil Armstrong's "one small step" was noted throughout the world

Drawing of Four-Node Network

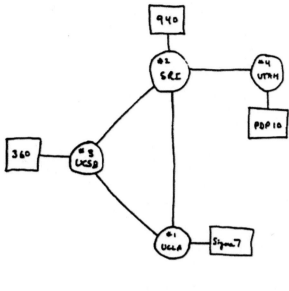

THE ARPA NETWORK

DEC 1969

4 NODES

Source: Courtesy of Computer History Museum.

as one of the great achievements of humanity, no one outside of ARPA was aware that a new, world-changing medium had just been born.[15]

Connecting Incompatible Networks

As ARPAnet increasingly expanded to universities, other networks were formed. Each of these small networks worked well in its own limited and defined sphere, but they could not communicate with one another. How could they be linked together?

The answer came from work done by Bob Kahn and Vint Cerf. The pair envisioned a box, or gateway, that would serve as a translator for all the various incompatible networks. The individual networks would talk to the gateways using a common set of rules, or "protocols." Their protocol was known as **TCP/IP**. TCP stands for transmission control protocol, which controls how data are sent out on the Internet. IP stands for internet protocol, which provides the address for each computer on the internet. The term *internet* was coined in 1973 as an abbreviation for "internetworking of networks." As academics started making personal use of the internet, nonacademics became interested in computer communication and started buying access to network services through companies such as CompuServe, Prodigy, and AOL.[16]

With all the public and commercial traffic flowing on the internet, next-generation networks are now under construction to serve the same purpose as ARPAnet—to provide academics and other researchers with high-speed links to computers around the world, especially the limited number of supercomputers. These new and improved networks have the potential to move data ten to twenty times faster than the conventional internet, given ideal conditions. Their primary advantage is that they make possible video and interactive applications that are of much higher quality. For example, students at medical schools in different parts of the country can view an interactive medical simulation simultaneously using the new network, something that would have been impossible with the older, slower lines. As of 2018, more than 562 member organizations, including universities, corporations, government agencies, and nonprofits, belonged to the Internet2 consortium, one of the leading next-generation networks, which connected to a broader, ninety-four-thousand-institution community spread across more than one hundred countries.[17]

With the coming of networks, and especially the internetworking standards, computers were transformed. Bob Taylor, who helped oversee the creation of ARPAnet, said, "Computers were first born as arithmetic engines, but my own view . . . is that they're much more interesting and powerful as communication devices because they mediate human-to-human communication."[18] The thing that makes computer-based communication so powerful is that it includes virtually every level of communication, from the interpersonal communication of email and instant messaging to the mass communication of the World Wide Web.

Email

Although its original purpose was the sharing of resources, the most important factor in the development of the internet was **electronic mail (email)**, defined simply as a message sent from one computer user to another across a network. Primitive email existed prior to the internet, but people could send messages only to other users on the same physical computer. There was no way to send a message from one computer to another.

In 1972, ARPAnet's Ray Tomlinson wrote a simple file-transfer program that could send a message from one system to another.[19] When the software that operated ARPAnet was updated, Tomlinson's email application was sent out over the net so that everyone would have the same materials. Tomlinson also created the form of address using the @ symbol. It was a way of saying, "This is a message for a person 'at' a particular computer." The other reason was that the @ symbol did not appear in users' names or locations. It was the one symbol that meant what Tomlinson wanted it to mean and that was not already in use.[20] Even with all the growth online communication has undergone throughout the decades, email continues to be one of the most important online applications for the largest number of people, even if it isn't as trendy as newer technologies.

Texting and Direct Messaging

Interpersonal communication on the internet has expanded beyond email through a variety of texting and "chat" services accessed through mobile phones or other mobile devices. These originated with text messages that could be sent using Short Message Service, or SMS. The protocol for sending these messages over mobile networks first went online in 1992, and by 2010, it was the most widely used application on mobile phones.[21] While SMS is convenient and can be used as a way of connecting to numerous social media networks, there are also alternative ways of sending instant messages, or ways of engaging in instantaneous communication with others over online and mobile networks. The granddaddy of these was AOL's Instant Messenger (AIM). At one point in the 1990s, it seemed as though AIM was everywhere. But as the former dial-up internet giant gradually lost relevance, it also neglected the development of its **instant messaging (IM)** product. On December 15, 2017, following a twenty-year run, AOL shut down AIM.[22] In the late 2010s, the two most popular apps in this category belong to Facebook—Facebook Messenger and the globally popular WhatsApp.[23] (You can read more about the rise and fall of AOL in Chapter 3.)

Tim Berners-Lee: Inventor of the World Wide Web

Until 1990, using the internet for anything more than email was a challenge. Information was scattered about in various places, with no easy way to access it. All that changed with the invention of the World Wide Web by British physicist Tim Berners-Lee. Berners-Lee, who built on the ideas of several internet pioneers, created the software that allows the internet to work as a medium of mass communication. He developed a system that is easy to use, allows users to access any type of information, and has a simplified single addressing system for accessing any document located on the web anywhere in the world.

The idea of the web dates to the 1960s. In 1968, Stanford researcher Doug Engelbart staged a demonstration of his vision of an interactive computer. He used a pair of computer terminals in an "online" session that included word-processing documents, hypertext documents, and live video images (sent over closed-circuit analog lines). Engelbart was ahead of his time and largely ignored, but his work was the first expression of what would come with Macintosh, Microsoft Windows, and videoconferencing.[24]

Another early vision of the web, more philosophical than technical, came from Ted Nelson. Nelson described a form of "nonsequential writing" that he called **hypertext**—material formatted to contain links that allow the reader to move easily from one section to another and from document to document. The most used hypertext documents are web pages.

When programmer Berners-Lee was a child, his parents owned a Victorian-era advice book called *Enquire Within Upon Everything*. What would it be like, Berners-Lee wondered, if there really was a book that contained everything you might want to know? In 1980, he made his first attempt to create such a resource by writing a program called "Enquire" to organize documents, lists of people, and projects on his computer. The hypertext program would let him find and connect any of his documents. Although Enquire was limited to Berners-Lee's computer, the young

British physicist thought about the possibilities of the program extending beyond his own computer to every computer in the world:

> Suppose all the information stored on computers everywhere were linked. . . . Suppose I could program my computer to create a space in which anything could be linked to anything. All the bits of information in every computer . . . on the planet would be available to me and to anyone else. There would be a single, global information space.[25]

▲ Tim Berners-Lee is the British physicist who created the World Wide Web software as a side project while working at the CERN high-energy physics lab in Switzerland.

Berners-Lee was never asked to create the web; he simply thought it would be a good idea for researchers to be able to find documents they needed regardless of which computer those documents resided on. In 1989, he returned to his Enquire idea and started writing the software for a system he called the **World Wide Web**, which allows users to view and link documents located anywhere in the world using standard software.

By 1990, the European Organization for Nuclear Research (CERN), where Berners-Lee was working at the time, had the first web server and a simple browser. (A web server is a program that makes web pages available on the internet. A browser is a program for viewing web pages.)

The World Wide Web has three major components:

1. The **uniform resource locator (URL)**—the address of content placed on the web. An example is www.mysite.com.

2. The **hypertext transfer protocol (http)**—the standard set of rules used by web servers and browsers for sending and receiving text, graphics, or anything else on a website. When you type http://, you are telling your web browser to use this protocol or set of rules.

3. The **hypertext markup language (HTML)**—the programming language used to create web pages. It consists of all the tags (brief computer commands) that say how text ought to be presented, where graphics should be placed, and what links should be included.

Although the web has grown immensely in complexity since it was invented, these three basic elements remain central to how it operates.

Berners-Lee released the web software in the summer of 1991 on several internet newsgroups. These early users helped him test and debug the program and made suggestions for improvement, and the web started spreading around the world.

Openness and Accessibility on the Internet

Whereas Berners-Lee developed the web on a NeXT computer system, the development of browsers for a wide range of computers was done on a volunteer basis by people around the world. These individuals were willing to share their work, but language barriers sometimes posed a problem. One of the early browsers had documentation only in Finnish. (You can read more about Steve Jobs and the NeXT computers in Chapter 3.)

The most surprising thing about the World Wide Web may be that it was developed almost entirely as a collaborative, nonprofit venture. "What amazed me during the early days was the enormous amount of free energy that went into developing that technology," said Michael Folk, one of the early web developers. "People from all over the world contributed huge amounts of time and ideas in a surprisingly noncompetitive, collaborative way."[26]

Zhang Peng/Getty Images

Although the World Wide Web has grown far beyond what anyone could have imagined and has changed immeasurably, it is still shaped by the basic vision of Berners-Lee. His goal was to create a completely decentralized system for sharing information that would have no central hub. With no central control, the whole system could scale—that is, grow almost indefinitely—yet still work properly. Berners-Lee was looking for a system in which any computer could link to any other computer: "The power of a hypertext link is that it can link to absolutely anything. That's the fundamental concept."[27]

▲ Mobile devices, such as the one being used by this Uygur woman in a Chinese bazaar, bring internet access to developing areas without easy access to traditional computers.

The success of the World Wide Web illustrates one of the major strengths of the internet: Although users can buy a web browser or web server, the basic technology is free. According to Dave Walden, who worked on the original ARPAnet software,

> [Berners-Lee] brought out something, he gave it to a few of his friends, they tried it, they saw that it was good, and he gave it away. It went all over the world. That's how the World Wide Web standard came on the world.[28]

The next time you go surfing on the web, look for evidence of the principles—openness and accessibility—on which it is based:

- Information of all kinds should be available through the same window, or information space. This means that you don't have to use one program to look up phone numbers and another to find the news.

- All documents on the web must be equally accessible.

- There must be a single address that will take users to a document.

- Users should be able to link to any document at any space.

- Users should be able to access any type of material from any type of computer.

- Users should be able to create whatever types of relationships between information that they want to. It should be possible to link a document to any other document.

- The web should be a tool not just for information, but also for collaboration. It is designed for interaction, as well as publication.

- There is no central control of the web.

- The web software should be available free to anyone who wants to use it.

Before 1993, the internet and the World Wide Web belonged primarily to university and military personnel who had used ARPAnet. But in his history of the internet, *Nerds 2.0.1*, Stephen Segaller notes that three things happened during the early 1990s to turn the internet into a significant social force: The World Wide Web code was posted to the internet, commercial users were allowed onto the net for the first time, and the first easy-to-use graphical web browser was written and posted to the net. With these changes, the internet outgrew its military and research origins and became a public medium.

Searching on the World Wide Web

Although Berners-Lee had created a browser as part of the original World Wide Web, it was limited in terms of the computers it would run on, and it could not display anything other than text. **Mosaic**, the first easy-to-use graphical web browser, was created by a group of

What is the first thing we do when we wake up? For many of us, it involves checking our phone and clicking through Facebook, Twitter, Instagram, and Snapchat.

student programmers led by Marc Andreessen at the University of Illinois at Urbana-Champaign. The developers wanted to create a tool that would make it easier to find things on the Internet and that would provide an incentive to put information on the web. As with the original web software, Mosaic was posted on the internet, free for users to download. More than one million users downloaded Mosaic in 1993 (the year it was released), and Andreessen, then twenty-one and a graduate, founded Netscape Communications.[29]

One issue that frequently brings conflict to Google is discussion about how they shape their searches. Google fields close to four million searches per minute about virtually any subject you can think about. The *Wall Street Journal* wrote that the Google search engine has "arguably the most powerful lines of computer code in the global economy, controlling how much of the world accesses information found on the Internet, and the starting point for billions of dollars of commerce."[30] The idea behind Google is that an impartial algorithm will calculate which results will show up first in search results, or at least show up first after the results that are paid advertising. (Take a look back at Chapter 3 to review Google's business model.)

The problem Google faces is that every time they tweak their algorithms, companies do their best to make their websites match what Google is looking for in an effort to game the system. Research by the *Wall Street Journal* found the following about Google's search process:

- Google's software tends to favor big businesses over smaller ones. Google also seems to favor Amazon.com and Facebook.

- Google helps shape how search happens by adjusting their autocomplete suggestions and their quickly appearing information boxes. Autocomplete is designed to avoid suggesting searches on problematic topics such as abortion or immigration.

- Google has thousands of contractors who work constantly at assessing the quality of the company's searches.

- Google is constantly fighting against "bad actors" who try to game the search results. This includes work on attempting to avoid deliberately misleading information and fight spam.

The issue of which websites would be emphasized in search results has been a problem for the company since its start in the late 1980s. Founders Larry Page and Sergey Brin wrote back in 1988 that "The importance of a Web page is an inherently subjective matter, which depends on the [reader's] interests, knowledge and attitudes."[31]

Over the years, Google has had continued criticism that its search results are politically biased, particularly on topics such as abortion. Pro-choice organizations complain that crisis pregnancy centers, which counsel women against having an abortion, show up in searches for places that perform abortions. Pro-life activists complain that abortion and women's health provider Planned Parenthood shows up in too many of the searches related to abortion.

The question of whether the internet's search capability is a news medium is significant because various governments around the world want to put limits on internet searching. And companies such as Google, Microsoft, and Yahoo all seem willing to build limits into their portals as part of the price of doing business in countries that have more restrictions on free speech than the United States. Sometimes the censorship of searches is relatively noncontroversial, such as France's attempts to make Yahoo filter out all references to Nazi paraphernalia.[32]

But even though major tech companies would love to have access to the massive Chinese market, they are largely blocked from doing business there. Google was blocked starting in 2010 when it allowed Chinese users access to its uncensored search engine. Facebook and Twitter have been blocked since 2009, though apparently President Donald Trump was able to tweet during his visit to China in 2017.[33]

Going Mobile

At more than thirty years old, the World Wide Web, even in the age of mobile apps, is still a major part of how we go online. And over that time, our access to computers and computer-based media has changed dramatically. If we go back to 1983 in the years before the World Wide Web, a Harris poll found that 10 percent of adults had a home computer and that 14 percent of that small number had a modem to go online using a slow landline phone connection. (If you solve out that story problem, you find that 1.4 percent of American adults were online that year.) Berners-Lee launched the earliest version of the web in 1989, and by 1995, 14 percent of American adults had internet access, primarily using dial-up. But perhaps more significantly, 42 percent of Americans had not even heard of the internet.[34]

By the year 2000, 37 percent of us were online, but only 3 percent had the fast, always-on broadband connection. **Broadband service**, such as a cable modem from a cable television provider or a digital subscriber line (DSL) from a phone company, offers connections that are many times faster than dial-up service. But broadband offers more than just increased connection speed. With a broadband connection, subscribers are connected to the net whenever their computer is turned on. This means that they don't have to download their email; it's always there. It means that things such as online radio, instant messaging, and streaming video are easily accessible.

A study by the Pew Research Center found that 90 percent of American adults go online, with 81 percent on daily and 28 percent on "almost constantly."[35] By 2020, 85 percent of Americans age twelve or older had smartphones and so were online in at least one way or another.[36] And in its own way, the move to mobile connectivity is just as revolutionary as the move from dial-up to broadband. For while broadband gave us "always on" connections, mobile internet gives us "anytime, anywhere" access to information.[37]

Mobile Apps. Back in 2010, *Wired* magazine ran a bright red cover with large black type proclaiming "The Web Is Dead." Chris Anderson, the same man who is responsible for the book *The Long Tail*, was arguing that the age of open-standard web pages was on the decline, leading the way to going online with specialized mobile apps. He wrote,

> You wake up and check your email on your bedside iPad—that's one app. During breakfast you browse Facebook, Twitter, and *The New York Times*—three more apps. On the way to the office, you listen to a podcast on your smartphone. Another app. . . . At the end of the day, you come home, make dinner while listening to Pandora, play some games on Xbox Live, and watch a movie on Netflix's streaming service.
> You've spent the day on the Internet—but not on the Web.[38]

Now, a decade later, much of what Anderson predicted has come true. Apps are a big part of how we interact online. Especially a few apps like Facebook, Twitter, and Snapchat—our social media. On the other hand, much of our interaction online is done through the mobile web—scaled-back versions of websites designed to work on everything from a nine-inch iPad screen, to a giant seven-inch Samsung phone, down to the smallest four-inch smartphone.

Apps are clearly important, but they are not necessarily an either/or proposition with the web. The Pew Research Center's 2018 "Digital News Fact Sheet" notes that all forty of the top digital news sites have a presence on Facebook, Twitter, YouTube, and Instagram.[39]

What there can be no doubt about is that mobile devices are becoming the dominant way of going online. Just look at where the money is coming from online. In 2015, of the top fifty newspapers, forty-four had more mobile traffic than desktop computers; of the top national TV news outlets, all eight of eight had more mobile than desktop traffic, and for the top forty **digital native** publishers (those that don't have a legacy media component), thirty-eight had more mobile traffic.[40]

Online Media: Blogs, Podcasts, and Streaming

When Berners-Lee created the World Wide Web, he viewed it not just as a convenient and inexpensive place to access published materials, but also as a forum where people could interact and create their own materials. "We ought to be able not only to find any kind of document on the Web, but also to create any kind of document, easily," he wrote in his history of the web. "We should be able not only to follow links, but to create them—between all sorts of media. We should be able not only to interact with other people, but to create with other people."[41]

Blogs are in many ways a throwback to the early days of magazine publishing when authors wrote without expecting to be paid. While there are subsidized blogs, the vast majority are run simply to give the writers a forum.[42]

I made the case earlier in this book that blogs can be almost as mainstream as what we consider to be the mainstream media. (Remember Secret 2—There are no mainstream media.) One test of the importance of a news source is whether it is included in the LexisNexis online news database. LexisNexis is part of a giant subscription service that gives clients access to the full text of major newspapers, magazines, financial reports, and court documents. As of 2006, LexisNexis started including text from selected blogs, including NPR's *Planet Money* economics blog and *Goats and Soda*, a global health and development blog.[43]

Berners-Lee's original idea was that every web browser would also be an editor that ordinary people could use to create content as well as to view it—a vision that the early web browsers did not support. But the late 1990s brought a new development called the **weblog** (or **blog** for short), which is a collection of links and commentary in hypertext that can be created and posted on the internet with relatively little effort. Blogs can be public diaries, collections of photos, or commentaries on the news. They often also allow readers to comment on and annotate what the owner has posted.

A prominent example of the influence of bloggers came when Dan Rather, on the CBS news-magazine *60 Minutes II*, reported on a set of memos that seemed to show that President George W. Bush's superior officer had been critical of his service in the Air National Guard. The story ran a couple of months before the 2004 election, and it drew immediate criticism from the conservative blogs *Power Line* and *Little Green Footballs*. The bloggers pointed out inconsistencies in the typefaces used in the memos, suggesting that they looked more like the product of a modern word processor than that of a 1970s vintage typewriter. They also raised questions about the motives and honesty of the source of the documents. Criticisms coming from these and other blogs led to Rather stepping down as the anchor of the *CBS Evening News*.[44]

Blogs have also given readers different perspectives on stories than they might receive otherwise from independent voices. Obsessed Apple blogger John Gruber runs *Daring Fireball*, which Recode calls "the world's most powerful one-man media company." Gruber publishes tech and business news about Apple, comments on related issues, and discusses whatever else he wants to. Gruber makes his decisions about what to write about based on the idea that his audience is himself. "It's somebody out there who's exactly like me and isn't writing Daring Fireball," he said.[45] Everest and Himalayan climbing blogger Alan Arnette is one of the world's leading sources on news about Himalayan mountaineering, and he posts daily updates during the peak climbing season. Aside from delivering information you would have a hard time finding anywhere else, Arnette uses his blog to raise money and awareness about Alzheimer's disease. If you do a search on Arnette while people are summiting in the Himalayas, you will find him being quoted in newspapers from Minneapolis to Nepal to Borneo to London. (He's also personally summited Everest and K2.)

HUMANS OF NEW YORK

Brandon Stanton

This is one of the thousands of portraits Brandon Stanton has shot and posted online as part of his *Humans of New York* blogging project.

Back in 2010, Brandon Stanton was a young bond trader working in Chicago. He had a semiprofessional camera and spent some of his free time taking photos around Chicago. Then he lost his job and suddenly had a lot more free time, so he started taking a lot more photos. "Instead of updating my resume and looking for a similar job, I decided to forget about money and have a go at something I really enjoyed."[46]

After traveling around taking photos in a number of U.S. cities, he moved to New York City with the goal of taking ten thousand portraits of ordinary people. Anyone who has tried going up to random people on the street and asking them if he or she can take their picture knows how hard that can be. The project came to be known as *Humans of New York*, and Stanton posted his best photos, along with a short caption/story, on Facebook and Tumblr. It took about a year, but finally he started getting followers, and talk. His blog got some positive comments from Tumblr founder David Karp, but the *Washington Post* says that most of the credit for *Humans of New York*'s fifteen million followers goes to Stanton himself.

In a 2014 speech in Ireland, Stanton said it's all about being willing to just go up and talk to people:

> The way I figured this out was just by doing it 10,000 times and getting beaten down, beaten down, beaten down, beaten down. There was no way I'm the best photographer in the world, no way that I'm the best journalist in the world, but I have approached over 10,000 people on the streets of what is stereotypically . . . one of the colder cities in the world and have asked them for their photograph. So I'm thinking by about this time I might be just about the best in the world at stopping random people on the street and getting them to let me take their photograph.[47]

Stanton's blog posts for years took a standard format—they have a photo of one or two people along with a quote that tells a very short story about the person(s). But during the COVID-19 pandemic in the spring of 2020, Stanton took to collecting cheerful stories from people. He sent a message to the twenty-eight million people who follow him on his varied platforms and asked them to submit their most uplifting stories. He then interviewed the people he wanted to feature through FaceTime.[48]

While *Humans of New York* clearly exists and is shared on social media, it also illustrates the importance of social interaction outside of the online component. As Stanton says, the thing that makes *Humans* such a success is not the brilliant quality of the photos or writing, but the fact that he is socially interacting with all these people. Karp said, "It's become this community effort where people actually send in stories about the dude that makes them a bagel every morning who just always has a great story to tell or the dude with an epic mustache that I see walking down the street every day. They send in these stories about these people and Brandon goes, finds them [and] takes these gorgeous portraits of them, and uploads them with that story that led him to that person."[49]

Since his start in 2010, Stanton has traveled around the world taking *Humans* photos in a range of countries including Iran and Pakistan.

You can see the entire blog on Facebook or at www.humansofnewyork.com.

. . . .

WHO is the source?

Who is Brandon Stanton? What did he do before he was a photographer?

WHAT is he doing?

Of whom is Stanton taking photos? How does he present them?

WHAT evidence is there?

How does Stanton find the people he takes photos of? How does he get their cooperation? How is his work on the *Humans of New York* project social media?

WHAT do you and your friends think about this?

Take a look at several of Stanton's photographs and read the captions that go with them. Which one is a favorite of yours? Why? How does it capture your attention? Have you ever tried to go up to strangers to try to interview them or take their photograph? Was it easy or hard? Why? If you want, you can try doing your own *Humans* photos and post them through your social media channels.

Longtail Content

The internet, through blogs, podcasts, and user-video sites such as YouTube, has opened up the options for long-tail news that doesn't get out through legacy (or mainstream) channels. Take the concept of **citizen journalism**. Often when we talk about citizen journalism, we are talking about a newspaper-like blog that posts reports about hyperlocal issues, such as neighborhood events or elementary school sports. These provide valuable alternatives to stories carried in traditional newspapers or on local television news. But they have more in common with the old-time community newspapers that ran stories about who had dinner with whom than with cutting-edge journalism.

But amateur cell phone video shared through sites such as YouTube can lead to ordinary citizens taking video that has national implications. When Minneapolis police arrested George Floyd on May 25, 2020, on suspicion of using a counterfeit $20 bill to buy cigarettes, there were a number of people outside the convenience store watching. Several of those bystanders recorded the eight minutes and 15 seconds while an officer pinned the Black man to the ground with a knee on his neck. Floyd eventually died of neck compression injuries. The white officer who held Floyd down was charged with third degree murder, second degree murder and second-degree manslaughter. Three more officers were charged with aiding and abetting second degree murder.[50]

As the host of videos of Floyd's death at the hands of police spread (including some from security cameras), so did the Black Lives Matter protests. The *New York Times* reports that in the month-and-a half following Floyd's death there were protests in at least 140 cities and that the National Guard was called out in at least 21 states.[51] While protests during the day were typically peaceful, late at night violence erupted in a number of cities when police wearing riot gear tried to disperse the crowds with tear gas, pepper balls, and other less-lethal munitions. These protests were covered by reporters working for regular media outlets who were sometimes attacked by police along with protesters. (For more on the attacks on journalists, see Chapter 14.) But there were also participants recording cell-phone video and sharing them through social media. These social media channels also allowed for misleading videos to spread as well. For example, a video seen more than 4 million times on Twitter claimed to show an FBI agent being arrested and then released. In reality, the video was a year old and showed the arrest and release of a someone who was mistaken for a wanted man. Another video claimed to show a US police building on fire; in reality the video was from 2015 and showed an explosion in Tianjin, China.[52] These deceptive videos made it hard for people seeking information about the protests to know what was real and what was fake.

The first use of the internet by the movie industry was to promote films through brochure-like web pages. Then came *The Blair Witch Project*, which showed how interaction on the web could draw in viewers (see Chapter 7). This has evolved into the internet being used as the screening venue for short films. And now film sites on the web have become the minor leagues of the movie and television industry. Aspiring filmmakers first establish themselves with a short, low-cost internet film in the hope that someone in the industry will notice them.[53] Of course, on user-generated content sites, such as YouTube, the short films can be beyond low budget.

Another thing the internet can do is air films that may be too avant-garde for conventional media. The streaming service Fandor serves up an eclectic mix of art house film, vintage B movies, and offbeat documentaries. But *New York Times* film critic Glenn Kenny says what really makes the streaming site stand out is its interesting menu structure. Look for action/adventure, and you'll see subchoices of "Martial Arts," "Sword and Sandal," "Wilderness," and "Treasure

Eagle vs Shark (2007)/Photofest

▲ *Eagle vs Shark* director Taika Waititi, center, on the set with stars Loren Horsley (left) and Jemaine Clement (right). Waititi would go on to make the blockbuster *Thor: Ragnarok*, but this earlier indie film can be streamed on Fandor.

Hunting." The viewer can also search by running time of the movie or year of release. The choices here are clearly different from what pops up on Netflix or Amazon Prime. On the front page as this is being written is a promo for the 2007 New Zealand comedy *Eagle vs Shark* by Taika Waititi, who burst onto the world stage in 2017 with *Thor: Ragnarok*.[54]

But, of course, as we discussed in Chapter 8, online is the place for watching mainstream television and movie programming from services such as Netflix, Hulu, Amazon Prime and Disney+. And during the COVID-19 pandemic, movies that would normally have opened in theaters have been instead offered as premium video on demand. Programs can be had through streaming video podcasts and digital downloads of movies and television shows through online services such as iTunes or Amazon.com. From there, users can view their video on computers, smartphones, tablets, or smart televisions. Back in 2000, Martin French, who worked for the internet film site MeTV, put it this way: "Let's be honest, nobody wants to sit in front of the PC and [watch movies]. It's not a comfortable position."[55] Obviously, people are willing to view video on their computers, tablets, and even smartphones. It is true that alternative devices have gotten better, but there is an ongoing cultural change on how people view video.

The Internet and Society: Hacker Ethic

Despite having its roots in the world of military research, the internet works primarily to permit the independent use of computers. The earliest users of time-sharing computer systems, in which several people on separate terminals could share a single computer, started seeing these large institutional computers as "theirs." Stewart Brand, author of the *Whole Earth Catalog*, said that users soon began to understand how they could use computers for their own purposes:

> Kennedy had said, "Ask not what your country can do for you. Ask rather what you can do for your country." . . . Basically we were saying, "Ask not what your country can do for you. Do it yourself." You just tried stuff and you did it yourself. You didn't ask permission.[56]

This would become the rallying cry of the internet: Take control of it for yourself. This attitude sent shock waves throughout the media industry because it transformed the model of mass communication from one in which a minimal number of producers delivered news, entertainment, and culture to a public whose choices were limited. Instead, it became one in which consumers can choose for themselves what news they want to learn about, what movies they want to see, what music they will listen to, and when they will do so.

This environment of uncontrolled information is not all bliss, however. Some critics point out that the same giant media companies that dominated the older forms of media produce much of the content available on the internet. Others complain that information on the internet is uncontrolled, unreliable, and often unsuitable for young people to view.

As a young man, Steve Jobs saw programming computers as a way of rebelling against and controlling an increasingly technological world. Jobs and Steve Wozniak, the cofounders of Apple, built electronic "blue boxes" that let them place long-distance phone calls for free by bypassing AT&T's control system. Beyond allowing the two to steal phone service and play an occasional prank, the boxes taught Jobs that technology could empower individuals:

Courtesy of O'Reilly Media

▲ Author and journalist Steven Levy laid out the principles of hacker culture in his 1984 book *Hackers*, written years before the internet became a popular mass medium.

What we learned was that we could build something ourselves that could control billions of dollars' worth of infrastructure in the world . . . . We could build a little thing that could control a giant thing. That was an incredible lesson.[57]

Jobs's attitude embodied what is known as the **hacker ethic**. The ethic is summed up in Steven Levy's book *Hackers*, originally published in 1984, before the internet was a public medium and before many of the major internet tools, most notably the World Wide Web, had been developed. (Levy uses the term *hackers* to refer to people who like programming computers and using them to their fullest potential. He prefers using *digital trespassers* to refer to people who break into institutional computers. It appears, however, that many of the "true" hackers are often also digital trespassers.)

Understanding the hacker ethic is critical to understanding the development of the internet because its values shaped so many of the new medium's developers. Levy lists four key principles of the hacker ethic:[58]

1. "Access to computers—and anything which might teach you something about the way the world works—should be unlimited and total." Hackers want to obtain programs, data, and computers, and they do not respect rules that keep them from these tools. They believe that they should be able to directly control any computer system they can find; what's more, they believe that they can probably do a better job of running the system than the people who own it.

2. "All information wants to be free." This translates into a disregard for copyright law. Hackers believe that all information should be available to anyone who wants to make use of it. This was at the heart of file-sharing pioneer Napster and user-video site YouTube. If you have music, photographs, artwork, writings, or programs on your hard drive, why shouldn't you be able to share them? And if those same things exist on other computers, why shouldn't you be able to access them? This idea of universally shared information is at the heart of Berners-Lee's design of the World Wide Web.

3. "Mistrust authority—promote decentralization." The hacker culture distrusts centralized bureaucratic authority. Bureaucracies hide information and make rules controlling who can have access to it. So the best way to keep information free is to keep it out in the open.

4. You should be judged by your skills and not by "bogus criteria such as degrees, age, race, or position." On the internet, traditional measures of individuals, such as age, education, sex, or income, matter less than they do under most other conditions because people are able to create identities for themselves that may or may not correspond with their actual identities. In essence, this is an extension of the multiple roles and identities people have always had. You can simultaneously be a teacher, a parent, a spouse, and a child. On the internet, users can further extend their identities, changing their sex, race, and background.

The application of the values of the hacker ethic to the internet in general provides an example of Secret 3—Everything from the margin moves to the center.

Hacking the 2016 Presidential Election

One of the most enduring controversies over the 2016 presidential election is the role that Russian hacking played in the results of the election. As you may recall, Hillary Clinton won the popular vote by nearly three million votes, but Donald Trump won the all-important electoral vote 306–232.[59] He did so because of the votes of eighty thousand in three states— Michigan, Pennsylvania, and Wisconsin.[60] So the question of what may have affected that small number of votes looms large.

While the story of what happened during the 2016 election is still being debated, several things are relatively well understood:

- The Russian digital propaganda company the Internet Research Agency set up fake Facebook and Twitter accounts that attempted to promote messages of dissent on issues such as LGBT issues, race, immigration, and gun rights. Some of these accounts had actual people behind them while others were automated bots that republished and amplified news that matched their programming.

- Russian news organizations *Russia Today* (*RT*) and *Sputnik* spread false stories on social media both through regular messages and paid ads. Both organizations have now been banned from advertising on Twitter.

- Russian hackers broke into Democratic National Committee computer networks and stole thousands of emails and other documents. They then released this through websites they controlled and Julian Assange's WikiLeaks. While these documents did not have any radical secrets, they did show the ugly infighting that occurs in every political operation.

- Russian hackers also broke into voter registration systems in thirty-nine states. While they attempted to modify some of the records, there is no evidence that they changed any actual votes.[61]

Figuring out what the Russians did is substantially easier than deciding what sort of effect the digital meddling had. *New Yorker* journalist Adrian Chen, often held up as an expert on the Russian hacking, writes that we should not overstate the effectiveness of the campaign by a group of Russians who barely spoke English. "[It] ignores people's tendency to share information they already agree with; and it sees evidence, in the spread of that information among self-interested groups, of some grand design by a mastermind propagandist."[62]

Election (and baseball) statistical journalist Nate Silver, at his *FiveThirtyEight* blog, cautions giving too much credit to the Russian hacking/interference in the election, writing that former FBI director James Comey's letter to Congress coming out the week before the election about Hillary Clinton's email investigation likely swayed more voters. (Does that number, 538, sound familiar? That is the number of electoral votes there are in our presidential election system.) Silver argues that Russian interference is hard to track in terms of importance because it was not just one thing. But mostly he argues that the Russian efforts were relatively small compared to the campaign as a whole. The Russian effort spent about $1.25 million a month, while the Trump campaign and associated organizations spent $617 million overall, and the Clinton campaign and her supporters spent $1.2 billion. Nevertheless, Silver notes that the themes of the Russian efforts matched those of the reasons that Clinton lost. The belief that Clinton was dishonest and untrustworthy were boosted by Russian-supported hashtags like #Hillary4Prison. The hacking of the Democratic National Committee's computer network and the subsequent release of emails were also important.[63]

The Notion of Cyberspace

The word *cyberspace* is used extensively to describe the internet and the interactions that take place there. But the word predates common use of the internet and the shared culture it has created. The word *cybernetics* (from the Greek *kybernetes*, meaning "pilot" or "governor") has been in use since 1948 to refer to a science of communication and control theory. Science-fiction writer William Gibson is generally credited with coupling the prefix *cyber* to the word *space* in his 1984 novel *Neuromancer*, although the authoritative *Oxford English Dictionary* (see Chapter 4) notes that Gibson originally used the word in a magazine story in 1982. Gibson defines cyberspace in this way: "Cyberspace is where the bank keeps your money. It's where a long-distance telephone call happens. It's this ubiquitous, non-physical place where increasingly a lot of what we think of as our civilization takes place."[64] Gibson sees cyberspace and the culture of the internet as an expression of the hippie ideals of freedom and self-expression: "Tired as I am with all the hype about the Internet and the info highway, I suspect that from a future perspective it will be on a par with the invention of the city as a force in human culture."[65]

The Internet and Society: Our Online World

Before the 1900s, it was relatively easy to define community: The community was made up of the people you interacted with every day. But the growth of the mass media led to changes in our understanding of community. People no longer need to be face-to-face with each other to interact. Larry Tesler, who helped develop the idea of computer communities at the Xerox PARC research center and at Apple Computer, has said that

> when we were human beings in small tribes hunting and gathering, everybody you had to deal with was somebody you saw every day. We're a species that's based on communication with our entire tribe. As the population grew and people had to split up into smaller tribes and separate, they got to the point where they would never see each other for their whole lives. The Internet is the first technology that lets us have many-to-many communication with anybody on the planet. In a sense, it's brought us back to something we lost thousands of years ago. So one reason I think the Internet's taken off so fast is that we always needed it. And we finally have it.[66]

In *The Victorian Internet*, author Tom Standage argues that the nineteenth-century telegraph was also a significant global development, serving many of the same purposes as the internet at the end of the twentieth century and the beginning of the twenty-first. According to him, the telegraph was "a world-wide communications network whose cables spanned continents and oceans, [and] it revolutionized business practice, gave rise to new forms of crime, and inundated its users with a deluge of information."[67]

The telegraph system was followed by both radio and the telephone as media that could tie large areas of the world together. While the earliest components of the internet were in use by 1969, the net was limited largely to interpersonal communication until 1991, when Berners-Lee released the World Wide Web as an easy and uniform way to access material on the internet. Although the internet owes a historical debt to the early telegraph and telephone systems, it has grown into a new medium unlike any other because it is the only one that incorporates elements of interpersonal, group, and mass communication. The unique nature of the internet, especially in a global context, poses new moral dilemmas concerning national boundaries, corporate control, freedom of the press, and the rights of individuals. As you read about global media in different countries later in this book, keep in mind some of these issues.

When Tesler claims that the internet allows people to interact with others anywhere on the planet, he overstates the case. Worldwide, approximately 46 percent of the population has internet access.[68] In developing countries, that number can average 35 percent, compared to 82 percent of the population in developed nations.[69] But the spread of mobile technology is helping bring change. Sub-Saharan Africa has the lowest percentage of people online, with only 20 percent having access, but that represents a 111 percent increase since 2010. This growth is coming because people are now getting access via phones using mobile broadband. And that technology is allowing for the 40 percent growth rate in Africa. Companies like Facebook and Google are putting substantial effort into bringing inexpensive over-the-air internet services to poorer areas.[70]

Even in the United States, access to a high-quality internet connection is not universal. Although there are not large systemic differences in access based on race and ethnicity, research by Pew shows that access to high-speed broadband connections go up as people's education levels and income increase. Urban people are also more likely to have broadband than people in rural settings.[71]

Conflicts Over Digital Media

For all the benefits associated with the web, the new medium has been criticized on a few fronts. For one thing, a great deal of material on the web is inappropriate for children. Another criticism is that web surfers and mobile users give up their privacy going online. Finally, it is argued that people spend so much time with their virtual communities and friends that they forget about their real lives.

Controlling Content on the Web.

The World Wide Web differs from all other media in that it is essentially an open forum where anyone can publish anything. More importantly, anyone can access anything he or she wants to. Because of this lack of control, unsupervised web surfing is not particularly suitable for children. As computers and the internet came to classrooms in the 1990s, parents and teachers became concerned about the possibility of students viewing pornography, hate speech, or even instructions on how to build a homemade bomb.

One solution to this problem is the use of filtering software, which can block access to certain kinds of material. This approach has been successful to a degree, but no filtering scheme can block all offensive material and still allow access to a full range of sites. For example, in 1998, the Loudoun County, Virginia, public libraries installed filtering software. The software successfully blocked pornographic material, but it also blocked sites with information on sex education, breast cancer, and gay rights.[72] The fundamental problem with trying to control information on the net is that the network of networks was designed specifically to overcome blocks and breakdowns. Once information is on the net, it is virtually impossible to stop it from spreading. Net pioneer John Gilmore summed up the issue neatly: "The Net interprets censorship as damage and routes around it."[73]

Attendees use a smartphone to take a selfie during an independence celebration in Nairobi, Kenya. People in developing countries like Kenya are most likely to go online using mobile devices.

Privacy and the Web.

A consumer walking into a conventional bookstore can wander from aisle to aisle, picking up titles of interest. After leaving the store, no one knows what books the consumer looked at. But when that same consumer shops at the online bookstore Amazon.com, the store keeps track of everything looked at. The Amazon software will then make recommendations to the shopper according to previous searches and purchases. Is this a great convenience or a serious loss of privacy?

As we discussed in the opening vignette, online users give up their privacy every time they fire-up their browser or app. Each time they fill out a form, join a group, or buy something, information (name, address, interests, etc.) is stored so that the owner of the site will know more about its visitors. On mobile devices, the mobile advertising ID helps advertisers, websites, and apps know about who is connecting with a given company. Websites make use of tiny files called **cookies** to identify website visitors and potentially track their actions on the web. Cookies may identify users so that they don't have to reenter their names and passwords. Or, as Amazon's cookies do, they might keep track of which types of items a visitor likes to look at. Cookies are generally designed to assist users as they visit one particular website, but they can also be used to track users' web-surfing habits or to provide evidence of what sites they have visited.

Website developers can use cookies to tailor sites to a particular visitor. For example, a news site could use information from a cookie to provide the scores of your favorite teams, quotes for the stocks in your portfolio, or reviews of the style of music you like. This tailoring to individual tastes could take a more sinister cast, however. Web creator Berners-Lee speculates that cookies could even be used to tailor propaganda to match the biases of the viewer:

Imagine an individual visiting the webpage of a political candidate, or a controversial company. With a quick check of that person's record, the politician or company can serve up just the right mix of propaganda that will warm that particular person's heart—and tactfully suppress points he or she might object to.[74]

Convergence of Old and New Media

There is lots of talk these days about convergence and new media, such as why the web will replace the old dead-tree media (newspapers and magazines), broadcast media, and other formats as the main source for news. New media synergy, we are told, will bring together the depth of text with an abundance of photos, audio, and video. You get all the advantages of the old media in one package.

There are signs that this is happening. NPR (formerly National Public Radio) launched its new NPR.org website in July 2009 with the goal of enabling journalists to present photos, video, audio, and written stories to go with streaming copies and transcripts of all the stories that have aired on NPR since May 2005. The site also makes these resources available on mobile media, such as the iPhone and Android.[75]

Convergence is also delivering media that would not be available otherwise. As will be discussed in Chapter 11, the Arab news channel Al Jazeera started its English-language service in November 2006, but it had trouble finding any U.S. cable or satellite services willing to carry it. For the time being, Americans who are interested in news from Al Jazeera must do so primarily over the internet or using their social media service AJ+.

Sometimes you get reverse synergy—the worst of the old and new media in one new package. A prime example of reverse synergy happened in 2008 when Bloomberg's online financial news service posted a six-year-old news story about United Airlines (UAL) filing for bankruptcy. The story was true—it was just six years out of date. What happened was this: An undated story about UAL's 2002 bankruptcy filing showed up on a Google search on "bankruptcy 2008" done by a reporter working for Income Securities Advisor. The story from the South Florida *Sun-Sentinel* dated back to December 10, 2002, when UAL did file for bankruptcy. The reporter who performed the search posted the story to Bloomberg News. In response to the story, investors started dumping their shares in UAL, dropping the stock from $12.17 a share to approximately $3 a share. Not realizing what had happened, UAL was baffled by the tanking of its stock, but it quickly posted an online denial of the story. By the time the market closed, UAL stock was back up to $10.92.[76]

What can we learn from this? Think about Secret 7—There is no "they." The story that sent the stock price crashing was a single story from a single website. Wouldn't you think that if a major corporation had filed for bankruptcy twice in six years the story would be playing on every major news site, not just a single Florida paper that had no local connection to the story? At the risk of oversimplifying things, the story was posted because someone—a "they"—said it was so. This resulted in a huge destruction of wealth, albeit a temporary one, because of a story that had no truth value and apparently was posted completely by accident.

Everything Is Data

We are moving into an age where media are increasingly being delivered digitally. And that means we will be moving away from old channels like cable television, paper, or cellular phone service and moving into the use of data services.

Think about it—how often do you come close to using up your allocation of cell phone minutes? Maybe you do not even have a limit on minutes anymore. The same is likely true of text messages (i.e., SMS).

But what about when it comes to data? Ah, that is a different story. How long do you get into the month before you start getting warning notes from your provider that you have used 50 percent, 75 percent, or 90 percent of your data allocation? Of course, your mobile provider is always quite happy to sell you another bucket of data.

Think about all the things you use data for on your mobile device: streaming audio and video, social media, games, maybe even a little old-school email. You might also be sending photos and video back upstream through Snapchat, Instagram, or Periscope.

If you are on an iPhone, you likely burn through a lot of data using FaceTime to make your audio and video calls (though if you're smart about it, you're using Wi-Fi whenever possible). And everyone is burning through data one way or another with Skype.

Over in the world of the television, we are seeing this transformation as well. Right now, at least if you are old, you think of TV as something that comes in through cable or down from the skies via satellite. If you are really old (or poor), you think of it as something that comes in over the air through an antenna.

But as we discussed in Chapter 8, increasingly we are getting our video programming from streaming services. When I ask my students about the most recent programming they watched on television, the most common answer (apart from the World Series broadcast) was Netflix. Now Netflix is a streaming service that you get over the internet using data. Netflix is just one of many sources of streaming video: Hulu, CBS's All Access, Amazon Prime, and the list goes on.

Apple has offered a streaming box for several years called Apple TV that the late Jobs used to refer to as a hobby. But with the release of the newest version of it, Apple seems to be taking it much more seriously—with the idea that the new Apple TV could serve as a substitute to your cable or satellite service—assuming you have a big bucket of data to support it.[77]

CHAPTER REVIEW

CHAPTER SUMMARY ▶▶

The internet arose in the late 1960s out of efforts to share expensive computer resources provided by the military to universities across the United States. The initial network, called ARPAnet, went online for the first time in the fall of 1969. The network operated using packet switching, a method of transferring information that breaks down messages into small packets that are transmitted separately across the network and reassembled once they are received. Through email and file sharing, ARPAnet soon became a tool used by academics to collaborate and communicate across the country.

As the number of incompatible networks grew in the 1970s, Bob Kahn and Vint Cerf developed the TCP/IP protocols that allowed the networks to communicate with each other. In 1983, ARPAnet started using the TCP/IP protocols. This is commonly seen as the true beginning of the internet.

The internet is unique among the mass media in allowing interpersonal communication through email and instant messaging and group communication through email, instant messaging, SMS, the World Wide Web, search, mobile apps, blogs, podcasts, and streaming media.

The World Wide Web was developed in 1989 by British physicist Tim Berners-Lee while he was working at the European Organization for Nuclear Research in Switzerland. His goal was to produce a decentralized system for creating and sharing documents anywhere in the world. The web has three major components: the uniform resource locator (URL), the hypertext transfer protocol (http), and the hypertext markup language

(HTML). Berners-Lee published the code for the World Wide Web on the internet in 1991 for anyone in the world to use at no cost.

The internet in general and the web in particular were based on a set of values known as the hacker ethic. This ethic holds that information should be freely distributed and that individuals should have as much control over computers as possible.

The World Wide Web has turned the internet into a major mass medium that provides news, entertainment, and community interaction. The web offers a mix of content providers, including traditional media companies, new media companies offering publications available only on the web, **aggregator sites** that offer help in navigating the web, and individuals who have something they want to say.

Mobile devices are increasingly becoming the dominant way for people to go online, with 85 percent owning smartphones, and users are replacing open access web pages with closed access through apps.

The web has been criticized for elevating rumors to the level of news, making inappropriate material available to children, collecting private information about users, and creating a false sense of intimacy and interaction among users. This can be seen with the Russian hacking of the 2016 U.S. presidential election.

Over the past several years, the transmission of media content has been moving from channels of legacy media into those of online digital media, allowing people to access content when and where they want to.

KEY TERMS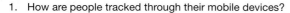

mobile advertising ID   215

internet   216

packet switching   217

ARPAnet   217

TCP/IP   218

electronic mail (email)   218

instant messaging (IM)   219

hypertext   219

World Wide Web   220

uniform resource locator (URL)   220

hypertext transfer protocol (http)   220

hypertext markup language (HTML)   220

Mosaic   221

broadband service   223

digital native   224

weblog (blog)   224

citizen journalism   226

hacker ethic   227

cookies   231

aggregator sites   233

REVIEW QUESTIONS ▸▸

1. How are people tracked through their mobile devices?

2. How was our first nationwide interactive computing network built?

3. How does interacting online differ when you do it through an app rather than through the World Wide Web?

4. What does your author mean when he writes "Everything is data"? What kind of transformation is taking place in the legacy media industry as more media are transmitted digitally?

FreeCell

Flo Period & O

CHAPTER 10

SOCIAL MEDIA AND VIDEO GAMES

Becoming Part of the Story

You may have seen the heartwarming story about Carson King, a young man who held up a sign at a 2019 University of Iowa/Iowa State football game soliciting money to buy a case of Busch Light beer. The sign, seen on ESPN's *College GameDay*, went viral on social media and King initially brought in more than $600 in contributions. (But stay with us; that number's going to grow.) And while the story will end fine for King, it will not for everyone else involved.

Once King realized how much money he had collected through the online money transfer service Venmo, he decided he needed to do something good with his windfall. When he announced he was going to donate the money to University of Iowa Stead Family Children's Hospital, Anheuser Busch (AB) and Venmo both pledged to match the money he had raised. Contributions continued to pour in, and the total amount raised rapidly exceeded $1 million. (That number's also going to grow.) AB was discussing using King as an influencer, perhaps even putting his face on beer cans.[1]

The *Des Moines Register*, a leading Iowa newspaper, had written about King while the story was breaking, and there was so much interest in King and his generosity that the paper decided to do a full-on profile. In reporter Aaron Calvin's article, most of what he wrote was complimentary. But toward the end of the story, Calvin discussed a pair of racist jokes King had posted on Twitter as a teenager. Before publishing the story, Calvin called King to talk about the tweets. King expressed regret to the reporter, and before the story was published, King spoke with local TV stations about the tweets. King made no complaints about the paper's background check on his social media profiles or about how the *Register* had treated him.

Unsurprisingly, once news of King's racist posts broke the folks at Busch Light rapidly distanced themselves from him, though they still agreed to make their pledged contribution to the children's hospital. The decision by Anheuser Bush to cut ties with King led to the event planners at the Iowa Oktoberfest in Waterloo to remove Busch Light from their tap list for the annual festival.[2] On top of the backlash against the *Des Moines Register* article, Iowa Governor Kim Reynolds made a decision to declare September 28 Carson King Day and praised his "message of generosity."[3]

But the story did not end there as reporter Calvin, who provided a sympathetic article about King (but did mention

King's offensive tweets), would experience a full-on assault from some Iowans and later other parts of the country. First, the *Des Moines Register* let Calvin go after the paper received hundreds of complaints about him and the story. Calvin said he felt as if the newspaper had abandoned him, even though he was following standard editorial practice for social media research. (Ironically, and as we have seen with many social media accounts, it turned out that Calvin also had a few questionable tweets in his feed from years ago.) Later, after news about the published tweets got out into the mainstream media, Calvin soon experienced attacks and vitriol against him that spread through mostly conservative media outlets. Also, in an all too familiar story regarding internet trolls, the reporter started receiving death threats for publishing King's racist tweets.[4]

There are a host of questions raised by this extraordinary story. For example,

- When should reporters dig into a subject's social media history? And what should they do with what they find?

- What do you think the reasons were for why people acted so strongly to King's two offensive tweets being reported in the newspaper?

- Do you agree with the way the newspaper handled the fallout from the article? Should the reported have been fired?

- Have you ever been on the receiving end of trolls or social media backlash?

The story did end well for the University of Iowa Children's Hospital, which received more than $2.9 million from King's beer fundraiser. In the end, King donated all the money he raised and only used enough to buy his original fundraiser request: one case of Busch Light beer.[5]

King and Calvin are far from the only people to have their lives changed by making ill-considered posts to social media. *Guardians of the Galaxy* movie franchise director James Gunn was fired by Disney in July 2018 when a number of offensive tweets he posted dating back to 2009 were brought to people's attention by alt-right activist Mike Cernovich who dug them out and started publicizing them.[6] The tweets have since been deleted. Gunn had also received criticism over some of his online writings from the feminist geek culture website *The Mary Sue* back as early as 2012. Gunn made full apologies for what he had posted, expressing regret at his "totally failed and unfortunate efforts to be provocative."[7]

Washington Post columnist Megan McArdle asks how we should deal with cases like Gunn's in the future:

> We don't have a statute of limitations for murder, of course, and I'm not advocating a blanket amnesty for heinous offenses. . . . But people who merely made dumb jokes should be offered the chance to apologize and to start with a clean slate, rather than seeing their lives wrecked over ephemeral missteps.[8]

It can be alarming how quickly things can escalate on social media to completely change a person's life for good or ill. These relatively new online services allow us to communicate in what feels like a one-on-one manner while we are sharing our messages with much of the online world. Video games have reached much the same point with online connectivity that allows our virtual avatars to interact with a range of imaginary worlds inhabited by very real people. In this chapter we will consider how these intensely interactive media developed and how they have shaped the world in which we now all live.

Social Media: Sharing Our Lives Online

Like so much of the media, social networks (also known as **social media**) are a central part of how we live (remember Secret 1—The media are essential components of our lives). While time and distance used to be barriers to communication, these can now be crossed with relative ease if you have access to some basic online technology, whether through desktop computers or mobile devices. We think of mobile phones as a transformational technology, but the social networks we can access through these phones can transform things even further.

What is a social network? According to researchers M. Chethan and Mohan Ramanathan, "Social networks connect individuals or groups over a common platform. Once connected, the human tendency to share information or chat (talk?) trivia becomes the driving force, creating a mind-boggling amount of information and traffic."[9] What do social media have that makes them social? Chethan and Ramanathan write that there are five basic characteristics that make social media social:

1. **User-generated content**—Social networks are not websites where you go just to consume content; you go there to create it. This content can include written words, photos, podcasts, and streaming audio and video.

2. **Comments**—The communication does not just flow from one creator to other consumers. Everyone who is active on the social network is commenting on what others are posting. This interaction can range from extensive online debates to things as simple as "liking" a photo on Facebook.

3. **Tagging**—People tag, or mark, photos and text in which they are featured. They can also tag ideas or keywords within their posts, such as the hashtags in Twitter. Although the

hashtag is now seen as an essential part of Twitter culture, it was more than a year after the service started that the hashtag was first created as an organizing principle on social media.[10]

4. **Social networking**—People are able to share what they post online with groups of friends or like-minded people. These can be groups of friends on Facebook, stories on Snapchat, or followers on the simple blogging service Tumblr.

5. **Customization**—People can make their social network pages unique. For example, on your Facebook page, you get to choose a small profile photo and a larger "cover" photo. On your Twitter page, you get a small "avatar" image, and you can set the colors and background.

Among the most popular social networks are YouTube, the video sharing service; Facebook, the giant of the field; Instagram, where everyone is sharing their photos; Snapchat, where younger people communicate; pinboard site Pinterest; the professionally oriented LinkedIn; microblogging site Twitter; the global messaging service WhatsApp; and the growing Chinese video sharing service TikTok.[11]

While we often think about social media as being primarily for recreational or social purposes, they can also be used by businesses and organizations for collaboration, public relations, and crowdsourcing—a fancy term for getting other people to do your homework. Remember, though, it is not just these most popular media channels that are social. As Secret 5 reminds us—All media are social.

YouTube

YouTube was founded by three friends who were early employees at Elon Musk's internet payment company PayPal. When eBay bought out PayPal in 2002, Chad Hurley, Steven Chen, and Jawed Karim had their chance to try something new.[12] The three got the idea for YouTube after a dinner party at Chen's house where many of the guests, who were shooting video using video cameras or cell phones, wanted to share their videos.

"We found it very easy to share the photos with one another," Chen says. "But when we tried to share the movies, and we tried to e-mail the movies, they kept getting rejected, bounced back. . . . This was going to be more and more of a problem for different people."[13]

"We saw an opportunity to help people with video," Hurley said. "People have access to devices that have video capability from digital cameras to cell phones and don't have an easy way to share those clips with one another. So, we went about simplifying this process to empower everyone with the ability to use video online."[14]

The following year, Google bought out the founders, and YouTube has grown into the biggest video-sharing site online. And while much of the content now is entertainment programming put up to make money with advertising, the roots of the social video-sharing site that it started as are still there. YouTube is the most popular social media network, used by 91 percent of people ages eighteen to twenty-nine.[15] (See Table 10.1.)

Facebook

As anyone who has seen the movie *The Social Network* knows, Mark Zuckerberg created Facebook while he was a student at Harvard back in 2004. As a child, Zuckerberg created a simple messaging

▼ TABLE 10.1

Top Social Media Sites, 2020

Channel	Age 12+	Age 12–34
YouTube	73% (U.S. adults)	91% (age 18–29)
Facebook	63%	64%
Instagram	41%	68%
Snapchat	31%	61%
Pinterest	29%	32%
LinkedIn	22%	22%
Twitter	22%	29%
WhatsApp	20%	29%
TikTok	11%	25%

Source: "Who Uses YouTube, WhatsApp and Reddit." *Pew Research Center,* June 12, 2019, http://www.pewresearch.org/internet/chart/who-uses-youtube-whatsapp-and-reddit/; Edison Research, "The Infinite Dial 2020," http://www.edisonresearch.com/wp-content/uploads/2020/03/The-Infinite-Dial-2020-from-Edison-Research-and-Triton-Digital.pdf.

Note: YouTube data is from 2019. Both Instagram and WhatsApp are owned by Facebook.

program that solved the problem of how his father's front office could announce that a dental patient had arrived. Instead of playing computer games, he created them, according to a profile of him that ran in the *New Yorker*.

While there is controversy as to who developed the idea of Facebook, there can be little doubt that Zuckerberg turned the concept into an incredibly popular tool for communicating with friends. He told journalist Jose Antonio Vargas (whom we will talk about further in Chapter 15) that when he was in college, he and his friends would speculate about how people would use the internet. "We'd say, 'Isn't it obvious that everyone was going to be on the Internet?'" he said. "'Isn't it, like, inevitable that there would be a giant social network of people?' It was something that we expected to happen."[16] As of 2020, more than 63 percent of Americans age twelve and older were on Facebook, and more than 2.4 billion people were active on Facebook worldwide, making it far and away the biggest conventional social network.[17] (YouTube may be bigger, but it is much more limited in what services it provides.) Facebook differs from much of the web and has more in common with the old AOL than with the web in general. It is a "walled garden" where people can play games, share articles, and post cute videos of cats. Central to Facebook is the idea that advertisers will be able to reach exactly the consumers that they want to based on information people have shared on Facebook. Even if you try to limit what Facebook can know about you, it still can discover quite a bit. Even if you turn off location tracking, Facebook can generally figure out where you are based on your IP address. And Facebook can use information from your browsing outside of Facebook to target ads at you. (You can read more about Facebook and concerns over its privacy policies at the beginning of Chapter 3.)

Social media groups can be a difficult place to be during times of social change and conflict because it forces us to confront things we may not like about our family, friends, and social groups. During the spring of 2020, Facebook groups covering topics ranging from being entrepreneurs and moms to long-distance motorcycle riders to local communities melted down over opinions about the COVID-19 pandemic and the Black Lives Matter protests following the death of George Floyd while being arrested by Minneapolis police. Moderators of these forums often have no training on how to handle name calling and rancorous debate, yet they must try to keep the peace.

Facebook has posted resources for moderators and some guidelines of its own, but critics say even Facebook itself does not follow its rules. Ashley Carman, writing for the *Verge*, notes that people are leaving groups when moderators point out that political content is banned.[18] Consider the example of a group for fans of the musician Hozier. Hozier has personally posted a great deal to his own social media sites about Black Lives Matter. But the fan group is not allowed to discuss these same political issues. Those who still want to talk politics have been invited to take their discussion elsewhere.

Lisa Lake / Contributor / Getty Images

▲ Irish musician, singer, songwriter Hozier is active on social media where he discusses political and social issues. But supporters of Hozier have been told by the people who run a fan page for him on Facebook to keep their political comments off the site.

Instagram

Instagram was born on July 16, 2010, and for all the photo-sharing site's evolution and growth into a social media powerhouse, in some ways, it has not changed that much. The very first post was by cofounder Mike Krieger with a filtered image of a marina shot through a window. The second was a workplace photo of cofounder Kevin Systrom. Later in the evening, there was a photo of beer and dinner, puppies, and people having fun for the evening. Everything except the selfie![19]

Instagram changed a lot over the following years, adding video, full frame as an option to the original square photo, and an ever-increasing number of filters. One important change has been the addition of tools to make it clearer when social media stars are putting up sponsored posts where they are being paid to feature a product in their photo.[20] The other big change happened in 2012 when Facebook paid $1 billion for Instagram. At the time, Instagram only had thirty million users and no revenue. By 2019, however, it had more than one billion monthly users, and it is expected to account for 30 percent of Facebook's advertising revenue in 2020.[21] It also paved the way for Facebook to buy the global messaging app WhatsApp and the virtual reality company Oculus.[22]

Like Snapchat, Instagram is much more heavily used by young people than adults (see Table 10.1). Instagram users also are likely to visit the site frequently.[23]

Snapchat

Snapchat is one of the most popular social media channels among young people, but once you get out of that demographic, its usage falls off. The instant message and photo-sharing service is used by 61 percent of Americans ages twelve to thirty-four, but only 31 percent of those ages twelve and up use Snapchat.[24] To those who use it, however, it is incredibly popular, with 71 percent of its young users visiting it multiple times a day.[25]

While Snapchat is wildly popular among young social media users, it has had trouble making money. Part of the reason is that its stripped-down design makes it harder to use for those who are not on it several times a day. Although Snapchat has a significant audience with 229 million daily global users, it is still an order of magnitude smaller than the 2-billion-subscriber Facebook.[26] *New York Times* reporter Kevin Roose writes that it was Snapchat's differences from Facebook that always made it stand out, with its auto-disappearing photos and messages. It was, as Roose writes, "temporary instead of permanent, private instead of public, candid instead of rehearsed."[27]

Although Snapchat is seen primarily as a youth-oriented social media service, forty-year-old California congressman Eric Swalwell, who live streamed a Democratic anti-gun sit-in on the House floor using Periscope, uses the app to connect with constituents. Unlike most politicians, Swalwell does his snapping himself rather than relying on his staff. Swalwell started sharing short videos, photos, and details about his daily life in a format where the material would be gone in a day to connect with younger voters. "I realized that so many of our constituents were on Snapchat," he told the *Hill.* "It wasn't just young people, but their parents had figured out that's where their kids are."[28]

Twitter

In 2006, three college dropouts developed Twitter, a medium that combines elements of mobile text messaging, online instant messaging, and a good dose of blogging. By 2017, it had more than 330 million people answering the question, "What are you doing?"[29] Evan Williams, Jack Dorsey, and Biz Stone started the microblogging Twitter service as a project while they were working for the podcasting company Odeo.[30] Twitter is designed to let people communicate with their friends, family, and coworkers using messages no longer than 140 characters. The little messages, known as tweets, can be delivered to your friends, your acquaintances, or anyone in the world who can be bothered to read them. You can send and receive tweets as emails, on Facebook, through a widget on a web page, or on your cell phone as text messages.

Technology consultant Charlene Li told the *Sunday Times* of London that Twitter can be valuable to businesses because they can use it to set up a two-way relationship with their customers, creating a sense of interaction. At a time when many consumers decide not to watch television commercials by fast-forwarding

Jack Dorsey, "twttr sketch" from Flickr. Licensed under CC BY 2.0, https://creativecommons.org/licenses/by/2.0/.

▲ Jack Dorsey's original sketch of what would become Twitter. In this version, he called it stat.us.

through them using their DVRs, they are still willing to receive messages, such as electronic coupons. "Twitter is a great platform to push out those messages," Li said. "I don't mind Starbucks making an announcement on my Twitter page but I don't want them in my inbox."[31]

In November 2017, Twitter made its biggest change to its microblogging service by doubling the maximum character count from 140 to 280. Twitter reports that the increased length did not cause most people to write longer tweets, but it did increase levels of traffic and engagement.[32] Later in this chapter we'll look at the controversies at Twitter over labeling potentially deceptive or dangerous tweets from prominent politicians.

TikTok

TikTok is the latest hot social media channel, used primarily for sharing short videos. While it might on the surface appear to be like Vine or other short video services, the difference is that TikTok is owned by a Chinese company that has a history of political censorship. TikTok is a relatively new social media channel, and during the winter of 2019/2020, it was the top app downloaded from the iOS store for Apple phones. During the first quarter of 2019, the app was downloaded an estimated 220 million times from the Apple app store and Google Play. And, as media scholar Michael Socolow points out, in September 2019, TikTok was the number one advertiser on Snapchat and the number two advertiser on YouTube.[33]

What concerns Socolow is not young people's infatuation with the quirky music videos on the service but the fact that few people realize that TikTok operates within Chinese censorship rules (see Chapter 11). How strongly the Chinese censor TikTok is not entirely clear. The *Guardian* newspaper published rules indicating that TikTok censored references to the Tiananmen Square massacre, Tibetan and Taiwanese independence, and banned religious group Falun Gong. And news about the recent protests about Chinese control of Hong Kong have been barely seen on the service. TikTok also took a blow to its reputation when it was discovered they were hosting beheading and other terrorist videos set to popular music.

In February 2019, the Federal Trade Commission fined TikTok $5.7 million for improperly collecting information about children under age thirteen.[34] In response to the fine, TikTok has been rolling out a series of new controls including keeping users under age thirteen from sharing, tagging, or creating videos. Another control disabled direct messages for children under age sixteen to help prevent online predators from contacting young people. Finally, there is a new feature that lets parents pair their account with that of their children under age thirteen to limit their screen time and put other controls on what they can view.[35]

The avowed goal of TikTok is for people to share things that cause them joy, and so it tends not to promote videos on more serious subjects, especially politics. In a practice known as "shadow banning," videos stay up on users' home pages, but they don't show up in TikTok's video feeds.

TikTok is notable for having more content moderation than any other social media channel. TikTok's algorithms tend to like people who put up a lot of content that is similar to what they've done in the past and what other people are doing; it likes remixing.[36] As of the fall of 2020, President Donald Trump was pushing for the Chinese owners of TikTok to sell the video-sharing service to an American-owned company.

Development of Video Games

Computers are tools we work with many (too many) hours of the day, but at their most powerful, they are channels for interaction—with ourselves, with others, and with the programmer's imagination. That interaction can make it feel like the computer is alive, that it is intelligent. British mathematician Alan Turing, who used an early computer to help break the German Enigma code during World War II, wanted to create an artificially intelligent machine that was good enough at interacting with us that we could no longer tell whether we were dealing with a person or with a machine. This would come to be known as the **Turing Test**.[47]

SHOULD THE PRESIDENT BE ACTIVE ON SOCIAL MEDIA?

OLIVIER MORIN / Contributor / Getty Images

A year following his election to the White House, real estate developer and former reality television host Donald Trump credited his use of social media, and Twitter in particular, for getting him elected. The president told Maria Bartiromo at Fox Business Network, "I doubt I would be here if it weren't for social media, to be honest with you."[37] Trump said he liked using Twitter because he could respond immediately and directly to his critics: "So when somebody says something about me, I am able to go bing, bing, bing, and I take care of it. The other way I would never get the word out."[38]

Communications professor David Gerzof Richard says President Trump has made a major transformation, going to social media rather than news media to get his messages out. "President Trump uses the platform to tell his story, his way," he said. "There is no editorial board, no fact checkers, no advisers, not filters—just a direct conduit to tens of millions of followers."[39]

Trump's effective use of Twitter harkens back to the work of Canadian economist and media theorist Harold Innis who wrote in the 1950s that new media that are biased toward rapid distribution of information rather than lasting a long time will tend to upset the social order.[40] (You can read more about Innis and his ideas back in Chapter 4.)

President Trump's most popular tweet of 2017 was of a video from 2007 that had Trump body slamming someone at WWE's WrestleMania. The video had been altered so that the man Trump slammed had his head replaced with a CNN logo. The tweet was discussed on the Sunday morning talk shows, and so it got amplification from the legacy media.

His second most popular tweet was part of an exchange of insults between the president and the head of North Korea.

President Trump wrote, "Why would Kim Jong-un insult me by calling me 'old,' when I would NEVER call him 'short and fat?' Oh well, I try so hard to be his friend—and maybe someday that will happen!"[41]

The president's use of a social media channel to handle much of his public communication has been controversial at a number of levels. In addition to his reputation for saying anything he wants to on social media, President Trump has had a history of blocking people who are critical of him. That means that not only does he not see what his critics post, but his critics can't see or comment on his posts.

In May 2018, federal district court judge Naomi Reice Buchwald ruled that President Trump's Twitter feed is a public forum, and so therefore he cannot block people from seeing or interacting with it. Judge Buchwald had previously suggested that if the president or other politicians did not want to see what critics were saying, they could "mute" them. Muting controls what the president would see but not what his followers would see.[42] This has First Amendment implications because presidential tweets are likely official government communication that must be freely available to everyone.

Social media channels have attracted criticism for giving powerful politicians like President Trump special treatment. Facebook, for example, has an official policy of not correcting politicians who put up deceptive content on their pages. "It is not our role to intervene when politicians speak," said Nick Clegg, Facebook's vice president of global affairs. "We do not submit speech by politicians to our independent fact-checkers, and we generally allow it on the platform even when it would otherwise breach our normal content rules."[43] Facebook has had a controversial fact-checking system in place since 2016, but there have been complaints about who the fact-checkers are and that Facebook will sometimes yield to political pressure on controversial topics.

The conflict came to the forefront when President Trump put a post on both Facebook and Twitter during the nationwide Black Lives Matter protests in late May 2020 that "when the looting starts, the shooting starts." President Trump said he was unaware of the phrase's racist history, but he kept the comment posted. Facebook did nothing with the post.[44] Twitter CEO Jack Dorsey had his company put a warning label on a tweet with the same text but did not take the post down.[45] Earlier that month, Twitter added a fact-checking label to a tweet from the president that advanced an unsupported conspiracy theory that MSNBC morning news host Joe Scarborough had murdered a young woman in his office more than two decades ago. In response to Twitter's action, the president

(Continued)

(Continued)

signed an executive order that attempts to take away protections from social media channels that they get under the Communications Decency Act of 1996.[46]

. . . .

WHO is the source?

Who is Donald Trump? How does he differ from other people on social media?

WHAT is he saying?

What is President Trump saying on Twitter and social media? Why is what he is saying controversial?

WHAT evidence is there?

Should presidents be able to block people on Twitter? Why or why not? Why is it different from you blocking someone you don't like? Should the president and other prominent politicians be allowed to violate rules that everyone else has to follow? Why or why not?

WHAT do you and your friends think about this?

Do you think that the president of the United States should be on Twitter? Why or why not? Is that an appropriate place for him to comment on world affairs or to criticize people he does not like?

▲ Mathematician and early computer scientist Alan Turing got little recognition during his life and immediately following his death in part because his work was secret but also because he was gay at a time when that was illegal in Great Britain. Turing is now honored with this statue at Bletchley Park where he worked on breaking the Germans' Enigma code.

Education Images / Contributor / Getty Images

Turing believed that having a computer play and win at chess would be a good way of demonstrating that intelligence, and though he was able to write a program to play chess, none of the computers of his time in the 1940s were capable of running the program. Much of what Turing did during his lifetime was classified Top Secret because of its importance for cryptography, and when he died in 1954, few people knew who he was or why he mattered.

Another reason Turing's role in developing our understanding of computers was initially neglected was because he was gay at a time when it was criminal in his native Britain to be homosexual. He was arrested in 1952 when the police came to his house to investigate a burglary, and Turing confessed to having a physical relationship with a man. He was arrested for "gross indecency" and was forced to undergo chemical castration by taking female hormones. Two years after his arrest, he died of cyanide poisoning, a death police ruled a suicide. He did not get an obituary in the *New York Times* until 2019 as part of a series to recognize people who had been neglected at the time of their deaths.[48]

What is quite likely the world's first video game to be demonstrated was in 1958 at an open house at Brookhaven National Laboratory in Long Island, New York. The *Tennis for Two* game was created by William Higinbotham, who had previously worked on the Manhattan Project nuclear bomb effort. It was displayed again in 1959, but its only lasting influence came from the people who saw this ancestor of *Pong*.

Then in 1961, a group of students at the Massachusetts Institute of Technology (MIT) got access to a $120,000 PDP-1 minicomputer and used it to write the two-player spaceship battle game called *Spacewar!*, complete with accurate physics and a star to provide gravity. The game became instantly popular with anyone who could get late night access to the computer, and Tristan Donovan writes in his history of video games that the students considered trying to sell the game. But the fact that it required a $120,000 computer to run made the commercial possibilities rather limited. So instead, they just gave it away.[49] Despite not being for sale (or perhaps because of that), *Spacewar!* moved rapidly around the country to wherever there were students working on a PDP-1 computer.

While the whiz kids at MIT were able to come up with a cool early video game to play on an expensive computer, the trick would be coming up with a way of presenting a simple dots-on-a-screen video game that could be constructed with inexpensive off-the-shelf electronic parts. That is what engineer Ralph Baer did when he and the company he worked for patented a device that could move dots around on a conventional home television set. Baer's employer, Sanders Associates, licensed the hardware to Magnavox, which sold this ping pong game and its variants as the Magnavox Odyssey system. It was a black-and-white system that came with colored overlays to place on the television screen to give the player a more interesting playing field.[50] Though Baer and Sanders Associates do not get a lot of discussion in video game history compared to Atari and Nintendo, both companies ended up having to license Baer's patent.

Atari Popularizes Video Games

The first company to really popularize video games was Atari, founded by Nolan Bushnell. The company got its start with a coin-operated arcade version of *Spacewar!* But the game was too complex to easily explain to people first encountering it in a bar or arcade and was not a financial success. The game that really put the company on the map was **Pong**. Al Alcorn was an engineer hired by Bushnell to create a knock-off of Baer's Magnavox game system. Bushnell called his initial company Syzygy (the astronomical term for when three planets line up) but changed it to **Atari** when he discovered Syzygy was already taken. Atari was the equivalent of "checkmate" in the ancient Chinese strategy board game *Go*.

Alcorn designed what would become the *Pong* arcade game using off-the-shelf parts and an inexpensive television set installed in an orange painted wooden box with a pair of knobs to control the paddles. Alcorn and Bushnell decided to test it out at a nearby bar—Andy Capp's Tavern. A week or so later, the bar manager called Alcorn to tell him the *Pong* machine wasn't working. Alcorn went to the bar to investigate and discovered that the coin box, actually an old coffee can, was full of at least $100 worth of quarters. The arcade game wouldn't work because customers couldn't put one more coin into it. The fix? Replace the small coffee can with a bigger milk carton.

Part of the game's success came from how simple it was to play. The production version would have three instructions on it:

- Deposit quarter

- Ball will serve automatically

- Avoid missing ball for high score

These first-generation video game arcade machines were bringing in roughly three-to-five times as much money as existing electro-mechanical pinball machines would. Back in 1972 these simple, non-computerized arcade video games were something radically new. Leslie Berlin, in his book *Troublemakers: Silicon Valley's Coming of Age*, wrote, "Most Americans had only seen screens display images sent from a broadcast network or projected from slides or a reel of film. *Pong* was different. It was interactive, viewer-commanded television."[51]

Atari engineer Harold Lee thought the company could make a home version of *Pong* that would be affordable using a design that could fit on a single integrated circuit chip. Atari would sell it through the Sears department and catalog store starting in 1974, and it was an instant hit. "It was the first time people have been able to talk back to their television set, and to make it do what they want it to do," Bushnell said. "It gives you a sense of control, whereas before all you could do was sit and watch channels."[52]

While *Pong* and its many variants brought the first primitive video games into the home, it was Atari's 2600 that really launched the home video game console market. The console was not cheap, costing $199 at its introduction in 1977. It came with *Combat*, a home version of the arcade game *Tank*. In order to afford such a massive project, Bushnell had to sell his company to Warner Communications for $28 million in 1976. (Warner Communications would go on to merge with Time Inc. to form Time Warner and is now at the core of WarnerMedia owned by tele-communications giant AT&T. For more on the history of WarnerMedia, turn back to Chapter 3 on the media business.) Bushnell's sale of Atari to Warner was also part of the common trend in the media industry where founders have to sell their small companies to a media giant in order to succeed. Yet another example of Secret 4—Nothing is new: Everything that happened in the past will happen again. East Coast corporate culture ended up being too much for the laid-back Bushnell, and in 1978, he left the company he founded, with manufacturing executive Ray Kassar being brought in to take over running the consumer division of Atari.

The Atari 2600 was not the first home video game console to make use of games burned into memory cartridges, but it was the first to be a big success. One of the main reasons Atari did so well was that there was quickly a big library of game cartridges available for it, including Warren Robinett's *Adventure* that plays a major role in the movie version of *Ready Player One*. Others included *Space Invaders*, *Pitfall*, and *Missile Command*. While these games seem primitive by today's standards, there is still an active interest in these vintage games, and mini-consoles containing a large library of preinstalled games from the time can be bought at discount stores. Other competitors from this time include ColecoVision, that brought *Donkey Kong* home, and Mattel's Intellivision.

By 1983, there were too many game cartridges being pushed out the door that were just plain bad, including one from Atari based on the hit movie *E.T. The Extra-Terrestrial* that virtually no one wanted to buy. And with that, the sale of home video games dropped from nearly $12 billion a year at its peak to just $360 million in 1985.[53] This left the industry ready for a reboot.

The other problem the Atari 2600 faced was the growing popularity of the VCR. Like video games, the VCR gave people control over their television sets, letting them shape what they wanted to consume. Rob Fulop, a game programmer, said, "All of a sudden you could see a movie at home whenever. It was amazing. Kids were watching and taping movies, computer games weren't what they did anymore."[54]

Importance of Arcades

Secret 5—All media are social—is emphatically true of video games. In the 1970s and early 1980s, when all the best games were in arcades, young people would gather there to meet with their friends, flirt, eat snacks, and yes, play video games. The 1970s were a time when enclosed shopping malls were getting to be big, and arcades were getting to be a significant part of them. This was a time when video games were getting more sophisticated, in large part because of a new type of integrated circuit—the microprocessor. These "computers on a chip" meant that game designers no longer needed to build all the circuits from scratch to make their games work. They could just write a program and run it through the game console's microprocessor.

How important were arcade machines during this era? They went from $50 million in dropped quarters in 1978 to a startling $900 million in 1981.[55] By way of comparison, the top ten grossing movies of 1981 brought in approximately $530 million.[56] Even at this early date, video games were starting to give movies a run for their money as a dominant force in youth culture. And by 1982, the combined home video game and arcade business was worth more than $5 billion a year.[57]

▲ Video game arcades had to start offering more immersive experiences such as this race car simulation in order to compete with the high quality of home consoles from the 1990s on to the present day.

The games themselves were not the only part of this. Guidebooks on how to beat the games filled the bestseller lists. The *Battlezone 3D* tank simulator inspired a group of retired Army generals to ask Atari to make a version of the game to help teach soldiers how to drive the Bradley Infantry Fighting Vehicle.

Video games, both then and now, have stereotypically (if not actually) appealed strongly to males with their conflict and violent themes. But when the bright yellow Pac-Man who gobbled up dots, fruits, and ghosts appeared on the scene in 1980, suddenly game manufacturers realized there was a bigger audience out there. "We decided to change the demographic by designing games that could appeal to women and thus to couples, therefore making game centers desirable places to go on a date," said Toru Iwatani, *Pac-Man*'s designer.[58] Iwatani started looking for imagery that would connect to eating, something of universal appeal, and when he found a picture of a pizza with a slice taken out of it, he knew he had his new character. For the overall design of the game, he built on the Japanese kawaii esthetic used in the Hello Kitty line of merchandise.

When *Pac-Man* hit, it hit big. The arcade games were everywhere, even places that didn't usually have game machines. There was an ABC-TV cartoon series. There were lunch boxes. There were sleeping bags. There were bumper stickers. There was even the hit song *Pac-Man Fever* that sold more than a million copies in 1982. MTV, which at the time was a music video network, had Pac-Man Day. And when *Pac-Man* came home to the Atari 2600, it sold more than twelve million copies globally. (Never mind the fact that the 2600 version was not very good. The game required more video capability than the first generation system could provide.)

Nintendo Revives Home Console Market

In 1889, Fusajiro Yamauchi founded the Marufuku Company to make and distribute Japanese playing cards. Then in 1951, Marufuku changed its name to Nintendo, a word meaning "leave luck to heaven."[59] So when Nintendo kicked off the next video game console surge in the United States in 1985 with its Nintendo Entertainment System, or NES, it was a nearly one hundred-year-old Japanese company trying to establish a foothold in the home video game market following the success of its *Donkey* Kong and *Super Mario Bros.* arcade games.

Nintendo made sure they didn't repeat the Atari 2600 problems of poor quality games by requiring that Nintendo approve and manufacture every cartridge for the system. Like the movies of the 1940s and 1950s, Nintendo had a set of rules for their games that were reminiscent of the Hays Production Code (see Chapter 7). While video games on other platforms got a lot of attention and sales from sparking controversy, Nintendo wanted their systems to be a place parents felt good about their children spending time. While Nintendo's obsessive control of every stage of game production gave the company the appearance of wanting to wring every dime out of the process, it was more a matter of the company wanting to make sure they never had a fiasco like the late Atari games.

Among the early games was *Super Mario Bros.*, a game still popular more than thirty-five years later. Japanese game designer Shigeru Miyamoto was in many ways responsible for the success of the NES, having created the *Donkey Kong* series, the *Super Mario Bros.* series, and the *Legend of Zelda* series.[60]

Nintendo faced competition from both Atari and Japanese competitor Sega. But while Sega would continue to find some level of success, Atari, after going through multiple owners, was never going to be a major player in home systems again.

The late 1980s brought new consoles, some more powerful—the Super NES and the Sega Genesis—as well as a simple, low-end system that would open up a whole new market for gaming: the Nintendo Game Boy. This portable system that was the size of an old pocket radio, had a small monochrome display, but it could go anywhere, it was inexpensive, and it came with the insanely popular *Tetris* as the packed-in game. The Game Boy would lead to the Game Boy Color, Game Boy Advance, as well as the Nintendo DS and 3DS, which would be among the bestselling systems ever. They also had the first cable and then wireless connections so that friends could play against each other on a pair of the systems, making them more social.

Sony PlayStation and Microsoft Xbox

All of the systems so far have generally used a two-dimensional perspective, something that changed with the Sony PlayStation (PS) family of disc-based systems. The PS was not the first system to use 3D polygon graphics, but it was the first to have substantial sales, setting up Sony to be one of the dominant system manufacturers. In its prime, the original PlayStation outsold all of its competitors combined. One line of games that really helped it become such a hit was the *Tomb Raider* series. Game designer Toby Gard wanted to make an Indiana Jones–style game without having to license intellectual property from Lucasfilm. So instead Gard created Lara Croft as the archaeologist heroine. With her tight, scant wardrobe and adolescent-male-fantasy body, Croft could hardly be considered a feminist icon, but she was transformative for games. *Tomb Raider* sold PS systems, Donovan writes, and the game tapped into the "girl power" movement of the late 1990s.[61] The games ended up being successful enough to lead to three movies based on them.

Sony has continued upping the processing power of its system, with the PlayStation 5 being announced while this book was in production. Sony, as a major maker of other media equipment, has always been on the forefront of game disc technology. The original PlayStation used CDs as the game storage medium, the PS2 used DVDs and could double as a DVD player, and the PS3 upped the ante using Blu-ray discs.

Computer software giant Microsoft has found success going after primarily an older audience with sports and first-person shooter games. The Xbox was initially released in the United States for the 2001 Christmas season, not long after the 9/11 terrorist attacks, and it became an instant hit with his first-person shooter *Halo*. Microsoft helped maintain this with the launch of its online game play system Xbox Live a year later. The Xbox was built on Microsoft's personal computer expertise, and the hardware was seen as being particularly good. Also the Xbox was built from the beginning for online play.

Nintendo figured out that it couldn't compete with Sony or Microsoft for technical prowess, so instead it focused on making video games that would be fun for everyone to play. They did this with their Wii system and its unconventional wave-wands-in-the-air control method, and even more so with their portable/console hybrid Switch system that became a runaway hit during the COVID-19 pandemic of 2020.[62] Part of what made the Switch so successful was its social *Animal Crossing: New Horizons* life simulation game set on islands with cute animal inhabitants. We will learn more about this game later in the chapter.

Conflicts Over Video Games

Like movies, comic books, and rock 'n' roll, video games have been subject to a lot of fear and criticism—sometimes when they have deliberately provoked it. One of the earliest to get people upset was a 1976 driving game called *Death Race* in which the player would attempt to run over stick-figure people with a car to score points. Once the person was hit, they turned into tombstones. The reason for creating the game was not particularly to generate controversy but rather to reuse some demolition derby–themed game design. *Death Race* immediately started upsetting critics, with a mother in Seattle complaining that "the game was teaching people to run over and kill people."[63] This led to the game being denounced by the National Safety Council and on news shows like CBS' *Sixty Minutes*. The fuss over the game also helped make it a hit for Exidy Games.

There have also been games that were designed to be deliberately offensive and grab negative media attention as a marketing strategy. One of the most notable of these was the Atari 2600 rape-themed game *Custer's Revenge* from a publisher run by a pornographic filmmaker. (Games like *Custer's Revenge* were part of what prompted Nintendo's tight control of all its system's games.)

The fighting game *Mortal Kombat* was deliberately provocative, but unlike *Custer's Revenge* it was an exciting fighting game that featured outrageous violence to go with good game play. It was disturbing enough to prompt former Senator Joseph Lieberman (D/I-CT) to hold congressional hearings. These hearings reflected the distrust parents had about video games. Donovan wrote in his history of video games, "It was a distrust that reflected the historical pattern of new forms of media or entertainment viewed—at least initially—with suspicion."[64] In response to these hearings, the video game industry came up with a ratings system not unlike those used for movies

and television that would be implemented by the industry itself, not the government, which would have likely been an unconstitutional limit on free speech. Not surprisingly, the other outcome was that *Mortal Kombat* sold even better than ever. The age rating system also allowed Nintendo to start selling games that were not appropriate for children because they would have the age rating on them. Donovan notes that the new rating system actually made it easier to get violence into games, not harder.

No discussion of video game history would be complete without looking at the *Grand Theft Auto* (*GTA*) franchise, one of the most controversial and immersive video game series ever. In the game, you play a person of dubious background who runs around a big city committing a wide range of crimes. The games can be played as a series of missions you need to complete or it can simply be freeform where you get to explore the city, stealing cars and other vehicles as needed. The revolution of the game was that it had very few limits. There wasn't a right way to go—you could drive down any street, enter every store, beat and rob any pedestrian, though if you commit enough crimes in a single area, you'll soon have the police after you.

"Giving players freedom of choice was our main goal," said Todd Howard, executive producer of the series. "To have the game react to you and remove as many boundaries as possible to what you can do. I think that players often start a new game by trying things, asking the game 'can I do this?' and the more the game says 'yes' the better."[65]

The depth of work that went into these games was substantial; before selling fourteen million copies in 2008, *Grand Theft Auto IV* took four years of work by a team of approximately 150 people to create what Donovan called "the video game equivalent of a James Cameron blockbuster [movie]."[66] But the crime-based gameplay also attracted substantial criticism. Former Democratic senator and presidential candidate Hillary Rodham Clinton called for a Federal Trade Commission investigation into the series after players discovered that the so-called 'Hot Coffee' secret code would unlock the ability of characters to have sex within the *GTA* universe that had been dropped from the game. But because of development issues, the code was deactivated instead of deleted. The game was rated "M" for mature, classified as appropriate for players ages seventeen years and older. But Clinton noted that statistics released by the National Institute on Media and the Family found that 50 percent of boys between ages seven and fourteen were able to buy M-rated games.[67]

Pokémon

If *Grand Theft Auto* represented video games at their most violent, disruptive, and controversial, Nintendo's **Pokémon** was perhaps the most friendly, wholesome, combat-based game series. In it, the Pokémon trainer collects cute "pocket monsters" they use to engage in combat with other trainers. But rather than fighting to the death, the defeated Pokémon would merely faint and need time to recover. Launched in Japan in 1996, it was an instant success, followed by hit animated series, a manga comic book series, and a trading card game. *Pokémon* encourage social interaction among players. They could trade the pocket monsters with each other by using link cables and later wireless connections, or by trading the cards. Bookstores in the early 2000s would often host play sessions for the card games on weekends. When *Pokémon* arrived in the United States in 1998, it initially sold 2.5 million game cartridges, along with 850,000 sets of trading cards, and even an animated movie that premiered in 1999 that would earn more than $160 million. In a strange twist, Republican presidential candidate Herman Cain acknowledged and endorsed some of the values from *Pokémon* when he quoted from the theme song from one of the movies when he withdrew from the campaign in 2012:

The *Grand Theft Auto* series is one of the most successful and controversial franchises in the world of video games. The immersive game lets a player live out a life as a criminal in a fictionalized city, engaging in robbery, carjacking, and murder, all while traveling wherever they want to within the fictionalized versions of major American cities. The games are as expensive to produce (and can be as profitable) as a blockbuster Hollywood movie.

"Life can be a challenge. Life can seem impossible. It's never easy when there's so much on the line. But you and I can make a difference. There's a mission just for you and me. Just look inside and you will find just what you can do."[68]

Pokémon in all of its various incarnations has made an indelible imprint on both video games and popular culture. In addition to all the versions listed above, in 2016 the mobile game developer released a phone-based **augmented reality** game called *Pokémon Go*. In it, would be trainers traveled around in the real world, catching animated Pokémon with their smartphones in an electronic/real-life hybrid scavenger hunt. Like the popular battle royale game *Fortnite*, *Pokémon Go* is a free-play game where players can buy cosmetic upgrades and access special events with in-game purchases. The game also has advertising within it where sponsors, such as Starbucks or Sprint stores, have special locations where players could find special Pokémon along with branded merchandise. Players sometimes engaged in inappropriate behavior while playing, such as looking for Pokémon at Washington's Holocaust Museum or the former Auschwitz concentration camp.[69]

Video Games as Mass Communication

In my own media literacy class, I used to raise the question as to whether video games and video game consoles count as mass communication and whether they are a new mass medium. I think the answer is a definite yes, for several reasons.[70]

Video game consoles are media content delivery devices. The PlayStation 2 was a DVD player as well as a game console, and the PlayStation 3 was among the early Blu-ray players. Microsoft's Xbox One is now pitching itself as a general-purpose media entertainment hub that can be used to stream television programs and movies, play video games, and stream video game play back onto the internet.[71] Video games, like television shows or movies, have stars. They have mascots. The most prominent of these is Super Mario, who has been a force in the gaming world for Nintendo since 1981, but the list also includes characters such as Sonic the Hedgehog for Sega, *Pokémon*'s Pikachu, and *Halo*'s Master Chief for the Microsoft Xbox.

Video games are a new venue for advertising. Just like newspapers, magazines, and websites are funded by ad revenue, many game publishers are turning to the advertising world to help manage costs. Companies such as IGA Worldwide are devoted entirely to securing deals for businesses to advertise in games, which have a near-perfect saturation in the eighteen- to thirty-four age market. When Barack Obama was making his first run for the presidency back in 2008, he advertised in video games—the first presidential candidate ever to do so.[72] Video games, now more than ever, are the site of entire communities. One needs only to look to online-specific games, such as *World of Warcraft*, or to online versions of console games, such as the *Halo* or *Call of Duty* series. The concept of online communities has become commonplace today. Now, instead of gathering around the water cooler to discuss the latest news or entertainment item, people are using Bluetooth headsets to talk to friends and family while playing capture the flag or fighting bosses to help their character rise to the next level.[73] (We will learn more about this later in the chapter.)

Video games can be more profitable than the movies. In 2013, the controversial video game *Grand Theft Auto V* was released. By 2018, it had sold at least ninety million copies at an estimated price of $60 a copy. That means that over five years the game has earned more than $6 billion.[74]

Keith Tsuji / Stringer / Getty Images

▲ In the spring of 2019, Pikachu starred in the first live-action Pokémon movie, *Detective Pikachu*. Actor Ryan Reynolds of *Deadpool* fame provided the voice and facial motion capture acting for the little yellow pocket monster.

Compare that with the movie global box office phenomenon *Avatar* from 2009 that grossed nearly $2.8 billion. In fact, if you combine that with James Cameron's other global box office hit, *Titanic*, which brought in $2.2 billion, *Grand Theft Auto V* still brought in more money.[75] In 2015, the movie industry had a record year when it came to total box office dollars, hitting more than $11 billion for the North American market. This was a year with really big movies being released, including *Jurassic World*, *Avengers: Age of Ultron*, and *Star Wars Episode VII: The Force Awakens*. But video game software sales were $16.5 billion for the U.S. market. And that is not including system sales—just the games themselves. Total video game revenue topped $23 billion. (As *Fortune* magazine notes, while sales of games systems are important, software sales are considered the best measure of success in the gaming industry.[76])

Video games are protected by the First Amendment. A U.S. Supreme Court ruling in 2011 determined that states cannot pass laws that restrict the sale of video games to minors. (This does not, however, limit the right of the industry to set standards for who can buy which games.) The case *Brown v. Entertainment Merchants Association* struck down a California law that prohibited the sale of video games to minors that depict "killing, maiming, dismembering or sexually assaulting an image of a human being."[77] The opinion from conservative justice Antonin Scalia stated that while these games may be disgusting, "disgust is not a valid basis for restricting expression."

Given all this, it is hard not to see video games as a mass medium or a form of mass communication. According to the Pew Research Center, 97 percent of teens aged twelve to seventeen play video games in one form or another, with fully 50 percent reporting having played "yesterday." Of those who play video games, 86 percent play on consoles, 73 percent play on computers, and 60 percent play on portable game systems.[78] Among adults aged eighteen and older, 53 percent play video games, and 21 percent play daily. Computers are the most popular place for older users to play video games; consoles are more common among younger players.[79]

Video Games as a Spectator Sport

Video games are no longer just something you play. They are now a legitimate spectator sport. Back in the summer of 2014, a fish named Grayson captured the attention of gaming fans nationwide by playing the video games *Pokémon Red* and *Pokémon Blue* on a Game Boy emulator using a motion sensor aimed at his fish tank. That a pair of technically oriented college students in New York would rig some equipment to allow their fish to randomly play a video game is not surprising. The fact that as many as twenty-two thousand people at a time would watch the fish play *Pokémon* using the video game streaming service Twitch is kind of amazing.[80]

▲ Opening weekend for the eSports arena at Caesars Entertainment Studios in Las Vegas, Nevada.

After some initial uncertainty, video game manufacturers have gotten on board with their games being streamed and viewed. In fact, the latest consoles from Sony and Xbox (Microsoft) are designed to stream on Twitch. In May 2014, stories originating in the entertainment press came out saying that Google was preparing to buy video game streaming service Twitch, but in the end, online retail giant Amazon bought the company for $970 million.[81] Twitch was founded in 2011 as an outgrowth of the live-streaming video site Justin.tv, and it now has more than 15 million daily viewers watching an average of 106 minutes of live gaming, and around 2.2 million gamers streaming their play monthly.[82] Amazon's purchase of the video game streaming service is part of its larger commitment to gaming. It has an in-house gaming studio, and is one of the largest video game vendors in the world. (Note that while Amazon paid close to $1 billion for Twitch, legacy news provider the *Washington Post* sold for only $250 million to Amazon founder Jeff Bezos.)

Among the most popular games to watch streaming are the so-called **battle royale games**. What is a battle royale? Video game streamer Aaron Blackman, whom you met back in Chapter 1, compares them to the competition in *the Hunger Games,* where one hundred players enter a digital arena to fight to the death until only one player or team is left standing. In the spring of 2018, the most popular of these was the free-to-play game *Fortnite* found on the PC, PlayStation 4, and Xbox One.[83]

At the time, Blackman writes, the most popular *Fortnite* streamer was Tyler Blevins, also known as "Ninja." A former pro gamer, Ninja had been streaming since 2011. Canadian rapper and fellow gamer Drake noticed his stellar play, and the two began to plan to play *Fortnite* one night. On March 14, 2018, the two began streaming *Fortnite* together without any fanfare or lead-up promotion. Word spread quickly about the matchup over Twitter, and the pair set a record for concurrent viewing with 628,000 people watching the stream live. As the evening progressed, rapper Travis Scott and Pittsburgh Steelers wide receiver JuJu Smith-Schuster joined in.

Then in April, Ninja hosted a live night of *Fortnite* at the new eSports Arena at the Luxor Hotel in Las Vegas. Fans paid $75 to enter and were promised a spot in two of the evening's ten games. Ninja played in each of the ten games and paid $2,500 to the last player standing in each game. He also paid a $2,500 bounty to whoever killed his character in each game. The live stream on Twitch broke his old record with more than 667,000 viewers at its peak. As of late April 2018, Ninja had more than 202,000 Twitch subscribers, each paying $5 a month that gets split between Ninja and Twitch. That means that Ninja is making more than $500,000 a month to stream video games.

Broadcast of live video game play is not limited to long-tail channels like Twitch, however. In 2016, for the second year in a row, cable giant ESPN skipped showing traditional physical sports during prime time on an April Sunday night. Instead of showing an NBA game, viewers instead watched ten college students competing in the Grand Final round of the Heroes of the Dorm tournament, playing for a chance at free college tuition. The tournament began with more than four hundred teams from universities across the country and ended with students from Arizona State winning up to $75,000 each in tuition for the rest of their college careers. Hulu is also streaming four eSports shows including commentary, tournament highlights, and competitions. Both Hulu and ESPN are interested in getting some of the attention Twitch is getting with the broadcast of **eSports** (that is, organized team competition in video games for spectators), thus illustrating Secret 3—Everything from the margin moves to the center.[84] As was discussed in Chapter 8, during the COVID-19 pandemic sports shutdown, sports broadcasters turned to airing eSports featuring professional athletes competing in video game versions of their regular sports.

Video Games in Contemporary Culture

Since the COVID-19 pandemic took hold in the United States in March 2020, your author has been working from home teaching classes, doing department work, and interacting with my family across the country and the world through a variety of chat and video meeting software. It got to be such a part of my life that I even installed a green screen in my basement office so I could reliably replace the mess behind my desk with a superimposed professional-looking image supplied by my university. It was also a time where my wife and I could not go to movies, concerts or the touring Broadway shows we had tickets for. But we were able to watch streaming concerts from some of our favorite musicians, including Wild Ponies as discussed in Chapter 6.

But video chat and social media were not the only vehicles people have been using during this time of social distancing. Video game platforms have been used for everything from meetings, to weddings, to concerts. The social simulation game *Animal Crossing: New Horizons* has been an enormous success during the spring of 2020, selling thirteen million copies in the first six weeks and prompted a nationwide shortage of Nintendo Switch systems to play it on. In the game, players set up their own island where they have a small society that can interact with other islands online.

Twitch streamer Nick Fiondella plays *Animal Crossing* for his 170,000 followers, and he says it is popular in part because it is relaxing and gives people opportunities to meet and interact with other online players of the game.[85]

That potential for online interaction has found a lot of uses beyond game play. New York Congressperson (and video gamer) Alexandria Ocasio-Cortez (D-NY), who is often referred to as AOC, bought a Switch and a copy *Animal Crossing* for herself, and soon started paying visits to some of her supporters through the game. Justin Mirsky, who used to live in AOC's district, sent an access code to the congresswoman on Twitter when she said she wanted to visit a few people's islands to say hello. He was then surprised to see that AOC was "flying" in to his island's airport for a visit. They talked for a bit via keyboards, AOC left a gift of virtual fruit, and she signed a note on the island's bulletin board.[86]

Video game developer Rami Ismail is Muslim and because of the pandemic he could not gather with friends in their homes for the breaking of the daylight fast in the evening during the holy month of Ramadan. While others gathered via video meeting services like Zoom, Ismail decided to bring in seven guests each evening to a table on his *Animal Crossing* island. Ismail got such a strong response to his invitation to his followers on Twitter that he had to set up an electronic calendar to manage his guests. Imran Khan, a *Washington Post* reporter attended one of these gatherings and discussed the nature of the virtual breaking of the fast. "I think the main thing about *Animal Crossing* is that it's a place," Ismail told Kahn. "*Animal Crossing* is tied to the real-time clock and the date of the user. So, the moon is the moon, right? Ramadan is based on the lunar calendar, *Animal Crossing* reflects the real moon, and you can talk about the moon above while in the game. The sunrise itself is about to start in the game while we're talking. It's a place and a time."[87]

Online video game platforms have also been used as concert venues. Rapper Scott did a series of live performances within the game *Fortnite* in April 2020. Players could arrive for the show up to thirty minutes ahead of time to pick out where they wanted to sit to listen and watch. Those who attended also got a concert-themed glider they could use in playing the game.[88] The video game *Minecraft* went one better, having an entire music festival online called Nether Meant run by virtual events producer Open Pit. Open Pit recreated the Brooklyn venue Elsewhere and renamed it Elsewither. Fans could watch the show through video game streaming service Twitch or by logging directly into *Minecraft*. People attending directly through the game could wander through the venue and communicate through a massive group chat.[89]

During the COVID-19 pandemic in the spring of 2020, Nintendo Switch video game systems became almost impossible to find in stores in part because of the huge popularity of the social simulation game *Animal Crossing: New Horizons*.

The Sims 4, the latest installment of EA's simulation game, introduced a new update that allows unprecedented gender customization options. Players can now create avatar characters with any type of physique, walk style, and tone of voice and then accessorize them in any way they choose—regardless of gender.

Diversity and Representation in Video Games

Video games have traditionally not been a hot spot for representational diversity. The characters in games are typically portrayed as white, male heterosexuals (to the degree that sexual orientation factors into gaming characters). A 2015 study by media research company Nielsen (the folks who do the television ratings) found that lesbian/gay/bisexual/transgender (LGBT) and Asian American gamers feel that they have limited opportunities to create game characters who represent them in real life (IRL).[90]

▼ TABLE 10.2

Percentage of Consumers Who Play Video Games

Demographic	Users
LGBT	65%
Heterosexual	63%
Asian American	81%
African American	71%
Non-Hispanic whites	61%
Hispanics	55%
Men	68%
Women	56%

Source: "How Diverse Are Video Gamers—and the Characters They Play?" Nielsen, March 24, 2015, http://www.nielsen.com/us/en/insights/news/2015/how-diverse-are-video-gamers-and-the-characters-they-play.html.

Among LGBT gamers, 65 percent do not feel that all sexual orientations are given adequate opportunity for representation, while only 28 percent of heterosexual gamers feel that opportunity is lacking. Asian American gamers are much more likely to feel video game characters are not inclusive than are Hispanic, African American, and non-Hispanic whites.

Interestingly enough, LGBT consumers are slightly more likely to play video games than are heterosexual consumers, and Asian American consumers are more likely to game than all other ethnicities. For the percentages of various populations who play video games, see Table 10.2.

There are, of course, games that are exceptions. The Xbox series *Saints Row* has in some editions of the game allowed for a wide range of body diversity, including extensive variation in body weight and level of masculinity and femininity. Comic artist Kiva Bay, an obese woman who has a nonbinary approach to gender identity, writes that having the opportunity to truly create a character in an open-world game who really represented her was liberating and life affirming. She wrote, "In *Saints Row 2*, I am not a hero. But I am me. . . . And that's a powerful feeling that I should get to have more often."[91] One game that has engendered a high level of controversy is the survival game *Rust*. The game has always randomized character features such as skin color, limb length, and other characteristics we won't get into here. All of the characters in the game, however, were male. That is, they were up until the spring of 2016 when the game designers gave many players a female avatar to play with, whether they wanted the gender swap or not.

Developers Garry Newman and Taylor Reynolds addressed the sometimes ugly complaints about the gender swap on their blog:

> We understand that this is a sore subject for a lot of people. We understand that you may now be a gender that you don't identify with in real-life. We understand that this causes you distress and makes you not want to play the game anymore. Technically nothing has changed, since half the population was already living with those feelings. The only difference is that whether you feel like this now is decided by your [game ID] instead of your real-life gender.[92]

(We will learn more about gender and online conflict in Chapter 15.)

CHAPTER REVIEW

CHAPTER SUMMARY ▶▶

A growing part of online interaction is through social media, which is defined as media that allows for user-created content, comments, tagging, and social networking.

Among the most popular social networks are the video sharing service YouTube, giant of the field Facebook, photo-sharing service Instagram, the youth-oriented disappearing message service Snapchat, microblogging site Twitter, and the growing Chinese video sharing service TikTok. Facebook controls a large portion of social media traffic by also owning Instagram and the WhatsApp global messaging service.

Video games are an emerging part of modern mass media that have been recognized by the U.S. Supreme Court as deserving full First Amendment protection. Video games got their start in national labs and college campuses in the 1960s where there were early computers for people to experiment with. *Spacewar!* and *Tennis for Two* were two of these early examples. Atari, founded by engineer Nolan Bushnell, was the first successful American video game company that made both arcade games and the massively successful Atari 2600 home console. It's market collapsed in the early 1980s due to oversaturation and poor quality control for games. Arcades became a major part of youth culture in the 1980s, though they faded to the background as home systems got better. Japanese game company Nintendo revived the American console market in 1985 when it introduced the NES home system. Later successful consoles include the Sony PlayStation series and Microsoft's Xbox systems.

Video games have been a source of controversy for a range of reasons, including violent, bloody, and sexual content. Politicians have held government hearings about these games which led to the industry creating an age-based rating system similar to that used for movies and television programming.

Video games have become a dominant part of the pop culture entertainment world, outearning legacy media such as movies and music. In addition to being a popular activity, video games, in the form of eSports, are also a spectator event now. Online video games have become important venues for social interaction and even for concerts and festivals. Like most media, video games have faced criticism for their lack of diversity.

KEY TERMS ▶▶

social media   238

Turing Test   242

Pong   245

Atari   245

Pokémon   249

augmented reality   250

battle royale games   252

eSports   252

REVIEW QUESTIONS ▶▶

1. How can old social media messages come back to hurt people long after they've been written?

2. What are three of the factors that make "social media" social?

3. Why did the Atari company collapse as the leader in home video games in the early 1980s? What did Nintendo do to avoid the same mistakes Atari made?

4. Why might video game makers want their games to be attacked by critics for being too extreme and violent?

5. Explain two different reasons video games could be considered mass communication.

6. Are eSports really sporting events? Why or why not?

7. How do people socially interact through online video games?

CHAPTER 11

GLOBAL MEDIA

Communication Around the World

Ivor Prickett/Panos

Marie Colvin Murdered in Syria

For twenty-six years, Marie Colvin of the *Sunday Times* of London reported from any place bad things were happening—the Middle East, Africa, Chechnya, the Balkans, South Asia. Longtime *New Yorker* editor David Remnick wrote that Colvin was always recognizable when she showed up on CNN, wearing her signature black eye patch she acquired after losing her left eye from a grenade attack during the civil war in Sri Lanka in 2001.

Colvin was a report-the-facts journalist who had no patience with claiming all sides were equal. One night in late February 2012, she was reporting about the death of a child during artillery attacks on the city of Homs in Syria by the forces of President Bashar al-Assad. Colvin reported,

> These are the twenty-eight thousand civilians, men, women, and children, hiding, being shelled, defenseless. The little baby is one of two children who died today. One of the children being injured every day. That baby will move more people to think, "What is going on, and why is no one stopping this murder in Homs that is happening every day?"[1]

Remnick writes there was "cool but profound rage in her voice." Colvin went on to say more about Assad's forces: "It's a complete and utter lie they're only going after terrorists. The Syrian Army is simply shelling a city of cold, starving civilians."

No statement of opinion. No waffling. Just the facts on the ground.

Remnick says it was Colvin who taught him how to be a foreign correspondent when he was covering the West Bank city of Jenin following an Israeli military incursion. The morning after Remnick watched the report by Colvin from Syria, he woke up to the news that the reporter had died from rocket fire.

Six years later, Colvin's family would document in a wrongful death suit against the Syrian government that the military was deliberately targeting the building she and French photojournalist Rémi Ochlik were in. According to a Syrian defector, the military intelligence officer who ordered the shelling reportedly said, "Marie Colvin was a dog, and now she's dead. Let the Americans help her now."[2]

The lawsuit by Colvin's family states that the attack that killed her was part of a Syrian campaign to stop coverage of the civil war by killing or arresting journalists who could reach worldwide audiences.[3] The Syrian government argues that journalists who went into rebel-held areas were violating the law. Assad told NBC News in 2016, "It's a war and she came illegally to Syria, she worked with the terrorists, and because she came illegally, she's been responsible for everything that befell on her."[4]

The *Washington Post*'s Pulitzer Prize–winning reporter Dana Priest wrote, "Her bravery was legendary. In the 1991 Iraq War, she stayed behind enemy lines. In 1999, when others fled, she remained in East Timor (an island nation in South Asia) to document the 1,000 refugees in a U.N. compound under attack by government-backed militias. . . . Her black eye patch symbolized her fearlessness and commitment to telling the story of civilians who, she reminded her worried friends and readers, 'endure far more than I ever will.'"[5]

Being a war correspondent is never an easy job, but CNN's Christiane Amanpour says that women war correspondents should not be singled out because they are women reporters. They are reporters, full stop. Certainly, Colvin would support Amanpour's case that women are as tough as (or tougher than) any men. When Colvin was

LEARNING OBJECTIVES

After studying this chapter, you will be able to

1 Explain why the authors of *Four Theories of the Press* believed that the nature of the press depends on the political and social structures of the society it serves

2 Describe how the British Broadcasting Company (BBC) got its start and what role it played during World War II

3 Describe the violent acts perpetrated against journalists in Central and South America

4 Explain the effects the Arab Spring had on the safety of journalists and media coverage in the Middle East

5 Identify and describe the two most effective censorship tools governments in Africa have used to repress freedom of the press

6 Describe who controls the media in Russia and how they do so

7 Identify a type of media censorship that is used for each of the following three countries: India, China, and Japan

in Afghanistan in 2002, she was still working at relearning how to handle stairs after losing her left eye and acquiring her black eye patch. She also had one with sparkly beads given to her by the author of *Bridget Jones's Diary*. She called that her "party patch." "I never though in my life I'd be the woman with the patch. But there you are, life changes."[6]

To Colvin, the story about wars is not as much about battles, strategy, or technology as it is about people. Colvin expressed a thought not that different from that of Charlottesville photographer Ryan Kelly (whom we will read about in Chapter 15) about feeling guilty because she can escape the trauma she is covering. She said she sometimes feels "like a fake because . . . I get to go home." Though she also understood that sometimes you can't leave it behind, something was brought home to her when her second ex-husband, also a war correspondent, took his own life. "A brutal reminder of seeing too much," she said.[7]

But Colvin did not stop seeing things. In 1999, she stayed on in East Timor during its transition to independence from Indonesia, trying to bring attention to the Timorese women and children who were being massacred by militiamen with machetes. Then, in 2001, she was bringing attention to five hundred thousand civilians being denied food and medical care during the Sri Lankan civil war. That was when grenade shrapnel took her left eye.[8]

In a speech Colvin gave in London in 2010 honoring journalists who died reporting from war zones, she said,

> Covering a war means going to places torn by chaos, destruction, and death, and trying to bear witness. It means trying to find the truth in a sandstorm of propaganda when armies, tribes, or terrorists clash. And yes, it means taking risks, not just for yourself but often for the people who work closely with you. . . . We go to remote war zones to report what is happening. The public have a right to know what our government, and our armed forces, are doing in our name. . . . You can't get that information without going to places where people are being shot at, and others are shooting at you.[9]

The notion of being able to print or broadcast almost any kind of news is central to the ideal of free speech in the United States and the democracies of the West. But different countries and cultures have differing ideas as to what constitutes the proper form for the media to take. And just because something is legally available in a country does not mean that people will in practice actually have access to it. In this chapter, we look at ideals of how the media ought to behave and how the media function in different societies around the world. Finally, we consider what it means to live in a world with such a wide range of media.

Media Ideals Around the World

Stay up to date on the latest in media by visiting the author's blog at **ralphehanson.com**

So far in this book, we have primarily discussed the development of the media in economically developed democracies. But the relationship among politicians, citizens, and the press can take vastly different forms in other nations, depending on the country's culture, government, and level of development.

In 1956, three journalism professors from the University of Illinois—Fred S. Siebert, Theodore Peterson, and Wilbur Schramm—outlined what they considered to be the major forms the press could take around the world in *Four Theories of the Press*. They built their argument around two basic value-oriented theories of how the press ought to behave: authoritarian and libertarian.

They then created two variations on these: Soviet/communist and social responsibility.[10] The authors argue that the nature of the press depends on the political and social structures of the society it serves. In other words, the structure and function of the press mirror the society it portrays. Since 1956, however, much has changed. The Cold War has ended, and the Soviet Union has collapsed. We have gone from talking about the influence of the press to talking about the influence of the media. The media industry has come to be dominated by a limited number of large owners. We have seen the rise of the internet, which allows many more voices to be heard, though they can easily get lost in all the digital noise. And the importance of developing nations is being increasingly recognized.

In response to these changes, and many others, scholars started questioning whether the ideas from the book needed to be revisited. John C. Nerone and his contributing authors—also all from the University of Illinois—did just that in 1995 with *Last Rights: Revisiting* Four Theories of the Press. As they pointed out,

> When Four Theories was written, many U.S. newspapers carried ads for segregated housing, it was still legal in a number of states for a husband to divorce his wife for being a bad housekeeper, and no one had ever seen what the earth looked like from outer space.[11]

Nerone and his colleagues suggested several things that contemporary readers of *Four Theories* should think about. Most important of these was that the four theories were not a timeless set of categories. Rather, they were a critique set within a particular time period that reflected the politics and economics of the day. Other critics have suggested that there should be a fifth theory of the press—development theory—to deal with countries that are in the process of building modern economies.[12] In this section, we look at the four original theories, along with development theory, and see how well they apply to press systems today.

Authoritarian Theory

The **authoritarian theory** is the oldest theory of the press. It says that the role of the press is to be a servant of the government, not a servant of the citizenry. Authoritarian theory has its roots in royal control of societies during the era when the printing press was first developed. Monarchs were believed to derive their authority to rule directly from God, and therefore they had the right and responsibility to control all aspects of society, including the printing press. Rulers felt that the proper role of the press was to provide the public with the information the rulers deemed appropriate. Keep in mind that the reach of the press was still fairly limited because relatively few people were literate. So the monarch gave formal permission to the publisher, who in return had a monopoly on the publishing business.

Today, countries that are developing mass media often start by taking an authoritarian approach. Authoritarian rule is also practiced in most totalitarian states, which seek to control the press along with all other aspects of social life.

Authoritarian control of the press is carried out by the following means:

- Giving permits to only certain printers—However, as the number of trained printers grows and an increasingly literate public demands more and more printed materials, the ability of the government to control "outlaw" printers can become problematic.

- Prosecuting anyone who violates generally accepted standards for the press.

Totalitarian governments have been ruthless in controlling the press through arrests, torture, arson, and imprisonment, along with more subtle methods such as controlling the availability of the internet. In the Democratic Republic of the Congo (DRC), the government shuts down access to the internet anytime opposition protest marches are held. The DRC's National Intelligence Agency also shut down a television station located in Bukavu in the eastern part of the country and arrested a journalist with a news website for interviewing an opposition political figure.[13] Since 2009, strong antiterrorism laws have forced journalists in Ethiopia to self-censor to avoid arrest. In 2014, six newspapers were closed and thirty journalists were forced into exile, and in February 2018, the government declared a new state of emergency that could be used to arrest journalists and ban the public from watching specified broadcast media.[14]

The DRC is a prime example of a country operating under an authoritarian model of the press, and was ranked 150th out of 180 in 2020 by the World Press Freedom Index. In addition to murders and threats against journalists, community radio stations received threats for broadcasting Ebola prevention messages since the outbreak there began in 2018.[15]

Nerone's major critique of authoritarian theory is that it is more a description of the procedures a government uses to control the press than a philosophy of press behavior.[16]

Communist Theory

Although the Soviet Union no longer exists, a variety of governments around the world, including those in China, Cuba, and Vietnam, continue to hold communist ideals. The **communist theory** of the press is similar to the authoritarian theory but goes a step further. Instead of just being a servant of the government, the press is run by the government to serve the government's own needs. The communist press is supposedly free to publish the truth. However, in the Soviet Union the press was not free, nor did it speak the truth. The communist view is that there is only one valid political and social philosophy, so there is no need for competing "false" ideals to be portrayed in the media. Moreover, communists argue that the American press is no freer than the communist press because the American media serve the needs of capitalist owners rather than those of society. Communist media theory proposes the following principles:

▲ A journalist from the Democratic Republic of the Congo broadcasts live to his audience from Brussels, Belgium, on a major political agreement being hashed out between opposition parties in the DRC in June 2016.

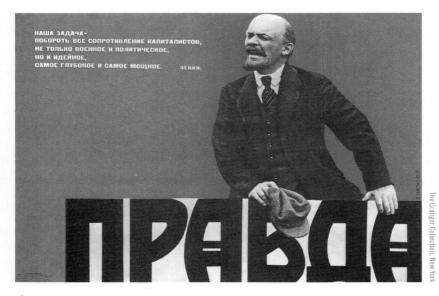

THIERRY CHARLIER/AFP/Getty Images

The Granger Collection, New York

▲ This 1968 Soviet propaganda poster depicting Vladimir Ilyich Ulyanov, better known as Lenin, reads: "Pravda: Our task is to overcome capitalist resistance—not only military and political resistance, but ideological resistance, which is the most profound and powerful."

- The media are an instrument of the government and the Communist Party—An independent press is undesirable and should be suppressed.

- The media should be closely tied to other sources of government power and authority—In the United States, the executive, legislative, and judicial branches of the government serve as checks and balances on each other, all overseen by the press. But communist theory holds that all elements of the state, including the press, should work toward a common goal.

- The media's main purpose is to act as a tool for government propaganda.

The communist notion of absolute right and wrong leaves no room for the media to debate the proper role of government. The press is not a watchdog, but rather a supporter of the Communist Party's efforts to create a perfect state. Since the responsibility for enforcing this truth lies within the leadership of the state, the leadership should control the mass media. So the role of the press is to put forward the official party line. This is almost directly counter to the Western notion of the press as an outside observer keeping watch on the government.[17]

Vietnam is an example of a country operating under the communist theory of the press. All of the media in Vietnam are required to follow the Communist Party's dictates, with online independent journalist/bloggers as the only source of unfiltered information. But even those are highly controlled, with bloggers facing long prison sentences for engaging in "activities aimed at overthrowing the government" and "anti-state propaganda." As of 2020, Vietnam was ranked 175th out of 180 countries by the World Press Freedom Index.[18]

In *Last Rights*, the authors point out that what we've been referring to as "the communist theory" was supposed to represent a generalized Marxist response to libertarian theory (discussed below) but really represented the Soviet approach at a given time.[19] The communist theory of the press was an ideal that Soviet communists never came even close to obtaining. The Soviets may have had an ideal of a communist press, but in reality it was generally just authoritarian controls. The only time the Soviet media came close to acting as a force for the people and not just for those in power was under the leadership of Mikhail Gorbachev in the 1980s during his campaign for *glasnost*, or openness. Glasnost allowed citizens and the media to express their opposition to the official government position and to criticize corrupt local leaders. Since then, however, the Russian media have gone back to a level of authoritarian control, as we discuss later in this chapter.

Libertarian Theory

The opposite of authoritarian theory is **libertarian theory**. In this view, the press does not belong to the government but is instead a separate institution that belongs to the people and serves as an independent observer of the government. Libertarian philosophy views people as moral beings who can tell the difference between truthfulness and falsity. Because of this, they need a free and open press so that they can decide for themselves what is true and what is false. The libertarian theory thus holds that there must be a marketplace of ideas in which both true and false statements can compete for the hearts and minds of audience members. This is the basic idea of the First Amendment to the U.S. Constitution.[20] Libertarian theory is the basis of free speech in the democracies of the West and is the most well-developed of the theories in *Four Theories*.[21]

Most noncommunist countries pay at least lip service to the libertarian ideal of the press, although many do not adhere to it. Again, even in the United States, there tends to be much more government control of the broadcast media than of print.

The free press of a libertarian society is based on the following principles:

- People want to know the truth and be guided by it.

- The only way to arrive at the truth is for ideas to be freely and openly discussed.

- Different people will have different opinions, and everyone must be allowed to develop his or her own.

- The most rational ideas will be the most accepted.

In the libertarian view, the major functions of the press are to inform, entertain, and advertise (to support itself). Overall, though, the goal of the media is to help people discover the truth. The press should be free of government control, and every idea, no matter how crazy or offensive, should be allowed a forum for expression. As Siebert et al. wrote in *Four Theories*, the ideal is "to

Ira L. Black – Corbis / Contributor / Getty Images

▲ In a country with a libertarian theory of the press, journalists are supposed to be free to cover protests against the government, such as this one in New York City where large numbers of people gathered to protest the killing of George Floyd while he was being arrested by Minneapolis, Minnesota, police.

let the public at large be subjected to a barrage of information and opinion, some of it possibly true, some of it possibly false, and some of it containing elements of both."[22] A key problem with libertarian media theory is that it assumes that the primary threat to freedom of speech and communication comes from the government rather than from the marketplace. Under the American system, the voices that are profitable to present will be heard much more loudly than those that do not produce a profit. The ideas that attract advertising revenue and sales draw much more attention from the press than do those about the poor or disenfranchised. Hence we hear more in the news about the stock market than about job programs for the unemployed. *Four Theories* argues that the free market is the ultimate in freedom, rather than media owned by "community groups, nonprofit corporations, universities, religious groups, and municipalities."[23] The debate is framed in terms of external controls rather than access. There is a presumption that the ideal of freedom is corporate or individual ownership with no government intervention.

As of 2020, the United States was ranked 45th out of 180 countries, up from its lowest rating ever of 48th, in the World Press Freedom Index. Despite leading the country of the First Amendment, President Donald Trump has declared the press an "enemy of the American people," and he routinely refers to what journalists publish as "fake news." Journalists have also been facing arrest for covering protests, something that started before the 2016 election. You can read more about this in Chapter 14 with the story about the *Washington Post*'s Wes Lowery getting arrested for covering the Ferguson, Missouri, protests.[24] And in the late spring of 2020, more than one hundred journalists were attacked, assaulted, or arrested in less than two days while covering national protests about the death of an unarmed Black man in police custody in Minneapolis, Minnesota.[25]

Social Responsibility Theory

The **social responsibility theory** of the press is an outgrowth of libertarian theory. This theory is based on the concern that, although it may be free from interference by the government, the press can still be controlled by corporate interests. For example, in principle, anyone can start up a newspaper, but in reality, it is an expensive and difficult proposition. Moreover, only a limited number of radio and television station licenses are available. So, although the government does not control the press in a free society, the control exercised by a limited number of corporations and individuals can be as effective as that of any government. Social responsibility theory says that the high level of concentrated power in the hands of the media requires that they be socially responsible in covering all sides of controversial issues and providing voters with all the information they need to make considered choices. If the press is not sufficiently vigilant, it is the duty of some representative of the public to force it to be responsible.[26]

Under social responsibility theory, the press is obliged to serve several social functions:

- Provide the news and information needed to make the political system work

- Give the public the information needed for self-governance

- Serve as an overseer of the government

- Serve the economic function of bringing together buyers and sellers through advertising

- Provide entertainment

- Be profitable enough to avoid outside pressures

Social responsibility theory essentially advocates nonauthoritarian media controls. France, Israel, and Sweden all operate under some form of social responsibility controls. The governments own and operate television channels, and the programming tends to promote the government's point of view.[27] The alternative is for the press to be in the hands of private business, which may allow for more political views but limits the media to carrying programming that is profitable. Government ownership frees the media from the constraint of having to make a profit.

Sweden, which ranks extremely high at #4 on the World Press Freedom Index, operates under a social responsibility system. It is the home of one of the world's oldest press freedom laws, dating back to 1776, and it has a media ombudsman to handle complains about print, TV, radio, and online media.[28]

The social responsibility theory was a response to the Hutchins Commission report from the late 1940s on the social responsibility of the press, which we discuss in Chapter 15. However, it does describe an approach to the press that is common in the world, for example, in the Israeli press, which we discuss later. The press does not necessarily like the idea that it has responsibilities to go with the freedoms it claims. The question really is, to whom does the freedom of the press belong? Is it to a corporate institution, or is it to people with voices wanting to be heard? Does giving a voice to one limit the voice of the other? Should we automatically favor the rights of those who can afford the press over those who cannot?[29]

▲ In the nineteenth century, the telegraph served to transmit news across the United States and around the world far faster than any vehicle could travel. It was the first step toward the creation of global electronic media.

Norms for the Press in the Twenty-First Century

Perhaps the biggest problem with these normative theories of the press is that it may take two or more of them to describe a given country's media system. For example, theocratic countries whose media operate under a strong social responsibility theory may incorporate elements of the communist media theory, substituting the values of the state religion for those of the Communist Party.

Several authors have suggested a fifth theory of the press, **development theory**, to address the special needs of emerging nations, whose governments may feel that they need to restrict freedom of the press in order to promote industry, national identity, and partnerships with neighboring nations. Media theorist Denis McQuail writes that less developed societies undergoing the transition from colonial rule to independence have different needs than do developed nations, such as those of North America and Western Europe. These developing nations "lack the money, infrastructure, skills, and audiences to sustain a free-market media system."[30] Thus, in many cases, leaders in those nations resort to using authoritarian controls. In May 2007, for example, then Venezuelan president Hugo Chávez revoked the broadcast license of the country's oldest and most watched television network, Radio Caracas Televisión, or RCTV. The network had been severely critical of Chávez and his administration, and lifting the network's broadcast license effectively silenced it. Chávez's efforts have been continued since Nicolás Maduro was elected president in 2013. A 2010 law allows the government to censor any content "calling the legitimately constituted authority into question." Print media also frequently suffer from unexplained newsprint shortages.[31]

Nerone and the contributing authors of *Last Rights*[32] say that *Four Theories of the Press*[33] was a map of the world's media drawn at a specific time—the mid-1950s. And although it was a good map for its day, it was limited by what could be seen at that time and does not take into account the massive transformations that have taken place since then—the fall of communism, the end of the Cold War, globalization, and media consolidation. So they ask, "Do we need to draw a new map?" Or the even bigger question: "Can we draw a new map?"[34] This new map will need to deal with the issues surrounding the press in developing nations, as well as the norms surrounding the controlled press in many Islamic nations.

Going Global: Media Standards Around the World

There is a presumption that a direct connection exists between a country's media system and its political system. Central to this presumption is the idea that a free press is essential for a functional democracy. But what constitutes a free press? Broadcasters in countries with commercially run media, such as the United States, presume that the freest press is that run by private-sector corporate control. Broadcasters in countries with strong traditions of public ownership, such as the United Kingdom, might argue that the commercial broadcasters are beholden to stockholders and advertisers and are no freer than the media in totalitarian states.

Alan Wells suggests that the four theories of the press might be replaced by five dimensions over which media could be rated:

- Control—Who controls the media system? This could be the state, a public corporation, a private enterprise, or corporate sponsorship.

- Finance—How do broadcasters pay the bills? Options include license fees, taxes, advertising, private subsidies, subscription charges, or a combination of these.

- Programming goals—What are the media trying to accomplish with their programming? Providing entertainment, educating the audience, selling products, promoting cultural goals, promoting a political ideology, or just putting up the cheapest possible imported material is each a possible programming goal.

- Target audience—For whom are the media producing and distributing content? These could be social or economic elites, the masses, or specialized/targeted audiences.

- Feedback mechanism—How do media organizations hear back from their audiences? Such feedback could be in the form of field reports, audience participation rates, polls and ratings, or response from critics and sponsors.[35]

As you can see, these five properties can be combined in an endless number of ways to describe a wide range of media systems. As we travel around the world looking at the various approaches to running the media, think about how these properties are being applied. You might also consider which of the normative theories of the press discussed previously would apply.

Are We Really Living in a Media World?

Marshall McLuhan is often better known for his catchphrases than for what he actually wrote. Aside from "the medium is the message," discussed in Chapter 2, he is best known for popularizing the term *global village*. He first used it in his 1962 book, *The Gutenberg Galaxy: The Making of Typographic Man*, in which he discusses how electronic media, primarily radio and television, help people live and interact globally. Since the rise of the internet, it would seem that we are truly living in a world where we can interact with people in any place at any time. But this global village may be largely an illusion.

There is no question that through our media—what McLuhan would call the extension of our senses—we are able to travel to places we could never reach otherwise. In an IMAX theater, we can travel to the bottom of the ocean off the Grand Banks near Newfoundland and visit the wreck of the *Titanic*. Through the photos from the Mars rovers *Curiosity*, *Spirit*, and *Opportunity*, we can see into the craters on a distant planet. On a more down-to-earth scale, our electronic media take us into war zones, into the aftermath of disasters, and to celebrations in cities or countries we would likely never visit. But are we really becoming members of a global village, or are we just sightseers who get a glimpse of something we can't really understand?

Media reporter Ken Auletta, whose work we have discussed extensively elsewhere in this book, suggests that perhaps there is not a single wired global village, but rather hundreds or thousands of them, "each broadcasting in its own language, with its own anchor and news team, its own weather and sports and local slant."[36] Communications scholar W. Russell Neuman suggests that McLuhan's global village concept is misleading: "McLuhan envisioned Americans seeing what was going on live in an African village. But Americans may not want to watch that. And perhaps vice versa."[37]

Media in Canada, Western Europe, and Great Britain

Canada, Western Europe, and Great Britain have liberal democracies that have free speech and media that are relatively free to criticize their governments. But their media differ in significant ways from the media in the United States, if only because the United States has the largest media industry in the world.

Around the world, countries implement regulations requiring broadcasters to carry a certain level of national-produced material. These policies can put a country at odds with trade agreements which call for products to flow freely, for example, across the borders of Canada, the United States, and Mexico.

Broadcasting in the countries of the European Union (EU) used to be dominated by state-run monopolies until the 1980s and 1990s, when commercial alternatives became more common. With this switch, broadcasters started moving away from subsidies to advertising revenues. But even the commercial stations remain heavily regulated and have strong controls and guidelines on the amounts and placement of advertisements. In Europe, part of the drive to privatize broadcasting was due to pirate radio stations located offshore on ships that broadcast into the countries.

Canada has a free press patterned in part on the U.S. model but modified by a desire to preserve Canadian culture in the face of the massive U.S. media industry. Canada can be characterized as a country with a large geographic area offset by a relatively small population, which makes media transmission relatively expensive. Canada's vastness means that it has strongly regional media, amplified by the fact that both English and French are official languages.

One area of resentment has been the somewhat one-way direction of media influence from the United States. As one major Canadian mass communication text points out,

> In Canada, more American television programming is available to the vast majority of Canadians than is Canadian programming. On most Canadian commercial radio stations, more American material is available to listeners than Canadian material. On virtually all magazine racks in Canada more American magazines are available to the reader than Canadian magazines, in spite of the fact that about 2,000 magazines are published in Canada. More American authors than Canadian authors are read by the average Canadian school child.[38]

Orphan Black/Photofest

▲ Thanks to the success of *Orphan Black*, Canada is now a noted producer of television rather than just being a friendly location to film programming.

Despite these issues, the Canadian media industry has been seeing growth. Canada's recording industry has been increasing steadily for the past two decades, as has the book publishing industry. The Canadian film industry has benefited from U.S. movie and television productions shooting north of the border, with Canada now being the second-largest producer of television programming in the world, after the United States. The movie and TV industry in Canada generated $12 billion in gross domestic product in 2017.[39] (This is also known as "screen-based production.") To protect and enhance Canada's media industry, the government has put in place a number of "Canadian content" regulations requiring broadcasters to carry a certain level of Canadian-produced material. For example, programming on Canadian radio must be at least 35 percent domestically produced. Canadian television attracted widespread attention in spring 2007 when the Canadian Broadcasting Corporation put a sitcom on the air called *Little Mosque on the Prairie*, which follows the travails of a rural Muslim community in small-town Canada.[40] (No, I'm not making this up. It was a hit series in Canada that ran six seasons through 2012, and it is available for rent on Amazon Prime and iTunes. Several episodes have also been available on DailyMotion.)

The problem Canada faces is that the United States' largest export is not wheat or steel but rather media content. Nevertheless, Canada has worked hard at maintaining its cultural production, exporting media content produced by authors such as Margaret Atwood and Douglas Coupland; filmmakers such as James Cameron and Jason Reitman; actors including Ryan Reynolds, Ryan Gosling, and Rachel McAdams; and musicians such as Drake, The Weeknd, deadmau5, and—of course—Justin Bieber.[41]

Canada is ranked 16th on the World Press Freedom Index. It has been working with the United Kingdom on the Media Freedom Coalition, creating an international alliance committed to defending press freedom. It has also passed a federal shield law protecting journalists from having to reveal confidential sources.[42]

Western Europe covers a wide range of countries, from Spain and Portugal up through France, Germany, and Scandinavia. Many of these nations are members of the European Union.[43] Cable television is common in some regions, such as Belgium and Germany, while satellite programming is more common in Scandinavia.

The top five countries in the 2020 World Press Freedom Index are all from Scandinavia and northern Europe, a group of countries that have dominated previous reports. They are as follows:

1. Norway

2. Finland

3. Denmark

4. Sweden

5. The Netherlands

All of these countries have a commitment to free expression and many have provisions to safeguard journalists. Norway has topped the list for four years straight, and yet it is still conducting a comprehensive review of concerns about free speech issues that includes looking at levels of public participation, slowing the spread of fake news, and limiting hate speech.[44]

Broadcasting in France typifies the European approach, with networks having a strong public service obligation and a desire to preserve French culture from foreign encroachment. According to broadcast scholar Matthew Rusher, "Each country in Western Europe seeks to preserve its own culture and language and sees the foreign produced programming on the international channels as a threat to its cultural integrity."[45] These stations want to attract audiences and make money, but they also want to preserve their distinctive national culture.

Globally, the British Broadcasting Corporation (BBC) may well be the best-known non-U.S. broadcaster. Britain, a pioneer in broadcasting from its earliest days, used radio to reach out to its far-flung empire, which once covered a quarter of the globe.[46] The BBC was created as a public service in the 1920s. In the 1930s, it started broadcasting on the shortwave radio band, which allowed its signals to extend around the world. During World War II, the BBC was the international voice of opposition to the Nazis, broadcasting in more than forty languages, including French, Danish, and Hindi.[47] Listening to BBC broadcasts in Nazi-occupied Europe was a punishable offense.

As of 2017, the BBC's World Service network had an audience of approximately 155 million on radio, 39 million online, and 110 million on television, including both news and entertainment programming.[48] The BBC notes that "the World Service Group is going from strength to strength in both developed and developing markets, with the single biggest audience for any country in the USA (30m), and with more than a third of the total audience on the African continent (100m), the biggest BBC audience ever seen on any continent."

While the BBC started out as a radio service, the network has always been willing to experiment with new channels of communication, which currently means social and mobile media. These include a new Africa page on the BBC website, a Thai news stream on Facebook, and an emergency Ebola news service in Africa over the WhatsApp chat service. What is more, the BBC has redesigned all its websites in twenty-seven languages to be easily read on mobile devices. Even a legacy media outlet as old as the BBC has reached the point where all media are social (Secret 5), and online media are mobile media (Secret 6).

The BBC's international reach can be seen with the program *Focus on Africa*. For a continent that depends on radio as its primary medium of mass communication, the BBC provides a reliable source of news that is not censored by local governments. To avoid charges of being a colonial voice of white Britain in Black Africa, most of the reporting on the show is done by African journalists. *Focus on Africa* is such an important source of news that it is often rebroadcast on local African stations, sometimes just by taking a shortwave radio and holding it up to the station's microphone.[49]

The BBC operates under a public service model in which audience members pay the cost of the programming through equipment licensing fees. Although the BBC is the best known of the British broadcasters, it also competes with several commercial channels, though these channels have not had the worldwide influence of the BBC. Wells argues that the public service orientation of the BBC has helped it deliver more innovative and less bland programming than the American commercial model. (It should, however, be pointed out that international viewers only see the best of the BBC's programming, missing out on the more routine soap operas and game shows.[50])

Media are pervasive throughout Western Europe, with almost every household owning at least one television set and close to half owning two or more. Most homes also have a radio, and two-thirds have VCRs. Computers and the internet are not as pervasive as in the United States; roughly one-third of homes in Western Europe have a personal computer. The big change in European media is the growth of privately owned television channels. As recently as 1990, Europe had only 47 national stations; by 2012, there were more than 11,000 channels available in Europe, including 8,270 in the European Union.[51] As we discussed in Chapter 5, European newspapers tend to take a more obvious political point of view than the detached, objective approach of U.S. papers. These papers have a clearly understood viewpoint designed to appeal to members of particular political parties.[52] While newspaper readership is higher in Europe than anywhere else in the world, papers in European countries are still facing the same kinds of declines experienced by those in North America.

Charlie Hebdo, the Danish Cartoons, and Terrorism

On January 15, 2015, three masked gunmen attacked and killed at least twelve people at the Paris offices of the satirical newspaper *Charlie Hebdo* in what was one of the deadliest attacks on journalists ever.

Charlie Hebdo is known for its controversial covers and provocative cartoons, which often skewer religion and politics of every stripe. One of the paper's most famous covers published shortly after its offices were firebombed in 2011 depicts a male *Charlie Hebdo* cartoonist giving a slobbery open-mouth kiss to a bearded man in traditional Muslim garb.[53] (We are not reprinting any of the *Charlie Hebdo* cartoons here, but you can see links to a number of them at a blog post that goes with this section. Even trying to describe some of the cartoons would go beyond the standards at SAGE.)

The killings were allegedly provoked by cartoons published in the paper that depicted the Prophet Muhammad and mocked the leader of the Islamic State (also known as ISIS). It is

▲ The murder of cartoonists and journalists at the satirical French newspaper *Charlie Hebdo* inspired a wide range of tributes, including this one made of pens and candles spelling 'Je Suis Charlie' in tribute at the Place de la Republique (Republic Square) in Paris, France.

important to remember, however, as Ezra Klein at *Vox* points out, that we do not need to try to analyze whether the paper was being too provocative. The attack was an act of terrorism and act of violence, not a response to a legitimate provocation. It should also be noted that *Charlie Hebdo* describes itself as a "secular and atheist newspaper" and routinely publishes material that is offensive to every major world religion.[54]

This explains, in part, why many U.S. news outlets did not reprint any of the *Charlie Hebdo* covers. Mark Memmott, writing for NPR's *The Two-Way* blog, said that NPR did not reprint any of the magazine's covers in part because they would give viewers the mistaken idea that the cartoons inside the publication are not as graphic as they actually are:

> Photos showing just a few of the magazine's covers could lead viewers to mistakenly conclude that *Charlie Hebdo* is only a bit edgier than other satirical publications. But a comprehensive display of *Charlie Hebdo*'s work would require posting images that go well beyond most news organizations' standards regarding offensive material.[55]

In essence, Memmott is arguing that to give readers a realistic view of what the cartoons are like would require violating NPR's rules for decency. The *New York Times* also declined to publish any of the most offensive *Charlie Hebdo* cartoons, including all of those that depicted the Prophet Muhammad. Margaret Sullivan, who was at the time the public editor at the *Times*, wrote in her column that while she understood the paper's reasons for not publishing the explicitly offensive cartoons that the magazine had run previously, she questioned why the paper had not run the cover from the week following the attack that showed a crying Muhammad holding a sign that loosely translated to "Sorry Charlie."[56]

The attacks in Paris bring back to mind the rioting and attacks that followed the publication (and republication) of the cartoons depicting the Prophet Muhammad in the Danish newspaper *Jyllands-Posten*. A Pew Research Center poll back in June 2006, at the time of the response to the Danish cartoons, asked whether Americans thought that the controversy was more about "Western disrespect" or "Muslim intolerance." Not surprisingly, Americans (by a 3-to-1 margin) blamed the problems on Muslim intolerance.[57]

The Danish cartoons were drawn in a range of styles. One made fun of the editors of *Jyllands-Posten* for trying to provoke attention, another put a Danish anti-immigration politician in a police lineup, and one portrayed the Prophet with a bomb in his turban with a quote from the Koran printed on the front.[58] At the time the cartoons were published, they drew relatively little attention. But in the winter of 2006, a number of European and American newspapers reprinted the cartoons. Following these reprints came rioting throughout the Middle East that led to dozens of deaths.[59]

So why was half the world infuriated over cartoons published in a conservative Danish newspaper? The answer is both simple and complex. At the heart of the controversy is Islam's prohibition on depicting the Prophet Muhammad. According to news accounts, it is a sin for a Muslim to create such an image and the "ultimate sort of insult" for a non-Muslim to do so. The *Washington Post*'s culture critic Philip Kennicott gives a compelling explanation of why the cartoons were so controversial and why he believes that publishing them was a bad idea:

> They were created as a provocation—Islam generally forbids the making of images of its highest prophet—in a conservative newspaper, which wanted to make a point about freedom of speech in a liberal, secular Western democracy. Depending on your point of view, it was a stick in the eye meant to provoke debate, or just a stick in the eye.[60]

He points out that we would be unlikely to see many cartoons quite that offensive toward Christianity in the United States:

> No serious American newspaper would commission images of Jesus that were solely designed to offend Christians. And if one did, the reaction would be swift and certain. Politicians would take to the floors of Congress and call down thunder on the malefactors. Some Christians would react with fury and boycotts and flaming e-mails that couldn't be printed in a family newspaper; others would react with sadness, prayer, and earnest letters to the editor. There would be mayhem, though it is unlikely that semiautomatic weapons would be brandished in the streets.[61]

The response to the cartoons was massive: At least four people were killed when Afghan troops fired on demonstrators, the cartoonists themselves went into hiding for fear of being killed, two Jordanian newspaper editors who reprinted the cartoons were arrested, the cartoons were banned in South Africa and the editor who published them there received death threats, and protesters burned the Danish embassy in Beirut. American commentators have written lengthy pieces on the controversy, the effects of which still linger. As recently as 2012, a Somali man who attacked one of the cartoonists was sentenced to ten years in prison.[62]

While many American news outlets did not reprint the Danish cartoons, the *Philadelphia Inquirer* did reprint the most offensive of the images. Muslims in the Philadelphia area responded by picketing the paper, thus illustrating the commonsense idea that the proper response to offensive speech is more speech, not less. In fact, *Inquirer* editor Amanda Bennett said of the protesters, "Neither I nor the newspaper meant any disrespect to their religion or their prophet. I told them I was actually really proud of them for exercising their right to freedom of speech."[63] The cartoons also ran in the University of Illinois student paper, the *Daily Illini*, which sparked debate about the issue on the campus and led to peaceful protests.

But far more papers decided against running the cartoons. The *Boston Globe*, in an editorial, explained the paper's reasoning:

> Depicting Mohammed wearing a turban in the form of a bomb with a sputtering fuse is no less hurtful to most Muslims than Nazi caricatures of Jews or Ku Klux Klan caricatures of blacks are to those victims of intolerance. That is why the Danish cartoons will not be reproduced on these pages.[64]

Privacy Law in Europe

When Britain's beloved Princess Diana died in a car crash on August 30, 1997, the entire world mourned, and many people in Europe and the United States blamed the accident on overly aggressive photographers chasing the car in which she was riding. Although evidence soon came to light that Diana's driver had been drunk at the time, the high-speed chase through the streets of Paris brought the privacy rights of the rich and famous to the forefront of the public's attention.[65] France has relatively strict privacy laws that proclaim "each individual has the right to require respect for his private life. . . . Privacy revolves around the secrecy of one's intimate life and the right to oppose investigation and revelation of this domain."[66] This protects against coverage of a person's family life, sexual activity or orientation, illness, and private leisure activities. The person suing does not need to show that he or she has been damaged; the law presumes that invasion of privacy, by its very nature, is damaging.

Despite the strength of the restrictions, the penalties for violating the laws are relatively mild.[67] Most fines are under $50,000, and the French press views them largely as a cost of doing business. Although the law also allows the courts to confiscate the publications containing the offending photographs, in practice the courts almost never do so.[68] Whereas France has relatively strict laws, until recently, British law did not recognize an individual's right to privacy. For example, in 1987, British actor Gorden Kaye suffered a serious head injury in an accident. Kaye was subsequently interviewed while he was semiconscious and recovering from brain surgery. The British courts ruled that the only thing legally wrong with the article was that it implied that the actor had consented to the interview. Thus, the article was published without penalty.[69] In 2000, the British Parliament put into law the Human Rights Act, which requires the press to observe a "proper balance" between privacy and publicity.[70]

In the spring of 2018, the European Union started enforcing one of the toughest online privacy rules in the world—the General Data Protection Regulation (GDPR).[71] The law requires that

- Companies be clear about how their customers' data are being handled. They also must have permission before they can use it.

- Online advertising can only target you if you give your consent. This means that on European websites and apps you will be less likely to see the ads that target you because you are a twenty-one-year-old woman from Stockholm, Sweden, who likes electronic dance music and Coca-Cola Light (as Diet Coke is known in Europe).

- You can ask companies about what information they have on you and require them to delete it if you request. This could include things like your shopping history tied to your credit card or loyalty program. (There is an example in Chapter 12 of targeting pregnant women based on their buying habits.)

- Most visibly, companies had to have new, clear, and understandable privacy policies. This is why you got a flood of new privacy policy notices in your email inbox in May 2018, even if you lived in the United States. Any company that does business in Europe has to follow the rules, so just to be on the safe side, companies sent the notice out to all of their customers.

In January 2019, France fined Google nearly $57 million for violating the new data privacy rules. This was the first major case brought against one of the United States' tech giants under the new law. Google was penalized for failing to disclose to consumers how their personal information was being collected and how it was being used. Google had also failed to get user permission to show them personalized ads.[72]

European "Right to Be Forgotten" Laws. In 2014, the European Court of Justice ruled that people who live in the EU have a right to purge search engine results they consider to be out of date or irrelevant. The "right to be forgotten" ruling requires that Google and other search providers present the edited search results on any search conducted from within any of the countries covered by the ruling.[73]

The "right to be forgotten" ruling does not force anyone to take down the offending material; it only forces them to omit it from search results. According to the *New York Times*, these requests have included removing links to news articles, a link to a mass shooter's published manifesto, and an unkind slideshow that called a reality TV star "an annoying, unbearable nag."[74]

As of February 2018, Google had received more than 655,000 "right to be forgotten" requests demanding the removal of nearly 2.5 million links and honored about 43 percent of them. What did people want deleted from search results? One-third of the requests were for "social media and directory services that contained personal information." One-fifth of them were for news articles or government websites, generally containing information about the person's legal history.[75]

The editing of results will be done on searches within the European Union, but not in the United States or other countries outside the EU.

Key Changes Under the EU's General Data Protection Regulation (GDPR)

Source: Based on information located at "GDPR Key Changes" on the EU GDPR website.

Media in Central and Latin America

Most of Latin American commercial broadcasting is dominated by North American, Mexican, and Brazilian programming. Brazil and Mexico have among the largest and most sophisticated broadcasting operations of any nation in the world. In fact, Mexico and Brazil export culture back to the United States through sports programming and the extremely popular telenovelas. Latin American broadcasters tend to follow the American for-profit model rather than the BBC's public-service orientation. One reason for the larger scope of South American broadcasting is that, unlike Africa (which we discuss shortly), Latin America has only two dominant languages to deal with—Spanish and Portuguese.[76] Since the 1990s, Latin American governments have become more stable and less repressive, and the economies of these countries have grown. All these factors have contributed to the growth of the media industry in Latin America. Unlike in much of the world, newspaper circulation has been growing in Latin America, with more than one thousand newspapers being published and daily readership exceeding one hundred million.[77] Journalists in Central and South America do face threats of violence, however, coming from organized crime and paramilitary groups, and to a lesser extent from the government.[78]

Journalists working in Mexico have faced violence and murder covering crime and corruption. Mexican journalist Javier Valdez was killed when he was shot near the newspaper he founded. The *Washington Post* reports that he was the fifth reporter in Mexico murdered in 2017. By the

▲ In March 2018, protesters in Sinaloa, Mexico, march to denounce the assassination of Mexican journalist Javier Valdez one year earlier and to call for justice for him and other journalists killed in the professional line of duty. In 2017, more journalists were killed in Mexico than in any other country.

end of the year, a total of eleven journalists would be killed, the most in any single country, including Syria.[79] In a speech he gave in 2011, Valdez said, "To do journalism is to walk on an invisible line drawn by the bad guys—who are in drug trafficking and in government—in a field strewn with explosives. This is what most of the country is living through. One must protect oneself from everything and everyone, and there do not seem to be options or salvation, and often there is no one to turn to."[80] Valdez's specialty was reporting on the human toll of violence in Mexico.

The World Press Freedom Index points out that for a country that is not at war, Mexico is one of the world's deadliest countries for journalists and the media. The report ranks Mexico at 143rd out of 180 countries, which it blames in part on "collusion between officials and organized crime."[81] As of June of 2020, twenty-one journalists have been killed in Mexico since 2018.

Media in Islamic Countries and the Middle East

The press in the Middle East seems to straddle the fence between social responsibility and authoritarian media control. For example, although Israel is a modern, liberal democracy, reporters there are required to submit stories on sensitive military issues to the government for approval.[82] During the 1991 Persian Gulf War, all news coming out of Israel via commercial media had to be cleared by military censors. Israeli authorities are also quick to control the dissident Palestinian press.

Even aside from the activities of the terrorist group ISIS (the Islamic State of Iraq and Syria) in the country, Syria was is one of the world's most dangerous countries for journalists, according to the group Reporters Without Borders. Between 2011 and 2018, 141 news workers were killed there, and 75 were taken prisoner or hostage.[83] For 2020, Syria was ranked 174th out of 180 countries in terms of press freedom.[84]

Along with Colvin's death by rocket fire in Syria in 2012, one of the highest-profile deaths in Syria was that of American journalist/photographer James Foley, who was beheaded by Islamic State militants in August 2014 after having been held hostage since November 2012. This was not the first time Foley had been taken prisoner. He had previously been held prisoner by Libyan soldiers loyal to Libyan leader Moammar Gadhafi.[85] Even before the recent revolutions and violence in Syria and Libya, the press there was under authoritarian control at best. Jordan and Egypt both tightened their controls on the press after the Arab Spring movement in 2011.[86] Along with the official state-controlled media, many Arab nations also have *Al-Hayat*, a regional Arabic newspaper published in London, and the **Al Jazeera** satellite channel, which originates in Qatar. The other alternative is to listen to news from a neighboring Arab state, which will not hesitate to criticize the government of its neighbor. By listening to a range of reports, one can gain a more complete picture of the news.[87]

On July 22, 2014, *Washington Post* Iran correspondent Jason Rezaian was arrested by Iranian authorities, along with his wife, Yeganeh Salehi, an Iranian citizen who was also a reporter for a United Arab Emirates paper. Rezaian was taken to Iran's notorious Evin Prison where he was kept in solitary confinement for months. He was eventually held captive for more than five hundred days until he and three other prisoners were swapped for seven people imprisoned or charged in the United States. Salehi had been released on bail.[88] Imprisoned nearly five months before finally being charged during a closed court hearing without having an attorney, Rezaian's captivity was the longest in Iran since the 1979 Islamic revolution. Almost a year after being arrested, Rezaian was tried on charges of "espionage, 'collaborating with hostile governments,' 'propaganda against the establishment,' and allegations that he gathered information 'about internal and foreign policy.'"[89]

The *Washington Post*, under the leadership of executive editor Martin Baron, petitioned the United Nations for "urgent action" to get his release. Baron and other *Post* editors quickly met with U.S. government officials, including Vice President Joe Biden and Secretary of State John Kerry. But for Baron and the rest of the people at the *Post*, getting information out of the U.S. government was challenging. "All along, the administration was reluctant to get into a lot of details with us," Baron said. Administration officials "remained concerned throughout, to the very end, that if they provided us details it would somehow end up being public."[90]

Up to the very last minute before Rezaian left Iran, whether he would actually get out was in question. As the jet left Iranian airspace, the former prisoners were served champagne and chocolate. *Post* owner and Amazon founder Jeff Bezos met Rezaian and his family once the Swiss plane landed in Germany, and brought them back to the United States in his private plane.[91] Iran has not been an easy place for journalists, both foreign and domestic, to work. At the time of Rezaian's release, there were still at least nineteen other "reporters, cartoonists and editors" being held by the government there.[92] In February 2018, two Iranian reporters working for a Sufi news website were badly beaten and arrested. Iran is currently ranked 173rd out of 180 by the 2020 World Press Freedom Index.[93]

Satellite and internet delivery have vastly changed media in the Middle East, and they bypass authoritarian rule. During the 1991 Persian Gulf War, people in the Middle East received news from CNN, which they believed was being censored by the U.S. government. But Western media are not that influential in Arab-speaking countries. First, not everyone speaks English or French, the languages typically spoken on international channels. And the middle class, as well as members of Islamist movements in the Middle East, have an understandable thirst for regional media.[94]

Kai Hafez, a scholar at American University in Cairo, has distinguished three types of press in the Arab world: the "mobilized press," which is controlled by the government to promote the government; the "loyalist press," which is run by private industry but is supportive of people in power, especially those who can control access to resources such as paper and electricity; and finally the "diverse press," which is relatively free.[95]

Many of these countries espouse freedom of the press, and the level of criticism of the government that a country tolerates varies from administration to administration, from year to year. However, even in countries without an Islamist government, it can be a crime to "insult" the country, which puts definite limits on what can be reported.

The Importance of "Small" Media

Long before we spoke of social media, so-called **small media** were significant channels for small-scale communication. Small media include fax machines, photocopy machines, and video cameras, along with computers, blogs, and mobile social media, such as Twitter and SMS text messages. Hafez has written about the importance of alternative independent media—of which small media are a crucial component—in the Middle East. Although Palestinian media in the West Bank have been subject to Israeli censorship, Palestinians have been able to use the web to post accounts and images of demonstrations and violence that bypass government censorship.[96]

During the Arab Spring protests and revolutions of 2011, social and mobile media were frequently credited as both a source of news about the protests and an organizing tool for the protesters. These small media alternatives have taken the spot formerly occupied by cheaply produced short-run magazines. The alternative-independent media provide for a range of voices, even in countries such as Iran that have strict Islamic control of the mainstream media (which shows us that, even in other parts of the world, Secret 2—There are no mainstream media—still holds).

Religion professor Fred Strickert notes that while the Israelis and Palestinians are still capable of manipulating the news, the internet allows for the expression of a wider range of views:

> Yes, the Palestinian Authority can still censor damaging video footage, as it did in the case of the mob lynching of two Israeli soldiers, and the Israeli government can put its spin on the news. But the truth is on the Internet for anyone who cares to find it.[97]

Whereas legacy media using internet and satellite delivery receive a great deal of popular attention, the small media have also done a good job of transmitting messages outside the realm of censorship. Following the disputed Iranian presidential elections in 2009 (discussed in Chapter 10), the Iranian government began to crack down on news media, going so far as to kick reporters out of the country.[98] The government blocked many forms of social media, reduced internet speed to block online video, shut down mobile phone towers, and threatened retaliation against those who used new media, such as mobile phones and the internet, to transmit information out of Iran. Legacy media, including CNN, Fox News, MSNBC, and even the BBC, had to turn to online video, blogs, and Twitter feeds of questionable reliability to report on what was happening within Iran. As social media expert Gaurav Mishra points out, mobile phone–based social media are increasingly going to be the medium through which news breaks.[99]

Old and New Media in the Islamic World

Media in the Arab world are heavily controlled by the government, though the presence of satellite broadcasting and mobile technology is challenging governmental control. Until recently, it has been very difficult to get a handle on media use in the Middle East. But in 2013, researchers with Northwestern University in Qatar started taking a long-term, in-depth look at how people in Egypt, Jordan, Lebanon, Qatar, the Kingdom of Saudi Arabia, Tunisia, and the United Arab Emirates used and thought about a full range of media, the social and political climate in their countries, and the state of freedom of expression. (Not every country has full data for every year.) The "Media Use in the Middle East" study does not look at the same issues each year. For example, in 2015, the focus was on use of entertainment media and leisure time.[100] The countries included in the study have varied slightly over the years.

The 2019 edition of the study found a decline in the percentage of people using almost all media since the first year of the study in 2013, except for the internet, which increased. Some of these declines were modest while others were more significant. Television use dropped from 98 percent to 86 percent; offline radio use dropped from 52 percent to 38 percent; and newspaper readership dropped the most, going from 42 percent to 16 percent. Internet usage, on the other hand, jumped from 55 percent to 86 percent.[101] (See Figure 11.2.)

In the Arab world, online media are most definitely mobile media (Secret 6), with a higher percentage of people going online with their phones rather than their desktop or laptop computers. Smartphones are used to go online by 96 percent of those surveyed, while computers were used by only 53 percent.[102]

For Syrian refugees attempting to escape from fighting in the area, smartphones are often the only media they have. Budget Android phones can be purchased for under £100, and second-generation iPhones can be found for approximately £25.

▲ Refugees from Syria and elsewhere in the Middle East recharge their mobile phones and other devices at a central charging station in a camp in Moria, Greece, in the spring of 2016. For many of the refugees, mobile phones are the only channel for communication they have access to.

NurPhoto/NurPhoto via Getty Images

Popularity of Various Media in the Middle East

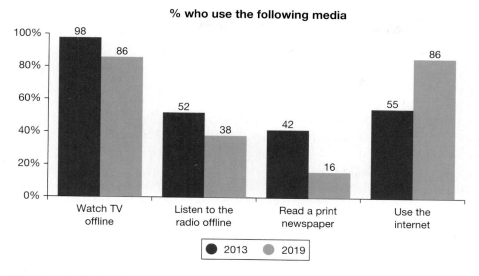

% who use the following media

Source: Data are from Everette E. Dennis, Justin D. Martin, and Robb Wood, "Media Use in the Middle East, 2017," Northwestern University in Qatar, 2017, http://www.mideastmedia.org

Social media are everywhere, but the popularity of different products varies. The texting and message sharing app WhatsApp was the most popular with 75 percent of internet users using it. (WhatsApp is particularly good for texting across national borders.) Facebook was close behind at 71 percent and Instagram a distant third at 42 percent. Snapchat and Twitter were at 24 percent and 22 percent, respectively.[103]

Egypt, which is more secular than much of the Arab world, has a large media industry and produces movies, music, and television programming for much of the Arab and Islamic world.[104] Access to television, especially direct-broadcast satellite signals, varies significantly throughout the Islamic nations of the Middle East. The Saudi Arabian monarchy built a substantial television network in the 1960s, in part to respond to anti-Saudi broadcasts coming into the country from Egypt. In March 1994, Saudi Arabia officially banned ownership of satellite receivers to satisfy religious conservatives who objected to Western programming. The ban has not been enforced, however, and both the dishes and the receivers are readily available.

In the words of Reporters Without Borders, Saudi Arabia permits no independent media. In its 2020 World Press Freedom Index, the group states that Saudi journalists are watched closely, even when they are outside of the country, as the murder of *Washington Post* journalist Jamal Khashoggi in Turkey in 2018 illustrates. (For more on Khashoggi, see Chapter 5.) Journalists who discuss political issues can be charged with "blasphemy, 'insulting religion,' 'inciting chaos,' 'jeopardizing national unity,' or 'harming the image and reputation of the king and he state.'"[105] The kingdom was ranked 170th out of 180 countries for press freedom.

Al Jazeera

The most significant of the advertising-supported channels is Al Jazeera.[106] Broadcast via satellite from the small Arab country of Qatar since 1997, the channel is not censored by the government.[107] Al Jazeera has carried interviews with everyone from Osama bin Laden to Colin Powell and has been criticized for doing so by both the United States and Arab countries. During the current war in Iraq, Al Jazeera came to worldwide attention, presenting an Arab point of view to the fighting between the United States and Iraq. It has a regular audience of forty million, which dwarfs CNN or Fox in scope.[108]

In the Arab Middle East, satellite news channels that can cross over national borders are clearly the top source of international news, and Al Jazeera is the most popular of the many Arab-language satellite channels. It is the most watched, or perhaps the most important, though many claim to dislike the controversial channel. According to NPR's *On the Media*, a recent survey shows that only 10 percent of Arabs who have access to satellite TV never watch Al Jazeera. In Iraq, the Saudi Arabia–based Al Arabiya is popular. But American channel Alhurra is clearly the last choice, with 53 percent saying they never watch it. Interestingly enough, the Hezbollah channel, Al-Manar, is similarly unpopular.[109] Although some observers accuse Al Jazeera of being a pro-Arab propaganda channel, others have described it as the CNN of the Arab world. Perhaps neither label is completely fair or completely accurate. It would seem instead that Al Jazeera is committed to presenting an Arab view of the world. That is, it works at telling the news accurately, but it tells it from a clear point of view. (Interestingly enough, taking a page from the American media synergy playbook, there is also an Al Jazeera sports channel.) What makes Al Jazeera interesting is that while its headquarters are in Qatar, it tends to take a broad Arab point of view, rather than that of one particular country. Too often, all Arab or Muslim countries are seen in the West as being the same, rather than having distinctly different views. It's easy for Americans to forget that Iraq and Iran were at war with each other for at least ten years.[110] Al Jazeera was founded by Sheikh Hamad bin Khalifa al-Thani, the emir of Qatar, in an effort to diversify his nation's economy. He started the satellite news channel following the failure of a 1994 BBC experiment with an Arab-language, Saudi-financed station. Hiring 120 of the unemployed journalists from the project gave Al Jazeera its start. Although Western governments have been highly critical of Al Jazeera, the network has carried criticism of Qatar's government, the Palestinian Authority, the Jordanian government, the Kuwaiti government, and the Israeli government.[111]

Al Jazeera journalists certainly don't receive special treatment by Arab governments. In fact, they are often targeted for the in-depth reporting. Three reporters for Al Jazeera, Peter Greste, Baher Mohamed, and Mohamed Fahmy, were arrested in December 2013, and were convicted of multiple offenses against the Egyptian government in the summer of 2014. Fahmy and Mohamed received presidential pardons and were released in September 2015 for the Muslim holiday of Eid al-Adha. Greste was released in February 2015 and sent back to his native Australia, apparently without having charges dropped.[112]

Media in Africa

The African continent provides a prime example of the range of approaches to development media theory—from a strong social responsibility approach to out-and-out authoritarian controls. The mass media first came to Africa through the European colonial powers; they were created to serve the needs of the colonists. Newspapers and early broadcast stations covered only white news and ignored Black Africans, or else treated them as "subhuman beings."[113] After independence, colonial media continued to exist in some countries, whereas in other countries the press was taken over by the new governments, which did not permit private media. Although the media were serving a new population, they continued to focus on the needs of the elite.

Africa is still largely rural, and its smaller towns often do not have newspapers. However, according to Tawana Kupe, a media scholar from Zimbabwe and South Africa, most countries have a dominant daily newspaper that is distributed primarily in the capital city. Newspaper circulation is limited by high levels of poverty and illiteracy.[114] Radio is the most important medium in Africa, but both radios and the batteries to run them are expensive, and transmission equipment often is not good enough to reach an entire country. Television is not available in many countries. Even where there are broadcasts, television can be received only where there is reliable electrical service, primarily in urban areas. Most of the programming consists of old European, American, and Australian reruns. Although many African countries seek to use television and radio to foster development by teaching people how to improve their standard of living, most of the development programming consists of speeches by politicians calling for development.

Reporters Without Borders writes that Africa has a wide range of press freedom within its many countries, "from Senegal and its lively newspapers to Eritrea and Djibouti, where there are no privately owned media at all."[115] One of the most effective censorship tools governments there have found is to simply shut off the internet in strategic regions. Another technique has been to pass "vague and draconian" rules that can be used to do pretty much anything those in power want.

The Committee to Protect Journalists (CPJ) reports that many of the countries embrace a development theory of the press. A 2011 report from the CPJ notes that many African leaders are claiming that they cannot achieve what they say are contradictory goals of balancing economic and social stability with freedom of the press. This approach goes so far as to shape how sports are covered. A star Cameroonian soccer player complained to a Senegalese reporter after the journalist raised a critical question about the team's play, saying, "You journalists, certain journalists like you, you who do not want Africa to advance, you who do not want Cameroon to advance, you are always negative. Try to change a little."[116]

Cléa Kahn-Sriber of Reporters Without Borders said that press freedom is "grim" in sub-Saharan Africa: "Several countries have lapsed into conflict or have continued to be in a conflict situation. . . . And over the whole continent we see that the issue of security and the fight against terrorism is often an argument that is being used by governments to justify a crackdown on the press."[117]

Language continues to be an issue for African media. Many African nations use the former colonial language (typically French or English) in their nation-building efforts, but this tends to be the language of the educated class, not of the majority of the people.[118] Except in Kenya and Tanzania, which have a Swahili press, virtually no major newspapers are published in African languages.

It is tempting in the West to view Africa as something akin to South America, but unlike South America, Africa as a continent does not share common languages or cultures. Africa is exceedingly culturally diverse, with more languages spoken there than on any other continent in the world.[119] Politically, many of the countries are dominated by single-party or military governments, though there are notable exceptions, such as South Africa, Mali, and Ghana.

South Africa was the first country in sub-Saharan Africa to have radio, and today it has the best-developed system in that area of the world. Most of the country's radio is handled by the South African Broadcasting Corporation. Following heavy censorship in South Africa during the apartheid era, the South African press in the early twenty-first century has an organization of publishers, journalists, and members of the public that can reprimand newspapers when necessary. A committee made up of lawyers and media professionals regulates the broadcast industry.[120] South African television broadcasts in seven different languages: English, Afrikaans, northern and southern Sotho, Tswana, Xhosa, and Zulu. As you can see, language is a big barrier when you consider the linguistic diversity within just a single country—South Africa has eleven language groups. African media experts Osabuohien P. Amienyi and Gerard Igyor recognize this dilemma: "This plurality [of languages] presents broadcasting with the dilemma of how to fulfill the natural desire of every community to be addressed in its own language or dialect."[121]

REUTERS/David Rae Morris

▲ South Africa's vibrant pop music scene has gained fans around the world. Groups such as the Mahotella Queens, pictured here, and Ladysmith Black Mambazo routinely draw crowds in the United States and Europe.

If stations hope to reach a large group with a single language, they are likely going to have to transmit in the languages of the colonial whites, typically English, French, Portuguese, or Spanish. This furthers the problem of programming that will be accessible primarily to urban elites and not the rural population who need the service the most.

South Africa is ranked 31st in the 2020 World Press Freedom Index, higher than the United Kingdom (35th), South Korea (42nd), or the United States (45th). When South Africa broke out of apartheid with its new constitution in 1996, it put in place protections for press freedom.

South Africa has also been a major source of inspiration for Western pop music. Among the Western musicians who have worked at bringing African music to the forefront of American pop culture are Paul Simon, Peter Gabriel, and Talking Heads frontman David Byrne.[122] Simon, a singer and songwriter, was captivated by the sounds of South Africa's township jive and in 1985 traveled to Johannesburg to record there with artists such as Miriam Makeba.[123] This collaboration resulted in the best-selling album *Graceland* and a world tour. Township jive emerged as a style during the apartheid era in South Africa. The music combines traditional African drumming and rhythms with Western instruments to create a unique musical style. Among the South African musicians who have found success in the West are the a cappella men's choir Ladysmith Black Mambazo, the group Mahlathini and the Mahotella Queens, and musician Johnny Clegg and his band Juluka. Groups such as Bongo Maffin have combined the South African pop music style with rhythm and blues, reggae, and rap.[124] African pop music is no newcomer to the United States. In 1961, the Tokens recorded a hit single, "The Lion Sleeps Tonight," which was based on an African chant.[125]

One thing that has inhibited world music's popularity in the United States is the language barrier, though language differences have not stopped people in other countries from listening to American music. "People around the world have been listening to American and British music for the last thirty years, very often not understanding the words but enjoying the ways people put things together," says producer D. A. "Jumbo" Vanrenen. "As Third World artists have access to the same recording studios, it's becoming easier to present their music in a clear way. Language becomes less important. People go for the dance rhythms and the fine quality of people's vocals."[126] You can hear this branch of world music on Public Radio International's Afropop Worldwide or on the BBC's world music programming.

Alexander Nemenov/Getty Images

▲ Russian president Vladimir Putin is rarely, if ever, challenged by the Russian media. News outlets in the former Soviet country are dominated by government control.

Media in Russia and the Former Soviet Republics

Media developed slowly in the old Soviet Union if for no other reason than the vast scale of its empire, which covered one-sixth of the world at its peak, inhibited its development. Along with the more conventional media, such as radio, people in the Soviet Union made use of alternative media, such as sending broadcasts out over phone lines that would then be played in communities over a loudspeaker system. Under communism, there was no ideal of an independent press. The goal of newspapers and broadcasters was to support the goals of communism, not to be detached and critical external observers. Janis E. Overlock, who specializes in study of the media of the old Soviet empire, describes the problem:

One of the main problems of the media in the countries of the former Soviet Union is a basic lack of understanding of the role of the media in a democracy. After years of Soviet domination, many of the governments as well as journalists view the media as a propaganda tool for the government.[127]

She further explains that even if the government professes a belief in the free press, that freedom simply doesn't exist within the culture.[128]

Since the collapse of the Soviet Union in 1991, the Russian press has had a troubled existence. Although many of the media are now in private hands, they are not necessarily free of government control, and they experience extremely high levels of self-censorship. The independent media in Russia are owned by a small group of businesspeople who support the government and want to maintain control of their own media monopolies.

Russian media scholar Nataliya Rostova told the *Huffington Post* that Russian president Vladimir Putin keeps tight control over the Russian media, appointing the editors and managers of all major media outlets either officially or unofficially. "The editors and directors have so-called weekly meetings with the presidential administration to talk about the upcoming events, what will be significant in the next week, what the administration wants to cover," she said. "Additionally, media outlets are dependent on state funding and the TV advertising market is almost monopolized as well."[129]

Journalists who have been too critical of the Russian government have found themselves dead under mysterious circumstances. In April 2018, Russian journalist Maksim Borodin died after falling from his apartment's fifth-story balcony. Police say his apartment was locked from the inside and that they are not treating his death as suspicious.[130] In 2017, the *Washington Post* ran a story on ten critics of Putin who died violently or in suspicious circumstances, including several who were journalists.[131] Russia was ranked 149th in the 2020 World Press Freedom Index.[132] The 2018 report states that there are at least five journalists currently being detained by the government along with many bloggers.[133]

Russian media has also been suspected of being involved in international propaganda efforts to affect elections in multiple Western nations. As we discussed in Chapter 10, Russian news organizations Russia Today (RT) and Sputnik spread false stories on social media during the 2016 U.S. presidential election through both regular messages and paid ads.[134]

Media in Asia

Although Asia has many countries and cultures, in most of its nations, the broadcast media are either government controlled or run by public corporations. In many of these countries, we see a development philosophy for the media, in which broadcasters are expected to work to support the economic and social development goals of the government.

India, China, and Japan stand apart from the rest of the continent as major media forces. Communist and former Soviet bloc countries, such as North Korea, continue to operate under the old Soviet-style communist model. Southeast Asia, which includes countries such as Indonesia, Malaysia, and the Philippines, tends to operate under a development philosophy. This can be seen in Malaysia, where the Ministry of Communications and Multimedia sets guidelines on how broadcasters can portray Malaysian education, art, culture, and identity.[135]

Newspapers are big business in India, with a daily circulation of seventy-two million, second only to China, which circulates eighty-five million copies a day. As of 2020, India has more than 17,000 newspapers, 100,000 magazines, 178 television news channels, and countless websites and social media pages. A report on Indian media estimates that 90 percent of India's population has access to a radio set. Print media in India are heavily supported by advertising, and hitting a balance between serving the public and making advertisers happy is a major issue.[136]

The big newspapers in India face the same sort of competitive pressures from newer media that U.S. papers do, community newspapers dealing with local issues are seen as a growth industry.[137] All India Radio (AIR) is the dominant radio service and the exclusive source of radio news and public affairs programming. There are broadcast television stations in India, but the television market is dominated by cable and satellite networks.

Subhendu Sarkar/Getty Images

When a group of terrorists killed 171 people and held the city of Mumbai, India, hostage for more than sixty hours, local journalists had to figure out how to respond to the story.[138] Arnab Goswami, then chief editor of *Times Now*, India's largest satellite news channel, said that the Indian government got very nervous about media coverage of the attacks, fearing that the reports were helping the terrorists. At one point, during the early phases of the attacks, the government shut down television news for forty-five minutes. But Goswami said that when the government cut off the news flow, the response from viewers was

▲ At a time when numerous American newspapers are downsizing, the Indian newspaper industry is booming. Local print newspapers saw double-digit growth in 2017.

massive, massive. . . . Every single phone was ringing. People were watching us so closely that if we were off for five seconds they would react, because cable and satellite television is largely the only form of receiving information at a time like this.[139]

Despite being the world's largest democracy, India is ranked at 142 out of 180 countries in the 2020 World Press Freedom Index. Reporters Without Borders writes that there are active hate campaigns on social media directed against reporters, and journalists have been targeted with criminal prosecutions.[140] Censorship has been on the rise in India under the government of Prime Minister Narendra Modi. As an example, on March 6, 2020, the Media One television station serving five million viewers got cut off the air for forty-eight hours because the government decided it didn't like how the station had covered mob attacks on Muslims in New Delhi. Modi came to power in 2014 and has worked hard to control the news media, especially broadcasters.[141]

Journalists in the Kashmir and Chhattisgarh regions face both censorship and physical violence from a variety of sources, including police and security forces, criminal groups, and political party supporters.[142] The Kashmir Valley region, where more than seven million people live, had its internet completely shut down by the federal government for nearly six months. This was at the same time the government revoked Kashmir's statehood and cut off all mobile and landline connections. Since late January 2020, the government has given people in the region limited internet availability that gives slow mobile access to approximately three hundred government approved websites. The government said the online shutdown was put in place to prevent violent protests.[143]

In the past, Chinese media was traditionally described as unapologetically political and propagandistic. Until the 1970s and 1980s, the media in China were proud of this distinction. At the time, the role of the media was not to entertain or market products; instead, they promoted public policies, such as water conservation programs; provided education to rural areas; and mobilized the public after natural disasters or industrial accidents.[144]

Over the past thirty years, Chinese media offerings and availability have changed rapidly. In 1978, China had fewer than one television set per hundred people. As of 2010, China had become the world's largest television market with more than 378 million households with television, and more than 180 million homes with multichannel television (i.e., cable/satellite). The average household watches approximately twenty-one hours per week. While international channels have only limited availability in China, local stations can get foreign programming blocks to put on the air.[145] The number of newspapers has similarly expanded, from 42 papers in 1968, most of which were run by the Communist Party, to approximately 1,900 newspapers in 2016.[146]

In China, as in the United States, online media are mobile media (Secret 6). As of 2011, China had more than 920 million mobile phone users. Of these, 100 million are registered with an app store, indicating that they use their phone for accessing the internet, and 35 million use mobile payments. China also has more than 640 million total people who are actively online.[147]

Mobile phones serve as a major channel for the flow of news. Chinese phone users tend to upgrade their phones frequently, so new mobile technology spreads through the country rapidly.[148] (For more about social media and China, see Chapter 10.)

China is ranked 177th out of 180 by the 2020 World Press Freedom Index, just above the bottom three of Eritrea, Turkmenistan, and North Korea.[149] China is famous for its so-called Great Firewall that monitors all internet traffic going in and out of the country. When your author was there in 2013, there was no access to Facebook or other social media sites, Google was censored, and many news sites and blogs could not be accessed. "Making unauthorized criticisms" is against the law. The government was detaining more than one hundred journalists and bloggers as of 2020 under dangerous conditions. In 2017, Nobel Peace Prize winner Liu Xiaobo and dissident blogger Yang Tongyan both died of cancer that was left untreated while the Chinese government was holding them.[150]

▲ A woman cycles past a building covered in portraits of Chinese president Xi Jinping in Shanghai. Dissident Chang Ping says relatives have been abducted after he was linked to a letter criticizing the president.

When looking at the major media players in Asia, Japan is a critical component. Japan is in many ways the technological heart of our modern media world. Many of our essential electronic media devices come from Japan. Broadcasting started in the country in 1925 and was run by the government for the next twenty-five years. In the era after World War II, U.S. policy helped shape what Japan offered, which became a mix of public and commercial broadcasting.[151] NHK is Japan's public broadcasting corporation, and it provides both domestic and international service. It is financed through a fee that all television owners must pay. Japan has relatively high levels of television broadcast viewership. The biggest difference between Japanese and U.S. broadcasting is that Japan has a much more even balance between commercial and public broadcasting.

Japan ranks 66th on the World Press Freedom Index. While Japan in general has an open and free press, journalists cannot always fulfill that promise, Reporters Without Borders writes, "because of the influence of tradition and business interests." There are also problems with Japanese nationalist groups harassing journalists who try to cover "antipatriotic" topics like the Fukushima Daiichi nuclear plant disaster.[152]

The most popular category of magazines in Japan is not fashion, lifestyle, or hobbies; it is manga, or comic books. The word *manga* means comics or amusing drawings, and according to *Publishers Weekly*, the genre accounts for 40 percent of all books and magazines published in Japan. In the United States, manga-style comics are most popular with teenage boys and tend to feature action stories. Some examples are *Yu-Gi-Oh!*, *Pokémon*, and *Sailor Moon*. In Japan, manga cover just about every magazine genre. Douglas Wolk, who has covered manga in the United States, writes, "There are hundreds of manga for girls and for boys, men's manga and women's manga, romance manga, political manga, baseball manga, mah-jongg manga, and more."[153] Plots can range from the story of a teenage girl who becomes a superhero after using magic eye shadow to one that describes the aftermath of the atomic bombing of Hiroshima. There is even one that gives advice on how to get a divorce. Manga targeted at adults often contain violent or pornographic imagery.

Manga started out in the tenth century as illustrated Buddhist scrolls. By the seventeenth century, silk-bound books created using woodblock printing and featuring text and drawings about actors and actresses became popular. Current manga can be the size of a small telephone book.[155] Estimates suggest that 95 percent of Japan's population reads manga on a regular basis.[156]

The United States has been accused of imposing its culture on the world by exporting media products, but the same charges have been leveled against Japan, especially by other Asian

HOW FREE ARE THE WORLD'S MEDIA TO REPORT THE NEWS?

As discussed in several spots earlier in this chapter, every year, the group Reporters Without Borders for Freedom of Information issues a report on the state of press freedom around the world. In it, the organization analyzes the degree of freedom that "journalists, news media, and netizens" have in 180 countries. Among the items quantified by the study are cultural pluralism, media independence, self-censorship, legislative framework, transparency, infrastructure, and the level of violence targeted against journalists. Countries gain points for things that discourage or limit freedom of the press, and they have points deducted for behavior that encourages free speech. In the 2020 study, scores were on a scale from 0 to 100 with Norway, Finland, and Denmark ranked in the top three for freedom of speech, all with scores between 7.84 and 8.13. The countries in last place all had scores between 83.50 and 85.82, and included Eritrea, Turkmenistan, and North Korea. And how did the United States score? Take a look at the report's summary. You might be surprised at where it was ranked. (Hint: We talked about the United States' ranking back in the section of this chapter on the four theories of the press.[154])

You can see the complete report here: https://rsf.org/en/world-press-freedom-index

WHO is the source?

Who are Reporters Without Borders? What do they do?

WHAT do they say?

Which three nations had the best records on freedom of the press? Which three nations were at the bottom of the list? Where did the United States fall in the rankings? Was it up or down from the previous year?

WHAT evidence is there?

For each of the countries you have listed above, why did it get the rating it did? How does each country behave as a democracy (or an authoritarian state)?

HOW do you and your classmates feel about the rankings?

How would you describe each of the highest- and lowest-ranked countries' approaches to freedom of speech and of the press? Based on what you have read, how would you describe the United States' approach to freedom of the press? What do you think about the rankings? Are they fair? Why or why not?

countries. However, attempts to keep comics out of those countries have only led to the publication of pirate editions.[157] Manga have a history of popularity in the United States. They are based primarily on books connected to anime cartoon programs. Featuring characters with spiky hair, big heads, and big eyes, young people sees manga as exciting, dynamic, and sexy. Many American translations of Japanese manga are printed to be read from the back of the book to the front, just as they would be in Japan. Why? In part because it's cheaper than redoing the pages in the American front-to-back style, but also because teen readers see the reverse style as cool.[158] Manga characters have also shown up in video games and on a wide range of products, such as clothing and plush toys. Manga's popularity in the United States is also an example of Secret 3— Everything from the margin moves to the center.

CHAPTER REVIEW

CHAPTER SUMMARY ▶▶

Not all countries take the same approach to the relationship between the government and the press. This relationship can take a variety of forms, depending on the form of government and the culture of the country. Theories of the press include the authoritarian, communist, libertarian, social responsibility, and development theories. Although these normative theories of the press still have considerable value today, they have to be reexamined in terms of how the world has changed since they were first discussed in the 1950s. An alternative to the normative theories of the press is to look at the media dimensions of control, finance, programming goals, target audience, and feedback mechanisms.

Media theorist Marshall McLuhan suggested in the 1960s that the world would become a global village, linked together through electronic media. Although these media have become far more pervasive today than when McLuhan was writing, it is unclear whether they are bringing the world together or breaking it up into a series of disconnected villages.

Media in Western democracies generally operate under a combination of libertarian and social responsibility theories. Many countries have free speech as a goal but are concerned about preserving their national cultures from the power of the American media industry. Several of the European countries have substantially stronger privacy laws than the United States, including "right to be forgotten" regulations that can control what can appear in online searches.

Latin America has a vibrant media industry, especially in Brazil and Mexico. These countries export Spanish-language programming, especially sports programs and telenovelas, to the United States.

The electronic media have a powerful presence in the Middle East, and satellite television can bypass national borders and bring outside content into otherwise closed media systems. The most popular source of news in the Arab-speaking countries of the Middle East is the satellite news channel Al Jazeera. Small media also have a significant presence in the Middle East because of their ability to bypass official government censorship. This area of the world has tended to be a dangerous area for journalists, with many being killed or imprisoned.

Media in Africa face a number of problems, including the lack of a common language, poor economies, and a lack of newsprint and reliable electricity.

While the news media in the old Soviet Union were designed to serve the needs of the government and the Communist Party, they went through a brief period of relative freedom in the 1980s. Since that time, the government has cracked down on free speech. The Russian press has no tradition of freedom and tends to engage in strong self-censorship to avoid persecution. Numerous journalists who have been critical of the government have died under suspicious circumstances.

Media in much of Asia tend to follow either a social responsibility theory or development theory, depending on the region. The major exception is Japan, which has strong public and private broadcasting businesses. Japan also exports content and media technology to the West and to the rest of the world. China operates under strong communist or authoritarian controls that tightly regulate what can be broadcast, printed, or transmitted over the internet.

KEY TERMS ▶▶

authoritarian theory   259

communist theory   260

libertarian theory   261

social responsibility theory   262

development theory   263

Al Jazeera   272

small media   273

REVIEW QUESTIONS ▶▶

1. Who was Marie Colvin? What was her approach to covering wars? How did she die?

2. Why do some people think there should be a development theory to go with the original four theories of the press? What do critics say is wrong with that theory?

3. How does freedom of speech in the United States differ from that in Canada or France?

4. How do media in Africa differ from media in South America?

5. Why are social media and small media important in the Middle East?

6. Why is it that Russians have low or no expectations of freedom of the press?

7. Why does India, as the world's largest democracy, have such a low ranking for freedom of the press?

PART IV

STRATEGIC COMMUNICATION

CHAPTER 12

ADVERTISING

Selling a Message

Youth is both the advantage and the disadvantage of trying to target advertising to digital natives— the young people who have grown up with mobile phones, tablets, and always-on internet. YouTube stars in their teens and twenties like PewDiePie, Logan Paul, and his brother Jake Paul can attract huge numbers of young viewers through videos, photos, and other brief online content. PewDiePie got his start by shouting while playing his way through video games; Logan Paul does stunts, pranks, and raps; and Jake Paul has been grabbing attention as of late by boxing with other YouTubers. But these notorious young men have now been supplanted in the public's attention by an eight-year-old boy who unboxes toys and proceeds to play with them. Toy influencer Ryan Kaji now has twenty-four million YouTube subscribers and reportedly made $26 million in 2019 with his online empire. Ryan first took the lead in 2018, earning $22 million, slightly more than the $21.5 million the previous leader Jake Paul made.[1]

Ryan first emerged in the public eye back in 2015 at the age of four with a series of roughly five-minute toy unboxing videos on YouTube under the name *Ryan ToysReview*. Unboxing videos, for the uninitiated, are where the presenter opens a toy's box, takes the toy out, and then plays with it.

One of these early videos has Ryan sleeping in his Disney Lightning McQueen bed next to a kid-sized chair featuring a vehicle from the Pixar *Cars* movies. Ryan's mother wakes him up to open a giant Lightning McQueen Egg full of 100+ Disney car and plane toys, with him squealing with excitement as he goes through all the contents. There are subtitles as required to understand Ryan's preschool-aged voice. Since first being posted on July 1, 2015, the video has been viewed more than 1 billion times. That is *billion* with a *b*.

As Ryan's channel grew in popularity, his parents Shion and Loan Kaji started working with Semaphore, an "influencer-focused wealth-management company" that helped the family become a juggernaut of branded toothbrushes, toys, and marketing partnerships including Colgate, Nickelodeon, Bonkers Toys, Roku, and Walmart.[2]

How does a YouTube star like Ryan make money? Ryan has a YouTube channel called *Ryan's World* (formerly *Ryan ToysReview*) where his parents post unboxing videos starring their son. These bring in revenue from advertising, product placement, and marketing partnerships. Ryan's popularity on YouTube has helped him also establish a presence on legacy media like the youth-oriented Nickelodeon

cable TV channel where he hosts *Ryan's Mystery Playdate*. The Nickelodeon show is produced by Pocket.watch, a company that manages a group of young influencers like Ryan.[3] Chris M. Williams, founder and CEO of Pocket.watch told *Variety*, "We specialize in identifying these stars who can be truly global, massive franchises."[4] Finally, Ryan has his own line of products.

Most of the episodes of Ryan's show feature at least one paid message targeted at preschoolers, a group child advocates argue is too young to know they are being marketed to. Josh Golin, executive director of the Campaign for a Commercial-Free Childhood tells the *New York Times,* "A 5-year-old isn't going to understand that Ryan's talking about the toys because Target is paying him to talk about the toys. There may be some disclosure, but disclosure isn't meaningful to a child that young."[5] Television has long had rules with the force of law that regulate the content of children's shows as well as separating shows from commercials. As an example, Nickelodeon's popular *Paw Patrol* is not allowed to feature ads for Paw Patrol toys.[6] But those same restrictions do not apply to online content. While the Federal Trade Commission (FTC) has guidelines for disclosure of sponsorship for online video, these do not have any force of law and there is no punishment for those who violate them.

The Truth in Advertising watchdog group filed a complaint with the Federal Trade Commission that Ryan's ToysReview, an earlier version of his channel, is deceptively promoting "a multitude of products to millions of preschool-aged children."[7] Truth in Advertising complains that the notices about paid content are "inadequate" being brief voiceovers or small-print disclaimers.

Although press coverage loves to make it Ryan's show, *Ryan's World*, and before that *Ryan ToysReview*, is really a product of his parents, who defend the ethics of their program. "We strictly follow all platforms' terms of service and all existing laws and regulations, including advertising disclosure requirements," said Shion Kaji, Ryan's father. "As the streaming space continues to quickly grow and evolve, we support efforts by lawmakers, industry representatives and regulators such as the FTC to continuously evaluate and update existing guidelines and lay new ground rules to protect both viewers and creators."

Toy unboxing videos are tremendously popular, making up twenty of the top one hundred channels on YouTube.[8] This, unsurprisingly, has led to criticism of kids' obsession with these videos that goes beyond just the issue of separating commercial messages from the entertainment or informative part of the programming. Activist Emma Worrollo, a mother of two, argues that unboxing videos are addictive to children. "It is capturing the eyeballs of kids around the world who are drawn in by the surprise-and-reveal format," she told the BBC. "This content has no narrative, no characters and no ending, which means it is hard for a young child to switch off or engage with it in a meaningful way. The experience is hypnotic and many parents report a negative impact on behavior when young children view this type of content."[9]

Not all media scholars and critics see unboxing videos as problematic. Children's media researcher David Craig tells *Vox*, "I believe this is a larger developmental misunderstanding; your children have grown up on these social networks, they know much more than you think they do. In the minds of kids, more likely, the blurred lines are able to exist. There is little to suggest that kids are watching these videos to covet toys. They are really just socializing and playing virtually with kids online."[10] He goes on to say that the concern over unboxing videos matches the "moral panic" over video games back in the 1990s. In other words, this is yet another example of Secret 5—Nothing is new: Everything that happened in the past will happen again.

Although advertising has been a part of American media since the 1700s, the challenge today is to get consumers to pay attention to the messages that pay for so much of the media we receive. In this chapter, we look at the development of the advertising industry in the United States, the major players in the advertising process, and the influence advertising has had on contemporary culture.

Creation of the Advertising Industry

It is fair to say that without the advertising industry the media industry may not even exist—or at least it would not be nearly as profitable as it is. Advertising is an almost inescapable element of the media. The American Marketing Association defines **advertising** as "any paid form of nonpersonal communication about an organization, product, service, or idea by an identified sponsor."[11] Advertisements are the commercial messages that pay for an article about cardiovascular health in *Prevention*, an editorial about foreign policy in the *New York Times*, and the block of *Rolling Stones* hits on the local classic rock radio station.

Advertising makes possible the vast array of inexpensive media available worldwide. But there is more to advertising than just cheap media. Advertising drives the size and diversity of the world's economy by telling consumers the multimedia functions they can perform by using a new computer, the image they will project by wearing a brand of clothing or driving a particular car, or the eating pleasure and health benefits they will experience by sampling a new variety of breakfast cereal. Advertising has been a key element of the American economy and culture of consumption and acquisition for more than one hundred years and has existed since before the United States was a nation. With the pervasiveness and importance of advertising in our society, we see once again Secret 1—The media are essential components of our lives.

The earliest American advertising was published in newspapers and was targeted at a narrow, elite audience, just as the papers themselves were. Advertising was not a major source of income for the early papers, but it was still important. The *Boston News-Letter*, one of the first successful colonial newspapers, solicited advertising as early as 1704. Most ads were simple announcements of what a merchant or shop had for sale. There was little point in promoting products because most manufacturers produced similar goods. Consumers judged the quality of the goods they bought by inspecting them and considering the reputation of the individual merchant. There were no brand names.[12]

Major societal changes had to occur before advertising could become a significant social force. The most important of these changes was the Industrial Revolution. The 1800s were a period of rapid **industrialization**, in which work done by hand using muscle or water power in small shops was replaced by mass production of goods in large factories that used steam power or, later, electricity. Industrialization brought about the mass production of low-cost, standardized products that had never been available before. Due to advances in transportation, these goods could be manufactured in a single location and then distributed over a wide area. Personal conversations between shop owners and their customers began to be replaced by sales messages placed in newspapers and magazines or posted on signs. Standardized goods were sold using standardized messages—advertisements. The mass production of consumer goods was developing along with the mass production of messages promoting those goods. Advertising grew explosively during this period as the responsibility for transmitting marketing information passed into the hands of the media.[13]

Along with industrialization, the nineteenth century was characterized by **modernization**, the social process by which people go from being born with an identity and a role in life to being able to decide who they want to be, where they want to live, what they want to do, and how they want to present themselves to the world.

As more products became widely available, thanks to industrialization, advertising was used to promote the products and what they stood for. People could now adopt a certain style and purchase the items necessary to portray that style to others—the clothes they wore, the food they served, the soap they washed with, and so forth. Each of these goods was associated with an image that was supposed to rub off on its user. How did people learn about these meanings? Through the advertising that gave meaning to the products.[14]

Media historian Michael Schudson has written that in modern societies people believe they can satisfy their social needs by buying and using mass-produced goods.[15] The late 1800s brought department stores that received new merchandise frequently and then sold it quickly, in contrast to the older dry-goods and clothing stores, which might receive new goods twice a year. As people moved into new urban centers in search of jobs in the factories, their old family identities had little meaning. This allowed them to create a new identity for themselves through the products they chose. For example, in the 1920s, people started to buy more ready-made clothes rather than sewing clothes for themselves. This ready-made clothing, which they learned about through advertisements, allowed them to be fashionable and "modern" and to "put on" the identity that went with the clothes.

The Growth of Brand Names

With the growth of industry allowing more production and the construction of transcontinental railroads and steamships making possible better distribution, increasingly prepackaged consumer goods came on the market, ready to be promoted through advertising. Among the first were patent medicines—manufactured remedies that often consisted primarily of alcohol and laudanum (opium). Instead of being shipped to stores in large containers and bottled at

Library of Congress

▲ Manufacturers of patent medicines promising cures for almost anything—internal ailments, weight gain or weight loss, debility, the common cold—were among the biggest of the early national advertisers.

the point of sale, these products arrived bottled and ready to be sold to the consumer. These were the first products of the **economy of abundance**, in which there are as many or more goods available as there are people who want to buy them.[16]

Brand-name goods became popular at the end of the nineteenth century. A **brand name** is a word or phrase attached to prepackaged consumer goods so that they can be better promoted to the public through advertising. In a highly mobile society, these standardized, branded products became a source of stability for consumers. The idea of stability coming from a brand-name product has persisted into the twenty-first century. For example, wherever they are, weary travelers are likely to stop for a meal at a familiar and comfortable landmark, such as a Starbucks or KFC.[17]

The development of brand-name goods was a driving force behind the growth of advertising. Brands were necessary to distinguish the new mass-produced products from one another. The names made it possible for people to ask for goods produced by a specific manufacturer, and advertising let people know what these brands were and what they stood for.

Quaker Oats, which was among the first prepackaged cereals, was typical of early brand-name products. It was sold in a multicolored box illustrated with the trademarked "man in Quaker garb." The cereal was a product of consistently high quality that was manufactured in Cedar Rapids, Iowa, and distributed to the entire country. Wherever you purchased the product, it would be the same. Quaker Oats promoted its trademark everywhere, including "on billboards, streetcars, newspapers, calendars, magazines, blotters, cookbooks, Sunday church bulletins, metal signs on rural fences, company-sponsored cooking schools, free samples given away house-to-house, booths at county fairs and expositions."[18]

Thomas J. Barratt developed the first branded soap. "Any fool can make soap," he commented. "It takes a clever man to sell it."[19] Barratt created the Pears' Soap brand and promoted it with outdoor and newsprint ads asking, "Have you had your Pears' today?" Other versions included "How do you spell soap? Why, P-E-A-R-S', of course," and "GOOD MORNING! Have you used Pears' Soap?" Pears' became one of the most talked-about brands of its era and was even mentioned by prominent writers, such as Mark Twain. The Pears' Soap catchphrases were the "I'm lovin' it," "Keeps on going and going," or "Just do it" of their day.

Advertising-Supported Media

The growth of products that needed advertising to succeed brought about a similar growth in advertising-supported media. Beginning in the 1830s, newspapers became much easier and cheaper to produce due to the availability of inexpensive wood-pulp paper and the steam-powered rotary press. The new penny papers (see Chapter 5) were sold to large numbers of people. These large audiences appealed to advertisers, so newspapers moved from subscription revenue to advertising revenue as their primary form of support. The change was dramatic. Instead of merely tolerating advertising, newspapers began to encourage it and even created special advertising sections to seek it out.

Magazines also started out with an uneasy relationship with advertising. In the 1800s, publications such as *Harper's* ran only limited advertising in an attempt to preserve their elite image. Another reason early magazines carried little advertising was that their circulation was national, whereas most advertising was done in local publications. Because there were few national brands at the time, few companies wanted or needed to reach a national audience.

Once manufacturers needed to reach the magazines' national audiences, the economics of magazine publishing changed. No longer were publishers selling magazines to subscribers;

Library of Congress

▲ Pears' Soap was one of the earliest national brands. Pears' ads encouraged consumers to ask not for soap, but for Pears'.

instead, they were selling subscribers to advertisers. The *Ladies' Home Journal*, which was published from 1887 to 2014, was designed specifically as a medium for consumer advertising.[20] Publisher Cyrus H. K. Curtis put it this way in a speech to advertisers:

> Do you know why we publish the *Ladies' Home Journal*? The editor thinks it is for the benefit of American women. That is an illusion, but a very proper one for him to have. But I will tell you; the real reason, the publisher's reason, is to give you people who manufacture things that American women want and buy a chance to tell them about your products.[21]

Curtis also used advertising to promote his magazine and build its circulation. When *Ladies' Home Journal* closed in 2014, it was not for lack of circulation—it still had more than three million subscribers—but the fact that advertisers had lost interest in the magazine's somewhat older readership.

Although the radio industry flirted with revenue options such as taxes and profits from selling radios, it soon became clear that the only way to make enough money to pay for top-notch entertainers and make a profit was to sell advertising. William Paley founded the CBS radio network after he saw how successful radio advertising was for his family's cigar company (see Chapter 6). Paley understood that good programming could attract a large audience that advertisers would want to reach. Sponsors frequently bought not just advertising time, but the entire program. This gave rise to shows such as the *Maxwell House Coffee Time*, the *Lucky Strike Dance Orchestra*, and the *General Motors Family Party*.

There was never any debate about whether television would be driven by advertising. Television grew quickly in the 1950s, and advertisers recognized its potential as a powerful tool for reaching all Americans. By 1960, 90 percent of all homes had television sets.[22] As with the rest of the media, television's "product" is the audience watching its programs. Thus, the primary purpose of the Super Bowl, from television's point of view, is not to choose a professional football champion but rather to deliver 45 percent of the American audience to advertisers for one evening each year. Robert Niles, a network marketing executive, echoed Curtis's promise to deliver an audience to American manufacturers almost a century earlier when he stated, "We're in the business of selling audiences to advertisers. [The sponsors] come to us asking for women 18 to 49 and adults 25 to 54 and we try to deliver."[23]

The Ladies Home Journal/Kellogg's Rice Krispies

▲ The food industry found an ideal medium for getting its message across in magazines like *Ladies' Home Journal*. The rapid expansion of Kellogg's in the early twentieth century was, in large part, due to mass advertisements like the one above.

Consumer Advertising. **Local advertising** attempts to induce people to go to a local store or business to buy a product or service, whether it be a new Toyota truck, a gallon of milk, or a travel agent's services. These ads announce the product or service and its price and tell consumers where they can buy it. The local ad is also looking for immediate, direct action. Thus, a **direct-action message** is designed to get consumers to purchase a product or engage in a behavior. For example, "Hurry down, these prices won't last, buy today!"

National advertising is designed to build demand for a nationally available product or service, but it does not send consumers out to a particular store to buy a can of Pepsi, a DVD, or a bag of cat food. National advertising assumes that the consumer knows where to buy the product or service or can be told in a local ad where and how to do so. The national advertiser is also more patient and can wait for consumers to take action. Thus, an **indirect-action message** is designed to build the image of and demand for a product. Perhaps a consumer won't buy a new washing machine this week, but he will eventually, and that's when he should buy a Maytag.

Advocacy ads are intended to promote a particular point of view rather than a product. In 2014, for example, food and biotechnology companies spent more than $25 million on ads in successful efforts to defeat state laws in Colorado and Oregon that would require the labeling of food containing genetically modified organisms (GMOs).[24] U.S. unions and businesses have fought foreign competition with advocacy ads. Companies express their concerns directly to the public through advocacy ads, bypassing traditional news channels. Such advertising has a long history in the United States, dating back to 1908, when AT&T ran a campaign arguing that it was natural that the phone company should be a monopoly.

Some of the most iconic advertising in the United States comes not from business, but from long series of **public service ads** created by the Advertising Council. The Ad Council got its start as the War Advertising Council back in 1942 with such memorable messages as the Rosie the Riveter "We Can Do It" campaign, which was designed to promote women working in factories producing goods for the war effort. The best-known creation of the Ad Council is likely Smokey Bear, who has stayed on message for more than sixty-five years, telling members of the public that only they can prevent forest fires. He is the second-most-recognized image in the United States, falling just behind Santa Claus. What is more, generations of children have taken great joy in delivering his basic message of fire prevention to their parents and other adults. Other prominent Ad Council campaigns include the 1971 "Crying Indian" antipollution campaign, a 2011 campaign encouraging fathers to "Take time to be a dad today," and McGruff the Crime Dog taking "a bite out of crime."[25]

The editorial and opinion pages of the prestigious national newspapers are popular spots for placing advocacy ads. This is partly due to the credibility associated with appearing on those pages and partly because it's a good place to reach the target audience of influential decision makers. These ads might, for example, support or oppose a piece of legislation. Sometimes the target of an advocacy ad in the *Washington Post* might be senators or representatives who are being reminded of the support they have received in the past from a given company or industry.[26]

In trade advertising, **business-to-business (trade) ads** promote products directly to other businesses rather than to the consumer market. Business-to-business advertising is a critical part of the advertising industry. Consider the fact that General Electric earns 80 percent of its revenue from nonconsumer business.[27] Business customers can be reached through trade magazines, such as *Electronic Engineering Times*; business-oriented cable news channels, such as CNBC; or local weekly business newspapers.

The Advertising Business

Advertising is a multifaceted business that involves four major groups. First, there is the client, the person or company that has a product or an idea to promote. Then, there is the advertising agency or department that researches

▲ A public service ad shares information about the Zika virus at a Florida town hall.

the market, creates the advertising, and places it in the media. Next, there is the medium, be it television, the internet, a newspaper, a magazine, or some other medium, that carries the advertisement. Finally, there's the audience, the people who see or hear the advertisement, whom the client hopes to influence.[28]

For a product to be successful in the marketplace, all four of these groups must work together successfully. There must be a good product backed by advertisements that have a strong sales message delivered through well-chosen media to an appropriate audience. If any part of this process is flawed or seriously miscalculated, the product is likely to fail.

The Client

The first component of advertising is the client, the company with something to sell. The client may want to increase awareness of a new product, encourage people to use an existing product more often, build a positive image of a product, convince users of competitors' products to switch brands, promote a benefit of a product, or demonstrate some new use for a product. The 3M Company increased sales of its Scotch brand cellophane tape by suggesting other uses for the product beyond repairing torn paper. Arm & Hammer baking soda's original purpose was to make cakes rise, but the company also increased sales by promoting the product as a cleaner and deodorizer. One of Arm & Hammer's best ads tells consumers to buy a box of baking soda and pour it down the drain to clean and deodorize the sink. The company was suggesting that people buy its product to throw it away! Arm & Hammer's research showed that people used baking soda to freshen laundry and to brush their teeth, so the company introduced detergent and toothpaste enhanced with baking soda.[29] Begun in 1993 on behalf of the California Milk Processor Board, the "Got Milk?" advertising campaign succeeded at boosting milk sales and has become one of America's longest-running and most celebrated ad series. The "Got Milk" ads ran both in California and nationally until 2014, when the national milk promotion board decided to focus on milk's protein content in its advertising. But the campaign does still live on in California more than twenty years after it started.[30]

For details on America's top advertisers, look at Table 12.1.

For a product to be successful, it needs more than a good advertising campaign. It also needs to be a good product at the right price and must be available for consumers to buy. When Sony launched its PlayStation 2 video game system, it did relatively little initial advertising and held off releasing popular games because it could not manufacture enough of the consoles to satisfy public demand. Customers were ready and willing to buy, but the product simply was not available.[31] Once there was enough of the product, Sony started advertising.

No amount of advertising can save a product that the public just doesn't want to buy, as Coca-Cola discovered when it launched New Coke more than thirty years ago in 1985. Coca-Cola spent $4 million on research that seemed to indicate that consumers would like the new formula better than the original recipe. But consumers reacted to the change with anger and frustration, and Coca-Cola eventually had to bring back the old drink under the name Coca-Cola Classic.[32] The research may have shown what people liked best in blind taste tests, but the company missed a couple of key points. For example, consumers did like the sweeter formula of New Coke, but only in small samples. When they drank an entire serving of Coke, their feelings for and against the new formula were much stronger.

▼ TABLE 12.1

Top Ten Advertised Brands in United States

Rank	Brand, Marketer	2017 U.S. Spending (in millions)
1	Geico Berkshire Hathaway	$1,400
2	Verizon Verizon Communications	$943
3	Ford Ford Motor Co.	$894
4	Chevrolet General Motors Co.	$817
5	T-Mobile Deutsche Telekom	$777
6	Apple Apple	$713
7	Samsung Samsung Electronics	$699
8	McDonald's McDonald's Corp.	$687
9	AT&T AT&T	$632
10	Progressive Progressive Corp.	$622

Source: Data from "Marketing Fact Pack 2019," *Ad Age*, http://adage.com/d/resources/resources/whitepaper/marketing-fact-pack-2019.

The research didn't take into account how people felt about the product, what meaning they assigned to it, and the fond memories they associated with it.[33] What the research missed was "the abiding emotional attachment" Coke drinkers had for the product in its familiar form.[34] As one Coke executive put it, "We did not know what we were selling. We are not selling a soft drink. We are selling a little tiny piece of people's lives."[35]

The Agency

The advertising profession originated in the 1840s when agents started selling ad space to clients in the new advertising-supported newspapers. At first, the advertising agents worked directly for the newspapers, but before long, they became more like brokers dealing in advertising space for multiple publications. George Rowell, the leading advertising agent of the 1860s and 1870s, was the first agent to buy large amounts of newspaper advertising space wholesale and sell it to his customers as they needed it. Rowell was also the first to publish a directory of newspaper circulation numbers, thus providing clients with an independent source of this vital information. Before Rowell's innovation, newspapers could, and did, lie about the size of their circulation.

The early agents earned a 15 percent commission on the space they sold for the newspapers. This is why advertising agencies were traditionally paid by commission on the media space and time they sold; initially, that was all they were selling.[36]

Before long, advertising agents moved beyond just selling space in the media. Their clients wanted help developing the ads for the space they were purchasing. In 1868, twenty-one-year-old Francis W. Ayer opened N. W. Ayer and Son (giving his father a 50 percent share in the company and the lead name), one of the first agencies to write copy, put together the artwork for an ad, and plan campaigns. The agency recognized that providing the associated services that would make advertising easier for clients would help the agency sell more space for the media.

Gradually, ad agencies came to represent their clients rather than the media in which they sold advertising space. This shift resulted from the **open contract**, which enabled the agency to provide advertising space in any publication (and eventually on broadcast outlets as well) rather than only a few. The agent was now handling the advertising services for the client, not selling space for the media.[37]

In the 1920s and 1930s, advertisers increasingly recognized that there were different market segments and that ads should be tailored to those segments. Agencies also realized that they needed to use a different mix of media for each of their target audiences. Eventually, they began offering clients three major services: research, creative activity, and media planning.

Agencies typically use research throughout the entire advertising campaign. The initial research activity is aimed at identifying the characteristics of the target audience and what those people are looking for in a product. Ads are then tested to see how well members of the target audience respond to them. After the campaign, the agency will evaluate its success. How many people remembered seeing the ad? How many people clipped the coupon or called the phone number? How much did sales go up or down?

The process starts with objectives. What does the client want to accomplish with the ads? These objectives could be increasing sales, increasing awareness, or getting people to clip a coupon or make a phone call. The agency may also study characteristics of the product's target audience, a process that is discussed later in the chapter.

Finally, the agency may test the ads itself, either as a pretest before the ads are run or as a recall test after the campaign. One problem advertising researchers face is that the people they want to reach may be unwilling to participate in the research. And the people who are willing to participate may be trying to give the agency the answers they are looking for. Although advertising research continues to be a powerful tool for reducing uncertainty, it is still a difficult process at best.[38]

There is more to marketing a product than advertising, but advertising is the most visible aspect of marketing, and it has to provide what legendary advertising executive David Ogilvy called **the big idea**—an advertising concept that will grab people's attention, make them take notice, make them remember, and, most important, make them take action. Leo Burnett, founder of one of the nation's biggest agencies, agrees with Ogilvy:

> The word "idea" is loosely used in our business to cover anything from a headline to a TV technique. [But] I feel that a real idea has a power of its own and a life of its own. It goes beyond ads and campaigns. Properly employed, it is often the secret of capturing the imagination of great masses of people and winning "the battle for the uncommitted mind," which is what our business really is about.[39]

In advertising, a tension often exists between creativity and salesmanship. An ad may do a great job of grabbing people's attention and generating talk, but if the ad doesn't have a solid sales message, consumers will not remember the product or give serious thought to buying it. Several ads have done a great job of grabbing the public's attention. But have they done a good job of promoting the product? Have they built the value of the brand?

Consider Anheuser-Busch back in 2009. Its brand Bud Light (the most popular beer in the United States) was launching its Bud Light Lime beer in cans. (Previously it had only been available in bottles.) Anheuser-Busch promoted the launch with an online ad that had people talking about "getting it in the can"—as in a suburban housewife confessing, "I never thought I'd enjoy getting it in the can as much as I do." The crude sex joke attracted a lot of talk and attention from the advertising press. But it's not clear what the message did to promote the brand or increase sales.[40]

Adman Hank Seiden puts it this way: "All good advertising consists of both idea and execution. All bad advertising consists of just execution."[41] Ogilvy believed that all advertising should be created to sell a product or promote a message. It does not exist to be innovative, exciting, creative, or entertaining. Good ads may be all of those things, but the central principle is that they must achieve the client's goals:

> A good advertisement is one which sells the product without drawing attention to itself. It should rivet the reader's attention on the product. Instead of saying, "What a clever advertisement," the reader says, "I never knew that before. I must try this product."[42]

For products that are similar, the **brand image** attached to them is often critical. This image gives a brand and the associated product a personality or identity and helps it stand out from the pack. Ogilvy once headed a campaign to give Hathaway shirts a personality when the company's competitor, Arrow, was spending almost a hundred times more on advertising than Hathaway, a smaller company, could. Ogilvy's solution was to buy a black eye patch in a drugstore for $1.50. A model wearing the eye patch was shown conducting an orchestra, driving a tractor, and sailing a boat. This simple bit of brand identity boosted Hathaway out of 116 years of obscurity and turned it into a leading brand.

Ogilvy argues that at the heart of all advertising is an appeal based on facts that are of interest to consumers. As he wrote in the early 1960s, "The consumer isn't a moron. . . . You insult her intelligence if you assume that a mere slogan and a few vapid adjectives will persuade her to buy anything. She wants all the information you can give her."[43]

For print ads, the most important element is the headline, because five times as many people read the headline as read the rest of the copy. This means that 80 percent of the ad's effectiveness comes from the headline. The headline must tell readers whom the ad is for, what the product is, what the product does for the consumer, and why he or she should buy it. That is a lot of responsibility for eight to fifteen words. Ogilvy says that the most powerful headline words are *free* and *new*. Other words favored by Ogilvy are *how to, suddenly, now, announcing, introducing, it's here, just arrived, important development, improvement, amazing, sensational, remarkable, revolutionary, startling, miracle, magic, offer, quick, easy, wanted, challenge, advice to, the truth about, compare, bargain, hurry,* [and] *last chance.*[44]

Although these phrases are overused, they do work. Look at what Ogilvy considered to be the greatest headline he ever wrote: "At Sixty Miles an Hour the Loudest Noise in the New Rolls-Royce Comes from the Electric Clock." It uses the word *new*, it contains a fact that also sells a benefit, and it is true.

Media planning involves figuring out which media to use, buying the media at the best rates, and then evaluating how effective the purchase was. It is the least glamorous part of the advertising business, but it is central to a successful campaign. No matter how brilliant the idea or how beautiful the execution, if the ad does not reach the target audience, it can't accomplish anything. Typically, advertisers try to pick a mix of media that will deliver the highest percentage of the target audience at the lowest cost per thousand views, or **CPM**. (M is the Roman numeral for one thousand.) Selecting the right media involves identifying the audience for the ad and knowing which media these consumers use.[45]

Advertising agencies have grown immensely since their modest start selling newspaper advertising space. According to *Ad Age*'s 2018 advertising agency report, the nine-hundred-plus agencies studied had their income grow in 2016 by 4.4 percent from the previous year to reach a total of $46.8 billion. (That figure included advertising, media, digital marketing services, health care communication, and public relations.) Work for digital media now dominates the business, accounting for 46.6 percent of all U.S. advertising agency revenue in 2016. Keep in mind that this is just the portion of the income that goes to the agency. This figure does not include the amount that goes to pay the media for advertising time and space. According to *Ad Age*'s 2018 annual report, advertisers were on track to spend $204 billion on advertising in the United States using media for which the size of the audience is measured. (This does not include, for example, direct-mail advertising.) Of that, television accounted for the largest share ($78.9 billion), followed by online ($31.9 billion), magazines with $18.8 billion, newspapers with $12.2 billion, radio with $7.9 billion, and outdoor and cinema with $5.6 billion.[46]

Several major trends have emerged in the agency business since the 1980s. One trend is toward the purchase of independent agencies and small groups of agencies by larger holding companies. The biggest of these are WPP, Omnicom Group, Publicis Groupe, and Interpublic Group of Companies.[47] A second trend is a shift toward greater specialization of agency functions. One agency may do research and creative work, whereas another agency (known as a media buyer) develops the media plan and buys the time and space. Because of this specialization, agencies are moving from the commission structure to charging fees for their services. After all, if an agency is just doing creative work, it cannot charge a commission on media space that it isn't buying.[48]

The Media

The third group in the advertising business is made up of the media that carry advertisements. These include newspapers, magazines, radio, television, outdoor sites such as billboards and public buses, and digital. Advertisers pay these outlets (buy space) to run their ads in their publications.

The two media that do not receive large amounts of advertising revenue are movies and books, although movies are increasingly using paid product placements and theaters run advertisements before showing movies. Postal regulations pose a barrier to advertising in books because materials containing advertising cannot be shipped using the post office's inexpensive book rate. But advertising scholar James Twitchell suggests that as delivery options expand through companies such as FedEx and UPS, advertising in books may become commonplace, especially in expensive academic books.[49]

This textbook does not yet contain advertisements in its pages, but you probably found a few advertising pieces for credit cards or magazine subscriptions in the bag the bookstore clerk gave you. In Table 12.2, you can see the relative importance of different media to the top two hundred leading national advertisers in the United States.

Print Advertising. Newspapers were the original advertising medium, but they have been suffering major declines in advertising revenue. Between 2007 and 2015, ad revenue declined by more than 61 percent. Some of this was due to the recent recession, but advertising analyst Ken Doctor says that much of it is coming from newspapers failing to make the digital transformation: "Despite uneven digital ad results reported by newspaper and magazine companies, it's not that the money isn't there—they just haven't transitioned their businesses enough to compete for it."[50] According to the Pew Research Center's "State of the News Media 2015" report, newspapers' digital advertising has been growing, but not enough to compensate for the drop in print advertising.[51]

Nevertheless, newspapers remain an advertising medium, carrying most of the local advertising and a significant amount of national advertising. They allow advertisers to present detailed information (such as grocery prices) that would be confusing on radio or television, and they give audience members plenty of time to interpret the information. Newspaper ads make it easy to include coupons, web addresses, and 800 numbers that readers can clip and save. They also allow advertisers to target not only specific cities, but also specific areas of the city (this is known as **zoned coverage**). Cities typically have only one or two newspapers, so advertisers can cover the entire market with a single purchase. Finally, newspapers allow advertisers to buy space at the last minute.[52]

Magazines are still an excellent medium for reaching a specific niche audience. Before the 1950s, general-interest magazines were the best way to reach a mass, national audience. Since the 1960s, however, that role has fallen to television. The response of magazines has been to seek ever narrower audiences—there are magazines for motorcyclists, computer users, young women, retired people, knitters, and video game players. Whatever audience an advertiser wants to reach, it is likely to find a magazine to help it do so. For business advertisers, magazines may be the only alternative to direct mail for reaching their target audiences. Magazines offer higher print quality than newspapers do but have a much longer lead time, so magazine advertising requires careful planning. The advertising market for magazines has been changing during the past decade. While the number of ad pages sold has been falling, the revenue from digital sources, such as websites and mobile apps, has been growing.[53]

Outdoor ads or "out of home advertising" catch people in a captive environment—such as being in a car surrounded by slow-moving traffic on the way to work—but they are limited to short, simple messages. The biggest change to have happened to outdoor advertising is the advent of the digital billboard. Essentially giant video screens, digital billboards display a static image that stays up for six to eight seconds before shifting to a new image. Digital billboards can include changing information, such as time or temperature, or even the day's television schedule for a local station.[54] In major cities, there are transit signs—posters on bus stop shelters, on subway platforms, and on the buses and in the subway cars themselves. Ads have also been placed in the bottom of golf holes so that you see them when you pick up your ball. Overall, $5.6 billion

▼ TABLE 12.2

Ad Spending Totals for All Advertisers in Measured Media

Measured Media	2017 Spending (in billions)
Television	$74.4
Digital (search, display, mobile web)	$28.3
Magazines	$16.6
Newspapers	$11.8
Radio	$7.6
Outdoor and cinema	$5.6

Source: "Marketing Fact Pack 2019," *Ad Age*, http://adage.com/d/resources/system/files/resource/Neustar%20Marketing%20Fact%20Pack%202019.pdf.

mauritius images GmbH / Alamy Stock Photo

▲ Advertising in printed form requires careful selection of both words and images that will go into newspapers, magazines, and "out-of-home" ads such as billboards or transit signs.

The entire cityscape of New York has become sponsored, product-placed, and wrapped in logos.

was spent on outdoor advertising in 2016.[55] Overall, billboards dominate outdoor advertising, accounting for 65 percent of the spending, with transit signs making up 18.1 percent, street furniture 5.5 percent, and place-based outdoor advertising 11.4 percent.[56] New York City's Times Square is one of the most valuable places in the United States for outdoor advertisements because of the large number of people who pass through it each day, its frequent coverage on television, and the nearly constant presence of tourists who are photographing the area.[57]

TV and Radio Advertising. Radio has enabled advertisers to broadcast their message repeatedly and to target a narrow audience for decades. Advertisers can choose stations with programming aimed at teens, women ages twenty-five to fifty-four, young adult males, Spanish speakers, or almost any other demographic group. Like outdoor advertising, radio ads can be highly effective in big cities where advertisers can reach a captive audience in their cars during the morning and afternoon commutes, which are known as **drive time**. Radio also offers a short lead time and relatively low costs.

Television is still a popular medium in this country. Although the most popular television shows remain an appealing place to advertise to a general, national audience, the remote control, the mute button, and the proliferation of cable channels have made it difficult to get viewers to pay attention to commercials. The audience for broadcast television has been declining, but the Big Four networks (see Chapter 8) can still reach a mass audience quickly and effectively. Television offers sound, motion, and visuals. A drawback, however, is that many of the best advertising time slots on the networks, such as those during the Super Bowl, are sold nearly a year in advance. There is also the problem of viewers channel surfing during commercial breaks or skipping commercials using the fast-forward button on their DVRs.

The new television environment allows targeted advertising, such as ads aimed at the youth market on MTV or The CW, the Hispanic market on Univision, or the African American market on BET. For local television advertising, there are independent stations along with the network affiliates. In many communities, local advertisers can buy time on a range of cable stations with local commercial breaks as well. The biggest problem facing television advertisers is that of clutter, which is discussed later in this chapter.

Digital advertising has been the fastest-growing segment of the advertising market, increasing by double-digit percentages for several years. During the recession in 2009, online advertising saw its first decline since the dot-com bubble burst in 2002 and sent numerous web properties into bankruptcy.[58] But since then, online advertising has resumed its rapid growth. A study by *eMarketer* found that in 2013 American consumers spent more time with digital media than with television for the first time. More recent data estimate that Americans spend an average of four hours and eleven minutes a day with television, but that they spend five hours and forty-five minutes with all digital media combined. *eMarketer* defines digital media as all online, mobile, and streaming services.[59]

The growth of use of digital media comes heavily from the growth of mobile devices. Time spent with digital media (which includes desktop/laptop computers, nonvoice mobile and other connected devices) was expected to be five hours and fifty-three minutes in 2017, and of that time, three hours and seventeen minutes came from nonvoice use of mobile phones (i.e., not talking on them).[60] (So we see once again Secret 6—Online media are mobile media.)

Digital advertising has the advantage of being able to closely target consumers. As an example, when your author visits websites that contain advertising, ads for motorcycle accessories often appear because the cookies in his browser history tell the ad server that he is interested in motorcycles. And we all expect that kind of behavior with online ads. But sometimes, as marketing professional David Berkowitz points out, that level of knowledge about us seems a little creepy. Berkowitz asks you to suppose you are searching for a camera using the web browser on your smartphone. You bring up an ad from Target for a camera you're interested in. The ad can tell that you already have the Target shopping app on your phone, so it automatically sends you the appropriate page on the app to view the camera you are searching for. The question then becomes: Are you creeped out by the fact that an ad on a web page knows what apps you have installed on your phone? Or do you like the fact that the ad is smart enough to redirect you to an app you already have on your phone?[61] (For more on digital advertising, look ahead to the section of the chapter on long-tail advertising.)

The Audience

As we talked about in the opening vignette of this chapter, the audience is made up of the people advertisers want to reach with their messages. The audience is also the central "product" that media sell to advertisers. In yet another example of **targeting**, advertisers try to make a particular product appeal to a narrowly defined group. Ads for Starburst candies, for example, target the teen and preteen audiences, whereas ads for Godiva chocolates target upscale adult women. The people appearing in an ad are chosen carefully to make members of the target audience say, "This is a product made for someone like me."

As with other types of media, such as radio and television, audience members for advertising are often defined by the "graphics": demographics, geographics, and psychographics. As you may recall from Chapter 2, demographics are the measurable characteristics of the audience, such as age, income, sex, and marital status, whereas geographics involve measurements of where people live. Psychographics combine demographics with measurements of psychological characteristics, such as attitudes, opinions, and interests.[62]

In advertising, it is not enough to know the demographics of the client's target audience (age, income, sex, etc.). Advertisers also want to know what the target audience dreams about, aspires to, and feels. These are the topics covered by psychographic research.

The term *psychographics* was first used in the 1960s to refer to a measure of consumer psychology. Depending on the project, researchers may look at a person's lifestyle, relationship to the product, and personality traits.[63]

Emanuel Demby, one of the first users of the term, defines psychographics as psychological, sociological, and anthropological data that are used to segment a market into relevant groupings. The way the income variable is conceived is more sophisticated than just grouping markets by income levels. Demby argues that it is just as important to know whether someone's income is increasing, decreasing, or remaining stable as it is to know the person's actual income. Why? Because how things are going in people's lives will say something about how they see themselves. If advertisers understand how members of the target audience see themselves, they can craft ads that will more readily appeal to the target.[64]

The best-known psychographic segmentation is VALS™, developed by SRI International and currently owned and operated by Strategic Business Insights. VALS classifies people into one of eight consumer groups according to their primary motivation and level of resources. Resources are the tangible and intangible things that people draw on to express themselves as a consumer, such as: their education, finances, level of curiosity, and self-confidence, among other factors. Primary motivation is the person's approach to life. Ideals-motivated consumers ("Thinkers" and "Believers") are guided by knowledge and principles; achievement-motivated consumers ("Achievers" and "Strivers") look for products that will demonstrate their status and success to others; and self-expression-motivated consumers ("Experiencers" and "Makers") seek action and independence.

▲ Following the Super Bowl success of PuppyMonkeyBaby, Mountain Dew Kickstart released another bizarre ad with a slew of dancing animals, including a mosquito, a frog, and a twerking cat.

At the top of the VALS framework are Innovators, described as being "successful, sophisticated, take-charge people with high self-esteem." These are people who have established careers and value the image of a product as "an expression of their taste, independence, and personality." At the bottom of the VALS framework are the survivors, who have few resources and believe "the world is changing too quickly." VALS describes them as cautious consumers with little to spend but with high brand loyalty.[65]

How might a company use psychographics and these personality types to target its advertising? As an example, a Minnesota medical center used VALS to identify and understand consumers who were interested in and able to afford cosmetic surgery. The resulting ad campaign targeted to these individuals was purportedly so successful that the clinic was fully booked.

To see targeting in action, we can look at some real-world examples. The first example discusses the targeting of a product (Mountain Dew); the second, a particular audience (gays and lesbians); and the third, some instances of targeting failures.

Some products are easier to sell than others; for example, advertising soft drinks can be a particular challenge because all the drinks are basically the same thing—sweetened carbonated water and a small amount of flavoring—with just a few variations, such as regular or diet, caffeinated or caffeine free. Since the products are so similar, the key to promoting the brand is selling not just a drink but an entire attitude and approach to life, thus making the product appeal to a particular audience. Television scholar Joshua Meyrowitz describes the basic message of a diet soda commercial as "Drink this and you'll be beautiful and have beautiful friends to play volleyball with on the beach."[66]

Mountain Dew has existed as a product since the 1940s and has always projected a rebellious and irreverent image, according to Scott Moffitt, who was director of marketing:

> We have a great unity of message and purpose that has been consistent over time about what we are and what we aren't. The brand is all about exhilaration and energy, and you see that in all that we do, from advertising and community to grassroots programs and our sports-minded focus. We have a very crystal clear, vivid positioning.[67]

In keeping with its young, energetic image, Mountain Dew sponsors events such as ESPN's X Games because they project the same image the soft drink does. It also goes after heavy consumers who drink three or more cans of Mountain Dew a day.

Mountain Dew now holds a coveted spot among the top four or five soft drinks, behind Coke, Pepsi, and Diet Coke, but it started out as a bar mix consisting of lemon-lime juice, orange juice, low carbonation, and caffeine. It cultivated a hillbilly image and logo and was billed as "zero-proof hillbilly moonshine." In the 1960s, Pepsi bought the brand and started giving it more of a hip image. Following a period of confused advertising images in the 1980s, Mountain Dew came into its own in 1992. Bill Bruce, who was the creative director on the Mountain Dew account, describes Mountain Dew's coming-of-age process:

> Seattle grunge music was happening at the time. Extreme sports were happening. So there was this subculture that we wanted to tap into. The idea was to show the most extreme things. We created these four characters, the Dew Dudes, who represented what was happening at the time musically and culturally.[68]

This approach was first used with Diet Mountain Dew, but given its success, it eventually became the central theme of the entire campaign.

The ongoing challenge to Mountain Dew as it grows in popularity is to maintain its edginess and youth appeal so that it can maintain both its sales and its image. Most recently, Mountain Dew has been trying to engage young urban consumers. (In marketing speak, urban marketing means reaching out to African American and Latino consumers.) The company's goal is to go beyond the rural markets where Mountain Dew has been enormously successful into the cities where it has traditionally sold less well. Mountain Dew is doing this by featuring hip-hop performers Lil Wayne; Tyler, The Creator; and Rick Ross. (It should be noted that some of the ads to come out of this campaign have backfired for the soft drink maker by offending virtually everyone with racist and misogynistic story lines.[69])

One audience that advertisers are increasingly targeting is the gay and lesbian market. Gays are desirable as a market to advertisers because they are perceived to be relatively upscale and highly educated.[70] "Because they primarily don't have children and there is one income for each person in the household, you are talking about a population with large sums of disposable income that non-gay families with children wouldn't have," says Rick Dean of the research firm Overlooked Opinions.[71]

As early as 1994, vodka producer Absolut was among the first major companies to place ads in gay publications, including *Out* and the *Advocate*.[72] In addition to advertising in gay publications, companies are using same-sex couples in ads. Some advertisers have gone further, experimenting with gay-specific ads. Hyatt Hotels and Resorts has targeted the gay and lesbian market since the late 1990s and has depicted same-sex couples in its messages.[73]

The Hallmark Channel sparked a small controversy in 2019 when it started running a series of ads from wedding planning company Zola that featured both heterosexual and lesbian couples kissing. The family-oriented cable channel pulled the ads with lesbian couples following complaints from the conservative activist group One Million Moms. Messages on the organization's website said, "Shame on Hallmark for airing commercials with same-sex couples," and "Such content goes against Christian and conservative values that are important to your primary audience." Hallmark's pulling of the ads prompted an immediate backlash from gay rights group GLAAD. Hallmark eventually apologized and reinstated the Zola ads. "The [Hallmark] team has been agonizing over this decision as we've seen the hurt it has unintentionally caused," said Hallmark Cards Inc. Chief Executive Mike Perry in a statement. "We are truly sorry for the hurt and disappointment this has caused."

Gay couples, along with interracial couples, have increasingly become a part of mainstream advertising and have sparked controversy from critics. In 2016, clothing chain Old Navy featured a young interracial couple and their son in a Tweet, provoking complaints from people opposed to Black and white people getting married and having children.[74] The tweet also generated support for the brand's inclusiveness. With these examples, we see once again Secret 3— Everything from the margin moves to the center.

Old Navy Official @OldNavy — Follow

Oh, happy day! Our #ThankYouEvent is finally here. Take 30% off your entire purchase: oldnvy.me/1LUMNBd

RETWEETS 7,118   LIKES 20,449

8:00 AM - 29 Apr 2016

7.1K   20K

Twitter/@OldNavy

▲ This interracial family in an Old Navy promotional tweet wouldn't seem to be controversial, but it attracted a wide range of responses from people who delighted in seeing an ad that represented people like themselves to people who claimed the ad was promoting ending the white race.

TARGET'S TARGETING

In the age of online shopping and digital information, it's easy to get paranoid about how much vendors know about us. You want to get creeped out? Start paying attention to the recommendations that Amazon makes to you based on what you've previously looked at and purchased.

But taking all your shopping to a brick-and-mortar department store won't help preserve your privacy. Exhibit number one? Target figured out that a high school girl was pregnant and started sending her direct-mail coupons for maternity products before her father knew anything was going on.[75]

How did Target know the young woman was pregnant? It seems that pregnant women have very predictable buying patterns. Sometime during the second trimester, four to six months into the pregnancy, pregnant women start buying things such as prenatal vitamins and maternity clothing. Once a woman starts buying these products, she's likely to be giving birth in three to six months.

According to Charles Duhigg, author of the book *The Power of Habit: Why We Do What We Do in Life and Business*, Target tracks every consumer who comes to its stores with a unique number tied to his or her credit or debit card. Using this number, Target knows what pattern of products every consumer buys. This information is then paired with data about the consumer that are purchased by the store, says Target statistician Andrew Pole. Before long, the store knows a lot of information about a customer, including preferred purchases, address, income, race, and even estimated earnings.[76]

So our high school student was buying the right combination of cocoa butter lotions, soaps, and mineral supplements that told Target there was an 86 percent likelihood she was pregnant. So Target started sending her coupons for the products people expecting babies are likely to buy.

When these coupons showed up in the mail, the young woman's father got upset and went to his local Target to complain to the manager. "My daughter got this in the mail!" the father told the manager. "She's still in high school, and you're sending her coupons for baby clothes and cribs? Are you trying to encourage her to get pregnant?"

The manager apologized repeatedly to the father. Then the father had an interesting discussion with his daughter. A few days later, when the manager called to apologize again, it was the father who had to apologize. His daughter was pregnant, but she hadn't told him.

Obviously, Pole's system of evaluating the young woman's purchases worked as intended. But how were he and his employer going to deal with the backlash from consumers who just figured out how much the company knew about them?

"If we send someone a catalog and say, 'Congratulations on your first child!' and they've never told us they're pregnant, that's going to make some people uncomfortable," Pole told Duhigg. This led Target to work on figuring out how to get its ads delivered to pregnant women without the women knowing they were being targeted. As Duhigg puts it, "How do you take advantage of someone's habits without letting them know you're studying their lives?"

The solution ended up being fairly simple. Target mails out coupon books to consumers based on their purchasing history all the time. Usually, those coupons don't upset people. So the secret, according to a Target executive, was to mix the pregnancy product coupons in with a collection of other innocuous coupons that hid the fact that Target knew the woman was pregnant.

"We found out that as long as a pregnant woman thinks she hasn't been spied on, she'll use the coupons," the executive said. "As long as we don't spook her, it works."

WHO is the source?

Who are Charles Duhigg and Andrew Pole, and what do they do?

WHAT are they saying?

How is Target using consumer buying habits to target them with advertising?

WHAT evidence is there?

How predictable are consumers? Does their spending indicate important life milestones? How do consumers react to businesses knowing so much about them?

WHAT do you and your friends think about this?

How do you feel about advertisers using your purchasing and online behavior to target you? Do you find that helpful or creepy? Or maybe a combination of both? Have you ever felt targeted in a way that completely missed who you are? Do you ever change your behavior so you don't get tracked and targeted by marketers?

Contemporary Culture in Advertising

Advertising is much more than a part of the marketing and media business; it is a central element of American culture. Children sing advertising jingles the way they once sang nursery rhymes. In the 1970s, the music from a Coca-Cola commercial even became a hit single, "I'd Like to Teach the World to Sing."

Critics argue that advertising places a burden on society by raising the cost of merchandise and inducing people to buy things they do not need. The American Association of Advertising Agencies has defended the ad business, claiming that there are four common misconceptions about the industry:[77]

▲ In 1962, McDonald's replaced its "Speedee" the hamburger man symbol with the Golden Arches logo, and a year later, the company sold its billionth hamburger. Years of successful advertising have made the McDonald's Golden Arches one of the most easily recognizable symbols in the world.

1. Advertising makes you buy things you do not want—The industry responds by saying that no one can make you buy things you don't want. People are free to do as they please.

2. Advertising makes things cost more—Advertisers claim that advertising builds demand for products, which can then be manufactured in larger quantities, more efficiently, and at a lower cost. (This defense ignores the idea of the prestige brand, however. Advertising does not make a bar of Clinique soap cost more to produce, but the premium image attached to the soap allows the company to charge more for it. Consumers apparently want to be able to buy better, more expensive products.)

3. Advertising helps sell bad products—The industry responds that a good ad may lead people to buy a product once, but it won't sustain demand for a product they don't like. In fact, the industry argues that good advertising for a bad product will kill the product faster than if it had not had a good campaign behind it. M. Night Shyamalan, director of the movies *The Sixth Sense* and *Signs*, says that with enough advertising studios can buy a good opening weekend for a movie, but only good word-of-mouth reports by fans will make the movie a long-term success.[78]

4. Advertising is a waste of money—The ad industry counters that advertising strengthens the economy by helping to move products through the marketplace and supporting the mass media.

When critics complain that there are too many ads on television, few would be quicker to agree than advertising agencies and their clients. They are concerned about the huge number of commercials and other messages—collectively referred to as **clutter**—that compete for consumer attention between programs.

Advertisers dislike clutter because the more ads and nonprogram messages there are on television, the less attention viewers will pay to any given message. A study conducted by the Cable Television Advertising Bureau (now the Video Advertising Bureau) found that viewers are much more likely to remember the first ad in a group (called a pod) than the fourth or fifth.[79] The clutter problem is not limited to television; each day, the average American adult is exposed to as many as 360 advertisements, of which perhaps 150 will receive at least minimal notice. (Many of the rest will be completely missed through using technology like fast-forwarding on the DVR.[80])

According to a study commissioned by advertising agencies and their clients, clutter is reaching record levels. In 2005, U.S. network television averaged about fifteen minutes of advertising and promotional clutter per hour during prime time.[81] Cable television rates were even higher, with MTV averaging sixteen minutes and thirteen seconds of clutter per hour. In 2010, cable channel Spike may have set a record for clutter with a single commercial pod running ten minutes during an episode of *Entourage*.[82]

Clutter is generally defined as anything that is not part of the program itself: ads, public service announcements, network promotions, and other gaps between programs.

Broadcast and cable networks are experimenting with cutting back on the number of commercials they carry. NBCUniversal announced in the spring of 2018 that it planned to cut the number of commercials it shows across all its networks by 20 percent in the fall of 2018. During prime-time original programming, the network planned to reduce advertising time by 10 percent for the 2018–2019 TV season. Among the changes the networks will be doing is trying to better match ads to the content of the programs to make them more relevant to their audience members. Time Warner's Turner networks and Viacom networks are planning similar changes. This means, of course, that if the networks are going to keep their revenues steady, advertisers are going to need to pay more for this smaller amount of ad time. Fox Broadcasting considered getting its commercial load down to two minutes per hour by 2020. Among the ways it might do so is by offering six-second-long commercials. According to data from television measurement firm Nielsen, in 2017 the average ad time per hour was thirteen minutes on broadcast TV and sixteen minutes on cable.[83]

Breaking through the clutter is a continuing challenge for advertisers, who have come up with a variety of solutions to the problem. Tire company Goodyear breaks through the clutter by putting its message on the Goodyear Blimp, which flies over sporting and other entertainment events that draw large audiences.[84] Drug companies fight clutter by using celebrities in their advertisements. NBA star Alonzo Mourning talked about the anemia drug Procrit, which is used to treat a kidney disorder that almost ended his career; and actress Lorraine Bracco, who played a psychiatrist on *The Sopranos*, discussed depression in ads for drugs manufactured by Pfizer Inc.[85]

Debunking Subliminal Advertising

With all the concern about advertising clutter, it is ironic that there is substantial public concern about **subliminal advertising**—messages that are allegedly embedded so deeply in an ad that they cannot be perceived consciously. The concept has been popularized by several writers, but no research has ever been done to demonstrate that advertising audiences can be influenced by messages they don't perceive consciously.

Although there is no evidence that it works and little evidence that any advertisers try to create ads with hidden messages, much of the public believes that subliminal advertising is used and is effective. A survey published in 1993 found that among people who were familiar with the concept of subliminal advertising, 72 percent thought it was effective.[86] The concept of subliminal advertising came to public attention in 1957, when Jim Vicary, a market researcher, claimed to have exposed movie audiences to the commands "drink Coca-Cola" and "eat popcorn" flashed on the screen so quickly (less than three-hundredths of a second) that they could not be perceived consciously. Vicary claimed that popcorn sales increased by an average of 57.5 percent and Coke sales went up 18.1 percent. Vicary claimed that people could be influenced strongly by things they didn't see. It turned out, however, that Vicary had not conducted the tests but had simply made up the statistics on increased sales of popcorn and Coke. Throughout 1957 and early 1958, Vicary collected more than $4 million in consulting fees; in June 1958, he disappeared. Despite the fact that this most famous of subliminal marketing studies was a total fraud, it still moved the concept from the margin to the center, demonstrating Secret 3.

In 1970, Wilson Bryan Key, a university professor in Canada, revived the idea of subliminal advertising. While looking at a photo in an article in *Esquire*, he thought he saw an image of a phallus. Key made a career of arguing that Madison Avenue hides images of death, fear, and sex in advertisements to increase sales.[87] It is unclear how these hidden images are supposed to influence viewers, who presumably are ignoring the clutter of overt advertising.

When Advertisements Are More Important Than the Program

Sometimes television ads are as interesting as the programs during which they appear. Commentators have even argued that people sometimes stay tuned to a boring Super Bowl broadcast just to see the commercials. Ridley Scott, best known as the director of blockbuster movies such as *Prometheus*, *The Martian*, and *Blade Runner*, made a name for himself by directing the 1984 Super Bowl commercial that introduced Apple's Macintosh computer. Scott's commercial, known as "1984," changed the world of advertising. Not only is it one of the most talked-about commercials of all time, but it also showed that good commercials can be more memorable than the shows they accompany.[88]

1984, Apple, Inc. "1984

▲ Famed director Ridley Scott created the iconic "1984" commercial to introduce the 1984 Super Bowl audience to Apple's new Macintosh computer. At the time it was produced it was the most expensive commercial ever made; it was also one of the most memorable.

The commercial, created by the Chiat/Day agency, was a success on several levels. It portrayed a dramatic image of a young woman athlete rebelling against an Orwellian "Big Brother" situation. It generated talk among the hundred million viewers who saw it, and it transmitted the central message that Apple wanted to get across: that there was an alternative to what was perceived at the time as the all-encompassing power of IBM (a role that has since been taken over by Microsoft).[89]

The commercial aired once on network television during the third quarter of the Super Bowl. After the Super Bowl, the commercial was broadcast free on the Big Three network news shows, and the trade magazine *Ad Age* named it the commercial of the decade. Steve Hayden, who wrote the spot while employed at Chiat/Day, says that the agency wanted to sum up the whole philosophy of the computer in one commercial: "We thought of it as an ideology, a value set. It was a way of letting the whole world access the power of computing and letting them talk to one another."[90]

Ironically, the commercial almost did not run at all. When it was previewed for Apple's board of directors, several members were horrified by it and wanted the spot scrapped. John O'Toole, former president of the American Association of Advertising Agencies, explained the significance of the ad as follows:

> What "1984" as a commercial for Apple really signified was the first time somebody could put a great deal of production money into a single commercial and run it only once and get tremendous benefit from running it only once. It took great coordination with PR. It was really event marketing, with sales promotion and PR built in. That was the beginning of the new era of integrated marketing communications.[91]

As we saw in the chapter opener, few aspects of advertising raise more concerns than commercials and marketing messages targeted at children. Yet children (and, through them, their parents) are a highly desirable audience and market for advertisers. If your parents tell you that there were not as many commercials targeted at children when they were young, they're right. In 1983, companies were spending $100 million a year to reach children. But by 2008, spending on advertising directed at children had grown to $17 billion a year. That means that marketers are spending 170 times more today to reach children than they were a generation ago.[92]

An FTC study published in 1978 under the title "Television Advertising to Children" found that children between the ages of two and eleven see approximately twenty thousand television commercials a year—that's the equivalent of about three hours a week, or slightly less than half an hour per day. The study was highly controversial at the time because it called for bans (never implemented) on all advertising in programs for which a "significant" portion of the audience was under the age of eight and on television ads for sugary foods targeted at children ages eight to eleven.[93]

Marketing to children in the twenty-first century goes far beyond the traditional print and thirty-second television ads. Companies are instead pouring money into product placement, in-school programs, mobile phone ads, and video games.[94] In 2006, the advertising industry revised its guidelines for advertising to children for the first time in thirty-two years. The new guidelines require companies to distinguish between advertising and programming content, show mealtime foods as part of a single balanced meal rather than as part of a larger balanced diet, and identify when online games contain advertising.[95]

Advertising to children in general has been controversial for years, but as of late the criticism has become more focused on children's food ads. In a nutshell, a recent research study conducted by the Institute of Medicine found the following, in respect to food preferences and diets:

- There is strong evidence that television advertising influences the food and beverage preferences of children ages 2–11 years. There is insufficient evidence about its influence on the preferences of teens ages 12–18 years.

- There is moderate evidence that television advertising influences the food and beverage beliefs of children ages 2–11 years. There is insufficient evidence about its influence on the beliefs of teens ages 12–18 years.

- There is strong evidence that television advertising influences the short-term consumption of children ages 2–11 years. There is insufficient evidence about its influence on the short-term consumption of teens ages 12–18 years.

- There is moderate evidence that television advertising influences the usual dietary intake of younger children ages 2–5 years and weak evidence that it influences the usual dietary intake of older children ages 6–11 years. There is also weak evidence that it does not influence the usual dietary intake of teens ages 12–18 years.[96]

The Long Tail and the Future of Advertising

Online advertising has grown dramatically in recent years, going from 3.8 percent of U.S. advertising spending in 2000 to 35.1 percent in 2017. This shows the rising importance of online and social media advertising with ads that hit highly targeted audiences through the long tail.[97]

Among the best known of the long-tail advertising tools are Google's AdWords and AdSense programs. Rather than buying a particular website, advertisers instead buy certain keywords, which place their ads next to particular content. Under AdWords, when surfers do a Google search that includes the keyword, the ad appears next to the search result. With AdSense, websites have a code on them that searches the content of the site and puts ads relevant to the subject matter next to the content posted there. So, if I had AdSense on my site and wrote about DVDs in a blog entry, ads for retailers that sold DVD players would start coming up. The advertisers pay for each person who clicks on the served-up ad, with a portion of the money going to the owner of the site where the ad appeared.[98] Although this tool can be used to market any product, it is especially useful for advertising long-tail media. If I were trying to sell punk polka CDs, for example, I would try to maximize the return on my advertising money by reaching only people who were already reading about punk polka bands. Google also supports its Android mobile device operating system software with advertising sales.[99]

One of the big problems with internet advertising is documenting how many people have clicked on the ad. Major advertisers have complained that "click fraud" drives up their cost of online advertising. The owner of a website with online ads may pay friends to click on the ads repeatedly to generate more page views and hence more income.[100] Or competitors of a particular advertiser will click on that advertiser's ad to run up his bill.[101] There are even automated programs known as clickbots or hitbots that will click away twenty-four hours a day, running up the bill for advertisers.

Google dominates the $130 billion digital advertising market, controlling much of the technology that connects major advertisers such as Procter & Gamble to publishers such as ESPN .com. A paper published in 2020 estimates that Google takes in about 40 cents of every dollar spent on advertising between the advertiser and the eventual publisher.[102]

Social Marketing

A common practice in advertising is to use celebrities to deliver their advertisement. Advertisers have found that having a credible personality show endorsement of a product boosts its sales. This has a long history of drug companies using medical professionals and shoe companies using athletes like LeBron James or Michael Jordan to endorse their products. But now this has moved out of the realm of just traditional celebrities into the world of social media stars.

As we discussed in the opening vignette, companies are paying prominent social media personalities, commonly known as **influencers**, to feature their products on Twitter, Facebook, Snapchat, and Instagram. One influencer, Danielle Bernstein, posts photos of herself daily in stylish apparel. Some of these photos are of her wearing what she was just planning to wear, but others are sponsored by companies that pay her from $5,000 to $15,000 for featuring their product in her photos. Among her clients are Lancôme and Virgin Hotels. The magazine *Harper's Bazaar* estimated that once she reached more than a million followers, she could ask for as much as $100,000 per post[103] (as of this writing, she has 2.4 million followers).

In 2017, Instagram developed a standard "Paid partnership" to be posted at the top of all sponsored posts. In addition to giving audience members more information, it gives the paid sponsor access to the reach and engagement data attached to the post that the influencer has.[104]

The FTC has had largely unenforced guidelines requiring influencers and brands to disclose their relationships, but as of this writing in the spring of 2020, the commission is considering taking these guidelines and turning them into formal rules that would have civil penalties.[105]

As we discussed in the section of this chapter on native advertising, however, new FTC regulations could be coming that would require social media figures to disclose when they are getting paid for promoting products.

Celebrities outside of the world of social media, such as musicians Beyoncé and Justin Bieber, and those who are famous for being famous, such as the Kardashian/Jenner clan, make substantial parts of the income by promoting products on social media platforms, such as Facebook, Instagram, and Twitter.

YouTube guidelines require that a box be checked to acknowledge that content is paid promotion. Edgar Alvarez, writing for the blog *Engadget*, says that influencers may note that they were sent a product by the manufacturer but make no mention of any payment. Warner Bros. was forced to disclose its payments to YouTubers, including the wildly-popular PewDiePie, for posting positive video game reviews online.

Something that can particularly complicate the disclosure is that influencers can be "brand ambassadors" for companies, where essentially everything they post is a promotional message. For example, YouTuber and filmmaker Casey Neistat, with 12.1 million subscribers, produced a film showing off the capabilities of the video camera on a new Samsung phone. While he clearly announced that the film was entirely shot using a Galaxy 8, he did not note that he was being paid as a representative of Samsung. As of this writing, the film has had 5.2 million views. *Engadget* reports that while brand ambassadors do not have to label their content as advertisements, they do need "to be fully transparent about their business partnership with any company."[106] This illustrates, as do all the examples in this section, Secret 5—All media are social.

Companies wanting to avoid many of the controversies surrounding influencers might choose to use a virtual one. Miquela, who posts on Instagram as "lilmiquela," has millions of followers. She has photos, videos, and songs. What she does not have is a human body or mind—she is a completely digital individual. While an unnamed human provides her voice, her voice is heavily processed, like it is for many contemporary pop stars. Kara Weber, president of Brud, the company that produces/programs Miquela, told *Variety*, "Miquela has cultivated a passionate fandom and now finds herself in the unique position of both reflecting and influencing culture. There are unprecedented opportunities for high-fidelity virtual characters to push the bounds of what we've seen in any content and advertising to date."[107]

With the rise of new advertising media, including computers connected to the internet, mobile phone screens, and video games, the older media, such as television, newspapers, and magazines, are going to be facing substantial challenges.

Integrated Marketing Communication

One response to the rapidly changing marketing environment advertisers are facing is **integrated marketing communication**, or **IMC**. The idea is that there should be an overall communication strategy for reaching key audiences and that this strategy can be carried out using advertising, public relations, sales promotion, and interactive media. Dating back to the 1980s and 1990s, IMC is a long-term approach to building the value of a brand or an organization.[108] (We'll take a more in-depth look at IMC in Chapter 13 when we talk about how Coca-Cola has marketed its Coca-Cola Freestyle machines.)

In addition to making online payment systems, electric cars, batteries for home electric storage, solar power shingles, reusable rocket ships, and (possibly) a high-speed transcontinental subway system, engineer and entrepreneur Elon Musk has done a great job of building himself up as a brand. And he has done it by using a wide range of media to grab the public's and the media's attention through his use of IMC.

Musk made his first fortune by founding electronic payment system PayPal. The money he made selling PayPal to eBay has helped him develop a wide range of high-tech businesses. His company Tesla makes high-performance all-electric cars. After getting started in the electric car business, Musk realized he also needed to be in the battery business—because if he wanted to make enough batteries to make the cost low enough to make his cars affordable, he needed more ways to sell batteries. So he developed the Powerwall, a high-powered battery that can charge with solar power during the day to provide electricity at night. He founded SpaceX to build the Falcon reusable rocket system to make launching satellites, and eventually humans, into space more affordable. He also wants to create a high-speed vacuum-based subway system that would speed people between cities.[109]

Musk does not rely on traditional advertising to promote his products. Instead, he tries to make people excited about them through a wide range of communication strategies. Instead of worrying about his company's Super Bowl ad, Musk launched his personal Tesla Roadster into space using the powerful SpaceX Falcon Heavy rocket. With the Falcon Heavy's test flight, he could have put anything in it, a block of iron, to serve as a simulated payload. But instead he put his personal Tesla Roadster convertible. Then, in the Roadster with its top down, there sat a Starman dummy wearing a SpaceX prototype space suit behind the wheel. And with that, he built a connection between his SpaceX space launch brand and his Tesla electric car brand.[110]

With people around the world watching the most powerful rocket launched in decades, the video supplied by SpaceX showed the Roadster and its Starman dummy on its way toward Mars.

The SpaceX video based on the launch livestream has attracted more than 15 million views. An edited video from SpaceX about the launch has had 22 million views. The video of the launch posted by the *Guardian* has had more than 1.2 million views. Another version of the video posted by the Canadian Broadcasting Corporation had 2.2 million views, and the video showing the Falcon Heavy's twin side boosters landing side by side picked up yet another 2.2 million views. As of this writing, Musk's Roadster has traveled 154 million miles, has gone past the orbit of Mars and is headed back in the general direction of Earth's orbit.[111]

That simple substitution of a car for a block of iron created global sensation. A search of news stories about the launch found more than 130,000 links ranging from *Florida Today*, to Space.com, to every major news organization.

Adweek journalist David Griner writes, "While the launch was clearly one of the most dramatic moments of livestreaming in recent memory, it's the live YouTube feed of Musk's own cherry-red Roadster circling the Earth that will perhaps generate the biggest publicity boost for Musk's emerging electric-car company. With a famously nonexistent ad budget, Tesla just secured a place in auto marketing history."[112] It should be noted that while all the media attention was achieved at minimal cost, it did require a $500 million rocket development program.

From Advertorials to Native Advertising

Back in 1950, legendary adman Ogilvy created one of the best examples of an ad trying to masquerade as magazine editorial content. The "Guinness Guide to Oysters" gave readers a delicious look at Atlantic oysters and suggested that a Guinness Extra Stout would go great with them. As Brian Clark wrote in his advertising column at the website Say Daily, "I don't even like oysters, and this sounds amazing right now."[113] Ogilvy's Guinness and oysters ad is oftentimes held up as the real start of the **advertorial**—a paid message where the advertisement blends in with the surrounding materials in the magazine, newspaper, or website. While advertorials have been around for more than sixty years, a new version known as native advertising has emerged. Native ads are essentially a more sophisticated form of sponsored content that "matches a publication's editorial standards while meeting the audience's expectations."[114] (They are also an example of Secret 4—Nothing is new: Everything that happened in the past will happen again.) Many prestige media companies—including the *Atlantic*, the *Washington Post*, and the *New York Times*—are making use of native ads, especially on their websites.[115]

While ads designed to look like editorial content are nothing new, having the publication's editorial staff producing articles appearing as sponsored content is breaking down the old barrier between "church and state"—the blurred line between the business side and the content side of a publication.[116] This line is fuzzy enough that according to a 2015 study published in the *Journal of Advertising*, only about 8 percent of subjects in an experiment could rightly identify native ads as paid marketing messages.[117] In an effort to help

▲ Billionaire entrepreneur Elon Musk excels at getting free attention for his brands. In this case, he launched one of his all-electric Tesla convertibles into space on top of the Falcon Heavy rocket with a Starman dummy clad in a SpaceX space suit. The Roadster is currently on its way to Mars and beyond.

▲ "Gildan Try Outs: Three guys try on their dad's underwear and give us their thoughts," Onion Labs, August 3, 2017, https://www.youtube.com/watch?v=E3KjTqAAsrA.

reduce this confusion, the FTC has put together new guidelines requiring online publishers to more clearly label native ads in a way that consumers will understand.[118] Globally, native advertising is growing rapidly, going from $30.9 billion in 2015 to an estimated $59.35 billion in 2018.[119]

The big challenge to both the advertiser and the publication is that the content of native ads needs to really match the style and standards of the hosting publication. When the Gildan underwear company wanted to create a modern image for its men's briefs to differentiate them from the "tighty whities" underwear worn by young men's dads, it turned to Onion Labs, the native advertising agency from the *Onion* news parody website. A pair of videos produced by Onion Labs showed the young men trying on their dad's underwear and finding the experience both unpleasant and unsettling. One young man wore his dad's underwear for seventy-two hours, and he started donating money to public radio and taking up fly-fishing.[120]

Native ads can go horribly wrong, however, when the content of the article or ad doesn't match the standards of the hosting publication. One of the most notorious examples came from 2013 when the *Atlantic* ran a sponsored article on its website extolling the opening of twelve new Scientology churches. Along with the article, which seemed to be at odds with content from the *Atlantic*, the comments section following the article appeared to have nothing but positive comments about Scientology. Comments on most articles at the site are both positive and negative. After the article was up less than twelve hours, it was pulled from the website, and the next day an apology was posted that began,

> We screwed up. It shouldn't have taken a wave of constructive criticism—but it has—to alert us that we've made a mistake, possibly several mistakes. We now realize that as we explored new forms of digital advertising, we failed to update the policies that must govern the decisions we make along the way.[121]

The *Atlantic* followed up that apology two weeks later with new guidelines for how it would handle sponsored content in the future.[122]

Is Anyone Watching Television Ads?

There is only a fixed amount of money available for advertising and marketing products. And as companies move their advertising dollars to new media—online for ads and streaming content and to mobile phone screens—there will be less money for older media, such as television. If that were not enough, television is grappling with declining audience sizes and new technologies, such as DVRs, which allow viewers to skip watching commercials altogether. As of 2017, DVRs were in approximately 53 percent of American households.[123]

The broadcast networks are responding to this threat in various ways. CBS is selling web ads as a package with broadcast ads. These are not the simple banner ads of the 1990s; they are video ads that come before streaming web content. Sneaker manufacturer Converse used its broadcast ads to get consumers to generate short videos featuring Converse sneakers, and the company then featured the videos on its website.[124]

Mobile Advertising

Mobile devices like smartphones and tablets have become the latest frontier for advertising, with their bright color screens and their ubiquitous use among the notoriously hard-to-reach population of adults aged eighteen to thirty-four. Although many companies are simply using banner ads to go with wireless web content, others are creating interactive apps to promote their products.

Despite having small screens, cell phones have several key advantages to advertisers. They are always on, they are always with the person who owns them, and the phone belongs to an identifiable individual. This lets advertisers send out highly targeted messages that can contain time-sensitive offers. Another popular use of mobile phone advertising is to get consumers to participate in activities such as voting for contestants on reality shows.[125] According to *Ad Age*, mobile advertising has been growing dramatically in recent years, going from $31.6 billion in 2015 to a projected $77.1 billion in 2020.[126] The magazine goes on to estimate that mobile advertising will account for two-thirds of online advertising that same year.[127] As this clearly shows, online media are mobile media—Secret 6.

Advertising consultant Kathryn Koegel said she learned a lot about mobile advertising being done around the world when she served as a judge of the GSMA Global Mobile Awards. What did she discover? That folks are doing much more interesting and creative things globally using simpler tools than marketers are in the United States.[128]

The problem, Koegel claims, is that in the United States advertisers are obsessed with fancy iPhone apps that really do not do much to promote the brand. What Koegel found globally was that companies promoted involvement using simple SMS text messages and creative approaches that led to publicly visible activity.

She points to the winning mobile campaign from the competition—one that sells Cornetto ice cream in Turkey through the use of a video game projected on the wall of a building in Taksim, Turkey's answer to Times Square. People compete by controlling game characters on the side of the building using text messages from their phones. If they complete the task, they win free ice cream that is collected on the spot.

The lesson from Koegel is not that there is anything wrong with mobile apps; you just want to make sure that you have clear goals for what you are trying to accomplish with them. What kind of mobile marketing could you think up?

Product Placement

Product placement has long been with us. When Paul Newman drank a beer in the 1981 movie *Absence of Malice*, it was a Budweiser. And when Steve McQueen played cop Frank Bullitt back in 1968, he chased criminals through San Francisco in a Ford Mustang GT. But in recent years, product placement has gotten considerably more sophisticated, rising occasionally to the level known as plot placement, branded entertainment, or **product integration**, in which the product or service being promoted is not only seen, but central to the story.[129]

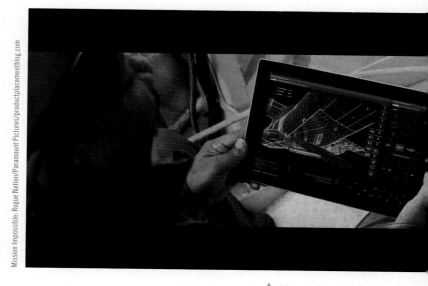

▲ Microsoft has used product integration in *Mission: Impossible* to feature the company's Surface tablet computer.

One of the forces driving the growth of this expanded form of product placement is that multitasking consumers are increasingly ignoring television ads by skipping past them on the DVR, surfing other channels during commercial breaks, or leaving the room to get a snack.[130]

The biggest challenge to product placement is making it seem natural rather than intrusive, as intrusive placement tends to put off consumers, according to *New York Times* advertising columnist Stuart Elliott. That may be why so much of the product placement is in reality shows, where the use of products as rewards and prizes makes them fit in better.

There seem to be no limits now to which products can get placed in prime-time programs. Pregnancy was an unmentionable topic on television in the 1950s, but pregnancy tests have shown up frequently in product placements in shows ranging from *Gossip Girl* to *Sex and the City*.[131]

Television and movie writers have rebelled against product integration, complaining that it interferes with their creative integrity; they have also called for getting a cut of the placement income if they're going to be writing the placements into the stories. Patric Verrone, president of a movie and broadcast writers' union, explained why writers are concerned about product integration: "Product placement is simply putting a branded box of cereal on the kitchen table in a show. Product

Chick-fil-A, Inc. ✔
@ChickfilA

Bun + Chicken + Pickles = all the ♥ for the original.

Bun
Chicken
+ Pickles
Love

8:15 AM · Aug 19, 2019 · Sprinklr

7K Retweets   **22.2K** Likes

▲ Chick-Fil-A's tweet in response to the Popeyes chicken sandwich craze in 2019.

▼ To which Popeyes responded with a rather cheeky tweet.

Popeyes Chicken ✔
@PopeyesChicken

... y'all good?

Chick-fil-A, Inc. ✔ @ChickfilA · Aug 19, 2019
Bun + Chicken + Pickles = all the ♥ for the original.

Bun
Chicken
+ Pickles
Love

10:58 AM · Aug 19, 2019 · Twitter Web App

91.6K Retweets   **311.7K** Likes

integration is having the characters talk about the crunchy deliciousness of the cereal."[132]

Social Chicken Sandwiches

One of the most intense recent social marketing battles was a corporate fight over . . . chicken sandwiches.

The Chick-fil-A chicken sandwich empire has long had connections to social conservatism. And while the company founder's connection to evangelical causes and "closed on Sunday" business model has brought it criticism, those same factors have made it a favorite on the political and religious right, along with all the people who simply like their sandwiches.[133]

So, Chick-fil-A has long been the default winner in the battle of the chicken sandwiches. Despite massive corporate efforts, McDonald's has not been able to create a break-out chicken product since the ubiquitous Chicken McNuggets went national back in 1983.

Kentucky Fried Chicken has the most mass-market fried chicken stores, but they have always been known much more for their bone-in chicken and strips than for their sandwiches. Note that while there are more KFC stores, Chick-fil-A sells a lot more chicken.[134]

The same was true of Popeyes Louisiana Kitchen until the summer of 2019. Popeyes has long had soul food sensibilities and has been built around the concept of spicy chicken. On August 12, 2019, Popeye's introduced their chicken sandwich, available in both spicy and regular forms, to the world, and the world went crazy. Soon after the announcement there were hours-long lines extending out the doors of every restaurant. Chick-fil-A could not let this shot on their bow pass, and so as a proper twenty-first century company, they tweeted (see top left). To which Popeyes responded, rather cheekily, with a tweet of their own (see bottom left).

The difference in response on Twitter was remarkable—Chick-fil-A as of this writing got around 22,000 "likes" while Popeyes got more than 310,000. The Popeyes sandwich proved to be so popular that before the end of the month the company had sold out of the product. But the social media battle didn't completely quiet down. At one point, Popeyes suggested to customers they could bring a bun to the restaurant and place a pair of chicken strips into it.[135]

Popeyes brought the sandwich back to the market on November 3, 2019—National Sandwich Day—which happened to be on a Sunday, when its rival Chick-fil-A is closed.

In mid-November of 2019, Chick-fil-A surprised both supporters and critics by announcing that their charitable foundation was going to change its giving pattern and no longer contribute to a pair of charities that had been perceived as anti-LGBTQ. Much of the response to this change came from the political right, who viewed the new policy as a betrayal of the company's conservative supporters.[136] See the tweet from former Arkansas governor Mike Huckabee on this page.

Other players in the fast food battlefield have tried to rise to relevance through all of this, with McDonald's trying for a Chick-fil-A sandwich clone in a pair of markets receiving only minimal attention. Wendy's sassy Twitter account generated a fair amount of notice a couple of years ago when then sixteen-year-old Carter Wilkerson got the chain to give him free chicken nuggets for a year when he got a tweet about the crispy product shared more than 3.6 million times, setting a record for Twitter.[137]

An important thing to remember through all of this is that the chicken sandwich wars are primarily about telling a story online about something that is easy to buy and enjoy. It's not really about the food. David Portalatin, a food industry analyst, told the *Washington Post*, "This whole thing is not about chicken sandwiches. It's about the virality of the story. And it's a reflection of the performance of chains like Chick-fil-A."[138]

Of course, not all the buzz was about mass-market chicken. As the narrative over the Popeyes sandwich was escalating, musician Bri Hall responded by tweeting about the Washington, DC, restaurant Roaming Rooster's chicken sandwich.

Her tweet went viral, bringing in long lines for the restaurant and its four food trucks. Roaming Rooster repaid Hall with a promise of free chicken for life.

Gov. Mike Huckabee ✔
@GovMikeHuckabee

In Aug 2012, I coordinated a national @ChickfilA Appreciation Day after they were being bullied by militant hate groups. Millions showed up. Today, @ChickfilA betrayed loyal customers for $$. I regret believing they would stay true to convictions of founder Truett Cathey. Sad.

10:22 AM · Nov 18, 2019 · Twitter Web App

3.9K Retweets   **10.5K** Likes

Twitter/@GovMikeHuckabee

LA HARA (Breaker of Combs)
@BriHallOfficial

While Popeyes is cool and all if you live in the DMV area you should check out Roaming Rooster in DC. It's Black owned, and the founder Mike is Ethiopian born. He grew the family business from a food truck and has always been kind

1:08 PM · Aug 26, 2019 · Twitter for iPhone

19.7K Retweets   **45.6K** Likes

Twitter/@BriHallOfficial

CHAPTER REVIEW

CHAPTER SUMMARY ▶▶

Advertisements are paid messages about an organization, a product, a service, or an idea that appear in the mass media. Advertising provides numerous benefits to society, including making media less expensive and contributing to a large and diverse economy. While advertising has existed in the United States since colonial times, it was industrialization, urbanization, and the growth of national transportation networks in the nineteenth century that allowed it to become a major industry. Advertising transformed the media industry from one supported primarily by subscribers to one supported by advertising revenues. Publishers (and later broadcasters) were no longer sellers of content to audience members; they were now sellers of audiences to advertisers.

Advertising can be broken down into consumer advertising, advocacy advertising, and trade (business-to-business) advertising, according to the audience the client is attempting to reach and the idea or product it is trying to sell. The advertising industry encompasses four main groups: the client who has something to advertise, the advertising agency or department that creates the advertising, the media that carry the ads, and the audiences targeted by the advertisements.

Advertisers use a variety of strategies to reach their audiences. They may attempt to understand the needs, wants, and motivations of audience members through psychographic research. They also target products to specific demographic groups. Targeting can provoke controversy both by people being offended by companies acknowledging the importance of audiences such as gay/lesbian families and by companies gathering what critics see as excessive information about consumers.

Critics argue that advertising raises the cost of merchandise, that many ads are tasteless, and that ads can exploit young people and other vulnerable audiences. Advertisers join the critics in complaining that there are too many advertisements in the media, creating the problem referred to as clutter. Although there have been complaints of advertisers embedding subliminal messages in ads, there is no evidence that such messages have been used or that they are effective. Advertising directed at children has been seen as problematic because young people are not able to understand the differences between paid messages and editorial/entertainment content.

Advertising is going through a period of significant change as new technology emerges that allows consumers to bypass viewing commercials on television. But technology is also providing numerous new venues for advertising, including the internet and mobile devices. Companies are increasingly making use of integrated marketing communication strategies that bring together multiple forms of marketing communication to promote their brands. Advertisers are also looking at promoting their products through elaborately developed product placement and social marketing. Online celebrities known as influencers are a prominent part of social marketing, reaching out with paid messages that are often indistinguishable from noncommercial content.

KEY TERMS ▶▶

advertising 288

industrialization 289

modernization 289

economy of abundance 290

brand name 290

local advertising 291

direct-action message 291

national advertising 291

indirect-action message 292

advocacy ads 292

public service ads 292

business-to-business (trade) ads 292

open contract 294

the big idea 295

brand image 295

media planning 296

CPM 296

zoned coverage 297

drive time 298

targeting 299

clutter 303

subliminal advertising 304

influencers 307

integrated marketing communication (IMC) 308

advertorial 309

product integration 311

REVIEW QUESTIONS ▶▶

1. Is it fair to young children to target them with persuasive messages like toy unboxing videos?

2. What had to happen socially in the nineteenth century for advertising to become an important part of our culture?

3. How can advertisers grab the attention of consumers when there are so many competing advertisements they are being exposed to?

4. How did Apple's "1984" commercial introducing the Macintosh transform Super Bowl advertising?

5. How does integrated marketing communication differ from traditional advertising?

Jeff Kravitz / Contributor / Getty Images

CHAPTER 13

PUBLIC RELATIONS

Interactions, Relationships, and the News

Tide, "Gronk knows that Ride PODS® are for DOING LAUNDRY. Nothing else." January 12, 2018. Retrieved from YouTube at https://www.youtube.com/watch?v=-DrC_PF_3Lg.

As we discussed in the opening to Chapter 12, young people can do a good job of attracting bad attention online with videos showing them doing stupid things. In 2013, teens were posting videos of themselves attempting to eat a tablespoon of pure spice in sixty seconds for the Cinnamon Challenge. In the summer of 2014, there was the more admirable Ice Bucket Challenge where people dumped a bucket of ice water over their heads to help raise money to fight Lou Gehrig's disease, or ALS. (To be fair, that one had plenty of full-fledged adults participating, including former Fox News host Shep Smith and MSNBC host Rachel Maddow.) In 2016, there were videos of the Mannequin Challenge where young people tried to stay frozen in action like, you guessed it, a mannequin.

What did all of these have in common? They all involved young people doing a silly, sometimes dangerous stunt while recording a video of it to post online.[1] (They are also all an example of Secret 4—Nothing is new: Everything that happened in the past will happen again.)

Few of these have been as directly dangerous, however, as the one that became popular in 2017 and 2018—the so-called Tide Pod Challenge that involves people attempting to eat (really just bite into) pods filled with highly concentrated and toxic laundry detergent. As the *PBS NewsHour* pointed out, the challengers do not actually eat the detergent. If they did, they could suffer chemical burns in their throats, esophagi, or lungs. They could also make themselves violently ill to their stomachs. They could give themselves breathing problems for the rest of their lives. They could die.[2]

No one is clear exactly where the Tide Pod Challenge came from. Procter & Gamble (P&G), the consumer product giant that makes Tide, dealt with a small outbreak of young people biting into the laundry pods for fun back in 2015. At the time, satire site *The Onion* posted a mock opinion piece from the point of view of a toddler who wanted to eat one. But it wasn't until 2017 that making videos of the activity became popular.[3] That was also when the *College Humor* website got 3.5 million views of a video titled "Don't Eat the Laundry Pods. (Seriously. They're Poison.)"[4] *Vox* reports that this was followed with memes of celebrity chef Gordon Ramsay talking about how tasty they were, fights in postapocalyptic grocery stores over the last bag of pods, and baking pizzas with laundry pod toppings. *The Onion* even had a follow-up parody announcement that Tide had introduced a new sour-apple-flavored laundry pod.[5]

After studying this chapter, you will be able to

1 Identify the two key founders of modern public relations and describe their individual contributions to the PR industry

2 Describe the three major functions of public relations

3 Identify four ways companies use media to communicate with their internal publics

4 Describe two examples of how the internet has made public relations more difficult

5 Explain the way PR plays a significant role in what is presented as news in the media

6 Identify the three things Dr. Martin Luther King Jr. said needed to be combined in the media to eliminate segregation laws

Both P&G and YouTube jumped in quickly to issue statements telling people not to deliberately eat the pods. One press release from P&G stated that the company is "deeply concerned about conversations related to intentional and improper use of liquid laundry packs. Laundry packs are made to clean clothes. They should not be played with, whatever the circumstances, even if meant as a joke. Like all household cleaning products, they must be used properly and stored safely."[6] P&G also got both YouTube and Facebook to take down the Tide Pod Challenge videos whenever they found them.

Of course, P&G didn't really expect to reach teens with its serious and responsible news messages. For that, the company turned to NFL football star Rob Gronkowski, who had previously made Super Bowl commercials for Tide. Gronkowski's message in the online video was direct. "What the heck is going on, people? Use Tide pods for washing, not eating. Do not eat." If that was not clear enough, at one point in the video he says, "No, no, no, no."[7] The video went viral and inspired a range of other videos mocking the whole idea of the challenge. Rapper and actor Ice-T made a very direct public service announcement that aired during the *Tonight Show* where the *Law & Order: SVU* star said in his monotone, "Stop eating laundry detergent dumb f——s."[8]

Tide also responded directly through social media to consumers who were reaching out to the company. When a consumer posted a tweet that said, "Help @tide I ate a tide pod because I lost a bet and now I feel like I'm burning a hole in my stomach," Tide responded quickly with a tweet saying, "Contact your doctor or your local poison control center. When you are feeling better, please call us at . . . We're open M–F from 9–6 ET."[9]

But the Tide Pod Challenge was only a small part of the problem—though it has been the most visible part. As early as 2012, the Centers for Disease Control and Prevention called poisoning by detergent pods an emerging health crisis, with poison control centers reporting 7,700 cases among children age five and under for that year.[10] Between 2012 and 2017, two children and six adults died from eating the packets, though apparently none of them were participating in the challenge.[11]

Tide responded to the original problem of small children biting into the packets by creating educational materials for parents and caregivers, putting the pods in more child-resistant packaging, and adding a bitter flavor to the wrapper that surrounds the detergent.[12]

Public relations practitioner Blair Nicole Natasi, writing for *Forbes*, says that one thing that helped P&G was that the Tide Pod Challenge was not a self-inflicted PR crisis. Tide long had warning labels on its packaging telling people not to ingest the packs or let them get into their eyes. Once the challenge started appearing on social media, the company wasted no time in responding with the message that the pods were for laundry only. Finally, Natasi writes that in addition to responding to young people, P&G worked at making the broader public aware of the problem.[13]

Marketing professor Robert Field praised P&G for not apologizing for the bad actions of consumers. "They validated public concerns, yet made it clear they don't consider themselves responsible," he said.[14]

As we will see later in the chapter, one of the key ways of promoting the image you want of your institution is making sure you are doing a good job of telling your story publicly before bad narratives get started. In addition to examining the development of the PR industry, we discuss how the PR process works, the various publics that organizations need to work with, and how public relations professionals have used public relations to protect and advance their employers' interests.

The Growth of Public Relations

Stay up to date on the latest in media by visiting the author's blog at **ralphehanson.com**

The field of **public relations** (also called PR) has had an uneven image in the United States. (The term *public relations* is discussed more extensively later in this chapter.) In his book on corporate public relations, Marvin Olasky noted that practitioners have been called "high-paid errand boys and buffers for management."[15] Other names have been less flattering. Despite such criticisms, public relations plays a critical role in industry, government, and nonprofit organizations. These organizations need to deal with the people who work for them, invest in them, are served by them, contribute to them, regulate them, or buy from them. They need to interact with the world. Ultimately, that is what public relations is all about: relating with a wide range of publics. A **public** is a group of people who share a common set of interests. An internal public is made up of people within the organization. An external public is made up of people outside the organization.

The origins of public relations go back as far as the American Revolution, with pamphlets distributed to the public, such as Thomas Paine's *Common Sense*, which built up the case for the colonies' break with England. In the early 1800s, famed author Washington Irving used publicity to build excitement for his latest book. But the PR profession is generally seen as having grown out of the Industrial Revolution. As companies and their accompanying bureaucracies grew, so did the need to manage their image.[16] Advances in communications also made publicity campaigns more feasible. It was not until the penny press of the 1830s and 1840s produced widespread newspaper circulation that publicity began to be particularly effective. Circus entrepreneur P. T. Barnum raised publicity to a fine art, building interest in his shows by writing letters to the editor under fake names and accusing himself of fraud. Thus, this early publicity process, known as **press agentry**, was a one-way form of public relations that involved sending material from the press agent to the media with little opportunity for interaction and feedback. Press agentry was used to support causes such as temperance with speakers, books, and songs. It was also practiced effectively by the abolitionist movement.

As noted in the previous paragraph, press agentry consisted of one-way communication. For the most part, press agents before the 1920s worked at building publicity for their clients rather than managing or creating a specific image. Standard Oil's efforts in the 1890s were typical of the time. The oil giant's advertising agency sent out news articles as paid advertisements, but the agency paid for the ads only if they looked like articles or editorials.[17] In the early years of the twentieth century, however, companies started realizing that they needed to respond to criticism from various populist and progressive political groups and to muckraking investigative reports by magazines such as *McClure's* (see Chapter 5).

The first major users of public relations were railroads, which had numerous reasons for working on their images.[18] In the 1870s, many railroads wanted to divide freight traffic among themselves according to predetermined percentages so as to avoid competition. The railroads did not want criticism of their monopolistic practices in the press, so they bribed reporters and editors, either by making cash payoffs or, more subtly, by giving free passes for travel on the railroad to cooperative members of the press. The Illinois Central Railroad realized that praise of the railroads coming from academics would do more good and be more persuasive than puffery coming from the industry itself, so it funded university research on the railroads, the findings of which could then be quoted by the press.

Like the railroads, the utility and telephone industries saw the value of public relations. Chicago Edison argued to both the government and the public that providing electricity was a "natural monopoly" and should not be open to competition. In the early 1900s, AT&T required newspapers in which it advertised to run positive articles about its actions. Both the utilities and the phone company used publicity firms to write articles and editorials promoting the companies' points of view that were placed in newspapers around the country.

Ivy Lee, one of the two key founders of modern public relations, brought to the business a strong understanding of both economics and psychology. Lee recognized that the public often reacted more strongly to symbols and phrases than to rational arguments, and he built his campaigns around the importance of symbolism.[19] He also saw that it was important to put a human face on corporations.[20]

Lee was the first PR professional to deal with crisis management, and although *spin control* did not become a popular term until the 1980s, he was practicing it as early as 1910. Lee wanted to do much more for his clients than just send out favorable publicity; he wanted to manipulate public opinion in favor of his clients. That meant actively working with the press.

Among the problems faced by the railroads was reporting on accidents. The accepted practice of the industry in the late 1800s was either to cover up accidents or to bribe reporters not to write about them. Lee suggested that it might be in the railroads' best interests to deal with the press openly. When his client, the Pennsylvania Railroad, had a wreck, Lee invited reporters to visit the scene of the accident at the company's expense. After they arrived, he helped them report on the story. Company officials were amazed to see that the publicity they received when they cooperated with the press was a vast improvement over what they received when they fought with it.[21]

Lee also recognized the importance of telling the truth. Although the arguments he presented clearly supported his clients' viewpoints, Lee was always careful to be accurate in any factual claims. This was not so much because telling the truth was right or moral as because doing so was effective.[22] Lee once told oil giant John D. Rockefeller Jr., "Tell the truth because sooner or later the public will

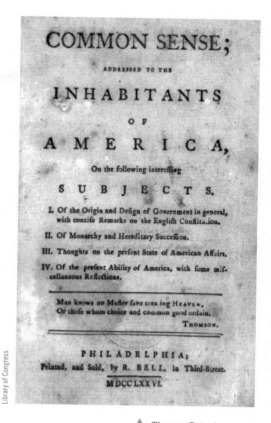

Thomas Paine's famous *Common Sense* pamphlet is an example of an early public relations effort. It was used to build the case for the American Revolution.

▲ Circus promoter P. T. Barnum built publicity for his shows through posters such as this one, as well as by staging protests and complaints about his circus.

find it out anyway. And if the public doesn't like what you are doing, change your policies and bring them into line with what the people want."[23] In 1902, American coal mine operators were facing a strike. The mine owners ignored the press, but the unionized miners worked with reporters to their advantage, and due to this the public strongly supported the workers. When the mine owners faced another strike in 1906, they hired Lee's publicity firm, Parker and Lee.[24] Lee convinced the mine operators that they could no longer ignore public opinion. A former business reporter, he started giving newspapers all the information they asked for. Supplied with clear and accurate statements from the mine owners, reporters started writing stories that were considerably less antagonistic to them.

At about this time, Lee developed his "Declaration of Principles," which outlined how he thought public relations ought to be carried out. These principles can be summarized quite simply: Openly and honestly supply accurate and timely news to the press.[25] Lee himself suffered from bad public relations late in his career: In the 1930s, he was accused of being a Nazi propagandist because he had worked for the German Dye Trust. The damage to his reputation from this association came at least in part from the many enemies he had made over the course of his career.[26]

Along with Ivy Lee, the other founder of public relations was Edward L. Bernays, who was the first person to apply social-scientific research techniques to the field. Bernays, a nephew of Sigmund Freud, promoted the use of psychology to manipulate public opinion, a technique that he called **engineering consent**:

This phrase means, quite simply, the use of an engineering approach—that is, action based only on thorough knowledge of the situation and on the application of scientific principles and tried practices in the task of getting people to support ideas and programs. Any person or organization depends ultimately on public approval and is therefore faced with the problem of engineering the public's consent to a program or goal.[27]

In addition to promoting his clients, Bernays actively promoted the concept of public relations as a profession. To that end, he wrote the first books on the practice, *Crystallizing Public Opinion* (1923) and *Propaganda* (1928). In 1923, Bernays taught the first course in public relations, which he offered at New York University.

Like Lee, Bernays recognized the importance of the crowd in modern life. He found that the best way to influence the public was to arrange for messages to be delivered by credible sources. "If you can influence the leaders, either with or without their conscious cooperation, you automatically influence the group which they sway," he commented.[28] While the guaranteed influence of leaders over groups may be a bit of an overstatement, the use of credible or admired individuals to speak on behalf of a company is certainly central to public relations.

World War I: The Federal Government Starts Using Public Relations

The years 1914–1918 were a period of major growth for public relations. According to Bernays, during this time governments figured out how important persuasive communication could be to mobilize popular support for a major war: "Ideas and their dissemination became weapons and words became bullets."[33] The U.S. government used public relations extensively during

FALSE REPORTS GARNER PUBLICITY

Fake news is not always about politics. Back in 1939, a young actress by the name of Rita Hayworth was trying to become a household name, and her press agent, the legendary Henry Rogers, was willing to do whatever it took to make her a Hollywood star. One of these efforts was putting out a made-up press release naming Hayworth the winner of a nonexistent "best-dressed off-screen actress" contest held by a nonexistent group. That story landed Hayworth a big photo story in *Look* magazine (a competitor of *Life*) and launched the actress's career.[29]

Getty Images/ Bob Landry

Emporio Armani, 2011 Fall-Winter Campaign

Truthfulness is not always the first priority when it comes to entertainment publicity. Actress Rita Hayworth in the 1930s and singer Rihanna in the 2010s had their publicity agents pull similar stunts and claim that the performers had won imaginary awards for their appearances.

Why do we care? Because it happened again.

More recently, British newspaper the *Daily Mail* ran a story proclaiming that singer Rihanna's ad campaign for Armani undies had won an award from *Ad Age* magazine for being the sexiest of the year. The writers even quoted *Ad Age* as saying, "It's Rihanna at her sexiest. She's never looked this good." They also added, "She's in amazing shape and the pictures are stunning."[30] (As a side note, the "they" in the attribution should have been a tip-off that there was not really a source behind the story. Remember Secret 7—There is no "they.")

Even Rihanna tweeted about the award. The only problem? As press blogger Jim Romenesko points out, *Ad Age* did not actually give out an award for the sexiest ad. That is why none of the stories about it (including those from the *Huffington Post*, the *Hindustan Times*, the *Global Grind*, and others) had links back to *Ad Age*.[31]

The actual source of the story? A company called TNI Press Ltd. that writes stories for British tabloids and is the source for several recent stories extolling Rihanna's sexiness. In his *New York Times* obituary, Rogers was quoted as saying in 1987, "If I did now what I did then, I'd be barred from every news media outlet."[32]

Hmmm . . . maybe not. Think about Secret 4—Nothing is new: Everything that happened in the past will happen again.

As a side note, at the time this story was spreading, your author ran a Google search on Rihanna's Armani ad and found twenty-four media stories about it but only one link to the actual correction. When it comes to celebrity gossip—gossip likely put forward by the celebrity himself or herself—do we really care whether it's true?

WHO are the sources?

What is the *Daily Mail*? What kind of stories does it run? Who was Henry Rogers?

WHAT are they saying?

What did Henry Rogers do for Rita Hayworth? What did the *Daily Mail* do for Rihanna? What connection is there between Rogers and the Rihanna story?

WHAT evidence is there?

What evidence did the *Daily Mail* have that the Rihanna story was true? How about the news sites that reprinted the story? What could these publications have done to check the story before they published it? What do you and your classmates think about fabricated celebrity stories?

WHY do you think that the *Daily Mail* ran the story with photos about Rihanna?

Do you think that it cared whether or not the story was true? Was there any difference between what the *Daily Mail* did for Rihanna and what Henry Rogers did for Rita Hayworth? Do you and your friends have any faith in the truth of tabloid stories about celebrities?

To Bernays, the chief characteristic distinguishing public relations from the press agentry of the past was that public relations was a two-way interaction between individuals and organizations—communication that involved listening as well as speaking. Bernays wrote that by the 1920s it had become clear to practitioners that words alone did not constitute public relations; there had to be actions to go with the words.

World War I. Within a week of the U.S. entry into the war, President Woodrow Wilson established the Committee on Public Information (CPI) under the direction of George Creel, the former editor of the *Rocky Mountain News*. The committee operated from April 6, 1917, until June 30, 1919, building American support for the war. Although the committee lacked many of the modern tools of mass communication—radio was still in its infancy and the movie industry was just taking its first steps—it was still able to use advertising, billboards, and posters, as well as newspaper opinion pieces, articles, and pamphlets.

The committee also used interpersonal channels. It enlisted seventy-five thousand "Four-Minute Men" who took the committee's messages to churches and civic groups by delivering four-minute speeches. Research conducted in the 1940s later proved the effectiveness of this technique by confirming that people often turn to individuals they know and trust when they are looking for guidance about an important topic. So if an organization wants to influence a particular public, the best way to do so may be to use influential local individuals, along with the mass media.[34] Bernays referred to this process as **opinion leadership**—using "journalists, politicians, businessmen, scientists, professional men, authors, society leaders, teachers, actors, women of fashion and so on" to deliver influential messages to the public.[35]

Woodrow Wilson's use of public relations was not limited to the war effort. He was the first president to hold regular press conferences, and under Wilson the Federal Trade Commission used publicity to force the food industry to adopt more sanitary practices.

The federal government turned to public relations once again during World War II. The Office of War Information served much the same purpose that the CPI had during World War I. The main difference was that the new group was able to use talking films and radio to supplement the print and interpersonal communications used by the CPI.

Public Relations Becomes a Profession

During the 1940s and 1950s, public relations continued to grow as a profession, and colleges and universities began offering degrees in the field. Advances in polling made it easier to measure public opinion, and clients began to realize that PR firms could help shape how people felt about companies and issues. Clients were also looking for help in making use of the emerging medium of television.

Throughout the 1960s, the media grew more critical of both business and government as the United States became caught up in the Vietnam War, the civil rights movement, the student and women's movements, environmentalism, and consumerism (for example, groups such as Ralph Nader's consumer activist organization). This trend continued into the 1970s with the rise of Watergate-inspired investigative reporting. It was a time when institutions had to actively manage their images, and they realized the importance of communicating with individuals, businesses, governments, and social organizations.[36]

Library of Congress

▲ The Committee on Public Information had seventy-five thousand "Four-Minute Men" who gave brief speeches about World War I to churches and civic groups across the United States.

The Business of Public Relations

There is a popular misconception among students that public relations primarily involves talking and meeting with people. Although it certainly includes these elements, there is much more to the profession. Public relations is the job of managing an organization's image through planning, research, communication, and assessment.

Edward Bernays described three major functions of public relations:

1. Informing—Sending out information to a variety of publics, ranging from the people who work in a company's office to its customers on the other side of the world. An example of information would be a press release announcing a new product line to stores that sell the company's products.

2. Persuading—Attempting to induce members of various publics to change their attitudes or actions toward an idea, product, or institution. An example of persuasion would be a campaign to persuade a company's customers to write or call their congressman to persuade them to remove a tax on the company's product.

3. Integrating—Attempting to bring publics and institutions together with a shared set of goals, actions, and attitudes. An example of an integrative event would be a charity auction designed to raise funds for a park in the city where the company has its offices as the company works to become a vital part of the community.[37]

Bernays saw public relations as a public good, necessary for the proper functioning of society. He argued that society was moving too fast and becoming too complex for the average person to cope with and that the only hope for a functional society was to merge public and private interests through public relations.

This two-way model of interaction between the institution and its publics is the central notion of modern public relations, which can be defined as "the management function that establishes and maintains mutually beneficial relationships between an organization and the publics on whom its success or failure depends."[38] This definition has three basic segments:

1. Public relations is a management function. This means that it is central to the running of a company or organization and not merely a tool of the marketing department.

2. Public relations establishes mutually beneficial relationships. This means that public relations is an interaction that should benefit both sides—the organization and the public(s).

3. Companies depend on various publics to succeed. One of the primary reasons PR campaigns fail is that they neglect these relationships and consider only the company's point of view.

One mistake companies must avoid is to assume that glib communication can be a substitute for real action when solving a public problem. This can be seen clearly in the case of the film industry in the 1920s and 1930s. As discussed in Chapter 7, during that period movies were being criticized for their immorality. Industry leaders responded by hiring former U.S. postmaster Will Hays to supervise the moral content of movies. Throughout the 1920s, Hays preached a message of corporate responsibility to the press, but the industry made no significant changes in response to criticism of the portrayal of sex, violence, and drug use in the movies.[39]

By 1934, critics had had enough of soothing words without action, and the Catholic Legion of Decency started a movie boycott. With the threat of government censorship growing, the movie industry finally adopted a production code that put strict limits on what directors could portray. Public relations historian Marvin Olasky argues that if the movie industry had dealt with its critics in a meaningful way in the 1920s, it might have avoided the restrictions forced on it in the 1930s.[40]

The Public Relations Process

Although there are a few different ways of looking at the PR process, we are going to look at it using a model known as ROPES: research, objectives, programming, evaluation, and stewardship.[41]

1. Research—Researching the opportunities, problems, or issues the organization is facing

2. Objectives—Setting specific and measurable objectives for the PR campaign

3. Programming—Planning and implementing the activities necessary to carry out the objectives

4. Evaluation—Testing the messages and techniques before using them, monitoring the programming while it's being delivered, and measuring the results of the programming

5. Stewardship—Maintaining the relationships created through the previous steps

Central to the ROPES process is the notion that public relations is concerned primarily with creating, developing, and nurturing relationships between an organization and its key publics.[42] To see how this process is carried out, let's look at how P&G used public relations to both discourage misuse of the Tide laundry pods and protect the value of the United States' best-selling liquid laundry detergent brand as we discussed earlier in this chapter.[43]

Research. P&G, the owner of the Tide brand, from the time of the initial launch of Tide laundry pods in 2012 up through the present day, needed to encourage the safe use of its product without overreacting to every accidental or deliberate misuse of the pods. To do so, the company monitored social media and news reports about them as well as public health reports. During the first year after the pods' release, P&G learned that toddlers were biting into the brightly colored, soft pods and making themselves sick, as were some older people suffering from cognitive disabilities or mental illness. A couple of years later, reports started to surface of teenagers attempting to eat the pods on a dare. Finally, in 2017 and 2018, news reports and social media showed young people were posting videos of themselves engaging in what they called the Tide Pod Challenge.[44]

Through media monitoring, P&G found that it clearly had a problem with small children innocently biting into the toxic product. In 2014 and 2015, the company found a low level of teen abuse of the pods but decided that it would do more harm than good in publicizing the abuse. When the Tide Pod Challenge surfaced and started going viral, the PR professionals working with P&G knew they needed to respond in a significant way.

Objectives. A successful PR campaign depends on a clear definition of what the client wants to accomplish. This requires having clearly measurable objectives for the campaign. It also involves working to solve the problem with changes to the product in addition to communicating with various publics. P&G's objectives over a multiyear period included the following:

- Maintaining the trust of its customers

- Encouraging safe storage and use of the pods

- Discouraging the attempted eating of the laundry pods

- Discouraging teens from engaging in stunts with the pods and sharing it on social media

- Preventing negative word of mouth through social media[45]

Programming. P&G put together several phases of product updates and communication to respond to the problems of safety and abuse.

- For the problem with toddlers biting into the pods, P&G decided early on to make changes to the product, most significantly by adding a strong bitter taste to the coating on the pods. The company also strengthened the effectiveness of the child-resistant packaging the pods came in. Finally, P&G improved and publicized the safety information that came with the product and was available online.[46]

- To deal with the social media-driven fad of posting videos of the Tide Pod Challenge, P&G made an online public service announcement featuring the New England Patriots' Rob Gronkowski telling teens, "No, no, no, no," about biting the pods. The company also worked with YouTube and Facebook to take down the Tide Pod Challenge videos. Additionally, the company launched a more conventional communication campaign to get across the idea that laundry pods were a cleaning product that needed to be treated carefully and with respect. Finally, P&G worked with an industry organization to produce educational materials to be distributed at colleges and universities.[47]

Evaluation. Evaluation of the campaign showed that it was effective in a number of ways. Analysis of poison control center reports showed that the number of accidental injuries from the pods stayed at a relatively stable number even as sales of the product drastically increased. The combination of communication and product changes was effective. The anti–Tide Pod Challenge campaign was also successful. The Gronkowski video was retweeted more than fifty thousand times and liked more than one hundred thousand times. Gronkowski also tweeted the video from his account, collecting an additional nine thousand retweets and twenty-nine thousand likes. The video also got more than forty-four thousand views on Facebook. In addition, the meme-like video inspired the production of several other videos that mocked the whole idea of biting into the pods. Efforts to work with YouTube and Facebook were also successful in getting the pod-eating videos removed from social media.[48]

Marketing professor Americus Reed praised the efforts by P&G and its agencies: "From the perspective of brand crisis assessment, I think Tide did everything that you're supposed to do. . . . You have to validate concerns. You have to show action. And you have to control the narrative."[49] By speaking out early and taking definitive action, P&G has protected one of its most important brands.

Stewardship. P&G made its response to the Tide laundry pod crisis part of its overall communication plan. Tide had always had safety warnings on its packaging and child-resistant packaging. The response simply had the company reinforcing its previous actions. When P&G's public relations agency produced the "No, no, no, no" video, it used Gronkowski, whom it had previously used in Super Bowl commercials, thus making the message part of its overall campaign. The company then continued to monitor social media and to respond to any reports of accidental or deliberate ingestion of the laundry pods.

The Publics

The term *public relations* seems to imply that there is a single monolithic group of people—"the public"—with whom the client needs to communicate. But, in reality, there are many such groups, since a public is any group of people who share a common set of interests.[50] These could include a company's employees, customers, stockholders, government regulators, or even people who live in the community where a new factory is to be built. In general, however, these publics can be divided into two main groups: internal publics and external publics.

An important audience for companies, and one that is easy to forget, is the internal public—the people who work for the company. Not only are good relations with employees important for morale and responsiveness, but employees are also an important informal source of news about the company. Through email, chat rooms, phone calls, and media contacts, employees are a central part of a company's communication environment.[51] For P&G, internal publics would include their management, employees, and communication professionals.

Corporations and other organizations use a variety of media to communicate with their internal publics. In the case of employees and managers, this communication can be done through something as simple as a weekly email or as elaborate as a four-color company newspaper. But internal communication is not limited to simple written materials. Web video, closed-circuit television, and even satellite conferences can be used to bring important news to employees. When the Three Mile Island nuclear plant suffered a major accident in 1979, a neighboring utility used videotaped programs to help its employees learn more about nuclear power. This form of education decreased the likelihood that the employees would spread misleading information when they talked with friends and family members.[52] Many organizations have started **intranets**, which are computer networks that are open only to members of that organization. Such a network can be used as an internal news source, a collection of corporate documents, or even an interactive communication channel.[53]

Whereas internal publics are well known to an organization, the range of external publics is far larger and relatively less well known. The press is one of the most important external publics because it is through the press that organizations communicate to many of their publics. Building a good relationship with the press is critical. Public relations practitioners as early as Ivy Lee and Edward Bernays found that working with the press during good times would lead to better relations during bad times.[54] Ian Monk, a British journalist turned PR practitioner, says that the relationships he built up as a reporter help him immensely in the PR business: "I deal with former colleagues and protégés all the time, and the relationships I have already built with them are invaluable."[55] For P&G, external publics would include customers, social media companies, and state legislators. The company communicated with people misusing the product one-on-one over social media and on a larger scale with online videos and websites. It also communicated using packaging materials.[56]

Media relations can be defined as two-way interactions with members of the press. Typically, media relations involve the placement of unpaid messages within the standard programming or news content of the medium. Good media relations, ultimately, are good relations with the public at large. A positive image with the press will often become a positive image with the general public. And a company that the public likes to begin with tends to weather a crisis much better than one that is disliked. According to PR practitioner Susanne Courtney, "Corporate PR is about building up an 'equity' account with groups like the investment community, customers, media, employees and others that a company may need to draw on in a time of need."[57] Presenting a company to the press is the most visible part of public relations. Press conferences, feature stories for the trade press, photographs, news releases, and streaming video are all tools that PR practitioners use to help manage the messages they send out to various publics through the media. Sometimes the press activities of an agency may be subtler. A PR firm may encourage a prominent leader to write an opinion piece favorable to its client's point of view for publication on the editorial page of a major newspaper. Or it may arrange for a reporter to interview a company president. Or it may simply provide useful background material to reporters.

For P&G, the company communicated with the press through communication professionals, such as spokespersons Jessica Mason and Petra Renck.[58] P&G CEO David Taylor also sent out a press release in which he wrote, "Let's all take a moment to talk with the young people in our lives and let them know that their life and health matter more than clicks, views and likes. Please help them understand that this is no laughing matter."[59]

Crisis Communication

Nothing tests an organization's PR ability more than a **crisis**, an event perceived by the public as being damaging to the organization's reputation or image. Al Tortorella, an executive with Ogilvy Public Relations Worldwide, says, "A crisis is what the media says it is."[60] What he means is that a problem can be defined as a crisis when it becomes public and begins to be perceived as a crisis. This means that it is possible to prevent a problem from becoming a crisis, but companies should never count on problems being kept secret; they need to have a plan for handling them if they turn into crises.

Boeing has long been the world's largest airplane manufacturer, but in 2018, it entered into a public relations crisis that could pose an existential threat to the company. Within a six-month

period, two of Boeing's 737 MAX aircraft crashed. The first was from Lion Air out of Indonesia that went into the ocean in October of 2018, killing all 189 people on board; the second was an Ethiopian Airlines plane that crashed shortly after takeoff, killing all 157 people on board.[61] Not long after, the Federal Aviation Administration (FAA) grounded all 737 MAX planes until the cause of the accidents was identified and any problems with the planes were solved.

Dennis Muilenburg, CEO of Boeing, took a week to speak out publicly following the second crash in March of 2019. Kara Alaimo, writing for Bloomberg, says that even if Muilenburg didn't have any answers, "He should have immediately expressed sympathy for the victims and their loved ones, then pledged to provide the public with more information as soon as possible." She goes on to say that companies must respond quickly to a crisis if they want to protect their reputation.[62]

Muilenburg eventually issued a pre-recorded apology twenty-six days after the second crash with an acknowledgment that sensors had malfunctioned in the same way on both of the 737 MAX planes. The slow response made airlines distrustful of Boeing, says crisis communication expert Helio Fred Garcia. This led the airlines to cancel orders for more of the planes. While the manufacturer acknowledged there were problems with the plane's flight software, it continued to defend the plane as having a solid design and suggested that the pilots might not have been following proper emergency procedures.[63]

▲ Airplane manufacturer Boeing has had a serious problem with its popular 737 MAX planes crashing, likely due to bad software in the control systems. Through slow and poorly thought out communication discussing the flaws, the company made its problem worse by making its various publics lose faith in the company..

As Boeing works to solve the software problems that apparently caused the planes to crash, it continues to have further public relations problems. In January of 2020, emails from Boeing employees were turned over to congressional investigators in which employees "mocked federal rules, talked about deceiving regulators and joked about potential flaws in the 737 MAX as it was being developed," according to the *New York Times*.[64]

As of this writing in May of 2020, the 737 MAX planes are still grounded globally, and Boeing is facing large numbers of cancelled plane orders (both from the 737 MAX problem and the difficulties the COVID-19 pandemic is presenting to the airlines).[65]

As the company goes forward, they have a range of people with whom they need to successfully communicate. At the most obvious level are the flying public who must be convinced that the planes are safe. But just as important are the governments that regulate their planes, airlines that buy their planes, and the pilots who must be willing to put their lives on the line flying the planes.

▲ Protesters gather at the Starbucks location in Center City, Philadelphia, Pennsylvania, in April 2018, where days earlier two Black men were arrested while waiting for a friend to arrive at the shop. The arrest prompted controversy after video of the incident became viral, and soon afterward Starbucks launched a crisis communication campaign. As part of its response, the company closed eight thousand stores in the United States for several hours to provide its employees with racial bias training.

Principles of Crisis Communication.

What should a company do when it faces a crisis? In general, it should communicate promptly and honestly with all its publics. More specifically, there are five principles of crisis communication:[66]

1. Be prepared—The most important principle is to have a crisis plan. For every company, there are certain things that are unlikely to happen but would be enormously damaging if they did. Such events could, if serious enough, put the existence of the company at risk by damaging its most important assets: its credibility and reputation.[67] Airlines should have a plan in the event of a plane crash; universities should have plans in the event of an academic or athletic scandal; a factory should be prepared for a chemical spill. These events might be unlikely to occur, but they can, and we should be prepared for them.

2. Be honest—One of the problems with lying is that liars are often caught. Cover-ups almost always end up being exposed, and the cover-up looks worse than the original problem. Instead, get the story out and over with quickly. President Richard Nixon's lies about the break-in at the Democratic Party's headquarters in the Watergate building created far more problems for him than did the actual burglary itself. For President Bill Clinton, lying about his relationship with Monica Lewinsky was infinitely more damaging to his reputation than was their affair.[68] Public relations consultant Bob Wilkerson says, "The truth is going to get out. I want it out of my lips. It's bad enough I've had an incident. It's even worse if it looks like I was trying to cover up."[69]

3. Apologize, and mean it—The company should respond with real action, not just words. In 2006, motorcycle manufacturer Yamaha got caught claiming that its new middle-weight sport bike had an engine that would rev up to 17,500 rpm. This was significantly higher than any competing motorcycle. It turned out that both the tachometer and the marketing department were a little optimistic because the motorcycle's true redline was 16,200 rpm. In real life, this discrepancy probably doesn't matter much. But when complaints about the overstated redline started surfacing on the internet, Yamaha made a simple decision to completely neutralize the crisis. The company sent a letter to everyone who had bought the motorcycle, apologized for the discrepancy, and offered to buy back the bike—including tax, setup, and interest—no questions asked.[70] In addition to having done the right thing, Yamaha squelched the crisis immediately and kept it from damaging the company's otherwise good reputation with motorcyclists.

4. Move quickly—Public relations critics say that how a company reacts in the first few hours after a crisis occurs will determine how the crisis is perceived from that point on. "All crises have a window of opportunity to gain control of 45 minutes to 12 hours," says crisis communication expert Paul Shrivastava.[71] Beyond that point, people will have already decided what they think about the crisis, and once they have made up their minds, they are reluctant to change them. In the past, companies could build their response around the time the morning newspapers were published or the nightly news was broadcast, but cable news channels and newspaper websites can publish news at any time, and social media will spread unfounded and unverified speculations that traditional news outlets might avoid. Bad news can also spread rapidly online.[72] Even when things move quickly, the company still needs to act carefully. Crisis management decisions are much more difficult to make than conventional decisions because they deal with things that have important consequences. They also need to be made quickly, while the whole world watches.[73]

5. Communicate with the press and other constituencies—These include the company's own employees and management, stockholders, government regulators, and customers, as well as the press. It was immediate communication with all publics that helped minimize Yamaha's problems with its advertising misinformation.

The application of these principles can be seen in two examples of crisis communication that are discussed in the following subsections. In the first, the company handled both the physical response and the communication response almost perfectly and emerged from the crisis with a good market position and a stronger image than it started with. In the second, mishandled communications led to a blot on the company's reputation that has endured for more than thirty years.

The Tylenol Scare. In September 1982, the consumer products giant Johnson & Johnson faced a crisis that could have destroyed one of its most important brands, Tylenol. Seven people in the

Chicago area died after taking cyanide-laced Extra Strength Tylenol capsules. The deaths set off what the *New York Times* called "the biggest consumer product scare in history."[74] (The perpetrator was never caught.) But Johnson & Johnson, with the help of PR agency Burson-Marsteller, managed to preserve the brand and the company's reputation with a combination of appropriate ethical action and good public relations.

The first thing the company did right was to be entirely honest with the media and public. The praise it subsequently received for its openness improved its image.[75] The next thing the company did right was to take immediate action in response to the tampering. As soon as Johnson & Johnson learned of the problem, it immediately stopped advertising the product and took it off the market in Chicago.[76] Throughout the crisis, Burson-Marsteller conducted nightly telephone surveys to measure public opinion. When those polls showed that the public feared that other Tylenol capsules might be tampered with, Johnson & Johnson took the product off the market nationwide.[77] The company was perceived as acting responsibly, and in fact it was acting responsibly.

Johnson & Johnson had clearly won the first PR battle and was being perceived as a responsible company that had been the victim of a vicious attack. The second battle was the campaign to rebuild trust in the Tylenol brand.

In November 1982, Johnson & Johnson announced the relaunch of Extra Strength Tylenol with the news that the product would now be sold in a triple-sealed container. Along with the expected marketing support, Johnson & Johnson engaged in an extensive PR campaign that utilized educational advertising, media appearances, and personal contacts.

The company sent out more than two thousand sales representatives to meet with major retailers and doctors. An advertising campaign informed people about the new tamper-resistant packaging, and Johnson & Johnson announced the relaunch of the brand in a thirty-city teleconference delivered via satellite. Simultaneously, it held a press conference that was attended by nearly six hundred journalists. Finally, Johnson & Johnson's CEO, James Burke, appeared on both *60 Minutes* and the daytime talk program *The Phil Donahue Show.*

The campaign was a success. Before the crisis, Tylenol had had a 37 percent share of the pain reliever market; this number dropped to 7 percent during the tampering scare. But within a month of the relaunch, Tylenol was back to 28 percent of the market, and it eventually regained its status as the industry leader.[78] Johnson & Johnson succeeded in protecting its brand and reputation for a number of reasons. First, few people blamed the company for the tampering; the fault appeared to lie with an individual beyond the span of the company's control. Second, the company acted quickly and responsibly in the interests of consumers. It was also open with its various publics, freely admitting what it did and didn't know. Finally, the company actively worked through the difficult situation and engaged the press by viewing it as an ally instead of as an adversary.

The *Exxon Valdez* and BP Oil Spills. On March 24, 1989, the oil tanker *Exxon Valdez* ran aground in Alaska's Prince William Sound, spilling 240,000 barrels of crude oil into the ocean. This oil soon washed up on shore, coating beaches, birds, and sea life in an environmentally sensitive area. Exxon spent more than $2 billion on the cleanup of the oil spill, but it still ended up with a tarnished image. Former reporter and network news president William Small notes that no company ever spent as much as Exxon did following the oil spill and still came out looking so bad.[79]

AP Photo/Jim Mone

▲ Johnson & Johnson had to handle the recall of millions of containers of Tylenol in 1982 after tainted capsules led to the deaths of seven people in the Chicago area.

▲ Despite the lessons learned after the catastrophic *Exxon Valdez* oil spill that had occurred twenty-one years earlier, the BP oil company seemed ill-prepared to deal with its wide range of publics following the 2010 Deepwater Horizon spill in the Gulf of Mexico.

Benjamin Lowy/Getty Images

Exxon's post-spill image problem had numerous causes that illustrate the difference between Johnson & Johnson's response to a crisis and Exxon's:

1. Perception of fault—Unlike the Tylenol tampering case, Exxon was considered at fault for the oil spill. Exxon's first problem was that it was the company's tanker that had run aground. It is difficult from a PR point of view to defend a company that has done something wrong.[80]

2. Lack of effective crisis plan—Exxon never developed a crisis plan for dealing with such a serious oil spill. Although Exxon shared responsibility with the Coast Guard for the lack of proper facilities, the fact that it did not have cleanup equipment in Alaska forced it to shoulder the blame after the spill.[81]

3. Failure to take immediate control—Exxon did not take immediate control of the flow of information. Not until a week after the spill did Exxon's CEO, Lawrence Rawl, make public comments. Meanwhile, numerous heartbreaking images of fouled wildlife started coming from the area. Almost all the press coverage of the spill was negative. In fact, Exxon made it actively difficult for reporters to get the company's point of view. The company's initial response was reportedly handled by a one-person PR office in Houston that had trouble coping with all the requests for information. Moreover, Exxon held all its news briefings for reporters in Valdez, Alaska, which had limited communication channels, instead of in a more accessible location, such as New York.[82]

4. Failure to accept responsibility immediately— Exxon didn't initially accept ethical responsibility for the spill and apologize. The company started off by trying to spread the blame, claiming that the Coast Guard, Alaska environmental officials, and the weather were also responsible. Whether or not these claims were valid, the press and the public saw Exxon as responsible. As one Alaska official put it, "I would suggest it's Exxon's tanker that ran up on the rocks."[83]

The final blow to Exxon's image came in the fall after the oil spill, when a memo from a company official was leaked to the press. The memo said that Exxon would end the cleanup effort whenever it chose to, that it would do nothing in the winter, and that it did not promise to return in the spring. The memo made the company look arrogant and uncaring.[84] Exxon eventually accepted responsibility for the oil spill and the cleanup, but by then the company's image was damaged irrevocably.

Even more that thirty years after the accident, the *Exxon Valdez* remained the standard to which environmental disasters were compared. Your author conducted a Google News search in May 2020 and found more than twenty new stories mentioning the *Exxon Valdez* oil spill published in a variety of news outlets.

When the Deepwater Horizon oil rig that was drilling for the London-based BP PLC exploded and sank in the Gulf of Mexico during the summer of 2010, triggering the world's largest oil spill, people immediately began comparing it to the Exxon spill. Critics contrasted BP's cleanup efforts to Exxon's, but they also compared public relations responses. Of course, the current media world, full of online social media, blogs, and multiple 24/7 cable channels, that faced

BP was very different from the one Exxon had to deal with. Yet the issues facing the two oil companies remained similar: Both tried to focus on technological issues rather than the effects on people, and both tried to shift blame away from themselves and onto others. But most of all, it appears that neither company had a plan to deal with a major oil spill.

Communications professor Kathleen Fearn-Banks told the *New York Times* blog *Greenwire*, "BP never had a plan in place for the worst-case scenario or they would have put it in place. I don't think it's a question of money. . . . They absolutely don't know what to do at all."[85] (This is a prime example of Secret 4—Nothing is new: Everything that happened in the past will happen again.)

Public Relations Goes Online

In the late 1980s and early 1990s, the PR industry acquired a new friend and enemy—the internet. The internet gave PR practitioners a new way to research and to distribute information, but it also provided a powerful new channel for the spreading of rumors that had the potential to develop into crises.

Among many other things, the internet has given the PR industry a new tool. Now companies can distribute press releases, background information, and photos to the media through email and websites. If a company's website or social media feed has a good reputation, it can become the first place reporters go to for information. Since reporters often start by going online to research articles, placing statistics and facts on a website can affect the way a company is covered.

Online has also given companies a means of bypassing the traditional media and communicating directly with various publics. Customers, stockholders, and even critics may go to a company's website in search of information. A website also ensures that a company's point of view is being presented the way the company intends it to be. Along with having a good website, companies need to make sure that their site will show up at the top of the list of search results for their company. It can be embarrassing if a company's critics appear above the company itself in a web search.[86] The internet also allows companies to find out what people are saying about them. Many organizations monitor social media to see what complaints and kudos are coming their way. Public relations practitioners may join chats and discussion groups to help shape what is being said about their clients. Of course, with millions of websites and social media accounts in existence, just finding out what is being said about a company can be a massive undertaking.[87] The internet gives critics access to the world without the checks and balances of traditional journalism. Prior to the internet, the only way to reach a broad, general audience was through the professional media, which might not always be a fan of your company but would probably treat you fairly. Many internet sites can be biased or don't engage in editorial oversight or fact-checking.

Crisis management consultant Jonathan Bernstein says that online media create significant new PR challenges. He writes that organizations need to consider the following:

Once a crisis hits the Internet, it can't be contained. It used to be that a local news story would stay local. Now, once a story is posted online by a newspaper or television station, it's gone national. The Internet makes it easy for critics to leak confidential information to reporters and others. This can include not just reports of confidential information, but also images of original documents or recordings of phone calls. In the absence of good information, rumors will flourish online. Of course, this problem isn't unique to the Internet. Anytime an organization doesn't provide creditable information, rumors and gossip will spread person-to-person to fill the gap.[88]

But the internet can accelerate the process by which rumors travel. These considerations perfectly illustrate the importance of Secret 5—All media are social.

Social Media—Interacting Directly With Your Publics

One of the great challenges that online media bring to the public relations business is that they are a continually moving target. Just when PR professionals think they have blogs and the web figured out, along comes the rise of social media such as Facebook, Twitter, Pinterest, and Instagram. Social media expert Pamela Seiple has written that PR professionals need to realize that social media are an opportunity for interactions with various publics, not just a channel to send out information. She notes that, through social media, stories about your company's brand can spread and mutate at a much faster rate than in the past: "If your company is not participating in social media today, it's missing an opportunity to spread its message and missing valuable—and even damaging—conversations that could be taking place about your brand." One of the most important uses for social media, according to Seiple, is building ongoing relationships with publics, including customers, vendors, opinion makers, and the press, something we discussed back in Chapter 10.[89]

In the winter of 2014, Kraft Foods was facing a minor shortage of Velveeta, its gooey cheese product that is a central ingredient in many sports fans' queso dip for Super Bowl and playoff watch parties. And with that, Kraft had a minor crisis on its hands. In some ways, it was a good problem to have—consumers wanted more of its iconic product than the company could supply, which demonstrated that its marketing efforts promoting making salsa and cheese dip were successful. But how would the company respond to its customers and stores? How would it interact with its publics?[90]

As word of the shortage spread, Twitter users started lamenting it. Among the early tweets collected by *People* magazine's *Great Ideas* blog were those pictured below.[91]

Kraft built on this social media response in a few ways. The company promoted the use of the #Cheesepocalype hashtag and built a Cheesepocalpyse website that mapped out reports of Velveeta shortages using Twitter reports from across the country. The company also used its Tumblr blog, which normally suggested humorous uses for Velveeta, to officially announce the shortage.[92]

So, what did Kraft and Velveeta get out of the Cheesepocalypse social media campaign? According to *Ad Age*'s Jack Neff, the brand got a huge amount of free publicity—publicity that was likely out of proportion to the "crisis." (The shortage was only of one packaging size.) But Kraft marketing executive Cannon Koo points out the #Cheesepocalypse hashtag helped the company identify its so-called "super-consumers," the people who consume the most of the brand. Super-consumers are the folks who make up about 10 percent of the buyers for any brand, but account for anywhere from 30 to 70 percent of the brand's sales. Information about how these super-consumers use Velveeta has helped the company increase its sales.[93]

Beyond the social media content itself, the active discussion drew a large amount of news media and blog coverage of Velveeta. Websites from Michigan to Alabama wrote about the Cheesepocalypse. The publicity generated was not always positive, with an Alabama news blog mocking the Kraft Velveeta shortage map, saying, "Hopefully folks in severe areas of Alabama and across the country will learn to function without Velveeta. If they use it to make dips, mac and cheese casseroles, melt on burgers etc., maybe they will rethink those recipes and substitute a healthier, real food option."[94]

Kraft's promotion of the Cheesepocalypse is at the core of how social media can be effectively used in public relations. Social media are not just new ways to push marketing information; they are a great tool for interacting with and getting to know the people who love a product best. In the case

▲ Fans of Velveeta got online to talk about the spot shortages of the product using hashtags on Twitter. One of the most popular ones was #VelveetaShortage.

of Velveeta, Kraft got to know the product's super-consumers better and helped them share recipes and new ways to use the soft cheese product. (Kraft's effective use of social media to interact with its consumers and turn what could have been a problem into a big plus for the brand is a great example of Secret 2—There are no mainstream media. In this case, interactive social media were far more important to Kraft than legacy media were, which also illustrates Secret 5—All media are social.)

Domino's: Fighting Back Against Social Media. It used to be that the worst media publicity a company had to worry about was a scathing story by an investigative journalist on a program such as *60 Minutes*. But today a corporation's worst PR nightmare can come from amateur-produced mobile phone video posted on video-sharing sites, such as YouTube, and then publicized through social media sites, such as Twitter. That's what Domino's Pizza discovered in April 2009 when two employees in Conover, North Carolina, posted a video showing one of them putting cheese up his nose and then placing it on a sandwich, blowing his nose on a sandwich, and farting on a sandwich. The other employee narrated the video with comments:

> In about five minutes it'll be sent out on delivery where somebody will be eating these, yes, eating them, and little did they know that cheese was in his nose and that there was some lethal gas that ended up on their salami.[95]

Once the video was posted on YouTube, word about it spread rapidly online through Twitter and other social media, and the video quickly racked up more than one million views.

The Domino's Pizza chain attempted to respond quickly and responsibly, but it may have spoken out too late in the rapidly changing online environment. The company responded publicly to the video within forty-eight hours of finding out about it, reportedly delaying its response to keep from drawing further attention to the video. Domino's eventual response included a YouTube video featuring company president Patrick Doyle, a complete cleaning of the store where the video was shot, and a revision of the company's hiring practices. The company also started a Twitter account with which to respond to customers.[96] Richard Levick of the PR firm Levick Strategic Communications told *Ad Age* that Domino's handled the crisis well after its initial delay in responding: "After the first 24 hours, they were largely textbook. They started a Twitter account, separated themselves from the villains, shut down the store, apologized, went to their demographic, went to YouTube—I think all of that is great."[97]

Levick said that companies need to do several things to prepare for online crisis communication:

- Identify your crisis team—This includes PR professionals, lawyers, and digital communication specialists.

- Imagine your nightmare scenarios—Make sure that you have the online resources so that when a crisis hits and people start searching for information, they come to your website first.

- Track the blogosphere and other social media—Make sure you know what people are saying about you, and be responsive to the people who are talking about your company.

- Don't wait—You have a very limited time to respond.[98]

Following the posting of the video, the two employees were identified by bloggers, arrested, and charged with distributing prohibited foods. Although the Domino's Pizza chain has largely recovered from the crisis created by the video, the North Carolina store where the video was shot has not. After closing briefly for cleaning following the posting of the video, the store closed for good five months later.[99] Note that while this story was covered by legacy media, it really moved through social media, thus illustrating Secret 5—All media are social. The Domino's story is also an illustration of Secret 6—Online media are mobile media.

IMC & Coca-Cola Freestyle

Coca-Cola is a big company. Really big. It has more than 450 brands in 200 countries selling more than 1.6 billion servings of their products a day. So how does a company that has built its reputation on serving you the exact same thing again and again anywhere in the world adapt to a culture where people want to have everything customized to their personal taste?[100]

Think about what happened back in 1985 when the company tried to change the basic formula for Coke, as we discussed in Chapter 12, and consumers responded with anger and frustration.[101] As one Coke executive put it, "We did not know what we were selling. We are not selling a soft drink. We are selling a little tiny piece of people's lives."[102] So how does a company address the problem of "Don't change anything" but also "Give me exactly what I want, even if it's different from everyone else"? How does Coke continue to make its drinks be a part of people's lives?

The answer to that question is the Coca-Cola Freestyle machine, though you may not recognize it by that name, which Coke has been promoting through integrated marketing communication (IMC). As you remember from Chapter 12, IMC is how companies reach their key audiences using advertising, public relations, sales promotion, and interactive media. While Coke has certainly used traditional advertising and PR techniques to promote this product, its big push has been to engage directly with consumers and their feelings toward it.

▲ The new Coca-Cola Freestyle vending machine allows consumers to mix different flavors to suit individual preferences, and businesses can also program custom drinks for their stores. The machines collect those data and send them over the internet back to beverage companies and restaurants to help them understand consumer habits.

When Scott Cuppari, global marketing director for Coca-Cola Freestyle, spoke to a group of public relations college students back in 2015, he largely drew blank stares from his audience when he mentioned the name. Then he said, "If I ask, 'Have you seen the touch-screen Coke machine where you get a hundred plus drinks?' then lots of hands shoot up."[103] He also referred to it as "the coolest drink machine," and the "Coke machine of the future." Even though few people knew the brand name, the product itself has been in development since at least 2005. David Butler, the company's vice president for global design back in 2009, had a remarkably simple goal for his project—he wanted to "sell more stuff." The Coca-Cola Freestyle machine was the solution to that goal.

The Freestyle machine does a variety of things. Instead of having the standard five-gallon bags of syrup, it instead has forty-six-ounce cartridges of highly concentrated drink mix. It also can track what people are drinking and when. As an example, during preliminary testing of the Freestyle machine, it showed that in an Atlanta location, Caffeine-Free Diet Coke was the third best-selling drink after 4:00 p.m.[104]

The Coca-Cola Freestyle machines are part of the so-called **Internet of Things**, that is, noncomputer devices that surround our lives that collect data and transmit them over the internet. The Freestyle machines, for example, can tell the company what students are drinking on campus right before popular television shows come on the air.[105] In addition to letting customers choose their own mixes and tracking what and when those mixes are bought, the Freestyle machines can give fast-food businesses their own custom drinks. In May 2017, burger chain Jack in the Box offered its own signature drink, "Jumpin' Jack Splash," a mix of "refreshing fruity flavors." What the Freestyle machine brings to the party is that there is no separate cartridge of syrup for each drink, only the recipe the machine needs to follow for mixing existing concentrates.[106] This capability also lets the machines dispense celebrity remixes. Olympic bobsled champion Elana Meyers Taylor had "Bobsled Rush" with "a smooth, delectable ride of cherry-raspberry sweetness" and "Bobsled Triumph," which let fans "celebrate a triumph over thirst with hints of orange and vanilla goodness."[107]

A new version of the machine that may be in stores by the time you read this will have Bluetooth connectivity so you can use the Coca-Cola Freestyle app on your phone to deliver your own custom drink. This connectivity will also let Coke know who is ordering each drink mix as well as what and when they are drinking it.

Toward the close of his speech to PR students, Cuppari pointed out that Coca-Cola Freestyle is about more than letting customers having it "just my way." It is also providing more choices to people who traditionally have not had choices. He notes that his diabetic son loves that Coca-Cola Freestyle gives him eighty separate choices of sugar-free drinks instead of just one or two from traditional fountain beverage machines.[108]

Public Relations and Society

This chapter has so far looked at public relations largely from the point of view of either PR firms or their clients. But it is also useful to look at it from the public's perspective. Public relations shapes the news we receive through newspapers, magazines, television, radio, and even the internet. In the form of "spin control," it attempts to shape our view of politicians and public policy, and it is also a central component of social movements.

Public relations plays a significant role in what is presented as news in the media. Sociologists David Altheide and Robert Snow argue that public relations is an integral part of the news business because most of the events—including crime and disaster reporting—covered by the media were created by PR practitioners to obtain coverage for their clients.[109] Just how much of the news originates with public relations?

Depending on how it is measured, anywhere from 40 to 90 percent of all news starts out as public relations. The *Columbia Journalism Review* tried to narrow this down by studying an issue of the *Wall Street Journal*. The researchers selected 111 stories from the paper. The companies mentioned in the stories were then contacted and asked to send a copy of their original press releases. The researchers found that 72 percent of the stories they were able to analyze were based almost exclusively on material from a press release. The study estimated that 45 percent of all the stories in the *Wall Street Journal* that day had been based on press releases, and that 27 percent of the actual news space was devoted to press releases.[110] The newspaper's executive editor estimated that 90 percent of the stories in the paper started with a company's announcement.

How does this happen? Think about a typical news day. Most news coming from Washington, DC, involves a press conference, a speech, a press release, or an event created specifically to be covered by the media. A scientific report on an environmental issue is published, and both environmentalists and industry groups hold press conferences to provide background information. A bank robber is arrested, and the police hold a media briefing. Even a basketball game will be reported using statistics provided by the sports information office and quotes from an official postgame interview session hosted for the media.

Although a lot of news may originate in PR efforts, executives and other individuals covered by the media sometimes have an exaggerated sense of what public relations can accomplish. One movie studio boss reportedly told an applicant for a PR position, "Your responsibility will be, if

Drew Angerer / Staff / Getty Images

▲ Press Secretary Kayleigh McEnany is responsible for making sure that President Donald Trump gets his message out to reporters in a way that portrays the administration in the best possible light.

I step out of my limousine and my pants fall down, you make sure that no one gets a photo to the press."[111] That's a guarantee no PR practitioner can make.

Along with the general public and media, the various levels of government are major external publics. Some PR firms have government relations departments, through which the firms represent their clients before the federal government, federal agencies, state legislatures, and even municipal bodies. As businesses face increasing government regulation, they have increased their efforts to work with government to shape legislation and regulations that are favorable to their interests.[112] Government relations includes lobbying for laws that will best meet the needs of the organization, as well as simply building goodwill with legislators and regulatory bodies. The Center for Responsive Politics, a nonpartisan research group that studies the influence of money on elections and public policy, estimates that, in 2017, there were 11,529 active, registered lobbyists in Washington who spent approximately $3.37 billion trying to influence the federal government on policy issues.[113] But that figure, as big as it is, only tells part of the story. Work by the Sunlight Foundation, another nonprofit focused on open government, found that for every dollar spent on reported lobbying, another dollar was spent on influencing activities that didn't meet the narrow legal definition of lobbying that was required to be reported. Thus, the total amount spent on "government relations" in 2013 would be estimated to be $6.44 billion.[114]

The government itself is a major practitioner of public relations. All elected federal officials have a press secretary, and many have a communications director. The various agencies themselves have PR offices. The role of the political press secretary is a challenging one, as the spokesperson must serve his or her boss while still dealing honestly with the press and the public. Sometimes this involves being evasive, as reporter Betsy Rothstein discusses somewhat satirically in Box 13.1. As one congressional press secretary told Washington, DC, paper the *Hill*,

> It is a matter of practice and experience and being able to steer a conversation toward issues you are looking to advance. . . . The golden rule is you don't answer the question you are asked, you answer the question you want to answer.[115]

Lanny Davis, who advised President Bill Clinton on damage control, says that when the press and the public are interested in an issue, the spokesperson only has one option: "Tell the truth, tell it all, tell it early, tell it yourself."[116] During the Monica Lewinsky sex scandal, President Clinton ignored the "tell the truth" rule, and the scandal stuck with him throughout the remainder of his second term in office.[117] Conservative opinion writer Jennifer Rubin writes that President Donald Trump's press secretary Sarah Huckabee Sanders suffered from severe credibility problems throughout her first year on the job for misleading the White House press corps. Sanders would routinely deny that senior advisers were going to be fired, right until the moment that they were fired. She also repeatedly denied that the president had knowledge of payments made on his behalf to adult film star Stormy Daniels, up until the point that President Trump acknowledged the payments. Rubin writes, "[I]t's not enough to tell the media and the country 'I didn't know better'—it's her job to know better and answer with authority."[118]

The U.S. military has been actively involved in public relations since World War I.

▼ BOX 13.1

"Tricks of the Trade" for Government Press Secretaries

Hill reporter Betsy Rothstein lists the following somewhat tongue-in-cheek "tricks of the trade" press secretaries use in dealing with reporters they do not want to talk to:

- Say "I will call you back" and then do not.
- Repeat the same phrase over and over.
- Try to talk the reporter out of writing the story.
- Act brusque and distant.
- Do not return phone calls until the day after the deadline.
- Talk in short sentences.
- Act as though you are in a hurry and need to get off the phone as soon as possible.

Source: Betsy Rothstein, "Capital Living: The Fine Art of Flacking," *Hill*, February 22, 2006.

Although the military's initial PR efforts were intended to recruit volunteers, they were also interacting with the press. Today the American Forces Radio and Television Service provides internal public relations in the form of radio and television broadcasts for service people overseas. There are also public information activities and community relations for the areas surrounding military bases.[119]

Spin Control: A More Personal Form of Public Relations

A new kind of public relations, known as spin control, has risen to the forefront since the 1970s. Rather than simply providing press releases, events, and background information, so-called spin doctors attempt to influence how a story will be portrayed and discussed. Newspaper columnist and former speechwriter William Safire suggests that the word *spin* came from the idea of spinning a yarn—that is, telling a story. It may also have a sports connotation, as in putting a spin on a tennis or billiard ball.[120]

John Scanlon, the late New York City publicist, was often cited as a top spin doctor. He was acquainted with many members of the national press corps and would call them when he considered a story unbalanced—or at least contrary to his client's interests. He also sent out frequent mailings to influential people in which he presented his point of view regarding events in the news. Scanlon's goal was not so much to give information to the press as to influence how stories were interpreted—that is, to control the spin put on them.

Here are some of the things spin doctors do:

- Selectively leak information in advance, hoping that reporters will pay more attention to it than to information received later.

- Contact members of the press immediately after an event to get them to adopt the desired spin or interpretation of the event.

- Push the idea that there are always two sides to every story. According to Scanlon, "What seems to be true is not necessarily the case when we look at it and we dissect it and we take it apart, and we turn it around and we look at it from a different perspective."[121]

Public Relations and the Civil Rights Movement

Not all public relations is practiced by professionals working for large agencies. As numerous political activists have shown, public relations can be an effective tool for social change as well. In 2005, the farm labor group Coalition of Immokalee Workers won a battle with Yum! Brands, the parent company of Taco Bell, over rights and pay for migrant workers. The laborers engaged in a work boycott against Taco Bell's produce farmers, held an extended hunger strike to draw attention to their cause, carried out a 230-mile protest walk, and organized a consumer boycott against Taco Bell. Despite the fact that migrant farmworkers are typically seen as a relatively powerless group, the workers were able to force a change in the fast-food business.[122]

Civil rights leader Martin Luther King Jr. displayed a brilliant understanding of public relations throughout the campaign to integrate the South in the 1950s and 1960s. King knew that it would take a combination of action, words, and visibility in the media to eliminate segregation laws and integrate lunch counters, restrooms, water fountains, and businesses. He practiced public relations in churches, hotel rooms, and even jail.

In 1963, King and the Southern Christian Leadership Conference, a civil rights group, wanted to do something highly visible that would let the entire nation see the evils of segregation. The goal of the campaign was to hold nonviolent demonstrations and acts of resistance that would force segregated stores and businesses to be opened to African Americans.

King and his colleagues picked Birmingham, Alabama, as one of their targets, in part because the city's police commissioner was Eugene "Bull" Connor. Connor was a racist who could be counted on to attack peaceful marchers. King's campaign was called Project C, for *confrontation*, and it included press conferences, leaflets, and demonstrations in front of hundreds of reporters and photographers. Starting in April 1963, African American volunteers marched in the streets, held sit-ins at segregated lunch counters, and boycotted local businesses. As the protests started, so did the arrests. The story was covered by the *New York Times* and the *Washington Post*. King and his colleagues knew that all the protests in the world would be ineffective if they were not covered by the press and that being beaten up by police would accomplish little if no photographers were present to document the event.

David Halberstam, who was a newspaper reporter in the South at the time, commented on the civil rights leaders' understanding of public relations:

> The key was to lure the beast of segregation out in the open. Casting was critical: King and his aides were learning that they needed to find the right venue, a place where the resistance was likely to be fierce, and the right local official to play the villain. Neither was a problem: King had no trouble finding men like . . . Bull Connor, who were in their own way looking for him, just as he was looking for them.[123]

On Good Friday, King and Ralph Abernathy joined in the marching so that they would be arrested. While King was in jail, he wrote the "Letter from Birmingham Jail," which was smuggled out and published as a brochure. His eloquent words, given added force by having been written in jail, were reprinted across the country.

After King was released, he and his followers raised the stakes. Adults would no longer march and be arrested; instead, children became the vanguard of the movement. The images, which appeared in print media throughout the world, were riveting. In his biography of King, Stephen Oates wrote, "Millions of readers in America—and millions overseas—stared at pictures of police dogs lunging at young marchers, of firemen raking them with jet streams, of club-wielding cops pinning a Negro woman to the ground."[124] King faced criticism for allowing young people to face the dangers of marching in Birmingham. But he responded promptly by criticizing the white press, asking the reporters where they had been "during the centuries when our segregated social system had been misusing and abusing Negro children."[125] Although there was rioting in Birmingham and King's brother's house was bombed, the campaign was ultimately successful. Business owners took down the "WHITE" and "COLORED" signs from drinking fountains and bathrooms, and African Americans could eat at the lunch counters and sit on the buses. The successful protest in Birmingham set the stage for the march on Washington in August 1963, during which King gave his famous "I Have a Dream" speech.[126]

The use of public relations techniques to advance civil rights certainly did not end in the 1960s. Professional athletes have been speaking out through the media, wearing jerseys with topical messages, and kneeling during the national anthem, along with other peaceful, yet visible protests to bring attention to civil rights issues. On August 26, 2020, the Milwaukee Bucks brought the National Basketball Association playoffs to a halt by refusing to take the court for a game against the Orlando Magic to protest the police shooting of Jacob Blake in nearby Kenosha, Wisconsin. The Milwaukee Brewers also refused to play their Major League Baseball game against the Cincinnati Reds the same day. This boycott/strike quickly spread, with multiple NBA, MLB, Women's NBA and Major League Soccer games being postponed. Bucks guard George Hill, reading a team statement to the press, said, "When we take the court and represent Milwaukee and Wisconsin, we are expected to play at a high level, give maximum effort and hold each other accountable. We hold ourselves to that standard, and in this moment we are demanding the same from lawmakers and law enforcement."[127]

The message in support of Black Lives Matter was not just coming from players. Buck's senior vice president Alex Larsy tweeted out, "Some things are bigger than basketball. The stand taken today by the players and org shows that we're fed up. Enough is enough. Change needs to happen. I'm incredibly proud of our guys and we stand 100% behind our players ready to assist and bring about real change."[128]

CHAPTER REVIEW

CHAPTER SUMMARY ▶▶

Public relations developed out of the press agentry of the late 1800s. Publicity firms used one-way communication, deceptive techniques, and bribery. By the beginning of the twentieth century, large corporations such as railroads and utilities realized that they needed to develop more sophisticated relationships with the press if they hoped to control their images.

Ivy Lee and Edward L. Bernays are generally considered to be the founders of public relations as a profession. Lee was among the first press agents to recognize that dealing with the press promptly and truthfully was the best way to obtain positive coverage for his clients. In 1906, he codified this approach in his "Declaration of Principles." Bernays wrote the first book about public relations and taught the first college course on the subject.

During World War I, the federal government realized the value of public relations and used a variety of techniques to build support for U.S. participation in the war. Public relations continued to grow as a profession as businesses became increasingly regulated and the public began to distrust both businesses and the government.

Public relations can be seen as performing three main functions: informing, persuading, and integrating (bringing together)

publics, both internal and external. Among the most important publics are the media. Effective public relations generally includes both communication and action. The PR process consists of five steps of the ROPES model: (1) **researching** the problem or opportunity, (2) setting measurable **objectives**, (3) **programming** the communication activities needed to achieve the objectives, (4) **evaluating** the success of the activities, and (5) successfully **stewarding** the relationships created through the campaign. Successful companies work at communicating with their internal, external and media publics during both good times and times of crisis. In order to survive crises, companies must be prepared, be honest, apologize sincerely when needed, move quickly, and communicate with their various publics.

The rise of the internet and instantaneous communication not controlled by major media has forced the public relations industry to speed up its rate of response to problems and to deal with a wider range of problems. Like advertising, public relations can make effective use of the integrated marketing communication process. Public relations is used by a wide range of organizations, including corporations, the government, and activist groups.

KEY TERMS ▶▶

public relations (PR)   318
public   318
press agentry   318

engineering consent   320
opinion leadership   322
intranets   326

media relations   326
crisis   326
Internet of Things   334

REVIEW QUESTIONS ▶▶

1. How did Procter & Gamble use public relations to fight the accidental and deliberate misuse of Tide laundry packs?

2. How does professional public relations differ from press agentry?

3. Name and explain two ways to mess up responding to a crisis affecting your organization.

4. How does interacting with your publics through social media differ from going through legacy media?

5. How did Martin Luther King Jr. make good use of public relations techniques during the Good Friday march in Birmingham, Alabama?

6. How did Coca-Cola use IMC techniques to deal with consumer demand for more choices of beverages?

PART V

REGULATION
AND CONTROL
OF THE MEDIA

MEDIA LAW

Free Speech and Fairness

Pittsburg, Kansas, is not a city that shows up much in the national media. Before the first week of April 2017, there had only been about four mentions of the city in the *Washington Post* during the past decade. One was when Pulitzer Prize–winning poet James Tate died in 2015. (Tate got his bachelor's degree from Kansas State College there in 1965.) Before that, it was when Pittsburg State University wide receiver John Brown was drafted by the Arizona Cardinals in 2014. There were also brief mentions of the death of a judge who had been born there and the fact that an unnamed Fortune 500 CEO had been born there.

But on Wednesday, April 5, 2017, the most read story on the *Washington Post*'s website was about a group of Pittsburg High School (PHS) students who discovered through dogged journalistic research that their high school's newly hired principal had questionable educational credentials. That story, reported in the school paper, the *Booster Redux*, on Friday, March 31, resulted in the new principal, Amy Robertson, resigning her post following a school board meeting on Tuesday evening of that week.

Seventeen-year-old Connor Balthazar told the *Washington Post* that "there were some things that just didn't quite add up" about Robertson. Reporting on the story was done by a team of six high school students.[1] In their story, the students wrote,

> The Booster Redux Staff typically introduces each new administrator at PHS with a news story. During the interview process with Robertson, the Booster staff found inconsistencies in Robertson's credentials. The staff presented these concerns to Pittsburg Community School superintendent Destry Brown, who encouraged the Booster reporters to reach out to Robertson.
>
> On March 16, the Booster staff held a conference call with the incoming principal. Booster adviser Emily Smith and Brown were also present. During the call, Robertson presented incomplete answers, conflicting dates and inconsistencies in her responses.
>
> After the conference call interview, the staff conducted further research online and by phone interview to confirm her credentials. These are the findings.[2]

And what a set of findings they were. Robertson claimed to have a master's degree and PhD from Corllins University in Stockton, California, but the students' research showed no signs in property records that there had ever been a university by that name in Stockton, no U.S. Department of Education records documenting the university, no sign of an active website of the university, and an online article that referred to Corllins University as a diploma mill. Robertson also claimed to have a Bachelor of Fine Arts degree in theater arts from Tulsa University. While TU is a very real school, the students found that it has never offered a BFA in theater.

PHS senior Trina Paul, part of the reporting team, told the *Kansas City Star* that the students were just concerned about Robertson's credentials. "She was going to be the head of our school, and we wanted to be assured that she was qualified and had the proper credentials. We stumbled on some things that most might not consider legitimate credentials."[3]

In the end, the students published the story and nervously awaited the results. The school superintendent dismissed the students' story the next day, saying the district had hired the best candidate. But then . . . the school board scheduled a special meeting to discuss the story. The *Wichita Eagle* reported that award-winning journalism teacher Emily Smith, the students' adviser, was even concerned she might be fired.[4]

Instead, the word came out that the new principal had resigned. When the school board met, most of the meeting was done in executive session to discuss the resignation. But when it was over, a parent stood up and told the board that the students were owed an answer about what happened because they were the ones who had found out the new principal was being deceptive.

Smith had to recuse herself on this story, she told the *Washington Post*, because she had been on the search committee that had hired Robertson.[5] But the students did receive help from a range of state and national journalists and experts. Smith is understandably proud of what her high school students have accomplished: "Everybody kept telling them, 'stop poking your nose where it doesn't belong.' They were at a loss that something that was so easy for them to see was waiting to be noticed by adults."[6]

Once their story was published and Robertson resigned, PHS journalism students started getting national attention for their work. The following day, the students got calls from *Good Morning America*, the *Washington Post*, and the *New York Times*. There were tweets and retweets from a number of top national journalists including *Boston Globe* Spotlight team reporter Todd Wallack, *Washington Post* executive editor Marty Baron, and *Washington Post* political reporter David Fahrenthold.[7] The students were even invited to be the guests of the *Huffington Post* at the White House Correspondents' Association dinner.

In the end, the superintendent bought pizza for the students and thanked them for their work. Smith had told the students, "This is probably going to be the hardest thing you do in your life because you're doing the right thing and it's not always easy and it's not always popular."[8] During a summer high school journalism camp at Kansas State University, the paper's adviser said, "I would say some people were really supportive, and they think it was great and they support the kids. [But] most people were really mad because they said we made everyone look really bad."[9]

In many states, the school superintendent would have had the authority to stop the students from publishing the story as a result of the U.S. Supreme Court's *Hazelwood School District v. Kuhlmeier* decision that ruled that high school newspapers have only minimal protection with the First Amendment. Kansas high school students, however, are also protected by the Kansas Student Publications Act that puts tight restrictions on when administrators can censor student papers.[10] (You can read more about this later in the chapter in the section on free speech and students.)

In this chapter, we look at the laws that both protect and restrict our privacy, our freedom of speech, and our freedom of the press. We start by examining the First Amendment to the U.S. Constitution, which established a minimally restrictive system of media law. We then look at media law in terms of how it protects individuals through laws governing libel, invasion of privacy, and the right to a fair trial. Next, we look at the controls that can be placed on the press, including requirements that the press tell the truth, restraints on publication, and regulation of obscenity. We then look at how the broadcast industry is regulated by the government in a somewhat stricter fashion than the rest of the media. Finally, we close out with regulation of online media.

The Development of a Free Press

Stay up to date on the latest in media by visiting the author's blog at **ralphehanson.com**

The First Amendment to the U.S. Constitution is at the core of all U.S. laws concerning the media. It simply says that

> Congress shall make no law respecting an establishment of religion, or prohibiting the free exercise thereof; or abridging the freedom of speech, or of the press; or the right of the people peaceably to assemble, and to petition the Government for a redress of grievances.

Although the First Amendment states that "Congress shall make no law," the U.S. Supreme Court has long upheld certain limits on both speech and the press. People do not have "the right to say anything they please, any way they please, anywhere or under any circumstances."[11] Let us look at how the notion of freedom of expression and of the press has developed and what regulations and restrictions the government can place on that freedom.

According to First Amendment scholar Fred Cate, the First Amendment is an essential component of a representative democracy because a democracy cannot function unless the people have the right to discuss matters of public concern freely and openly. It is through free and open speech that change takes place within society. The First Amendment does not just protect popular or conventional ideas; it protects all forms of expression, including offensive ideas. Even some level of false expression is allowed because the truth is not always clear. Thus, the solution to the expression of dangerous ideas is to permit more, rather than less, communication.[12] The most basic right guaranteed by the First Amendment is freedom of speech without constraint by the government. The right of freedom of the press is an extension of the rights of individuals to express themselves.[13] In addition to its explicit mention of the press and speech, the First Amendment provides a wide range of other rights, including freedom of religious practice, the right to assemble, and the right to petition the government.

The Granger Collection, New York

▲ The Bill of Rights, ratified in 1791, established protection for all forms of expression, not just popular ideas.

The Roots of American Free Speech

Speech was not always free in the American colonies. Colonial newspapers were published under licenses granted by the British colonial government, with the phrase "Published by Authority" printed at the top of each edition. This notice implied that the British government approved of what was being published, and editors violated that approval at their peril. For example, John Peter Zenger and his wife, Anna Catherine Zenger, were independent editors, printers, and small-business owners in the American colonies. Zenger started his *New York Journal* in 1733 and, like many editors of that time, was soon in trouble with the authorities. Zenger accused Governor William Cosby of political corruption for replacing New York Supreme Court justices with whom he disagreed.[14] The governor retaliated by throwing Zenger in jail on a charge of seditious libel (writing things critical of the government). When the case went to trial in 1735, Zenger, who was represented by prominent lawyer Andrew Hamilton, defended himself against the charge by claiming that what he had written was the truth. The shocked judge argued that the truth of the statement did not matter. But Zenger and Hamilton refused to back down, and the jury found Zenger not guilty, thus establishing truth as a defense against libel. While her husband was in prison, Anna Catherine took over the operation of the paper, thus becoming one of the first women newspaper publishers in the country.[15]

Limits on Free Speech

In 1791, the states ratified the first ten amendments to the Constitution, commonly known as the Bill of Rights. But making the Bill of Rights a part of the Constitution did not end the government's efforts to limit a person's right to freedom of expression. In 1798, just seven years after the ratification of the Bill of Rights, Congress passed, and President John Adams signed, the **Alien and Sedition Acts**. These laws punished anyone who published "false, scandalous, or malicious writings against the government of the United States, or either house of the Congress of the United States, or the President of the United States" with substantial fines, jail time, or deportation. The notoriously thin-skinned President Adams was a member of the Federalist Party, and the laws were passed primarily to silence supporters of his opponent Thomas Jefferson, a member of the Democratic Republican Party. Among those prosecuted under the acts was James Callender, a journalist who supported Jefferson and had exposed Federalist Treasury Secretary Alexander Hamilton's extra-marital affair with Maria

Reynolds. (Yes, the musical Hamilton even finds its way into the media law chapter.) Another was Vermont Congressman Matthew Lyon, who wrote that President Adams was "swallowed up in a continual grasp for power, in an unbounded thirst for ridiculous pomp, foolish adulation and selfish avarice."[16] All those charged under the acts were eventually pardoned by Jefferson when he became president.[17]

Sedition became a crime once again during World War I, when more than 1,900 people were prosecuted under sedition statutes for criticizing the government, the military draft, or U.S. involvement in the war. Following the war, some but not all of the anti–free speech provisions were repealed.[18] Then, in 1940, during the run-up to U.S. involvement in World War II, Congress passed the Smith Act, which made it a crime to advocate the violent overthrow of the government or to belong to a group that advocated the violent overthrow of the government. The central purpose of the act was to suppress the Communist Party of the United States.[19]

The Post-9/11 Era. Forty-five days after the September 11, 2001, terrorist attacks, Congress passed the USA PATRIOT Act, its name an acronym that stands for "Uniting and Strengthening America by Providing Appropriate Tools Required to Intercept and Obstruct Terrorism."[20] The PATRIOT Act follows in the tradition of previous wartime laws in changing the balance point between maximizing our civil liberties and protecting the United States from perceived threats. The act is one more example of Secret 4—Nothing is new: Everything that happened in the past will happen again.

The law permitted a host of activities by the Justice Department, including the placing of wiretaps and increased domestic surveillance, and it also widened the definition of what constitutes terrorism. Most of the objections to the act fall under the Fourth Amendment to the U.S. Constitution, which protects against "unreasonable searches and seizures."[21] But there are First Amendment implications as well. One of the biggest is that Section 215 of the act allows the Federal Bureau of Investigation (FBI) to examine individuals' media use by obtaining "library records, health-care records, logs of Internet service providers and other documents and papers."[22]

Jameel Jaffer of the American Civil Liberties Union (ACLU) says the fact that people may be watched can keep them from looking at things they might otherwise view: "If people think that the government is looking over their shoulders to see what books they are reading or what Web sites they are visiting, many are not going to read those books or visit those Web sites."[23] The law also makes it a crime for anyone to provide "expert assistance" to any group designated as a terrorist organization, even if there is no evidence that the advice leads to further terrorism.

▲ The National Security Agency has used a broad understanding of the PATRIOT Act Section 215 to justify collecting voice mail and email data on almost any U.S. citizen.

Most controversial was the provision that people served with PATRIOT Act warrants could not tell anyone that they had received them. That is, anyone served with a PATRIOT Act warrant lost his or her free speech rights when it came to discussing the warrant. Since the act was originally passed in 2001, it has undergone changes that have scaled back the limits on free speech. The most important of these changes is that people served with warrants under the act now have permission to consult an attorney.

The PATRIOT Act has also been used to identify journalists' confidential sources. Brian Ross and Richard Esposito of ABC News wrote in their blog, the *Blotter*, that the federal government was tracking the phone numbers they called after they reported on the Central Intelligence Agency's (CIA's) secret prisons in Romania and Poland.[24] Ross charges that this tracking of his calls was done under Section 215 of the act. "It's a provision of the Patriot Act designed to fight terrorism—and it's being used to fight journalists," Ross said. "That's really what it comes down to."[25]

While there had been a variety of reports about potential misuse of Section 215 similar to those from Ross, the world learned the extent of the collection of "metadata" in a series of stories from the *Guardian* newspaper based on documents leaked by former National Security Agency (NSA) contractor Edward Snowden. As you may recall from Chapter 2, Snowden revealed that the NSA had been collecting bulk information that showed "who called whom, the date, time, duration and frequency of calls for millions of Americans who are not suspected of any crimes."[26] These data do not include the content of the calls, but just the metadata alone could establish someone's political activities, health issues, or personal relationships. The PATRIOT Act underwent a fairly substantial revision with the passage of the USA FREEDOM (Uniting and Strengthening America by Fulfilling Rights and Ending Eavesdropping, Dragnet-Collection and Online Monitoring) Act in June 2015. Among the changes was an end to the NSA's practice of bulk collection of phone data of millions of Americans. A coalition of liberal Democrats and libertarian-thinking Republicans passed the revisions.[27]

Libel and Protection of Individuals

Although the press is censored only rarely in the United States, individuals do have a right to protect themselves from being harmed by the media. Rather than exercising prior restraint to prevent the press from printing or broadcasting potentially damaging material, U.S. law allows individuals to sue the press for any damage they feel they have suffered. Protection of individuals from the press focuses on three main issues: libel, invasion of privacy, and the right to a fair trial.

In general, the press cannot be restricted from publishing something, but it can be held accountable for what it does publish. This is accomplished primarily through libel law. **Libel** is any published statement that unjustifiably exposes someone to ridicule or contempt. In general, for a statement to be libelous, it needs to contain three elements: defamation, identification, and publication.

1. Defamation—To defame is to damage a person's reputation in some way. This can involve calling someone, for example, a criminal, a communist, or a drunk. If a student newspaper ran an article falsely accusing Dr. Smith, a journalism professor, of selling an A grade in his Introduction to Mass Communication class for $100, Dr. Smith would probably have been defamed.

2. Identification—No person can sue for libel unless the defamation can be proved to apply to him or her; another reader or viewer must agree that the comment applies to the person who is suing. Just leaving that person's name out of the article isn't enough. If a person can be identified, he or she can sue. Going back to the example of Dr. Smith, suppose that the article did not mention his name but merely said that the teacher of the Introduction to Mass Communication course at Big State University was taking bribes for grades. If Dr. Smith was the only person teaching the course at Big State U, he would have been identified.

3. Publication—To be libelous, the statement must be published or broadcast and seen by someone other than the author and the person who was defamed.[28]

How can the media defend themselves against libel suits? After all, much of what gets printed or broadcast in the news has the potential to damage a person's reputation. There are at least two approaches. When an article is genuinely false and defamatory, the media look to a landmark 1960s case, *New York Times Co. v. Sullivan*, which is discussed later in this chapter. First, let us look at approaches that are used when the material in an article is true, privileged, or a statement of opinion.

Truth, Privilege, and Opinion

The Zenger case from the early 1700s established truth as an absolute defense against libel. It is not always an effective defense, however, because the truth is not always clear. In the article about Dr. Smith, it may well be true that a student accused Dr. Smith of selling grades, but it would be much more difficult to prove that Dr. Smith actually sold the grades.

Asserting privilege is a much better defense than truth in a libel case. As a legal defense against libel, **privilege** is the idea that statements made in government meetings, in court, or in government documents cannot be used as the basis for a libel suit. What is more, any fair and accurate report of what happened at the meeting, in court, or in a government document is also protected from libel.[29] For example, the privilege defense protects a reporter who is covering a murder trial. The journalist is privileged to give a fair and accurate report of any testimony, no matter how inflammatory, without fear of being sued.

Opinions are neither true nor false, so a statement of opinion cannot be used as the basis of a libel suit. Calling someone an idiot or a jerk would probably not be considered libelous; both words are expressions of opinion. Editorial cartoons, parodies, and reviews are all generally considered to be opinion and are given broad latitude in their protection from libel. But remember that, to be protected, statements need to be clear expressions of opinion. An article that states, "Dr. Smith, in my opinion, is selling grades," would most likely be considered libelous: Claiming that a fact is a statement of opinion does not protect the writer.

New York Times Co. v. Sullivan

The defenses of truth, privilege, and opinion arise from the notion that the press has published something it is entitled to publish. But there are times when the press gets a story wrong, runs an advertisement containing factual errors, or makes a mistake in a headline. In these cases, the press is likely to look to the 1964 case of *New York Times Co. v. Sullivan*.[30]

The 1960s were a period of racial unrest in the United States, marked by protests and rioting over efforts to integrate schools, lunch counters, and other public facilities, with white segregationists claiming that the national media were interfering with local issues that were none of their business.[31]

On March 29, 1960, a civil rights group ran a full-page ad in the *New York Times* to raise money for Dr. Martin Luther King Jr. The ad included the names of numerous well-known individuals, such as Harry Belafonte, Marlon Brando, Nat King Cole, Jackie Robinson, and former first lady Eleanor Roosevelt, and was paid for by the Union Advertising Service for the Committee to Defend Martin Luther King and the Struggle for Freedom in the South.[32] Among the sections of the ad that created trouble was the following:

> In Montgomery, Alabama, after students sang "My Country 'Tis of Thee" on the State Capitol steps, their leaders were expelled from the school, and truck-loads of police armed with shotguns and teargas ringed the Alabama State College Campus. When the entire student body protested to state authorities by refusing to reregister, their dining hall was padlocked in an attempt to starve them into submission.[33]

This passage contained several false statements. The students did not sing "My Country 'Tis of Thee," and the police did not literally surround the building.

Although Montgomery police commissioner L. B. Sullivan, who was in charge of the police department, was not mentioned by name in the advertisement, he felt that any accusations against the police department were accusations against him. He also charged that the advertisement contained numerous factual errors. He asked the *Times* to retract the ad, but the paper responded that it did not see how the ad reflected negatively on Sullivan's reputation. So Sullivan filed suit, joining eleven other libel cases that were pending against the *Times*.[34] In the initial three-day trial, the *Times* admitted that the ad contained errors, but friends of Sullivan testified that they did not think less of him as a result because they did not believe what they had read in the ad. Nevertheless, the judge instructed the jury that they could presume that the material in the ad was libelous and that it had damaged Sullivan's reputation. The jury returned a verdict in favor of Sullivan, awarding him $500,000 in damages. The verdict was upheld by the Alabama Supreme Court.

The case then went before the U.S. Supreme Court, which reversed the lower courts with a sweeping ruling in favor of the *Times*. The Court could have overturned the lower court judgment simply by ruling that Sullivan had not been identified in the ad or by saying that Sullivan's reputation had not suffered any damage. But it decided instead to use the case to consider whether the public had the right to criticize the government.[35] The Court ruled that it was not enough to protect true statements; false statements against public officials made in good faith should also be protected.

records of rights.org

▲ This is the ad from the Committee to Defend Martin Luther King and the Struggle for Freedom in the South that was printed in the *New York Times* that led Police Commissioner L. B. Sullivan to sue the paper for libel.

With the Sullivan case, the Court established a new standard for libel. It ruled that public officials would have to show that the media had acted with **actual malice** and displayed a reckless disregard for the truth or falsity of a published account. In the Sullivan case, the Court ruled, the paper had not acted with malice; at worst it had been negligent. One of the goals of the Court's judgment was to help protect against self-censorship—to prevent publications from being so afraid of making a mistake that they would not print anything that might be controversial. The Court was attempting to balance the right of a public official to protect his or her reputation versus a critic's right to speak out against that official.

While the Sullivan case has been considered the standard for charges of libel by public officials since 1964, United States Supreme Court Justice Clarence Thomas wrote in an opinion in February 2019 that the court's decisions in the case "were policy-driven decisions masquerading as constitutional law." He wrote that instead states should be allowed to decide on their own how to strike "an acceptable balance between encouraging robust public discourse and providing a meaningful remedy for reputational harm."[36] Thomas did not get any support from his fellow justices for that opinion.

Libel and Public Figures

In 1967, the Supreme Court extended the actual malice standard to apply to public figures as well as public officials. The theory behind this extension of the Sullivan standard was that these people have voluntarily exposed themselves to public scrutiny and thus to the threat of being libeled.

The standard was settled by the case of *Gertz v. Robert Welch Inc.* in 1974.[37] The John Birch Society's magazine had run an article accusing Elmer Gertz of being a communist. The question was whether Gertz, an attorney, was a public figure. The Court ruled that private individuals deserve more protection because they have not voluntarily submitted themselves for public attention and because they are less able than public figures to defend themselves.[38]

Libel and Social Media

In general, there are few differences in the standard for libel between legacy media and social media. The big difference is that legacy media have a legal staff to advise writers when they are writing or broadcasting something that could be problematic; people on Twitter or Facebook rarely do. Also, as attorney Ellyn Angelotti points out, social media like Twitter make publishing potentially defamatory content much easier.[39] Finally, while newspapers or broadcasters are typically responsible for what they publish because they actively control what goes out in their name, social media sites themselves are not responsible for what people post using their service. In January 2014, the first Twitter libel case to be settled dealt with a tweet posted by singer/celebrity Courtney Love that suggested one of her attorneys had been "bought off." The jury in the case ruled in favor of Love and against her attorney. The jury ruled that Love's tweet contained false information but that she didn't know that it was false.[40] (Note to students: Don't assume that other juries would rule the same way!) Be sure to look back at Chapters 9 and 10 for more about online and social media legal issues.

Recent Libel Cases

The most high-profile libel case in the United States in recent years was against *Rolling Stone* magazine for a story about an alleged gang rape by members of a fraternity on the University of Virginia campus and the supposed callous response by university administrators. The magazine and journalist Sabrina Rubin Erdely were sued by a university administrator, a group of fraternity members, and three members of the fraternity. The associate dean who had been accused in the story of being indifferent to the rape allegations in the story received an award of $3 million, the fraternity was awarded $1.65 million, and the fraternity members received an undisclosed amount. Erdely testified during the trial that after the story was published in 2014 she no longer trusted her source for the story and the magazine should issue a retraction.[41]

Nicholas Sandmann, a student at Covington Catholic High School in Covington, Kentucky, sued multiple news outlets, including the *Washington Post* and CNN, for libel for how he was portrayed in stories about an interaction he had with a Native American activist on the steps of the Lincoln Memorial during an antiabortion march in 2019. Sandmann was in a group of students, many of whom were wearing red "Make American Great Again" hats, when he encountered Native American activist Nathan Phillips. Videos and stories about the encounter prompted a national debate over what happened when the two met. Phillips said that Sandmann had blocked him from walking forward. Sandmann said he had acted respectfully and had not blocked Phillips. CNN reported in January 2020 that it had settled with Sandmann for an undisclosed amount. The *Washington Post* reports that news organizations in the past have settled defamation claims rather than take them to trial because the expenses of the cases can be so high. The federal judge in the suit against the *Post* had initially dismissed all thirty-three of the published statements in the lawsuit, but he eventually reinstated three of them. As of this writing, the case had not gone to trial.[42,43]

▲ United States Supreme Court Justice Clarence Thomas wrote in an opinion in February of 2019 that the court's decision in *New York Times Co. v. Sullivan* "were policy-driven decisions masquerading as constitutional law."

Pool / Getty Images

Invasion of Privacy

What magazines do you subscribe to? What books do you check out from the library? How much money do you have in the bank? What movies have you rented from the video store? What do you buy at the grocery store? Why did you see the doctor last week? Are you uncomfortable with these questions? Most people would like to keep such information private.[44] With all this information potentially available, what legal expectation do people have of maintaining a private life in the information age? The Constitution offers no explicit protection of privacy, but a right to privacy has been implied, and the issue shows up in several ways. The "freedom to associate" clause of the First Amendment prevents the government from requiring a group to release its membership list to the public. It also protects the right of an individual to possess any type of literature in the privacy of his or her own home. The Fourth Amendment limits searches and seizures, and the Fourteenth Amendment limits disclosure of personal information. In cases involving privacy, the courts try to balance an individual's right to protect his or her privacy and reputation versus the public's interest in a news or feature story that the press might publish.

In general, legal protection exists for four types of invasion of privacy:

1. Intrusion

2. Embarrassment

3. False light

4. Misappropriation[45]

Intrusion is invasion of privacy by physical trespass into a space surrounding a person's body or onto property under his or her control. Reporters and photographers are not allowed to go onto private property to collect news without the permission of the owner, but in some cases, the newsgathering function and the right of the public to know can conflict with the rights associated with private property. For example, a reporter and a photographer were sued for intrusion when they pretended to be patients at a private California medical clinic that was being run by a plumber practicing medicine without a license. Their visit to the clinic was ruled to be trespass, but the story won numerous prizes and resulted in the clinic's being shut down.[46]

The courts have generally held that undercover reporting is legal, if not necessarily ethical, if it does not involve trespass. (For more about intrusion, see the section on the Food Lion case later in this chapter.)

Sometimes reporters come across true information that is so embarrassing and private that a person has reason to expect that it will not be published, especially if he or she is not well known. In general, **embarrassment** cases are difficult to win. If the information is true, it will often be considered newsworthy, which is the press's strongest defense in privacy cases.

One of the best-known embarrassment cases arose in 1975, when Oliver "Bill" Sipple, a former U.S. Marine, helped save President Gerald R. Ford by knocking aside Sara Jane Moore's gun as she attempted to shoot the president. Two days later, a columnist for the *San Francisco Chronicle* implied that Sipple was gay. Sipple sued the *Chronicle* for giving unwanted publicity to that information. The court ruled against Sipple, however, because he had been written about in gay magazines and had marched in gay pride parades. The court also ruled that the information about Sipple was legitimate news.

So, when is something that is private not newsworthy? On October 13, 1961, an Alabama woman went into a fun house at the local county fair. As she came out, an air jet blew her skirt up, exposing her underwear, and a photographer from the local newspaper took her picture. The woman was recognized by friends and relatives, who teased her about the picture. She called the paper at least twice but received no sympathy. The paper's editor says that had he apologized at that point, the case would have likely ended. But he didn't, and the woman sued and won.[47] What distinguishes *Daily Times Democrat v. Graham* from the Sipple case? Sipple had just saved the president's life and hence was a part of the news. In the Alabama case, however, the woman had done nothing to make herself newsworthy.

The most spectacular invasion of privacy case in recent years is that between Hulk Hogan and the gossip website *Gawker*. Hogan was a professional wrestler who had been quite famous back in the late 1980s and 1990s. In the 2000s, he had sex with a friend's wife, and the friend recorded them on video. (The friend, it should be noted, was radio shock jock Bubba the Love Sponge, and yes, that is his legal name.) Someone sent a copy of the video to *Gawker*, which published it. Hogan sued *Gawker* for invasion of privacy, and initially a judge ruled in favor of *Gawker*, ruling that the video did not have to be taken down, given Hogan's public persona and his public discussion of his sex life. But then the case got complicated. Tech billionaire Peter Thiel, who hated *Gawker* for outing him as gay several years earlier, financed Hogan's appeal

▲ Hulk Hogan, whose real name is Terry Bollea, testified in his case against the website *Gawker* in March 2016 in St. Petersburg, Florida. Bollea took legal action against *Gawker* in a $100 million lawsuit for releasing a video of him having sex with his best friend's wife. Hogan's appeal, it was later revealed, was financed by billionaire Peter Thiel, who allegedly was motivated by a grudge against *Gawker*.

of the verdict. This time, the case went before a jury, and Hogan won a judgment of $115 million, enough to force *Gawker* owner Nick Denton to sell his media company in 2016 to Spanish-language broadcaster Univision Communications. When Thiel's involvement in the case was revealed, it became clear that he had financed the appeal in order to seek revenge on Denton and *Gawker*.[48]

False light is similar to libel, and people who file libel suits often simultaneously file false light suits. False light doesn't really seem to be an invasion of privacy, but that's how the law treats it.[49] False light occurs when a journalist publishes untrue statements that alter an individual's public image in a way that he or she cannot control. The *Cleveland Plain Dealer* lost a false light suit when reporter Joe Eszterhas (who later became famous for writing the screenplay for the movie *Basic Instinct*) described a poverty-stricken widow whose husband had been killed in a bridge collapse several months earlier in West Virginia—even though he had neither met nor spoken with the woman. He wrote,

> Margaret Cantrell will talk neither about what happened nor about how they are doing. She wears the same mask of non-expression she wore at the funeral. She is a proud woman. Her world has changed. She says that after it happened, the people in town offered to help them out with money and they refused to take it.[50]

Regardless of whether the woman's reputation was damaged, the portrayal was clearly false because Eszterhas had never been in contact with her. False light often arises more from context than from a deliberate attempt to deceive. For example, a television story about street prostitution might show men and women walking down the street, with the implication that the women are prostitutes and the men are their customers. ABC television settled multiple lawsuits over just such a story (though without admitting guilt).

The final form of invasion of privacy is quite different from the preceding three. **Misappropriation** is using a person's name or image for commercial purposes without his or her permission. The right to control the commercial use of their names and images is of great importance to athletes and celebrities, who may make more money from endorsements than they do from competing or acting. For example, in 1997, basketball legend Michael Jordan earned $31.3 million in pay from the Chicago Bulls but more than $40 million from endorsements.[51] Clearly, it is in Jordan's economic and financial interest to control the use of his name and image.

What of the paparazzi armed with telephoto lenses who make a business out of stalking celebrities? Television and movie star Jennifer Aniston has filed numerous invasion-of-privacy lawsuits to stop distribution or publication of topless photos taken of her. It is not clear how a court would rule on her cases, as most of them have been settled out of court. Aniston has used a range of legal strategies in her cases, including copyright infringement, intrusion, and misappropriation.[52] (She apparently did not have a problem with her officially sanctioned top-less photo that ran on the cover of *GQ* magazine in 2005, at the same time one of her lawsuits was in progress.[53]) In 2009, California governor Arnold Schwarzenegger signed a bill into law that allows lawsuits against media outlets that publish photos shot illegally. In general, free-lance photographers can be sued for violating privacy laws, but the publications that buy their photos have been shielded from liability. Free-speech advocates argue that California's law could interfere with legitimate newsgathering. Legal experts have questioned whether California's law is enforceable because it can be difficult to prove when and where a photo was taken.[54]

Social Media and Privacy

If we were to go ask Captain Obvious whether we had any right to privacy with things we post to social media sites, he would immediately reply, "Duh, no, it's meant to be shared, obviously." And from a practical point of view, he would be correct—once anything is posted to the internet, it is bound to go public. If you want to keep something secret, don't post it. But from a legal point of view, you do have some protection. According to a 2012 ruling by the District Court of New Jersey, if you post something that is available only to a select group of people (i.e., "friends"), you may have a reasonable expectation of privacy. On the other hand, a 2009 California Court of Appeals ruling found that someone who posted a series of complaints about her hometown on Myspace had no grounds to sue for invasion of privacy when her comments were republished in a local newspaper.[55]

Privacy and Your Smartphone

How private is the content of your smartphone? If you have a recent iPhone with the latest operating system on it, pretty darn private. So private that even Apple's engineers could not get in and read your private messages, even if they wanted to. Which they do not.

The level of privacy in iPhones became a national controversy in the winter of 2016, when the FBI wanted to get access to an iPhone used by a married couple who killed fourteen people and injured twenty-two others when they attacked a county employee holiday party in San Bernardino, California. The FBI was hoping the phone might contain information about motives for the attack and whether Islamic extremist groups had influenced the couple.

The FBI could not get the access code from the attacker and owner of the phone—he was dead, shot by police. Investigators also could not simply guess at the four-digit access code. Apple's software shuts down the phone if someone guesses unsuccessfully at the passcode a given number of times. Under some settings, the phone will erase itself if you guess wrong too many times.[56]

The FBI wanted Apple to write a new, special version of the phone's iOS operating system that would disable all the anti-guessing features so the feds could rapidly do a brute-force attack to break into the phone. When Apple refused to do so, the FBI got a federal court order mandating that Apple comply. Apple again refused. Apple's CEO Tim Cook, in an open letter to the company's customers, wrote,

Smartphones, led by iPhone, have become an essential part of our lives. People use them to store an incredible amount of personal information, from our private conversations to our photos, our music, our notes, our calendars and contacts, our financial information and health data, even where we have been and where we are going.

LUCY NICHOLSON / Stringer / Getty Images

▲ Former *Cleveland Plain Dealer* reporter Joe Eszterhas, shown here at a book signing years later, lost a 1974 false light suit for a story where he described a poverty-stricken widow whose husband had been killed in a bridge collapse several months earlier in West Virginia—even though he had neither met nor spoken with the woman.

All that information needs to be protected from hackers and criminals who want to access it, steal it, and use it without our knowledge or permission. . . . Compromising the security of our personal information can ultimately put our personal safety at risk. That is why encryption has become so important to all of us. . . . We have even put that data out of our own reach, because we believe the contents of your iPhone are none of our business.[57]

Cook wrote that while he and Apple were horrified by the terrorist attack and wanted to help the FBI, they were unwilling to create a back door past the iPhone's security system. Apple put the new, enhanced security on the phone because the company had a history of cooperating with the government in unlocking dozens of phones in the post-9/11 era. Apple, along with most other major tech companies, was revealed to be turning over supposedly secure data to the government in the name of protecting national security.[58]

The case ended with neither the FBI nor Apple backing down. Instead, the FBI apparently hired a hacker who managed to find a way into the one specific phone, reportedly at a cost of more than $1 million, though the FBI refused to be specific.[59] In a separate case, in April 2018, police tried to use the fingerprint of a man they had shot and killed to unlock his phone. The police held the corpse's finger up to the phone's sensor, but they were not able to get into the phone. Law professor Charles Rose told the *Tampa Bay Times* that while what the police did was legal (you don't have a right to privacy after you are dead), "it really doesn't pass the smell test."[60]

Free Press/Fair Trial

The right to a free press often conflicts with the right to a fair trial. The Sixth Amendment to the U.S. Constitution guarantees accused individuals the right to be tried by an impartial jury, and the Fourteenth Amendment requires that criminal defendants be tried fairly before an unprejudiced jury. Supreme Court justice Hugo Black wrote that "free speech and fair trials are two of the most cherished policies of our civilization, and it would be a trying task to choose between them."[61] Over the years, there have been repeated charges that pretrial publicity interferes with the ability to select an impartial jury and that media coverage turns trials into circuses. These complaints became particularly loud during O. J. Simpson's 1994 murder trial, which attracted an inordinate amount of media attention. Media scholar Matthew D. Bunker argues that the conflict between a free press and a fair trial does not require that one right be sacrificed for another. Instead, he suggests that creative decisions by judges can lead to fair trials and open media coverage at the same time.[62] The general rule is that the First Amendment must be upheld unless there is a compelling state interest in regulating the speech. If speech is regulated, it must be done in the least restrictive way possible. The reasoning is that there should be no official version of the truth. Instead, people should be able to put forward contrasting ideas that compete for attention.

One of the most spectacular collisions between the right to a free press and the right to a fair trial involved the murder trial of Dr. Sam Sheppard. The case, later fictionalized in the television series and movie *The Fugitive*, involved the murder of Sheppard's wife, Marilyn, who was found beaten to death in their home in 1954. In his defense, Sheppard, a prominent Cleveland doctor, claimed to have been awakened by his wife's screams and to have fought with his wife's attacker, who left him unconscious.

Sheppard's story did not convince the police, and he soon became the leading suspect in his wife's murder. Reporters found out that Sheppard had been having an affair with a woman named Susan Hayes. A newspaper headline demanded, "Why Isn't Sam Sheppard in Jail?" As the trial began, the Cleveland newspapers printed the names and addresses of prospective jurors, along with their pictures. Jurors were also allowed to view the media during the trial, despite a "suggestion" by the judge that they avoid doing so.

Sheppard was convicted of murder, but his conviction was overturned by the U.S. Supreme Court, and he was given a new trial. This time he was acquitted. The Court, in *Sheppard v.*

Maxwell,[63] said that the "carnival atmosphere" surrounding Sheppard's trial had denied him due process. But the Court also noted that it was the judge's responsibility to make sure the defendant received a fair trial. If stopping coverage of the trial was not an option, what could the courts do to avoid this problem? The Court suggested a number of possibilities:[64]

- Put a gag order on participants in the trial to keep them from talking to the press in the first place (although the press would be free to report on anything that happened in the courtroom itself).

- Sequester the jury.

- Postpone the trial until the publicity dies down.

- Change the venue for the trial.

- Order a new trial.

Beyond the Sheppard case, the most important free press/fair trial case during the past thirty years is undoubtedly the Timothy McVeigh trial for the 1995 bombing of the Oklahoma City Alfred P. Murrah Federal Building that resulted in the death of 168 victims, including numerous children and eight federal agents. Chad F. Nye, in his book *Journalism and Justice in the Oklahoma City Bombing Trials*, found eleven major areas of free press/fair trial law to emerge from the case, including the following:

- Concerns about pretrial publicity in a case that affected directly or indirectly almost every family in the Oklahoma City area.

- The challenges of handling access for a huge press corps that produced more than 1,700 newspaper stories and more than 900 broadcast stories.

- The challenge of getting access to the trial for the people of Oklahoma City after the trial was moved to Denver, Colorado, because the defense argued that McVeigh and his accused collaborator Terry Nichols could not get a fair trial in Oklahoma. The judge ordered the court to have a closed-circuit television feed setup that would bring the trial from the Denver courtroom into an auditorium in Oklahoma City where family members of the victims could see and hear testimony. The judge also allowed journalists who couldn't get into the courtroom itself to listen to an audio feed of the trial, as long as they promised not to record or rebroadcast any of the testimony.

In the end, U.S. District Judge Richard Match kept everyone involved in the trial under tight control that satisfied both the rights of the accused and the rights of the public and the press to observe the trial.[65]

Cameras in the Courtroom

While there is no question that reporters and the public are entitled to view trials, there has been considerable debate over whether television and other cameras ought to be allowed in

Staff Sergeant Preston Chasteen/Department of Defense

▲ The bombing of the Alfred P. Murrah Federal Building in Oklahoma City on April 19, 1995, is the deadliest act of homegrown terrorism in U.S. history, resulting in the deaths of 168 people.

SHOULD LEGAL PROTECTIONS EXTEND TO OFFENSIVE SPEECH?

The Westboro Baptist Church (WBC) of Topeka, Kansas, has made itself infamous during the past decade by picketing the funerals of U.S. servicemen and women, as well as other high-profile funerals, carrying signs proclaiming "GOD HATES FAGS" and "THANK GOD FOR DEAD SOLDIERS." The church, which is not connected to any other Baptist denomination, is generally described as being mainly composed of the extended family of its founder and former leader, the late Fred Phelps. The church argues that God is punishing the United States for homosexuality, and its members picket the funerals to draw attention to their group.[66] (Phelps died in March 2014, but the WBC has continued with its pickets reportedly under the leadership of nonrelative Steve Drain.[67])

In 2006, members of the Phelps family brought their pickets to the funeral of Lance Cpl. Matthew Snyder, who was killed in Iraq. The protesters were reportedly kept approximately one thousand feet away from the church where the funeral was being held. Then, a week later, a member of the WBC posted an "epic" to the church's website that told a disparaging story about Snyder and his family, claiming that Snyder's parents raised him to "defy his creator" and that they taught him that "God was a liar." Albert Snyder, Matthew's father, sued Phelps for intentional infliction of emotional distress and invasion of privacy. He was initially awarded an $11 million judgment, but that judgment was later reduced to $5 million by the judge. The case was then reversed by the federal appeals court, based in part on the Supreme Court's ruling in *Hustler v. Falwell* that even speech that was "gross and repugnant in the eye of most" was still protected.[68]

When the case of *Snyder v. Phelps* reached the U.S. Supreme Court, there was an extensive public debate over the rights of the Phelps family to free speech versus the rights of the Snyder family to bury their son in peace.

During arguments before the court, the attorney for the Snyder family testified, "We're talking about a funeral. If the context is ever going to matter, it has to matter in the context of a funeral. Mr. Snyder simply wanted to bury his son in a private, dignified manner."[69] In response, Margie J. Phelps, daughter of Fred Phelps, argued that there is no constitutional law to keep her from exploiting a funeral for her cause. She told the court that "when I hear the language of 'exploiting the bereavement,' I look for: What is the principle of law that comes from this court? This notion of exploiting, it has no definition in a principle of law that would guide people as to when they could or could not."[70]

The Court eventually ruled in favor of the Phelps family's right to protest in an 8–1 decision, holding that the Phelps family had followed local laws and stayed the required

What is your first reaction to this photo? Does it shock and anger you? Why or why not? Should members of groups such as the Westboro Baptist Church have the right to picket near a soldier's funeral?

Douglas Graham/Roll Call via Getty Images

thousand feet away from the funeral. Chief Justice John Roberts, writing for the majority, said that "speech is powerful. It can stir people to action, move them to tears of both joy and sorrow, and—as it did here—inflict great pain. On the facts before us, we cannot react to that pain by punishing the speaker. As a Nation we have chosen a different course—to protect even hurtful speech on public issues to ensure that we do not stifle public debate."[71]

In an odd twist, the WBC picketed the funeral of Supreme Court justice Antonin Scalia, who had voted with the majority in the *Snyder v. Phelps* case in favor of the church's right to picket.[72]

· ·

WHO are they?

Who is Fred Phelps? Who is Albert Snyder?

WHAT did they say?

Why did Snyder sue Phelps and the Westboro Baptist Church? Why do Phelps and his family picket veterans' funerals?

WHAT evidence is there?

What grounds would the Court have had for ruling in favor of Snyder? What grounds did the Court have for ruling in favor of Phelps?

WHAT do you and your classmates think?

Do you agree with how the Court ruled in the Phelps case? Why or why not? What would the consequences be for free speech if the Court had ruled against Phelps? What can communities do (if anything) about the WBC protests? Do you think people have a right to protest at or near funerals?

the courtroom. The central argument in favor of allowing cameras is that the right to an open trial belongs to the public, not to the participants in the trial. Steven Brill, founder of the cable network Court TV (now truTV), argues that television coverage of trials

> offer[s] the public the chance to see the legal system at work and to judge with their own eyes whether it has performed properly. [It] can heighten public understanding of the system, counter rumors and speculation, and provide important insurance against abuses of defendants' rights.[73]

Movie cameras were first allowed in courtrooms in 1917. But in 1935, when Bruno Richard Hauptmann was on trial for the kidnapping and murder of aviator Charles Lindbergh's baby, the trial became a media circus. As a result, in 1937, a general ban was placed on movie and still photography in courtrooms. The fraud trial of the flamboyant Texas financier Billie Sol Estes in 1965 led to a Supreme Court decision that the time had not yet come for cameras to be allowed in the courtroom. But the Court went on to say that this might change when cameras became smaller and less intrusive.

In the 1970s and 1980s, electronic technology led to small, remote-controlled cameras. In 1977, the Florida Supreme Court started experimenting with allowing televised coverage of state court proceedings; by 1981, twenty-nine states had laws allowing partial television access.[74] By 1999, the vast majority of states had begun to allow cameras in their courtrooms under certain circumstances, although the judge generally retained the discretion to control when they could be used. Most states limit coverage of jurors, and many allow witnesses to refuse to be shown on television.[75] Experiments conducted in Illinois and Minnesota in the 2010s found that in general television cameras in the courtroom were not particularly disruptive. In fact, a Minnesota judge reported that she forgot the cameras were there.[76] A judge in Illinois commented that the courts couldn't use what happened in the circus-like televised Simpson murder trial because that case was "an aberration."[77] The one place cameras have not been allowed into is the U.S. Supreme Court. However, members of Congress and the judiciary have argued that the public should be able to watch the Supreme Court hear oral arguments on important cases, such as the constitutionality of President Barack Obama's health care reform law.[78]

Controlling the Press

Despite the First Amendment, Congress has repeatedly placed restrictions on speech and the press. These restrictions include bans on false advertising, libel, perjury, obscenity, reporting troop movements during time of war, and solicitation of murder.[79] Let us look at some of these limits in detail as illustrations of Secret 4—Nothing is new: Everything that happened in the past will happen again.

In the United States of America, the law clearly states that the press can be held responsible for printing material that is libelous or invades a person's privacy. But can that same law require that the press behave ethically? Or honestly? Journalists certainly should behave ethically, but can the law *require* them to keep a promise or tell the truth? This question has been tested in several cases. For example, in 1982, Republican Wheelock Whitney was running for governor of Minnesota. With just one week to go before the election, the campaign discovered that the Democratic candidate for lieutenant governor had been arrested and convicted of a minor theft eleven years earlier. What could Whitney's campaign managers have done with this information? Simply revealing it to the public would have made them look as if they were engaging in a smear campaign. Instead, they hired local public relations practitioner Dan Cohen to leak the information to the press. Cohen spoke to a series of reporters, offering them a deal:

> I have some documents which may or may not relate to a candidate in the upcoming election, and if you will give me a promise of confidentiality—that is, that I will be treated as an anonymous source, that my name will not appear in any material in connection with

this, and you will also agree that you're not going to pursue with me a question of who my source is—then I'll furnish you with the documents.[80]

Four reporters from the Minneapolis/St. Paul media agreed to Cohen's terms, and all received copies of the court documents. But once they had the documents, the media responded in three different ways. Television station WCCO decided not to run a story at all. The Associated Press distributed a brief story outlining the charges against the candidate that did not identify Cohen as the source of the story. But against the wishes of their reporters, both the *Star Tribune* and the *Pioneer Press*, the Twin Cities' leading newspapers, ran stories that identified Cohen as the source of the story. In the end, the Democratic candidates won handily, and the information about the lieutenant governor seemed to have no effect on the election. There was, however, fallout for Cohen: He was immediately fired by his employer, who did not want to risk offending the new administration that Cohen had helped attack.

Cohen then sued the newspapers, which led to the trial of *Cohen v. Cowles Media*. He argued that the newspapers had entered a verbal contract with him, exchanging a promise of confidentiality in return for the information he provided. The newspapers argued that they had done nothing wrong by printing Cohen's name. Instead, they had simply printed a true and accurate story about dirty tricks during a political campaign. Although the papers clearly broke an agreement with Cohen, they said that they were entitled to do so because they were printing the truth, which was protected by the First Amendment.

The trial court found in favor of Cohen and awarded him $200,000 in damages for being fired, as well as punitive damages of $500,000. The state court of appeals, however, struck down the punitive damages. When the case reached the U.S. Supreme Court, the justices ruled by a 5–4 vote that the First Amendment did not excuse the media from having to live up to the contracts into which they entered.[81] Given the long battle over whether reporters should have to reveal their confidential sources, this is an example of Secret 4—Nothing is new: Everything that happened in the past will happen again.

Controversy over the verdict arose within the press. Although it was the source who sued the press, the conflict lay primarily between editors and reporters. Could editors overrule promises made by reporters? The local reporters' union started urging reporters not to reveal their confidential sources to their editors unless the sources agreed to it. The newspaper publishers argued that the courts ought not to make judgments about journalistic ethics. In some instances, the courts have not punished the press for deceptive behavior. For example, in 1992, the ABC television newsmagazine *Primetime Live* sent undercover reporters Lynn Dale and Susan Barnett to apply for jobs as food handlers at a Food Lion grocery store. The network had been tipped off by disgruntled union officials that the store had been cleaning, bleaching, and repackaging beef, chicken, and fish that had passed its freshness date. The reporters (who did not reveal their true occupation) wore hidden microphones and cameras to document the store's misconduct. When the story ran, ABC charged that Food Lion had mixed old hamburger with new, sold improperly packaged chicken, and engaged in other unsanitary practices.[82]

Food Lion sued ABC, but not for libel as might be expected. Instead, it sued the network and producers for résumé fraud and trespass. Although the story was substantially true, Food Lion was trying to punish ABC for its aggressive—some would say unethical—reporting techniques. In the initial trial, Food Lion won its case and was awarded $5.5 million in damages. (We will talk more about the ethics of reporters lying in Chapter 15.) But the judge reduced the award to $316,402, saying that $5.5 million was excessive for lying on a job application and entering a closed area of the store. With this case, we see a major corporation trying to stop a news organization from reporting news the company would rather keep secret, providing another example of Secret 4—Nothing is new: Everything that happened in the past will happen again.

The U.S. Court of Appeals for the Fourth Circuit reduced the damages to a symbolic $2: $1 for trespass and $1 for breach of loyalty (food handlers not serving their employer properly).[83]

The court made it clear that this was not really a résumé fraud or trespass case, but a libel suit in disguise (in which truth would be an absolute defense). Food Lion argued that the broadcast had damaged its reputation and that it deserved compensation, but the court held that the reporters' only offense was lying on their résumés. The judgment, although technically ruling against ABC with the award of symbolic damages, preserved the right of journalists to report truthful information.

Prior Restraint

The most extreme and least accepted form of control of the press in the United States is **prior restraint**, a judicial order that stops a media organization from publishing a story or image. In the American colonies, prior restraint was the rule rather than the exception. All newspapers were published by the approval of the Crown; if they did not have that permission, they could not publish. But since the ratification of the First Amendment, in only a handful of cases have stories been barred from being published or broadcast. The landmark case on prior restraint is the 1931 case of *Near v. Minnesota*. Jay Near was the publisher of the *Saturday Press*, a racist, anti-Semitic newspaper. Among other things, Near used his paper to charge that the police were controlled by a "Jewish gangster" and therefore were not going after gamblers and bootleggers. A Minnesota court stopped publication of the paper, using a state law allowing prosecutors to suppress publications that were "malicious, scandalous, and defamatory."

On appeal, the U.S. Supreme Court ruled that the government did not have the right to suppress an entire publication merely because it was offensive. Instead, the Court said that the government could engage in prior restraint only to suppress the publication of military information during time of war, incitement to overthrow the government, or obscenity. Since none of Near's material fell into those categories, he could not be restrained from publishing it. The case established a major precedent: Although obscenity and publication of military secrets were not protected by the First Amendment, virtually everything else, no matter how offensive, was.[84] As we have seen multiple times in this chapter, just because people in positions of power or authority want to see a story suppressed does not give them the right to do so, illustrating Secret 4—Nothing is new: Everything that happened in the past will happen again.

The Pentagon Papers.
The second major case of prior restraint arose in 1971, when the federal government tried to suppress newspaper stories about a top-secret, forty-seven-volume report with the irresistible title "History of U.S. Decision-Making Process on Vietnam Policy." The report, which came to be known as the Pentagon Papers, contained extensive background information about how the United States had become involved in the Vietnam War, going as far back as the Truman administration's assistance to France in its colonial war in Indochina. Along with this lengthy commentary were copies of the original documents on which the report was based.[85]

One of the authors of the report was Daniel Ellsberg, a former U.S. Marine who worked for the RAND Corporation think tank. Although he made only minor contributions to the massive report, he was one of the few familiar with its entire contents. Ellsberg became convinced that if the report was publicized, the public outcry would bring the war to a quicker end. So he started leaking copies of the papers to members of Congress and a few academics. Finally, in March 1971, he gave *New York Times* reporter Neil Sheehan nearly seven thousand pages from the report, withholding only the four "diplomatic" volumes, which he thought should be kept confidential.

Sheehan headed a team of reporters from the *New York Times* that read and verified what was in the papers. There was considerable debate at the *Times* about the ethics of publishing the papers.

On June 13, 1971, after three months of work, the *New York Times* started publishing stories about the Pentagon Papers. On June 14, President Richard Nixon's attorney general asked the paper to stop publishing the information, but it politely declined to do so. On June 15, the third installment of the series was published, and the Justice Department obtained a restraining order against the *Times* to prevent it from publishing any additional stories. It was, as journalist

▲ Daniel Ellsberg (left) was cleared of espionage charges for leaking copies of a top-secret Pentagon report to the press after it was revealed that the Nixon administration had authorized a break-in of Ellsberg's psychiatrist's office.

ASSOCIATED PRESS/AP Images

Sanford Ungar put it, "the first time in the nation's history that a newspaper was restrained in advance by a court from publishing a specific article."[86] Ellsberg started looking for another news organization to cover the story. All three of the major broadcast networks turned him down, but the *Washington Post* was eager to obtain a copy of the papers. Lawyers for the *Post* cautioned the paper not to run the stories because the *Times* had already received a court order not to publish. But to *Washington Post* managing editor Ben Bradlee, not publishing was unthinkable—a violation of what journalism was all about: "Not publishing the information when we had it would be like not saving a drowning man, or not telling the truth."[87] So on June 18, the *Post* published its first Pentagon Papers story, and on June 19, the government obtained a restraining order against the *Post*.

At this point, the documents and stories were spreading across the country. Although approximately twenty newspapers published articles based on the Pentagon Papers, only four were taken to court: the *New York Times*, the *Washington Post*, the *Boston Globe*, and the *St. Louis Post-Dispatch*.[88] The U.S. Supreme Court heard arguments on the restraining orders on June 26, and voted 6–3 to allow the newspapers to resume publishing their stories. Justice Potter Stewart raised the central issue in the case: Did the publication of the Pentagon Papers pose "such a grave and immediate danger as to justify prior restraint?" Stewart said that it did not: "The only effective restraint upon executive policy and power . . . may lie in an informed and enlightened citizenry—in an informed and critical public opinion that alone can here protect the values of democratic government."[89] Justice William O. Douglas wrote that one of the primary goals of the First Amendment is to stop the government from covering up embarrassing information. In fact, the reason the First Amendment was ratified in the first place was to put a stop to random charges of seditious libel against people who were exposing embarrassing information about the government. The court pointed out that the government had been engaging in activism, not analysis, when it sought to control the release of the Pentagon Papers.

Now, more than forty-five years later, the lessons of *New York Times Co. v. United States*[90] (informally known as the Pentagon Papers case) are still relevant. While the Pentagon Papers were classified as "top secret," the secrets they contained were embarrassing political secrets, not dangerous military secrets.[91] In 1989, Erwin Griswold, who had argued the government's case before the Supreme Court, said that he had "never seen any trace of a threat to the national security" from publication of the papers.[92] But what about Ellsberg, the man who leaked copies of the Pentagon Papers to the press? The legality of Ellsberg's releasing the documents was never really resolved. Ellsberg was indicted on charges of conspiracy, misappropriation of government property, and violating the Espionage Act. But the court eventually declared a mistrial and dismissed the charges against him after it was revealed that the Nixon administration had Ellsberg's psychiatrist's office burglarized and made illegal recordings of the sessions there. In recent years, Ellsberg has spoken out against the Persian Gulf War and the invasion of Iraq.[93] In the Pentagon Papers case, the newspapers were desperately trying to publish their articles. But eight years later, author Howard Morland and the *Progressive* magazine wanted to have an article censored.

Morland was an Air Force pilot turned antinuclear activist who maintained that the government was concealing details about how hydrogen bombs operate—not for security reasons but to stifle public opposition to the weapon. Morland used unclassified documents and interviews with scientists to write an article explaining how these weapons of mass destruction worked. Morland and the *Progressive* knew that censorship would transform the article from an obscure piece in a radical magazine into a cause célèbre that would receive nationwide publicity.

They got their wish. A former professor of Morland's submitted an early draft of the article to the U.S. Department of Energy (DOE), which manages nuclear material in the United States. In addition, the magazine's editor sent the article and drawings to the DOE to have them checked for accuracy. On March 1, 1979, a district court judge in Wisconsin issued a temporary restraining order against the *Progressive* because the article presented a "clear and present danger" to the United States.

It initially appeared that the government might have a good case against Morland and the *Progressive*. The *Near* case (discussed earlier in this chapter) had established that the government could censor a publication that published "the sailing dates of transports or the number and location of troops." Although the types of information involved in national security had changed since *Near*, the same argument might be made—that the article would compromise national security by giving away military secrets. (It should be noted that although the article explained how a hydrogen bomb worked, it did not provide instructions for building one.)

Central to the *Progressive*'s defense was the argument that there were no secrets in the article because all the material it contained was available from nonclassified sources. The government argued that Morland's organization of the material into an article made it a security problem.[94] While the *Progressive* case was under appeal, a number of people started working on similar articles. *Milwaukee Journal Sentinel* reporter Joe Manning re-created Morland's research and published a two-part story that covered the three "secrets" from Morland's article in simple terms. Then nuclear hobbyist Charles Hansen wrote an eighteen-page letter to the editor of the *Madison Press Connection* that outlined much the same information as Morland's article. On September 17, 1979, the day after the Hansen letter appeared, the government dropped its case, declaring that its attempt to suppress the information was "meaningless, superfluous, unnecessary, inconsequent."[95] The *Progressive* finally ran Morland's article in November 1979 under the headline "The H-Bomb Secret: How We Got It, Why We're Telling It," but it was a somewhat hollow victory for the magazine.[96] Its editors had gotten the attention they sought, but unfortunately for them, everyone saw the case as a freedom-of-the-press issue—not the important debate over nuclear weapons they were hoping for.

The Pentagon Papers and *Progressive* cases have two important implications. The first is that much information that the government would like to believe is secret is public knowledge. The second is that in a free and open society it is exceedingly difficult to keep information secret that determined people want to make public. And with the addition of the internet to the range of available media, virtually anyone can publish any information widely and easily. Although it is still possible to punish individuals and media corporations after the fact for publishing or broadcasting inappropriate material, prior restraint is becoming virtually impossible in the United States and the Western democracies.

Journalists and the Police

As we discussed back in Chapter 9, in the spring of 2020, Minneapolis police arrested George Floyd, a forty-six-year-old Black man after a convenience store clerk accused him of passing a counterfeit $20 bill. During the arrest, a police officer kneeled on Floyd's neck using all his weight as three other officers looked on. During the time he was pinned down, Floyd called out that he could not breathe. Floyd died later that day of neck compression injuries he sustained during the arrest, according to the medical examiner. As of this writing, all four officers were fired and the officer who held down Floyd with his knee has been charged with third-degree murder, second-degree murder, and second-degree manslaughter.[97] During the nationwide

▲ CNN journalist Omar Jimenez was arrested, along with his crew, on live television while reporting on protests and rioting that took place following the police killing of George Floyd in Minneapolis, Minnesota. Jimenez was just one of many journalists arrested or attacked by police during the protests across the country.

protests and riots in the following weeks, multiple journalists were arrested while trying to cover the events. One of the most visible was CNN reporter Omar Jimenez, who is Black, and his crew who were arrested on live TV while reporting from Minneapolis. In addition to those who were arrested, many journalists were also attacked by police with pepper balls, rubber bullets, and other riot control munitions.[98] Freelance photographer Linda Tirado was blinded in her left eye after being shot with a foam bullet by police while covering a confrontation between protestors and law enforcement in Minneapolis on May 29. Tirado had been wearing press credentials along with goggles to protect her eyes, but the bullet shattered her protective gear.[99] "I was aiming my next shot, put my camera down for a second and then my face exploded," she told the *New York Times*. "I immediately felt blood and was screaming, 'I'm press! I'm press!'"[100] The only good news for Tirado was that she was blinded in her left eye, but she uses her right eye to take pictures.

As of June 10, 2020, the U.S. Press Freedom Tracker reports that there have been more than four hundred total press freedom incidents including the following:[101]

- More than fifty-eight arrests
- Fifty-four attacks by police officers
- Fifty-two tear gassings
- Thirty-one pepper sprayings
- Eighty-seven rubber bullet/projectiles

These arrests are similar to what was happening back on August 13, 2014, when then *Washington Post* reporter Wesley Lowery was sitting in a McDonald's restaurant in Ferguson, Missouri, working on a story about the protests and violence in Ferguson over the death of Michael Brown. Brown was an unarmed Black man who was shot and killed by Ferguson police. Brown's death set off nights of protests, looting, and killing in the St. Louis suburb. The McDonald's was a popular place with journalists that night, with the availability of food, tables to work on, and Wi-Fi to file stories with.

A story from the *Washington Post* reported that after initially telling reporters they were fine staying in the restaurant, police returned and told reporters they had to leave. Lowery started packing up his belongings, but while he did so, he also started recording a video with his phone. As he was preparing to leave, Lowery said he was shoved up against a soda machine, cuffed, and arrested. Lowery told the *Post*,

> This is probably the single point at which I've been more afraid than at any point. More afraid than the tear gas and rubber bullets, more afraid during the riot police. I know of too many instances where someone who was not resisting arrest was assaulted or killed.[102]

Huffington Post reporter Ryan Reilly was also arrested. Within half an hour of being taken to a holding cell, all the arrested members of the media were released without charges being filed.

But nearly a year later, both Reilly and Lowery were charged with trespassing and interfering with a police officer.[103] Close to forty news organizations signed a letter from the Reporters Committee for Freedom of the Press that condemned the charges against the reporters. It said,

"The fact that these journalists were kept from doing their jobs was troublesome enough. But the fact that your office—after having time to reflect on police actions for a full year—has chosen to pursue criminal prosecution now is astonishing."[104] Not all news organizations were sympathetic toward Reilly and Lowery. John Nolte, writing for the strongly conservative website Breitbart .com, said, "Left-wing *Washington Post* activist Wesley Lowery (who identifies as a journalist) has been charged officially in St. Louis County of trespassing and interfering with a police officer."[105]

Nearly two years after they were arrested, charges against the reporters were dropped.[106]

Many states have **shield laws** that protect journalists from having to testify in court (and divulge sources) under certain circumstances, but there is currently no federal shield law in place. Many journalists are lobbying strongly for one.

The U.S. Senate has been considering bills creating a federal shield law for several years. The 2014 version of the bill easily passed out of the Judiciary Committee, but was never put up for a vote of the full Senate.[107] Some journalists find shield laws of concern because they seem to define who is a journalist—and is thus protected—while excluding others who are not considered journalists. First Amendment attorney David Bodney says, "Any attempt to legislate the scope of our First Amendment rights is unsettling business."[108] Despite these concerns, Bodney does support the proposed federal law.

Since the 1960s, several journalists have been either fined or sent to jail for refusing to testify in federal courts. These have included journalists who witnessed drug crimes or the actions of the Black Panther Party and some who interviewed murder suspects.

In 2005, journalists Matt Cooper and Judith Miller faced fines and jail time for refusing to testify to a federal grand jury about who had leaked information to them about the identity of a covert CIA officer. Both were eventually granted permission to testify by the source they sought to protect, vice presidential adviser I. Lewis "Scooter" Libby Jr. *Time* magazine's Cooper testified without serving jail time after his employer ordered him to do so. *New York Times* reporter Miller went to jail for eighty-five days for refusing to testify in the same case. Miller finally accepted the release by Libby from her promise of confidentiality and testified.[109]

Free Speech and Students

Do the rights that protect adult journalists also protect student reporters working on high school newspapers? More than twenty-five years ago, the U.S. Supreme Court decided the answer is no. In 1988, a group of high school students in Hazelwood, Missouri, sued the school system because their principal had barred articles about pregnancy and divorce from the student newspaper. The Supreme Court in *Hazelwood v. Kuhlmeier*[110] ruled that a principal could censor a student newspaper when it was produced as part of a class. It wrote,

> The First Amendment rights of students in the public schools are not automatically co-extensive with the rights of adults in other settings. . . . A school need not tolerate student speech that is inconsistent with its "basic educational mission," even though the government could not censor similar speech outside the school.[111]

The Court ruled that the student newspaper is a classroom exercise rather than a vehicle for free speech, and hence administrators may censor any content that is "reasonably related to legitimate pedagogical concerns."[112]

One way students have reacted against this censorship is by starting web-based newspapers that are not sponsored by the school. In addition, at least eleven states have passed laws that restore to high school students the rights they had prior to the *Hazelwood* decision. These laws limit the circumstances under which student newspapers can be censored, generally allowing articles to be banned only if they are "libelous, obscene, or will create a substantial disruption of school activities."[113] Interestingly enough, in both 2016 and 2017, the Walter Cronkite New Voices Act that restored the rights to student journalists they had lost in the *Hazelwood* case has been passed by the Missouri House. According to the bill, student journalists are responsible for the content of their newspapers "unless such material is libelous, an invasion of privacy, a violation of the law or incites students to create a clear and present danger." The bill has yet to make it through the state senate, however.[114]

There have also been several cases that dealt with schools trying to limit the free speech of students in other venues. Some schools have attempted to limit what students can post to either blogs or social networking sites such as Facebook and Myspace. Three middle school students in the Chicago area were suspended after they posted "obscene and threatening" comments about a teacher in their blog. Schools in the Washington, DC, area have banned students from using their school-provided email accounts to register with Facebook.[115] And a student in Indiana was expelled from high school for a grammar joke laced with the "*F* word" that he tweeted late at night from what he claims was his own computer.[116] Student Joseph Frederick was suspended from a Juneau, Alaska, high school in 2002 by the principal, Deborah Morse, for holding up a giant sign saying "BONG HiTS 4 JESUS" across the street from his high school as the Olympic torch passed through his town.[117] The school district in the case claims that the student was promoting drug use. The student responded, "I wasn't trying to say anything about drugs. I was just trying to say something. I wanted to use my right to free speech, and I did it."[118] The case, known as *Morse v. Frederick*, was heard by the U.S. Supreme Court in 2007. The Court ruled on June 25, 2007, that principals could punish speech that could "reasonably be viewed" as promoting the use of illegal drugs.[119]

Interestingly enough, the student received support from the ACLU, gay rights advocates, and the Christian Legal Society (CLS). (The CLS and gay rights groups were concerned that other school districts might use the case as a way of limiting speech about religious or gay rights issues.)

Many students may not be aware that their rights are being limited or what their rights entail. A survey of more than one hundred thousand high-school-aged students found that three-fourths of them believed incorrectly that flag burning was a crime. The survey also found that 36 percent of students said newspapers should get government permission before publishing stories and that 32 percent said the press has "too much freedom to do what it wants."[120]

Obscenity

The *Near* case, in addition to allowing prior restraint of sensitive military information, established that obscene material is not protected by the First Amendment. The term **obscenity** describes sexually explicit material that is legally prohibited from being published. This raises the question of what kinds of material can be considered obscene. Finding the answer has proved difficult, both for the courts and for society.[121]

Clay Good/ZUMA

▲ Student Joseph Frederick was suspended from his high school in 2002 for displaying a sign reading "BONG HiTS 4 JESUS." The U.S. Supreme Court supported his suspension in a 5–4 ruling.

Roth v. United States. The Supreme Court made its first contemporary attempt to answer the question of what constitutes obscenity in 1957 in *Roth v. United States*.[122] Samuel Roth, who ran a business selling sexually explicit books, photos, and magazines, had been convicted of mailing obscene material through the U.S. Postal Service. He appealed his case to the U.S. Supreme Court, which eventually upheld his conviction. But more important, the Court used the case to start establishing standards for what was and was not protected by the First Amendment. The *Roth* case reaffirmed that the courts could regulate obscenity and that obscenity is not protected by the First Amendment. But the justices also cautioned that "sex and obscenity are not synonymous."[123]

With *Roth*, the court established a three-part test to help determine whether something is obscene: "Whether to the average person, applying contemporary community standards, the dominant theme of the material taken as a whole appeals to prurient interests."[124] The three parts of this test can be analyzed as follows:

1. The standard for obscenity is set by individual "community standards" using the view of an "average person." This means that neither the most liberal nor the most conservative view should be used, nor should there be a national standard.

2. The work must be "taken as a whole." It is not enough for there to be a single sexually explicit section; the work as a whole must be explicit to be obscene.

3. The work must appeal to "prurient interests." This is the most difficult point. Prurient interest means, according to the Court, an "exacerbated, morbid or perverted" interest in nudity, sex, or excretory functions.[125]

Miller v. California. The standards established in the *Roth* case were refined with the Supreme Court's ruling in *Miller v. California*. Like Roth, Miller had been convicted of sending obscene material through the mail. The *Miller* case upheld the basic standard from *Roth* but had further impact in two key areas. The first is that states have used this ruling to ban child pornography, and many states have added laws that ban other types of content.

The second key aspect of *Miller* is it held that material that has "serious literary, artistic, political, or scientific value" cannot be banned. This protects, for example, information about sexual health and birth control. It also protects erotic literature, such as D. H. Lawrence's novel *Lady Chatterley's Lover*. Miller also reaffirmed that local communities could set their own standards. There is not an expectation, the Court said, that "the people of Maine or Mississippi accept public depiction of conduct found tolerable in Las Vegas or New York City."[126]

Obscenity in the Information Age. The *Roth* and *Miller* standards both assume that obscene material is being sold at a particular location in a particular community. Neither case anticipated the problems raised by the growth of the internet and satellite television. What can the courts do about sexually explicit material that is located on a web server in New York City but is viewed by a person in Morgantown, West Virginia? Attorney Rieko Mashima's piece in *Computer Lawyer* explains the problem: "On the Internet, which is available to a nationwide audience, a sender of information can neither control where it will be downloaded or through which places it will travel, nor tailor contents for different communities."[127]

Pay-per-view cable and satellite television provide a similar problem. In 1999, Larry W. Peterman, owner of a video store in Provo, Utah, was charged with renting obscene films and appeared to be headed to jail. Then his lawyer came up with the idea of recording all the erotic movies that could be seen on pay-per-view at the Provo Marriott Hotel across the street from the courtroom. A little more research found that far more people in Provo were buying adult movies from cable and satellite providers and in hotels than from Peterman's video store. The jury promptly acquitted Peterman on all charges.[128] The courts have yet to rule definitively on how to handle local control of pornography delivered by satellite or internet, although Congress made an attempt to do so with the Telecommunications Act of 1996, discussed later in this chapter. And as of 2004, the FCC started cracking down on what it called "indecent" communication on broadcast television, as discussed in Chapter 8.

Copyright and Regulation of the Media Industry

The print media have been largely unregulated throughout the history of the United States beyond copyright and fair use provisions. But broadcast media have been necessarily controlled from the beginning, for two reasons: Radio and television stations have to meet certain technical standards to keep from interfering with each other's broadcasts, and the government has an interest in making sure that the limited number of broadcast frequencies available are used in the public interest. Let us look at how these controls of the media industry have been applied. Creators of books, newspapers, magazines, music, and other media products have been protected from having their works appropriated by others since the first U.S. copyright law was passed in 1790. In the law's original form, works were protected for fourteen years, and copyright could be renewed for an additional fourteen years. This protection was extended only to U.S. authors and artists, however. It was not until the 1890s that copyright was extended to works by authors and artists from other countries. Under the leadership of Barbara Ringer in the 1960s and 1970s, the length of copyright was increased from the original twenty-eight years to fifty years after the creator's death for an individual copyright. In 1998, the Copyright Term Extension Act extended individual copyright to seventy years after the creator's death and extended corporate copyright to ninety-five years. Why ninety-five years for the corporate copyright? If not for that extension, Mickey Mouse would have entered the public domain in 2003.[129] The 1998 Digital Millennium Copyright Act expanded the copyright on materials that are recorded digitally, such as electronic books, CDs, and DVDs.

It has long been illegal to distribute duplicate copies of electronic material without permission, but the act also makes it a crime to produce software or hardware designed to break the copy protection on movies, music, or other software. The act leaves users in an odd position: It is legal to make a backup copy of a DVD movie for personal use, but it is illegal to use a computer program that will make a copy of the protected movie.[130] In 2002, a group led by Stanford University law professor Lawrence Lessig created an alternative set of copyright licenses known as Creative Commons that allow authors and artists to reserve a limited set of rights for a creative work without using all the restrictions of a conventional copyright. For example, a photographer can license his or her photo so that anyone can use the image without permission if he or she attributes the photo to the original creator. The main advantage of Creative Commons is that it allows creators a middle ground between full copyright and placing their work in the public domain.[131]

You can read more about court rulings on several musical copyright issues, including Led Zeppelin's "Stairway to Heaven, along with multimedia looks at the subject, on my blog at www.ralphehanson.com/?s=copyright.

▲ Stanford University law professor Lawrence Lessig led the group that created the alternative copyright licenses known as Creative Commons.

Riccardo S. Savi/Getty Images

The Rise and Fall of Broadcast Regulation

Broadcast regulation began with the Radio Act of 1912, passed immediately after the sinking of the *Titanic*. But this regulation dealt only with point-to-point communication, such as ship-to-shore radio. Meanwhile, commercial broadcasting got its start in 1920 when radio station KDKA went on the air in Pittsburgh. By 1925, broadcasters were calling for regulation by the government to bring stability to the new industry.

The Radio Act of 1927 created the Federal Radio Commission. This act was also the first to charge broadcast stations with acting in the "public interest, convenience, and necessity." With the Communications Act of 1934, the Radio Commission evolved into the Federal Communications Commission (FCC). The 1934 act brought all electronic communication, wired and wireless, under the control of the FCC, but the basic tenets of the 1927 act remained in place:[132]

- The airwaves are licensed to broadcasters, but the broadcasters do not own them.

- The FCC has the power to regulate broadcasters to ensure that they act in the public interest.

- The FCC can tell broadcasters what frequencies and power to use and where their transmitters can be located.

Mandating Fairness on the Air. In addition to attempting to regulate the murky area of indecency, the FCC has regulated how broadcasters handle political campaigns and controversial issues. The FCC's **equal time provision** requires broadcast stations to make equivalent amounts of broadcast time available to all candidates running for public office. The rule does not require stations to provide time to candidates; it requires them only to ensure that all candidates have equal access. So if a station sells time to one candidate, it must be willing to sell an equal amount of similarly valuable time to all candidates who can afford it. The rule also states that if a station gives free non-news time to one candidate, it must provide similar amounts of free time to all candidates. The purpose of the rule is to prevent stations from favoring one candidate over another while making use of a valuable public resource.[133]

The equal time provision has been subject to controversy in cases where candidates have sought to run ads that are either offensive or libelous. Because stations cannot edit or censor anything in political advertisements, the FCC has ruled that broadcasters are not responsible for libelous statements made in political ads. There has also been conflict over explicit antiabortion ads. In 1992 and 1994, some stations channeled the graphic messages and images contained in such ads to a "safe harbor" time between midnight and 6:00 a.m., when children were unlikely to see them. Indiana congressional candidate Michael Bailey objected to the channeling, saying that the explicit ads were an essential part of his campaign; he persuaded stations to run the ads during prime time, although the stations ran disclaimers before many of them. The FCC has since said that ads dealing with abortion could be channeled into the "safe harbor" time periods.[134] There are limits to what candidates can do. When *Hustler* publisher Larry Flynt declared that he would run for president and would broadcast pornographic campaign commercials under the equal time provision, the FCC said that the "no censorship" clause would not apply to "obscene or indecent political announcements."

More controversial than the equal time provision was the **fairness doctrine**. Under this 1949 rule, stations were required to cover controversial issues of public interest and to present contrasting views on those issues. The fairness doctrine required not that stations give the same amount of time to all sides of an issue, but rather that they "afford reasonable opportunity for the discussion of conflicting views on issues of public importance."[135]

The major objection to the fairness doctrine was that stations might avoid covering controversial issues because they did not want to present extreme viewpoints or cover every aspect of an issue. For example, stations would argue that they did not want to cover issues dealing with racism for fear of having to give the Ku Klux Klan an opportunity to participate. Critics argued that the public suffered because they received no coverage of issues rather than every possible variation.

A 1985 study by the FCC found that the fairness doctrine tended to inhibit free speech and was no longer needed because of new media outlets such as cable television. Moreover, the FCC had to deal with thousands of complaints filed under the rule each year. Following publication of the 1985 study, the FCC essentially stopped enforcing the fairness doctrine, and it was repealed in 1987.[136] Despite this, radio talk show hosts such as Rush Limbaugh continued to argue that the federal government was considering bringing back the fairness doctrine in order to silence conservative commentators.[137] In a strange footnote, the FCC announced in the summer of 2011 that it was finally taking the language that authorized the fairness doctrine out of its regulation book. Why was it still listed there despite being repealed in 1987? Technically, it was still the rule even though the FCC had voted against its enforcement nearly twenty-five years earlier.[138]

The Telecommunications Act of 1996. The Telecommunications Act of 1996 has been called the biggest reform of broadcast regulation since the formation of the FCC in 1934. The section of the Telecommunications Act that attracted the most attention was the one calling for the creation of the V-chip, which allows parents to electronically block material with a particular content rating. But the greatest impact the act has had is that it relaxed most of the rules that restricted how many broadcast stations a particular company can own. This led to the rapid turnover of many broadcast properties and an increasing concentration of ownership, completing a trend that began in the 1970s and 1980s.[139] (For more about concentration of media ownership, see Chapter 3.)

In addition to calling for the V-chip, the Communications Decency Act provision of the Telecommunications Act of 1996 attempted to regulate the internet in a similar way to the regulation of broadcasting.

Figuring out what kind of medium the internet is from a legal standpoint has been a problem for both Congress and the courts. On the one hand, the internet looks something like television because it comes in over a wire and is displayed on a screen, and many websites are maintained by the same companies that operate television networks. On the other hand, the internet can be seen as more like a newspaper or magazine. There's a great deal of print on the internet, and newspapers have a strong presence there. Also, the number of channels on the internet is not limited, as is the case with broadcast or even cable television. But, unlike both television and print, the internet has strong elements of interpersonal communication, resembling the telephone network in this respect. There is no central authority controlling what can and cannot be said on the internet.

Some observers argue that perhaps regulation of the internet should model regulation of the telephone system. Others say the internet might qualify as an open public forum, without any need for regulation at all.[140] In reality, the internet has elements of all these media—radio, broadcast and cable television, telephone, newspapers, and magazines. The companies that provide high-speed internet service to the home are regulated to a degree, as are phone and cable television companies. First Amendment protection for media sites on the web is similar to that given to print media. Individuals have the same levels of responsibility for what they say through the internet as they do anywhere else. In general, internet bulletin boards and chat rooms are treated in much the same way as telephone communication. The people posting to the bulletin boards, not the company providing internet access, are responsible for what they say, just as a phone company is not responsible for a libelous or defamatory phone call or fax sent over its lines.

The many levels of communication on the internet make it extremely difficult to control. The Communications Decency Act attempted to ban internet messages that are "obscene, lewd, lascivious, filthy, or indecent." The law was opposed by the American Library Association, the Electronic Frontier Foundation (an electronic communication rights group), and the ACLU, among others. Although the law banned only the transmission of indecent messages to minors, it seemed impossible to keep minors out of discussions involving adults.

In 1997, the Supreme Court struck down the Communications Decency Act as an unconstitutional limit on the free speech of adults. It ruled that the possibility of a minor being present in a chat room did not remove the adults' First Amendment rights. Justice John Paul Stevens wrote in the majority opinion, "The interest in encouraging freedom of expression in a democratic society outweighs any theoretical but unproven benefit of censorship."[141] The only certainty is that Congress will continue to consider how to regulate communication on the internet.

Since 1997, attempts have been made to pass new legislation that would control "indecent" content on the web without infringing on the free speech of adults.[142] You can read more about regulation of the internet in Chapter 10.

Net Neutrality. If you ever want to spark an argument about communication technology, bring up the topic of **net neutrality**. The term was originated by Columbia University law professor (and popular author) Tim Wu in a 2003 paper about online discrimination, and he defines a neutral network as an "Internet that does not favor one application (say, the world wide web), over others (say, email)."[143]

▲ Protester Mike Adkins joins proponents of an open and unregulated internet in a protest in February 2018 in Washington, DC, part of a "net neutrality day of action."

When the idea first came up, some internet providers, including Comcast and AT&T, were doing a variety of things to control their customers' use of the internet including banning them from using virtual private networks (VPNs), banning them from using Wi-Fi routers, and selectively slowing service to the peer-to-peer file-sharing network BitTorrent. (BitTorrent was heavily used for sharing pirated video and audio, but it also had legal uses.) Wu argued that existing broadband providers tended to limit new technologies that would improve the internet overall. So, he called for creating a level playing field for content providers in a world where there are a limited number of internet service providers.[144]

In 2015, the Obama-era FCC put in place comprehensive net neutrality rules that were opposed by all the major telecommunication companies. The rules were upheld by a lower court and were in the process of being appealed to the U.S. Supreme Court when the Trump-era FCC started rescinding the Obama-era rules. In December 2017, the FCC threw out all of the Obama-era regulations. The new regulations let the carriers manage their networks as they please, but it does require them to disclose what their policies and procedures are.[145]

This has the potential to allow internet providers to charge companies such as Netflix, Hulu, or Facebook a premium to have better/faster service than competitors. Given that 61 percent of Americans (and 87 percent of rural Americans) have no more than one high-speed internet provider, most people can't choose to change providers if they don't like their current one.[146] The Internet Association, which represents companies like Google and Facebook, argues that net neutrality is vital or internet providers will give preferential treatment either to those who will pay or to companies they own.[147] As an example, Comcast is the nation's leading internet provider and also owns content company NBCUniversal.

While internet broadband and mobile phone providers such as Verizon and Comcast say that they have no intention of either throttling certain companies on their service or charging companies extra for higher-speed service, what will actually happen remains to be seen.[148] AT&T, which owns media conglomerate WarnerMedia, has said that it will not count time spent streaming its HBO Max video service against its mobile data caps, while streaming programming from competing services, such as Netflix and Disney+, will burn up customers' data. That gives AT&T mobile customers a strong incentive to do as much of their mobile viewing as possible on networks owned by AT&T.[149]

CHAPTER REVIEW

CHAPTER SUMMARY ▶▶

The First Amendment to the U.S. Constitution says that

> Congress shall make no law respecting an establishment of religion, or prohibiting the free exercise thereof; or abridging the freedom of speech, or of the press; or the right of the people peaceably to assemble, and to petition the Government for a redress of grievances.

This statement is at the core of all media law in the United States. The purpose of the amendment is to protect the free and open discussion necessary to a democratic society. Although the First Amendment guarantees the right of free speech, Congress has passed several laws that limit this freedom. These include the Alien and Sedition Acts of 1798; the Espionage Act of 1917; the Smith Act of 1940; the USA PATRIOT Act of 2001; and laws controlling libel, invasion of privacy, publication of military secrets, and obscenity.

The rights of individuals are protected from actions of the media through libel law, invasion of privacy law, and guarantees of a fair trial. Libel is a statement that unjustifiably exposes someone to ridicule or contempt. For a statement to be libelous, it must include defamation, identification, and publication. In general, the media are allowed to publish defamatory material that is true, privileged, or a statement of opinion. *New York Times Co. v. Sullivan* established that public officials seeking to win a libel suit must show that the media acted with actual malice in publishing a false defamatory statement.

There are four basic forms of invasion of privacy: intrusion, embarrassment, false light, and misappropriation. In some cases, journalists can defend themselves against charges of invasion of privacy by showing that the story in question was newsworthy. There is often a conflict between an individual's right to a fair trial and the press's right to cover that trial. The Supreme Court has generally ruled that the judge, not the press, is responsible for guaranteeing the defendant a fair trial. The Court has also ruled that protection of the right to a fair trial should require as few limits on the freedom of the press as possible. This can be done by imposing gag orders, sequestering the jury, postponing or changing the venue of a trial, or ordering a new trial.

Since 1977, courts in the United States have been experimenting with allowing cameras in the courtroom. Proponents of such a policy argue that televising trials allows the public to better understand how the justice system works. Opponents argue that cameras are intrusive and turn trials into media circuses.

Although the press is subject to the same laws as society as a whole, it is protected from censorship in most cases. The government is allowed to prevent publication of certain information only if the material is obscene or gives away military secrets during time of war. There have been only three major cases involving prior restraint: *Near v. Minnesota*, the Pentagon Papers case, and the *Progressive* H-bomb story. High school newspapers published as a classroom activity are not afforded the same level of protection, however. The courts have ruled the First Amendment does not protect obscenity, and they have established that the standard for obscenity will be set using state law and local community standards.

Journalists are not generally required by law to tell the truth to people they are interacting with while reporting a story, and they can be required to keep a verbal promise of confidentiality that they give to a source. While many states have shield laws that protect journalists from being forced to testify in court about their work, there is not a federal law protecting journalists from having to testify. Journalists have also been arrested and threatened with charges for reporting in areas where there is rioting and other forms of civil disobedience.

Copyright law has protected the creators of creative works in the United States since 1790. Copyright law has been updated in recent years to extend the length of copyright on commercially valuable works. There have also been provisions added to the law to make it easier for people to make fair use of copyright materials.

The broadcast media traditionally have been regulated much more heavily than the print media because they make use of the public airwaves. They are regulated both for technical reasons and to ensure that they serve the public interest. Major legislation controlling the broadcast media was passed in 1927, 1934, and 1996. Standards for regulating the internet are still evolving, but they appear to be more similar to print regulations than to broadcast ones.

KEY TERMS ▶▶

Alien and Sedition Acts   345

libel   347

privilege   348

actual malice   349

intrusion   351

embarrassment   351

false light   352

misappropriation   352

prior restraint   359

shield laws   363

obscenity   364

equal time provision   367

fairness doctrine   367

net neutrality   369

REVIEW QUESTIONS ▶▶

1. What rights to free speech do high school students have? Does it vary from state to state? Why?

2. How has the USA PATRIOT Act changed the freedoms for Americans since 9/11? How did the USA FREEDOM Act change the PATRIOT Act?

3. Why did the U.S. Supreme Court rule that public officials needed to meet a higher standard to win a libel suit than ordinary people do?

4. According to the U.S. Supreme Court, why do student publications have fewer First Amendment rights than do publications created by adults? What have states done in response to this?

5. What is net neutrality? Why should you care about it? What is the status of net neutrality in the United States?

CHAPTER 15

MEDIA ETHICS

Truthfulness, Fairness, and Standards of Decency

Trump: Why Allow Immigrants from 'Shithole Countries'?

In bluntly vulgar language, President Donald Trump questioned the U.S. would accept more immigrants from Haiti and "shithole countries" in Africa rather than places like Norway.

By Associated Press

Presidents and other politicians using bad language is nothing new.

Lyndon Johnson was famous for his coarse language, with one of his most famous examples being, "I do know the difference between chicken sh-- and chicken salad." He knew, however, that his profanity was never going to find its way into print.

Vice President Joe Biden was known to let his enthusiasm get the best of him at times. At the signing ceremony for the Affordable Care Act, Biden was heard telling President Barack Obama, "This is a big f---ing deal." President Obama got some static for calling his opponent Mitt Romney a "bullsh---er" in *Rolling Stone* magazine. Neither made much of a splash.

It was really President Richard Nixon who forced the press into dealing with how to report profanity. Nixon recorded every conversation in his office, and when the Watergate hearings made those tapes public, many people were shocked to hear the torrent of bad language pouring out of his mouth. When transcripts of the tapes were published, they did not contain the troubling words; instead, they were always replaced with the now iconic phrase "expletive deleted."[1]

In 2004, Vice President Richard Cheney got into an argument on the Senate floor with Senator Patrick Leahy (D-VT). Their heated discussion ended with Cheney telling Leahy to "f--- yourself." What was unusual was that the *Washington Post* reported the language without bleeping it out, apparently because he had used it to attack a senator on the Senate floor.[2]

This was the first time the *Washington Post* had used the actual *F* word since publishing the Kenneth Starr report in 1998. Before that, a search of the archives only showed two occasions when the paper had used that word.[3] NPR chose not to use the word, instead saying that the vice president used a "vulgar epithet."

President George W. Bush was caught on tape at a dinner in Russia talking to British Prime Minister Tony Blair saying, "See, the irony is that what they need to do is get Syria to get Hezbollah to stop doing this s---, and it's over." There was little fuss over this quote in 2006 as it was not said in a particularly public setting, and it was seen a fairly honest statement of the situation he was discussing in

LEARNING OBJECTIVES

After studying this chapter, you will be able to

1 Identify and describe the two approaches to judging journalistic ethics that Franklin Foer suggests

2 Describe at least two factors to weigh when considering a lie according to the Bock model and identify the major ethical problem related to truth-telling

3 Explain how a newspaper's error and subsequent apology became a springboard for discussion in its community

4 Describe at least two examples of how advertisers attempted to influence programming on television

5 Explain why it took media outlets so long to report on the Flint, Michigan, water crisis

Lebanon. In this case, the *Washington Post* did not deem it necessary to quote the actual word.[4]

But in January 2018, President Donald Trump generated a lot of news after making some highly offensive and obscene remarks about the country of Haiti, the continent of Africa, and presumably several countries in Central America. The report in the *Washington Post* read this way:

Trump derides protections for immigrants from "shithole" countries

President Trump grew frustrated with lawmakers Thursday in the Oval Office when they discussed protecting immigrants from Haiti, El Salvador and African countries as part of a bipartisan immigration deal, according to several people briefed on the meeting.

"Why are we having all these people from shithole countries come here?" Trump said, according to these people, referring to countries mentioned by the lawmakers.

Trump then suggested that the United States should instead bring more people from countries such as Norway, whose prime minister he met with Wednesday. The president, according to a White House official, also suggested he would be open to more immigrants from Asian countries because he felt that they help the United States economically.

In addition, the president singled out Haiti, telling lawmakers that immigrants from that country must be left out of any deal, these people said.

"Why do we need more Haitians?" Trump said, according to people familiar with the meeting. "Take them out."[5]

There has been considerable debate over what is appropriate and inappropriate for the press to do when the president or a member of his cabinet uses offensive language, especially to express an offensive idea or point of view. Marty Baron, executive editor of the *Washington Post*, told the *Washingtonian*,

When the president says it, we'll use it verbatim. . . . That's our policy. We discussed it quickly, but there was no debate.[6]

CNN used the full vulgarity on its chyron, in a way the network has not generally done. On the day the news was breaking, Fox News did not use the vulgarity itself on its home page, but on the actual story used "s---hole" in the headline. For the record, Fox News also reported at the time that it had independently confirmed the president's statements. The *New York Times* declined to use the word in the headline, but did in its story.

NPR initially did not use the word, referring to it as a "vulgarity," but as the story progressed, the public radio network decided to use the word sparingly—approximately once an hour.[7] MSNBC's use of the term varied depending on the host. Some used it repeatedly, while Rachel Maddow used the actual word quite sparingly, as is her usual practice with offensive language on the show.

The vehemently anti-Trump *New York Daily News* had perhaps the most creative approach, using an emoji-based cartoon to get its message across.

Twitter, of course, was exploding with excitement over how the media were reporting this story, but the best tweet, and one of the few that really got at the main ethical issue here, was from Karen Attiah, global opinion editor from the *Washington Post*, who wrote, "I hope every media outlet that is going to produce outraged pieces about Trump's 'shithole' comments takes a long and hard look at its coverage of black and brown countries."[8]

In this chapter, we look at and attempt to understand why media practitioners behave the way they do and how the media-consuming public can judge their behavior.

Stay up to date on the latest in media by visiting the author's blog at ralphehanson.com

Ethical Principles and Decision Making

The words *morality* and *ethics* are often used interchangeably, but they are distinctly different concepts. Media ethics scholars Philip Patterson and Lee Wilkins explain that **morals** refer to a religious or philosophical code of behavior that may or may not be rational. **Ethics**, by contrast, come from the ancient Greek study of the rational way to decide what is good for individuals or society. A moral decision depends on the values held by an individual, but an ethical decision should be explainable to others in a way that they will appreciate, regardless of whether they accept it. In short, ethics consist of the ways in which we make choices between competing moral principles.[9]

Journalists in the United States have a wealth of competing ethical principles to draw on beyond the basic Judeo-Christian values that constitute the core of American morality. (This is not to deny that there are many other significant religious traditions in the United States. But a recent survey of journalists showed that they come overwhelmingly from either Christian or Jewish households.[10]) Franklin Foer, writing in the *New Republic*, suggests that there are two approaches to judging journalistic ethics. The first considers the journalist's process of producing the product. If the process has moral failings, such as conflicts of interest, then the product will be flawed. The other approach, which he advocates, suggests that the product itself should be judged. Apart from the process of production, what can be said about the ethical quality of the outcome?[11] Media leaders must examine the major ethical principles affecting journalism (all of which fall within Foer's two categories), consider how they might be applied to journalistic decision making, and look at a contemporary model for deciding between competing ethical principles.

Aristotle: Virtue and the Golden Mean

The Greek philosopher Aristotle was a student of Plato and the tutor of Alexander the Great. Although he lived more than 2,300 years ago (approximately 350 BC), his writings on ethics, logic, natural science, psychology, politics, and the arts contain insights that are still relevant, especially his comments on ethics and human endeavor. Aristotle argued that the ultimate goal of all human effort is "the good," and the ultimate good is happiness. To Aristotle, achieving happiness involved striking a balance, a "just-right point between excess and defect."[12] Popularizers have labeled this valued midpoint the **golden mean**.

The classic example of the golden mean is courage, which strikes a balance between the inaction and timidity of cowardice and the recklessness of foolhardiness, both of which are unacceptable behaviors. The example of courage also illustrates how the acceptable ethical middle ground is not a single defined place, but its parameters depend on the abilities and strengths of the individual.[13] To behave ethically, according to Aristotle, individuals must

- Know what they are doing
- Select their action with a moral reason
- Act out of good character

In other words, Aristotle emphasized the character and the intent of the actor and how those determine the way in which he or she acts.

Media ethics scholar David L. Martinson cautions journalists not to take an overly simplistic view of the golden mean and assume that it refers only to compromise. Instead, they must recognize that finding the mean requires virtue. Martinson writes,

A virtuous journalist is one who communicates truthfully in a manner which will enable the reader or listener to better understand the reality of the community, nation, and world in which he or she lives. In that communication, the journalist will show respect for human dignity and individual circumstances.[14]

To test this principle, consider the photo of Marcus Martin flying through the air after being hit by a car at a white nationalist riot in Charlottesville, Virginia, discussed in the "Test Your Visual Media Literacy" box. A newspaper editor trying to decide whether to run this disturbing photo might want to hit a mean between sensitivity and the need to report what happened. One extreme would be not running the photo at all; the other would be running a graphic image of the victims of the driver of the car that plowed through a crowd of counterprotesters writhing in pain. A possible middle ground would consist of running the photo of the hit taking place. Other forms of balance might be reducing the size of the photo so that it would have less impact than a large photo and placing it on an inside page rather than on the front of the sports page. The decision to run the photo could also be justified by the argument that the editor was acting out of good character by feeling an obligation to help readers understand what happened during the riot.

Kant: The Categorical Imperative

German philosopher Immanuel Kant published his most important writings during the final decades of the eighteenth century. Kant differed from Aristotle in that Kant suggested that morality lies in the act itself and not in the character of the actor or the intent behind the action.

"IT WAS SUCH A VIOLENT COLLISION"

August 12, 2017, was Ryan Kelly's last day on the job for the *Daily Progress*, the newspaper for Charlottesville, Virginia. He was getting ready to move on to be the digital and social media coordinator for Ardent Craft Ales. But he picked that Saturday as his last day so he wouldn't leave the paper shorthanded on the day a big white nationalist protest was scheduled.[15] "The journalist in me wanted to be there," Kelly told the National Press Photographers Association (NPPA) magazine.

The Unite the Right demonstration had come to town in part because Lee Park, home of a statue of Confederate general Robert E. Lee, had been renamed Emancipation Park. The night before the demonstration, there had been a torch-lit march through town. The day of the demonstration, the protest never got properly started because a riot broke out between the white nationalists and a group of counterprotesters.

The rioters did not like the press. One protester attacked reporters with pepper spray while others splashed liquid on them or threw eggs. One African American reporter was punched by a demonstrator wearing a T-shirt with a photo of Hitler on it.[16]

Kelly was out in the street, but he stepped onto the sidewalk about twenty seconds or so before the car driven by James Alex Fields Jr. came roaring up. The car ran through the counterprotesters, killing one person and injuring nineteen others.[17]

Kelly says he just started documenting the scene: "It was pure reflex. Years of photojournalism experience had prepared me to react instinctively, and it was more muscle memory than intentional composition that led to those photos."[18] The photo itself is a frozen moment of action. Kelly told NPR,

> You see sunglasses and shoes and cellphones that aren't connected to people's hands or feet or heads. You see water spraying. There's just a lot of violent, violent details coming through in ways that you don't normally experience in everyday life. . . . It was such a violent collision. He was travelling so fast down the road when he collided with the crowd.

Afterward, Kelly and his editor Wesley Hester reviewed the images he had downloaded to his laptop to decide which ones to transmit. They saw the image of people being thrown into the air and knew that while the photo was disturbing and graphic, it told the news.[19]

The photo had an immediate impact, distributed nationwide by the Associated Press. Then, in April 2018, it was announced that Kelly had won the Pulitzer Prize for spot photography. The citation read, "For a chilling image that reflected the photographer's reflexes and concentration in

ASSOCIATED PRESS

capturing the moment of impact of a car attack during a racially charged protest in Charlottesville, Virginia."[20]

Taking a photo that grabbed the nation's attention and made him famous did not make Kelly happy, however. "It almost feels like a bad dream at this point," he told the NPPA.[21]

"This is journalism, I understand that. But being recognized with awards and especially the Pulitzer, they're an incredible honor, but I was constantly reminded that it came at the expense of someone's life and injuries and emotional trauma and PTSD for lots of people."[22]

"I'm just happy I could have done my job in that moment despite the fact that I wish it had never happened to begin with."[23] He added, "I would die a happy man if I never witness anything like I saw on Saturday."[24]

. . . .

WHAT does this photo say?

What does this photo of the car hitting Marcus Martin say? What news value does it have? Does it tell you anything important about the white nationalists who marched in Charlottesville?

WHY was this photo published?

Why do you think newspapers and websites published this photo? Why would editors decide not to publish the photo?

HOW do you and your classmates interpret this photo?

How does this photo make you feel? Does it change your understanding of the riots in Charlottesville? Are still images any better or worse than video? Does it matter whether the photo or video has explicit gore? Does that make it any less disturbing? You will have the opportunity to think about this photo and revisit these questions as you work your way through the first portion of this chapter.

He also put forward the Judeo-Christian value of seeing people as ends, never as a means to an end. In short, Kant emphasized that you cannot use people to achieve your goals.

Kant's ethics begin with the notion that we can reason and hence are able to base our actions on moral reasoning. Because of this, people are responsible for their own actions and are obliged to act in a moral way.

The basic summary of Kant's **categorical imperative**, written in the 1780s, states, "Act as if the maxim of your action were to become through your will a universal law of nature."[25] In simpler terms, Kant asks people to consider what would be the result of everyone acting the same way they themselves wish to act. Kant does not worry particularly about the consequences of an action; rather, he looks at the act itself. This does not mean that Kant doesn't consider outcomes important; it means only that he believes unethical behavior cannot be justified by its possibly desirable outcomes.

In the case of the riot photo, the philosopher might ask what moral decision the photographer made. The photographer's decision was to tell the truth about what happened during the riot. Would we be willing to accept the consequences of everyone telling the truth? What problems might arise out of a position of absolute truth?

John Stuart Mill: The Principle of Utility

In the movie *Star Trek II: The Wrath of Khan*, the emotionless Spock performs a rational yet selfless act. He saves the crew of the starship U.S.S. *Enterprise* by entering a reactor room to prevent an explosion that would have killed everyone on board the ship. But in doing so, he absorbs a lethal dose of radiation. As he dies, he justifies his actions to his friends with the maxim, "The needs of the many outweigh the needs of the few, or the one." In this moment, Spock sums up the central tenet of the nineteenth-century ethical philosopher John Stuart Mill's **principle of utility**: the greatest good for the greatest number.

Mill did not create the idea of utility, but he did do a great deal to refine and promote the philosophy known as utilitarianism. Mill wrote that the consequences of actions are important in deciding what is ethical: "An act's rightness is [a] desirable end."[26] Looking back to the Aristotelian notion of happiness as the ultimate public good, utilitarianism holds that which is virtuous is that which provides the greatest happiness for the greatest number. Or, looked at another way, that which causes the least pain is best. The challenge in applying this principle is that the same act can cause both happiness and pain. NBC News faced extensive criticism when it decided to air excerpts from a multimedia disk created by Seung-hui Cho, who shot and killed thirty-two students and faculty at Virginia Tech in April 2007. Family and friends of the victims said that they felt victimized all over again when they saw the video. NBC News president Steve Kapas said the network ran the excerpts from the disk so that the public might better understand what had happened. "This is as close as we'll ever come to being in the mind of a killer," he said.[27] The network accepted the additional suffering it caused a smaller number of people who knew the victims in order to accomplish the greater good of informing the public at large.

Mill also held that some forms of pleasure or happiness are morally superior to others. He suggested that actions and decisions that improve the lot of society as a whole may be superior to those that merely provide the most physical or emotional pleasure.[28] Employing utilitarian reasoning, an editor might decide to run the photo of the attack even though it is painful to see for the people who were involved because it would help people around the country understand what happened. As Kelly put it with respect to his own photo of the Charlottesville attack, "Maybe seeing the horror of what an attack like that looks like, it might shock folks into an understanding that they wouldn't have had if it weren't for that photo."[29]

London Stereoscopic Company - Hulton Archive

▲ John Stuart Mill has been called "the most influential English-speaking philosopher of the nineteenth century." He explored the individual's right to have freedom of thought, opinion, and action in society.

John Rawls: The Veil of Ignorance

Contemporary philosopher John Rawls builds on the ideas of utilitarianism. His argument is that which is just is also that which is fair:

> First: Each person is to have an equal right to the most extensive basic liberty compatible with a similar liberty for others. . . .

> Second: Social and economic inequalities are to be arranged so that they are both (a) reasonably expected to be to everyone's advantage, and (b) attached to positions and offices open to all.[30]

To decide what is fair, the journalist must hide behind Rawls's **veil of ignorance**, a principle of ethics that says that justice emerges when we make decisions without considering the status of the people involved and without considering where we personally fall in the social system. In other words, we should not ask, "How does this affect me?" Behind this veil, everyone is equal. Journalists following this principle would not question whether they or their subjects were powerful or powerless, rich or poor, Black or white, male or female.

Reporters deciding how to treat sources should make the same decision whether they like or dislike the person. They should imagine how they would want to be treated if they were the source and would have to live with the outcome of the story. The value of freedom of the press must be considered on an equal level with the protection of individual privacy, as reporters behind the veil of ignorance do not know whether they are a reporter or a source.[31] It is difficult to say what a photo editor would decide to do with the riot photo using the veil of ignorance. Photographer Kelly acknowledges that the photo brought him national honor and attention, especially when he won the Pulitzer Prize for it. On the other hand, he said he could easily imagine how painful seeing the image showing up repeatedly could be for the people whom the driver hit. "That picture just went all over the world and it keeps popping up in the news and it would've made sense to me if they were unhappy about it, unhappy about the constant reminders of pain and the fact that Heather [Heyer] died and so many were injured."[32]

Hutchins Commission: Social Responsibility Ethics

In 1947, widespread concerns about the ethical behavior of the press led Henry Luce, the founder of *Time* magazine, to form a commission to study the responsibility of the press in the United States. Chaired by scholar Robert M. Hutchins, the commission concluded that the First Amendment, by itself, might not be enough to protect the free speech rights of the public because a small number of corporations controlled a large number of the available communication outlets. Although the government might not be limiting free speech, corporations might do so. The report reached two major conclusions:

1. The press has a responsibility to give voice to the public and to society.

2. The free press was not living up to that responsibility to the public because of its need to serve its commercial masters.

The social responsibility theory of the press, holding that the press has an ethical obligation to society, arose from the Hutchins report. (This theory is discussed further in Chapter 11.) The Hutchins Commission listed five requirements for a responsible press:

1. The media should provide a truthful, comprehensive, and intelligent account of the day's events in a context that gives them meaning.

2. The media should serve as a forum for the exchange of comment and criticism (that is, the press should present the full range of thought and criticism).

3. The media should project a representative picture of the constituent groups within the society.

4. The media should present and clarify the goals and values of the society.

5. The media should provide full access to the day's news.

Today, the range of long-tail media, including blogs and podcasts, allows both professional and citizen journalists to bypass legacy media (traditional big media) and go directly to the public, though it is hard for the long-tail news outlets to have the impact that a newspaper or television station can. Nevertheless, this is one more example of Secret 2—There are no mainstream media.

Using a social responsibility approach, running the photo of the automobile attack can be defended, assuming that it is run with the goal of giving readers a better understanding of what happened during the riots in Charlottesville.

The Bok Model for Ethical Decision Making

Given the many competing ethical principles journalists must consider, it can be difficult to decide what is right or wrong, as our consideration of the decision about running a disturbing photo illustrates. But contemporary ethicist Sissela Bok provides a straightforward three-step model for analyzing an ethical situation:

1. Consult your conscience—How do you feel about the action? What does your conscience tell you is right?

2. Seek alternatives—Is there another way to achieve the same goal that will not raise ethical issues? Is there an expert to whom you can turn for advice?

3. Hold an imaginary ethical dialogue with everyone involved—Ask, "How will my action affect others?" Discuss the issues involved from the point of view of each of the people whom it will affect. Think about who will be involved: the source, the news consumer, the public at large, a special interest group, and so forth.[33]

In her book *Lying: Moral Choice in Public and Private Life*, Bok suggests consulting experts and holding a public dialogue. It may not be practical for a working reporter or editor to apply her method fully, but the basic approach of consulting one's conscience, considering alternatives, and taking the point of view of all affected parties is reasonable.[34]

Truthfulness and the News

Journalists have always claimed that they feel obliged to report the truth,[35] and reporters or editors who violate this commitment to truth have paid dearly. The *Washington Post*'s credibility suffered a major blow when the paper discovered in 1981 that a Pulitzer Prize–winning story about an eight-year-old heroin addict by reporter Janet Cooke was fabricated. In the spring of 2003, young *New York Times* reporter Jayson Blair created shock waves throughout the news business when it was revealed that he had fabricated or plagiarized at least thirty-six stories for the nation's most prestigious newspaper. The controversy concerns not only the poor behavior of particular journalists, but also the implications of that behavior for the publication and the resulting lack of trust in the institution. At issue, too, is the lack of commitment to the truth on the part of publications and editors that put exciting stories ahead of making sure those stories are true.

In her book on the nature of lying, Bok states that there are at least two factors to weigh when considering a lie. The first is whether the speaker is intending to transmit the truth or attempting to deceive people. The second is whether the statement itself is true or false. Bok argues that the major ethical problem related to truth-telling is intentionally deceiving people to "make them believe what we ourselves do not believe."[36] Media ethics scholar David Martinson argues that telling the truth entails more than just stating facts that are not false. Instead, the press needs to report "the truth about the fact." In the early 1950s, when Senator Joseph McCarthy—without any evidence—started accusing people of being communists, the press reported his charges without giving any indication that the charges he was making might be false or without conducting independent verification. It was true that McCarthy had made the statements, but the statements themselves were not true. Martinson suggests that the press too often asks whether the story is factually true instead of asking whether the story helps the public understand the truth.[37]

The truthfulness of nonfiction books has also been called into question. The best-known instance of fabrication in recent years has been James Frey's memoir, *A Million Little Pieces*. Published in 2003, *Pieces* was presented as a memoir about crime, violence, drugs, alcohol, and redemption. Despite some questions raised early on about its essential truthfulness, it was a wildly popular best seller, and many readers deeply identified with Frey.[38]

But in January 2006, muckraking investigative website The Smoking Gun (TSG) reported that the book was filled with exaggerations and "a million little lies."[39] TSG investigated Frey after the site had trouble finding a mug shot from one of Frey's numerous arrests portrayed in the book. (TSG has a big section devoted to celebrity mug shots.) What the site's researchers found in their investigation was that Frey either fabricated or grossly embellished the accounts of his involvement in a train accident that killed a girl, the time he spent in jail, and the details of a friend's suicide.[40] In another memoir, a former U.S. secretary of labor fabricated testimony that he supposedly had given before Congress.[41] And a prominent writer admitted including imagined conversations in a biography of Ted Kennedy. Presidential biographer Edmund Morris went so far as to insert himself as a fictional character in his biography of Ronald Reagan (a fact that he acknowledged in the introduction to the book).

In contrast, when late *New York Times* reporter David Carr wrote his memoir *Night of the Gun* about drugs, crime, alcohol, and single parenthood, he video recorded interviews with people he had interacted with over the years. In the book, he told things the way he remembered events and then also explained the way the people he interviewed remembered the same events. Carr, with his memoir, acknowledged the fact that a person's memory of how something happened could be faulty and was subject to change over time, something many memoir writers seem to have trouble admitting. (For several years, if you went to the index at the back of this book, you would find that Carr, in his role as the *New York Times'* media reporter, was one of the most cited people.) Carr died of cancer in February 2015.

Catching Fabrications

Except for tabloid stories about a space alien having Elvis's baby, articles in magazines and newspapers are generally assumed to be true, or at the very least based on fact. But occasionally that basic assumption is called into question.

Consider the following case: A twenty-five-year-old writer named Stephen Glass had written incredible stories for the *New Republic*, *Rolling Stone*, *George*, and *Harper's*. Other writers—some would say jealous colleagues—thought Glass's stories, with their customary "wow" opening paragraphs that set the scene, were too good to be true. Unfortunately, they were. In 1998, Glass was caught fabricating an article for the *New Republic* about teenage hackers, and his subsequent firing sent shock waves throughout the magazine industry.[42] Follow-up investigations suggested that Glass had fabricated material for dozens of articles without the magazines' fact-checkers catching on.

Said Charles Lane, then the editor of the *New Republic*, "I don't wish [Glass] ill. . . . I just don't want him to be in journalism."[43] After becoming the poster boy for bad journalism, Glass left the magazine business, went to law school, and wrote a novel. Following the critical and commercial failure of his novel, Glass has reportedly worked as a paralegal and as an occasional member of a Los Angeles comedy troupe.[44] How did Glass get away with his fabrications? First, the magazines did not conduct fact-checking as well as they should have. Second, Glass would submit articles late so that they couldn't be checked, and he would fabricate substantiation for them, such as a phony web page and voice mail message for the beleaguered high-tech company in the hacker story.[45] In an article for the political magazine *George*, Glass wrote a description of presidential advisor Vernon Jordan based on anonymous sources. He avoided the fact-checking by saying that his sources would be fired if they were contacted at work. After editors found out that Glass had been fabricating articles, fact-checkers discovered that the sources he had cited didn't exist. To be fair to the fact-checkers, their procedures were designed to catch mistakes, not outright fabrications.[46] One result of the fallout from Glass's fabrications was a renewed commitment to fact-checking at magazines; another was increased skepticism toward sensational stories, especially by young writers.

Lying About Who You Are. Former *Washington Post* reporter Jose Antonio Vargas was a successful young journalist. He was part of a reporting team that won a Pulitzer for covering the Virginia Tech massacre, he wrote a well-regarded profile of Facebook founder Mark Zuckerberg for the *New Yorker*, and he's written for numerous outlets around the country, including the *Huffington Post* and the *San Francisco Chronicle*.

The secret that Vargas kept until the summer of 2011 was that he is an undocumented immigrant who entered the United States illegally from the Philippines.

Vargas outed himself in a first-person article for *New York Times Magazine*. In it, he told the story of how he came to the United States as a twelve-year-old boy to live with his grandparents in California. He did not know that he had entered the country on forged papers until he took his supposed immigration status card to the Department of Motor Vehicles at age sixteen to get his driver's permit. There he was told that his card was fake and that he should not come back again.[47] As he told MSNBC's Maddow, Vargas's parents and grandparents intended for him to work shadow economy jobs until he could find a U.S. citizen to marry and get a permanent residency card that way. Only one problem: When Vargas was in high school, he came out publicly as being gay. So while he was out of the closet as a gay male, he remained secretive about his immigration status.[48] Vargas initially offered his story to the *Washington Post*, but the paper turned him down. Vargas then shopped it to *New York Times Magazine*, which jumped at the chance. The editors went so far as to "tear up" the completed magazine and put the Vargas story on the cover.[49] The story of Vargas and his outing of himself caused a fair amount of controversy in journalistic circles because Vargas had been lying about his immigration status for his entire adult life.[50] Phil Bronstein, who had hired Vargas to write for the *San Francisco Chronicle*, writes that he felt duped by Vargas, especially since Vargas wrote about the experiences of undocumented workers without mentioning that he was one himself. On the other hand, Bronstein hopes that Vargas's story may lead to meaningful immigration reform:

Alex Wong/Getty Images

▲ Pulitzer Prize–winning reporter Jose Antonio Vargas revealed in the summer of 2011 that he was an undocumented immigrant who entered the country illegally from the Philippines when he was a child.

> But if he can come out, the force of his story—both good reaction and bad—and his project just might lubricate the politically tarred-up wheels of government and help craft sane immigration policy. If it has that effect, we should forgive him his lies.[51]

At the heart of Vargas's story is this central ethical conflict: A journalist lying about his or her identity is always troubling for any reason, but if Vargas had not lied about who he was, he could not have been a reporter. This is, at its core, the definition of an ethical problem. Because ethics are all about what you do when no answer seems right, when all answers are problematic, when telling the whole truth stands in the way of telling any truth.

Disclosing Conflicts of Interest

Being fair and balanced are core journalistic values that have been discussed extensively in earlier chapters. At times, however, other factors can overwhelm that value, especially when the interests of the news organization's owners or the journalist him- or herself are in conflict with the values of balance and fairness. This problem of a conflict of corporate interest extends beyond suppressing stories; it also involves actively promoting the company's interests.

▲ Fox News Channel host Sean Hannity, shown here (right) interviewing Donald Trump Jr. in July 2017, did not disclose that he was a client of one of his guests, lawyer Michael Cohen, presenting a potential conflict of interest. Hannity disputes that Cohen was actually his lawyer, although Cohen stated in court documents that he was.

During the spring of 2018, Fox News host Sean Hannity had interviewed President Donald Trump's attorney Michael Cohen on several occasions on his top-rated evening show. He criticized the fact that federal agents had raided Cohen's office and home. The problem for Hannity is that he had not disclosed that he had also been a client of Cohen's, something that got revealed in court after the raid. Hannity's response was twofold. First, he said he does not need to follow journalistic ethics because he is a talk show host, not a journalist. The difficulty with this is that sometimes he says he's a journalist, an opinion journalist, or an advocacy journalist. His second claim of innocence is that Cohen was not really his lawyer. "I never retained his services, I never received an invoice, I never paid Michael Cohen for legal fees," Hannity said. "I did have occasional brief conversations with Michael Cohen—he's a great attorney—about legal questions I had."[52] (Nevertheless, Cohen listed Hannity as one of his three clients.[53]) This undisclosed relationship that Hannity had with a source could be considered a conflict of interest.

Another example comes from the *Washington Post*. The paper is owned by Jeff Bezos, the same billionaire (and richest person in the world) who is the CEO and major stockholder for Amazon.com. To deal with this conflict of interest, reporters at the *Post* mention that Bezos owns the paper every time they report on Amazon. Traditionally, such conflicts of interest are recognized when reporters give favorable coverage to a company in which they have an interest or to a person who is their friend. Or a conflict could involve the negative coverage of someone they dislike. With the growth in size and concentration of media companies in the past decade, an increasing issue is conflict of interest by the owners themselves. Newspapers always claim that they keep the business side of their operations separate from the newsroom, but it is sometimes hard for the public to see things that way.

Recognizing Fake News Is Consumer Responsibility

You know how you have always been warned about being careful when something seems too good to be true? That is never more the case than when you see a story online and say to yourself, "YES! This is exactly how I thought it would be."[54]

Take, for example, the following story from the *Seattle Tribune*:

BREAKING: Trump's Android Device Believed to Be Source of Recent White House Leaks

If you've recently seen the hashtag #DitchTheDevice trending on social media, it's because, according to several private intelligence reports, the source of the multiple recent leaks within the White House is President Trump's unsecured Android device.

Throughout the past several weeks President Trump and his administration have expressed extreme frustration over the multiple leaks provided to members of the press from inside the White House.

The recent leaks range from information regarding his executive orders (before he issued them), fighting and chaos among White House staffers, classified conversations with foreign leaders (specifically Australian Prime Minister Malcolm Turnbull & Mexican President Enrique Peña Nieto), White House staffers conducting meetings in the dark because they can't figure out how the lights work, and President Trump wandering the White House in his bathrobe.[55]

In March 2017, the story showed up repeatedly on social media, posted by people who dislike President Trump and love the thought that the leaks from his administration are coming from hackers who had compromised his Android smartphone. But the savvy reader should be able to quickly recognize this as a fabrication—fake news, if you will.

First of all, the kinds of documents that were necessary for the leaks that had come from the Trump administration are not the kind that would be likely to be stored on a smartphone by a guy who is not particularly tech savvy. (This is not a criticism of President Trump—merely a statement of fact. He does not use either a computer or a particularly modern smartphone; nor have most of our other presidents.)

The story also smelled because it was a little too pat; it has a bit too much schadenfreude about it: "Wouldn't it be so appropriate if Trump were being done in by the phone he uses to send out all those early morning tweets?" The story simply matched too many of the fantasies of Trump critics.

So the first step a suspicious reader should do is look for information about the site. At the *Seattle Tribune*, it was on the Disclaimer page on the website, as clear as day:

> The Seattle Tribune is a news and entertainment satire web publication. The Seattle Tribune may or may not use real names, often in semi-real or mostly fictitious ways. All news articles contained within The Seattle Tribune are fictional and presumably satirical news.

Now, that is not a completely honest statement. The story about President Trump and his phone was not funny in a satirical way—it was clearly "fake news," complete with links to real stories. It was designed to attract readers drawn to an appealing story, so that those people would see the ads on the *Tribune*'s pages, and hopefully click on them.

You should also notice that this publication had a name that sounded a lot like a very reliable news source, the *Seattle Times*. But this was the *Seattle Tribune*, a name chosen most likely to deliberately confuse unsuspecting readers.

So when you are thinking about posting links to stories on Facebook that make you angry or self-satisfied, why not look for reputable stories from reliable news sources instead of leaping to the clickbait made-up stories. Think back to the chart from Chapter 5 of reliable and unreliable news sources, and try to pick stories that run on the most reliable and least partisan sources. And remember Secret 5—All media are social.

Photos and the Truth

Photos seem to be at the heart of many of the most troubling ethical cases that journalists face. Whether it is showing live television video of the shooting at Columbine High School, moments of private grief following a drunk-driving accident, or the horrors of September 11, 2001, editors have always had to strike a balance between sensitivity toward readers, consideration for sources, and dedication to reporting the news accurately. Now they also have new tools, like Adobe Photoshop, that allow them to manipulate photos digitally, sometimes producing quite different images from those they started with.

Photographs have always been prone to manipulation. Photographers choose their films, lenses, and angles with a particular image in mind. Darkroom techniques extended the photographer's ability to control the image. But now photographs are altered electronically in ways that can be almost undetectable. In fact, all photos published today are manipulated digitally in terms of size, shape, color, and contrast. For example, the light and dark contrasts in many of the photos in this book have been adjusted in preparation for the printing process so that they will look better.

So the question becomes "How much manipulation is too much?" Keep in mind that there are several issues here:

- What is an acceptable level of photo manipulation?

- Should viewers know to what degree a photo has been altered?

- Does intentionally making changes in a photo change the viewer's response to the image?

▼ BOX 15.1

Standards for Digital Photo Manipulation

The *Charlotte Observer* has put together an extremely specific set of guidelines for how digital photos can be edited. Among its criteria are the following:

- "Dodging and burning," similar to what could be done in a conventional darkroom, are acceptable.

- Colors cannot be changed.

- Backgrounds cannot be eliminated or "aggressively toned."

- The original unedited image files need to be downloaded.

- Digital retouching (cloning) can be used only to remove things such as dust spots on the image.

- The only time these rules can be violated is with a photo illustration that is clearly labeled as such and can be clearly seen as an illustration.

Source: Kenny Irby, "*Charlotte Observer* Photo Correction/Editing Guidelines," *Poynter*, September 25, 2003.

In 2008, there was an intense discussion on an online photojournalism bulletin board about a college newspaper advisor who insisted that a photographer needed to make the sky bluer in a photo of a Martin Luther King Day march. Most of the photographers on the bulletin board were outraged at the demand, saying that deepening the sky's color would be completely unethical. But how many photographers, seeing the pale winter sky, would have boosted the blue in the sky without a moment's thought? Or if the photo had been taken in the predigital era, how many photographers would have chosen to shoot with Kodak's Kodachrome film, which is known for giving intensely vibrant colors?[56]

On a similar, simple level, a photographer at the *Charleston Gazette* was disciplined for removing a television station's logo from a reporter's microphone. After the altered photo was noticed and commented on by West Virginia radio personality Hoppy Kercheval, the *Gazette* published an apology on Facebook along with the unaltered image:

A Gazette photographer went outside the boundaries of our standards when he obscured the name of a television station on a microphone in today's front-page photo. Other than the photographer, no one at the Gazette was aware of what had taken place with the photo. Our photographers know that it is unacceptable to alter reality in news photos. The photographer believed his action helped direct the focus of the photo to the subject. He was wrong to do so. This is a singular incident. Disciplinary action will be taken to ensure it doesn't happen again.[57]

Photo manipulation by magazines first came to the public's attention in 1982, when *National Geographic*'s editors "moved" one of the Egyptian pyramids so that a photo of the pyramids would fit on the magazine's cover. The change had no lasting moral significance—a similar effect could have been created by having the photographer reshoot the picture from a slightly different angle—but it forced the magazine industry to confront the implications of journalists altering images.[58] (See Box 15.1.)

Conflicts over digital manipulation of photographs emerge on a regular basis. In June 2006, *El Nuevo Herald*, the leading Spanish-language paper in the United States, ran a photo that appeared to show four Cuban prostitutes soliciting tourists in Havana while two police officers looked on. The only problem was that the hookers weren't actually there—they had been added digitally by an editor.[59] In another case, a *Los Angeles Times* photographer was fired in 2003 after he combined two images of a U.S. soldier supervising a group of refugees in Iraq to make the image more dramatic. But sometimes the alterations are on a smaller scale and are intended to help rather than to deceive. After a terrorist bombing of a train in Spain, some newspapers digitally removed a severed arm lying next to the tracks because they felt the image was too horrifying for a family newspaper.

Mistakes and Consequences in the News

All communicators, such as journalists, news anchors, and so on, should realize that they will not always make the right decision; mistakes will be made, and they will get facts wrong. Some of these errors will be relatively small and unnoticed by all but a very few. Others will be larger and can pose an existential threat to the communicator's organization. So, while it is certainly correct to avoid as many mistakes and ethical misjudgments as possible, communicators also need to be prepared to deal with the consequences of their actions.

Apologies are a hard thing for the media to handle. Too often they take the form of "If anyone was offended, we're sorry you feel that way," which is so weak that it lacks almost all meaning. Other times they can trivialize the seriousness of the error. But sometimes an apology can serve as a springboard for discussion about the original issue.

That is what happened in the fall of 2010, when the *Portland Press Herald* in Maine ran a long, thoughtful story on its front page about the local observance of the end of the Muslim holy month of Ramadan. What would normally be considered a relatively noncontroversial story became extremely controversial because this year the final day of Ramadan fell on September 11. Topping things off for the paper was the fact that it planned to run all its September 11 anniversary stories in the September 12 Sunday paper. The response was instantaneous and furious. Letter writers, emailers, and callers were uniformly upset that the paper did not have a story on the front page about the 9/11 anniversary. And many were upset that there was a story about Ramadan on the front page that day. On Sunday, September 12, the day the paper planned to give extensive coverage of the 9/11 anniversary, the paper ran the following apology:

> We made a news decision on Friday that offended many readers and we sincerely apologize for it.
>
> Many saw Saturday's front-page story and photo regarding the local observance of the end of Ramadan as offensive, particularly on the day, September 11, when our nation and the world were paying tribute to those who died in the 9/11 terrorist attacks nine years ago.
>
> We have acknowledged that we erred by at least not offering balance to the story and its prominent position on the front page.
>
> What you are reading today was the planned coverage of the 9/11 events. We believed that the day after the anniversary would be the appropriate occasion to provide extensive new coverage of the events and observances conducted locally and elsewhere.

In hindsight, it is clear that we should have handled this differently and with greater sensitivity toward the painful memories stirred by the anniversary of 9/11.[60]

But the apology was not the end of the story. Why not? Because some people read that apology as saying there was a connection between peaceful practitioners of Islam in the United States and the terrorists who attacked the nation back in 2001.

That was the central theme of a story that ran soon after on NPR's *On the Media* (OTM). In the story, OTM's Bob Garfield had a somewhat confrontational interview with Richard Connor, the *Press Herald*'s editor and publisher. In the interview, Garfield tried to get Connor to acknowledge that the apology made the "connection between Islam and radical Islamic terrorists." Connor refused to do so. If you listen to the program, several things become clear: Connor had obviously had a bad week and was tired of being criticized by all sides about his paper's coverage of the issue, and Garfield was just as clearly trying to hold Connor accountable for what he had to say.[61] All this led to a follow-up to the September 12 apology that Connor published on September 19 that didn't receive as much attention. Connor wrote,

> I have failed my writing hero, E. B. White, whose guiding principle, outlined in the classic "Elements of Style," was: "Omit needless words."

> If I'd followed that rule last week, I would have responded to criticism of our newspaper on 9/11 with this:

> "Our coverage of the conclusion of the local Ramadan observance was excellent and we are proud of it. We did not adequately cover 9/11 on the 9/11 anniversary, which also should have been front-page news, in my opinion."

> Why would I have omitted the other words in last week's column?

> Their lack of precision led to mischaracterization and misunderstanding. They were used to prove the maxim that a lie travels faster than truth. Mostly they allowed those with a personal ax to grind or a political agenda to advance to twist and misinterpret.

> I meant to apologize for what we did not print—front-page coverage of 9/11 on the anniversary of a day that stirs deep and unhealed wounds. I was in no way apologizing for what we did print in a deservedly prominent position—a striking photo of our local Muslim community in prayer.[62]

What Connor says here is what he probably should have said the previous week—that the paper did a good job of covering Ramadan and a bad job of covering the September 11 anniversary on September 11. This apology is particularly good because it does not talk about "who might have been offended," but rather talks about the quality of judgments made at the paper.

When News Moves Too Fast: Kobe Bryant's Death

The United Press International news agency has long been known for its motto, "Get it first, but first get it right."[63] That motto highlights the complications that journalists face when dealing with rapidly breaking news. And it was readily apparent on January 26, 2020, when basketball legend Kobe Bryant and his daughter were killed in a helicopter crash. As is so often the case, the initial reports were inconsistent with conflicting details. Sometimes it was from a rush to report while other times events simply overtook reporting that has already gone out.

Washington Post media columnist Margaret Sullivan writes that much of the early news about Bryant's death was inaccurate, including a tweet from President Trump that had the wrong number of people killed, the BBC showing a video clip of LeBron James instead of Bryant, and the Twitter trending page about Bryant's death that had a photo of the recently deceased sexual predator Jeffrey Epstein. The *Los Angeles Times*, on the other hand, acknowledged their uncertainty about what had happened in a tweet that read, "We are aware of reports about Kobe Bryant and are currently investigating. We will update here as soon as we can confirm anything."[64]

Other problems came up dealing more with issues of timing than accuracy.

Britain's *Guardian* newspaper got caught when they had a tweet pre-scheduled to go out on that Sunday announcing that Kobe Bryant had been knocked out of third place on the NBA all-time scoring list by LeBron James. The *Guardian* handled this awkward gaff with grace, tweeting,

> We apologise unreservedly for the tweeted story about Kobe Bryant losing his third place in the NBA all-time scoring list.
>
> It had been scheduled earlier in the day before we knew of the sad death of Kobe Bryant. The tweet should not have gone out—and has now been deleted.[65]

More controversial were a series of tweets sent out by *Washington Post* political reporter Felicia Sonmez who shared a link to an older, accurate, story at another media outlet about the rape allegations against Bryant as the details about his death were coming out. Within an hour, the reporter got more than 10,000 comments and emails critiquing her with abuse and death threats for sharing the story. The reporter eventually deleted the tweets. Not long after, the *Washington Post* put her on administrative leave, saying, "Her tweets displayed poor judgment that undermined the work of her colleagues."[66] *Post* management was also critical for her tweets being outside of her coverage area.

Washington Post media critic Erik Wemple disagreed with management, writing that all the reporter did was tweet out a link to an excellent story from the *Daily Beast* that gave the history of the charges against Bryant, explained why they got dropped, and discussed how Bryant settled the subsequent civil lawsuit. Wemple defended Sonmez, noting that if reporters would normally get suspended for tweeting about subjects outside of their assigned area, "the entire newsroom should be on administrative leave." Wemple investigated what the *Post*'s social media guidelines said. This is what he found:

- Be informative. Social media encourages sharing of the human experience, but we should balance personal information with useful information.

- Fact-check. Information on social networks needs to be verified like any other information. Work to verify the authenticity of people and organizations before attributing acts or quotes to them.

- Take ownership. If you mistakenly retweet or forward erroneous information, correct your mistake in a subsequent tweet/update and make an effort to provide a more accurate link.[67]

There Is No "They": Sago Mine Disaster

Few journalistic mistakes have been as cruel as the headlines that ran in newspapers across the country on Wednesday, January 4, 2006. The papers trumpeted that all the coal miners trapped in West Virginia's Sago Mine had been found alive after having been trapped for two days below ground, when, in reality, all but one of the thirteen had died.

In the early morning hours of Monday, January 2, an explosion, likely triggered by lightning, trapped thirteen miners deep below ground in the Sago Mine. About 9:00 p.m. Tuesday, the first body was discovered in the mine, according to a timeline in the *Washington Post*.[68] At 11:45 p.m., one miner was found alive more than two miles into the tunnel.

At this point, confusion reigned. According to the *Post*, at 12:18 a.m., the rescue command center heard a report from a rescue worker that twelve miners were found alive. Apparently, this early report was overheard and spread instantly through a crowd that had been praying for a miracle. Church bells started ringing. People cried, sang, and cheered.

Newspapers and television news outlets across the United States struggled with tight deadlines and inaccurate information during the Sago Mine disaster in West Virginia. Though initial stories reported that some miners survived, the tragic truth was that twelve of them had died.

According to the *Charleston Daily Mail*, then West Virginia governor Joe Manchin had come out to the mine to wait with family members and had asked for confirmation of the good news. Although he did not get the confirmation, Manchin said he was quickly caught up by the joyous mood: "We went out with the people and they said, 'They found them.' We got swept up in this celebration. I said, 'The miracle of all miracles has happened.'"[69] A statement from the governor would seem to signal some level of official confirmation. But within the next half hour, reports started coming into the command center that only one miner was alive—reports that were not passed on to families or the press until nearly 3:00 a.m.

Morning papers, such as the *Charleston Gazette* in West Virginia and Denver's now-defunct *Rocky Mountain News*, started printing around midnight (if not a little earlier). Newspapers must make really tough calls on a breaking story, and unlike television, they leave a permanent reminder of the times that they get a story wrong. For example, the early edition of the *Rocky Mountain News* carried the headline "They're Alive." The headline was corrected in the final edition.

National papers also had problems with the story. *USA Today*, which has perhaps the best national distribution of any newspaper in the country, devoted one-third of its front page to the rescue story on Wednesday. On Thursday, the press started an intense examination of how the story was botched.

According to industry newsweekly *Editor & Publisher*, the *Inter-Mountain*, an eleven-thousand-circulation afternoon daily out of Elkins, West Virginia, managed to get the story right, not only in its print edition but also on its website. *Editor & Publisher* quoted *Inter-Mountain* editor Linda Skidmore's account of the paper's handling of the story: "I feel lucky that we are an afternoon paper and we have the staff that we do. We had a reporter there all night at the scene and I was on the phone with her the whole time." Skidmore also described how the false story started snowballing:

> I was on the phone with [reporter Becky Wagoner] and I was hearing things on CNN and FOX that she was not hearing there. . . . She heard that the miners were alive just before it was broadcast, around midnight. She talked about hearing church bells ringing and people yelling in jubilation—but nothing official.[70]

"We heard that they were found alive through CNN, then it snowballed to ABC, then FOX and it was like a house afire," recalled Wagoner, who said she was at the media information center set up by the mine's operator, International Coal Group Inc., when the reports spread. "A lot of the media left to go to the church where family members were located, but I stayed put because this was where every official news conference was given—and we never got anything official here," she said. "Something was not right. Then we were hearing reports that 12 ambulances had gone in [to the mine area] but only one was coming out. There was so much hype that no one considered the fact that there was no [official] update."[71]

Then a resident of West Virginia, I went to bed Tuesday night with reports on the internet announcing that the miners had been found alive. When I sat down to breakfast and my local paper on Wednesday morning, though, it was immediately obvious that something was wrong with the story. The report from the Associated Press read,

> Twelve miners caught in an explosion in a coal mine were found alive Tuesday night, more than 41 hours after the blast, family members and Gov. Joe Manchin III said.
>
> Bells at a church where relatives had been gathering rang out as family members ran out screaming in jubilation.
>
> Relatives yelled, "They're alive!"
>
> Manchin said rescuers told him the miners were found.
>
> "They told us they have 12 alive," Manchin said. "We have some people that are going to need some medical attention."
>
> A few minutes after word came, the throng, several hundred strong, broke into a chorus of the hymn "How Great Thou Art," in a chilly, night air.[72]

What clues tipped me off? How could a reader, reading between the lines, tell there were problems with the story?

There were no official sources cited, other than the governor. Why didn't reporters also quote a source from the coal company?

When the governor made his statement, he noted, "They told us . . ." Not a name—just "they." My high school journalism teacher Judith Funk always took us to task about that word, asking, "Who's 'they'?" And the Sago story is probably one of the saddest examples of Secret 7— There is no "they."

Later, the story said, "The company did not immediately confirm the news."

There were no details on the miners' condition or where they were found.

In short, the story read like it was passing along secondhand accounts. How did the press go so wrong with this story?

- There was the understandable problem of midnight deadlines. It is very difficult to handle a breaking story under these circumstances. But news organizations certainly could have been clearer in emphasizing the unconfirmed nature of the information in their reports.

- News organizations have gotten way too comfortable passing on unconfirmed stories that originate in the realm of blogs and rumors because they are afraid of being "scooped." No longer does a story have to be true; it just must be true that the story is out there. When we are dealing with rumors about misconduct by politicians, whose realities are more subject to interpretation, perhaps this is OK (though I don't really think so). But when we are talking about the lives of ordinary people, this irresponsibility just does not cut it.

- The facts of the news did not match the story reporters were looking for. Journalists, especially the national press, were looking for a "miracle story," in which people's prayers would be answered and everything would turn out fine. When reporters thought they found that story, they reported it. Tragically, that was not the way the story turned out.

So, what can journalists do to make sure this doesn't happen again? *USA Today*'s Mark Memmott, speaking as part of a panel at West Virginia University on the press coverage of Sago, said,

Our responsibility was to ask a lot of questions and be incredibly careful about attributions and sourcing, and to make sure we told people not just about what we knew, but what we didn't know. We had not seen anybody come out of that mine. We hadn't really talked to anybody who knew what was going on inside there. We had heard from family members, who had heard from somebody else, who in some cases could not even tell reporters on the scene exactly who it was they had heard it from.[73]

Ethics Enforcement

How should the media address ethical issues? Are such issues the responsibility of the individual journalist? Of his or her editor? Should there be a single person in charge of ethics? Perhaps a code of ethics, applied properly, could provide sufficient guidance. In reality, various methods are used. This section looks briefly at some of the choices for systematically handling ethics issues.

The Ombudsman. The **ombudsman**, also known as the reader's representative or audience advocate, takes the point of view of those who purchase or consume the news. Sanders LaMont, former ombudsman for the *Sacramento Bee*, argues that the ombudsman is an essential part of the journalism ethics process because the ombudsman connects the news consumer with the news outlet, be it a magazine, newspaper, website, radio station, or cable news operation.

The term *ombudsman* is derived from the word for a person who mediated between citizens and the government in Sweden in the early 1800s. Since that time, it has been used to describe anyone who mediates between two groups. News ombudsmen have a variety of tasks to perform:

- Listening to the concerns of readers or audience members—Readers tend to be enthusiastic about someone taking their point of view, whereas newsroom employees may be less so. Kenneth Starck, a former ombudsman for Iowa's *Cedar Rapids Gazette*, told *American Journalism Review*, "News organizations need individuals who can withdraw from the bustle of the newsroom and get some perspective on performance by communicating—thoughtfully, intelligently, empathetically—with people who care enough to offer their views to the organization."[74]

- Writing a regular column or commentary—The ombudsmen at news outlets such as the *New York Times* and NPR have regular commentaries posted online and sometimes within the news pages or broadcast.

- Writing a regular memo for the news staff—The *Washington Post*'s former ombudsman wrote a blog on a regular basis that praises and criticizes the staff; he also wrote a column for the Sunday editorial page.[75] Until the summer of 2003, the *New York Times* did not have an ombudsman because management believed that the job should be done by the editors. However, following the scandal surrounding reporter Blair's fabrications, publisher Arthur Sulzberger Jr. appointed two editors to function as ombudsmen and enforce newsroom standards.[76] Although the position of ombudsman has been in a decline in recent years, these internal media critics continue to serve an important function. Poynter's ethicist Kelly McBride points to several examples:[77]

  o ESPN's Don Ohlmeyer discussed *The Decision*, the controversial program the sports channel carried about LeBron James's decision in 2010 to move from Cleveland to Miami.

  o NPR's Edward Schumacher-Matos wrote a thirty-five-thousand-word critique of the network's 2011 investigative series on foster care for Native American children in South Dakota.

Despite the decline in the number of news organizations with ombudsmen, Simon Dumenco, writing in *Ad Age*, suggests that these reader representatives are less necessary because excellent press criticism sites are available online.[78]

Codes of Ethics. News organizations have a variety of codes of ethics to consider. The Society of Professional Journalists has an extended code of ethics with three main principles:

1. Seek truth and report it as fully as possible.

2. Act independently.

3. Minimize harm.

Beyond those principles and the accompanying code, the organization's ethics handbook contains a series of case studies and a collection of other codes of ethics to help journalists make ethical decisions. In their introduction, the authors argue that ethics are not merely a set of ideals; they are something journalists do that leads to good reporting.[79] Obviously, a single code of ethics cannot cover all the issues encountered by the many different news outlets in the United States. "Can you even hope to have a common set of standards for the *New York Times*, the *National Enquirer*, and *People* magazine?" asks journalism professor Alex S. Jones, writing in the *Columbia Journalism Review*.[80]

If codes of ethics are to be effective, they need to be more than static documents, according to Jeffrey L. Seglin, an ethics columnist for the *New York Times*. A code of ethics must be central to the way the news outlet does business on a daily basis.[81] Unless that is the case, ethics problems will continue to arise, Seglin warns. The *New York Times* management clearly had not followed up on a lower-level editor's complaints about Blair a year before the young reporter was caught fabricating and plagiarizing stories for the paper.

The *Cincinnati Enquirer* encountered trouble for an exposé it ran on the banana company Chiquita. The story may or may not have been accurate, but the highly critical article about the company's business practices was based on two thousand voice mail messages the reporter had listened to using stolen access codes. The paper ended up apologizing to the company and paid an out-of-court settlement of $14 million. But prior to writing the story, the reporter had signed a copy of the paper's corporate code of ethics each year.

In these and other cases, the people involved clearly knew that their behavior was wrong and that it violated their publications' codes of ethics.

Ethics and Persuasive Communication

Many of the items we see in the media are not messages created by members of the news staff, but rather persuasive images created by advertising and public relations (PR) professionals seeking to influence people's behavior. The question of what constitutes ethical behavior for people who are attempting to manipulate public opinion then arises.[82] There are several ethical issues concerning the advertising industry today, including truth in advertising and the level of control advertisers can expect to have over the news content surrounding their ads.

During World War II, the advertising industry formed the Advertising Council in response to charges of unethical behavior. The organization's purpose was to promote both advertising and business in general. One of its first functions was to help build support for wartime austerity. The Ad Council worked on a communication campaign to stop the hoarding of scarce resources, promote the buying of war bonds, and build morale. After the war, it worked on a variety of public interest campaigns to maintain the positive image the group had fostered during the war. In recent years, the Ad Council has been responsible for a wide range of memorable public service ads, most notably the "Just Say No" and "This Is Your Brain on Drugs" campaigns.[83]

Snapple claims to make its drinks from the "best stuff on earth." But what is the "best stuff"? Papa John's says "Better Ingredients. Better Pizza." Is this true? Just as important, do consumers expect such claims to be true?

Typically, ads for prescription drugs and medicines are held to high standards of truthfulness, whereas claims that one article of clothing is more fashionable than another are held to a much lower standard of proof. However, a dog food company was once required to prove that dogs really did prefer one brand over another by showing how much of two competing brands dogs would eat.[84] A number of groups keep tabs on honesty in ads. The Federal Trade Commission (FTC) investigates many complaints. In 2014, the FTC acted against a number of companies making deceptive claims about weight-loss supplements.[85] The National Advertising Division of the Council of Better Business Bureaus also investigates claims of false advertising. Says council representative Gunnar Waldman, "We care even about the seemingly frivolous or 'less-important' cases. The issues at stake—truth in advertising—are always broader than the products themselves."[86]

Advertising executive Michael Dweck says that claims of being "best" are dangerous: "So the only claims we'd make ought to be sufficiently humorous, exaggerated, and far-fetched that no one will take them seriously."[87] Chris Wall of advertising giant Ogilvy & Mather says that as long as companies are truthful in their ads, they have nothing to worry about: "The most powerful advertising tends to be fundamentally truthful anyway. The trick is finding an honest point of advocacy for a product and then presenting it in a way that moves people, catches their attention, that they remember."[88]

Sometimes concern about media content comes from advertisers rather than from critics of the media. Advertisers may want to control the kind of material that surrounds their messages, hoping to avoid stories that are critical of their products or simply to associate themselves with high-quality content. For example, a group of car dealers in California pulled all their advertising from the San Jose *Mercury News* after the paper ran an article that explained to buyers how to read the factory invoices on new cars so that they would be in a better negotiating position.[89] At other times, advertising boycotts are driven by advertisers who don't want to be associated with a program's political point of view. In 2012, at least forty-five advertisers pulled their sponsorship from *The Rush Limbaugh Show* when the popular conservative radio talk show host called a law student and birth control advocate a "slut" over the air.[90]

Occasionally companies want to know in advance what kind of content is going to be included in forthcoming issues of magazines so that they can decide whether to include their advertising with it. Some publishers view this simply as a way of keeping important advertisers informed about how their advertising will look. However, the American Society of Magazine Editors warns "that some advertisers may mistake an early warning as an open invitation to pressure the publisher or editor to alter, or even kill, the article in question."[91]

Advertisers have also attempted to influence programming on television. Finding "family-friendly" shows to sponsor on television, especially broadcast television, is becoming increasingly difficult. The hit program *Friends* delivered a huge audience for NBC, but it did so with racy story lines and risqué humor. Companies such as consumer product giant Johnson & Johnson want to sponsor shows that parents and children can watch together so that they'll see commercials for Band-Aids, baby powder, Motrin, and Mylanta. To combat this problem, Johnson & Johnson, along with companies such as Procter & Gamble, Coca-Cola, and Ford, formed a group called the ANA Alliance for Family Entertainment to promote the development of shows that are acceptable to the entire family (ANA stands for Association of National Advertisers). The group, which began back in 1998 as the Family Friendly Programming Forum, isn't boycotting or criticizing adult-oriented shows; it just wants to promote shows on which its members won't be embarrassed to advertise. In 2000, the first show whose development had been funded by the forum came on the air: *Gilmore Girls*.[92] Since then, the forum has been responsible for the development of shows such as *The New Adventures of Old Christine*, *Ugly Betty*, and *Friday*

Night Lights. It has also started partnering with YouTube in the production of family-friendly programming.[93]

Ethics in Public Relations

It is easy to joke about a lack of ethics in public relations, but PR firms ignore ethical behavior at their own peril. The Public Relations Society of America (PRSA), founded in 1948, established its own code of ethics in 1954 not only to improve the profession's behavior, but also to improve the industry's image at a time when practitioners were "generally . . . perceived as slick con artists." In its original form, the code said, "We pledge to conduct ourselves professionally, with truth, accuracy, fairness, and responsibility to the public." The code was substantially revised and clarified in 1999. (See Box 15.2.)

Conducting War Through Public Relations.
The ethical challenge of balancing the needs of truthfulness, the public interest, and the client's interests became a major issue for one PR firm during the 1991 Persian Gulf War. Foreign governments often hire PR firms to represent their interests in the United States, but few have hired a major firm to promote the nation's involvement in a war.[94]

Hill & Knowlton, the nation's largest PR firm at the time, was hired by Citizens for a Free Kuwait, a group made up of members of the Kuwaiti government. The campaign was designed to create sympathy for Kuwait, opposition to Iraq and Saddam Hussein, and support for U.S. involvement in fighting Iraq. The campaign followed a typical pattern of lobbying Congress, calling press conferences, sending out press releases, and producing video news releases.[95] What really attracted controversy and raised ethical questions throughout the industry was testimony that Hill & Knowlton arranged to have given before the Congressional Human Rights Caucus. This group of U.S. representatives held hearings on October 10, 1990, on the Iraqi invasion of Kuwait. The centerpiece of these hearings was the eyewitness testimony of a fifteen-year-old Kuwaiti girl identified only as Nayirah. Nayirah told the caucus that she had personally seen atrocities committed following the invasion:

> While I was there, I saw the Iraqi soldiers come into the hospital with guns, and go into the room where . . . babies were in incubators. They took the babies out of the incubators, took the incubators, and left the babies on the cold floor to die.[96]

Her testimony certainly was effective. President George H. W. Bush mentioned the "twenty-two babies 'thrown on the floor like firewood'" on six separate occasions.[97] Two years later, journalist John R. MacArthur revealed that Nayirah, who had not previously been identified, was actually the daughter of the Kuwaiti ambassador to the United States, who was a member of the Kuwaiti royal family. MacArthur, and others, charged that the incubator story was not true. Amnesty International found no evidence that the story was true, and ABC News reported that the story was "almost certainly false."[98] Since Nayirah's testimony had not been given under oath, no questions were raised about the legality of Hill & Knowlton's actions. The firm defended its actions on behalf of Citizens for a Free Kuwait, but the fact remains that it did not investigate Nayirah's claims to see if they were true.[99] Whether true or false, the testimony itself was certainly not enough to send the United States to war with Iraq; rather, it was a well-planned PR effort intended to make Iraq seem evil and Kuwait appear to be a victim in need of assistance.

Whom Do You Serve: The Client or the Public?
One of the most difficult ethical problems facing PR practitioners is the conflict between serving the client's interests and serving those of the public. David Martinson, a professor of journalism, argues that PR practitioners can internalize important ethical principles of honesty and serving the public interest by practicing them daily in small ways. Then, when the rare moral dilemmas arise, the practitioner is used to behaving in an ethical manner.[100]

Public Relations Society of America's Statement of Professional Values

The following is the Public Relations Society of America's Statement of Professional Values:

This statement presents the core values of PRSA members and, more broadly, of the public relations profession. These values provide the foundation for the Member Code of Ethics and set the industry standard for the professional practice of public relations. These values are the fundamental beliefs that guide our behaviors and decision-making process. We believe our professional values are vital to the integrity of the profession as a whole.

Advocacy

- We serve the public interest by acting as responsible advocates for those we represent. We provide a voice in the marketplace of ideas, facts, and viewpoints to aid informed public debate.

Honesty

- We adhere to the highest standards of accuracy and truth in advancing the interests of those we represent and in communicating with the public.

Expertise

- We acquire and responsibly use specialized knowledge and experience. We advance the profession through continued professional development, research, and education. We build mutual understanding, credibility, and relationships among a wide array of institutions and audiences.

Independence

- We provide objective counsel to those we represent. We are accountable for our actions.

Loyalty

- We are faithful to those we represent, while honoring our obligation to serve the public interest.

Fairness

- We deal fairly with clients, employers, competitors, peers, vendors, the media, and the general public. We respect all opinions and support the right of free expression.

Source: "PRSA Code of Ethics," Public Relations Society of America, https://www.prsa.org/about/ethics/prsa-code-of-ethics.

As noted earlier, Aristotle suggested that ethical behavior arises from a golden mean, or balance, between two extremes of behavior or belief. Does this mean that PR practitioners can strike a balance between lying and telling the truth? No. Martinson says that PR practitioners must always be fully committed to the truth, but that it is possible to compromise between serving the public's interests and serving the client's. The PR practitioner must serve the client's best interests, but not to the extent that his or her professional and ethical obligations to the public are compromised.

Media and Representation

At the end of the hit musical *Hamilton*, much of the cast is on the stage asking the question "Who lives, who dies, who tells your story?" Like the characters ranging from Vice President Aaron Burr to President George Washington to Hamilton's widow Eliza, we need to be asking ourselves not only how are we telling our stories, but whose stories get told? Media representation is an enormous issue in the news industry and popular culture because it determines who gets to see themselves being portrayed. Do we get to see people who look and sound like us, people who care about the same things we do? So, which stories get covered?

Long before it became a national story, the Flint, Michigan, water contamination crisis was an important local media story. Flint is an old industrial city with a population of about one hundred thousand people. It is poor, and the auto industry jobs that have left the city are not coming back. The city is predominantly Black.[101]

In the fall of 2013, Flint was suffering from severe financial problems. These were so serious that the city had lost the power of home governance and instead was being run by a state-appointed emergency manager. One way this manager found to reduce costs was to change the city's source of water from Detroit municipal water to water taken out of the Flint River.

Aside from any purity issues (of which there were several), the river water had high levels of chlorides in it, making it corrosive.[102] Among the first to discover Flint's water problem was a local General Motors (GM) plant, where employees realized that the local water was corroding car parts being produced at the factory. But in addition to corroding new car parts, that water was leeching lead and other heavy metals from lead-based water services leading up to the homes in Flint.[103] That water turned out to have such high levels of lead in it that, according to a group of Virginia Tech researchers, the liquid coming out of some local taps could be considered "toxic waste" by the Environmental Protection Agency.[104]

As early as May 2014, the *Flint Journal* local newspaper was running stories about "murky or foamy" water. By September, the paper was running stories about the boil advisories because of bacterial contamination. And by October, the *Journal* was reporting about the GM plant switching water suppliers because of the corrosion.

The reporting on Flint's water came from several news sources, including Curt Guyette, an investigative journalist working for the American Civil Liberties Union in Michigan. Guyette had been hired to investigate Michigan's emergency manager law. As he started digging, he found complaints about the "brownish smelly water" coming out of the household taps in Flint.[105]

It took a significant amount of time for the story to get out because it was almost too awful to believe. Guyette, in an interview with public radio's *On the Media*, said, "We would not be sitting here anyway talking about this now were it not first and foremost about the relentless efforts on the part of Flint's citizens who refused to believe the lie their government was telling them that their water was safe."

Michigan Radio, a public radio news service, started covering the story in June 2014 with news about complaints about the smell and taste of the city's water. In January 2015, a full year before the national media really started to pay attention to the story, Michigan Radio had a story about the fact that the city's water violated the Safe Drinking Water Act because the high level of chlorides was creating other problems with the water.[106]

Despite being an early reporter on the story, Michigan Radio journalist Steve Carmody is still unhappy about how long it took before he really broke the news. "It just gnaws on me that when people were saying they can't drink this water in May or June of 2014, I was taking 'Don't worry, it's safe' as an answer from state officials," he told *Columbia Journalism Review*. "It just sticks in my craw. I should have seen this earlier. That will bother me the rest of my career."[107]

The local ABC, CBS, NBC, and Fox television affiliates also aggressively covered the story of the *E. coli* bacterial contamination of the river water and General Motors' decision to stop using local water. In January 2015, the Detroit papers, the *Free Press* and the *Detroit News*, started covering the story as well, but after a month and a half of coverage, the story largely dropped away until September 2015. *Free Press* columnist Nancy Kaffer was credited with running multiple in-depth articles about the crisis.[108]

Most of the broadcast and cable news networks gave it sparse coverage until January 2016 except for *The Rachel Maddow Show*, which made the Flint water crisis a major ongoing story on the show starting in December 2015. Until the state of emergency was declared, *Media Matters* reports that Maddow provided more coverage of the story than all the other national television news organizations combined.[109]

Even after the story came to national attention and the state of Michigan declared a state of emergency in Flint, the city's water was still often undrinkable by the summer of 2016. Covering the story was a major commitment for Michigan Radio, with as many as six of its twenty-one staffers devoting time to covering the story. But Carmody says that the story will never really be over. He told *Columbia Journalism Review*, "I know on my very last day, I'm going to do a story about Flint water. Not because it's my last day, and I feel like I have to, or because it's an anniversary, but because it's still going to be hurting people in this community sixteen years from now."[110]

Sullivan, the former public editor for the *New York Times*, wrote in January 2016 that the *Times* dropped the ball when it came to reporting on the Flint water crisis. The paper had done stories on Flint's problems dating back to March 2015. But then it took the paper more than six months to do anything more with the story. Editors at the *Times* defended their level of coverage of the story, noting that increasing the number of reporters working in Flint would have resulted in them missing other important Midwest stories.[111]

Attacks on Women Through Online Media

The internet can be a scary place. Want to see how scary? Look at the comments that follow stories about the role of women in video games, comic books, or any other area of geek pop culture. Before too long, you are likely to encounter the terms *gamergate* and *social justice warriors* accompanied by harassing threats of rape and murder.

Gamergate, usually expressed as **#gamergate**, started out as an attack on female game developer Zoë Quinn, her text-based game *Depression Quest* that deals with her own experiences with depression, and her personal sex life. An ex-boyfriend of Quinn's published a series of long blog posts accusing Quinn of having affairs with five other men, some of whom worked in the gaming industry or games journalism. Quinn was being accused of using sex to promote her video game and to feminize the world of video gaming.

According to the blog *Gawker*, before long, the people behind #gamergate expanded their critique, claiming that their real concerns were about ethics in video game journalism, not the behavior of a specific female game developer.[112] So that brings us to the **social justice warriors**, or #SJW. According to the 2015 update of the *Oxford English Dictionary*, *social justice warrior* is an informal, derogatory noun referring to "a person who expresses or promotes socially progressive views." But to members of the #gamergate movement, SJWs are people promoting enhanced roles for women in geek culture.[113]

Members of the movement have been highly abusive to game developer Quinn and other women in the gaming community. Quinn had her home address and cell phone number posted online, along with her passwords and nude photos of her. She has had online threats from people saying they want to rape and then kill her. One person posted on Tumblr, "If I ever see you are doing a panel [*sic*] at an event I'm going to, I will literally kill you." Another wrote, "I'm not going

▲ Brianna Wu is a software engineer and head of development at Giant Spacekat, which makes games with female protagonists. Wu is one of three woman targeted for abuse and death threats by the gaming community after posting online about the misogyny in the gaming industry. She stands next to a poster of her video game characters.

▲ Actress Kelly Marie Tran, who played Rose Tico in *Star Wars: The Last Jedi*, deleted all of her posts from Instagram after months of social media harassment. Tran, one of the first women of color with a major role in *Star Wars*, received criticism for her looks, her Asian ethnicity, and her performance.[117] (Black actress Lupita Nyong'o plays the key character Maz Kanata in the new trilogy, but it is a motion-capture part where you never actually see the actress herself.) Daisy Ridley, who plays the lead character Rey in the new trilogy, left Instagram in 2017 because she found social media "bad for her mental health."[118]

to stop spreading your disgusting nudes around and making sure your life is a living hell until you either kill yourself or I rape you to death."[114]

Others receiving similar threats, or worse, include feminist gaming and culture critic Anita Sarkeesian (who helped publicize the Bechdel Test for the role of women in movies discussed in Chapter 7) and Brianna Wu, cofounder of game studio Giant Spacekat.

Caitlin Dewey, digital culture critic for the *Washington Post*, writes,

> Whatever Gamergate may have started as, it is now an Internet culture war. On one side are independent game-makers and critics, many of them women, who advocate for greater inclusion in gaming. On the other side of the equation are a motley alliance of vitriolic naysayers . . . people convinced they're being manipulated by a left-leaning and/or a corrupt press, and traditionalists who just don't want their games to change.[115]

Women in the gaming/comics/geek culture world are not the only ones subject to severe online harassment. Erin Andrews, who now works for Fox Sports, was working for ESPN in 2008. While she was traveling for the network to Nashville, she was secretly filmed while undressing. A year later, the video was posted online and widely shared.

In a lawsuit Andrews filed against the hotel where the recording took place, Andrews testified, "This happens every day of my life, either I get a tweet or somebody makes a comment in the paper or somebody sends me a still of the video to my Twitter or someone screams it at me in the stands and I'm right back to this."[116] Andrews has been widely harassed about the video and has even been accused of creating it herself as a publicity stunt.

Representation and the Movies

One of the major themes of this book has always been the importance of diversity in our media world, but that has been a central emphasis of recent revisions of this edition.

Media scholar George Gerbner, who developed cultivation analysis that we discussed back in Chapter 2, wrote in 1994,

> Middle-class, white male characters dominate in numbers and power. Women play one out of three characters. Young people comprise one-third and old one-fifth of their actual proportions of the population. Most other minorities are even more underrepresented. That cast sets the stage for stories of conflict, violence and the projection of white male prime-of-life power.[119]

▲ Patty Jenkins (right) directs Gal Gadot (left) in her starring role as *Wonder Woman* in 2017.

How much has changed since then? Both a lot and not as much as you might think.

Marvel's *Black Panther* has been an enormous success, sitting now at the number-three spot on the all-time domestic box office ranking, having brought in almost $700 million in North America. And at one level, this should be no surprise. The annual and all-time box office lists are full of Marvel movies. There are two *Avengers* movies in the all-time top ten along with a host of Marvel Cinematic Universe movies in the top fifty. But the one at the top was of a lesser-known Marvel hero in his debut film that does not feature other Avengers.

Why?

One explanation is that it told a different kind of story than we have gotten used to seeing. It was a story where the heroes, villains, stars, and supporting cast were almost all Black.

The director and the screenwriter were Black. The production designer was Black and female. The cinematographer was a woman. It was a story with its roots in a mythical African country. The characters being subtitled spoke Xhosa, an official language of South Africa. *Daily Show* host Trevor Noah, who voiced a computer in *Black Panther*, said in a monologue that hearing the language he grew up speaking in his native Johannesburg was an incredible experience. "There were subtitles, and I was like, I don't need subtitles! I don't need your subtitles! This is just for me right now! Nobody else listen! This reminds me of my mom."[120]

Dave Hollis, Disney's president of theatrical distribution, said, "It's clear that representation matters, and moviegoers have responded every time we've answered that demand. We are trying to make movies that resonate with a global audience, and that means making movies that allow people to see themselves represented on screen."[121]

For all the progress, representation still has a long way to go. The Color of Change report, "Race in the Writers' Room: How Hollywood Whitewashes the Stories That Shape America," that came out in 2017 found that only 4.8 percent of television writers were Black and that two-thirds of the shows for 2016–2017 had no Black writers on staff. The shows that did have substantial Black writing staffs were generally helmed by Black showrunners. Having people of color in management roles is important when it comes to trying to get diverse themes into stories. "I don't think it's appropriate for a nonwhite person to discuss race in normal writers' rooms because you're just too outnumbered, and people get too defensive," said one Black writer.[122]

Hollywood keeps needing reminders of how representation is good for business. In 2012, *The Hunger Games*, fronted by Jennifer Lawrence and based on the novel by Suzanne Collins, told a different, but very popular, kind of story about child soldiers. Jeremy Fuster, writing for the Hollywood blog the *Wrap*, argues that the success of *The Hunger Games* helped bring a host of female-fronted action movies like *Mad Max: Fury Road*, the new *Star Wars* movies, and *Wonder Woman* over in the DC Expanded Universe.[123]

Despite the success of movies like *Wonder Woman*, starring Israeli-born actress Gal Gadot and directed by Patty Jenkins, Hollywood is still sticking to movies told for and by men. According to a report in the entertainment industry trade magazine *Variety*, less than 15 percent of the producer deals in Hollywood are with women. "The value of women in the marketplace seems to be a lesson that continues to be learned," said Nina Jacobson, a producer on *The Hunger Games* series who has a deal with Fox. "It keeps needing to be reaffirmed every time it happens, such as with *Wonder Woman*.[124]

CHAPTER REVIEW

CHAPTER SUMMARY ▶▶

Media ethics are a complex topic because they deal with an institution that must do things that ordinary people in ordinary circumstances would not do. Media ethics draw on a range of philosophical principles, including basic Judeo-Christian values, Aristotle's ideas about virtue and balanced behaviors (the golden mean), Kant's categorical imperative, Mill's principle of utility, Rawls's veil of ignorance, and the Hutchins Commission's social responsibility ethics. One way contemporary journalists can resolve their ethical problems is by using the Bok model for ethical decision making.

Journalists, professional communicators, and news consumers face a range of ethical issues on a regular basis. Those issues include the following:

- Journalists need to make a commitment to telling the truth. This includes not giving false or made-up reports and telling truthful stories that are not intended to deceive the audience. This may require reporters to provide not only the facts but also the context surrounding them. Truthfulness requires a commitment not only from the journalist but also from the organization he or she works for.

- Both consumers and journalists need to recognize fake news and not perpetuate it by sharing it on social media

- Authenticity and appropriateness of photographs— Photos can be among the most controversial media materials, both because of their disturbing content and because they can be altered with digital editing tools.

- Conflicts of interest—The interests of a corporation that owns a news organization may sometimes be at odds with the nature of the news being reported. Journalists need to be careful not only to portray their parent company in an accurate light, but also to give no special favors to companies connected to the organization's parent company.

- Handling corrections and apologies as needed when journalists and other communicators either make mistakes, report before knowing all the facts, or behave inappropriately. Dealing with these may involve having an ombudsman or a code of ethics.

The advertising industry became concerned with protecting its image during World War II. Among the major ethical issues in advertising are the following:

- Truthfulness—How important is it that claims such as "Tastes great" or "It's the best" are demonstrably true?

- Taste—Is it appropriate for ads to attract attention by shocking audiences?

- Media control—Do advertisers have a right to control the editorial material that surrounds their advertisements?

In the public relations industry, practitioners need to work at balancing their clients' interests against those of the public at large. This can become problematic when a client is attempting to influence the public to support an issue, such as going to war.

The issue of fair representation of women, minorities, and communities not located in the coastal areas in the news and entertainment media is an ongoing problem. These include national media not paying attention to stories taking place in communities of color; attacks on women through online media; and underrepresentation of minority narratives in popular culture.

KEY TERMS ▶▶

morals 374	categorical imperative 377	ombudsman 390
ethics 374	principle of utility 377	#gamergate 396
golden mean 375	veil of ignorance 378	social justice warriors (#SJW) 396

REVIEW QUESTIONS ▶▶

1. How do newspapers and other news outlets make decisions about when to run vulgar or offensive language from politicians, such as the president or vice president?

2. How can two competing ethical principles lead us to making different ethical decisions?

3. Do reporters have an obligation to stay to report on protests and violence when police are telling them to leave the area? Why or why not? What factors might affect how you answer the question?

4. Should advertisers be able to shape the content of media they advertise in? Should they be able to veto ad placement next to certain types of content? Why or why not?

5. What was the #gamergate hashtag supposedly about, and how was it actually used?

6. Why does representation of women and people of color matter in entertainment media?

GLOSSARY

above the fold: A term used to refer to a prominent story; it comes from placement of a news story in a broadsheet newspaper above the fold in the middle of the front page.

actual malice: A reckless disregard for the truth or falsity of a published account; this became the standard for libel plaintiffs who were public figures or public officials after the Supreme Court's decision in *New York Times Co. v. Sullivan.*

advertising: Defined by the American Marketing Association as "any paid form of nonpersonal communication about an organization, product, service, or idea by an identified sponsor."

advertorial: Advertising materials in magazines designed to look like editorial content rather than paid advertising.

advocacy ads: Advertising designed to promote a particular point of view rather than a product or service. Can be sponsored by a government, corporation, trade association, or nonprofit organization.

agenda-setting theory: A theory of media effects that says that the media tell the public not what to think but rather what to think *about*—thus the terms of public discourse are set by what is covered in the media.

aggregator sites: Websites that offer help navigating the web by collecting information from various online sources and putting them in one place.

Al Jazeera: The largest and most viewed Arabic-language satellite news channel. It is run out of the country of Qatar and has a regular audience of forty million viewers.

Alien and Sedition Acts: Laws passed in 1798 that made it a crime to criticize the government of the United States.

alphabets: A form of writing in which letters represent individual sounds. Sound-based alphabet writing allows any word to be written using only a few dozen unique symbols.

analog recording: An electromechanical method of recording in which a sound is translated into analogous electrical signals that are then applied to a recording medium. Analog recording media included acetate or vinyl discs and magnetic tape.

ancillary, or secondary, markets: Movie revenue sources other than the domestic box office. These include foreign box office, video rights, and television rights, as well as tie-ins and product placements.

ARPAnet: The Advanced Research Projects Agency Network; the first nationwide computer network, which became the first major component of the internet.

Atari: An early video game company named after the equivalent of "checkmate" in the ancient Chinese strategy board game *Go.*

augmented reality: Where a computer or smartphone adds online imagery in real time to photos or videos of real life.

authoritarian theory: A theory of appropriate press behavior that says the role of the press is to be a servant of the government, not a servant of the citizenry.

battle royale games: A video game where one hundred players enter into a digital arena and the last player standing is the winner.

Bay Psalm Book: The first book published in North America by the Puritans in the Massachusetts Bay Colony. The book went through more than fifty editions and stayed in print for 125 years.

Big Four networks: The broadcast landscape we know today: the Big Three networks plus the Fox network.

Big Three networks: The original television broadcast networks: NBC, CBS, and ABC.

blacklist: A group of people banned from working in the movie industry in the late 1940s and 1950s because they were suspected of being communists or communist sympathizers. Some of them, such as a few screenwriters, were able to work under assumed names, but others never worked again in the industry.

block bookings: Requiring a theater owner to take a whole series of movies in order to get a few desirable, headliner films. This system was eventually found to violate antitrust laws.

blockbuster era: A period from the late 1970s to the present day in which movie studios make relatively expensive movies that have a large, predefined audience. These movies, usually chock-full of special effects, are packaged with cable deals and marketing tie-ins, and they can be extremely lucrative if they are able to attract large repeat audiences.

brand image: The image attached to a brand and the associated product that gives the product a personality or identity that makes it stand out from similar products and stick in the mind of the consumer.

brand name: A word or phrase attached to prepackaged consumer goods so that they can be better promoted to the general public through advertising and so that consumers can distinguish a given product from the competition.

brick-and-mortar stores: Stores that have a physical presence at which you can shop.

British invasion: The British take on classic American rock 'n' roll, blues, and R&B transformed rock 'n' roll and became internationally popular in the 1960s with groups such as the Beatles and, later, the Rolling Stones and the Who.

broadband service: A high-speed continuous connection to the internet using a cable modem from a cable television provider or a digital subscriber line from a phone company.

business-to-business (trade) ads: Advertising that promotes products and services directly to other businesses rather than to the general consumer market.

categorical imperative: Kant's idea of a moral obligation that we should act in a way in which we would be willing to have everyone else act; also known as the principle of universality.

chains: Corporations that control a significant number of newspapers and other media outlets.

channel: The medium used to transmit the encoded message.

citizen journalism: Journalism created by people other than professional journalists, often distributed over the internet.

clutter: The large number of commercials, advertising, and other nonprogramming messages and interruptions that compete for consumer attention on radio, television, and now the internet.

communication: How we socially interact at a number of levels through messages.

communist theory: A theory of appropriate press behavior that says the press is to be run by the government to serve the government's own needs.

community antenna television (CATV): An early form of cable television used to distribute broadcast channels in communities with poor television reception.

community press: Weekly and daily newspapers serving individual communities or suburbs instead of an entire metropolitan area.

compact disc (CD): A digital recording medium that came into common use in the early 1980s. CDs can hold approximately seventy minutes of digitally recorded music.

computer-generated imagery (CGI): Movie special effects created digitally using computers. Sometimes known as computer animation.

concept album: An album by a solo artist or group that contains related songs on a common theme or even a story, rather than a collection of unrelated hits or covers.

cookies: Tiny files that websites create to identify visitors and potentially track their actions on the site and the web.

correlation: The process of selecting, evaluating, and interpreting events to give structure to the news. The media assist the process of correlation by persuasive communication through editorials, commentary, advertising, and propaganda and by providing cues that indicate the importance of each news item.

country music: Originally referred to as hillbilly or "old-timey" music, this genre evolved out of Irish and Scottish folk music, Mississippi blues, and Christian gospel music and grew in the 1950s and 1960s with the so-called Nashville sound.

cover: Songs recorded (or covered) by someone other than the original artist. In the 1950s, it was common for white musicians to cover songs originally played by Black artists, but now artists commonly cover all genres of music.

CPM: Cost per thousand exposures to the target audience—a figure used in media planning evaluation.

crisis: Any situation that is perceived by the public as being damaging to the reputation or image of an organization. Not all problems develop into crises, but once a situation develops into a crisis, it can be damaging to an organization's reputation.

critical/cultural approach: Examining how meaning is created within society, who controls the media, and the roles the media play in our lives.

critical theory: A school of thought that grew out of the time period between World War I and World War II that addressed the connection between ideas and values, the context of the development of ideas, and the commodification of culture.

cultivation analysis: An approach to analyzing the effects of television viewing that argues that watching significant amounts of television alters the way an individual views the nature of the surrounding world.

cut the cord: Replacing traditional paid video services, such as cable or satellite television, with internet-based streaming video services.

decoding: The process of translating a signal from a mass medium into a form that the receiver can understand and then interpreting the meaning of the message itself.

demographics: The study of audience members' gender, race, ethnic background, income, education, age, educational attainment, and the like; a method typically used to analyze potential markets for products and programs.

development theory: A theory of appropriate press behavior that states that developing nations may need to implement press controls in order to promote industry, national identity, and partnerships with neighboring nations.

digital native: Online media that do not have a traditional legacy media component; online-only media.

digital recording: A method of recording sound—for example, that used to create CDs—that involves storing music in a computer-readable format known as binary information.

dime novels: Inexpensive paperback books that sold for as little as five cents (despite their name). They were especially popular during the Civil War era.

direct-action message: An advertising message designed to get consumers to go to a particular place to do something specific, such as purchasing a product, obtaining a service, or engaging in a behavior.

direct-broadcast satellite (DBS): A low-earth-orbit satellite that provides television programming via a small, pizza-sized satellite antenna; DBS is a competitor to cable TV.

disco: The name of the heavily produced techno club dance music of the 1970s, which grew out of the urban gay male subculture, with significant Black and Latino influences. In many ways, disco defined the look and feel of 1970s pop culture, fashion, and film.

domestic novels: Novels written in the nineteenth century by and for women that told the story of women who overcame tremendous problems to end up in prosperous middle-class homes.

drive time: The morning and afternoon commutes in urban areas; the captive audience makes this a popular time to advertise on radio.

e-book readers: Portable devices for viewing, and sometimes selling, electronic books and other texts. Among the most popular are the line of Amazon Kindles.

economy of abundance: An economy in which there are as many or more goods available as there are people who want to or have the means to buy them.

electronic mail (email): A message sent from one computer user to another across a network.

embarrassment: Invasion of privacy where a journalist publishes something that is true but embarrassing and not newsworthy about a person.

emojis: A word borrowed from Japanese that refers to small icons that are used to express ideas and emotions in SMS and social media messages.

encoding: The process of turning the sender's ideas into a message and preparing the message for transmission.

engineering consent: The application of the principles of psychology and motivation to influencing public opinion and creating public support for a particular position.

entertainment: Media communication intended primarily to amuse the audience.

equal time provision: An FCC policy that requires broadcast stations to make equivalent amounts of broadcast time available to all candidates running for public office.

eSports: Organized video game team competition for spectators.

ethics: A rational way of deciding what is good for individuals or society. Ethics provide a way to choose between competing moral principles and help people decide in cases where there is not a clear-cut right or wrong answer.

fairness doctrine: A former FCC policy that required television stations to "afford reasonable opportunity for the discussion of conflicting views on issues of public importance."

fake news: A term used to describe satirical news, mistakes and fabrications, partisan clickbait, foreign political manipulation, and general purpose media criticism.

false light: Invasion of privacy in which a journalist publishes untrue statements that alter a person's public image in a way that he or she cannot control.

feature-length film: A theatrical movie that runs more than one hour.

Federal Communications Commission (FCC): The federal agency charged with regulating telecommunications, including radio and television broadcasting.

font: All the characters of a typeface in a particular size and style. The term *font* is typically used interchangeably today with the word *typeface*.

format radio: A style of radio programming designed to appeal to a narrow, specific audience. Popular formats include country, contemporary hits, all talk, all sports, and oldies.

45-rpm disc: This record format was developed in the late 1940s by RCA. It had high-quality sound but held only about four minutes of music per side. It was the ideal format for marketing popular hit songs to teenagers, though.

#gamergate: A series of attacks on women in the video game industry that is framed as a critique of video gaming journalism ethics.

geographics: The study of where people live; a method typically used to analyze potential markets for products and programs.

girl groups: Musical groups composed of several women singers who harmonize together. Groups such as the Shirelles, the Ronettes, and the Shangri-Las, featuring female harmonies and high production values, were especially popular in the late 1950s and early 1960s.

golden age of radio: A period from the late 1920s until the 1940s, during which radio was the dominant medium for home entertainment.

golden mean: Aristotle's notion that ethical behavior comes from hitting a balance, a "just-right point between excess and defect."

gramophone: A machine invented by Emile Berliner that could play prerecorded sound on flat discs rather than cylinders.

group communication: Communication in which one person is communicating with an audience of two or more people. The roles of communicator and audience can be changing constantly.

hacker ethic: A set of values from the early days of interactive computing that holds that users should have absolute control over their computer systems and free access to all information contained on those computers. The hacker ethic shaped much of the development of the internet.

halftone: An image produced by a process in which photographs are broken down into a series of dots that appear in shades of gray on the printed page.

HD radio: Sometimes also referred to as high-definition radio, this technology provides listeners with CD-quality sound and the choice of multiple channels of programming, but it has not achieved a high level of popularity.

high-definition television (HDTV): A standard for high-quality digital broadcasting that features a high-resolution picture, wide-screen format, and enhanced sound.

high fidelity (hi-fi): A combination of technologies that allowed recordings to reproduce music more accurately, with higher high notes and deeper bass, than was possible with previous recording technologies.

hip-hop: A cultural movement that originated in the 1970s and 1980s that features four main elements: MCing, or rapping over music; DJing, or playing recorded music from multiple sources; B-boying, a style of dancing; and graffiti art.

Hollywood Ten: A group of ten writers and directors who refused to testify before the House Un-American Activities Committee about their political activities. They were among the first people in Hollywood to be blacklisted.

House Un-American Activities Committee: A congressional committee chaired by Parnell Thomas that held hearings on the influence of communism on Hollywood in 1947. These activities mirrored a wider effort to root out suspected communists in all walks of American life.

hypertext: Material in a format containing links that allow the reader to move easily from one section to another and from document to document. The most commonly used hypertext documents are web pages.

hypertext markup language (HTML): One of the three major components of the web; the programming language used to create and format web pages.

hypertext transfer protocol (http): One of the three major components of the web; a method of sending text, graphics, or anything else over the internet from a server to a web browser.

ideograph: An abstract symbol that stands for a word or phrase. The written forms of the Chinese, Korean, and Japanese languages make use of ideographs.

inclusive access: Where a textbook publisher licenses textbooks and other course materials to a school so that all students have access to them at a reduced cost.

indirect-action message: An advertising message designed to build the image of and demand for a product, without specifically urging that a particular action be taken at a particular time and place.

industrialization: The movement from work done by hand using muscle or water power in small shops to mass production of goods in factories that used energy sources such as steam power or electricity.

influencers: Social media personalities who use their status to promote products and brands as paid sponsors.

instant messaging (IM): Email systems that allow two or more users to chat with one another in real time, hold virtual meetings that span multiple cities or even countries, and keep track of which of their "buddies" are currently logged on to the system.

integrated marketing communication (IMC): An overall communication strategy for reaching key audiences using advertising, public relations, sales promotion, and interactive media.

internet: "A diverse set of independent networks, interlinked to provide its users with the appearance of a single, uniform network"; a mass medium like no other, incorporating elements of interpersonal, group, and mass communications.

Internet of Things: Noncomputer devices that surround our lives that collect data and transmit it over the internet.

interpersonal communication: Communication, either intentional or accidental, between two people. It can be verbal or nonverbal.

intranets: Computer networks designed to communicate with people within an organization. They are used to improve two-way internal communication and contain tools that allow for direct feedback. They are a tool for communicating with internal publics.

intrapersonal communication: Communication you have with yourself. How you assign meaning to the world around you.

intrusion: Invasion of privacy by physical trespass into a space surrounding a person's body or onto property under his or her control.

kinetoscope: An early peep show–like movie projection system developed by Thomas Edison that could be used only by an individual viewer.

legacy media: The traditional media, often owned by large corporations. These may include newspapers, magazines, book publishers, and television networks.

libel: A published statement that unjustifiably exposes someone to ridicule or contempt; for a statement to be libel, it must satisfy the three elements of defamation, identification, and publication.

libertarian theory: A theory of appropriate press behavior that says the press does not belong to the government but is instead a separate institution that belongs to the people and serves as an independent observer of the government.

Linotype: A typesetting machine that let an operator type at a keyboard rather than pick each letter out by hand. The Linotype was the standard for typesetting until phototypesetting became common in the 1970s.

local advertising: Advertising designed to get people to patronize local stores, businesses, or service providers.

local cable television systems: The companies that provide cable television service directly to consumers' homes.

long-playing record (LP): A record format introduced by Columbia Records in 1948. The more durable LP could reproduce twenty-three minutes of high-quality music on each of two sides and was a technological improvement over the 78-rpm record.

long tail: The portion of a distribution curve where a limited number of people are interested in buying a lot of different products.

mass communication: When an individual or institution uses technology to send a message to a large, mixed audience, most of whose members are not known to the sender.

mass media: The technological tools, or channels, used to transmit the messages of mass communication.

mean world syndrome: The perception of many heavy television watchers of violent programs that the world is a more dangerous and violent place than facts and statistics bear out.

media literacy: Audience members' understanding of the media industry's operation, the messages delivered by the media, the roles media play in society, and how audience members respond to these media and their messages.

media planning: The process central to a successful ad campaign of figuring out which media to use, buying the media at the best rates, and then evaluating how effective the purchase was.

media relations: Two-way interactions between PR professionals and members of the press. These can involve press conferences, press releases, video news releases, or interviews. Typically, media relations involve the placement of unpaid messages within the standard programming or news content of the medium.

message: The content being transmitted by the sender to the receiver.

misappropriation: Invasion of privacy by using a person's name or image for commercial purposes without his or her permission.

mobile advertising ID: A unique ID on mobile devices that allows advertisers to identify which device is accessing their information.

modernization: The process of change from a society in which people's identities and roles are fixed at birth to a society where people can decide who they want to be, where they want to live, what they want to do, and how they want to present themselves to the world.

morals: An individual's code of behavior based on religious or philosophical principles. Morals define right and wrong in ways that may or may not be rational.

Mosaic: The first easy-to-use graphical web browser, developed by a group of student programmers at the University of Illinois at Urbana-Champaign.

MP3: Short for Moving Picture Experts Group audio layer 3; a standard for compressing music from CDs or other digital recordings into computer files that can be easily exchanged on the internet.

multiplex: A group of movie theaters with anywhere from three to twenty screens that share a common box office and concession stand. Largely a suburban phenomenon at first, the multiplex replaced the old urban Art Deco movie palaces.

national advertising: Advertising designed to build demand for a nationally available product or service and that is not directing the consumer to local retail or service outlets.

net neutrality: Rules that would require internet service providers to give equal access to all online content providers.

network: A company that provides common programming to a large group of broadcast stations.

noise: Interference with the transmission of a message. This can take the form of semantic, mechanical, or environmental noise.

non-notated music: Music such as a folk song or jazz solo that does not exist in written form.

obscenity: Sexually explicit material that is legally prohibited from being published.

ombudsman: A representative of a publication's readers who takes the point of view of those who purchase or consume the news; also known as a reader's representative or audience advocate.

open contract: An arrangement that allows advertising agencies to sell space in any publication (and eventually on broadcast outlets as well) rather than just a limited few.

opinion leaders: Influential community members who invest substantial amounts of time learning about their own area of expertise, such as politics. Less well-informed friends and family members frequently turn to them for advice about the topic.

opinion leadership: A two-step process of persuasion that uses respected and influential individuals to deliver messages with the hope of influencing members of a community, rather than just relying on the mass media to deliver the message.

packet switching: A method for breaking up long messages into small pieces, or packets, and transmitting them independently across a computer network. Once the packets arrive at their destination, the receiving computer reassembles the message into its original form.

paper: A writing material made from cotton rags or wood pulp; invented by the Chinese between 240 BC and 105 BC.

papyrus: An early form of paper made from the papyrus reed, developed by the Egyptians around 3100 BC.

parchment: An early form of paper made from the skin of goats or sheep, which was more durable than papyrus.

penny press: Inexpensive, widely circulated papers that became popular in the nineteenth century. They were the first American media to be supported primarily through advertising revenue.

Pentagon Papers: A top-secret forty-seven, volume report commissioned by the Secretary of Defense to explain how the United States got involved and fought in the Vietnam War.

people meter: An electronic box used by the ratings company Nielsen Media Research to record which television shows people watch.

phonograph: An early sound-recording machine invented by Thomas Edison; the recorded material was played back on a cylinder.

phonography: A system of writing in which symbols stand for spoken sounds rather than objects or ideas. Among the most widely used phonographic alphabets are the Latin/Roman alphabet used in English and the Cyrillic alphabet used for writing Russian.

photojournalism: The use of photographs to portray the news in print.

pictograph: A prehistoric form of writing made up of paintings on rock or cave walls.

plus-sized model: A female fashion model who wears an average or larger clothing size.

podcast: An audio program produced as an MP3 compressed music file that can be listened to online at the listener's convenience or downloaded to a computer or an MP3 player. Podcasts sometimes contain video content as well.

Pokémon: A series of games and other media properties based on players collecting "pocket monsters" to compete against each other. They have been globally popular since being introduced in Japan in 1996.

Pong: A ping pong simulation that was the first commercially successful arcade video game.

press agentry: An early form of public relations that involved sending material from the press agent to the media with little opportunity for interaction and feedback. It often involved conduct that would be considered deceptive and unethical today.

principle of utility: John Stuart Mill's principle that ethical behavior arises from that which will provide the greatest good for the greatest number of people.

print on demand: A form of publishing in which the physical book is not printed until it's ordered, or until the distributor of the book prints additional copies in small batches.

prior restraint: A judicial order that stops a media organization from publishing or broadcasting a story or image.

privilege: A legal defense against libel that holds that statements made in government meetings, in court, or in government documents cannot be used as the basis for a libel suit.

producers: The people who put together the right mix of songs, songwriters, technicians, and performers to create an album; some observers argue that the producer is the key catalyst for a hit album.

product integration: The paid integration of a product or service into the central theme of media content. This is most common in television programming or movies, but it can be found in books, magazine articles, web pages, or even songs.

Production Code: The industry-imposed rules that controlled the content of movies from the 1930s until the current movie ratings system came into use in 1968.

proofs: The ready-to-print typeset pages sent to book authors for final corrections.

psychographics: A combination of demographics, lifestyle characteristics, and product usage; a method typically used to analyze potential markets for products and programs.

public: Any group of people who share a common set of interests and goals. These include *internal publics*, which are made up of people within the organization, and *external publics*, which consist of people outside the organization.

Public Broadcasting Service (PBS): A nonprofit broadcast network that provides a wide range of public service and educational programs. It is funded by government appropriations, private industry underwriting, and viewer support.

public relations (PR): "The management function that establishes and maintains mutually beneficial relationships between an organization and the publics on whom its success or failure depends."

public service ads: Advertising designed to promote the messages of nonprofit institutions and government agencies. The messages are typically produced and run without charge by advertising professionals and the media. Many of these ads are produced by the Ad Council.

publicity model: A model of the mass communication process that looks at how media attention can make a person, concept, or thing become important, regardless of what is said about it.

publishers: The companies that buy manuscripts from authors, turn them into books, and market them to the public.

race records: A term used by the recording industry prior to 1949 to refer to recordings by popular Black artists. It was later replaced by more racially neutral terms such as *R&B, soul,* and *urban contemporary*.

Radio Music Box memo: David Sarnoff's 1915 plan that outlined how radio could be used as a popular mass medium.

rap music: This genre arose out of the hip-hop culture in New York City in the 1970s and 1980s. It emerged from clubs where DJs played and remixed different records and sounds and then spoke (or rapped) over the top.

rating point: The percentage of the total potential television audience actually watching a particular show. One rating point indicates an audience of approximately 1.14 million viewers.

receiver: The audience for the mass communication message.

reception model: A critical theory model of the mass communication process that looks at how audience members derive and create meaning out of media content as they decode the messages.

ritual model: A model of the mass communication process that treats media use as an interactive ritual engaged in by audience members. It looks at how and why audience members (receivers) consume media messages.

rock 'n' roll: A style of music popularized on radio that combined elements of white hillbilly music and Black rhythm and blues.

rotary press: A steam-powered press invented in 1814 that could print many times faster than the older, hand-powered flat-bed presses.

satellite radio: The radio service provided by digital signal broadcast from a communications satellite. Supported by subscribers, this service covers a wider area than terrestrial radio and offers programming that is different from corporate-owned terrestrial stations. However, it is costly and doesn't provide local coverage, such as traffic and weather reports.

scriptoria: Copying rooms in monasteries where monks prepared early hand-copied books.

sender: The source of messages that go out through mass communication.

Sender Message Channel Receiver (SMCR) or transmission model: A dated model that is still useful in identifying the players in the mass communication process.

serial novels: Novels published and sold in single-chapter installments.

share: The percentage of television sets in use that are tuned to a particular show.

shield laws: Laws that give journalists special protection from having to testify in court about their stories and sources.

shock jock: A radio personality, such as Howard Stern, who attracts listeners by making outrageous and offensive comments on the air.

short head: The portion of a distribution curve where a large number of people are interested in buying a limited number of products.

small media: Alternative media, such as fax machines, photocopiers, video cameras, and personal websites, which are used to distribute news and information that might be suppressed by the government if published through traditional mass media channels.

soap operas: Serialized daytime dramas targeted primarily at women.

social justice warriors (#SJW): A negative term used within the #gamergate community and elsewhere to describe people who advocate for socially progressive causes, especially women's equality.

social learning theory: The process by which individuals learn by observing the behaviors of others and the consequences of those behaviors.

social media: Websites that allow users to generate content, comment, tag, and network with friends or other like-minded people.

social music: Music that people play and sing for one another in the home or other social settings. In the absence of radio, recordings, and, later, television, this was the means of hearing music most readily available to the largest number of people.

social responsibility theory: A theory of appropriate press behavior based on the concern that, although the press may be free from interference from the government, it can still be controlled by corporate interests; an outgrowth of libertarian theory.

socialization: The process of educating young people and new members about the values, social norms, and knowledge of a group or society.

standard digital television: A standard for digital broadcasting that allows six channels to fit in the broadcast frequency space occupied by a single analog signal.

status conferral: The process by which media coverage makes an individual gain prominence in the eyes of the public.

streaming audio: Audio programming transmitted over the internet.

studio system: A factory-like way of producing films that involved having all of the talent, including the actors and directors, working directly for the movie studios. The studios also had almost total control of the distribution system.

subliminal advertising: Messages that are allegedly embedded so deeply in an ad that they cannot be perceived consciously. There is no evidence that subliminal advertising is effective.

surveillance: How the media help us extend our senses to perceive more of the world surrounding us.

sweeps: The four times during the year that Nielsen Media Research measures the size of individual television station audiences.

symbolic interactionism: The process by which individuals produce meaning through interaction based on socially agreed-upon symbols.

synchronized soundtrack: Sound effects, music, and voices synchronized with the moving images in a movie.

synergy: Where the combined strength of two items is greater than the sum of their individual strengths. In the media business, synergy means that a large company can use the strengths of its various divisions to successfully market its content.

talkie: A movie with synchronized sound; these quickly replaced silent films.

targeting: The process of trying to make a particular product or service appeal to a narrowly defined group. Groups are often targeted using demographics, geographics, and psychographics.

TCP/IP: TCP stands for transmission control protocol, which controls how data are sent out on the internet; IP stands for internet protocol, which provides the address for each computer on the internet. These protocols provided common rules and translations so that incompatible computers could communicate with each other.

telegraph: The first system for using wires to send messages at a distance; invented by Samuel Morse in 1844.

telenovelas: Spanish-language soap operas popular in both Latin America and the United States.

television networks: The companies that provide programs to local stations around the country; the local affiliate stations choose which programs to carry.

terrestrial radio: AM and FM broadcast radio stations.

the big idea: The goal of every advertising campaign—an advertising concept that will grab people's attention and make them take notice, remember, and take action.

trade books: General-interest fiction and nonfiction books that are sold in hardback or large-format paperback editions.

Turing Test: A test developed by mathematician Alan Turing to see whether a person could distinguish whether they were interacting with a computer or a person. It is a test for artificial intelligence.

type mold: A mold in which a printer would pour molten lead to produce multiple, identical copies of a single letter without hand-carving each.

uniform resource locator (URL): One of the three major components of the web; the address of content placed on the web.

university and small presses: Small-scale publishers that issue a limited number of books covering specialized topics. They are often subsidized by a university or an organization.

uses and gratifications theory: An approach to studying mass communication that looks at the reasons why audience members choose to spend time with the media in terms of the wants and needs of the audience members that are being fulfilled.

veil of ignorance: John Rawls's principle of ethics that says that justice comes from making decisions that maximize liberty for all people and without considering which outcome will give us personally the biggest benefit.

video on demand (VOD): Television channels that allow consumers to order movies, news, or other programs at any time over fiber-optic lines.

videocassette recorder (VCR): A home videotape machine that allows viewers to make permanent copies of television shows and, thus, choose when they want to watch programs.

Watergate scandal: A burglary of the Democratic National Committee headquarters in the Watergate office and apartment building that was authorized by rogue White House staffers. Its subsequent cover-up led to the resignation of President Richard Nixon in 1974. Bob Woodward and Carl Bernstein, two reporters from the *Washington Post*, covered the Watergate scandal.

weblog (blog): A collection of links and commentary in hypertext form on the World Wide Web that can be created and posted on the internet with relatively little effort. Blogs can be public diaries, collections of photos, or commentaries on the news.

whitewashing: Casting white actors to play nonwhite characters or rewriting characters who were originally people of color to be white.

wireless telegraph: Guglielmo Marconi's name for his point-to-point communication tool that used radio waves to transmit messages.

World Wide Web: A system developed by Tim Berners-Lee that allows users to view and link documents located anywhere in the world using standard software.

yellow journalism: A style of sensationalistic journalism that grew out of the newspaper circulation battle between Joseph Pulitzer and William Randolph Hearst.

zoned coverage: When a newspaper targets news coverage or advertisements to a specific region of a city or market.

NOTES

CHAPTER 1

1. "A Guide to Coronavirus-Related Words," *Merriam-Webster*, March 18, 2020, http://www.merriam-webster.com/words-at-play/coronavirus-words-guide/covid-19.

2. Sui-lee Wee and Donald G. McNeil Jr., "China Identifies New Virus Causing Pneumonialike Illness," *New York Times*, January 9, 2020, http://www.nytimes.com/2020/01/08/health/china-pneumonia-outbreak-virus.html?searchResultPosition=1.

3. Liao Jun, "41 Cases of New Coronavirus Pneumonia Infected in Wuhan," *Xinhuanet*, January 11, 2020, http://www.xinhuanet.com/2020-01/11/c_1125448269.htm.

4. Marc Stein, "For Danilo Gallinari, the N.B.A. Shutdown Wasn't So Sudden," *New York Times*, March 15, 2020, http://www.nytimes.com/2020/03/15/sports/basketball/danilo-gallinari-italy.html.

5. Independent Auditor's Report, "National Collegiate Athletic Association and Subsidiaries," Deloitte, 2018.

6. Adrian Wojnarowski, "Sources: NBA, ESPN Working on Televising H-O-R-S-E Competition," *ESPN*, April 4, 2020, http://www.espn.com/nba/story/_/id/28995745/sources-nba-espn-working-televising-h-o-r-s-e-competition.

7. Richard Trenholm, "Marvel, James Bond and More: These Are the New Movie Release Dates for 2020 and 2021," *CNET*, April 2, 2020, http://www.cnet.com/news/coronavirus-movie-delays-2020-and-2021-blockbusters-postponed/; Sarah Whitten, "Disney Pixar's 'Onward' Coming to Digital and Disney+ Earlier Due to Coronavirus Outbreak," *CNBC*, March 20, 2020, http://www.cnbc.com/2020/03/20/disney-pixars-onward-coming-to-digital-and-disney-early.html; Brad Brevet, "Status Update On BoxOfficeMojo Amid COVID-19 Concerns," *Box Office Mojo*, March 17, 2020, http://www.boxofficemojo.com/article/ed2758804484/?ref_=bo_hm_hp.

8. Playbill Staff, "Broadway Goes Dark Amid Coronavirus Concerns." *Playbill*, March 12, 2020, http://www.playbill.com/article/broadway-goes-dark-amid-coronavirus-concerns.

9. Lucia Tonelli, "'Hamilton' Sing Along Alert: Stuck-at-Home Fans Can Submit Videos For a Chance to Be Part of #HamAtHome," *Town & Country*, March 25, 2020, http://www.townandcountrymag.com/leisure/arts-and-culture/a31929879/hamilton-casts-fans-for-saturday-night-on-broadway-video-coronavirus-initative/.

10. Aaron Blackman, personal communication with the author, December 30, 2019.

11. George Gerbner, "Mass Media and Human Communication Theory," in *Human Communication Theory: Original Essays*, ed. Frank E. X. Dance (New York: Holt, Rinehart, and Winston, 1967), 40–60.

12. Larry G. Ehrlich, *Fatal Words and Friendly Faces: Interpersonal Communication in the Twenty-First Century* (Lanham, MD: University Press of America, 2000), 82.

13. Aaron Blackman, personal communication with the author, December 30, 2019.

14. Denis McQuail, *McQuail's Mass Communication Theory*, 6th ed. (Thousand Oaks, CA: SAGE, 2010); Benjamin Compaine et al., eds., *Who Owns the Media?* (White Plains, NY: Knowledge Industry, 1982); Harold Lasswell, "The Structure and Function of Communication in Society," in *Mass Communications*, ed. Wilbur Schramm (Urbana: University of Illinois Press, 1960); Charles R. Wright, *Mass Communication: A Sociological Perspective*, 3rd ed. (New York: Random House, 1986).

15. Aaron Blackman, personal communication with the author, December 30, 2019.

16. W. James Potter, *Media Literacy*, 9th ed. (Thousand Oaks, CA: SAGE, 2019).

17. Ibid.

18. Ibid.

19. Dana Stevens, "*Wonder Woman*," *Slate*, June 1, 2017, http://www.slate.com/articles/arts/movies/2017/06/wonder_woman_starring_gal_gadot_reviewed.html.

20. Arthur Asa Berger, *Media Analysis Techniques*, 6th ed. (Thousand Oaks, CA: SAGE, 2019).

21. Elizabeth Findell, "In Dustup Over 'Wonder Woman' Screenings, Alamo Offers Men Free DVDs," *Austin American-Statesman*, August 7, 2017, https://www.statesman.com/article/20170808/NEWS/308089791.

22. Casey Rackman, "This Is for Everyone Who's Obsessed With Robin Wright in 'Wonder Woman,'" *BuzzFeed*, June 5, 2017, https://www.buzzfeed.com/caseyrackham/for-everyone-who-wants-to-be-robin-wright-in-wonder-woman?utm_term=.qc3P6KGM2#.ooNaPXDZY.

23. Potter, *Media Literacy*.

24. Richard Brody, "The Hard-Won Wisdom of 'Wonder Woman,'" *New Yorker*, June 6, 2017, https://www.newyorker.com/culture/richard-brody/the-hard-won-wisdom-of-wonder-woman.

25. Potter, *Media Literacy*.

26. Wright, *Mass Communication*.

27. McQuail, *McQuail's Mass Communication Theory*.

28. Daniel Victor, "Step Aside, Ellen DeGeneres: The New Retweet Champion Is a Nugget-Hungry Teenager," *New York Times*, May 9, 2017, https://www.nytimes.com/2017/05/09/technology/wendys-nuggets-twitter.html.

29. Frank Ahrens, "Anti-indecency Forces Opposed," *Washington Post*, March 26, 2005.

30. Shankar Vedantam, "Two Views of the Same News Find Opposite Biases," *Washington Post*, July 24, 2006.

31. McQuail, *McQuail's Mass Communication Theory*.

32. Neil Postman, *Amusing Ourselves to Death: Public Discourse in the Age of Show Business* (New York: Penguin Books, 1985).

33. Robert Nelson, "Television and the Public Decline of Public Discourse," *Civic Arts Review*, vol. 3 (1990): 1. Excerpt used with permission.

34. John Koblin, "Premature CBS Report of Tom Petty's Death Sets Off an Outpouring," *New York Times*, October 2, 2017,

https://www.nytimes.com/2017/10/02/business/media/tom-petty-cardiac-arrest.html.

35. "Internet/Broadband Fact Sheet," *Pew Research Center*, February 5, 2018, http://www.pewinternet.org/fact-sheet/internet-broadband/.

36. Katie Crowe, "Cartoonist Earns Readership, Freelance Deals With 'Girls With Slingshots' Strip," *Frederick News-Post*, April 26, 2013.

37. Anna Pearce, "The Transcontinental Disability Choir: Four Ways to Do It Right," *Bitch Media*, November 25, 2009, http://bitchmagazine.org/post/four-ways-to-do-it-right.

38. Crowe, "Cartoonist Earns Readership, Freelance Deals."

39. Alyssa Rosenberg, "Danielle Corsetto on the End of Her Long-Running Comic 'Girls With Slingshots,'" *Washington Post*, March 19, 2015, https://www.washingtonpost.com/news/act-four/wp/2015/03/19/danielle-corsetto-on-the-end-of-her-long-running-comic-girls-with-slingshots/.

40. Danielle Corsetto, "Patreon Is Basically Keeping Me Alive While I Figure Out What I'm Doing Next," *Patreon*, accessed May 7, 2018, https://www.patreon.com/girlswithslingshots.

41. Ben H. Bagdikian, *The New Media Monopoly* (Boston: Beacon Press, 2004).

42. Jenn Chen, "Important Instagram Stats You Need to Know for 2020," *Sprout Social*, January 23, 2020, https://sproutsocial.com/insights/instagram-stats/.

43. Linda Pershing and Margaret R. Yocom, "The Yellow Ribboning of the USA: Contested Meanings in the Construction of a Political Symbol," *Western Folklore* 55, no. 1 (1996); Jack Santino, "Yellow Ribbons and Seasonal Flags: The Folk Assemblage of War," *The Journal of American Folklore* 105, no. 415 (1992); George Mariscal, "In the Wake of the Gulf War: Untying the Yellow Ribbon," *Cultural Critique*, no. 19 (1991).

44. Brooke Gladstone, "Never the Same Mainstream Twice," *WNYC*, November 24, 2006, https://www.wnycstudios.org/podcasts/otm/segments/129641-never-the-same-mainstream-twice.

45. A. J. Katz, "2019 Ratings: Fox News Averages Largest Prime Time Audience Ever, Is No. 1 Basic Cable Network for the Year," *TVNewser*, January 2, 2020, www.adweek.com/tvnewser/2019-ratings-fox-news-averages-its-largest-prime-time-audience-ever-and-is-no-1-on-basic-cable/424382/; A. J. Katz, "2019 Ratings: CNN Finishes as a Top 10 Basic Cable Network for 3rd Straight Year," *TVNewser*, January 2, 2020, http://www.adweek.com/tvnewser/2019-ratings-cnn-remains-a-top-10-basic-cable-network-for-3rd-straight-year/424385/.

46. A. J. Katz, "Q4 Evening News Ratings: ABC World News Tonight Is No. 1 in Total Audience, NBC Nightly News Earns Tight Win in A25-54," *TVNewser*, January 3, 2020, http://www.adweek.com/tvnewser/q4-evening-news-ratings-abc-world-news-tonight-delivers-largest-total-audience-while-nbc-nightly-news-earns-tight-win-in-a25-54/424398/.

47. Jennifer Harper, "Hannity Ranked No. 1 Among the Top 100 Talk Radio Gods," *Washington Times*, June 6, 2019, http://www.washingtontimes.com/news/2019/jun/6/inside-the-beltway-talk-radio-gods-rank-sean-hanni/.

48. Daniel Middleton, *TheDiamondMinecart*, YouTube, www.youtube.com/user/TheDiamondMinecart/featured.

49. Todd Spangler, "YouTube Now Has 2 Billion Monthly Users, Who Watch 250 Million Hours on TV Screens Daily," *Variety*, May 3, 2019, https://variety.com/2019/digital/news/youtube-2-billion-users-tv-screen-watch-time-hours-1203204267/.

50. Daniel Fienberg, "'The Rocky Horror Picture Show: Let's Do the Time Warp Again': TV Review," *Hollywood Reporter*, October 17, 2016, https://www.hollywoodreporter.com/review/rocky-horror-picture-show-lets-938951.

51. Hal R. Varian, "File-Sharing Is the Latest Battleground in the Clash of Technology and Copyright," *New York Times*, April 7, 2005.

52. Erik Barnouw, *Tube of Plenty: The Evolution of American Television*, 2nd rev. ed. (New York: Oxford University Press, 1990).

53. Shearon A. Lowery and Melvin L. DeFleur, *Milestones in Mass Communication*, 3rd ed. (White Plains, NY: Longman, 1995).

54. Stan Soocher, *They Fought the Law: Rock Music Goes to Court* (New York: Schirmer Books, 1999).

55. Jesse Sheidlower, "If You Seek Amy's Ancestors," *Slate*, March 18, 2009, http://www.slate.com/id/2214106.

56. Wright, *Mass Communication*.

57. Ibid.; Robert K. Merton, "Patterns of Influence: A Study of Interpersonal Influence and of Communications Behavior in a Local Community," *Communications Research* 1949 (1948): 180–219.

58. Case McDermott, Twitter post, *Twitter*, October 2, 2017, 8:30 a.m., https://twitter.com/caseymcdermott/status/914830013425491968.

59. Andrew Perrin, "Digital Gap Between Rural and Nonrural America Persists," *Pew Research Center*, May 31, 2019, www.pewresearch.org/fact-tank/2019/05/31/digital-gap-between-rural-and-nonrural-america-persists/.

60. AllBlackBerry, "The Evolution of BlackBerry in Pictures," *CrackBerry*, October 1, 2007, https://crackberry.com/evolution-blackberry-pictures.

61. David Pogue, "Apple Waves Its Wand at the Phone," *New York Times*, January 11, 2007, https://www.nytimes.com/2007/01/11/technology/11pogue.html.

62. T-Mobile, "Exclusive T-Mobile Phone Boasts an Intuitive Touch Screen and QWERTY Keyboard, Plus Popular Google Products and Fresh, New Applications," September 23, 2008, https://newsroom.t-mobile.com/news-and-blogs/t-mobile-unveils-the-t-mobile-g1-the-first-phone-powered-by-android.htm.

63. Cecilia Kang, "Mobile Internet Use to Surge," *Washington Post*, February 6, 2013, https://www.washingtonpost.com/business/technology/mobile-internet-use-to-surge/2013/02/06/9eeaa086-6fdd-11e2-a050-b83a7b35c4b5_story.html?utm_term=.ad02c992568d.

64. Darrell M. West, "Ten Facts About Mobile Broadband," *Brookings*, December 8, 2011, https://www.brookings.edu/research/ten-facts-about-mobile-broadband/.

65. Todd Spangler, "YouTube Now Has 2 Billion Monthly Users, Who Watch 250 Million Hours on TV Screens Daily," *Variety*, May 3, 2019, https://variety.com/2019/digital/news/youtube-2-billion-users-tv-screen-watch-time-hours-1203204267/; J. Clement, "Facebook Users Worldwide 2020," *Statista*, April 30, 2020, http://www.statista.com/statistics/264810/number-of-monthly-active-facebook-users-worldwide/; Lucy Handley, "Super Bowl Draws Lowest TV Audience in More Than a Decade, Early Data Show," *CNBC*, February 5, 2019, www.cnbc.com/2019/02/05/super-bowl-draws-lowest-tv-audience-in-more-than-a-decade-nielsen.html.

66. Josh Constine, "Facebook Now Has 2 Billion Monthly Users . . . and Responsibility," *Techcrunch*, June 27, 2017, https://techcrunch.com/2017/06/27/facebook-2-billion-users/; Frank Pallotta and Brian Stelter, "Super Bowl 50 Audience Is Third Largest in TV History," *CNN*, February 8, 2016, http://money.cnn.com/2016/02/08/media/super-bowl-50-ratings/index.html.

67. Ellie Hensley, "Dan Cathy: Pinewood Atlanta Studios Hosting 'Largest Film Production Ever,'" *Atlanta Business Chronicle*, March 1, 2017, https://www.bizjournals.com/atlanta/news/2017/03/01/dan-cathy-pinewood-atlanta-studios-hosting.html.

CHAPTER 2

1. Megan Twohey, "Harvey Weinstein Is Fired After Sexual Harassment Reports," *New York Times*, October 8, 2017, https://www.nytimes.com/2017/10/08/business/harvey-weinstein-fired.html; Jodi Kantor and Megan Twohey, "Harvey Weinstein Paid Off Sexual Harassment Accusers for Decades," *New York Times*, October 5, 2017, https://www.nytimes.com/2017/10/05/us/harvey-weinstein-harassment-allegations.html.

2. Sarah Almukhtar, Michael Gold, and Larry Buchanan, "After Weinstein: 71 Men Accused of Sexual Misconduct and Their Fall From Power," *New York Times*, February 8, 2018, https://www.nytimes.com/interactive/2017/11/10/us/men-accused-sexual-misconduct-weinstein.html.

3. Bethonie Butler, "Matt Lauer Accused of Raping a Former Colleague in Ronan Farrow's New Book," *Washington Post*, October 9, 2019, https://www.washingtonpost.com/arts-entertainment/2019/10/09/matt-lauer-accused-raping-former-colleague-ronan-farrows-new-book/.

4. Brian Stelter, "Les Moonves Is Out at CBS After Harassment Allegations, Corporate Battle," *CNNMoney*, September 9, 2018, https://money.cnn.com/2018/09/09/media/les-moonves-cbs/index.html.

5. Kantor and Twohey, "Harvey Weinstein Paid Off Sexual Harassment Accusers for Decades."

6. Ibid.

7. Ramin Setoodeh, "Ashley Judd Reveals Sexual Harassment by Studio Mogul," *Variety*, October 6, 2015, http://variety.com/2015/film/news/ashley-judd-sexual-harassment-studio-mogul-shower-1201610666/.

8. Jan Ransom, "Harvey Weinstein Is Found Guilty of Sex Crimes in #MeToo Watershed," *New York Times*, February 24, 2020, http://www.nytimes.com/2020/02/24/nyregion/harvey-weinstein-trial-rape-verdict.html.

9. Jan Ransom, "Harvey Weinstein Wanted to Testify. His Lawyers Stopped Him," *New York Times*, February 11, 2020, http://www.nytimes.com/2020/02/11/nyregion/harvey-weinstein-trial.html?searchResultPosition=1.

10. W. James Potter, *Media Literacy*, 3rd ed. (Thousand Oaks, CA: SAGE, 2005).

11. Melvin L. DeFleur and Sandra Ball-Rokeach, *Theories of Mass Communication*, 5th ed. (New York: Longman, 1989); Ferdinand Tönnies, *Gemeinschaft und Gesellschaft*, trans. Charles P. Loomis (East Lansing: Michigan State University Press, 1957).

12. DeFleur and Ball-Rokeach, *Theories of Mass Communication*.

13. Stanley Rothman, "Introduction," in *The Mass Media in Liberal Democratic Societies*, ed. Stanley Rothman (New York: Paragon House, 1992).

14. DeFleur and Ball-Rokeach, *Theories of Mass Communication*.

15. Gerald Mast, "Introduction," in *The Movies in Our Midst: Documents in the Cultural History of Film in America*, ed. Gerald Mast (Chicago: University of Chicago Press, 1982).

16. Anthony A. Leiserowitz, "Day After Tomorrow. Study of Climate Change Risk Perception." *Environment*, (November 2004): 23–44.

17. Shearon A. Lowery and Melvin L. DeFleur, *Milestones in Mass Communication*, 3rd ed. (White Plains, NY: Longman, 1995).

18. Stephen Ansolabehere, Shanto Iyengar, and Adam Simon, "Shifting Perspectives on the Effects of Campaign Communication," in *Do the Media Govern? Politicians, Voters, and Reporters in America*, ed. Shanto Iyengar and Richard Reeves (Thousand Oaks, CA: SAGE, 1997).

19. Paul Lazarsfeld, Bernard Berelson, and Hazel Gaudet, *The People's Choice*, 3rd ed. (New York: Columbia University Press, 1968).

20. Brooke Gladstone, "Trail of Years," *On the Media*, February 23, 2007, http://www.onthemedia.org/transcripts/2007/02/23/07.

21. Ansolabehere et al., "Shifting Perspectives on the Effects of Campaign Communication."

22. Yan Su, "Exploring the Effect of Weibo Opinion Leaders on the Dynamics of Public Opinion in China," *Global Media China* 4, no. 4 (December 2019): 493–513, https://doi.org/10.1177/2059436419866012.

23. Sujin Choi, "The Two-Step Flow of Communication in Twitter-Based Public Forums," *Social Science Computer Review* 33, no. 6 (December 2015): 696–711, https://doi.org/10.1177/0894439314556599.

24. James W. Carey, *A Cultural Approach to Communication From Communication as Culture* (New York: Routledge, 1992).

25. Denis McQuail, *McQuail's Mass Communication Theory*, 6th ed. (Thousand Oaks, CA: SAGE, 2010).

26. DeFleur and Ball-Rokeach, *Theories of Mass Communication*; Denis McQuail, *McQuail's Mass Communication Theory*, 5th ed. (Thousand Oaks, CA: SAGE, 2005); Potter, *Media Literacy*.

27. Doris A. Graber, *Processing the News: How People Tame the Information Tide*, 2nd ed. (New York: Longman, 1988).

28. David Hinckley, "Rush and Sean Tops in Talk," *Daily News*, December 10, 2005.

29. Graber, *Processing the News*; Lazarsfeld et al., *People's Choice*.

30. Editorial Board, "Young Voters, Motivated Again," *New York Times*, February 21, 2016, http://www.nytimes.com/2016/02/22/opinion/young-voters-motivated-again.html.

31. Arthur Asa Berger, *Media Analysis Techniques*, 3rd ed. (Thousand Oaks, CA: SAGE, 2005).

32. Ibid.

33. Potter, *Media Literacy*.

34. Alex Ross, "A Field Guide to the Musical Leitmotifs of 'Star Wars,'" *New Yorker*, January 3, 2018, https://www.newyorker.com/culture/culture-desk/a-field-guide-to-the-musical-leitmotifs-of-star-wars.

35. Marshall McLuhan, *Understanding Media: The Extensions of Man* (New York: McGraw-Hill, 1964).

36. McQuail, *McQuail's Mass Communication Theory*, 6th ed.

37. Joshua Meyrowitz, "Shifting Worlds of Strangers: Medium Theory and Changes in 'Them' Versus 'Us,'" *Sociological Inquiry* 67, no. 1 (1997): 59–71.

38. Joshua Meyrowitz, *No Sense of Place* (New York: Oxford University Press, 1985).

39. McQuail, *McQuail's Mass Communication Theory*, 6th ed.

40. Jürgen Habermas, *The Theory of Communicative Action*, vol. 1, trans. Thomas McCarthy (Boston: Beacon Press, 1984).

41. Matthew Forney, "Testing Beijing's Limits: In the Quest for China's Lucrative—and Elusive—TV Market, Did Murdoch Bend the Rules?" *Time*, September 5, 2005; Ken Auletta, *Googled: The End of the World as We Know It* (New York: Penguin Press, 2009).

42. Ben H. Bagdikian, *The Media Monopoly*, 2nd ed. (Boston: Beacon Press, 1987), xvi.

43. Chris Anderson, *The Long Tail* (New York: Hyperion, 2006).

44. Potter, *Media Literacy*; Shearon A. Lowery and Melvin L. DeFleur, *Milestones in Mass Communication*, 3rd ed. (White Plains: Longman, 1995); McQuail, *McQuail's Mass Communication Theory*, 6th ed.

45. Elihu Katz, "The Two-Step Flow of Communication," in *Mass Communications*, ed. Wilbur Schramm (Urbana: University of Illinois Press, 1960).

46. Harold Lasswell, "The Structure and Function of Communication in Society," in *Mass Communications*, ed. Wilbur Schramm (Urbana: University of Illinois Press, 1960).

47. Robert K. Merton, *Social Theory and Social Structure*, enlarged ed. (New York: Free Press, 1968).

48. Lasswell, "The Structure and Function of Communication in Society."

49. Charles R. Wright, *Mass Communication: A Sociological Perspective*, 3rd ed. (New York: Random House, 1986).

50. Everette E. Dennis, Justin D. Martin, and Robb Wood, "Social Media: Sharing Information and Connecting Online Nearly Universal," in *Media Use in the Middle East, 2015* (Northwestern University in Qatar, 2015), April 15, 2015, http://www.mideastmedia.org/survey/2015/chapter/social-media.html#.

51. Travis M. Andrews, "Omarosa Manigault Newman: From the White House to the 'Big Brother' House," *Washington Post*, January 29, 2018, https://www.washingtonpost.com/news/morning-mix/wp/2018/01/29/omarosa-manigault-newman-from-the-white-house-to-the-big-brother-house/.

52. "Investors Now Go Online for Quotes, Advice," Pew Research Center for the People and the Press, June 11, 2000.

53. Wright, *Mass Communication*; Meyrowitz, *No Sense of Place*.

54. Meyrowitz, *No Sense of Place*.

55. Everett M. Rogers, William B. Hart, and James W. Dearing, "A Paradigmatic History of Agenda-Setting Research," in *Do the Media Govern?*, ed. Shanto Iyengar and Richard Reeves (Thousand Oaks, CA: SAGE, 1997).

56. Lowery and DeFleur, *Milestones in Mass Communication*.

57. Ibid.

58. Brian Stelter, "'Ashamed': Ex-PR Exec Justine Sacco Apologizes for AIDS in Africa Tweet," CNN.com, December 22, 2013, http://www.cnn.com/2013/12/22/world/sacco-offensive-tweet/index.html.

59. Albert Bandura, "Social Cognitive Theory of Mass Communication," in *Media Effects: Advances in Theory and Research*, ed. Jennings Bryant and Dolf Zillman (Hillsdale, NJ: Erlbaum, 1994).

60. Elihu Katz, Jay G. Blumler, and Michael Gurevitch, "Utilization of Mass Communication by the Individual," in *The Uses of Mass Communications: Current Perspectives on Gratifications Research*, ed. Jay G. Blumler and Elihu Katz (Thousand Oaks, CA: SAGE, 1974).

61. Berger, *Media Analysis Techniques*.

62. George Herbert Mead, *Mind, Self, and Society* (Chicago: University of Chicago Press, 1934).

63. Robert K. Merton, "The Thomas Theorem and the Matthew Effect," *Social Forces* 74, no. 2 (December 1, 1995): 379–422.

64. Michael J. Socolow, "The Hyped Panic Over 'War of the Worlds,'" *The Chronicle of Higher Education*, October 24, 2008; Wright, *Mass Communication*.

65. Joanne Ostrow, "Authority on Media Violence Says Don't Blame TV for Columbine," *Denver Post*, April 25, 1999.

66. George Gerbner et al., "Growing Up With Television: The Cultivation Perspective," in *Media Effects: Advances in Theory and Research*, ed. Jennings Bryant and Dolf Zillman (Hillsdale: Erlbaum, 1994).

67. Lowery and DeFleur, *Milestones in Mass Communication*, 278.

68. Gerbner et al., "Growing Up With Television."

69. Wilson Biographies, "Gerbner, George," *Wilson Web*, hwwilsonweb.com.

70. Ibid.

71. Stephen Eric Bronner, *Critical Theory: A Very Short Introduction* (New York: Oxford University Press, 2011), 106.

72. Ibid., 115.

73. Werner J. Severin and James W. Tankard, *Communication Theories: Origins, Methods, and Uses in the Mass Media*, 5th ed. (New York: Longman, 2001).

74. Lisa de Moraes, "Fighting Words From a Bantamweight," *Washington Post*, July 2, 1999; Eils Lotozo, "Getting Real: No Skinny Models in *Grace* Magazine," *Hamilton Spectator*, September 5, 2002.

75. Nicole Bitette, "Nina Agdal Calls Out Magazine That Body-Shamed Her for Not Being a Sample Size," *New York Daily News*, January 13, 2018, http://www.nydailynews.com/life-style/nina-agdal-calls-magazine-body-shaming-article-1.3755107.

76. Ana Colón, "Nina Agdal Spoke Out About Body Shaming in Fashion—and It Landed Her a New Campaign," *Glamour*, April 3, 2018, https://www.glamour.com/story/nina-agdal-aerie-real-campaign-interview.

77. Eric Schlabs, "Regulating Weight in the Fashion Industry," *The Regulatory Review*, July 27, 2016, http://www.theregreview.org/2016/07/27/schlabs-regulating-weight-in-the-fashion-industry/.

78. Stuart Elliott, "For Everyday Products, Ads Using the Everyday Woman," *New York Times*, August 17, 2005; Theresa Howard, "Dove Ads Enlist All Shapes, Styles, Sizes," *USA Today*, August 29, 2005; Rebecca Traister, "Move Over, Dove Ads: Nike's Posteriors and Scraped Knees Bring a Greater Dose of Reality to Marketing," *Chicago Sun-Times*, August 23, 2005.

79. Madeline Jones, "Plus Size Bodies, What Is Wrong With Them Anyway?" *PLUS Model Magazine*, January 8, 2012, http://plus-model-mag.com/2012/01/plus-size-bodies-what-is-wrong-with-them-anyway/.

80. Nicole Spector, "What Makes Someone 'Most Beautiful' Is Changing, Study Says," *NBC News*, October 11, 2017, http://www.nbcnews.com/better/health/how-beauty-standard-has-changed-1990-how-it-hasn-t-ncna809766.

81. Ibid

82. Cleve R. Wooston Jr., "A Photographer Unexpectedly Snapped Her Picture at Homecoming. Then, Modeling Agencies Called," *Washington Post*, October 31, 2017, https://www.washingtonpost.com/news/grade-point/wp/2017/10/31/a-photographer-unexpectedly-snapped-her-picture-at-homecoming-then-modeling-agencies-called/.

83. Janelle Okwodu, "How a Viral Photo Turned Anok Yai Into the Model of the Moment," *Vogue*, November 7, 2017, https://www.vogue.com/article/anok-yai-sudanese-model-viral-sensation-modeling-contract.

84. Alexander Breindel, "'Average' Photo Brings Teen Stardom," *Resource*, November 7, 2017, http://resourcemagonline.com/2017/11/average-photo-brings-teen-stardom/82278/.

85. Wooston, "A Photographer Unexpectedly Snapped Her Picture at Homecoming."

86. Sabrina Barr, "Anok Yai Becomes First Black Model to Open Prada Runway Show Since 1997," *Independent*, February 27, 2018, http://www.independent.co.uk/life-style/fashion/anok-yai-prada-open-show-black-model-milan-fashion-week-a8230361.html.

87. Katy Waldman, "Lena Dunham Responds to the *Vogue* Haters," *Slate*, January 17, 2014, www.slate.com/blogs/xx_factor/2014/01/17/lena_dunham_response_to_vogue_photoshop_criticism_fashion_magazines_are.html.

88. Jessica Roy, "Kate Winslet's Contract States L'Oréal Can't Retouch Her Photos," *Cut*, October 23, 2015, http://nymag.com/thecut/2015/10/kate-winslets-loral-contract-no-retouching.html.

89. Anna Davies, "People Are Getting Surgery to Look Like Their Snapchat Selfies." *BBC*, April 19, 2018, www.bbc.co.uk/bbcthree/article/9ca4f7c6-d2c3-4e25-862c-03aed9ec1082.

90. A. J. Willingham, "Social Media Filters Mess With Our Perceptions so Much, There's Now a Name for It." *CNN*, August 10, 2018, http://www.cnn.com/2018/08/10/health/snapchat-dysmorphia-cosmetic-surgery-social-media-trend-trnd/index.html.

91. Chiu, Allyson Chiu, "Patients Are Desperate to Resemble Their Doctored Selfies. Plastic Surgeons Alarmed by 'Snapchat Dysmorphia,'" *Washington Post*, August 6, 2018, http://www.washingtonpost.com/news/morning-mix/wp/2018/08/06/patients-are-desperate-to-resemble-their-doctored-selfies-plastic-surgeons-alarmed-by-snapchat-dysmorphia/.

CHAPTER 3

1. Jose Antonio Vargas, "The Face of Facebook," *New Yorker*, September 20, 2010, https://www.newyorker.com/magazine/2010/09/20/the-face-of-facebook.

2. Tony Romm and Craig Timberg, "Cambridge Analytica Shuts Down Amid Scandal Over Use of Facebook Data," *Washington Post*, May 2, 2018, https://www.washingtonpost.com/news/the-switch/wp/2018/05/02/cambridge-analytica-shuts-down-amid-scandal-over-use-of-facebook-data/.

3. Roger McNamee, "I Mentored Mark Zuckerberg. But I Can't Stay Silent," *Time*, January 17, 2019, https://time.com/5505441/mark-zuckerberg-mentor-facebook-downfall/.

4. Katherine Bindley, "Why Facebook Still Seems to Spy on You," *Wall Street Journal*, February 28, 2019, www.wsj.com/articles/facebook-ads-will-follow-you-even-when-your-privacy-settings-are-dialed-up-11551362400.

5. Ryan Tracy and Emily Glazer, "Facebook Settlement Expected to Mandate Privacy Committee," *Wall Street Journal*, July 22, 2019, http://www.wsj.com/articles/ftc-to-announce-5-billion-facebook-settlement-as-soon-as-this-week-11563816621?mod=djem10point.

6. J. Clement, "Facebook Users Worldwide as of 1st Quarter 2020," Statista, January 30, 2020, www.statista.com/statistics/264810/number-of-monthly-active-facebook-users-worldwide/.

7. J. Clement, "Most Popular Mobile Messaging Apps Worldwide as of October 2019," Statista, November 20, 2019, http://www.statista.com/statistics/258749/most-popular-global-mobile-messenger-apps/.

8. J. Clement, " Number of Monthly Active Twitter Users Worldwide From 1st Quarter 2020 to 1st Quarter 2019," Statista, August 14, 2019, http://www.statista.com/statistics/282087/number-of-monthly-active-twitter-users/.

9. D&B Hoovers, "Company Profile: Facebook, Inc.," http://www.hoovers.com/company-information/cs/company-profile.facebook_inc.f1fe73cc6a208e18.html.

10. D&B Hoovers, "Company Profile: Apple Inc.," http://www.hoovers.com/company-information/cs/company-profile.apple_inc.4c9baa063908dbd8.html; D&B Hoovers, "Company Profile: Alphabet Inc.," http://www.hoovers.com/company-information/cs/company-profile.alphabet_inc.67543c15188bf061.html; D&B Hoovers, "Company Profile: Comcast Corporation," http://www.hoovers.com/company-information/cs/company-profile.comcast_corporation.42bb142511eab416.html.

11. Ben Bagdikian, *The Information Machines: Their Impact on Men and the Media* (New York: Harper & Row, 1971).

12. John Tebbel, *The Media in America* (New York: Crowell, 1974).

13. Ibid.

14. Ibid.

15. Michael Schudson, *The Power of News* (Cambridge, MA: Harvard University Press, 1995).

16. Margaret A. Blanchard, ed., *History of the Mass Media in the United States* (Chicago: Fitzroy Dearborn, 1998).

17. Linda Werthheimer, ed., *Listening to America: Twenty-Five Years in the Life of a Nation, as Heard on National Public Radio* (Boston: Houghton Mifflin, 1995). NPR, "NPR Fact Sheet," https://www.npr.org/documents/about/press/NPR_Fact_Sheet.pdf; NPR, "Sponsor *Morning Edition*, the Nation's Number One Morning Drive Program."

18. Schudson, *Power of News*.

19. Jeanine Poggi, "Hulu Tops 28 Million Users, Announces New Binge-Watch Ad Format at NewFronts." *Ad Age*, May 1, 2019, https://adage.com/article/special-report-newfronts/hulu-tops-28-million-users-announces-new-binge-watch-ad-format-newfronts/2168261?utm_source=ad-age-digital-wednesday&utm_medium=email&utm_campaign=20190501&utm_content=hero-headline.

20. "Internet/Broadband Fact Sheet," *Pew Research Center*, February 5, 2018, http://www.pewinternet.org/fact-sheet/internet-broadband/; "Mobile Fact Sheet," *Pew Research Center*, February 5, 2018, http://www.pewinternet.org/fact-sheet/mobile/; Center for Technology, Media & Telecommunications, "Digital Media Trends Survey: A New World of Choice for Digital Consumers," 12th ed., Deloitte Insights, 2018, https://www2.deloitte.com/content/dam/insights/us/articles/4479_Digital-media-trends/4479_Digital_media%20trends_Exec%20Sum_vFINAL.pdf; "Average Circulation of the Wall Street journal as of July 2017 (in thousands)," Statista, https://www.statista.com/statistics/193788/average-paid-circulation-of-the-wall-street-journal/.

21. D&B Hoovers, "Company Profile: The Walt Disney Company," http://www.hoovers.com/company-information/cs/company-profile.the_walt_disney_company.432c15c5e0758b7d.html.

22. PBS, "Walt Disney's Life: Timeline," *American Experience*.

23. Richard Schickel, "Walt Disney," *Time*, December 7, 1998.

24. "The House of the Mouse," *New Internationalist*, December 1998.

25. Suzy Wetlaufer, "Common Sense and Conflict," *Harvard Business Review*, January/February 2000; Wilson Biographies, "Walt Disney," http://vweb.hwwilsonweb.com.

26. Ken Auletta, *The Highwaymen* (New York: Random House, 1997).

27. D&B Hoovers, "Company Profile: The Walt Disney Company."

28. Peter Schweizer and Rochelle Schweizer, *Disney: The Mouse Betrayed* (Washington, DC: Regnery, 1998); Robert F. Hartley, *Marketing Mistakes and Successes*, 7th ed. (New York: Wiley, 1998); Maureen Fan, "A Bumpy Ride for Disneyland in Hong Kong," *Washington Post*, November 20, 2006.

29. Steven Zeitchik, "Disney and Justice Dept. Reach Agreement, Smoothing the Way for Fox Acquisition," *Washington Post*, June

27, 2018, https://www.washingtonpost.com/news/business/wp/2018/06/27/disney-and-doj-reach-agreement-smoothing-the-way-for-fox-acquisition/?utm_term=.d6c0772cc5c1.

30. Bloomberg News, "Disney Is Dropping the Fox Name from 20th Century Studios." *Ad Age*, January 17, 2020, https://adage.com/article/bloomberg-news/disney-dropping-fox-name-20th-century-studios/2228526?utm_source=ad-age-digital-friday&utm_medium=email&utm_campaign=20200117&utm_content=hero-headline.

31. M. B., "What Is the Endgame for Disney+?" *The Economist*, November 11, 2019, http://www.economist.com/prospero/2019/11/11/what-is-the-endgame-for-disney-.

32. Frank Pallotta, "Disney CEO Bob Iger Is About to Take the Biggest Risk of His Career," *CNN*, November 8, 2019, https://www.cnn.com/2019/11/08/media/disney-bob-iger-risk-takers/index.html.

33. Jonathan Seff, "First Look: iTunes Store Movies: What You Need to Know." *Macworld*, September 21, 2006, http://www.macworld.com/article/1053017/itunesmovies.html.

34. Todd Spangler, "Disney Plus Signed Up 24 Million U.S. Subscribers in November and Took Bite Out of Netflix, Analysts Estimate," *Variety*, December 18, 2019, https://variety.com/2019/digital/news/disney-plus-24-million-us-subscribers-netflix-q4-churn-1203447210/.

35. M. B., "What Is the Endgame for Disney+?"

36. Steven Zeitchik, "In a Surprise Move, Disney Chief Executive Robert Iger Steps Down and Is Replaced by a Theme-park Lieutenant," *Washington Post*, February 25, 2020, http://www.washingtonpost.com/business/2020/02/25/disney-names-bob-chapek-ceo-robert-iger-become-executive-chairman/.

37. Wayne Friedman, "21st Century Fox to Be Fox Entertainment," *Television News Daily*, February 7, 2019, http://www.mediapost.com/publications/article/331637/21st-century-fox-to-be-fox-entertainment.html.

38. Brooks Barnes, "Disney Drops Fox From Names of Studios It Bought From Rupert Murdoch," *New York Times*, January 17, 2020, http://www.nytimes.com/2020/01/17/business/media/disney-fox-name.html.

39. "Fox Annual Report 2019," Fox Corporation, January 27, 2019.

40. Auletta, *Highwaymen*.

41. A. J. Katz, "The Top Cable Networks of April 2018," *AdWeek*, May 2, 2018, http://adweek.it/2rdSiWw.

42. James Rufus Koren, "Murdoch Family Becomes Second Largest Disney Shareholder With Fox Deal," *Los Angeles Times*, December 14, 2017, http://www.latimes.com/business/la-fi-disney-fox-sale-shareholder-20171214-story.html; Matthew Garrahan, "Murdoch Family to Hold Less Than 5% of Disney After Fox Sale," *Financial Times*, December 13, 2017, https://www.ft.com/content/5c52993a-e02c-11e7-a8a4-0a1e63a52f9c.

43. Jonathan Mahler and Jim Rutenberg, "Part 3: The Future of Fox: An Even More Powerful Political Weapon," *New York Times*, April 3, 2019, http://www.nytimes.com/interactive/2019/04/03/magazine/new-fox-corporation-disney-deal.html.

44. Jonathan Mahler and Jim Rutenberg, "Part 2: Inside the Succession Battle for the Murdoch Empire," *New York Times*, April 3, 2019, http://www.nytimes.com/interactive/2019/04/03/magazine/james-murdoch-lachlan-succession.html.

45. Brian Fung, "It's Official: AT&T–Time Warner Is a Done Deal," *Washington Post*, June 14, 2018, https://www.washingtonpost.com/news/the-switch/wp/2018/06/14/its-official-att-time-warner-is-a-done-deal/?noredirect=on&utm_term=.741566bc3c02.

46. Clair Atkinson, "Time Warner Is Now Warner Media, and a Lot of Executives Are Leaving," *NBC News*, June 15, 2018, https://www.nbcnews.com/card/time-warner-now-warner-media-lot-executives-are-leaving-n883781.

47. D&B Hoovers, "Company Profile: Warner Media, LLC"; Alger, *Megamedia*; AOL Time Warner, "2002 Annual Report."

48. D&B Hoovers, "Company Profile: Warner Media, LLC."

49. Joe Nocera, "RIP, Time Inc. It Was Fun While It Lasted," *Bloomberg*, November 27, 2017, https://www.bloomberg.com/view/articles/2017-11-27/rip-time-magazine-meredith-will-make-you-fade-away.

50. Alex Sherman, "John Stankey's Challenge: Making AT&T's $100 Billion Bet on Time Warner Pay Off," *CNBC*, June 7, 2019, http://www.cnbc.com/2019/06/07/john-stankey-warnermedia-ceo-one-year-profile-departures-silos.html.

51. Joan E. Solsman, "HBO Max Launches May 27: Discounts, Free Upgrades, Shows and Movies to Expect," *CNET*, October 30, 2019, http://www.cnet.com/news/hbo-max-launch-dates-prices-shows-movies-to-expect/.

52. D&B Hoovers, "Company Profile: Viacom Inc.," http://www.hoovers.com/company-information/cs/company-profile.viacom_inc.6747d8b05f13db09.html; D&B Hoovers, "Company Profile: CBS Corporation," http://www.hoovers.com/company-information/cs/company-profile.cbs_corporation.21bc71ea9265b776.html.

53. Rani Molla and Peter Kafka, "Here's the Chart That Explains Why CBS and Viacom Want to Merge," *Recode*, February 1, 2018, https://www.recode.net/2018/1/18/16906042/cbs-viacom-merger-media-market-landscape-streaming; William D. Cohan, "'Betrayal,' 'Blackmail,' and 'Elder Abuse'?: The Battle for Sumner Redstone's Affection—and Fortune—Gets Even Weirder," *Vanity Fair*, May 3, 2018, https://www.vanityfair.com/news/2018/05/sumner-redstone-shari-redstone-manuela-herzer-complaint.

54. Benjamin Mullin and Joe Flint, "Viacom–CBS Deal Drama Was Worthy of the Fall Lineup," *Wall Street Journal*, August 13, 2019, http://www.wsj.com/articles/behind-the-scenes-viacom-cbs-deal-drama-was-worthy-of-the-fall-lineup-11565729372.

55. Steven Zeitchik, "CBS, Viacom to Reunite, Hoping to Take on Disney and Netflix," *Washington Post*, August 13, 2019, http://www.washingtonpost.com/business/2019/08/13/cbs-viacom-reunite-hoping-take-disney-netflix/.

56. Edmund Lee, "CBS and Viacom to Reunite in Victory for Shari Redstone," *New York Times*, August 13, 2019, http://www.nytimes.com/2019/08/13/business/cbs-viacom-merger.html; D&B Hoovers, "Company Profile: The Walt Disney Company," https://www.dnb.com/business-directory/company-profiles.the_walt_disney_company.42cf1f7156420b0a5454d50d9a70043f.html.

57. Brian Steinberg, "Wall Street Has Mixed Response to Viacom–CBS Merger," *Variety*, August 13, 2019, https://variety.com/2019/biz/news/viacomcbs-merger-wall-street-response-1203301437/.

58. Bertelsmann, "Financial Figures," https://www.bertelsmann.com/investor-relations/bertelsmann-at-a-glance/financial-figures/.

59. Alger, *Megamedia*.

60. "New Chapter," *Economist*, February 10, 2001; D&B Hoovers, "Company Profile: Bertelsmann SE & Co. KGaA," http://www.hoovers.com/company-information/cs/company-profile.bertelsmann_se__co_kgaa.89b5c24e863d43d7.html.

61. Jack Ewing, "Bertelsmann's Creed: Inner Growth," *Businessweek*, March 17, 2005, http://www.bloomberg.com/

news/articles/2005-03-17/bertelsmanns-creed-inner-growth; Julie Bosman, "Penguin and Random House Merge, Saying Change Will Come Slowly," *New York Times*, July 1, 2013, http://www.nytimes.com/2013/07/02/business/media/merger-of -penguin-and-random-house-is-completed.html.

62. Frank Gibney Jr., "Napster Meister," *Time*, November 13, 2000; D&B Hoovers, "Company Profile: Bertelsmann SE & Co. KGaA."

63. Jack Ewing, "Bertelsmann's Slimmer Profile Generates Thinner Profits," *Businessweek*, September 6, 2006, http://www.bloomberg.com/news/articles/2006-09-05/bertelsmanns -slimmer-profile-generates-thinner-profits; Bertelsmann, "Annual Report 2017"; D&B Hoovers, "Company Profile: Bertelsmann SE & Co. KGaA."

64. D&B Hoovers, "Company Profile: Bertelsmann SE & Co. KGaA."

65. D&B Hoovers, "Company Profile: Comcast Corporation"; D&B Hoovers, "Company Profile: Alphabet Inc."

66. Alger, *Megamedia*.

67. Auletta, *Three Blind Mice: How the TV Networks Lost Their Way* (New York: Random House, 1991).

68. Howard Kurtz, "Comcast–NBC Deal Possible," *Washington Post*, October 1, 2009; Paul Tobin, "Vivendi Wants to Exit NBC, Deal Is Complex, CFO Says," *Bloomberg*, November 19, 2009, www.bloomberg.com; Shira Ovide and Amy Schatz, "Comcast–NBC Deal Would Draw Lengthy Scrutiny in Washington," *Wall Street Journal*, November 16, 2009; Brian Stelter and Tim Arango, "Comcast-NBC Deal Wins Federal Approval," *New York Times*, January 18, 2011, http://mediadecoder.blogs.nytimes.com/2011/01/18/f-c-c-approves -comcast-nbc-deal/.

69. Amy Chozick and Brian Stelter, "Comcast Buys Rest of NBC in Early Sale," *New York Times*, February 12, 2013, http://mediadecoder.blogs.nytimes.com/2013/02/12/comcast-buying -g-e-s-stake-in-nbcuniversal-for-16-7-billion/?_php=true&_ type=blogs&smid=tw-share&_r=0.

70. Meg James, "Comcast to Own All of Media Giant," *Los Angeles Times*, February 13, 2013, http://articles.latimes.com/2013/ feb/13/business/la-fi-ct-comcast-ge-20130213.

71. Wayne Friedman, "Comcast Q3 Sees More Video Subscriber Losses, Stronger Broadband Business," *Television News Daily*, October 25, 2019, http://www.mediapost.com/publications/ article/342419/comcast-q3-sees-more-video-subscriber -losses-stro.html?utm_source=newsletter&utm_ medium=email&utm_content=readmore& utm_campaign=115824&hashid=6mTu5Bmo GXoc5CFuFDoRPPm4utY.

72. D&B Hoovers, "Company Profile: Comcast Corporation"; D&B Hoovers, "Company Profile: NBCUniversal Media, LLC," http://www.hoovers.com/company-information/cs/company- profile.nbcuniversal_media_llc.109556adb7a28138.html.

73. D&B Hoovers, "Company Profile: Comcast Corporation"; George Szalai, "NBCUniversal to Acquire DreamWorks Animation in $3.8B Deal," *Hollywood Reporter*, April 28, 2016, http://www.hollywoodreporter.com/news/comcast-acquire -dreamworks-animation-888103.

74. D&B Hoovers, "Company Profile: Comcast Corporation."

75. Wayne Friedman, "Comcast Q3 Sees More Video Subscriber Losses, Stronger Broadband Business," October 24, 2019, *Television News Daily*, http://www.mediapost.com/publications/ article/342419/comcast-q3-sees-more-video-subscriber-losses -stro.html?utm_source=newsletter& utm_medium=email&utm_content=

76. Google, "Google News Help," https://support.google.com/news/ answer/106259?hl=en&ref_topic=2428790.

77. D&B Hoovers, "Company Profile: Alphabet Inc."

78. D&B Hoovers, "Company Profile: Alphabet Inc."

79. Google, "About: Google Doodles," https://www.google.com/ doodles/about.

80. Pamela Hutchinson, "Lotte Reiniger: Animated Film Pioneer and Standard-Bearer for Women," *Guardian*, June 2, 2016, http://www.theguardian.com/film/2016/jun/02/lotte-reiniger -the-pioneer-of-silhouette-animation-google-doodle.

81. "44th Anniversary of the Birth of Hip Hop," *Google*, August 11, 2017, https://www.google.com/doodles/44th-anniversary-of -the-birth-of-hip-hop.

82. Avi Selk, "18 Years of Google Doodles and the People Who Hate Them," *Washington Post*, April 2, 2018, https://www .washingtonpost.com/news/acts-of-faith/wp/2018/04/02/18 -years-of-google-doodles-and-the-people-who-hate- them/?utm_term=.32be94587dff.

83. U.S. Securities and Exchange Commission, "Form 10-K Annual Report for the Fiscal Year Ended December 31, 2017: Alphabet Inc."

84. Google, "About: Google Doodles."

85. Auletta, *Googled: The End of the World as We Know It* (New York: Penguin Press, 2009), 35.

86. Ibid., 38.

87. Tony Romm and Elizabeth Dwoskin, "FTC Approves Settlement with Google over YouTube Kids Privacy Violations," *Washington Post*, July 19, 2019, http://www.washingtonpost.com/ technology/2019/07/19/ftc-approves-settlement-with-google -over-youtube-kids-privacy-violations/.

88. Brent Kendall and John D. McKinnon, "Justice Department Is Preparing Antitrust Investigation of Google," *Wall Street Journal*, June 1, 2019, http://www.wsj.com/articles/justice -department-is-preparing-antitrust-investigation-of-google -11559348795?mod=hp_lead_pos1.

89. Margaret Sullivan, "Google and Facebook Sucked Profits from Newspapers. Publishers Are Finally Resisting," *Washington Post*, June 5, 2019, http://www.washingtonpost.com/lifestyle/style/ google-and-facebook-sucked-profits-from-newspapers-publishers -are-finally-resisting/2019/06/04/d5fa2aaa-86de-11e9-98c1 -e945ae5db8fb_story.html.

90. D&B Hoovers, "Company Profile: Apple Inc."

91. Peter Burrows and Ronald Grover, "Steve Jobs's Magic Kingdom," *Businessweek*, January 26, 2006.

92. Tim Berners-Lee, *Weaving the Web* (New York: HarperCollins, 1999).

93. D&B Hoovers, "Company Profile: Apple Inc."; John Markoff, "Oh, Yeah, He Also Sells Computers," *New York Times*, April 25, 2004.

94. Jefferson Graham, "Jobs Has a Knack for Getting His Way," *USA Today*, January 25, 2006.

95. D&B Hoovers, "Company Profile: Pixar," http://www .hoovers.com/company-information/cs/company-profile.pixar .e5d158d2aed147f3.html.

96. Burrows and Grover, "Steve Jobs's Magic Kingdom."

97. Auletta, *Googled*.

98. Brandon Keim, "Twitter Analysis: Massive Global Mourning for Steve Jobs (Infographic)," *Wired*, October 7, 2011, http://www .wired.com/epicenter/2011/10/global-mourning-for-steve-jobs/.

99. Timothy B. Lee, "How Google Passed Apple to Become the World's Most Valuable Company," *Vox*, May 12, 2016, http:// www.vox.com/2016/2/4/10911364/google-apple-most-valuable.

100. Paul R. La Monica, "Apple Inches Closer to $1 Trillion Market Value," *CNN Money*, May 7, 2018, http://money.cnn.com/2018/05/07/investing/apple-trillion-dollar-market-value/index.html, and Jack Nicas, "Apple reaches $2 trillion, punctuating big tech's grip," *New York Times*, Aug. 19, 2020, https://www.nytimes.com/2020/08/19/technology/apple-2-trillion.html.

101. Chris Anderson, *The Long Tail* (New York: Hyperion, 2006).

102. Ibid.

103. Ed Christman, "Walmart to Cut Its CD Stock by Nearly Half," *Billboard*, April 8, 2014.

104. Ed Christman, "Best Buy to Pull CDs, Target Threatens to Pay Labels for CDs Only When Customers Buy Them," *Billboard*, February 2, 2018, https://www.billboard.com/articles/business/8097929/best-buy-to-pull-cds-target-threatens-to-pay-labels-for-cds-only-when.

105. "Bill Patrizio Appointed as President and CEO of Napster," *Napster*, February 8, 2018, https://blog.napster.com/2018/02/08/bill-patrizio-appointed-as-president-and-ceo/.

106. Andrew Flanagan, "Where's the Long Tail? Spotify Touts Its Artist Discovery," *Billboard*, May 26, 2016, https://www.billboard.com/articles/business/7385830/wheres-the-long-tail-spotify-artist-discovery.

107. Ibid.; Napster, "About Us," https://us.napster.com/about.

108. Alina Selyukh, "Long Kept Secret, Amazon Says Number of Prime Customers Topped 100 Million," *NPR*, April 18, 2018, https://www.npr.org/sections/thetwo-way/2018/04/18/603750056/long-kept-secret-amazon-says-number-of-prime-customers-topped-100-million.

109. Ibid.

110. Ibid.

111. Ibid.

112. Michael Liedtke, "Now Starring on the Internet: YouTube.com," *USA Today*, April 9, 2006.

113. Charlie Rose, "A Conversation with the YouTube Co-Founders," August 11, 2006, https://charlierose.com/videos/13874.

114. D&B Hoovers, "Company Profile: Youtube, LLC," http://www.hoovers.com/company-information/cs/company-profile.youtube_llc.c21e009f1fe74a2c.html.

115. Todd Spangler, "YouTube Now Has 2 Billion Monthly Users, Who Watch 250 Million Hours on TV Screens Daily," *Variety*, May 3, 2019, https://variety.com/2019/digital/news/youtube-2-billion-users-tv-screen-watch-time-hours-1203204267/; Daisuke Wakabayashi, "YouTube Is a Big Business. Just How Big Is Anyone's Guess," *New York Times*, July 24, 2019, http://www.nytimes.com/2019/07/24/technology/youtube-financial-disclosure-google.html.

116. YouTube, "YouTube for Press," https://www.youtube.com/yt/press/statistics.html.

117. Rose, "A Conversation with the YouTube Co-Founders."

118. Diane Mermigas, "Mermigas on Media," *Hollywood Reporter*, October 24, 2006.

119. Ibid.

120. Ibid.

CHAPTER 4

1. Katy Waldman, "John Green Is a Hero of the Teen Internet. Is He to Blame for the Controversy Around Him?" *Slate*, July 7, 2015, http://www.slate.com/blogs/browbeat/2015/07/07/john_green_author_of_paper_towns_and_tfios_is_the_most_loved_and_hated_person.html; Alison Flood, "John Green: Having OCD Is an Ongoing Part of My Life," *Guardian*, October 14, 2017, http://www.theguardian.com/books/2017/oct/14/john-green-turtles-all-the-way-down-ocd-interview.

2. "Number of Stations by Format," *News Generation*, https://www.newsgeneration.com/broadcast-resources/number-of-stations-by-format/.

3. D&B Hoovers, "Company Profile: Twenty-First Century Fox, Inc.," http://www.hoovers.com/company-information/cs/company-profile.twenty-first_century_fox_inc.0b822046e0ab357c.html.

4. David Lindquist, "John Green's 'The Fault in Our Stars' Is a Play for the First Time, and It's Close to Home," *Indianapolis Star*, October 4, 2019, http://www.indystar.com/story/entertainment/arts/2019/10/03/john-greens-the-fault-our-stars-play-first-time/2434133001/?utm_source=oembed&utm_medium=onsite&utm_campaign=storylines&utm_content=news&utm_term=2730392002.

5. Annlee Ellingson, "SpaceX Plans to Spin off Starlink, Take It Public," *Bizjournals.com*, February 6, 2020, www.bizjournals.com/losangeles/news/2020/02/06/spacex-plans-to-spin-off-starlink-take-it-public.html.

6. Margaret Talbot, "The Teen Whisperer: How the Author of 'The Fault in Our Stars' Built an Ardent Army of Fans," *New Yorker*, https://www.newyorker.com/magazine/2014/06/09/the-teen-whisperer; Flood, "John Green."

7. David Lindquist, "'Vlogbrothers' John and Hank Green Plan Tour Stop in Carmel," *Indianapolis Star*, February 20, 2020, www.indystar.com/story/entertainment/arts/2020/02/14/john-green-plans-carmel-appearance-vlogbrothers-partner-hank/4762592002/.

8. Flood, "John Green."

9. Ibid.

10. Alexandra Alter, "John Green Tells a Story of Emotional Pain and Crippling Anxiety. His Own," *New York Times*, October 10, 2017, https://www.nytimes.com/2017/10/10/books/john-green-anxiety-obsessive-compulsive-disorder.html.

11. Ibid.

12. Ibid.

13. Talbot, "Teen Whisperer."

14. Waldman, "John Green Is a Hero of the Teen Internet."

15. Alter, "John Green Tells a Story of Emotional Pain and Crippling Anxiety."

16. James D. Hart, *The Popular Book: A History of America's Literary Taste* (New York: Oxford University Press, 1950).

17. Brian Feldman, "If Emojis Are the Future of Communication Then We're Screwed," *Cut*, April 11, 2016, http://nymag.com/thecut/2016/04/people-often-disagree-about-what-emoji-mean.html.

18. Katherine Connor Martin, "New Words Notes January 2018," *Oxford English Dictionary*, January 2018, https://public.oed.com/the-oed-today/recent-updates-to-the-oed/january-2018-update/new-words-notes-january-2018/.

19. Ibid.

20. Ibid.; Bill Katz, *Dahl's History of the Book*, 3rd English ed. (Metuchen, NJ: Scarecrow Press, 1995).

21. Katz, *Dahl's History of the Book*.

22. Ibid.; John J. Goldman and Eileen V. Quigley, "Gutenberg Bible Is Sold for Record $4.9 Million," *Los Angeles Times*, October 23, 1987, http://articles.latimes.com/1987-10-23/news/mn-10733_1_bids.

23. Katz, *Dahl's History of the Book*.

24. Ibid.

25. Stephen E. Ambrose, *Undaunted Courage* (New York: Simon & Schuster, 1996).

26. "Our Latest Update: April 2020," Oxford English Dictionary, https://public.oed.com/updates/.

27. Jonathan Dent, "It's Time to Kvell about Some Awesomesauce New Words: The OED January 2020 Update," Oxford English Dictionary, 2020, https://public.oed.com/blog/new-words-notes-for-january-2020/.

28. Katz, *Dahl's History of the Book*.

29. Hart, *Popular Book*.

30. Katz, *Dahl's History of the Book*.

31. Ibid.

32. Hart, *Popular Book*.

33. Ibid.

34. Katz, *Dahl's History of the Book*.

35. Chris Anderson, *The Long Tail* (New York: Hyperion, 2006).

36. Derek Haines, "How Many Kindle eBooks Are There on Amazon?" *Just Publishing Advice*, May 15, 2018, https://justpublishingadvice.com/how-many-kindle-ebooks-are-there/.

37. Katz, *Dahl's History of the Book*.

38. Doreen Carvajal, "Book Publishers Seek Global Reach and Grand Scale," *New York Times*, October 19, 1998.

39. "About Us," Penguin Random House, http://www.penguinrandomhouse.com/about-us/.

40. David Streitfeld, "Book Report," *Washington Post*, March 14, 1999.

41. Florence Shinkle, "University Presses Seize Upon a Silver Lining," *St. Louis Post-Dispatch*, October 12, 1998.

42. Jim Milliot and Claire Kirch, "Fast-Growing Independent Publishers, 2017," *Publishers Weekly*, April 7, 2017, https://www.publishersweekly.com/pw/by-topic/industry-news/publisher-news/article/73281-fast-growing-independent-publishers-2017.html.

43. Jim Milliot, "Cottage Door Press to Acquire Parragon Assets," *Publishers Weekly*, April 5, 2018, www.publishersweekly.com/pw/by-topic/industry-news/publisher-news/article/76512-cottage-door-press-to-acquire-parragon-assets.html.

44. Hannah Hess, "Senators Propose Rebranding GPO as Government Publishing Office," *Roll Call*, January 22, 2014, www.rollcall.com/news/senators_propose_rebranding_gpo_as_government_publishing_office-230308-1.html; Steve Vogel, "Marking JFK Anniversary, GPO Releases Digital Warren Commission Report," *Washington Post*, November 18, 2013, www.washingtonpost.com/blogs/federal-eye/wp/2013/11/18/marking-jfk-anniversary-gpo-releases-digital-warren-commission-report/.

45. Robert Kiely, "Armageddon, Complete and Uncut," *New York Times*, May 13, 1990, www.nytimes.com/books/97/03/09/lifetimes/king-stand.html.

46. Bureau of Labor Statistics, "Occupational Outlook Handbook: Writers and Authors," U.S. Department of Labor, https://www.bls.gov/ooh/media-and-communication/writers-and-authors.htm.

47. D&B Hoovers, "Company Profile: Ingram Book Group LLC," http://www.hoovers.com/company-information/cs/company-profile.ingram_book_group_llc.aaf76ac5e3fa7ef5.html; Ingram, "Book Distribution Worldwide," http://www.ingramcontent.com/publishers/distribution.

48. James Shapiro, "Wariness Greets the Latest Round in the Publishing Wars," *Chronicle of Higher Education*, November 27, 1998.

49. Jim Milliot, "PW's Top News Stories of 2019," *Publishers Weekly*, January 3, 2020, www.publishersweekly.com/pw/by-topic/industry-news/publisher-news/article/82094-pw-s-top-news-stories-of-2019.html.

50. Stuart Lauchlan, "B&N Nukes the NOOK With a 15 March Deadline for Customers to Save Content," *Diginomica*, March 7, 2016, http://diginomica.com/2016/03/07/bn-nukes-the-nook-with-a-15-march-deadline-for-customers-to-save-their-content/; Barnes & Noble, "Barnes & Noble Reports Fiscal 2018 Year-End Financial Results," *Business Wire*, June 21, 2018, https://www.businesswire.com/news/home/20180621005588/en/Barnes-Noble-Reports-Fiscal-2018-Year-End-Financial; D&B Hoovers, "Company Profile: Barnes & Noble Education Inc.," http://www.hoovers.com/company-information/cs/company-profile.barnes__noble_education_inc.7799ff43c256e6cb.html.

51. Jill Schlesinger, "Small Bookstores Are Booming after Nearly Being Wiped Out," *CBS News*, November 23, 2018, www.cbsnews.com/news/small-bookstores-are-booming-after-nearly-being-wiped-out-small-business-saturday/?fbclid=IwAR2rrz5PUWIHxioCdw2d1iEBK29b3OMVpMbBJJ2EOYzbMrqos1sq-AhtvjM.

52. Carmen Nobel, "How Independent Bookstores Thrived in Spite of Amazon," *Quartz*, November 26, 2017, https://qz.com/1135474/how-independent-bookstores-thrived-in-spite-of-amazon/.

53. Ryan Raffaelli, "Reframing Collective Identity in Response to Multiple Technological Discontinuities: The Novel Resurgence of Independent Bookstores," Harvard Business School, November 15, 2017.

54. J. Gerry Purdy, "Inside Mobile: Why eBooks and eBook Readers Will Eventually Succeed," *eWeek.com*, October 13, 2008, https://www.eweek.com/mobile/inside-mobile-why-ebooks-and-ebook-readers-will-eventually-succeed.

55. Doug Levy, "Amazon.com Amazes: On-line Gamble Pays Off With Rocketing Success," *USA Today*, December 24, 1998; Elisabeth Bumiller, "On-line Booksellers: A Tale of Two C.E.O.s," *New York Times*, December 8, 1998.

56. Noor Javed, "Digital Reader Meets Skeptics at Literary Fest," *Toronto Star*, September 29, 2008.

57. Gaby Del Valle, "The High Cost of College Textbooks, Explained," *Vox*, March 6, 2019, www.vox.com/the-goods/2019/3/6/18252322/college-textbooks-cost-expensive-pearson-cengage-mcgraw-hill.

58. Stephanie Zimmermann, "College Students' Latest Headache? Digital Access Fees on Top of Rising Textbook Prices," *Chicago Sun-Times*, September 13, 2019, https://chicago.suntimes.com/consumer-affairs/2019/9/13/20863263/college-students-textbook-savings-online-digital-access-code-cengage-mcgraw-hill-merger-student-debt.

59. David Gernon, "Students Are Spending Less on Books by Smart Buying," *CNBC*, August 8, 2017, https://www.cnbc.com/2017/08/08/one-smart-money-lesson-college-freshmen-can-learn-from-seniors.html.

60. Eric Johnson, "'The $300 Textbook Is Dead,' Says the CEO of Textbook Maker Pearson," *Vox*, August 2, 2019, https://www.vox.com/recode/2019/8/2/20750863/john-fallon-pearson-education-textbook-digital-aida-teachers-kara-swisher-recode-decode-podcast.

61. Marc Parry, "Students Get Savvier About Textbook Buying," *Chronicle of Higher Education*, January 27, 2013.

62. "Global E-Textbook Rental Market Growth Opportunities and Forecast 2017–2021," Orbis Research, November 17, 2017, http://orbisresearch.com/reports/index/global-e-textbook-rental-market-2017-2021.

63. Jennifer Howard, "For Many Students, Print Is Still King," *Chronicle of Higher Education*, January 27, 2013.

64. Zimmermann, "College Students' Latest Headache?"

65. Lindsay McKenzie, "'Inclusive Access' Takes Off," *Inside Higher Ed*, November 7, 2017, https://www.insidehighered.com/news/2017/11/07/inclusive-access-takes-model-college-textbook-sales.

66. Ibid.

67. Del Valle, "The High Cost of College Textbooks."

68. Lindsay McKenzie, "Messy Merger Forecast for 'McCengage'," *Inside Higher Ed*, February 19, 2020, www.insidehighered.com/news/2020/02/19/cengage-and-mcgraw-hill-navigate-challenging-merger-delay.

69. Hart, *Popular Book*.

70. Ibid., 93.

71. Katz, *Dahl's History of the Book*.

72. Romance Writers of America, "Romance Fiction Statistics."

73. Dana Flavelle, "Torstar Eyes Convergence," *Toronto Star*, May 3, 2001.

74. Jeff Ayers, "Janet Evanovich Works Hard at Her Easy-to-Read Stephanie Plum Novels," *Seattle Post-Intelligencer*, June 23, 2006.

75. Allen Pierleoni, "Doubling Up: With Her Wisecracking Heroines Stephanie Plum and Alexandra Barnaby, Novelist Janet Evanovich Is on the Move," *Sacramento Bee*, December 5, 2005.

76. Carol Memmott, "Janet Evanovich by the Numbers," *USA Today*, June 25, 2009; Rachel Donadio, "Promotional Intelligence," *New York Times*, March 21, 2006, www.nytimes.com/2006/05/21/books/review/21donadio.html?pagewanted=all&_r=0.

77. Julie Bosman, "A Classic Turns 50, and Parties Are Planned," *New York Times,* May 25, 2010.

78. Roger Cohen, "In Re: Marketing Parameters for Great American Novel," *New York Times*, March 25, 1990.

79. Jeff Gordinier, "Elvish Lives!" *Entertainment Weekly*, December 14, 2001.

80. Douglas A. Anderson, "Note on the Text," in *The Lord of the Rings*, J. R. R. Tolkien (New York: Houghton Mifflin, 1994); Brian Bethune, "The Lord of the Bookshelves," *Maclean's*, December 23, 2002; Gordinier, "Elvish Lives!"; Lev Grossman et al., "Feeding on Fantasy," *Time*, December 2, 2002; Karen Raugust, "Licensing Hotline," *Publishers Weekly*, July 2, 2001.

81. Library of Congress, "Selections From the Cuneiform Tablets Collection: About the Collection," http://international.loc.gov/intldl/cuneihtml/about.html; Katz, *Dahl's History of the Book*.

82. Katz, *Dahl's History of the Book*, 50.

83. Katz, *Dahl's History of the Book*.

84. St. Catherine's Monastery, "Library," http://www.sinaimonastery.com/index.php/en/library; Brigit Katz, "Lost Languages Discovered in One of the World's Oldest Continuously Run Libraries," *Smithsonian Magazine*, September 5, 2017, https://www.smithsonianmag.com/smart-news/long-lost-languages-found-manuscripts-egyptian-monastery-180964698/.

85. Katz, *Dahl's History of the Book*.

86. Katz, *Dahl's History of the Book*; American Library Association, "Number of Libraries in the United States," http://libguides.ala.org/numberoflibraries.

87. Omaha Public Library, "Book Clubs," https://omahalibrary.org/book-clubs/.

88. Kaitlyn Tiffany, "What Public Libraries Will Lose Without Net Neutrality," *Verge*, December 14, 2017, https://www.theverge.com/2017/12/14/16772582/public-libraries-net-neutrality-broadband-access-first-amendment.

89. American Library Association, "Top Ten Most Challenged Books Lists," http://www.ala.org/bbooks/frequentlychallengedbooks/top10.

90. Editorial Board, "Lust and Liberties," *Indianapolis Star*, October 5, 1998.

91. "Book Bans Bring Storm of Debate," *Omaha World-Herald*, September 28, 1998.

92. Chris Taylor, "The Truth About Banned Books Is Stranger Than You Think," *Mashable*, October 1, 2015, http://mashable.com/2015/10/01/banned-books-truth/.

93. Associated Press, "School District Pulls 'Mockingbird' from Reading List," October 13, 2017, *AL.com*, www.al.com/news/2017/10/mississippi_school_district_pu.html.

94. William Breyfogle, "Librarians See Banned Books Week as a Wake-Up Call to Society," *Milwaukee Journal Sentinel*, September 25, 1997.

95. George Takei, "George Takei Recounts Internment's Long Shadow," *High Country News*, November 11, 2019, www.hcn.org/issues/51.19/books-george-takei-recounts-internments-long-shadow?fbclid=IwAR1CkhHCUbpDKrIAnuGmv3bMdV2M81V_oo8NCkKGn_ZAuS2RU7Js7MOpsRU.

96. George Gene Gustines, "A Graphic Novel Remembers Attica," *New York Times*, February 14, 2020, www.nytimes.com/2020/02/14/books/big-black-stand-at-attica-graphic-novel.html.

97. Hart, *Popular Book*.

98. PBS, "Huck Finn Teacher's Guide: About the Book: *Adventures of Huckleberry Finn*," 2000, www.pbs.org/wgbh/cultureshock/teachers/huck/aboutbook.html.

99. Amy E. Schwartz, "Huck Finn Gets the Revisionist Treatment," *Washington Post*, January 10, 1996.

100. Paul Vallely, "They Will Not Be Silenced," *Independent*, February 14, 1998.

101. Barbara Crossette, "Iran Drops Rushdie Death Threat, and Britain Renews Teheran Ties," *New York Times*, September 25, 1998.

102. Douglas Jehl, "New Moves on Rushdie Exposing Iranian Rifts," *New York Times*, October 21, 1998.

103. "Author Banned by British Air," *New York Times*, September 26, 1998.

104. Sarah Lyall, "Rushdie, Free of Threat, Revels in 'Spontaneity,'" *New York Times*, September 26, 1998.

105. Henry Foy, "Rushdie Speech Cancelled Amid Death Threats, Protests," Reuters, January 24, 2012, http://in.reuters.com/article/india-rushdie-cancel-idINDEE80N0AT20120124.

106. Neal, "Sherry Jones Reacts to UK Jewel of Medina Firebombing," *GalleyCat*, September 28, 2008, http://www.adweek.com/galleycat/sherry-jones-reacts-to-uk-jewel-of-medina-firebombing/8806?red=as.

107. Vallely, "They Will Not Be Silenced"; "Write and Wrong—Taslima Has the Courage of Conviction," *Statesman* (India), October 22, 1998; Melvyn Bragg, "Forging Links With the Writers in Chains," *Times* (London), February 9, 1998.

108. Anderson, *Long Tail*, 40.

109. Jacob Weisberg, "Book End: How the Kindle Will Change the World," *Slate*, March 21, 2009.

110. Lauren Goode, "Amazon Finally Makes a Waterproof Kindle, After 10 Years of Kindles," *Verge*, October 11, 2017, https://www.theverge.com/2017/10/11/16453860/new-amazon-oasis-kindle-waterproof-10th-anniversary.

111. Ibid.

112. Jonathan Segura, "No More E-Books vs. Print Books Arguments, OK?," *NPR*, January 31, 2012, http://www

.npr.org/sections/monkeysee/2012/01/31/146140663/no-more-e-books-vs-print-books-arguments-ok.

113. Ibid.
114. Ezra Klein, "Will Books Survive eBooks?," *Washington Post*, May 20, 2011, https://www.washingtonpost.com/blogs/wonkblog/post/will-books-survive-ebooks/2011/05/19/AFHNqz7G_blog.html.
115. Michael Kozlowski, "Global Audiobook Trends and Statistics for 2018," *Good e-Reader*, December 17, 2018, https://goodereader.com/blog/audiobooks/global-audiobook-trends-and-statistics-for-2018.
116. Peter Schrag, *Test of Loyalty: Daniel Ellsberg and the Rituals of Secret Government* (New York: Simon & Schuster, 1974).
117. Janet Reitman, "Snowden and Greenwald: The Men Who Leaked the Secrets," *Rolling Stone*, December 4, 2013, www.rollingstone.com/politics/news/snowden-and-greenwald-the-men-who-leaked-the-secrets-20131204.
118. "Missing the Point of WikiLeaks," *Economist*, December 1, 2010, www.economist.com/blogs/democracyinamerica/2010/12/after_secrets; Marshall Soules, "Harold Adams Innis: The Bias of Communications & Monopolies of Power," *Malaspina University-College*, 2007, www.media-studies.ca/articles/innis.htm.
119. Harold Innis, *Empire and Communications* (Toronto: Dundurn, 2007).
120. Alexander John Watson, "Introduction to the Second Edition," in *The Bias of Communication*, 2nd ed., ed. Harold Innis (Toronto: University of Toronto, 2008).
121. Anderson, *Long Tail*.
122. Ingram, "Book Distribution Worldwide."
123. Jim Milliot, "Print Sales Up Again in 2017," *Publisher's Weekly*, January 5, 2018, https://www.publishersweekly.com/pw/by-topic/industry-news/bookselling/article/75760-print-sales-up-again-in-2017.html.

CHAPTER 5

1. Paul Farhi, "*Washington Post* to Be Sold to Jeff Bezos, the Founder of Amazon," *Washington Post*, August 5, 2013, http://www.washingtonpost.com/national/washington-post-to-be-sold-to-jeff-bezos/2013/08/05/ca537c9e-fe0c-11e2-9711-3708310f6f4d_story.html.
2. Paul Farhi, "Jeffrey Bezos, *Washington Post*'s Next Owner, Aims for a New 'Golden Era' at the Newspaper," *Washington Post*, September 3, 2013, http://www.washingtonpost.com/lifestyle/style/jeffrey-bezos-washington-posts-next-owner-aims-for-a-new-golden-era-at-the-newspaper/2013/09/02/30c00b60-13f6-11e3-b182-1b3bb2eb474c_story.html; Craig Timberg and Jia Lynn Yang, "The Sale of the *Washington Post*: How the Unthinkable Choice Became the Clear Path," *Washington Post*, August 6, 2013, http://www.washingtonpost.com/business/technology/2013/08/06/46216532-fed7-11e2-9711-3708310f6f4d_story.html.
3. Victor Luckerson, "Jeff Bezos Makes His First Major Move at the *Washington Post*," *Time*, March 19, 2014, http://www.time.com/30243/jeff-bezos-makes-his-first-major-move-at-the-washington-post/.
4. Kyle Pope, "Revolution at the *Washington Post*," *Columbia Journalism Review*, November 2016, http://www.cjr.org/q_and_a/washington_post_bezos_amazon_revolution.php.
5. Ken Doctor, "'Profitable' *Washington Post* Adding More Than Five Dozen Journalists," *POLITICO*, December 27, 2016, http://www.politico.com/media/story/2016/12/the-profitable-washington-post-adding-more-than-five-dozen-journalists-004900.
6. Pope, "Revolution."
7. Joe Pompeo, "'When Your Owner Is Richer Than God, It's Easier to Get Uppity': Discontent at the *Washington Post* as the Union Targets Jeff Bezos," *Vanity Fair*, June 2018, http://www.vanityfair.com/news/2018/06/washington-post-union-jeff-bezos.
8. Pete Vernon, "Trump's War on the *Washington Post*," *Columbia Journalism Review*, April 6, 2018, http://www.cjr.org/the_media_today/trump-amazon-bezos.php.
9. Paige Leskin, "Jeff Bezos' Nudes Were Reportedly Leaked When His Girlfriend Lauren Sanchez Sent Them to Her Brother, in a New Twist to the Dramatic Saga—Here's Everything We Know so Far," *Business Insider*, January 27, 2020, http://www.businessinsider.com/jeff-bezos-national-enquirer-investigation-timeline-2019-2.
10. Jim Rutenberg and Karen Weise, "Jeff Bezos Accuses *National Enquirer* of 'Extortion and Blackmail,'" *New York Times*, February 7, 2019, http://www.nytimes.com/2019/02/07/technology/jeff-bezos-sanchez-enquirer.html.
11. Brian McNair, *News and Journalism in the UK* (London: Routledge, 1994).
12. Bill Katz, *Dahl's History of the Book*, 3rd English ed. (Metuchen, NJ: Scarecrow Press, 1995).
13. James D. Hart, *The Popular Book: A History of America's Literary Taste* (New York: Oxford University Press, 1950).
14. Michael Schudson, *Discovering the News* (New York: Basic Books, 1978).
15. Katz, *Dahl's History of the Book*, 218.
16. Hazel Dicken-Garcia, *Journalistic Standards in Nineteenth-Century America* (Madison: University of Wisconsin Press, 1989).
17. Schudson, *Discovering the News*.
18. George H. Douglas, *The Golden Age of the Newspaper* (Westport, CT: Greenwood Press, 1999).
19. McNair, *News and Journalism in the UK*.
20. Ibid.
21. Schudson, *Discovering the News*, 60.
22. Dicken-Garcia, *Journalistic Standards in Nineteenth-Century America*, 52.
23. Kevin J. Delaney, "Bill Gates: If Anybody Says We Don't Need the Media, That's a Little Scary," *Quartz*, February 14, 2017, https://qz.com/909840/bill-gates-if-anybody-says-we-dont-need-the-media-thats-a-little-scary/.
24. Paul H. Weaver, *News and the Culture of Lying* (New York: Free Press, 1994).
25. George Juergens, *Joseph Pulitzer and the New York World* (Princeton, NJ: Princeton University Press, 1966).
26. Brooke Kroeger, *Nellie Bly: Daredevil, Reporter, Feminist* (New York: Times Books, 1994).
27. Ibid.
28. Michael L. Carlebach, *The Origins of Photojournalism in America* (Washington, DC: Smithsonian Institution Press, 1992).
29. James Playsted Wood, *Magazines in the United States*, 3rd ed. (New York: Ronald Press Company, 1971).
30. Louis Joughin, "Introduction," in *The Shame of the Cities*, ed. Lincoln Steffens (New York: Hill and Wang, 1957).
31. Wood, *Magazines in the United States*.
32. Ibid.
33. Vicki Goldberg, *Margaret Bourke-White* (New York: Harper & Row, 1986).
34. Ibid.

35. Ibid.
36. Ibid., 259.
37. D&B Hoovers, "Company Profile: Time Inc.," http://www.hoovers.com/company-information/cs/company-profile.time_inc.66ca6f856feacdea.html; David Carr and Ravi Somaiya, "Saddled With Debt, Time Inc. Sets a Lonely Course in a Shifting Market," *International New York Times*, June 10, 2014.
38. Joe Nocera, "RIP, Time, Inc. It Was Fun While It Lasted," *Bloomberg*, November 27, 2017, https://www.bloomberg.com/view/articles/2017-11-27/rip-time-magazine-meredith-will-make-you-fade-away.
39. William S. Paley, *As It Happened: A Memoir* (Garden City, NY: Doubleday, 1979).
40. Ben H. Bagdikian, *The New Media Monopoly* (Boston: Beacon Press, 2004).
41. Paley, *As It Happened*.
42. Edward Bliss, *Now the News: The Story of Broadcast Journalism* (New York: Columbia University Press, 1991).
43. Richard Zoglin, "Inside the World of CNN: How a Handful of News Executives Make Decisions Felt Round the World," *Time*, January 6, 1992.
44. Ken Auletta, *Three Blind Mice: How the TV Networks Lost Their Way* (New York: Random House, 1991).
45. Peter Johnson, "Fox News Enjoys New View—From the Top," *USA Today*, April 4, 2002.
46. Brian Lowry, "On Cable News, It's All Shoutmanship," *Los Angeles Times*, March 5, 2003; A. J. Katz, "The Top Cable Networks of April 2018," *TVNewser*, May 2, 2018, https://www.adweek.com/tvnewser/the-top-cable-networks-of-april-2018/363575.
47. Katerina Eva Matsa, "Fewer Americans Rely on TV News; What Type They Watch Varies by Who They Are," *Pew Research Center*, January 5, 2018, http://www.pewresearch.org/fact-tank/2018/01/05/fewer-americans-rely-on-tv-news-what-type-they-watch-varies-by-who-they-are/.
48. McNair, *News and Journalism in the UK*.
49. Bagdikian, *New Media Monopoly*.
50. "The State of the News Media 2016," *Pew Research Center*, June 15, 2016, https://www.journalism.org/2016/06/15/state-of-the-news-media-2016/2006/.
51. Michael Barthels, "Newspapers Fact Sheet," *Pew Research Center*, July 9, 2019, https://www.journalism.org/fact-sheet/newspapers/.
52. Ibid.
53. Jonathan O'Connell and Rachel Siegel, "America's Two Largest Newspaper Chains Are Joining Forces. Will It Save Either?" *Washington Post*, August 5, 2019, http://www.washingtonpost.com/business/2019/08/05/gannett-merge-with-gatehouse-media/.
54. Barbara Allen, "Gannett Layoffs Underway at Combined New Company," *Poynter*, February 28, 2020, www.poynter.org/business-work/2020/gannett-layoffs-underway-at-combined-new-company/.
55. Johnnie L. Roberts, "The Paperless Paper," *Newsweek*, October 28, 2008.
56. Sinéad O'Brien, "The Last of the Color Holdouts," *American Journalism Review*, December 1997, 15.
57. "Newspapers: Circulation at the Top 5 U.S. Newspapers Reporting Monday-Friday Averages," *Pew Research Center*, September 30, 2014, https://www.pewresearch.org/wp-content/uploads/sites/8/2017/05/state-of-the-news-media-report-2014-final.pdf.
58. James McCartney, "*USA Today* Grows Up," *American Journalism Review*, September 1997.
59. "Newspapers."
60. "USA Today," Nieman Journalism Lab, http://www.niemanlab.org/encyclo/usa-today/.
61. Rob Lenihan, "Marking *Times*'s Color Milestone," *Editor & Publisher* 131, no. 39 (1998).
62. D&B Hoovers, "Company Profile: The New York Times Company," http://www.hoovers.com/company-information/cs/company-profile.the_new_york_times_company.2aefe2f2b952d93c.html.
63. Mario R. Garcia, "Color for a New Millennium," *Editor & Publisher* 131, no. 39 (1998).
64. Ben Bradlee, *A Good Life: Newspapering and Other Adventures* (New York: Simon & Schuster, 1995).
65. Claire Atkinson, "The *Washington Post* Still Plays Catch-Up, but Is Gaining on the *Times*," *NBC News*, December 28, 2017, https://www.nbcnews.com/news/us-news/washington-post-still-plays-catch-gaining-times-n833236.
66. Charles Rappleye, "Are New Ideas Killing the *L.A. Times*?" *Columbia Journalism Review*, November/December 1994.
67. "Pulitzer Prizes for the *Los Angeles Times*," *Los Angeles Times*.
68. Jeremy Barr, "Journalists Boycott Disney Films After *L.A. Times* Snub," *Hollywood Reporter*, November 6, 2017, http://www.hollywoodreporter.com/news/journalists-boycott-disney-films-la-times-snub-1055338?utm_source=sailthru&utm_medium=email&utm_term=ABN_MorningMediaNewsfeed&utm_campaign=MorningMediaNewsfeed_Newsletter_2017110708&s_id=57e9a1372ddf9c7ef38aa7e8.
69. Sydney Ember and Brooks Barnes, "Disney Ends Ban on *Los Angeles Times* Amid Fierce Backlash," *New York Times*, November 7, 2017, https://www.nytimes.com/2017/11/07/business/disney-la-times.html; Emily VanDerWerff, Twitter post, November 7, 2017, 12:33 p.m., https://twitter.com/tvoti/status/927952033788735490.
70. Jock Lauterer, *Community Journalism: Relentlessly Local*, 3rd ed. (Chapel Hill: University of North Carolina Press, 2006)
71. Charles Bermant, "Hometown Newspapers Use Web to Strengthen Communities," *CNN*, August 21, 1998, http://www.cnn.com/TECH/computing/9808/21/hometown.idg/.
72. Michael Barthel, Jesse Holcomb, Jessica Mahone, and Amy Mitchell, "Civic Engagement Strongly Tied to Local News Habits," *Pew Research Center*, November 1, 2016, http://assets.pewresearch.org/wp-content/uploads/sites/13/2016/11/02163924/PJ_2016.11.02_Civic-Engagement_FINAL.pdf.
73. Erik Wemple, "*Storm Lake Times* Pulitzer Winner: 'They Give You 15 Grand. That's Worth It,'" *Washington Post*, April 10, 2017, https://www.washingtonpost.com/blogs/erik-wemple/wp/2017/04/10/storm-lake-times-pulitzer-winner-they-give-you-15-grand-thats-worth-it/?utm_term=.9ef48e885ec1.
74. Doris A. Graber, *Mass Media and American Politics*, 7th ed. (Washington, DC: CQ Press, 2006).
75. Ibid.
76. Ibid.
77. Herbert Gans, *Deciding What's News* (New York: Pantheon Books, 1979).
78. Emily Witt, "Calling B.S. in Parkland, Florida," *New Yorker*, February 17, 2018, https://www.newyorker.com/news/news-desk/three-days-in-parkland-florida.
79. Gans, *Deciding What's News*.
80. Stanley Rothman, "Introduction," in *The Mass Media in Liberal Democratic Societies*, ed. Stanley Rothman (New York: Paragon House, 1992).

81. Jay Rosen, "So Whaddaya Think: Should We Put Truthtelling Back Up There at Number One?" *PressThink*, January 12, 2012, http://pressthink.org/2012/01/so-whaddaya-think-should-we-put-truthtelling-back-up-there-at-number-one/.

82. Jay Rosen, "The View From Nowhere: Questions and Answers," *PressThink*, November 10, 2010, http://pressthink.org/2010/11/the-view-from-nowhere-questions-and-answers/.

83. Ibid.

84. Recode Staff, "Full Transcript: New York University Journalism Professor Jay Rosen," *Recode*, February 3, 2017, https://www.recode.net/2017/2/3/14503050/full-transcript-new-york-university-journalism-professor-jay-rosen-trump-facts.

85. Ibid.

86. Jeffrey Gottfried, Michael Barthel, and Amy Mitchell, "Trump, Clinton Voters Divided in the Main Source for Election News," *Pew Research Center*, January 18, 2017, http://www.journalism.org/2017/01/18/trump-clinton-voters-divided-in-their-main-source-for-election-news/.

87. Shawn Langlois, "How Does Your Favorite New Source Rate on the 'Truthiness' Scale? Consult This Chart," *MarketWatch*, December 17, 2016, https://www.marketwatch.com/story/how-does-your-favorite-news-source-rate-on-the-truthiness-scale-consult-this-chart-2016-12-15.

88. Ibid.

89. "1370 Journalists Killed Between 1992 and 2020," *Committee to Protect Journalists*, https://cpj.org/data/killed/?status=Killed&motiveConfirmed%5B%5D=Confirmed&type%5B%5D=Journalist&start_year=1992&end_year=2020&group_by=year.

90. Martin Baron, "Remarks by *Washington Post* Executive Editor Martin Baron at the 2018 Fourth Estate Awards," *Washington Post*, November 30, 2018, http://www.washingtonpost.com/amphtml/pr/2018/11/30/remarks-by-washington-post-executive-editor-martin-baron-fourth-estate-awards/?utm_term=.dbdcd245a543&__twitter_impression=true.

91. "Journalism in Syria, Impossible Job?" *Reporters Without Borders for Freedom of Information*, November 6, 2013, https://rsf.org/en/reports/journalism-syria-impossible-job; Elle Shearer, "In Syria, Freelancers Like James Foley Cover a Dangerous War Zone With No Front Lines," *Washington Post*, August 22, 2014, http://www.washingtonpost.com/opinions/in-syria-freelancers-like-ames-foley-covera-dangerous-war-zone-with-no-front-lines/2014/08/22/25e4bfda-295b-11e4-86ca-6f03cbd15c1a_story.html; Karen DeYoung and Adam Goldman, "Islamic State Claims It Executed American Photojournalist James Foley," *Washington Post*, August 20, 2014, http://www.washingtonpost.com/world/national-security/islamic-state-claims-it-beheaded-american-photojournalist-james-foley/2014/08/19/42e83970-27e6-11e4-86ca-6f03cbd15c1a_story.html.

92. "Two Photojournalists Killed in Libyan City of Misrata," *BBC News*, April 21, 2011, http://www.bbc.co.uk/news/uk-13151490.

93. David W. Dunlap, James Estrin, and Kerri Macdonald, "Parting Glance: Tim Hetherington," *New York Times*, April 20, 2011, https://lens.blogs.nytimes.com/2011/04/20/parting-glance-tim-hetherington/.

94. Derek Hawkins, "Army Combat Photographer Snapped One Last Picture—Seconds Before an Explosion Killed Her," *Washington Post*, May 3, 2017, https://www.washingtonpost.com/news/morning-mix/wp/2017/05/03/army-combat-photographer-snapped-one-last-picture-seconds-before-an-explosion-killed-her/?utm_term=.04483af4cea6.

95. "BBC's Alan Johnston Is Released," *BBC News,* July 4, 2007, http://news.bbc.co.uk/2/hi/6267928.stm.

96. Howard Kurtz, "Mission Impossible?" *Washington Post*, August 28, 2006, http://www.washingtonpost.com/wp-dyn/content/blog/2006/08/28/BL2006082800239.html.

97. Charles A. Simmons, *The African American Press* (Jefferson, NC: McFarland, 1998).

98. Ibid.

99. Roland E. Wolseley, *The Black Press, U.S.A.*, 2nd ed. (Ames: Iowa State University Press, 1990).

100. Simmons, *African American Press*.

101. Wolseley, *Black Press, U.S.A.*

102. Jessica Madore Fitch, "Four Companies Vying for *Chicago Defender*," *Chicago Sun-Times*, May 1, 2000; Jim Romenesko, "*Chicago Defender* Lays Off Top Editors, Falls Months Behind on Rent," *Poynter*, October 24, 2011, https://www.poynter.org/news/chicago-defender-lays-top-editors-falls-months-behind-rent.

103. Mitchell Armentrout, "'An Essential Force in American History,' *Chicago Defender* to Stop Print Publication," *Chicago Sun-Times*, July 5, 2019, https://chicago.suntimes.com/business/2019/7/5/20683442/chicago-defender-ends-print-edition-digital-only-platform.

104. "Trends and Facts on Hispanic and African-American News: State of the News Media," *Pew Research Center*, July 9, 2019, http://www.journalism.org/fact-sheet/hispanic-and-black-news-media/.

105. "El Nuevo Herald," *McClatchy,* 2016, http://www.mcclatchy.com/2012/06/27/2739/el-nuevo-herald.html; "Hispanic and African-American New Media Fact Sheet."

106. Brooke Gladstone, "Tale of Two *Heralds*," *WNYC*, October 6, 2006, http://www.wnyc.org/story/128569-tale-of-two-heralds/.

107. Eytan Avriel, "*NY Times* Publisher: Our Goal Is to Manage the Transition From Print to Internet," *Haaretz*, February 8, 2007.

108. "Future Forum," *Ad Age*, September 20, 1999.

109. Jennifer Saba, "All the News That's Fit to Swipe," *Breaking Views*, July 26, 2017, https://www.breakingviews.com/considered-view/new-york-times-could-risk-all-digital-bet/?utm_source=CNN+Media%3A+Reliable+Sources&utm_campaign=272bb71487-EMAIL_CAMPAIGN_2017_06_06&utm_medium=email&utm_term=0_e95cdc16a9-272bb71487-81549889.

110. Michael Meyer, "Brick by Brick," *Columbia Journalism Review*, June 26, 2014, http://www.cjr.org/cover_story/washington_post_jeff_bezos.php?page=all.

111. WashPostPR, "*Washington Post* Executive Editor Martin Baron on Journalism's Transition From Print to Digital," *Washington Post*, April 8, 2015, https://www.washingtonpost.com/pr/wp/2015/04/08/washington-post-executive-editor-martin-baron-on-journalisms-transition-from-print-to-digital/.

112. Ibid.

113. Jill Lepore, et al., "Does Journalism Have a Future?" *New Yorker*, January 28, 2019, http://www.newyorker.com/magazine/2019/01/28/does-journalism-have-a-future.

114. Laura Owen, "Most Americans Think That Local News Is Doing Well Financially, and Not Many Pay for It," *Nieman Lab*, March 26, 2019, http://www.niemanlab.org/2019/03/most-americans-think-that-local-news-is-doing-well-financially-and-not-many-pay-for-it/.

115. Julie Bosman, "How the Collapse of Local News Is Causing a 'National Crisis,'" *New York Times*, November 20, 2019, http://www.nytimes.com/2019/11/20/us/local-news-disappear-pen-america.html?smtyp=cur&smid=fb-nytimes.

116. Anna Clark, "How an Investigative Journalist Helped Prove a City Was Being Poisoned With Its Own Water," *Columbia Journalism Review*, November 3, 2015, http://www.cjr.org/united_states_project/flint_water_lead_curt_guyette_aclu_michigan.php.

117. Denise Robbins, "Analysis: How Michigan and National Reporters Covered the Flint Water Crisis," *Media Matters for America*, February 2, 2016, https://www.mediamatters.org/research/2016/02/02/analysis-how-michigan-and-national-reporters-co/208202.

118. Paul Donoughue, "Why All Your Favourite Songs Sound the Same," *ABC News* (Australia), January 22, 2018, www.abc.net.au/news/2018-01-16/why-all-your-favourite-songs-sound-the-same/9329180.

119. Jeremy Littau, "The Crisis Facing American Journalism Did Not Start With the Internet," *Slate*, January 26, 2019, https://slate.com/technology/2019/01/layoffs-at-media-organizations-the-roots-of-this-crisis-go-back-decades.html.

120. Adam Gabbatt, "US Newspapers Face 'Extinction-Level' Crisis as Covid-19 Hits Hard," *Guardian*, April 9, 2020, http://www.theguardian.com/media/2020/apr/09/coronavirus-us-newspapers-impact?CMP=share_btn_fb&fbclid=IwAR2te-Dp88QHubmZxjXjJRun0t-VzJW6vgZsvOHT1AHis6vqvD1l9lLJL2c.

121. Penelope Muse Abernathy, *The Expanding News Desert* (Chapel Hill: University of North Carolina Press, 2018), 1–104.

122. Ibid.

123. Wendy Guild Swearingen, "Halpern Takes on Graphic Narrative," *Buffalo Spree*, May 2017, http://www.buffalospree.com/Buffalo-Spree/May-2017/Halpern-takes-on-graphic-narrative/.

124. Michael Cavna, "Cartooning Pulitzer Goes to a Game Changer: An Electronic Comic Book by Two Creators," *Washington Post*, April 16, 2018, https://www.washingtonpost.com/news/comic-riffs/wp/2018/04/16/cartooning-pulitzer-goes-to-a-game-changer-an-electronic-comic-book-by-two-creators/.

125. Bruce Headlam, "*Times* Journalists Use Words, Photos, Graphics, and Video. And Now, a Comic Strip," *New York Times*, May 12, 2017, https://www.nytimes.com/2017/05/12/insider/times-journalists-use-words-photos-graphics-and-video-and-now-a-comic-strip.html.

126. Swearingen, "Halpern Takes on Graphic Narrative."

CHAPTER 6

1. Joe Coscarelli, "Kendrick Lamar Wins Pulitzer in 'Big Moment' for Hip-Hop," *New York Times*, April 16, 2018, https://www.nytimes.com/2018/04/16/arts/music/kendrick-lamar-pulitzer-prize-damn.html.

2. Michael Paulson, "Lin-Manuel Miranda, Creator and Star of 'Hamilton,' Grew Up on Hip-Hop and Show Tunes," *New York Times*, April 12, 2015, https://www.nytimes.com/2015/08/16/theater/lin-manuel-miranda-creator-and-star-of-hamilton-grew-up-on-hip-hop-and-show-tunes.html.

3. Ibid.

4. Anthony Tommasini and Jon Caramanica, "Exploring 'Hamilton' and Hip-Hop Steeped in Heritage," *New York Times*, August 27, 2015, https://www.nytimes.com/2015/08/30/theater/exploring-hamilton-and-hip-hop-steeped-in-heritage.html.

5. Ibid.

6. Mark Binelli, "'Hamilton' Creator Lin-Manuel Miranda: The *Rolling Stone* Interview," *Rolling Stone*, June 1, 2016, https://www.rollingstone.com/music/features/hamilton-creator-lin-manuel-miranda-the-rolling-stone-interview-20160601.

7. Ibid.

8. Daniel Kreps, "Lin-Manuel Miranda, Ben Platt Release New Song for March for Our Lives," *Rolling Stone*, March 19, 2018, https://www.rollingstone.com/music/news/lin-manuel-miranda-shares-new-song-for-march-for-our-lives-w518009; Sidney Madden, "Lin-Manuel Miranda's Latest Hamildrop Features Many Elizas," *NPR*, April 30, 2018, https://www.npr.org/sections/allsongs/2018/04/30/607065531/lin-manuel-mirandas-latest-hamildrop-features-all-the-elizabeths.

9. John Lynch, "For the First Time in History, Hip-Hop Has Surpassed Rock to Become the Most Popular Music Genre, According to Nielsen," *Business Insider*, January 4, 2018, http://www.businessinsider.com/hip-hop-passes-rock-most-popular-music-genre-nielsen-2018-1.

10. Kelly McBride, "NPR's New Public Editor: I Thought Listening to the News Would Be Easier." *NPR*, April 22, 2020, http://www.npr.org/sections/publiceditor/2020/04/22/839650891/nprs-new-public-editor-i-thought-listening-to-the-news-would-be-easier.

11. Neil Baldwin, *Edison: Inventing the Century* (New York: Hyperion, 1995).

12. Roland Gelatt, *The Fabulous Phonograph, 1877–1977* (New York: Macmillan, 1977).

13. Baldwin, *Edison*.

14. Gelatt, *Fabulous Phonograph*.

15. Ibid., 63.

16. Charles Hamm, "The Phonograph as Time-Machine" (paper presented at *The Phonograph and Our Musical Life*, Brooklyn College, New York, 1980).

17. Gelatt, *Fabulous Phonograph*.

18. Ken C. Pohlmann, "The Last Compact Disc," *Stereo Review*, May 1996.

19. Isaac Asimov, *Isaac Asimov's Biographical Encyclopedia of Science and Technology*, rev. ed. (New York: Avon Books, 1972).

20. Ibid.; Kenneth Bilby, *The General: David Sarnoff and the Rise of the Communications Industry* (New York: Harper & Row, 1986).

21. Bilby, *General*.

22. Ibid., 39.

23. Ibid.

24. Ibid.

25. Burton Paulu, *Television and Radio in the United Kingdom* (Minneapolis: University of Minnesota Press, 1981).

26. Ibid.

27. Lewis J. Paper, *Empire: William S. Paley and the Making of CBS* (New York: St. Martin's Press, 1987).

28. Muriel G. Cantor and Suzanne Pingree, *The Soap Opera*, ed. F. Gerald Kline, The Sage Commtext Series (Thousand Oaks, CA: SAGE, 1983).

29. Christine Fix, "*General Hospital* Celebrates 13,000 Episodes," *Soaps*, February 20, 2014, http://soaps.sheknows.com/general-hospital/news/37373/general-hospital-celebrates-13000-episodes.

30. Ibid.

31. Julius Lester, "Foreword," in *Playing the FM Band: A Personal Account of the Free Radio*, ed. Steve Post (New York: Viking Press, 1974), vii.

32. Nina Huntemann, "Corporate Interference: The Commercialization and Concentration of Radio Post the 1996

Telecommunications Act," *Journal of Communication Inquiry* 23, no. 4 (1999): 390–407.

33. Roy Bragg, "Clear Channel: Owning the Waves," *San Antonio Express-News*, February 4, 2003, 1; Kenneth Creech, *Electronic Media Law and Regulation*, 3rd ed. (Boston: Focal Press, 2000).

34. "House Members Call on FCC Inspector General to Investigate Hidden Studies on Media Consolidation," *US Fed News*, September 21, 2006.

35. L. A. Lorek, "FCC Review Could Clip Clear Channel; Commission Might Limit Ownership of Radio Stations," *San Antonio Express-News*, May 17, 2003, 1.

36. Seth Fiegerman, "End of an Era: Clear Channel Rebrands as iHeartMedia," *Mashable*, September 16, 2014, https://mashable.com/2014/09/16/clear-channel-iheartmedia/.

37. D&B Hoovers, "Company Profile: Iheartmedia, Inc.," https://www.dnb.com/business-directory/company-profiles.cc_media_holdings_inc.ab9301d5f8b46459ea80184bb5d056b3.html.

38. Debbie Weingarten, "America's Rural Radio Stations Are Vanishing—and Taking the Country's Soul with Them," *Guardian*, June 6, 2019, http://www.theguardian.com/tv-and-radio/2019/jun/06/radio-silence-how-the-disappearance-of-rural-stations-takes-americas-soul-with-them.

39. Jeff Smith, "Radio Automation," *Radio*, May 1, 2006, 22.

40. "Audio and Podcasting Fact Sheet," *Pew Research Center*, June 16, 2017, http://www.journalism.org/fact-sheet/audio-and-podcasting/?utm_content=buffer60d03&utm_medium=social&utm_source=twitter.com&utm_campaign=buffer; Jeremy Laukkonen, "The Problem with HD Radio," *Lifewire*, March 21, 2017, https://www.lifewire.com/problem-with-hd-radio-534510; Edison Research, "The Infinite Dial 2020," http://www.edisonresearch.com/wp-content/uploads/2020/03/The-Infinite-Dial-2020-from-Edison-Research-and-Triton-Digital.pdf.

41. Sirius XM Holdings Inc., "Investor Relations," http://investor.siriusxm.com/investor-overview/default.aspx#reports-tab4.

42. Cecilia Kang, "Liberty Extends $530 Million Loan to Bail Out Sirius XM," *Washington Post*, February 18, 2009; D&B Hoovers, "Company Profile: Liberty Media Corporation," http://www.hoovers.com/company-information/cs/company-profile.liberty_media_corporation.06a24bdf96f162ec.html.

43. Ana Marie Cox, "Howard Stern and the Satellite Wars," *Wired*, March 2005.

44. Libby Copeland, "Is Howard Stern Going Soft or Just Getting Sharper?" *Washington Post*, December 14, 2015, https://www.washingtonpost.com/lifestyle/is-howard-stern-going-soft-or-just-getting-sharper/2015/12/13/691d8cfe-9ddc-11e5-a3c5-c77f2cc5a43c_story.html.

45. Leonard Wiener, "Radio's Next Wave: 9 Kinds of Latin Music," *U.S. News & World Report*, August 2, 1999, 70.

46. Edison Research, "The Infinite Dial 2018," http://www.edisonresearch.com/infinite-dial-2018/.

47. Edison Research, "The Infinite Dial 2020."

48. Ibid.

49. "Which Smart Speaker Should You Buy?" *CNET*.

50. Adam Clark Estes, "Don't Buy Anyone an Echo," *Gizmodo*, December 5, 2017, https://gizmodo.com/dont-buy-anyone-an-echo-1820981732.

51. Matt Day, "Amazon Workers Are Listening to What You Tell Alexa," *Bloomberg*, April 10, 2019, http://www.bloomberg.com/news/articles/2019-04-10/is-anyone-listening-to-you-on-alexa-a-global-team-reviews-audio.

52. "Audio and Podcasting Fact Sheet."

53. Byron Acohido, "Radio to the MP3 Degree: Podcasting," *USA Today*, February 9, 2005; Marco R. della Cava, "Podcasting: It's All Over the Dial," *USA Today*, February 9, 2005; Erika Gonzalez, "Podcast Power: Diversity of Free Audio Programs Expands as Technology Catches On," *Rocky Mountain News*, September 23, 2005, 26D.

54. Benny Evangelista, "Jobs Announces iTunes Will Accommodate Podcasts," *San Francisco Chronicle*, May 23, 2005.

55. Nelson Branco, "Rob Cesternino Leads the Reality Tribe," *24 Hours Toronto*, November 25, 2015.

56. Mike Bloom, "How Rob Cesternino and 'Rob Has a Podcast' Changed the Face of *Survivor* Coverage," *Parade*, February 10, 2020, https://parade.com/993161/mikebloom/rob-cesternino-survivor-podcast-interview/.

57. Nelson Branco, "Rob Cesternino Leads the Reality Tribe."

58. Edison Research, "The Infinite Dial 2020;" "Audio and Podcasting Fact Sheet."

59. Ronald Byrnside, "The Formation of a Musical Style: Early Rock," in *Contemporary Music and Music Cultures*, ed. Charles Hamm, Bruno Nettl, and Ronald Byrnside (Englewood Cliffs, NJ: Prentice-Hall, 1975).

60. James Miller, *Flowers in the Dustbin: The Rise of Rock and Roll, 1947–1977* (New York: Simon & Schuster, 1999).

61. Gerald Early, *One Nation Under a Groove: Motown and American Culture* (Hopewell, NJ: Ecco Press, 1995).

62. Miller, *Flowers in the Dustbin*.

63. Ibid., 31.

64. Byrnside, "Formation of a Musical Style."

65. Miller, *Flowers in the Dustbin*.

66. Ibid., 72.

67. Ibid., 83.

68. Ibid., 105.

69. Ibid., 37.

70. Early, *One Nation Under a Groove*.

71. Ibid., 105.

72. Allan F. Moore, *The Beatles: Sgt. Pepper's Lonely Hearts Club Band* (Cambridge, UK: Cambridge University Press, 1997); Patricia Romanowski, Holly George-Warren, and Jon Pareles, eds., *The New Rolling Stone Encyclopedia of Rock & Roll*, completely revised and updated ed. (New York: Rolling Stone Press, 1995).

73. Moore, *Beatles*.

74. Early, *One Nation Under a Groove*.

75. Miller, *Flowers in the Dustbin*.

76. Moore, *Beatles*.

77. Christopher John Farley, "A Hitmaker and a Gentleman," *Time*, November 11, 1996, 90; "New Babyface/David E. Talbert Musical Set Premiering at Beacon Theater," *PR Newswire*, May 31, 2001; "Bio," Babyface, http://www.babyfacemusic.com/.

78. Romanowski et al., *New Rolling Stone Encyclopedia of Rock & Roll*.

79. Ibid.

80. Mickey Hess, ed., *Hip Hop in America: A Regional Guide* (New York: Greenwood Press, 2010), viii.

81. Hess, *Hip Hop in America*, xi.

82. Brian Longhurst, *Popular Music and Society* (Cambridge, UK: Polity Press, 1995).

83. Marina Terkourafi, *Language of Global Hip Hop* (London: Continuum International, 2010).

84. Laura Atallah, "This Syrian Rapper Risked Everything For Freedom. Now He Wants the World to Listen," *Huck*, August 7, 2017, https://www.huckmag.com/art-and-culture/music-2/syrian-rapper-berline-exile-mohammad-abu-hajar/.

85. Ibid.

86. Bruce Feiler, "Gone Country," *New Republic*, February 5, 1996, 19–20.

87. Bobby Reed, "'Murder' Numbers; Country Radio Makes a Killing—Is It Killing Country?" *Chicago Sun-Times*, October 8, 2000.

88. David Browne et al., "100 Greatest Country Artists of All Time," *Rolling Stone*, June 15, 2017, https://www.rollingstone.com/country/lists/100-greatest-country-artists-of-all-time-w486191.

89. Feiler, "Gone Country."

90. Ibid.

91. "Radio Today 2013: How America Listens to Radio," *Arbitron*, 2013, http://www.arbitron.com/downloads/Radio_Today_2013_execsum.pdf; Nielsen, "Tops of 2015: Audio," *Media and Entertainment*, December 17, 2015, http://www.nielsen.com/us/en/insights/news/2015/tops-of-2015-audio.html.

92. "Number of Stations by Format," *News Generation*, https://www.newsgeneration.com/broadcast-resources/number-of-stations-by-format/.

93. Richard Corliss, "Look Who's Talking," *Time*, January 23, 1995, 22–25.

94. Judy Rene Sims, "Talk, Talk, Talk: Opinion or Fact?" *Journalism History* 22 (Winter 1997): 173; Jeffrey Gottfried, Michael Barthel, Elisa Shearer, and Amy Mitchell, "The 2016 Presidential Campaign—A News Event That's Hard to Miss," *Pew Research Center*, February 4, 2016, http://www.journalism.org/2016/02/04/the-2016-presidential-campaign-a-news-event-thats-hard-to-miss/.

95. Corliss, "Look Who's Talking."

96. Brian Stelter, "For Conservative Radio, It's a New Dawn, Too," *New York Times*, December 22, 2008.

97. Jennifer Harper, "Hannity Ranked No. 1 Among the Top 100 Talk Radio Gods," *Washington Times*, June 6, 2019, www.washingtontimes.com/news/2019/jun/6/inside-the-beltway-talk-radio-gods-rank-sean-hanni/.

98. Rodney Ho, "Rush Limbaugh Tops Talkers Heavy Hundred for Ninth Year in Row," *Atlanta Journal-Constitution*, March 26, 2015, http://radiotvtalk.blog.ajc.com/2015/03/26/rush-limbaugh-tops-talkers-heavy-hundred-for-ninth-year-in-row/.

99. Copeland, "Is Howard Stern Going Soft?"; Polly Mosendz, "Opie and Anthony No More: Inside the Nasty Breakup of Radio's Most Notorious Shock Jocks," *Newsweek*, April 9, 2015, http://www.newsweek.com/opie-and-anthony-no-more-inside-nasty-break-radios-most-notorious-shock-jocks-321186; Ben Sisario, "Howard Stern and SiriusXM Sign New Deal for 5 Years," *New York Times*, December 15, 2015, http://www.nytimes.com/2015/12/16/business/media/howard-stern-and-siriusxm-reach-new-deal.html.

100. "Hispanic and African American News Media Fact Sheet," *Pew Research Center*, August 7, 2017, http://www.journalism.org/fact-sheet/hispanic-and-african-american-news-media/.

101. Arbitron, "Hispanic Radio Today," 2011 edition (Arbitron, 2011).

102. Della de Lafuente, "Look Who's Talking: Putting a Face on Hispanic Radio," *Adweek*, September 17, 2007.

103. "Audio and Podcasting Fact Sheet."

104. "Tops of 2019: Radio," *Nielsen*, December 18, 2018, http://www.nielsen.com/us/en/insights/article/2019/tops-of-2019-radio/.

105. Radio Ink, "ESPN Radio Shows Headed for TV Simulcast," *RadioInk*, March 20, 2018, https://radioink.com/2018/03/20/espn-radio-shows-headed-for-tv-simulcast/.

106. Joseph P. Kahn, "Macho in the Morning: 'Guy Talk,'" *Boston Globe*, September 7, 1999, A1.

107. Linda Werthheimer, ed., *Listening to America: Twenty-Five Years in the Life of a Nation, as Heard on National Public Radio* (Boston: Houghton Mifflin, 1995).

108. William Buzenberg, "The National Public Radio Idea," *Nieman Reports* 51, no. 2 (1997): 32.

109. "NPR Audience," *National Public Media*, http://nationalpublicmedia.com/npr/audience/; NPR, "NPR Fact Sheet," https://www.npr.org/documents/about/press/NPR_Fact_Sheet.pdf.

110. NPR, "NPR Fact Sheet"; NPR, NPR, "Sponsor *Morning Edition*, the Nation's Number One Morning Drive Program."

111. Brian Steinberg, "'Good Morning America' Bounces Back Against NBC's 'Today,'" *Variety*, January 23, 2018, http://variety.com/2018/tv/news/good-morning-america-today-tv-ratings-2-1202673687/.

112. NPR, "NPR Fact Sheet"; NPR, "Public Radio Finances," https://www.npr.org/about-npr/178660742/public-radio-finances.

113. "Audio and Podcasting Fact Sheet."

114. NPR, "NPR Fact Sheet."

115. Brian Longhurst, *Popular Music and Society* (Cambridge, UK: Polity Press, 1995).

116. Ken Auletta, *The Highwaymen* (New York: Random House, 1997), 293.

117. Richard Crawford, "Introduction: The Phonograph and the Scholar" (paper presented at *The Phonograph and Our Musical Life*, Brooklyn College, New York, 1980).

118. Chris Bonastia, "Sucking in the '70s," *New Republic*, January 30, 1995, 11–12.

119. Miller, *Flowers in the Dustbin*.

120. "The Walkman Man," *People*, October 18, 1999, 132.

121. RiShawn Biddle, "Personal Soundtracks," *Reason*, October 1999, 58–59.

122. Ibid.

123. Ibid.

124. "The State of the News Media 2009: Audio," *Pew Research Center*, https://assets.pewresearch.org/files/journalism/State-of-the-News-Media-Report-2009-FINAL.pdf.

125. Doug Williams, personal communication with the author, February 12, 2016.

126. Kevin Kelly, "The Technium: 1,000 True Fans," *KevinKelly.com*, March 4, 2008, https://kk.org/thetechnium/1000-true-fans/.

127. David Carr, "At Sundance, Kickstarter Resembled a Movie Studio, but Without the Egos," *New York Times*, January 30, 2012, https://mediadecoder.blogs.nytimes.com/2012/01/30/at-sundance-kickstarter-resembled-a-movie-studio-but-without-the-egos/?_php=true&_type=blogs&_r=0.

128. "Wild Ponies: Galax," Kickstarter, https://www.kickstarter.com/projects/wildponies/wild-ponies-galax.

129. Brendan Farrington, "Independent Musicians Turn to Social Media to Recoup Wages," Associated Press, April 16, 2020, https://apnews.com/e9d74420e020032f7c30775794afceff?fbclid=IwAR3AplG1ip5mx6VJyWFlIaJZvUkc6GvGwje9MULzXIYmMS1jr89eVStX3qo.

130. Joshua Friedlander, Mid-Year 2019 RIAA Music Revenues Report, *RIAA*, 2019, pp. 1–3, www.riaa.com/wp-content/uploads/2019/09/Mid-Year-2019-RIAA-Music-Revenues-Report.pdf.

131. Gael Fashingbauer Cooper, "Groovy! Vinyl Records Will Soon Outsell CDs for First Time since 1986," *CNET*,

September 7, 2019, www.cnet.com/news/vinyl-records-will
-soon-outsell-cds-for-the-first-time-since-1986/.

132. Keith Caulfield, "U.S. Vinyl Album Sales Hit Nielsen Music-
Era Record High in 2017," *Billboard*, January 3, 2018, https://
www.billboard.com/articles/columns/chart-beat/8085951/us
-vinyl-album-sales-nielsen-music-record-high-2017; Nielsen
Music, "2017 U.S. Music Year-End Report," *Nielsen*, https://
www.nielsen.com/us/en/insights/report/2018/2017-music-us
-year-end-report/#; Elias Leight, "Vinyl Is Poised to Outsell
CDs for the First Time Since 1986," *Rolling Stone*, January 16,
2020, http://www.rollingstone.com/music/music-news/vinyl-cds
-revenue-growth-riaa-880959/.

133. Stephanie McKay, "Vinyl Records Get Their Groove Back;
Record Store Day Celebrates Format's Return," *Edmonton
(Alberta) Journal*, April 20, 2013, D10.

134. Williams, personal communication.

CHAPTER 7

1. Richard Trenholm, "Marvel, James Bond and More: These Are
the New Movie Release Dates for 2020 and 2021," *CNET*, April
2, 2020, http://www.cnet.com/news/coronavirus-movie-delays
-2020-and-2021-blockbusters-postponed/.

2. Sarah Whitten, "Disney Pixar's 'Onward' Coming to Digital
and Disney+ Earlier Due to Coronavirus Outbreak," *CNBC*,
March 20, 2020, http://www.cnbc.com/2020/03/20/disney
-pixars-onward-coming-to-digital-and-disney-early.html.

3. Rebecca Rubin, "Does Anyone Win in AMC Theatres' Fight
With Universal Pictures?" *Variety*, April 30, 2020, http://www
.variety.com/2020/film/news/amc-theatres-universal-pictures
-dispute-movie-theaters-1234592899/.

4. Sophie Maerowitz, "What to Post On Social Media in a Global
Crisis: 7 Communicators Weigh In," *PRNEWS*, April 3, 2020,
http://www.prnewsonline.com/what-to-post-social-media
-covid-communications#.Xodd7ccR_Us.twitter.

5. Brent Lang, "Theater Owners Chief on Plans to Reopen
Cinemas After Coronavirus Crisis," *Variety*, April 29, 2020,
http://www.variety.com/2020/film/features/theaters-reopening
-plan-coronavirus-john-fithian-1234592228/.

6. Bryce Jensen, interview with the author, May 4, 2020.

7. Bryce Jensen, interview with the author, May 4, 2020.

8. Neil Baldwin, *Edison: Inventing the Century* (New York:
Hyperion, 1995).

9. Eadweard Muybridge, "The Attitudes of Animals in Motion
(1882)," in *The Movies in Our Midst: Documents in the Cultural
History of Film in America*, ed. Gerald Mast (Chicago: University
of Chicago Press, 1982).

10. Gerald Mast and Bruce F. Kawin, *A Brief History of the Movies*,
6th ed. (Needham Heights, MA: Allyn & Bacon, 1996); John
Fell, *A History of Films* (New York: Holt, Rinehart and Winston,
1979).

11. Mast and Kawin, *Brief History of the Movies*.

12. National Association for the Advancement of Colored People
Boston Branch, "Fighting a Vicious Film: Protest Against 'The
Birth of a Nation,'" in *The Movies in Our Midst: Documents in the
Cultural History of Film in America*, ed. Gerald Mast (Chicago:
University of Chicago Press, 1982).

13. Mast and Kawin, *Brief History of the Movies*.

14. Linda Arvidson Griffith, "When the Movies Were Young
(1925)," in *The Movies in Our Midst: Documents in the Cultural
History of Film in America*, ed. Gerald Mast (Chicago: University
of Chicago Press, 1982).

15. Gerald Mast, "Introduction," in *The Movies in Our Midst:
Documents in the Cultural History of Film in America*, ed. Gerald
Mast (Chicago: University of Chicago Press, 1982).

16. Mast and Kawin, *Brief History of the Movies*; *Fortune* Magazine
Staff, "Loew's Inc. (1939)," in *The Movies in Our Midst:
Documents in the Cultural History of Film in America*, ed. Gerald
Mast (Chicago: University of Chicago Press, 1982); New York
Center for Visual History, *American Cinema: The Studio System*
(Burlington, VT: Annenberg/CBP, 1994), videotape.

17. Steven Bach, *Final Cut: Dreams and Disaster in the Making of
"Heaven's Gate"* (New York: William Morrow, 1985).

18. Mast, "Introduction."

19. Fitzhugh Green, "A Soldier Falls," in *The Movies in Our Midst:
Documents in the Cultural History of Film in America*, ed. Gerald
Mast (Chicago: University of Chicago Press, 1982).

20. Douglas Gomery, "Warner Bros. Innovates Sound: A Business
History," in *The Movies in Our Midst: Documents in the Cultural
History of Film in America*, ed. Gerald Mast (Chicago: University
of Chicago Press, 1982).

21. Harry Geduld, "The Voice of the Vitaphone (1975)," in *The
Movies in Our Midst: Documents in the Cultural History of Film
in America*, ed. Gerald Mast (Chicago: University of Chicago
Press, 1982).

22. Ralph L. Henry, "The Cultural Influence of the 'Talkies,'"
in *The Movies in Our Midst: Documents in the Cultural History
of Film in America*, ed. Gerald Mast (Chicago: University of
Chicago Press, 1982), 291.

23. Gilbert Seldes, "Talkies' Progress (1929)," in *The Movies in Our
Midst: Documents in the Cultural History of Film in America*, ed.
Gerald Mast (Chicago: University of Chicago Press, 1982).

24. *United States v. Paramount Pictures, Inc.*, 334 U.S. 131 (1948).

25. Mast, "Introduction"; Michael Conant, "The Paramount Case
and Its Legal Background (1961)," in *The Movies in Our Midst:
Documents in the Cultural History of Film in America*, ed. Gerald
Mast (Chicago: University of Chicago Press, 1982).

26. House Un-American Activities Committee, "Hearings
Regarding the Communist Infiltration of the Motion-Picture-
Industry Activities in the United States (1947)," in *The Movies
in Our Midst: Documents in the Cultural History of Film in
America*, ed. Gerald Mast (Chicago: University of Chicago
Press, 1982).

27. Gordon Kahn, "Hollywood on Trial (1948)," in *The Movies in
Our Midst: Documents in the Cultural History of Film in America*,
ed. Gerald Mast (Chicago: University of Chicago Press, 1982).

28. John Cogley, "Report on Blacklisting," in *The Movies in Our
Midst: Documents in the Cultural History of Film in America*, ed.
Gerald Mast (Chicago: University of Chicago Press, 1982).

29. Leonard Maltin, ed., *Leonard Maltin's Movie and Video Guide*,
1997 ed. (New York: Signet, 2006).

30. Mast and Kawin, *Brief History of the Movies*.

31. Daniel Engber, "Will the 3-D Revival Go the Way of Pixar's
Up?" *Slate*, June 2, 2009, https://slate.com/culture/2009/06/will
-the-3-d-revival-go-the-way-of-pixar-s-up.html.

32. Will Greenwald and Jamie Lendino, "What Is 4K (Ultra HD)?"
PC Magazine, October 19, 2017, https://www.pcmag.com/
article2/0,2817,2412174,00.asp.

33. *Fortune* Magazine Staff, "Color and Sound on Film (1930),"
in *The Movies in Our Midst: Documents in the Cultural History
of Film in America*, ed. Gerald Mast (Chicago: University of
Chicago Press, 1982).

34. Gwilym Mumford, "'Max Max: Fury Road'—Black
and Chrome Edition Review—A Gem Drained of Color,"
Guardian, April 28, 2017, http://www.theguardian.com/

film/2017/apr/28/mad-max-fury-road-black-and-chrome-edition-review-george-miller.

35. Tom Philip, "'Logan: Noir' Makes the New Feel Old Again," *GQ*, May 18, 2017, https://www.gq.com/story/logan-noir-makes-the-new-feel-old-again.

36. Garth Jowett, *Movies as Mass Communication.*, book 4, The SAGE Commtext Series (Thousand Oaks, CA: SAGE, 1980).

37. Elwin Green, "Big Screen Boom Goes Bust; Rash of Theater Closings Raises the Question: What to Do With an Empty Multiplex," *Pittsburgh Post-Gazette*, August 4, 2005, C1; "Number of U.S. Movie Screens," *National Association of Theater Owners*, http://www.natoonline.org/data/us-movie-screens.

38. Thomas Schatz, "The Return of the Hollywood Studio System," in *Conglomerates and the Media*, ed. Eric Barnouw (New York: New Press, 1997).

39. Mast and Kawin, *Brief History of the Movies*.

40. Corey Chichizola, "Why Marvel Movies Are So Successful, According to 'Infinity War's' Paul Bettany," *Cinema Blend*, March 27, 2018, https://www.cinemablend.com/news/2393731/why-marvel-movies-are-so-successful-according-to-infinity-wars-paul-bettany.

41. "Top Lifetime Grosses," *Box Office Mojo*, https://www.boxofficemojo.com/chart/top_lifetime_gross/?ref_=bo_lnav_hm_shrt.

42. Leonard Klady, "Tara Torpedoes *Titanic* as the Real B.O. Champ," *Variety*, March 2–8, 1998.

43. Steven Zeitchik, "Is Netflix Killing the Movie Theater? Not so Fast," *Washington Post*, December 24, 2018, http://www.washingtonpost.com/business/is-netflix-killing-the-movie-theater-not-so-fast/2018/12/24/7a16dbf8-037a-11e9-8186-4ec26a485713_story.html.

44. Arthur Asa Berger, *Media Analysis Techniques*, 3rd ed. (Thousand Oaks, CA: SAGE, 2005).

45. Carol Cling, "Room With a View: Audiences Paying for IMAX Experience of Summer Blockbusters," *Las Vegas Review-Journal*, July 17, 2009; Scott Mendelson, "'Gravity' Passes $100M in IMAX," *Forbes*, February 7, 2014, http://www.forbes.com/sites/scottmendelson/2014/02/07/gravity-passes-100m-worldwide-in-imax/2/.

46. Jowett, *Movies as Mass Communication*, 127.

47. Anthony D'Alessandro, "Imax CEO Richard Gelfond on Large-Format Future: 'Avengers: Age of Ultron,' Rivals, TV Shows & Adult Fare," *Deadline*, April 21, 2015, http://deadline.com/2015/04/imax-richard-gelfond-interview-avengers-age-of-ultron-star-wars-force-awakens-game-of-thrones-1201413428/.

48. David Sims, "Why Hollywood Should Pay Attention to *Dunkirk*," *Atlantic*, July 10, 2017, https://www.theatlantic.com/entertainment/archive/2017/07/why-hollywood-should-pay-attention-to-dunkirk/533094/?ex_cid=SigDig; "*Avengers: Endgame* Was Filmed With IMAX Cameras," April 2, 2019, https://www.imax.com/news/avengers-endgame-was-filmed-with-imax-cameras.

49. Maria Bartiromo, "Bartiromo: IMAX CEO Gelfond Has Global Outlook," *USA Today*, July 22, 2014, http://www.usatoday.com/story/money/columnist/bartiromo/2014/07/21/movies-bartiromo-imax-gelfond/12821501/.

50. J. W. Elphinstone, "Watercooler: DVDs' Popularity Passes VCRs', New Year's Resolutions, Bad Publicity," Associated Press Financial Wire.

51. Dan Frost, "Consumers Changing DVD Buying Habits," *San Francisco Chronicle*, September 5, 2005, E1.

52. Sarah Whitten, "The Death of the DVD: Why Sales Dropped More Than 86% in 13 Years," *CNBC*, November 8, 2019, https://www.cnbc.com/2019/11/08/the-death-of-the-dvd-why-sales-dropped-more-than-86percent-in-13-years.html.

53. Scott Bowles, "'Sky Captain' Takes CGI to Limit," *USA Today*, September 14, 2004.

54. Larry Carroll, "Reaching for the Sky," *FilmStew.com*, January 30, 2004.

55. "*Sky Captain and the World of Tomorrow*," *Box Office Mojo*, http://boxofficemojo.com/movies/?id=skycaptain.htm.

56. "*300*," *Box Office Mojo*, http://boxofficemojo.com/movies/?id=300.htm.

57. Brandon Gray, "Hordes Drive '300' to Record," *Box Office Mojo*, March 12, 2007, http://boxofficemojo.com/news/?id=2268&p=.htm.

58. Variety Staff, "Half of Screens to Be Digital by 2013," *Variety*, November 12, 2007, https://variety.com/2007/film/news/half-of-screens-to-be-digital-by-2013-1117975781/?jwsource=cl.

59. Motion Picture Association of America, "2017 THEME Report."

60. Peter Suderman, "There's One Great Reason to See Quentin Tarantino's *The Hateful Eight* in Theaters," *Vox*, January 4, 2016, http://www.vox.com/2016/1/4/10707828/hateful-eight-70mm-roadshow.

61. Ben Kenigsberg, "Tarantino's 'The Hateful Eight' Resurrects Nearly Obsolete Technology," *New York Times*, November 11, 2015, http://www.nytimes.com/2015/11/12/movies/tarantinos-the-hateful-eight-resurrects-nearly-obsolete-technology.html.

62. Carolyn Giardina, "'Ready Player One' in 70mm Film Opens on 22 Screens," *Hollywood Reporter*, March 30, 2018, https://www.hollywoodreporter.com/behind-screen/ready-player-one-70mm-film-opens-22-screens-1098364.

63. Dade Hayes, "Bombs Away: Biz Disavows Duds," *Variety*, March 20–26, 2000, pp. 7–8.

64. "Movie Budgets," *Numbers*, https://www.the-numbers.com/movie/budgets/all.

65. Brooks Barnes, "With $218 Million Haul, 'Black Panther' Smashes Box Office Records," *New York Times*, February 18, 2018, https://www.nytimes.com/2018/02/18/movies/black-panther-box-office-records.html.

66. "Movie Budgets," *Numbers*.

67. Ray Subers, "Weekend Report: 'Stars' Align for 'Fault,' Cruise Misses with 'Edge,'" *Box Office Mojo*, June 8, 2014, http://www.boxofficemojo.com/news/?id=3855&p=.htm; "Domestic Box Office For 2014," *Box Office Mojo*, http://www.boxofficemojo.com/yearly/chart/?yr=2014&p=.htm.

68. Brad Brevet, "'Black Panther' Tops $600M Domestically While 'I Can Only Imagine' Surprises With $17M Debut," *Box Office Mojo*, March 18, 2018, https://www.boxofficemojo.com/article/ed4217439236/; "I Can Only Imagine," *Box Office Mojo*, http://www.boxofficemojo.com/movies/?id=icanonlyimagine.htm.

69. Susan Wloszczyna, "What Makes a Film a Phenom?" *USA Today*, May 12, 2006.

70. "Movie Budgets," *Numbers*; "*Ready Player One*," *Box Office Mojo*, http://www.boxofficemojo.com/movies/?id=readyplayerone.htm; "*The Post*," *Box Office Mojo*, http://www.boxofficemojo.com/movies/?id=untitledstevenspielberg.htm.

71. Michael Brice-Saddler, "Pence Said Georgia 'Ain't Hollywood,' and He's Right. More Box Office Hits Are Shot in Georgia," *Washington Post*, November 2, 2018, http://www.washingtonpost.com/business/2018/11/02/pence-said-georgia-aint-hollywood-hes-right-more-box-office-hits-are-shot-georgia/?utm_term=.76329ec954d8.

72. Steven Zeitchik, "Why Hollywood Isn't Actually in a Rush to Leave Georgia," *Washington Post*, May 31, 2019, http://www

.washingtonpost.com/business/2019/05/31/why-hollywood-isnt
-actually-rush-leave-georgia/?utm_term=.87b950cf2d54.

73. Nicquel Terry Ellis, "'Hollywood of the South:' After a Decade, Industry Leaders Succeed in Making Atlanta a Hub for Filmmakers of Color," *USA Today*, March 1, 2020, http://www .usatoday.com/story/news/2020/03/01/industry-leaders-say -tyler-perry-has-paved-the-way-for-filmmakers-of-color-to -succeed-in-georgia/4747702002/.

74. "Slumdog Millionaire," *Box Office Mojo*, https://boxofficemojo .com/movies/?id=slumdogmillionaire.htm.

75. Victoria Young, "Bolly Good Show," *Sun Herald*, June 30, 2002, 1.

76. Rani Singh, "Shah Rukh Khan—The Biggest Movie Star In the World," *Forbes*, December 26, 2015, https://www.forbes.com/ sites/ranisingh/2015/12/26/shah-rukh-khan-the-biggest-movie -star-in-the-world/.

77. Rama Lakshmi, "Hooray for Bollywood: Oscar Bid Lifts Hopes," *Washington Post*, March 24, 2002.

78. Young, "Bolly Good Show."

79. Elham Khatami, "Is Bollywood Coming to Hollywood?" *CNN*, February 23, 2009, http://www.cnn.com/2009/SHOWBIZ/ Movies/02/23/bollywood.hollywood/index.html.

80. Roger Ebert, "'Lagaan' Brings Out the Best of Bollywood," *Chicago Sun-Times*, June 7, 2002, 33.

81. Jeremy Fuster, "Will 'Black Panther' Finally Open Hollywood's Floodgates for More Diverse Studio Movies?" *Wrap*, February 21, 2018, https://www.thewrap.com/will-black-panther -blockbuster-hollywood-floodgates-studio/.

82. Fuster, "Will 'Black Panther' Finally Open Hollywood's Floodgates?"

83. Emily Yahr, "Audiences Show Up to Movies With People of Color. So Why Are #OscarsSoWhite Again?" *Washington Post*, January 14, 2016, https://www.washingtonpost.com/news/arts -and-entertainment/wp/2016/01/14/oscarssowhite-again/; Emily VanDerWerff, "Oscars 2016: The Nominees Are Blindingly White. Again," *Vox*, January 14, 2016, http://www.vox. com/2016/1/14/10767662/oscar-nominations-2016-so-white.

84. Yahr, "Audiences Show Up to Movies With People of Color."

85. Jessica Contrera, "Here's What the People Boycotting the Oscars Are Watching Instead," *Washington Post*, February 28, 2016, https://www.washingtonpost.com/news/arts -and-entertainment/wp/2016/02/28/heres-what-the-people -boycotting-the-oscars-are-watching-instead/.

86. Kickstarter, "'Hair Love' Oscar Shows a Route to Better Representation in Hollywood." *Medium*, February 11, 2020, https://medium.com/kickstarter/hair-love-oscar-shows-a-route -to-better-representation-in-hollywood-57033f4901b3.

87. Charles Solomon, "'Hair Love': 3 Men and a Little Girl (With a Lot of Curls)," *New York Times*, August 29, 2019, http://www.nytimes .com/2019/08/29/movies/hair-love.html?searchResultPosition=2.

88. Karen Attiah, "Why Chadwick Boseman's fight for African accents in 'Black Panther' was so important." Sept. 1, 2020, *The Washington Post*, https://www.washingtonpost.com/ opinions/2020/09/01/why-chadwick-bosemans-fight -african-accents-black-panther-was-so-important.

89. Manohla Dargis, Wesley Morris, and A. O. Scott, "Oscars So White? Or Oscars So Dumb? Discuss," *New York Times*, January 15, 2016, https://www.nytimes.com/2016/01/24/movies/ oscars-so-white-or-oscars-so-dumb-discuss.html.

90. VanDerWerff, "Oscars 2016."

91. Joey Nolfi, "People of Color Win Majority of Acting Oscars for the First Time in History," *Entertainment Weekly*, February 24, 2019, https://ew.com/oscars/2019/02/24/people-of-color-oscar -history/amp/?__twitter_impression=true.

92. Princess Weekes, "Disney+ Adds Disclaimer to Problematic Movies Citing 'Outdated Cultural Depictions,'" *The Mary Sue*, November 14, 2019, http://www.themarysue.com/disney-adds -disclaimer-to-problematic-movies-citing-outdated-cultural -depictions/.

93. THR Staff, "'Tom and Jerry' Cartoons Get 'Racial Prejudices' Disclaimer on iTunes," *Hollywood Reporter*, October 3, 2014, http://www.hollywoodreporter.com/news/ tom-jerry-cartoons-get-racial-737969.

94. Ana Swanson, "The Real Reason Matt Damon Was Brought in to Save Ancient China," *Washington Post*, August 9, 2016, https://www.washingtonpost.com/news/wonk/wp/2016/08/09/ the-real-reason-matt-damon-was-brought-in-to-save -ancient-china/?hpid=hp_hp-more-top-stories_mattdamon -0830pm%3Ahomepage%2Fstory.

95. Amanda Hess, "Asian-American Actors Are Fighting for Visibility. They Will Not Be Ignored," *New York Times*, May 25, 2016, http://www.nytimes.com/2016/05/29/movies/asian -american-actors-are-fighting-for-visibility-they-will-not-be -ignored.html.

96. Kyle Buchanan and Brooks Barnes, "'Parasite' Earns Best-Picture Oscar, First for a Movie Not in English," *New York Times*, February 10, 2020, http://www.nytimes.com/2020/02/09/ movies/parasite-movie-oscars-best-picture.html.

97. Lisa Katayama, "The Bechdel Test for Women in Movies," *Boing Boing*, July 22, 2010, http://www.boingboing. net/2010/07/22/the-bechdel-test-for.html; Rachel Sklar, "The Bechdel Test for Movies (and Media?)," *Mediaite*, July 22, 2010, http://www.mediaite.com/online/the-bechdel-test-for -movies-and-media/.

98. Jeff Guo, "Researchers Have Found a Major Problem With 'The Little Mermaid' and Other Disney Movies," *Washington Post*, January 25, 2016, https://www.washingtonpost.com/news/ wonk/wp/2016/01/25/researchers-have-discovered-a-major -problem-with-the-little-mermaid-and-other-disney-movies/.

99. John Collier, "Censorship and the National Board (1915)," in *The Movies in Our Midst: Documents in the Cultural History of Film in America*, ed. Gerald Mast (Chicago: University of Chicago Press, 1982).

100. Ellis Paxson Oberholtzer, "Sex Pictures (1922)," in *The Movies in Our Midst: Documents in the Cultural History of Film in America*, ed. Gerald Mast (Chicago: University of Chicago Press, 1982).

101. J. R. Rutland, "State Censorship of Motion Pictures," in *The Movies in Our Midst: Documents in the Cultural History of Film in America*, ed. Gerald Mast (Chicago: University of Chicago Press, 1982).

102. Mast and Kawin, *Brief History of the Movies*.

103. "The Sins of Hollywood (1922)," in *The Movies in Our Midst: Documents in the Cultural History of Film in America*, ed. Gerald Mast (Chicago: University of Chicago Press, 1982).

104. Motion Picture Producers and Distributors of America, "The Don'ts and Be Carefuls (1927)," in *The Movies in Our Midst: Documents in the Cultural History of Film in America*, ed. Gerald Mast (Chicago: University of Chicago Press, 1982).

105. Mast, "Introduction," xix.

106. Raymond Moley, "The Birth of the Production Code (1945)," in *The Movies in Our Midst: Documents in the Cultural History of Film in America*, ed. Gerald Mast (Chicago: University of Chicago Press, 1982).

107. Motion Picture Producers and Distributors of America, "The Motion Picture Production Code of 1930s," in *The Movies in Our Midst: Documents in the Cultural History of Film in America*, ed. Gerald Mast (Chicago: University of Chicago

Press, 1982); Amy Wallace, "MPAA's Dozen Judge Movies for Millions," *Los Angeles Times*, July 18, 1999, A1.

108. Charles Lyons, *The New Censors: Movies and the Culture Wars* (Philadelphia: Temple University Press, 1997).

109. Gary Arnold, "Between PG & R; Valenti Says New Rating Possible by Next Week," *Washington Post*, June 23, 1984, C1.

110. Ibid.

111. "Top Lifetime Grosses by MPAA Rating: G, Domestic," *Box Office Mojo*, http://www.boxofficemojo.com/alltime/domestic/ mpaa.htm?page=G&sort=rank&order=ASC&p=.htm; "Top Lifetime Grosses by MPAA Rating: R, Domestic," *Box Office Mojo*, http://www.boxofficemojo.com/alltime/domestic/mpaa .htm?page=R&sort=rank&order=ASC&p=.htm.

112. Conner Schwerdtfeger, "Why Logan Needed to Be Rated-R, According to James Mangold," *Cinema Blend*, https://www .cinemablend.com/news/2308982/why-logan-needed-to-be -rated-r-according-to-james-mangold.

113. Jerome Hellman, "Problems With Movie Ratings Go Beyond Categories," *Los Angeles Times*, August 23, 1999, F3.

114. Wallace, "MPAA's Dozen Judge Movies for Millions."

115. Ibid.

116. Pamela McClintock, "MPAA Tries to Remove NC-17 Stigma," *Variety*, March 10, 2007, https://variety.com/2007/ film/news/mpaa-tries-to-remove-nc-17-stigma-1117960864/.

117. Joan Graves, "Survey Shows 93% of Parents Find Film Ratings Helpful in Making Movie Choices," *Motion Picture Association of America*, November 30, 2015, http://www.mpaa .org/cara/#.Vll5rpMrI_U.

118. Chris Anderson, *The Long Tail* (New York: Hyperion, 2006), p. 110.

119. Chris Anderson, "Briefly Noted From Australia," *Long Tail*, December 22, 2006, http://www.longtail.com/the_long_ tail/2006/12/briefly_noted_f.html.

120. Richard Corliss, "Blair Witch Craft," *Time*, August 16, 1999, pp. 58–64; Timothy L. O'Brien, "The Curse of the Blair Witch," *Talk*, February 2002, p. 81.

121. Charlotte O'Sullivan, "Film: Hell Is Other People. We Should Know: The Makers of the *Blair Witch Project*, Ed Sanchez and Daniel Myrick, on the Nightmare of Collective Filmmaking," *Independent*, October 22, 1999, 13.

122. O'Brien, "Curse of the Blair Witch."

123. Glenn Whipp, "Searching for 'Blair Witch' a Decade Later," *Los Angeles Times*, July 11, 2009.

124. Ibid.

125. "Domestic Box Office Weeklies For 2020," *Box Office Mojo*, as of May 13, 2020, https://www.boxofficemojo.com/ weekly/.

126. Brandon Gray, "'Brokeback Mountain' Most Impressive of Tepid 2005," *Box Office Mojo*, February 25, 2006, http://www .boxofficemojo.com/news/?id=2012.

127. Michael Medved, "Hollywood's Disconnect," *USA Today*, July 25, 2005.

128. Tim Purtell, "Our Favorite Year," *Entertainment Weekly*, April 29, 1994.

129. Motion Picture Association of America, "2017 THEME Report."

130. Cogley, "Report on Blacklisting."

131. Motion Picture Association of America, "2017 THEME Report."

132. Zeitchik, "Is Netflix Killing the Movie Theater?"

133. R. T. Watson, "Trading Places: Global Box Office Dethroned by Spending on Home Entertainment." *Wall Street Journal*, March 21, 2019, http://www.wsj.com/articles/trading -places-global-box-office-dethroned-by-spending-on-home -entertainment-11553173204.

134. Justin McCarthy, "In U.S., Library Visits Outpaced Trips to Movies in 2019." *Gallup*, April 13, 2020, https://news.gallup .com/poll/284009/library-visits-outpaced-trips-movies -2019.aspx?fbclid=IwAR0Ue_iUFmQxk3OGecetOWhy 5RVsxtZWo2xk8pAd6VwvOXjm2cNDKc7Ovx4.

135. Schatz, "Return of the Hollywood Studio System."

136. "*Transformers: Revenge of the Fallen*," *Box Office Mojo*, http:// boxofficemojo.com/movies/?id=transformers2.htm.

137. "Digital Domain Collaborates With Michael Bay on 'Transformers: Revenge of the Fallen' Movie Tie-Ins," *CGArena*, January 7, 2009, http://www.cgarena.com/archives/ news/transformers_tieins.html.

138. Sarah Mahoney, "Kmart Launches Transformers Tie-In," *Marketing Daily–Media Post News*, June 1, 2009, http://www .mediapost.com/publications/article/107088/kmart-launches -transformers-tie-in.html.

139. Garrett Kessler, "2010 Camaro Stars in Transformers: Revenge of the Fallen, the Game," *Edmunds Inside Line*, June 30, 2009; "Latest Buzz: Chevrolet Unveils Camaro 'Transformers' Edition," *USA Today*, July 22, 2009, http://content.usatoday .com/communities/driveon/post/2009/07/68495117/1.

CHAPTER 8

1. Ben Cohen, Joshua Robinson, and Joe Flint, "Sports Industry Reels From Coronavirus Fallout," *Wall Street Journal*, March 29, 2020, http://www.wsj.com/articles/sports-industry-reels -from-coronavirus-fallout-11585517192?mod=djem10point.

2. Stephen Battaglio and Meg James, "No Summer Olympics in Tokyo. Why It Matters to NBC," *Los Angeles Times*, March 24, 2020, http://www.latimes.com/entertainment-arts/business/ story/2020-03-24/olympics-postponement-nbc-ad-sales -coronavirus.

3. Laine Higgins, "The Big Bill for Canceling March Madness Has Arrived at the NCAA," *Wall Street Journal*, March 26, 2020, http://www.wsj.com/articles/ncaa-schools-to-see-fewer -funds-next-year-11585256379?mod=article_inline.

4. Frank Pallotta, "What It's Like to Host ESPN's SportsCenter Without Sports," *CNN*, May 10, 2020, http://www.cnn .com/2020/05/10/media/espn-sportscenter-scott-van-pelt -coronavirus/index.html.

5. Lillian Rizzo and David Marcelis, "Live Sports Are Canceled. But Don't Expect a Cable-TV Refund," *Wall Street Journal*, April 18, 2020, http://www.wsj.com/articles/live-sports-are-canceled -but-dont-expect-a-cable-tv-refund-11587211201; Dan Gartland, "ESPN's NBA H-O-R-S-E Competition Was Tough to Watch," *Sports Illustrated*, April 13, 2020, http://www.si.com/extra -mustard/2020/04/13/espn-nba-horse-tournament-highlights.

6. Cohen, Robinson, and Flint, "Sports Industry Reels."

7. JR Radcliffe, "40 Years Ago, the First Live ESPN Game Ever Broadcast Was a Slow-Pitch Softball Game in Wisconsin. How Did It Happen?" *Milwaukee Journal Sentinel*, August 28, 2019, http://www.jsonline.com/story/sports/2019/08/28/e-60-espn -commemorates-its-first-broadcast-softball-game-lannon -wisconsin/1902053001/.

8. David Dugan, "Big Dreams, Small Screen," *WGBH Educational Foundation*, 1997.

9. Neil Postman, "Electrical Engineer Philo Farnsworth," *Time*, March 29, 1999, http://content.time.com/time/magazine/ article/0,9171,990620,00.html.

10. Ibid.

11. Erik Barnouw, *Tube of Plenty: The Evolution of American Television*, 2nd rev. ed. (New York: Oxford University Press, 1990).

12. Postman, "Electrical Engineer Philo Farnsworth."

13. Barnouw, *Tube of Plenty*.

14. John Carman, "The 20 Series That Changed the Tube," *San Francisco Chronicle*, May 24, 1998; Deborah Felder, *The 100 Most Influential Women of All Time: A Ranking Past and Present* (Secaucus, NJ: Carol Publishing Group, 1996); Douglas McGrath, "The Good, the Bad, the Lucy: A Legacy of Laughs; The Man Behind the Throne: Making the Case for Desi," *New York Times*, October 14, 2001.

15. Fred Kaplan, "Costs of High-Definition TV Make Its Future Look Fuzzy," *Boston Globe*, July 25, 2000.

16. Christopher Carey, "Ready or Not, High-Definition Television Starts on Sunday," *St. Louis Post-Dispatch*, November 1, 1998.

17. Patrick R. Parsons and Robert M. Frieden, *The Cable and Satellite Television Industries* (Needham Heights, MA: Allyn & Bacon, 1998).

18. Robert W. Crandall and Harold Furchtgott-Roth, *Cable TV: Regulation or Competition?* (Washington, DC: Brookings Institution, 1996).

19. Ibid.

20. Priscilla Painton, "The Taming of Ted Turner," *Time*, January 6, 1992.

21. Ibid.

22. "Prince of the Global Village," *Time*, January 6, 1992.

23. Parsons and Frieden, *Cable and Satellite Television Industries*.

24. Ken Auletta, *Three Blind Mice: How the TV Networks Lost Their Way* (New York: Random House, 1991).

25. Parsons and Frieden, *Cable and Satellite Television Industries*.

26. "Industry Data," NCTA, 2020, http://www.ncta.com/industry-data.

27. Barnouw, *Tube of Plenty*.

28. Wayne Friedman, "Dish Posts Gains in Total Pay TV Subs, Net Income," *MediaPost*, February 22, 2017, https://www.mediapost.com/publications/article/295682/dish-posts-gains-in-total-pay-tv-subs-net-income.html; Todd Spangler, "AT&T Loses Record 385,000 Traditional Pay-TV Subscribers in Q3, Posts Gains for DirecTV Now," *Variety*, October 24, 2017, https://variety.com/2017/biz/news/att-directv-q3-2017-record-pay-tv-loss-1202598165/.

29. Satellite Broadcasting & Communications Association, "Facts & Figures," April 10, 2012, www.sbca.com/receiver-network/industry-satellite-facts.htm; "Americans Cutting the Cable TV Cord at Increasing Pace," *eMarketer*, December 10, 2015, https://www.emarketer.com/Article/Americans-Cutting-Cable-TV-Cord-Increasing-Pace/1013327.

30. Mark Dawidziak, "Satellite Television Providers to Include Local Programming," *Plain Dealer*, December 17, 1999.

31. Spangler, "AT&T Loses Record 385,000 Traditional Pay-TV Subscribers."

32. J. W. Elphinstone, "Watercooler: DVDs' Popularity Passes VCRs', New Year's Resolutions, Bad Publicity," *Associated*, December 19, 2006; Megan Garber, "58% of Americans Still Have a VCR in Their Homes," *Atlantic*, January 8, 2014, http://www.theatlantic.com/technology/archive/2014/01/58-of-americans-still-have-a-vcr-in-their-homes/282859/.

33. Richard Mullins, "VCR's Demise Fast Forwards in Brave New World of DVDs," *Tampa Tribune*, December 20, 2006; Wayne Freidman, "As Streaming TV Rises, DVR Penetration Slows," *MediaPost*, December 9, 2013, http://www.mediapost.com/publications/article/215069/as-streaming-tv-rises-dvr-penetration-slows.html; DTVE Reporter, "US Netflix Use Tops DVR Ownership for the First Time," *Digital TV Europe*, March 7, 2017, https://www.digitaltveurope.com/2017/03/07/us-netflix-use-tops-dvr-ownership-for-the-first-time/.

34. Leichtman Research Group, "75% of US Households Have a DVR, Netflix, or Use On-Demand," *Leichtman Research Group*, January 2, 2015.

35. Joelle Tessler, "Senate OKs 4-Month Delay to Digital TV Changeover," *USA Today*, January 27, 2009; Leslie Cauley, "Switch to Digital Television (DTV) Went Remarkably Well," *USA Today*, June 15, 2009; Associated Press, "800,000 Callers Phone Digital TV Hotline," *USA Today*, June 14, 2009.

36. Paul Farhi, "A Defining Moment for TV? As Digital Broadcast Age Begins, the Outlook Is Far From Clear," *Washington Post*, November 1, 1998.

37. Ibid.

38. "Expansion Teams Count Too," *Research Notes*, 2Q 2017, https://www.leichtmanresearch.com/wp-content/uploads/2018/03/LRG-Research-Notes-2017-06.pdf.

39. Auletta, *Three Blind Mice*.

40. Anthony Smith, "Television as a Public Service Medium," in *Television: An International History*, ed. Anthony Smith (New York: Oxford University Press, 1995).

41. Laurence Jarvik, *PBS: Behind the Screen* (Rocklin, CA: Prima, 1997).

42. Ibid., 37.

43. Emily Steel, "'Sesame Street' to Air First on HBO for Next 5 Seasons," *New York Times*, August 13, 2015, http://www.nytimes.com/2015/08/14/business/media/sesame-street-heading-to-hbo-in-fall.html.

44. Ken Auletta, *The Highwaymen* (San Diego, CA: Harcourt Brace, 1998).

45. Michael Schneider, "Top Rated Shows of 2019: Super Bowl LIII, 'The Big Bang Theory,' 'Game of Thrones' Dominate," *Variety*, December 27, 2019, https://variety.com/2019/tv/news/top-rated-shows-2019-game-of-thrones-big-bang-theory-oscars-super-bowl-1203451363/.

46. "Intro to Nielsen Ratings: Basics and Definitions," *Spotted Ratings*, September 3, 2013, http://www.spottedratings.com/2013/09/intro-to-nielsen-ratings-basics-and.html.

47. David Lieberman, "Nielsen Pegs TV Households at 119.6M for 2017–18 Season," *Deadline*, August 25, 2017, http://deadline.com/2017/08/nielsen-pegs-tv-households-119-6m-2017-18-season-1202156331/.

48. James R. Walker and Douglas A. Ferguson, *The Broadcast Television Industry* (Needham Heights, MA: Allyn & Bacon, 1998).

49. Auletta, *Three Blind Mice*.

50. Ibid.

51. Derek Thompson, "ESPN Is Not Doomed," *Atlantic*, May 1, 2017, https://www.theatlantic.com/business/archive/2017/05/espn-layoffs-future/524922/.

52. Michael Schneider, "100 Most-Watched TV Shows of 2018–19: Winners and Losers," *Variety*, May 21, 2020, https://variety.com/2019/tv/news/most-watched-tv-shows-highest-rated-2018-2019-season-game-of-thrones-1203222287.

53. Cynthia Littleton and Daniel Holloway, "TV's Dead Zone: How the Cable Sector Is Killing Off Struggling Networks," *Variety*, March 21, 2017, https://variety.com/2017/tv/features/overcrowded-cable-sector-esquire-spike-fyi-1202012647/ and https://pmcvariety.files.wordpress.com/2017/03/0321_041-nu.pdf; Daily Kos Staff, "If You Have Cable, You Are Subsidizing Fox News. It Might Be Time to Cut the Cord.

Here's How," *Daily Kos*, March 31, 2020, www.dailykos.com/stories/2020/3/31/1933075/-If-you-have-cable-you-are-subsidizing-Fox-News-It-might-be-time-to-cut-the-cord-Here-s-how; Rizzo and Marcelis, "Live Sports Are Canceled. But Don't Expect a Cable-TV Refund."

54. Joe Flint, "Netflix Reveals New Data on Overseas Growth Amid Stiffer U.S. Competition," *Wall Street Journal*, December 16, 2019, www.wsj.com/articles/netflix-says-90-of-subscriber-growth-comes-from-overseas-11576532846?mod=djem10point; "Industry Data."

55. John Koblin, "Netflix's Opaque Disruption Annoys Rivals on TV," *New York Times*, January 17, 2016, http://www.nytimes.com/2016/01/18/business/media/disruption-by-netflix-irks-tv-foes.html?rref=collection%2Ftimestopic%2FNetflix%20Inc.

56. Robert P. Laurence, "NBC Program Executive Says Network Has Lagged on Ethnic Diversity," *San Diego Union-Tribune*, July 31, 1999.

57. Dave Itzkoff, "Why Hank Azaria Won't Play Apu on 'The Simpsons' Anymore," *New York Times*, February 25, 2020, https://www.nytimes.com/2020/02/25/arts/hank-azaria-simpsons-apu.html.

58. Fresh Air, "Actor Randall Park Says 'Fresh Off The Boat' Is Comedy Without the Cliché," *NPR*, October 14, 2015, www.npr.org/2015/10/14/448278570/actor-randall-park-says-fresh-off-the-boat-is-comedy-without-the-clich.

59. Kat Chow, "In Its Season Finale, 'Fresh Off The Boat' Is Still Wrestling with Authenticity," *NPR*, April 22, 2015, www.npr.org/sections/codeswitch/2015/04/22/401466130/in-its-season-finale-fresh-off-the-boat-is-still-wrestling-with-authenticity.

60. Meron Mogos, "Primetime Television: The New Color-Blind Medium?" *Huffington Post*, January 29, 2013, www.huffingtonpost.com/meron-mogos/diversity-in-primetime-tv_b_2574898.html.

61. "That's So Raven, Episode Guide" IMDb, http://www.imdb.com/title/tt0300865/; Personal communication, March 29, 2018.

62. Sarah Hughes, "American Television's Real Scandal," *Guardian*, October 22, 2012, http://www.theguardian.com/lifeandstyle/2012/oct/22/american-television-real-scandal.

63. Tonya Pendleton, "Kerry Washington Talks 'Scandal' Shocker and Why It's Great to Be a Black Woman on TV," *BlackAmericaWeb*, February 16, 2015, http://blackamericaweb.com/2015/02/16/kerry-washington-talks-scandal-shocker-and-why-its-great-to-be-a-black-women-on-tv/.

64. Madeline Berg, "Note to Networks: Diversity on TV Pays Off," *Forbes*, February 22, 2017, https://www.forbes.com/sites/maddieberg/2017/02/22/note-to-networks-diversity-on-tv-pays-off/#79a76ea03d0a.

65. Candice Roberts, "Guest Blog Post—Streaming and Mainstreaming: Spotlight on LGBT Media," *Living in a Media World*, May 9, 2018, https://www.ralphehanson.com/2018/05/09/guest-blog-post-streaming-and-mainstreaming-spotlight-on-lgbt-media/. Thanks to Dr. Roberts for her guest blog post at *Living in a Media World* on which this section is based.

66. Shadow and Act, "ABC Names Its First African American President—Channing Dungey," *IndieWire*, February 17, 2016.

67. "QuickFacts: United States," U.S. Census Bureau, 2019, http://www.census.gov/quickfacts/fact/table/US.

68. David Adams, "ABC, CBS, NBC, Fox . . . Univision?," *St. Petersburg Times*, June 5, 2005; Michael Schneider, "Novela Energizes Univision," *Variety*, October 4, 2009; Steve Baron, "Univision Network Out-Delivered at Least One English-Language Network on 6 Nights Last Week Among Adults 18–34," *TV by the Numbers*, September 1, 2015, http://tvbythenumbers.zap2it.com/2015/09/01/univision-network-out-delivered-at-least-one-english-language-network-on-6-nights-last-week-among-adults-18-34/; Amanda Kondolojy, "Univision Sets Milestone as No. 4 Network in February Sweeps Ahead of NBC in Key Demos," *TV by the Numbers*, February 27, 2013, https://tvbythenumbers.zap2it.com/2013/02/27/univision-sets-milestone-as-no-4-network-in-february-sweeps-ahead-of-nbc-in-key-demos/171192/; Michael Schneider, "Most Watched Television Networks: Ranking 2015's Winners and Losers," *TV Insider*, December 28, 2015, http://www.tvinsider.com/article/62572/most-watched-tv-networks-2015/; "State of the News Media 2015," *Pew Research Center*, April 29, 2015, https://assets.pewresearch.org/wp-content/uploads/sites/13/2017/05/30142603/state-of-the-news-media-report-2015-final.pdf; Rick Porter, "NBC and CBS Lead 2016–17 Season, and Congrats to NBC on Its '17–'18 Victory," *TV by the Numbers*, May 24, 2017, http://tvbythenumbers.zap2it.com/more-tv-news/nbc-and-cbs-lead-2016-17-season-and-congrats-to-nbc-on-its-17-18-victory/.

69. Cara Lombardo, Benjamin Mullin, and Miriam Gottfried, "Univision Suitor Seeks to Recruit CBS Chief to Front Bid," *Wall Street Journal*, January 28, 2020, http://www.wsj.com/articles/univision-suitor-seeks-to-recruit-cbs-chief-to-front-bid-11580256086?mod=djem10point.

70. Marcela Valdes, "Jorge Ramos Is Not Walter Cronkite," *New York Times*, August 31, 2015, http://www.nytimes.com/2015/08/31/magazine/jorge-ramos-is-not-walter-cronkite.html.

71. Lee Romney, "Markets: Univision Shares Drop Over Azteca News," *Los Angeles Times*, September 9, 2000.

72. Keach Hagey, "Inside Telemundo's Battle with Univision for American Hispanics," *Wall Street Journal*, March 16, 2018, https://www.wsj.com/articles/inside-telemundos-battle-with-univision-for-american-hispanics-1521198000.

73. Michael Schneider, "Most-Watched Television Networks: Ranking 2017's Winners and Losers," *Indiewire*, December 28, 2017, http://www.indiewire.com/2017/12/highest-network-ratings-2017-most-watched-hbo-cbs-espn-fx-msnbc-fox-news-1201911363/; BET Networks, "BET Networks Goes From the Altar to a Ratings Honeymoon as 'GUCCI MANE & KEYSHIA KA'OIR: THE MANE EVENT' Is Now the #1 Cable Series Premiere of the 2017/18 Season," *Business Wire*, October 18, 2017, https://www.businesswire.com/news/home/20171018006614/en/BET-Networks-Altar-Ratings-Honeymoon-"GUCCI-MANE.

74. Greg Braxton, "BET on the Past and Future of a Dream," *Los Angeles Times*, May 6, 2000.

75. BET Networks, "BET Networks Goes from the Altar to a Ratings Honeymoon."

76. Stuart Elliott, "General Motors Is Significantly Increasing Its Efforts to Aim Pitches at Black Consumers," *The New York Times*, September 23, 1999.

77. Barnouw, *Tube of Plenty*, 467.

78. Rani Molla, "Americans Are Spending More Time on Media Thanks to Multitasking," *Recode*, October 9, 2017, https://www.recode.net/2017/10/9/16447820/americans-time-spent-media-multitasking-emarketer.

79. "American Time Use Survey Summary," Bureau of Labor Statistics, June 27, 2017, https://www.bls.gov/news.release/atus.nr0.htm.

80. Robert Kubey and Mihaly Csikszentmihalyi, *Television and the Quality of Life: How Viewing Shapes Everyday Experience* (Hillsdale, NJ: Erlbaum, 1990).

81. Victoria J. Rideout, Ulla G. Foehr, and Donald F. Roberts, *Generation M2: Media in the Lives of 8–18 Year-Olds* (Menlo Park, CA: Henry J. Kaiser Family Foundation, 2010).

82. Kubey and Csikszentmihalyi, *Television and the Quality of Life.*

83. Shearon A. Lowery and Melvin L. DeFleur, *Milestones in Mass Communication*, 3rd ed. (White Plains, NY: Longman, 1995).

84. Terry Gross, "Actress Mary Tyler Moore," *NPR*, October 30, 1995, http://www.npr.org/templates/story/story.php?storyId=1108624.

85. Elizabeth Kolbert, "What's a Network TV Censor to Do?" *New York Times*, May 23, 1993.

86. Warren Berger, "Censorship in the Age of Anything Goes; Where Have You Gone, Standards and Practices?" *New York Times*, September 20, 1998.

87. Stephen Farber, "They Watch What We Watch," *New York Times*, May 7, 1989.

88. David Zurawik, "Ratings Deal Signed; TV: Starting Oct. 1, Symbols Will Give Parents More Clues About Content. Except on NBC," *Baltimore Sun*, July 11, 1997.

89. Joshua Meyrowitz, *No Sense of Place* (New York: Oxford University Press, 1985), 117.

90. William A. Henry III, "History as It Happens; Linking Leaders as Never Before, CNN Has Changed the Way the World Does Its Business," *Time*, January 6, 1992, 24–27.

91. Berger, "Censorship in the Age of Anything Goes."

92. " US-TV-MA (Sorted by Popularity Ascending)," IMDb, https://www.imdb.com/search/title?certificates=US:TV-MA.

93. Associated Press, "A Closer Look at Broadcast Indecency," *First Amendment Center*, March 23, 2004.

94. Ibid.

95. Brendan Sasso, "Supreme Court Won't Take Up Janet Jackson 'Wardrobe Malfunction' Case," *Hill*, June 29, 2012, https://thehill.com/blogs/hillicon-valley/technology/235629-supreme-court-wont-take-up-janet-jackson-case.

96. Frances Martel, "Wardrobe Malfunction! Nancy Grace Lets a Nipple Slip During DWTS Performance (NSFW)," *Mediaite*, September 26, 2011, www.mediaite.com/tv/wardrobe-malfunction-nancy-grace-lets-a-nipple-slip-during-dwts-performance/.

97. Associated Press, "Some Stations Hesitate to Air 9/11 Documentary," *First Amendment Center*, September 5, 2006; Lisa de Moraes, "Where Aired, 'Private Ryan' Draws a Crowd," *Washington Post*, November 13, 2004, http://www.washingtonpost.com/wp-dyn/articles/A46922-2004Nov12.html.

98. Associated Press, "'Saving Private Ryan' Not Indecent, FCC Rules," *First Amendment Center*, March 1, 2005.

99. Adam Sherwin, "Amateur 'Video Bloggers' Under Threat From EU Broadcast Rules," *Times* (London), October 17, 2006.

100. Gene Policinski, "Censorship in the Name of Decency?" *First Amendment Center*, September 5, 2006.

101. Crandall and Furchtgott-Roth, *Cable TV.*

102. David Liberman and Laura Petrecca, "Deal Has Some ABC Affiliates Feeling Uneasy," *USA Today*, October 12, 2005, http://www.usatoday.com/tech/products/services/2005-10-12-abc-ipod-iger_x.htm.

103. *Hoover's Company Records—In-Depth Records: Netflix Inc.* (Austin, Texas: Hoover's Inc., 2012).

104. Meg James, "HBO Says Its HBO Now Streaming Service Has 800,000 Paying Subscribers," *Los Angeles Times*, February 10, 2016, http://www.latimes.com/entertainment/envelope/cotown/la-et-ct-streaming-service-hbo-now-subscribers-20160210-story.html.

105. Farhad Manjoo, "Why Media Titans Would Be Wise Not to Overlook Netflix," *New York Times*, January 13, 2016, http://www.nytimes.com/2016/01/14/technology/why-media-titans-need-to-worry-about-netflix.html?rref=collection%2Ftimestopic%2FNetflix%20Inc.

106. Chris Lindahl, "'Hamilton' Is the Surest Way for Disney+ to Challenge Netflix at the Event-Streaming Game," *IndieWire*, May 12, 2020, www.indiewire.com/2020/05/hamilton-disney-plus-release-means-huge-subscriber-gains-1202230837/.

107. Prospero, "What Is the Endgame for Disney+?" *Economist*, November 11, 2019, http://www.economist.com/prospero/2019/11/11/what-is-the-endgame-for-disney-.

108. Jim Romenesko, "My Valentine's Day Break-Up With Comcast," *JimRomenesko.com*, April 17, 2012.

109. Josh Herr, "The Long, Slow Death of Cable Just Reached a Tipping Point," *Yahoo Finance*, March 12, 2015, http://finance.yahoo.com/news/long-slow-death-cable-just-152700220.html.

110. Todd Spangler, "CBS All Access Available to Amazon Prime Members in U.S. as Add-On Channel," *Variety*, January 5, 2018, https://variety.com/2018/digital/news/cbs-all-access-amazon-prime-channel-1202654346/.

111. Brian Fung, "Comcast Rolls Out Trial of New Plan: Unlimited Data for an Extra $35," *Washington Post*, November 2, 2015, https://www.washingtonpost.com/news/the-switch/wp/2015/11/02/your-phone-company-already-limits-your-data-your-cable-company-could-be-next/.

112. DTVE Reporter, "US Netflix Use Tops DVR Ownership for the First Time."

113. Luke Russert, Alex Moe, Halimah Abudullah, and Corky Siemaszko, "'Spirit of History': House Democrats Hold Sit-In on Gun Control," *NBC News*, June 22, 2016, https://www.nbcnews.com/news/us-news/house-democrats-hold-sit-gun-control-n597041.

114. Rep. Eric Swalwell, *Periscope*, https://www.pscp.tv/RepSwalwell/1DXxylkZMoyJM.

115. Russell Berman, "When House Democrats Turned Out the Lights on Republicans," *Atlantic*, June 22, 2016, http://www.theatlantic.com/politics/archive/2016/06/when-democrats-turned-out-the-lights-on-republicans/488321/.

116. Taylor Lorenz, "How Rep. Eric Swalwell Became the Snapchat King of Congress," *Hill*, April 27, 2016, http://thehill.com/homenews/news/277737-swalwell-snapchat; "Democratic Sit-In Over Gun Violence Continues," *C-SPAN*, June 22, 2016, https://www.c-span.org/video/?411624-1/democratic-sit-continues-house-adjournment-july-5&live=.

117. Erik Wemple, "Covering Sit-in by House Democrats, C-SPAN Makes History via Periscope," *Washington Post*, June 22, 2016, https://www.washingtonpost.com/blogs/erik-wemple/wp/2016/06/22/covering-sit-in-by-house-democrats-c-span-makes-history-via-periscope/.

118. Cecilia Kang and Will Hobson, "Periscope and Other New Apps Threaten TV's Golden Egg: Live Sports," *Washington Post*, May 5, 2015, https://www.washingtonpost.com/business/economy/new-apps-threaten-tv-networks-golden-egg-live-sports/2015/05/05/b5d0b836-f347-11e4-84a6-6d7c67c50db0_story.html; Garrett Sloane, "Pirated NFL, MLB Games Proliferate on Facebook Live," *AdAge*, August 21, 2017, https://adage.com/article/digital/nfl-mlb-games-found-pirated-facebook-live-streams/310176.

CHAPTER 9

1. Jane C. Timm, "Trump Says He's No Longer Taking Hydroxychloroquine," *NBC News*, May 25, 2020, http://www.nbcnews.com/politics/donald-trump/trump-says-he-s-no-longer-taking-hydroxychloroquine-n1214301.

2. "George Floyd Protests: Misleading Footage and Conspiracy Theories Spread Online" *BBC*, June 2, 2020, http://www.bbc.com/news/52877751; Daisuke Wakabayashi, Davey Alba, and Marc Tracy, "Bill Gates, at Odds with Trump on Virus, Becomes a Right-Wing Target," *New York Times*, April 17, 2020, https://www.nytimes.com/2020/04/17/technology/bill-gates-virus-conspiracy-theories.html.

3. Edison Research, "The Infinite Dial 2020," www.edisonresearch.com/wp-content/uploads/2020/03/The-Infinite-Dial-2020-from-Edison-Research-and-Triton-Digital.pdf; Ian Sherr, "Bill Gates Calls COVID-19 Vaccine Conspiracy Theories 'Stupid,' but Many Believe Them," *CNET*, June 4, 2020, http://www.cnet.com/news/bill-gates-calls-wrongful-covid-19-vaccine-conspiracy-theories-stupid-but-many-people-believe-them/; Drew Harwell, "Is Your Pregnancy App Sharing Your Intimate Data With Your Boss?" *Washington Post*, April 10, 2019, http://www.washingtonpost.com/technology/2019/04/10/tracking-your-pregnancy-an-app-may-be-more-public-than-you-think/?arc404=true.

4. Joseph Cox, "I Gave a Bounty Hunter $300. Then He Located Our Phone," *Vice*, January 8, 2019, https://www.vice.com/en_us/article/nepxbz/i-gave-a-bounty-hunter-300-dollars-located-phone-microbilt-zumigo-tmobile.

5. Joanna Stern, "iPhone Privacy Is Broken . . . and Apps Are to Blame," *Wall Street Journal*, May 31, 2019, http://www.wsj.com/articles/iphone-privacy-is-brokenand-apps-are-to-blame-11559316401?mod=hp_lead_pos8.

6. Marie C. Baca, "These Apps May Have Told Facebook About the Last Time You Had Sex," *Washington Post*, September 17, 2019, http://www.washingtonpost.com/technology/2019/09/10/these-apps-may-have-told-facebook-about-last-time-you-had-sex/; Harwell, "Is Your Pregnancy App Sharing Your Intimate Data With Your Boss?"

7. Geoffrey Fowler, "It's the Middle of the Night. Do You Know Who Your iPhone Is Talking To?" *Washington Post*, May 28, 2019, http://www.washingtonpost.com/technology/2019/05/28/its-middle-night-do-you-know-who-your-iphone-is-talking/.

8. Jennifer Valentino-DeVries, Natasha Singer, Michael H. Keller, and Aaron Krolik, "Your Apps Know Where You Were Last Night, and They're Not Keeping It Secret," *New York Times*, December 10, 2018, http://www.nytimes.com/interactive/2018/12/10/business/location-data-privacy-apps.html.

9. Stern, "iPhone Privacy Is Broken."

10. National Research Council, *The Internet's Coming of Age* (Washington, DC: The National Academies Press, 2001), 29.

11. "Scientist Who Transformed the Internet," *Irish Times*, June 24, 2000.

12. Peter Grier, "In the Beginning, There Was ARPANET," *Air Force Magazine*, January 1997, 66.

13. Barnaby J. Feder, "Donald W. Davies, 75, Dies; Helped Refine Data Networks," *New York Times*, June 4, 2000.

14. Katie Hafner and Matthew Lyon, *Where Wizards Stay Up Late* (New York: Simon & Schuster, 1996).

15. Ibid.

16. Ibid.

17. Joseph Gallivan, "A Bit More Backbone: Internet II Is in the Wings," *Independent*, February 25, 1997; Jeffrey R. Young, "Internet2 Spurs Equipment Upgrades, but Use in Research Remains Limited," *Chronicle of Higher Education*, August 13, 1999; "About Us," Internet2, http://www.Internet2.edu/about-us/.

18. Stephen Segaller, *Nerds 2.0.1: A Brief History of the Internet* (New York: TV Books, 1998).

19. Ibid.

20. Ibid.

21. Jamie Tolentino, "Why Are People Still Using SMS in 2015?" *TNW*, February 16, 2015, http://thenextweb.com/future-of-communications/2015/02/16/people-still-using-sms-2015/.

22. Josh Constine, "AOL Instant Messenger Is Shutting down After 20 Years," *Tech Crunch*, October 6, 2017, http://social.techcrunch.com/2017/10/06/aol-instant-messenger-shut-down/.

23. John Abbruzzese, "The Rise and Fall of AIM, the Breakthrough AOL Never Wanted," *Mashable*, April 15, 2014, http://mashable.com/2014/04/15/aim-history/.

24. Segaller, *Nerds 2.0.1*.

25. Tim Berners-Lee, *Weaving the Web* (New York: HarperCollins, 1999), 4.

26. Anick Jesdanun, "From Two Users to 7 Million, Web's Come a Long Way," *Associated Press*, December 24, 2000.

27. Segaller, *Nerds 2.0.1*, 288.

28. Ibid., 291.

29. Ibid.

30. Kirsten Grind, Sam Schechner, Robert McMillan, and John West, "How Google Interferes With Its Search Algorithms and Changes Your Results," *Wall Street Journal*, November 15, 2019, http://www.wsj.com/articles/how-google-interferes-with-its-search-algorithms-and-changes-your-results-11573823753?mod=djem10point.

31. Grind, et al., "How Google Interferes With Its Search Algorithms."

32. Peter Sayer, "Yahoo's Legal Battle Over Nazi Items Continues," *Infoworld*, August 24, 2004, http://www.infoworld.com/article/2664810/application-development/yahoo-s-legal-battle-over-nazi-items-continues.html.

33. Johnny Lieu, "China Reiterates Its Stance on Internet Regulation to Google and Facebook," *Mashable*, December 18, 2017, https://mashable.com/2017/12/18/china-censorship-reminder-Internet/; Colin Daileda, "Trump's Still Tweeting From China Even Through the Country's Twitter Ban," *Mashable*, November 8, 2017, https://mashable.com/2017/11/08/twitter-china-donald-trump/.

34. Susannah Fox and Lee Rainie, "The Web at 25 in the U.S.," *Pew Research Center*, February 27, 2014, https://www.pewresearch.org/internet/2014/02/27/the-web-at-25-in-the-u-s/.

35. Andrew Perrin and Madhu Kumar, "About Three-in-Ten U.S. Adults Say They Are 'Almost Constantly' Online," *Pew Research Center*, July 25, 2019, http://www.pewresearch.org/fact-tank/2019/07/25/americans-going-online-almost-constantly/.

36. Edison Research, "The Infinite Dial 2020."

37. "Three Technology Revolutions," *Pew Research Center*, https://www.pewresearch.org/internet/three-technology-revolutions/; "Mobile Phone Ownership Over Time," *Pew Research Center*, June 12, 2019, https://www.pewresearch.org/internet/fact-sheet/mobile/; Andrew Perrin and Maeve Duggan, "American's Internet Access: 2000–2015," *Pew Research Center*, June 26, 2015, https://www.pewresearch.org/internet/2015/06/26/americans-internet-access-2000-2015/; Monica Anderson, Andrew Perrin, and JingJing Jiang, "11% of Americans Don't Use the Internet. Who Are They?" *Pew Research Center*, March 5, 2018.

38. Chris Anderson and Michael Wolff, "The Web Is Dead. Long Live the Internet," *Wired*, August 17, 2010, http://www.wired.com/2010/08/ff_webrip/.

39. "Digital News Fact Sheet," *Pew Research Center*, June 6, 2018.

40. Amy Mitchell and Jesse Holcomb, "State of the News Media 2016," *Pew Research Center*, June 15, 2016, https://www.journalism.org/2016/06/15/state-of-the-news-media-2016/2010/.

41. Berners-Lee, *Weaving the Web.*
42. Austin Bunn, "Human Portals," *Brill's Content*, May 2001.
43. LexisNexis, "Blogs."
44. Howard Kurtz, "After Blogs Got Hits, CBS Got a Black Eye," *Washington Post*, September 20, 2004; Alessandra Stanley, "The TV Watch; Signing Off, Rather's Wish for Viewers Is Still 'Courage,'" *New York Times*, March 10, 2005.
45. Eric Johnson, "How Apple Obsessive John Gruber Built Daring Fireball, the World's Most Powerful One-Man Media Company," *Recode*, June 30, 2016, https://www.recode.net/2016/6/30/12053348/john-gruber-daring-fireball-apple-podcast-recode-media.
46. Michael E. Miller, "'Humans of New York': Obama's Comment Is Big Moment for Beloved, Controversial Blog," *Washington Post*, September 4, 2015, https://www.washingtonpost.com/news/morning-mix/wp/2015/09/04/humans-of-new-york-obamas-comment-is-big-moment-for-beloved-controversial-blog/?tid=pm_national_pop_b.
47. Ibid.
48. Kristyn Martin, "Coronavirus Social Distancing Rules Change How Humans of New York Tells Stories," *Yahoo*, March 19, 2020, http://www.yahoo.com/lifestyle/coronavirus-social-distancing-rules-humans-of-new-york-205759876.html.
49. Kathryn Dill, "Here's the Tumblr Founder's Favorite Tumblr (and Why It Matters)," *Inc.*, February 20, 2013, http://www.inc.com/kathryn-dill/whats-your-favorite-tumblr-founder-david-karp.html.
50. Evan Hill, Ainara Tiefenthäler, Christiaan Triebert, Drew Jordan, Haley Willis and Robin Stein, "How George Floyd Was Killed in Police Custody." May 31, 2020, *The New York Times*, https://www.nytimes.com/2020/05/31/us/george-floyd-investigation.html.
51. Derrick Bryson Taylor, "George Floyd Protests: A Timeline." July 10, 2020, *The New York Times*, https://www.nytimes.com/article/george-floyd-protests-timeline.html.
52. Flora Carmichael, Alistair Coleman, Joice Etutu, Jack Goodman, Shayan Sardarizadeh, Marianna Spring, Olga Robinson and Ben Strick, "George Floyd protests: Misleading footage and conspiracy theories spread online." BBC News, https://www.bbc.com/news/52877751.
53. Nazila Fathi, "In a Death Seen Around the World, a Symbol of Iranian Protests," *New York Times*, June 23, 2009.
54. Ibid.
55. Hiawatha Bray, "Finding a Way Around Iranian Censorship," *Boston Globe*, June 19, 2009.
56. Gary Gentile, "Hollywood Net Survivor: IFILM Hopes to Build Media Company," *Billings Gazette*, October 24, 2000, http://billingsgazette.com/business/technology/hollywood-net-survivor-ifilm-hopes-to-build-media-company-from/article_d8cf30d6-55c0-5c6b-a648-1e41c31a6f02.html.
57. Glenn Kenny, "Fandor: A Streaming Rabbit Hole Worth Falling Down," *New York Times*, April 7, 2017, https://www.nytimes.com/2017/04/07/movies/fandor-a-streaming-rabbit-hole-worth-falling-down.html.
58. Jon Healey, "Pay-Per-View Sites Offer New Options for Computer Movie-Viewing," *San Jose Mercury News*, May 21, 2000.
59. Segaller, *Nerds 2.0.1*, 125.
60. Ibid, 152.
61. Steven Levy, *Hackers* (New York: Penguin Books, 1994); Steven Levy, "The Day I Got Napsterized," *Newsweek*, May 28, 2001, 23–31.
62. "Presidential Election Results: Donald J. Trump Wins," *New York Times*, August 9, 2017, http://www.nytimes.com/elections/results/president.
63. Philip Bump, "Donald Trump Will Be President Thanks to 80,000 People in Three States," *Washington Post*, December 1, 2016, https://www.washingtonpost.com/news/the-fix/wp/2016/12/01/donald-trump-will-be-president-thanks-to-80000-people-in-three-states/.
64. Carol D. Leonnig, Tom Hamburger, and Rosalind S. Helderman, "Russian Firm Tied to Pro-Kremlin Propaganda Advertised on Facebook During Election," *Washington Post*, September 6, 2017, https://www.washingtonpost.com/politics/facebook-says-it-sold-political-ads-to-russian-company-during-2016-election/2017/09/06/32f01fd2-931e-11e7-89fa-bb822a46da5b_story.html; Greg Miller and Adam Entous, "Declassified Report Says Putin 'Ordered' Effort to Undermine Faith in U.S. Election and Help Trump," *Washington Post*, January 6, 2017, https://www.washingtonpost.com/world/national-security/intelligence-chiefs-expected-in-new-york-to-brief-trump-on-russian-hacking/2017/01/06/5f591416-d41a-11e6-9cb0-54ab630851e8_story.html; Raffi Khatchadourian, "Julian Assange, a Man Without a Country," *New Yorker*, August 21, 2017, https://www.newyorker.com/magazine/2017/08/21/julian-assange-a-man-without-a-country; Adrian Chen, "A So-Called Expert's Uneasy Dive Into the Trump-Russia Frenzy," *New Yorker*, February 22, 2018, https://www.newyorker.com/tech/elements/a-so-called-experts-uneasy-dive-into-the-trump-russia-frenzy; Selina Wang, "Twitter Finds 1,062 More Accounts Linked to Russian Agency," *Bloomberg*, January 19, 2018, https://www.bloomberg.com/news/articles/2018-01-19/twitter-finds-1-062-more-accounts-linked-to-russian-agency?ex_cid=SigDig; Garrett Sloane, "Facebook Says Content Wasn't the Problem With Russian Election-Season Ads," *Ad Age*, October 3, 2017, http://adage.com/article/digital/facebook-content-problem-foreign-ads/310739/.
65. Chen, "A So-Called Expert's Uneasy Dive."
66. Nate Silver, "How Much Did Russian Interference Affect the 2016 Election?" *FiveThirtyEight*, February 16, 2018, https://fivethirtyeight.com/features/how-much-did-russian-interference-affect-the-2016-election/.
67. Jamie Portman, "Confronting Cyberspace," *Calgary Herald*, June 11, 1995.
68. Ibid.
69. Segaller, *Nerds 2.0.1*, 359.
70. Thomas Standage, *The Victorian Internet* (New York: Berkley Books, 1998), xvii–xviii.
71. "Individuals Using the Internet (% of Population)," *World Bank*, https://data.worldbank.org/indicator/it.net.user.zs.
72. Salvador Rodriguez, "60% of World's Population Still Won't Have Internet by the End of 2014," *Los Angeles Times*, May 7, 2014, http://www.latimes.com/business/technology/la-fi-tn-60-world-population-3-billion-Internet-2014-20140507-story.html; "ICT Facts and Figures—the World in 2015," *ITU*.
73. Ibid.
74. Perrin and Duggan, "American's Internet Access: 2000–2015."
75. Berners-Lee, *Weaving the Web.*
76. Leslie Regan Shade, "Is There Free Speech on the Net? Censorship in the Global Information Infrastructure," in *Cultures of the Internet*, ed. Rob Shields (Thousand Oaks, CA: SAGE, 1996).
77. Berners-Lee, *Weaving the Web*, 80.
78. Daniel Jacobson, "API Update: New Transcript API and Much More," *NPR*, July 29, 2009, http://www.npr.org/blogs/inside/2009/07/api_update_transcript_api_and.html.
79. Frank Ahrens, "2002's News, Yesterday's Sell-Off," *Washington Post*, September 9, 2008.
80. Hayley Tsukayama, "Apple TV Review: If the Future of Television Is Apps, Sign Me Up," *Washington Post*, October 30, 2015, https://www.washingtonpost.com/news/the-switch/wp/2015/10/30/apple-tv-review-if-the-future-of-television-is-apps-sign-me-up/.

CHAPTER 10

1. Aaron Calvin, "Meet Carson King, the 'Iowa Legend' Who's Raised More Than $1 Million for Charity off of a Sign Asking for Beer Money," *Des Moines Register*, September 24, 2019, http://www.desmoinesregister.com/story/sports/college/iowa-state/football/2019/09/24/meet-carson-king-whos-raised-over-1-million-charity-asking-beer-money-childrens-hospital-tweet/2427538001/.

2. Tim Jamison, "Iowa Oktoberfest Pulls Busch Light Over Carson King Controversy," *Quad-City Times*, September 26, 2019, http://qctimes.com/news/state-and-regional/iowa/iowa-oktoberfest-pulls-busch-light-over-carson-king-controversy/article_1a5af2af-845b-5613-a872-bbea41c7b23b.html.

3. "This Saturday Is Now Carson King Day in Iowa, by Gubernatorial Decree," *Gazette*, September 25, 2019, http://www.thegazette.com/subject/news/government/this-saturday-is-now-carson-king-day-in-iowa-by-gubernatorial-decree-20190925.

4. Julia Reinstein, "The Reporter Fired in the Iowa Milkshake Duck Scandal Said He Feels 'Abandoned' by the *Des Moines Register*," *BuzzFeed*, September 30, 2019, http://www.buzzfeednews.com/article/juliareinstein/des-moines-register-iowa-reporter-fired-aaron-calvin-carson?utm_source=dynamic&utm_campaign=bfsharefacebook&ref=mobile_share&fbclid=IwAR1OvHgVCRPQ74YSCtt_tp1_5qttQFNjPnCuOy-OPaZX616hiYkYgayzYS8.

5. Vanessa Miller, "Carson King's UI Children's Hospital Campaign Reaches $2.95 Million," *Gazette*, October 1, 2019, http://www.thegazette.com/subject/news/carson-king-busch-light-childrens-hospital-fundraiser-3-million-iowa-state-university-of-iowa-20191001?utm_campaign=magnet&utm_source=entity_page&utm_medium=related_articles.

6. Ralph Hanson, "Is There Ever Grace for Being Stupid on Social Media?" *Living in a Media World*, April 15, 2020, http://www.ralphehanson.com/2018/07/28/is-there-ever-grace-for-being-stupid-on-social-media/.

7. Susana Polo, "So Here's the Slut-Shaming, Homophobic Post on Superheroes by . . . the Director of *Guardians of the Galaxy*," *The Mary Sue*, November 28, 2012, http://www.themarysue.com/james-gunnsuperhero-sex-post/.

8. Megan McArdle, "People Are Getting Fired for Old Bad Tweets. Here's How to Fix It," *Washington Post*, July 24, 2018, http://www.washingtonpost.com/opinions/we-need-a-statute-of-limitations-on-bad-tweets/2018/07/24/a84e335c-8f7d-11e8-b769-e3fff17f0689_story.html.

9. M. Chethan and Mohan Ramanathan, "Social Knowledge: The Technology Behind," in *Social Knowledge: Using Social Media to Know What You Know*, ed. John P. Girard and JoAnn L. Girard (Hershey, PA: Information Science Reference, 2011).

10. Matt Stevens, "As the Hashtag Celebrates Its 10th Birthday, Are We #Blessed?" *New York Times*, August 23, 2017, https://www.nytimes.com/2017/08/23/business/hashtag-anniversary-twitter.html.

11. "Who Uses YouTube, WhatsApp and Reddit," *Pew Research Center*, June 12, 2019, http://www.pewresearch.org/internet/chart/who-uses-youtube-whatsapp-and-reddit/; Edison Research, "The Infinite Dial 2020," http://www.edisonresearch.com/wp-content/uploads/2020/03/The-Infinite-Dial-2020-from-Edison-Research-and-Triton-Digital.pdf.

12. Richard Waters, "How to Get Seriously Rich in Two Easy Moves," *Financial Times*, October 10, 2006, 25.

13. *Charlie Rose*, "YouTube Co-founders," interview by Charlie Rose, PBS, August 11, 2006.

14. Ibid.

15. "Who Uses YouTube, WhatsApp and Reddit."

16. Jose Antonio Vargas, "Letter From Palo Alto: The Face of Facebook," *New Yorker*, September 13, 2010, http://www.newyorker.com/reporting/2010/09/20/100920fa_fact_vargas.

17. Edison Research, "The Infinite Dial 2020"; David Cohen, "2.1 Billion People Use Facebook's Family of Apps on a Daily Basis," *Adweek*, July 26, 2019, http://www.adweek.com/digital/2-1-billion-people-use-facebooks-family-of-apps-on-a-daily-basis/.

18. Ashley Carman, "Facebook Groups Are Falling Apart Over Black Lives Matter Posts," *Verge*, June 5, 2020, http://www.theverge.com/2020/6/5/21279319/facebook-group-moderation-black-lives-matter-movement.

19. Raisa Bruner, "A Brief History of Instagram's Fateful First Day," *Time*, July 16, 2016, http://time.com/4408374/instagram-anniversary/.

20. Anthony Ha, "Instagram Is Testing a New Way for Celebrities and Influencers to Identify Their Sponsored Posts," *Tech Crunch*, June 14, 2017, https://techcrunch.com/2017/06/14/instagram-sponsored-posts/.

21. Jenn Chen, "Important Instagram Stats You Need to Know for 2020," *Sprout Social*, May 6, 2020, http://sproutsocial.com/insights/instagram-stats/.

22. Kurt Wagner, "Here's Why Facebook's $1 Billion Instagram Acquisition Was Such a Big Deal," *Recode*, April 9, 2017, https://www.recode.net/2017/4/9/15235940/facebook-instagram-acquisition-anniversary.

23. Aaron Smith and Monica Anderson, "Social Media Use in 2018," *Pew Research Center*, March 1, 2018, http://www.pewinternet.org/2018/03/01/social-media-use-in-2018/.

24. Edison Research, "The Infinite Dial 2020."

25. Smith and Anderson, "Social Media Use in 2018."

26. J. Clement, "Snapchat Daily Active Users 2019," *Statista*, April 23, 2020, http://www.statista.com/statistics/545967/snapchat-app-dau/.

27. Kevin Roose, "Snapchat's New Test: Grow Like Facebook, Without the Baggage," *New York Times*, November 15, 2017, https://www.nytimes.com/2017/11/15/business/snapchats-new-test-grow-like-facebook-without-the-baggage.html.

28. Taylor Lorenz, "How Rep. Eric Swalwell Became the Snapchat King of Congress," *Hill*, April 27, 2016, http://thehill.com/homenews/news/277737-swalwell-snapchat.

29. Kevin Maney, "Short & Tweet," *Upstart*, February 11, 2009; Britney Fitzgerald, "Twitter Use Is on the Rise, Daily Use Doubles: Pew," *Huffington Post*, June 1, 2012, http://www.huffingtonpost.com/2012/06/01/twitter-use-stats-growth_n_1559716.html?ref=technology; "Company," Twitter, https://about.twitter.com/company.

30. Jon Swartz, "Twitter Has Millions Tweeting in Public Communication Service," *USA Today*, May 26, 2009.

31. Dominic Rushee, "What Makes Twitter Worth a Billion Dollars?" *Sunday Times*, September 27, 2009.

32. Jacob Kastrenakes, "Twitter Says People Are Tweeting More, but Not Longer, With 208-Character Limit," *Verge*, February 8, 2018, https://www.theverge.com/2018/2/8/16990308/twitter-280-character-tweet-length.

33. Michael J. Socolow, "The Trouble With TikTok," *POLITICO Magazine*, November 2, 2019, http://www.politico.com/magazine/story/2019/11/02/the-trouble-with-tiktok-229890.

34. Casey Newton, "The Mounting Pressures on TikTok," *Revue*, November 4, 2019, http://www.getrevue.co/profile/caseynewton/issues/the-mounting-pressures-on-tiktok-208003.

35. Jacob Kastrenakes, "TikTok Now Lets Parents Set Restrictions on Their Kids' Accounts," *Verge*, April 16, 2020, http://www

.theverge.com/2020/4/16/21222817/tiktok-family-pairing -linked-accounts.

36. Hannah Donovan and Geneviève Patterson, "How TikTok Decides Who to Make Famous," *TechCrunch*, February 17, 2020, https://techcrunch.com/2020/02/17/how-tiktok-decides -who-to-make-famous/.

37. Nolan D. McCaskill, "Trump Credits Social Media for His Election," *Politico*, October 20, 2017, https://www.politico.com/ story/2017/10/20/trump-social-media-election-244009.

38. Ibid.

39. S. A. Miller, "The Match Made in Heaven: Trump and Twitter," *Washington Times*, December 28, 2017, https://www .washingtontimes.com/news/2017/dec/28/donald-trumps -twitter-use-changed-presidential-pol/.

40. Nicholas Carr, "Why Trump Tweets (and Why We Listen)," *Politico*, January 26, 2018, https://www.politico.com/magazine/ story/2018/01/26/donald-trump-twitter-addiction-216530.

41. Tamara Keith, "From 'Covfefe' to Slamming CNN: Trump's Year in Tweets," *NPR*, December 20, 2017, https://www.npr .org/2017/12/20/571617079/a-year-of-the-trump-presidency-in -tweets.

42. John Herrman and Charlie Savage, "Trump's Blocking of Twitter Users Is Unconstitutional, Judge Says," *New York Times*, May 23, 2018, https://www.nytimes.com/2018/05/23/business/ media/trump-twitter-block.html.

43. Abby Ohlheiser, "The One Word That Lets Politicians Get Away with Breaking the Rules on Social Media," *Washington Post*, September 25, 2019, http://www.washingtonpost.com/ technology/2019/09/25/newsworthiness-one-word-that-lets -politicians-get-away-with-spreading-misinformation-social -media/.

44. Ohlheiser, "The One Word That Lets Politicians Get Away with Breaking the Rules."

45. Davey Alba, Kate Conger, and Raymond Zhong, "Twitter Adds Warnings to Trump and White House Tweets, Fueling Tensions," *New York Times*, May 29, 2020, http:// www.nytimes.com/2020/05/29/technology/trump-twitter -minneapolis-george-floyd.html?action=click&module= Spotlight&pgtype=Homepage.

46. Chip Stewart, "Guest Blog Post: Executive Orders and Social Media," *Living in a Media World*, June 1, 2020, http://www .ralphehanson.com/2020/05/30/guest-blog-post-executive -orders-social-media/.

47. Unless otherwise noted, the material from this history of video games is drawn from the following sources: Brian J. Wardyga, *The Video Games Textbook: History, Business, Technology* (Boca Raton, FL: CRC Press, 2018); Tristan Donovan, *Replay: The History of Video Games* (East Sussex, UK: Yellow Ant, 2010); Steven L. Kent, *The Ultimate History of Video Games* (New York: Three Rivers Press, 2001).

48. Alan Cowell, "Overlooked No More: Alan Turing, Condemned Code Breaker and Computer Visionary," *New York Times*, June 5, 2019, http://www.nytimes.com/2019/06/05/obituaries/alan -turing-overlooked.html.

49. Donovan, *Replay*.

50. Douglas Martin, "Ralph H. Baer, Inventor of First System for Home Video Games, Is Dead at 92," *New York Times*, December 7, 2014, http://www.nytimes.com/2014/12/08/ business/ralph-h-baer-dies-inventor-of-odyssey-first-system -for-home-video-games.html.

51. Leslie Berlin, "The Inside Story of 'Pong' and Nolan Bushnell's Early Days at Atari," *Wired*, November 15, 2017, http://www .wired.com/story/inside-story-of-pong-excerpt/.

52. Donovan, *Replay*.

53. Wardyga, *Video Games Textbook*.

54. Donovan, *Replay*.

55. Wardyga, *Video Games Textbook*.

56. "Domestic Box Office For 1981," *Box Office Mojo*, www .boxofficemojo.com/year/1981/.

57. Donovan, *Replay*.

58. Ibid.

59. Kent, *Ultimate History of Video Games*.

60. Wardyga, *Video Games Textbook*.

61. Donovan, *Replay*.

62. Tom Huddleston Jr., "How 'Animal Crossing'and the Coronavirus Pandemic Made the Nintendo Switch Fly Off Shelves," *CNBC*, June 2, 2020, http://www.cnbc .com/2020/06/02/nintendo-switch-animal-crossing-and -coronavirus-led-to-record-sales.html.

63. Donovan, *Replay*.

64. Ibid.

65. Ibid.

66. Ibid.

67. Raymond Hernandez, "Clinton Urges Inquiry Into Hidden Sex in Grand Theft Auto Game," *New York Times*, July 14, 2005, http://www.nytimes.com/2005/07/14/nyregion/clinton-urges -inquiry-into-hidden-sex-in-grand-theft-auto-game.html.

68. Chris Plante, "Herman Cain Breaks Five-Year Silence on Pokémon," *Verge*, July 19, 2016, http://www.theverge .com/2016/7/19/12227602/pokemon-go-nintnedo-herman -cain.

69. Mansoor Iqbal, "Pokémon GO Revenue and Usage Statistics (2020)," *Business of Apps*, June 23, 2020, http://www .businessofapps.com/data/pokemon-go-statistics/.

70. I would like to thank Charley Reed, a communications graduate student at the University of Nebraska at Omaha, for his research and work on the video game section of this chapter.

71. Andrew Edwards, "Video Games? Microsoft Pitches Xbox 360 as an Entertainment Hub," *Silicon Valley News*, June 4, 2012; Paul Tassi, "Twitch Starts Swinging YouTube-Like Copyright Sledgehammer [Updated]," *Forbes*, August 7, 2014, http://www .forbes.com/sites/insertcoin/2014/08/07/twitch-starts-swinging -youtube-like-copyright-sledgehammer/.

72. Jim Rutenberg, "Obama Aims TV Ads at Younger Voters," *New York Times*, October 8, 2008, https://thecaucus.blogs.nytimes .com/2008/10/08/obama-aims-tv-ads-at-younger-voters/.

73. Seth Schiesel, "Finding Community in Virtual Town Squares," *New York Times*, November 5, 2005.

74. Max Cherney, "This Violent Videogame Has Made More Money Than Any Movie Ever," *MarketWatch*, April 9, 2018, https://www.marketwatch.com/story/this-violent-videogame -has-made-more-money-than-any-movie-ever-2018-04-06.

75. "All Time Worldwide Box Office Grosses," *Box Office Mojo*, http://www.boxofficemojo.com/alltime/world/.

76. Pamela McClintock, "Global 2015 Box Office: Revenue Hits Record $38 Billion-Plus," *Hollywood Reporter*, January 3, 2016, http://www.hollywoodreporter.com/news/global-2015 -box-office-revenue-851749; Chris Morris, "Level Up! Video Game Industry Revenues Soar in 2015," *Fortune*, February 16, 2016, http://fortune.com/2016/02/16/video-game-industry -revenues-2015/.

77. Ken Paulson, "Court's Video-Game Ruling Shields Emerging Media," *First Amendment Center*, June 27, 2011.

78. Amanda Lenhart, Joseph Kahne, Ellen Middaugh, Alexandra Macgill, Chris Evans, and Jessica Vitak, "Teens, Video Games and Civics," *Pew Research Center*, September 16, 2008, https://

www.pewresearch.org/internet/2008/09/16/teens-video-games
-and-civics/.

79. Amanda Lenhart, Sydney Jones, and Alexandra Macgill, "Pew Internet Project Data Memo: Adults and Video Games," in *Pew Internet and American Life Project* (Washington, DC: Pew Foundation, 2008).

80. Dave Thier, "20,000 People Are Watching a Fish Play Pokémon on Twitch," *Forbes*, August 8, 2014, http://www.forbes.com/ sites/davidthier/2014/08/08/20000-people-are-watching-a -fish-play-pokemon/; Jason Koebler, "An Exclusive Interview With the Fish Playing Pokémon," *Motherboard*, August 8, 2014, https://www.vice.com/en_us/article/vvbzey/an-exclusive -interview-with-the-fish-playing-pokemon.

81. German Lopez, "Why Amazon Spent $970 Million to Buy Twitch," *Vox*, August 26, 2014, http://www.vox .com/2014/8/26/6067085/amazon-twitch-tv-video-games-live -streaming-league-of-legends-dota-2.

82. Mike Hume, "Travis Scott Will Go on a 'World Tour' inside Fortnite," *Washington Post*, April 20, 2020, http://www .washingtonpost.com/video-games/2020/04/20/travis-scott -fortnite-concert/.

83. Aaron Blackman, "Guest Blog Post: Ninja Reshapes Streaming Video Games in 2018," *Living in a Media* World, May 1, 2018, https://www.ralphehanson.com/2018/05/01/guest-blog-post -ninja-reshapes-streaming-video-games-in-2018/. Thanks to Aaron Blackman for his guest blog post at *Living in a Media World* on which this section is based.

84. The material on eSports is drawn from the guest post written by my colleague Aaron Blackman at "Heroes of the Dorm on ESPN 2," *Living in a Media World*, April 12, 2016, www .ralphehanson.com/2016/04/12/guest-blog-post-heroes-of-the -dorm-on-espn2/; Kellen Beck, "Premium eSports Shows Are Heading to Hulu," *Mashable*, October 9, 2017, https://mashable .com/2017/10/09/hulu-esports-esl/.

85. Huddleston,. How 'Animal Crossing' and the Coronavirus Pandemic Made the Nintendo Switch Fly Off Shelves.

86. Gene Park, "Alexandria Ocasio-Cortez Is Now Playing Animal Crossing. And She's Visiting Her Followers," *Washington Post*, May 8, 2020, http://www.washingtonpost.com/video -games/2020/05/07/alexandria-ocasio-cortez-is-now-playing -animal-crossing-shes-visiting-her-followers/.

87. Imran Khan, "In Extraordinary Times, Ramadan Finds a Place in Animal Crossing," *Washington Post*, May 15, 2020, http:// www.washingtonpost.com/video-games/2020/05/15/ramadan -animal-crossing/.

88. Hume, "Travis Scott Will Go on a 'World Tour' Inside Fortnite."

89. Travis Andrews, "Thousands Gathered Saturday for a Music Festival. Don't Worry: It Was in Minecraft," *Washington Post*, April 15, 2020, http://www.washingtonpost.com/ technology/2020/04/15/minecraft-music-festival-american -football-nether-meant/.

90. "How Diverse Are Video Gamers—and the Characters They Play?" *Nielsen*, March 24, 2015, http://www.nielsen.com/us/en/ insights/news/2015/how-diverse-are-video-gamers-and-the -characters-they-play.html.

91. Kiva Bay, "Fat Basement Dweller," *Medium*, December 8, 2015, https://medium.com/@kivabay/fat-basement-dweller -f49f12dd8ac3.

92. Leif Johnson, "This Game Is Forcing Some Players to Be Women, and They're Freaking Out," *Motherboard*, April 10, 2016, http://motherboard.vice.com/read/this-game-is-forcing -some-players-to-be-women-and-theyre-freaking-out.

CHAPTER 11

1. David Remnick, "Postscript: Marie Colvin, 1956–2012," *New Yorker*, February 22, 2012, https://www.newyorker.com/news/ news-desk/postscript-marie-colvin-1956-2012.

2. Anne Barnard, "Syrian Forces Aimed to Kill Journalists, U.S. Court Is Told," *New York Times*, April 9, 2018, https://www .nytimes.com/2018/04/09/world/middleeast/syria-marie-colvin -death.html.

3. Dana Priest, "War Reporter Marie Colvin Was Tracked, Targeted, and Killed by Assad's Forces, Family Says," *Washington Post*, July 9, 2016, https://www.washingtonpost .com/world/national-security/war-reporter-marie-colvin -was-tracked-targeted-and-killed-by-assads-forces-family -says/2016/07/09/62968844-453a-11e6-88d0-6adee48be8bc_ story.html?tid=sm_fb.

4. Barnard, "Syrian Forces Aimed to Kill Journalists."

5. Priest, "War Reporter Marie Colvin Was Tracked."

6. Evgenia Peretz, "The Girls at the Front," *Vanity Fair*, June 22, 2002, https://www.vanityfair.com/culture/2002/06/female-war -correspondents-200206.

7. Ibid.

8. Ibid.

9. Marie Colvin, "Marie Colvin: 'Our Mission Is to Report These Horrors of War With Accuracy and Without Prejudice,'" *Guardian*, February 22, 2012, https://www.theguardian.com/ commentisfree/2012/feb/22/marie-colvin-our-mission-is-to -speak-truth.

10. Fred S. Siebert, Theodore Peterson, and Wilbur Schramm, *Four Theories of the Press* (Urbana: University of Illinois Press, 1956).

11. John C. Nerone, ed., *Last Rights: Revisiting* Four Theories of the Press (Urbana and Chicago: University of Illinois Press, 1995), 153.

12. Denis McQuail, *McQuail's Mass Communication Theory*, 6th ed. (Thousand Oaks, CA: SAGE, 2010).

13. "DRC Intelligence Agents Shut Down TV Channel in Bukavu," *Reporters Without Borders*, March 23, 2018, https:// rsf.org/en/news/drc-intelligence-agents-shut-down-tv -channel-bukavu; "RSF Index 2018: Hatred of Journalism Threatens Democracies," *Reporters Without Borders*, https:// rsf.org/en/rsf-index-2018-hatred-journalism-threatens -democracies.

14. "RSF Index 2018."

15. "2020 World Press Freedom Index," Reporters Without Borders, 2020, https://rsf.org/en/ranking.

16. Nerone, *Last Rights*.

17. Siebert et al., *Four Theories of the Press*.

18. "2020 World Press Freedom Index."

19. Nerone, *Last Rights*.

20. Siebert et al., *Four Theories of the Press*.

21. Nerone, *Last Rights*.

22. Siebert et al., *Four Theories of the Press*.

23. Nerone, *Last Rights*.

24. "RSF Index 2018."

25. Ralph Hanson, "Living in a Media World," *Living in a Media World*, 2020, http://www.ralphehanson.com/.

26. Siebert et al., *Four Theories of the Press*.

27. Doris Graber, *Mass Media and American Politics*, 7th ed. (Washington, DC: CQ Press, 2006).

28. "2020 World Press Freedom Index."

29. Nerone, *Last Rights*.

30. McQuail, *McQuail's Mass Communication Theory*, 176.

31. Bob Garfield, "Pulling the Plug," *On the Media*, May 18, 2007, http://www.wnyc.org/story/129427-pulling-the-plug/; Associated Press, "Anti-Chavez TV Company Struggles to Survive," *San Diego Union-Tribune*, May 22, 2012, http://www.sandiegouniontribune.com/sdut-anti-chavez-tv-company-struggles-to-survive-2012may22-story.html; Silvia Higuera, "Venezuela's Supreme Court: Inter-American Court's Ruling on RCTV Is 'Unenforceable,'" *Journalism in the Americas Blog*, September 22, 2015, https://knightcenter.utexas.edu/blog/00-16310-venezuelas-supreme-court-inter-american-courts-ruling-rctv-unenforceable; "RSF Index 2018."

32. Nerone, *Last Rights.*

33. Siebert et al., *Four Theories of the Press.*

34. Nerone, *Last Rights.*

35. Alan Wells, "Introduction," in *World Broadcasting: A Comparative View*, ed. Alan Wells (Norwood, NJ: Ablex, 1996).

36. Ken Auletta, *The Highwaymen* (San Diego, CA: Harcourt Brace, 1998), 209.

37. Ibid., 209–210.

38. Rowland Lorimer and Mike Gasher, *Mass Communication in Canada*, 5th ed. (Don Mills, ON: Oxford University Press, 2004).

39. Ibid.; Brian Morton, "Feature Film Sector Slows as TV Production Ramps Up," *Vancouver Sun*, May 28, 2012, https://www.pressreader.com/canada/vancouver-sun/20120528/281822870848372; Toronto City Council Economic Development Committee, "Film and Television Industry Facts," *ACTRA Toronto*, April 2015, http://www.actratoronto.com/advocacy/industry-facts/; "Profile 2017: Economic Report on the Screen-Based Media Production Industry in Canada," *Canadian Media Producers Association*, https://telefilm.ca/wp-content/uploads/cmpa2017engfeb08.pdf.

40. Bob Garfield, "God Is Great (Funny, Too)," *On the Media*, May 18, 2007, http://www.wnyc.org/story/129430-god-is-great-funny-too/.

41. Ibid.

42. "2020 World Press Freedom Index."

43. Lorimer and Gasher, *Mass Communication in Canada.*

44. "2020 World Press Freedom Index."

45. Matthew Rusher, "Western Europe," in *World Broadcasting: A Comparative View*, ed. Alan Wells (Norwood, NJ: Ablex, 1996), 45.

46. Alan Wells, "United Kingdom," in *World Broadcasting: A Comparative View*, ed. Alan Wells (Norwood, NJ: Ablex, 1996).

47. Geoffrey Wheatcroft and Stephen Sandy, "Who Needs the BBC?" *Atlantic Monthly*, March 2001, 53.

48. "BBC's Combined Global Audience Revealed at 308 Million," *BBC*, May 21, 2015, https://www.bbc.co.uk/mediacentre/latestnews/2015/combined-global-audience.

49. "Africa's Dramas Played Out on the Beeb," *Economist*, January 16, 1999, 44.

50. Ibid.

51. Kevin Williams, *European Media Studies* (London: Hodder Arnold, 2005); "Facts & Figures," *Association of Commercial Television in Europe*, 2012, http://www.acte.be/; "Our Sector," *Association of Commercial Television in Europe*, https://acte.be/about-us/our-sector.

52. Graber, *Mass Media and American Politics.*

53. Brooke Gladstone, "On Je Suis Charlie," *On the Media*, January 9, 2015, http://www.wnyc.org/story/on-je-suis-charlie/#transcript.

54. Brian Love, "Refile-No Rule, No Regrets for French Cartoonists in Mohammad Storm," *Reuters*, September 19, 2012, http://www.reuters.com/article/film-protests-charlie-idUSL5E8KJE6320120919.

55. Mark Memmott, "Why You're Not Seeing Those 'Charlie Hebdo' Cartoons," *NPR*, January 10, 2015, http://www.npr.org/sections/thetwo-way/2015/01/10/376098073/why-youre-not-seeing-those-charlie-hebdo-cartoons.

56. Margaret Sullivan, "With New *Charlie Hebdo* Cover, News Value Should Have Prevailed," *New York Times*, January 14, 2015, https://publiceditor.blogs.nytimes.com/2015/01/14/with-new-charlie-hebdo-cover-news-value-should-have-prevailed/.

57. Aaron Blake, "How Do Americans Feel About Muhammad Cartoons?" *Washington Post*, January 7, 2015, https://www.washingtonpost.com/news/the-fix/wp/2015/01/07/how-do-americans-feel-about-muhammad-cartoons/.

58. Flemming Rose, "Why I Published Those Cartoons," *Washington Post*, February 19, 2006.

59. Daryl Cagle, "Two Kinds of Offensive Cartoonists," *Cagle Cartoons*, February 13, 2006, http://www.caglecartoons.com/column.asp?ColumnID=%7B3FA565D3-2A09-4772-8135-174B4DDF1AD4%7D.

60. Philip Kennicott, "Clash Over Cartoons Is a Caricature of Civilization," *Washington Post*, February 4, 2006.

61. Ibid.

62. Agence France-Presse, "Danish Cartoonist Attacker Has 10-Year Sentence Confirmed," *Vancouver Sun*, May 2, 2012.

63. Angela Charlton, "Depictions Put Press Freedoms to the Test," *Star-Ledger*, February 7, 2006.

64. Staff, "Forms of Intolerance," *Boston Globe*, February 4, 2006.

65. Christopher Dickey, Mark Hosenball, and Geoffrey Cowley, "A Needless Tragedy," *Newsweek*, September 22, 1997.

66. Larysa Pyk, "Legislative Update: Putting the Brakes on Paparazzi," *Journal of Art and Entertainment Law* 187, no. 9 (1998).

67. Associated Press, "Magazine Fined Over Picture of Diana and Dodi," *Ottawa Citizen*, April 29, 1998.

68. Ester Laushway, "What Price Privacy?" *Europe*, October 1997.

69. "Whose Life Is It Anyway?" *Economist*, March 9, 2002.

70. Jane Kirtley, "Privacy for Sale," *American Journalism Review*, March 2001.

71. Adam Satariano, "What the G.D.P.R, Europe's Tough New Data Law, Means for You," *New York Times*, May 6, 2018, https://www.nytimes.com/2018/05/06/technology/gdpr-european-privacy-law.html.

72. Tony Romm, "France Fines Google Nearly $57 Million for First Major Violation of New European Privacy Regime," *Washington Post*, January 21, 2019, http://www.washingtonpost.com/world/europe/france-fines-google-nearly-57-million-for-first-major-violation-of-new-european-privacy-regime/2019/01/21/89e7ee08-1d8f-11e9-a759-2b8541bbbe20_story.html.

73. Samuel Gibbs, "Google to Extend 'Right to Be Forgotten' to All Its Domains Accessed in EU," *Guardian*, February 11, 2016, https://www.theguardian.com/technology/2016/feb/11/google-extend-right-to-be-forgotten-googlecom.

74. Farhad Manjoo, "'Right to Be Forgotten' Online Could Spread," *New York Times*, August 5, 2015, http://www.nytimes.com/2015/08/06/technology/personaltech/right-to-be-forgotten-online-is-poised-to-spread.html.

75. David Meyer, "People Have Asked Google to Remove 2.4 Million Links About Them: Here's What They Want to Forget," *Fortune*, February 28, 2018, http://fortune.com/2018/02/28/google-right-to-be-forgotten-europe-reasons-eu/.

76. Donnalyn Pompper, "Latin America and the Caribbean," in *World Broadcasting: A Comparative View*, ed. Alan Wells (Norwood, NJ: Ablex, 1996).

77. Thomas L. McPhail, *Global Communication: Theories, Stakeholders, and Trends* (Malden, MA: Blackwell, 2006).

78. "2016 World Press Freedom Index – Leaders Paranoid About Journalists," Reporters Without Borders, https://rsf.org/en/news/2016-world-press-freedom-index-leaders-paranoid-about-journalists.

79. "1305 Journalists Killed Between 1992 and 2018," *Committee to Protect Journalists*.

80. Amanda Erickson, "'Where I Work . . . It Is Dangerous to Be Alive': A Slain Mexican Journalist's Prescient Speech," *Washington Post*, May 16, 2017, https://www.washingtonpost.com/news/worldviews/wp/2017/05/16/where-i-work-it-is-dangerous-to-be-alive-a-slain-mexican-journalists-prescient-speech/?hpid=hp_no-name_hp-in-the-news%3Apage%2Fin-the-news&utm_term=.46061fc03428.

81. "2020 World Press Freedom Index."

82. Nicole Gaouette, "Mideast's Clash of Images," *Christian Science Monitor*, October 21, 2000.

83. "141 Journalists Killed in Syria Between 2011 and 2018/Motive Confirmed," *Committee to Protect Journalists*, accessed June 22, 2020, https://cpj.org/data/killed/mideast/syria/?status=Killed&motiveConfirmed%5B%5D=Confirmed&type%5B%5D=Journalist&cc_fips%5B%5D=SY&start_year=2011&end_year=2018&group_by=location/.

84. "2020 World Press Freedom Index."

85. "Journalism in Syria, Impossible Job?" *Reporters Without Borders*, November 6, 2013, https://rsf.org/syrie-journalism-in-syria-impossible-job-06-11-2013,45424.html; Elle Shearer, "In Syria, Freelancers Like James Foley Covers a Dangerous War Zone with No Front Lines," *Washington Post*, August 22, 2014, www.washingtonpost.com/opinions/in-syria-freelancers-like-james-foley-covera-dangerous-war-zone-with-no-front-lines/2014/08/22/25e4bfda-295b-11e4-86ca-6f03cbd15c1a_story.html; Karen DeYoung and Adam Goldman, "Islamic State Claims It Executed American Photojournalist James Foley," *Washington Post*, August 20, 2014, http://www.washingtonpost.com/world/national-security/islamic-state-claims-it-beheaded-american-photojournalist-james-foley/2014/08/19/42e83970-27e6-11e4-86ca-6f03cbd15c1a_story.html.

86. "RSF Index 2018"; "122 Journalists Killed in Syria Between 2011 and 2018/Motive Confirmed."

87. Ibid.

88. Joby Warrick and Swati Sharma, "The Ordeal of *Post* Reporter Jason Rezaian," *Washington Post*, January 16, 2016, https://www.washingtonpost.com/world/the-washington-posts-jason-rezaian-has-now-spent-a-full-year-in-an-iranian-jail/2015/07/21/811bb46e-2cd7-11e5-bd33-395c05608059_story.html.

89. "2015 Prison Census: 199 Journalists Jailed Worldwide," *Committee to Protect Journalists*, December 1, 2015.

90. Karen DeYoung and Carol Morello, "Freeing a Reporter: Secret Diplomatic Talks and Private Back Channels," *Washington Post*, January 17, 2016, https://www.washingtonpost.com/world/national-security/freeing-jason-secret-diplomatic-talks-and-private-back-channels/2016/01/17/aaf01484-bc7d-11e5-829c-26ffb874a18d_story.html.

91. Andrew Roth, "*Post* Owner Jeff Bezos Flies Reporter Jason Rezaian to U.S. After Iran Release," *Washington Post*, January 22, 2016, https://www.washingtonpost.com/world/middle_east/post-reporter-rezaian-flies-to-us-after-release-by-iran-checkups-in-germany/2016/01/22/b47273ba-c09e-11e5-bcda-62a36b394160_story.html.

92. Editorial Board, "Iran's Appalling Treatment of Journalists Has Not Ended," *Washington Post*, January 24, 2016, https://www.washingtonpost.com/opinions/irans-appalling-treatment-of-journalists-has-not-ended/2016/01/24/58d8bc42-c131-11e5-bcda-62a36b394160_story.html.

93. "RSF Index 2020."

94. Kai Hafez, ed., *Mass Media, Politics, and Society in the Middle East* (Cresskill, NJ: Hampton Press, 2001).

95. Ibid.

96. Fred Strickert, "War on the Web," *Christian Century*, May 16, 2001.

97. Ibid.

98. I would like to thank Charley Reed, a communications graduate student at University of Nebraska at Omaha, for his research and work on the new media coverage of the Iranian protests section of this chapter.

99. Ali Arouzi, "Iran to Media: No Cameras Allowed," *World Blog*, June 16, 2009, http://worldblog.nbcnews.com/_news/2009/06/16/4376296-iran-to-media-no-cameras-allowed; Brian Stelter, "Journalism Rules Are Bent in News Coverage From Iran," *New York Times*, June 29, 2009; Brian Stelter, "In Coverage of Iran, Amateurs Take the Lead," *New York Times: Media Decoder*, June 17, 2009, https://mediadecoder.blogs.nytimes.com/2009/06/17/in-coverage-of-iran-amateurs-take-the-lead/; Gaurav Mishra, "The Digital News Lifecycle: Why Breaking News on Twitter Isn't News Anymore," *MSFS 556 at Georgetown University*, January 18, 2009.

100. Everette E. Dennis, Justin D. Martin, and Robb Wood, "Media Use in the Middle East, 2016," Northwestern University in Qatar, March 9, 2016, http://www.mideastmedia.org/survey/2016/.

101. "Media Use in the Middle East, 2019," Northwestern University in Qatar, 2020, http://www.mideastmedia.org/survey/2019/.

102. "Media Use in the Middle East, 2019."

103. "Media Use in the Middle East, 2019."

104. Hussein Y. Amin, "The Middle East and North Africa," in *World Broadcasting: A Comparative View*, ed. Alan Wells (Norwood, NJ: Ablex, 1996).

105. "2020 World Press Freedom Index."

106. Peter Feuilherade, "Analysis: Politics Affect Funding of Arab Satellite TV Stations," *BBC Monitoring International Reports* (2007).

107. Christophe Ayad, "Middle East Media Pluralism via Satellite," *UNESCO Courier*, January 2000.

108. Isabel Hilton, "'Al-Jazeera': And Now, the Other News," *New York Times*, March 6, 2005.

109. Brooke Gladstone, "Al-Nielsens," *On the Media*, December 16, 2005, https://www.wnycstudios.org/podcasts/otm/segments/128910-al-nielsens.

110. Mark Memmott, "Former Marine in Media Glare as He Joins Al-Jazeera," *USA Today*, September 28, 2005.

111. Hilton, "'Al-Jazeera.'"

112. "Al Jazeera Journalists Freed From Egypt Prison," *Al Jazeera*, September 23, 2015, http://www.aljazeera.com/news/2015/09/al-jazeera-journalists-pardoned-egypt-150923112113189.html.

113. Tawana Kupe, "New Forms of Cultural Identity in an African Society," *Innovation: The European Journal of Social Science* 8, no. 4 (1995).

114. Ibid.

115. "2020 World Press Freedom Index."

116. Mohamed Keita, "In Africa, Development Still Comes at Freedom's Expense," *Committee to Protect Journalists*, February 2012, www.cpj.org/2012/02/attacks-on-the-press-in-2011-in-africa-a-return-of.php.

117. Abu-Bakarr Jalloh, "Reporters Without Borders: 'Press Freedom in Africa Remains Grim,'" *Deutsche Welle*, http://www.dw.com/en/reporters-without-borders-press-freedom-in-africa-remains-grim/a-18423623.

118. Keita, "In Africa, Development Still Comes at Freedom's Expense."

119. Osabuohien P. Amienyi and Gerard Igyor, "Sub-Saharan Africa," in *World Broadcasting: A Comparative View*, ed. Alan Wells (Norwood, NJ: Ablex, 1996).

120. Jean Huteau, "Media Self-Control, the South's New Option," *UNESCO Courier*, April 2000.

121. Amienyi and Igyor, "Sub-Saharan Africa."

122. Richard Harrington, "'World Beat' Rattles Pop Music Scene," *Toronto Star*, June 18, 1988.

123. Jim Miller, "Simon's Spirit of Soweto," *Newsweek*, November 17, 1986.

124. Bob Young, "Bongo Maffin Sets Message to Dance Beat," *Boston Herald*, August 16, 2002.

125. Miller, "Simon's Spirit of Soweto."

126. Harrington, "'World Beat' Rattles Pop Music Scene."

127. Janis E. Overlock, "The Former Soviet Union and Eastern Europe," in *World Broadcasting: A Comparative View*, ed. Alan Wells (Norwood, NJ: Ablex, 1996), 95.

128. Ibid.

129. Eline Gordts, "Putin's Press: How Russia's President Controls the News," *Huffington Post*, October 24, 2015, http://www.huffingtonpost.com/entry/vladimir-putin-russia-news-media_us_56215944e4b0bce34700b1df.

130. Matthew Luxmoore, "Russian Journalist Who Reported on Secretive Paramilitary Dies," *New York Times*, April 16, 2018, https://www.nytimes.com/2018/04/16/world/europe/maksim-borodin-journalist-dead-russia.html?wpmm=1&wpisrc=nl_daily202.

131. David Filipov, "Here Are 10 Critics of Vladimir Putin Who Died Violently or in Suspicious Ways," *Washington Post*, March 23, 2017, https://www.washingtonpost.com/news/worldviews/wp/2017/03/23/here-are-ten-critics-of-vladimir-putin-who-died-violently-or-in-suspicious-ways/.

132. "2020 World Press Freedom Index."

133. "RSF Index 2018."

134. David Cohen, "*Russia Today* and *Sputnik* Can No Longer Advertise on Twitter," *Ad Week*, October 26, 2017, https://www.adweek.com/digital/russia-today-and-sputnik-can-no-longer-advertise-on-twitter/.

135. Hsiang-Wen Hsiao, "Asia," in *World Broadcasting: A Comparative View*, ed. Alan Wells (Norwood, NJ: Ablex, 1996).

136. BS Reporters, "DTH, Digital Cable Penetration to Drive TV Growth: Report," *Business Standard*, September 20, 2014, http://www.business-standard.com/article/companies/dth-digital-cable-penetration-to-drive-tv-growth-report-114092000020_1.html.

137. Uday Sahay, ed., *Making News: Handbook of Media in Contemporary India* (New Delhi: Oxford University Press, 2006).

138. Gaurav Mishra, "Social Media and Citizen Journalism in the 11/26 Mumbai Terror Attacks: A Case Study," *Gauravonomics*, November 28, 2008, http://www.gauravonomics.com/.

139. Brooke Gladstone, "Detailed Coverage," *On the Media*, December 5, 2008, http://www.wnyc.org/story/131229-detailed-coverage/.

140. "2020 World Press Freedom Index."

141. Ralph Hanson, "Media Twitter: On Bed Bugs, the NYT and Thin-Skinned Columnists," *Living in a Media World*, August 28, 2019, http://www.ralphehanson.com/2019/08/28/media-twitter-on-bed-bugs-the-nyt-and-thin-skinned-columnists/.

142. "World Press Freedom Index 2016."

143. Joanna Slater and Shams Irfan, "Internet Service Limps Back to Kashmir after Nearly Six-Month Blackout," *Washington Post*, January 27, 2020, http://www.washingtonpost.com/world/asia_pacific/internet-service-limps-back-to-kashmir-after-nearly-six-months-blackout/2020/01/27/298b34fe-40d2-11ea-abff-5ab1ba98b405_story.html.

144. Kenneth C. Petress, "China," in *World Broadcasting: A Comparative View*, ed. Alan Wells (Norwood, NJ: Ablex, 1996).

145. "China," *CASBAA*, http://www.casbaa.com/advertising/countries/china.

146. "China Profile—Media," *BBC News*, April 26, 2016, http://www.bbc.com/news/world-asia-pacific-13017881.

147. "China's Media Landscape," *AHK*, https://china.ahk.de/market-info/chinas-media-landscape.

148. Sarah Lacy, "Tudou: A Push Towards Mobile Video and Profits," *Washington Post*, November 7, 2009, http://www.washingtonpost.com/wp-dyn/content/article/2009/11/08/AR2009110801808.html.

149. "2020 World Press Freedom Index."

150. Ibid.

151. Hiroshi Tokinoya, "Japan," in *World Broadcasting: A Comparative View*, ed. Alan Wells (Norwood, NJ: Ablex, 1996).

152. "2020 World Press Freedom Index."

153. Douglas Wolk, "Manga, Anime Invade the U.S.," *Publishers Weekly*, March 12, 2001.

154. "2020 World Press Freedom Index."

155. Nicole Gaouette, "Get Your Manga Here," *Christian Science Monitor*, January 8, 1999.

156. Milton Mayfield et al., "Manga and the Pirates: Unlikely Allies for Strategic Growth," *Advanced Management Journal* 65, no. 3 (2000).

157. Ibid.

158. Calvin Reid, "Asian Comics Delight U.S. Readers," *Publishers Weekly*, December 23, 2002.

CHAPTER 12

1. Tiffany Hsu, "Popular YouTube Toy Review Channel Accused of Blurring Lines for Ads," *New York Times*, September 4, 2019, www.nytimes.com/2019/09/04/business/media/ryan-toysreview-youtube-ad-income.html.

2. Amanda Perelli, "The World's Top-Earning YouTube Star Is an 8-Year-Old Boy Who Made $22 Million in a Single Year Reviewing Toys," *Business Insider*, October 20, 2019, www.businessinsider.com/8-year-old-youtube-star-ryan-toysreview-made-22-million-2019-10.

3. Whyte, Alexandra. "Why Aren't There Laws Protecting Kid Influencers?" Kidscreen" Archive," August 12, 2019, http://kidscreen.com/2019/08/12/why-arent-there-laws-protecting-kid-influencers/.

4. Chavie Lieber, "Toy Unboxing Videos Have Taken Over YouTube. Some Experts Say They Exploit Kids," *Vox*, March

22, 2019, www.vox.com/the-goods/2019/3/22/18275767/toy -unboxing-videos-youtube-advertising-ethics.

5. Hsu, "Popular YouTube Toy Review Channel Accused of Blurring Lines."

6. Lieber, "Toy Unboxing Videos Have Taken Over YouTube."

7. Elizabeth Chuck, "Hit YouTube Channel Ryan ToysReview Accused of Deceiving Kids Into Watching Sponsored Content." *NBC News*, September 10, 2019, http://www.nbcnews.com/tech/ tech-news/hit-youtuber-ryan-toysreview-accused-deceiving -kids-watching-sponsored-content-n1052006.

8. Hsu, "Popular YouTube Toy Review Channel Accused of Blurring Lines."

9. Charlie Jones, "Should Children Watch Toy Unboxing Videos?" *BBC News*, December 9, 2019, http://www.bbc.com/news/uk -england-beds-bucks-herts-49975644.

10. Hsu, "Popular YouTube Toy Review Channel Accused of Blurring Lines."

11. George E. Belch and Michael A. Belch, *Advertising and Promotion: An Integrated Marketing Communications Perspective* (Boston: Irwin McGraw-Hill, 1998).

12. Pamela Walker Laird, *Advertising Progress* (Baltimore: Johns Hopkins University Press, 1998).

13. James W. Carey, "Advertising: An Institutional Approach," in *Advertising in Society*, ed. Roxanne Hoveland and Gary B. Wilcox (Lincolnwood, IL: NTC Business Books, 1989).

14. Laird, *Advertising Progress*.

15. Michael Schudson, "Historical Roots of Consumer Culture," in *Advertising in Society*, ed. Roxanne Hoveland and Gary B. Wilcox (Lincolnwood, IL: NTC Business Books, 1989).

16. Laird, *Advertising Progress*.

17. Carey, "Advertising."

18. Schudson, "Historical Roots of Consumer Culture."

19. Laird, *Advertising Progress*.

20. Michael Sebastian, "*Ladies' Home Journal* Ends Monthly Publication, Lays Off All Staff," *Ad Age*, April 24, 2014, https:// adage.com/article/media/ladies-home-journal-fold-131-years -print/292839/.

21. James B. Twitchell, *Adcult USA: The Triumph of Advertising in American Culture* (New York: Columbia University Press, 1996), 73.

22. Ibid.

23. Ibid., 93.

24. Suzanne Goldenberg, "Big Ag Spending Millions to Defeat GMO Labeling Campaigns," *AlterNet*, October 24, 2014, http://www.alternet.org/big-ag-spending-millions-defeat -gmo-labeling-campaigns; "Colorado Mandatory Labeling of GMOs Initiative, Proposition 105 (2014)," *Ballotpedia*, https:// ballotpedia.org/Colorado_Mandatory_Labeling_of_GMOs_ Initiative,_Proposition_105_(2014).

25. "Public Service Advertising That Changed a Nation," *Ad Council*, 2014; Karen Egolf, "Ad Council Offers New Responsible Fatherhood PSAs," *Ad Age*, June 15, 2011, http:// adage.com/article/goodworks/ad-council-offers-responsible -fatherhood-psas/228199/.

26. Eugene H. Fram, S. Prakash Sethi, and Nobuaki Namiki, "Newspaper Advocacy Advertising: Molder of Public Opinion," *USA Today Magazine*, July 1993, 90.

27. Belch and Belch, *Advertising and Promotion*.

28. Michael Schudson, "Advertising as Capitalist Realism," in *Advertising in Society*, ed. Roxanne Hoveland and Gary B. Wilcox (Lincolnwood, IL: NTC Business Books, 1989).

29. Herschell Gordon Lewis, *Advertising Age Handbook of Advertising* (Lincolnwood, IL: NTC Business Books, 1999).

30. E. J. Schultz, "'Got Milk' Dropped as National Milk Industry Changes Tactics," *Ad Age*, February 24, 2014, http://adage .com/article/news/milk-dropped-national-milk-industry -tactics/291819/.

31. Mike Snider, "Hunt for PlayStation 2 Becomes Easier for Shoppers," *USA Today*, March 22, 2001.

32. Nancy Giges, "Coke's Switch a Classic," in *Advertising Age: The Principles of Advertising at Work*, ed. Esther Thorson (Lincolnwood, IL: NTC Business Books, 1989).

33. Jack Honomichl, "Missing Ingredients in 'New' Coke's Research," in *Advertising Age: The Principles of Advertising at Work*, ed. Esther Thorson (Lincolnwood, IL: NTC Business Books, 1989).

34. Giges, "Coke's Switch a Classic."

35. Phil Edwards, "New Coke Debuted 30 Years Ago. Here's Why It Was a Sugary Fiasco," *Vox*, April 23, 2015, http://www.vox .com/2015/4/23/8472539/new-coke-cola-wars.

36. Schudson, "Historical Roots of Consumer Culture."

37. Laird, *Advertising Progress*.

38. Lewis, *Advertising Age Handbook of Advertising*.

39. C. Bruce Bartels, "Ad Agencies Must Look to Customers to Change," *Boston Business Journal*, December 30, 1994.

40. Dylan Matthews, "One in Five Beers Sold in America Is a Bud Light," *Vox*, April 16, 2014, www.vox.com/2014/4/16/5620170/ one-in-five-beers-sold-in-america-is-a-bud-light; Jeremy Mullman, "In Juvenile Bud Light Lime Spot, This Butt's for You," *Ad Age*, September 8, 2009, https://adage.com/article/ adages/juvenile-bud-lime-spot-butt-s/138877/.

41. Bartels, "Ad Agencies Must Look to Customers to Change."

42. David Ogilvy, *Confessions of an Advertising Man* (New York: Atheneum, 1963), 90.

43. Ibid., 96.

44. Ibid., 105.

45. Alf Nucifora, "Advertising 101: How to Get the Best Out of Your Media Buy," *Houston Business Journal*, October 16, 1998.

46. Bradley Johnson, "What's Up at Agencies? Revenue, Jobs, Stocks—and Digital," *Ad Age*, May 1, 2016, http://adage.com/ article/agency-news/agency-report-web-mainbar/303704/; "Marketing Fact Pack 2018," *Ad Age*, December 18, 2017.

47. Bradley Johnson, "Agency Report: U.S. Agency Revenue Jumped 7.7% in 2010," *Ad Age*, April 25, 2011, http://adage .com/article/agency-news/agency-report-u-s-agency-revenue -jumped-7-7-2010/227162/.

48. Esther Thorson, ed., *Advertising Age: The Principles of Advertising at Work* (Lincolnwood, IL: NTC Business Books, 1989).

49. Twitchell, *Adcult USA*.

50. Rick Edmonds, Emily Guskin, Tom Rosenstiel, and Amy Mitchell, "Newspapers: Building Digital Revenues Proves Painfully Slow," *Pew Research Center*, April 11, 2012, https:// www.pewresearch.org/wp-content/uploads/sites/8/2017/05/ State-of-the-News-Media-Report-2012-FINAL.pdf.

51. "State of the News Media 2015," *Pew Research Center*, April 29, 2015, https://assets.pewresearch.org/wp-content/uploads/ sites/13/2017/05/30142603/state-of-the-news-media-report -2015-final.pdf.

52. Lewis, *Advertising Age Handbook of Advertising*; "The State of the News Media 2009: Newspapers," *Pew Research Center*, https://assets.pewresearch.org/files/journalism/State-of-the -News-Media-Report-2009-FINAL.pdf.

53. Katerina-Eva Matsa, Jane Sasseen, and Amy Mitchell, "Magazines: Are Hopes for Tablets Overdone?" *Pew Research Center*, 2012.

54. "About Digital Billboard Technology," Outdoor Advertising Association of America, https://oaaa.org.

55. "Marketing Fact Pack 2018."

56. Twitchell, *Adcult USA*; Outdoor Advertising Association of America, "2017 YE: Total OOH Revenue $7.7 Billion (Printed and Digital)," http://oaaa.org/Portals/0/Public%20PDFs/F&F%20-%20OOH%20by%20Format%20Pie%20Chart%20-%20YE%202017.pdf.

57. Louise Story, "Times Sq. Ads Spread via Tourists' Cameras," *New York Times*, December 11, 2006.

58. Michael Learmonth, "Online Advertising Spending Expected to Be Down for 2009," *Ad Age*, October 19, 2009, https://adage.com/article/digital/online-advertising-spending-expected-2009/139785.

59. "Mobile Continues to Steal Share of US Adults' Daily Time Spent With Media," *eMarketer*, April 22, 2014, http://www.emarketer.com/Article/Mobile-Continues-Steal-Share-of-US-Adults-Daily-Time-Spent-with-Media/1010782.

60. "US Time Spent With Media," *eMarketer*, October 2017, http://www.emarketer.com/Report/US-Time-Spent-with-Media-eMarketers-Updated-Estimates-2017/2002142.

61. David Berkowitz, "The Converging Paths of Mobile Advertising," *Ad Age*, January 22, 2014, http://adage.com/article/digitalnext/converging-paths-mobile-advertising/291204/.

62. Rebecca Piirto Heath, "Psychographics: Q'est-Ce Que C'est," *Marketing Tools*, November/December 1995.

63. Emanuel H. Demby, "Psychographics Revisited: The Birth of a Technique," *Marketing Research* 6, no. 2 (1994).

64. "VALS," *Strategic Business Insights*, www.strategicbusinessinsights.com/vals/.

65. Ibid.

66. Joshua Meyrowitz, *No Sense of Place* (New York: Oxford University Press, 1985), 104.

67. Theresa Howard, "Being True to Dew," *Brandweek*, April 24, 2000.

68. Richard Linnett, "A New Dew; A Soft Drink Finds Deliverance," *Print*, November/December 2000.

69. Duane Stanford, "Mountain Dew Wants Some Street Cred," *Businessweek*, April 26, 2012, http://www.businessweek.com/articles/2012-04-26/mountain-dew-wants-some-street-cred; Christopher Heine, "Mountain Dew Fiasco Shows Brands Desperately Want Street Cred," *AdWeek*, May 1, 2013, http://www.adweek.com/news/advertising-branding/mountain-dew-fiasco-shows-brands-desperately-want-street-cred-149079.

70. Barbara Thau, "Courting the Gay Consumer," *HFN*, February 27, 2006.

71. Charles A. Jaffe, "Dealers Say Wooing Gay, Lesbian Customers Is Good Business," *Automotive News*, January 31, 1994.

72. Brett Chase, "Advertisements Land in Gay Publications," *Des Moines Business Record*, August 8, 1994.

73. Thau, "Courting the Gay Consumer"; "Marketing to Gay and Lesbian Consumers" (Rivendell Media, 2008).

74. "Old Navy Responds to Racist Trolls for an Ad With an Interracial Couple." *Digiday*, 2 May 2016, https://digiday.com/marketing/old-navy-interracial-couple-tweet/.

75. Kashmir Hill, "How Target Figured Out a Teen Girl Was Pregnant Before Her Father Did," *Forbes*, February 16, 2012, http://www.forbes.com/sites/kashmirhill/2012/02/16/how-target-figured-out-a-teen-girl-was-pregnant-before-her-father-did/.

76. Charles Duhigg, "How Companies Learn Your Secrets," *New York Times*, February 16, 2012, http://www.nytimes.com/2012/02/19/magazine/shopping-habits.html.

77. Kim Rotzoll, James E. Haefner, and Charles H. Sandage, "Advertising and the Classical Liberal World View," in *Advertising in Society*, ed. Roxanne Hoveland and Gary B. Wilcox (Lincolnwood, IL: NTC Business Books, 1989).

78. M. Night Shyamalan, *The Sixth Sense: A Conversation With M. Night Shyamalan* (Burbank, CA: Hollywood Pictures Home Video, 2000), DVD.

79. Chuck Ross, "NBC Blasts Beyond the 15-Minute Barrier," *Ad Age*, August 7, 2000.

80. "Network, Cable Messages Buried in Commercial Avalanche," *Chicago Sun-Times*, May 30, 2006.

81. Sheree Johnson, "New Research Sheds Light on Daily Ad Exposures," *SJ Insights*, September 29, 2014, https://sjinsights.net/2014/09/29/new-research-sheds-light-on-daily-ad-exposures/.

82. Brian Steinberg, "Spike's Supersized Ad Breaks Buck TV's Clutter-Busting Trend," *Ad Age*, September 13, 2010.

83. Jill Disis, "Fox Wants to Cut Commercial Time to 2 Minutes Per Hour," *CNN*, March 6, 2018, https://money.cnn.com/2018/03/06/media/fox-advertising-commercial-time/index.html; Jeanine Poggi, "NBC Universal Promises to Slash TV Commercials by 20 Percent," *Ad Age*, February 28, 2018, http://adage.com/article/media/nbcu-promises-reduce-tv-commercials-20-percent/312548/; Tony Maglio, "NBCUniversal to Cut Number of Commercials Across All Networks by 20 Percent," *Wrap*, February 28, 2018, https://www.thewrap.com/nbcuniversal-cut-number-commercials-across-networks-20-percent/.

84. Dick Morris, "Break Through the Clutter," *Chain Store Age*, December 2000.

85. Diedtra Henderson, "Rise of Celebrity Testimonials Spurs FDA Scrutiny," *Boston Globe*, October 30, 2005.

86. Martha Rogers and Christine A. Seiler, "The Answer Is No: A National Survey of Advertising Industry Practitioners and Their Clients About Whether They Use Subliminal Advertising," *Journal of Advertising Research* 34, no. 2 (1994).

87. J. Leo, "Hostility Among the Ice Cubes," *U.S. News & World Report*, July 15, 1991; J. Levine and J. L. Aber, "Search and Find," *Forbes*, September 2, 1991.

88. Tom O'Sullivan, "Ridley Scott Returns to Ads With Orange Blitz," *Marketing Week*, April 2, 1998.

89. Bob Garfield, "Breakthrough Product Gets Greatest TV Spot," *Ad Age*, January 10, 1994.

90. Bradley Johnson, "The Commercial, and the Product, That Changed Advertising," *Ad Age*, January 10, 1994.

91. Ibid.

92. Lenore Skenazy, "Keep Targeting Kids and the Parents Will Start Targeting You," *Ad Age*, May 19, 2008.

93. Thorson, *Advertising Age*; Carole Shifrin, "Ban on TV Ads to Children Is Proposed," *Washington Post*, February 25, 1978.

94. Caroline E. Mayer, "TV Ads Entice Kids to Overeat, Study Finds," *Washington Post*, December 7, 2005.

95. Annys Shin, "Ads Aimed at Children Get Tighter Scrutiny; Firms to Promote More Healthful Diet Choices," *Washington Post*, November 15, 2006.

96. J. Michael McGinnis, Jennifer Appleton Gootman, and Vivica I. Kraak, *Food Marketing to Children and Youth: Threat or Opportunity?* (Washington, DC: Institute of Medicine of the National Academies, 2005), https://www.books.nap.edu/openbook.php?record_id=11514&page=1.

97. "Marketing Fact Pack 2018."

98. Ibid.

99. Ken Auletta, *Googled: The End of the World as We Know It* (New York: Penguin Press, 2009).

100. Louise Story, "Marketers Demanding Better Count of the Clicks," *New York Times*, October 30, 2006.

101. Jefferson Graham, "Google to Experiment With Newspaper Ad Sales Online; Search Giant to Offer Print Options to Customer Base," *USA Today*, November 6, 2006.

102. "Google's Digital-Ad Dominance Is Harming Marketers and Publishers, Says New Study," *Ad Age*, May 18, 2020, https://adage.com/article/digital/googles-digital-ad-dominance-harming-marketers-and-publishers-says-new-study/2257576?utm_source=ad-age-digital&utm_medium=email&utm_campaign=20200518&utm_content=hero-headline.

103. Michael Sebastian, "Brands Pay This Instagrammer $15,000 to Include Their Products in a Picture," *Ad Age*, May 20, 2015, http://adage.com/article/digital/brands-pay-instagrammer-15-000-include-products-a-picture/298709/; Kayleen Schaefer, "How Bloggers Make Money on Instagram," *Harper's Bazaar*, May 20, 2015, http://www.harpersbazaar.com/fashion/trends/a10949/how-bloggers-make-money-on-instagram/.

104. Anthony Ha, "Instagram Is Testing a New Way for Celebrities and Influencers to Identify Their Sponsored Posts," *TechCrunch*, June 14, 2017, https://techcrunch.com/2017/06/14/instagram-sponsored-posts/.

105. Jason Aten, "The FTC Is About to Crack Down on Influencer Ads on Instagram, TikTok, and YouTube," *Inc.*, February 13, 2020, http://www.inc.com/jason-aten/the-ftc-is-about-to-crack-down-on-influencer-ads-on-instagram-tiktok-youtube.html.

106. Edgar Alvarez, "YouTube Stars Are Blurring the Lines Between Content and Ads," *Engadget*, March 6, 2020, http://www.engadget.com/2017-07-25-youtube-influencers-sponsored-videos.html.

107. Todd Spangler, "Miquela, the Uncanny CGI Virtual Influencer, Signs With CAA (EXCLUSIVE)," *Variety*, May 6, 2020, https://variety.com/2020/digital/news/miquela-virtual-influencer-signs-caa-1234599368/?fbclid=IwAR0EPWZqXpuv85T3139R2BxTdWMrF-ikQpw4F9z4JirevhNy4Ba-WD0gOsM.

108. Dawn Edmiston, "An Examination of Integrated Marketing Communication in U.S. Public Institutions of Higher Education," *International Journal of Educational Advancement* 8, no. 3/4 (2009).

109. Neil Strauss, "Elon Musk: The Architect of Tomorrow," *Rolling Stone*, November 15, 2017, https://www.rollingstone.com/culture/features/elon-musk-inventors-plans-for-outer-space-cars-finding-love-w511747.

110. Mark Wnek, "There's Advertising and Marketing, and Then There's Elon Musk," *Ad Age*, February 8, 2018, http://adage.com/article/special-report-super-bowl/advertising-marketing-elon-musk/312307/.

111. Andrew Gilman, "Too Early for the Tylenol Playbook to Work for Boeing's 737 Max," *PR Daily*, September 9, 2019, http://www.prdaily.com/too-early-for-the-tylenol-playbook-to-work-for-boeings-737-max/.

112. David Griner, "With a $0 Ad Budget, Tesla Just Pulled Off One of the Greatest Marketing Stunts Ever," *Ad Week*, February 7, 2018, https://www.adweek.com/brand-marketing/with-a-0-ad-budget-tesla-just-pulled-off-one-of-the-greatest-marketing-stunts-ever/.

113. Brian Clark, "Don't Waste Your Time With Native Advertising (Do This Instead)," *Say Daily*, February 27, 2014, https://www.saydaily.com/2014/02/dont-waste-your-time-with-native-advertising-do-this-instead.

114. Demian Farnworth, "Copyblogger's 2014 State of Native Advertising Report," *Copyblogger*, April 7, 2014, http://www.copyblogger.com/native-advertising-2014/.

115. Lucia Moses, "The *Washington Post*'s Native Ads Get Editorial Treatment Borrowing From the Newsroom," *Ad Week*, March 3, 2014, http://www.adweek.com/news/press/washington-posts-native-ads-get-editorial-treatment-156048.

116. Antony Young, "Native Advertising Is Making Media Brands Count for More, Not Less," *Ad Age*, May 29, 2013, https://adage.com/article/digitalnext/media-native-good-news/241727/.

117. Demian Farnworth, "12 Examples of Native Ads (and Why They Work)," *Copyblogger*, April 14, 2014, http://www.copyblogger.com/examples-of-native-ads/.

118. Erik Sass, "Consumers Can't Tell Native Ads From Editorial Content," *Media Post*, December 31, 2015, http://www.mediapost.com/publications/article/265789/consumers-cant-tell-native-ads-from-editorial-con.html.

119. Misbaah Mansuri, "Native Advertising Spends to Double Up Globally: Experts," *Exchange4Media*, December 28, 2017, http://www.exchange4media.com/advertising/native-advertising-spends-to-double-up-globally-experts_87772.html.

120. "Gildan: Not Your Dad's Underwear," *Onion Labs*.

121. Ibid.; Julie Moos, "The *Atlantic* Publishes Then Pulls Sponsored Content From Church of Scientology," *Poynter*, January 15, 2013, https://www.poynter.org/news/atlantic-publishes-then-pulls-sponsored-content-church-scientology.

122. Jeff Sonderman, "*Atlantic* Introduces Sponsored Content Guidelines That Address the Scientology Incident," *Poynter*, January 30, 2013, https://www.poynter.org/news/atlantic-introduces-sponsored-content-guidelines-address-scientology-incident.

123. DTVE Reporter, "US Netflix Use Tops DVR Ownership for the First Time," *Digital TVEurope*, March 7, 2017, https://www.digitaltveurope.com/2017/03/07/us-netflix-use-tops-dvr-ownership-for-the-first-time/.

124. Julie Bosman, "TV and Top Marketers Discuss the State of the Medium," *New York Times*, March 24, 2006; Julie Bosman, "A Match Made in Product Placement Heaven," *New York Times*, May 31, 2006.

125. Paul Davidson, "Ad Campaigns for Your Tiny Cellphone Screen Get Bigger: Marketers Leverage Growth in Text Messaging, Wireless Web," *USA Today*, August 9, 2006.

126. "Mobile Fact Pack," *Ad Age*, October 17, 2016, http://adage.com/d/resources/resources/whitepaper/mobile-fact-pack.

127. "Marketing Fact Pack 2018."

128. Kathryn Koegel, "Unilever Turkey's Cornetto Ice Cream Wins Global Media Awards," *Ad Age*, February 15, 2011, https://adage.com/article/global-news/mobile-marketing-campaigns-u-s/148886/.

129. Stuart Elliott, "More Products Get Roles in Shows, and Marketers Wonder If They're Getting Their Money's Worth," *New York Times*, March 29, 2005.

130. Ibid.

131. Andrew Adam Newman, "Once a Seldom-Heard Word, Pregnancy Is Now in the Spotlight," *New York Times*, April 2, 2009.

132. Doreen Carvajal, "Placing the Product in the Dialog, Too," *New York Times*, January 17, 2006.

133. Hannah Knowles, "Chick-Fil-A Had Big Plans for National Sandwich Day." *Washington Post*, November 1, 2019.

134. "Top 500 Chain Restaurant Report," *Technomic*, April 20, 2020, https://www.restaurantbusinessonline.com/top-500-chains.

135. Emily Heil, "Now Popeyes Is Trolling America by Inviting People to Make Their Own Chicken Sandwiches," *Washington Post*, September 12, 2019, http://www.washingtonpost.com/news/voraciously/wp/2019/09/12/now-popeyes-is-trolling-america-by-inviting-people-to-make-their-own-chicken-sandwiches/.

136. Emily Heil, "Chick-Fil-A Drops Donations That Angered LGBTQ Groups, and Conservative Leaders Cry Betrayal," *Washington Post*, November 18, 2019, http://www.washingtonpost.com/news/voraciously/wp/2019/11/18/chick-fil-a-drops-donations-that-angered-lgbt-groups-and-conservatives-cry-betrayal/.

137. Julie Jargon. "You Want Snark With Those Fries? No One Is Safe From Wendy's Tweets," *Wall Street Journal*, July 25, 2017, http://www.wsj.com/articles/you-want-snark-with-those-fries-no-one-is-safe-from-wendys-tweets-1500995026?mod=article_inline.

138. Laura Reiley, "In the Chicken Sandwich Wars, the Beef Burger Still Reigns Supreme," *Washington Post*, October 29, 2019, www.washingtonpost.com/business/2019/10/29/chicken-sandwich-wars-beef-burger-still-reigns-supreme/.

CHAPTER 13

1. Imani Moise and Sharon Terlep, "P&G Grapples With How to Stop a Tide Pods Meme," *Wall Street Journal*, January 20, 2018, https://www.wsj.com/articles/p-g-grapples-with-how-to-stop-a-tide-pods-meme-1516449600; Lindsey Bever, "Teens Are Daring Each Other to Eat Tide Pods. We Don't Need to Tell You That's a Bad Idea," *Washington Post*, January 17, 2018, https://www.washingtonpost.com/news/to-your-health/wp/2018/01/13/teens-are-daring-each-other-to-eat-tide-pods-we-dont-need-to-tell-you-thats-a-bad-idea/.

2. Laura Santhanam, "Kids Got Sick Eating Detergent Long Before the Tide Pod Challenge," *PBS NewsHour*, January 26, 2018, https://www.pbs.org/newshour/health/kids-got-sick-eating-detergent-long-before-the-tide-pod-challenge.

3. Bever, "Teens Are Daring Each Other to Eat Tide Pods."

4. "Don't Eat the Laundry Pods. (Seriously. They're Poison.)," *College Humor*, March 31, 2017, https://www.youtube.com/watch?v=pM6wanZOLtk.

5. Alex Abad-Santos, "Why People Are (Mostly) Joking About Eating Tide Pods," *Vox*, January 19, 2018, https://www.vox.com/2018/1/4/16841674/tide-pods-eating-meme-tide-pod-challenge.

6. Bever, "Teens Are Daring Each Other to Eat Tide Pods."

7. Diana Bradley, "Tide Unleashes Its Secret Weapon Against the Tide Pod Challenge: Gronk," *PR Week*, January 16, 2018, https://www.prweek.com/article/1454684; Bever, "Teens Are Daring Each Other to Eat Tide Pods."

8. Nicholas Rice, "Ice-T Drops by 'Tonight Show' With PSA Warning Teens About Dangers of Tide Pod Challenge," *Billboard*, January 25, 2018, https://www.billboard.com/articles/news/television/8096217/tonight-show-ice-t-tide-pod-challenge.

9. Michael O'Brien, "What We Can Learn From the Tide Pod Challenge Besides the Obvious," *Next Page*, February 1, 2018, https://gonextpage.com/2018/02/01/what-we-can-learn-from-the-tide-pod-challenge/.

10. Santhanam, "Kids Got Sick Eating Detergent Long Before the Tide Pod Challenge"; Tide, "At Tide Safety Comes First, and It Never Stops," https://tide.com/en-us/safety.

11. Abad-Santos, "Why People Are (Mostly) Joking About Eating Tide Pods."

12. O'Brien, "What We Can Learn From the Tide Pod Challenge Besides the Obvious."

13. Blair Nicole Nastasi, "Four PR Lessons to Learn From the Tide Pod Challenge," *Forbes*, March 26, 2018, https://www.forbes.com/sites/forbesagencycouncil/2018/03/26/four-pr-lessons-to-learn-from-the-tide-pod-challenge/.

14. "Brand Crisis Management: Responding to the Tide Pod Challenge," *Knowledge@Wharton*, January 25, 2018, http://knowledge.wharton.upenn.edu/article/fallout-tide-pod-challenge/.

15. Marvin N. Olasky, *Corporate Public Relations: A New Historical Perspective* (Hillsdale, NJ: Erlbaum, 1987).

16. Ibid.

17. Cynthia E. Clark, "Differences Between Public Relations and Corporate Social Responsibility: An Analysis," *Public Relations Review* 26, no. 3 (September 2000): 363–380.

18. Olasky, *Corporate Public Relations*.

19. Ibid.

20. H. Frazier Moore and Frank B. Kalupa, *Public Relations: Principles, Cases, and Problems*, 9th ed. (Homewood, IL: Irwin, 1985).

21. John C. Stauber and Sheldon Rampton, *Toxic Sludge Is Good for You: Lies, Damn Lies, and the Public Relations Industry* (Monroe, ME: Common Courage Press, 1995).

22. Olasky, *Corporate Public Relations*.

23. Ray Eldon Hiebert, *Courtier to the Crowd: The Story of Ivy Lee and the Development of Public Relations* (Ames: Iowa State University Press, 1966), 4–5.

24. Edward L. Bernays, *Public Relations* (Norman, OK: University of Oklahoma Press, 1952).

25. Hiebert, *Courtier to the Crowd*.

26. Ibid.

27. Bernays, *Public Relations*, 159.

28. Stauber and Rampton, *Toxic Sludge Is Good for You*.

29. Robert McG. Thomas Jr., "Henry Rogers, 82, Press Agent Who Built Hollywood Stars," *New York Times*, May 1, 1995, http://www.nytimes.com/1995/05/01/obituaries/henry-rogers-82-press-agent-who-built-hollywood-stars.html?src=pm.

30. Deborah Arthurs, "Rihanna's Steamy Armani Adverts Voted the Sexiest of 2011 (and Let's Not Forget Miranda Kerr's and Kate Moss Too)," *Daily Mail*, December 28, 2011, http://www.dailymail.co.uk/femail/article-2079455/Rihannas-steamy-Armani-adverts-voted-sexiest-2011.html.

31. Jim Romenesko, "Ad Age *Did Not* Name Rihanna's Armani Ad Year's Sexiest," *JimRomenesko.com*, December 30, 2011.

32. Thomas, "Henry Rogers, 82, Press Agent Who Built Hollywood Stars."

33. Bernays, *Public Relations*, 71.

34. Shearon A. Lowery and Melvin L. DeFleur, *Milestones in Mass Communication*, 3rd ed. (White Plains, NY: Longman, 1995).

35. Bernays, *Public Relations*, 73.

36. Moore and Kalupa, *Public Relations*.

37. Bernays, *Public Relations*.

38. Scott M. Cutlip, Allen H. Center, and Glen M. Broom, *Effective Public Relations* (Upper Saddle River, NJ: Prentice-Hall, 2000).

39. Raymond Moley, "The Birth of the Production Code (1945)," in *The Movies in Our Midst: Documents in the Cultural History of Film in America*, ed. Gerald Mast (Chicago, IL: University of Chicago Press, 1982).

40. Olasky, *Corporate Public Relations*.

41. Kathleen S. Kelly, "Stewardship; The Fifth Step in the Public Relations Process," in *Handbook of Public Relations*, ed. Robert Lawrence Heath and Gabriel M. Vasquez (Thousand Oaks, CA: SAGE, 2001).

42. Ibid.

43. Lucy Handley, "People Are Eating Tide Laundry Pods and This Is What Owner P&G Is Doing About It," *CNBC*, January 22, 2018, https://www.cnbc.com/2018/01/22/people-are-eating-tide-laundry-pods-and-this-is-what-pg-is-doing.html.

44. "Brand Crisis Management"; Moise and Terlep, "P&G Grapples With How to Stop a Tide Pods Meme."

45. "Brand Crisis Management"; Moise and Terlep, "P&G Grapples With How to Stop a Tide Pods Meme"; O'Brien, "What We Can Learn From the Tide Pod Challenge."

46. Shoroush Vosoughi, Deb Roy, and Sinan Aral, "The Spread of True and False News Online," *Science* 359, no. 6380 (March 9, 2018): 1146–1151, http://science.sciencemag.org/content/359/6380/1146.full; Abad-Santos, "Why People Are (Mostly) Joking About Eating Tide Pods."

47. O'Brien, "What We Can Learn From the Tide Pod Challenge"; Bradley, "Tide Unleashes Its Secret Weapon."

48. Bradley, "Tide Unleashes Its Secret Weapon"; "Brand Crisis Management."

49. "Brand Crisis Management"; Abad-Santos, "Why People Are (Mostly) Joking About Eating Tide Pods."

50. Moore and Kalupa, *Public Relations*.

51. Jerry Lazar, "Foot-in-Mouth Disease," *Electronic Business* 26, no. 6 (2000).

52. David P. Bianco, ed., *PR News Casebook: 1,000 Public Relations Case Studies* (Potomac, MD: Gale Research, 1993).

53. Karleen Murphy, "10 Common Intranet Complaints—and How to Resolve Them," *Ragan.com*, May 14, 2014, http://www.ragan.com/InternalCommunications/Articles/48317.aspx.

54. David E. Williams and Bolanle A. Olaniran, "Exxon's Decision-Making Flaws: The Hypervigilant Response to the *Valdez* Grounding," *Public Relations Review* 20, no. 1 (1994).

55. David McCormack, "The Pulling Power of the 'Dark Side,'" *Guardian*, January 22, 2007.

56. Bradley, "Tide Unleashes Its Secret Weapon"; Abad-Santos, "Why People Are (Mostly) Joking About Eating Tide Pods."

57. Susanne Courtney, "Measuring PR," *Marketing Magazine*, October 30, 2000.

58. Bever, "Teens Are Daring Each Other to Eat Tide Pods"; Nastasi, "Four PR Lessons to Learn."

59. David Taylor, "Safety Is No Laughing Matter," *P&G News*, January 22, 2018, http://news.pg.com/blog/KeepingUsSafe.

60. Lazar, "Foot-in-Mouth Disease."

61. Sinéad Baker. "Boeing's Response to the 737 Max Crisis Confused and Frightened People, Making It Hard to Believe Its Apologies, Experts Say," *Business Insider*, May 19, 2019, http://www.businessinsider.com/boeing-737-max-crisis-response-confusing-hard-to-trust-experts-2019-5.

62. Kara Alaimo, "What We Learned From 2019's Worst PR Disasters," Bloomberg, December 30, 2019, http://www.heraldnet.com/business/what-we-learned-from-2019s-worst-pr-disasters/.

63. Baker, "Boeing's Response to the 737 Max Crisis."

64. Natalie Kitroeff, "Boeing Employees Mocked F.A.A. and 'Clowns' Who Designed 737 Max," *New York Times*, January 9, 2020, http://www.nytimes.com/2020/01/09/business/boeing-737-messages.html.

65. Shannon Bond and Avie Schneider, "Trump Threatens to Shut Down Social Media After Twitter Adds Warning to His Tweets," *NPR*, May 27, 2020, http://www.npr.org/2020/05/27/863011399/trump-threatens-to-shut-down-social-media-after-twitter-adds-warning-on-his-twee?utm_source=dlvr.it&utm_medium=twitter.

66. William J. Small, "Exxon Valdez: How to Spend Billions and Still Get a Black Eye," *Public Relations Review* 17, no. 1 (1991).

67. Williams and Olaniran, "Exxon's Decision-Making Flaws."

68. Wayne L. Pines, "Myths of Crisis Management," *Public Relations Quarterly* 45, no. 3 (2000).

69. Lazar, "Foot-in-Mouth Disease."

70. Alex Edge, "Yamaha Offers Buyback Option for 2006 R6 Owners," *Motorcycle Daily*, February 14, 2006, http://www.motorcycledaily.com/2006/02/14february06_r6buyback/.

71. John Holusha, "Exxon's Public-Relations Problem," *New York Times*, April 21, 1989.

72. Dana James, "When Your Company Goes Code Blue," *Marketing News*, November 6, 2000.

73. Williams and Olaniran, "Exxon's Decision-Making Flaws."

74. N. R. Kleinfield, "Tylenol's Rapid Comeback," *New York Times*, September 17, 1983.

75. Moore and Kalupa, *Public Relations*.

76. Kleinfield, "Tylenol's Rapid Comeback."

77. Jeff Blyskal and Marie Blyskal, *PR: How the Public Relations Industry Writes the News* (New York: Morrow, 1985).

78. Ibid.; Kleinfield, "Tylenol's Rapid Comeback."

79. Small, "Exxon Valdez."

80. Holusha, "Exxon's Public-Relations Problem."

81. Williams and Olaniran, "Exxon's Decision-Making Flaws."

82. Holusha, "Exxon's Public-Relations Problem"; Small, "Exxon Valdez."

83. Williams and Olaniran, "Exxon's Decision-Making Flaws."

84. Small, "Exxon Valdez."

85. Anne C. Mulkern, "BP's PR Blunders Mirror Exxon's, Appear Destined for Record Book," *New York Times*, June 10, 2010, http://www.nytimes.com/gwire/2010/06/10/10greenwire-bps-pr-blunders-mirror-exxons-appear-destined-98819.html.

86. Jonathan Bernstein, "Crisis Manager University: My Top 5 Internet-Related Crisis Management Tips," http://www.bernsteincrisismanagement.com.

87. Carole M. Howard, "Technology and Tabloids: How the New Media World Is Changing Our Jobs," *Public Relations Quarterly* 45, no. 1 (2000).

88. Jonathan Bernstein, "Who Are These Bloggers, and Why Are They Saying Those Terrible Things?" *Associations Now*, October 2006.

89. Pamela Seiple, *How to Leverage Social Media for Public Relations Success*, (Cambridge, MA: HubSpot, 2012), https://cdn2.hubspot.net/hub/53/file-13204195-pdf/docs/hubspot_social_media_pr_ebook.pdf.

90. E. J. Schultz, "Dip Dilemma: Is Kraft Running Out of Velveeta?" *Ad Age*, January 7, 2014, http://adage.com/article/news/dip-dilemma-kraft-running-velveeta/290932/; Jenn Harris, "Kraft Confirms Velveeta Shortage, a.k.a. Cheesepocalypse," *Los Angeles Times*, January 10, 2014, http://www.latimes.com/food/dailydish/la-dd-velveeta-confirms-liquid-gold-cheesepocalypse-shortage-20140110-story.html.

91. "The #Cheesepocalypse Is Real: Your Reactions to the Velveeta Shortage," *People*, January 8, 2014, https://people.com/food/velveeta-shortage-cheesepocalypse/.

92. Harris, "Kraft Confirms Velveeta Shortage, a.k.a. Cheesepocalypse"; Sandi Moynihan, "#Cheesepocalypse: Surviving the Super Bowl Without Velveeta," *Washington Post*, February 1, 2014, http://www.washingtonpost.com/blogs/style-blog/wp/2014/02/01/cheesepocalypse-surviving-the-super-bowl-without-velveeta/.

93. Jack Neff, "How 'Cheesepocalypse' Helped Velveeta Bond With Its Biggest Fans," *Ad Age*, March 24, 2014, http://adage.com/article/media/cheesepocalypse-helped-velveeta-bond-biggest-fans/292297/?utm_source=daily_email&utm_medium=newsletter&utm_campaign=adage&ttl=1396317492.

94. Christie Dedman, "Why the Velveeta Cheesepocalypse Shortage May Be a Good Thing," *AL.com*, January 14, 2014, http://blog.al.com/bargain-mom/2014/01/why_the_velveeta_cheesepocalyp.html.

95. Stephanie Clifford, "Video Prank at Domino's Taints Brand," *New York Times*, April 16, 2009.

96. Emily Bryson York, "What Domino's Did Right—and Wrong—in Squelching Hubbub Over YouTube Video; Pizza Purveyor Faulted for Waiting to Respond but Did Well in the End," *Ad Age*, April 20, 2009.

97. Ibid.

98. Raymund Flandez, "Domino's Response Offers Lessons in Crisis Management," *Wall Street Journal*, April 20, 2009, http://blogs.wsj.com/independentstreet/2009/04/20/dominos-response-offers-lessons-in-crisis-management/.

99. Alice Gomstyn, "Brown's, Domino's and Beyond: Business Felled by Crime, Scandal," *ABC News*, October 1, 2009, http://abcnews.go.com/Business/browns-chicken-dominos-crimes-hurt-stores-restaurants/story?id=8706183.

100. Linda Tischler, "Pop Artist: David Butler," *Fast Company*, September 10, 2009, https://www.fastcompany.com/570/pop-artist-david-butler.

101. Phil Edwards, "New Coke Debuted 30 Years Ago. Here's Why It Was a Sugary Fiasco," *Vox*, April 23, 2015, http://www.vox.com/2015/4/23/8472539/new-coke-cola-wars.

102. Ibid.

103. Scott Cuppari, "The Integrated Marketing Communications of Coca-Cola Freestyle," filmed December 2015 at PRSSA 2015 National Conference, Atlanta, GA, video, 38:47, https://www.youtube.com/watch?time_continue=192&v=9xZ9HA7kcV8.

104. Tischler, "Pop Artist."

105. Joe Peters, "How IoT Is Changing Prototyping," *Best Techie*, February 21, 2018, https://www.besttechie.com/how-iot-is-changing-prototyping/.

106. Jack in the Box, "Jack in the Box Introduces New Signature Coca-Cola Freestyle Beverage, Jumpin' Jack Splash," *Business Wire*, May 22, 2017, https://www.businesswire.com/news/home/20170522005395/en/Jack-Box%EF%83%92-Introduces-New-Signature-Coca-Cola-Freestyle%EF%83%92.

107. Tom Spigolon, "Coke Unveils Custom Drink Mix Featuring Douglas Olympic Champion," *MDJOnline*, January 22, 2018, http://www.mdjonline.com/neighbor_newspapers/west_georgia/business/coke-unveils-custom-drink-mix-featuring-douglas-olympic-champion/article_ecf4564a-ff8a-11e7-8be8-9b3b9e81efb4.html.

108. Cuppari, "Integrated Marketing Communications of Coca-Cola Freestyle."

109. David L. Altheide and Robert P. Snow, *Media Worlds in the Postjournalism Era* (Hawthorne, NY: Aldine De Gruyter, 1991).

110. Blyskal and Blyskal, *PR*.

111. Dana Harris, "Flack Pack Hits Burnout Track," *Variety*, April 17–23, 2000.

112. Moore and Kalupa, *Public Relations*; Tim LaPira, "How Much Lobbying Is There in Washington? It's DOUBLE What You Think," *Sunlight Foundation*, November 25, 2013, http://sunlightfoundation.com/blog/2013/11/25/how-much-lobbying-is-there-in-washington-its-double-what-you-think/.

113. "Lobbying Database," *Open Secrets*, June 11, 2016, http://www.opensecrets.org/lobby/.

114. Moore and Kalupa, *Public Relations*; LaPira, "How Much Lobbying Is There in Washington?"

115. Betsy Rothstein, "Capital Living: The Fine Art of Flacking," *Hill*, February 22, 2006.

116. Ibid.

117. Betsy Rothstein, "Capital Living: Doing the Write Thing," *The Hill*, January 3, 2007.

118. Jennifer Rubin, "Sarah Huckabee Sanders Has Lost All Credibility," *Chicago Tribune*, May 4, 2018, http://www.chicagotribune.com/news/opinion/commentary/ct-sarah-huckabee-sanders-lies-20180504-story.html.

119. Moore and Kalupa, *Public Relations*.

120. Randy Sumpter and James Tankard, "The Spin Doctor: An Alternative View of Public Relations," *Public Relations Review* 20, no. 1 (1994).

121. Ibid.

122. Daniel Zwerdling, "Fast-Food Deal a Big Win for Small Migrants' Group," *NPR*, June 16, 2005, http://www.npr.org/templates/story/story.php?storyId=4706271.

123. David Halberstam, "And Now, Live From Little Rock," *Newsweek*, September 29, 1997.

124. Stephen B. Oates, *Let the Trumpet Sound* (New York: Harper & Row, 1982).

125. Ibid.

126. Martin Luther King Jr., *The Autobiography of Martin Luther King Jr.*, ed. Clayborne Carson (New York: Warner Books, 1998); Steven Kasher, *The Civil Rights Movement: A Photographic History, 1954–68* (New York: Abbeville Press, 1996).

127. Ben Golliver, "Sports come to a halt: NBA, WNBA, MLB, MLS postpone games as players protest Jacob Blake shooting." Aug. 26, 2020, *The Washington Post*, https://www.washingtonpost.com/sports/2020/08/26/bucks-boycott-nba-playoff-game/.

128. Alex Lasry. Twitter. Aug. 26, 2020, https://twitter.com/AlexanderLasry/status/1298722513304748032.

CHAPTER 14

1. Samantha Schmidt, "These High School Journalists Investigated a New Principal's Credentials. Days Later, She Resigned," *Washington Post*, April 5, 2017, https://www.washingtonpost.com/news/morning-mix/wp/2017/04/05/these-high-school-journalists-investigated-a-new-principals-credentials-days-later-she-resigned/.

2. Ralph Hanson, "High School Journalism Students in Pittsburgh, Kansas Take Down High School Principal With Questionable Credentials," *Living in a Media World*, April 6, 2017, https://www.ralphehanson.com/2017/04/06/high-school-journalism-students-in-pittsburg-kansas-take-down-high-school-principal-with-questionable-credentials/.

3. Mará Rose Williams, "New Pittsburg, Kan., High School Principal Resigns After Student Journalists Question Her Credentials," *Kansas City Star*, April 4, 2017, http://www.kansascity.com/news/local/article142682464.html.

4. Oliver Morrison, "How a Teacher Prepared Her Students to Take on the Adults and Win," *Wichita Eagle*, April 27, 2017, http://www.kansas.com/news/state/article147293239.html.

5. "Emily Smith From Pittsburg Named Jackie Engle Award Winner," *KSPAOnline*, April 21, 2015, https://www.kspaonline.org/news/2015/04/21/emily-smith-from-pittsburg-named-jackie-engel-award-winner/.

6. Schmidt, "These High School Journalists Investigated a New Principal's Credentials."

7. Hanson, "High School Journalism Students in Pittsburg, Kansas Take Down High School Principal."

8. Dylan Lysen, "Journalism Teacher Recounts Lack of Community Support for National Story," *Manhattan Mercury*,

July 18, 2017, https://themercury.com/news/journalism-teacher
-recounts-lack-of-community-support-for-national-story/
article_0cd1323c-243d-5850-b96d-6755d3211302.html.

9. Ibid.

10. Mike Hiestand, "Understanding 'Anti-Hazelwood' Laws,"
NSPA, http://studentpress.org/nspa/its-the-law-understanding
-anti-hazelwood-laws/.

11. Fred H. Cate, *Privacy in the Information Age* (Washington, DC:
Brookings Institution, 1997).

12. Ibid.

13. "Legal Information Institute," *Cornell University Law School*,
http://www.law.cornell.edu.

14. Kenneth Creech, *Electronic Media Law and Regulation*, 3rd ed.
(Boston: Focal Press, 2000).

15. Ben H. Bagdikian, "Not Just Another Business," *University of
Arizona*, 1996.

16. Ronald G. Shafer, "The Thin-Skinned President Who Made
It Illegal to Criticize His Office," *Washington Post*, September
8, 2018, http://www.washingtonpost.com/news/retropolis/
wp/2018/09/08/the-thin-skinned-president-who-made-it
-illegal-to-criticize-his-office/.

17. Herbert N. Foerstel, *Banned in the Media* (Westport, CT:
Greenwood Press, 1998).

18. Creech, *Electronic Media Law and Regulation*; Foerstel, *Banned
in the Media*.

19. Don R. Pember and Clay Calvert, *Mass Media Law*, 2005–2006
ed. (New York: McGraw-Hill, 2005).

20. David L. Hudson Jr., "Libraries and First Amendment,"
First Amendment Center, May 25, 2004, http://www.firstamendment
center.org/patriot-act.

21. Ibid.

22. Ibid.

23. Ibid.

24. Brian Ross and Richard Esposito, "Federal Source to ABC
News: We Know Who You're Calling," *ABC News*, May 17,
2006.

25. Patrick W. Gavin, "ABC's Ross: Anti-Terrorism Tools Turned
on Journos," *Adweek*, May 17, 2006, http://www.adweek
.com/fishbowldc/abcs-ross-anti-terrorism-tools-turned-on
-journos/3459.

26. Harley Geiger, "Issue Brief: Bulk Collection of Records Under
Section 215 of the PATRIOT Act," *Center for Democracy and
Technology*, February 10, 2014, https://cdt.org/blog/issue-brief
-bulk-collection-of-records-under-section-215-of-the-patriot
-act/.

27. Cindy Cohn and Dia Kayyali, "Understanding the New USA
FREEDOM Act: Questions, Concerns, and EFF's Decision to
Support the Bill," *Electronic Frontier Foundation*, August 7, 2014,
http://www.eff.org/deeplinks/2014/08/understanding-new
-usa-freedom-act-questions-concerns-and-effs-decision
-support; Erin Kelly, "Senate Approves USA Freedom Act,"
USA Today, June 2, 2015, http://www.usatoday.com/story/news/
politics/2015/06/02/patriot-act-usa-freedom-act-senate
-vote/28345747/.

28. Rodney A. Smolla, *Law of Defamation* (New York: Clark
Boardman Company, 1988).

29. Barbara Dill, *The Journalist's Handbook on Libel and Privacy*
(New York: Free Press, 1986).

30. 376 U.S. 254 (1964).

31. Dill, *Journalist's Handbook on Libel and Privacy*.

32. W. Wat Hopkins, *Actual Malice: Twenty-Five Years after* Times v.
Sullivan (New York: Praeger, 1989).

33. Ibid., 12.

34. Ibid.

35. Ibid.

36. Adam Liptak, "Justice Clarence Thomas Calls for
Reconsideration of Landmark Libel Ruling," *New York Times*,
February 19, 2019, http://www.nytimes.com/2019/02/19/us/
politics/clarence-thomas-first-amendment-libel.html.

37. 418 U.S. 323 (1974).

38. Dill, *Journalist's Handbook on Libel and Privacy*.

39. Ellyn Angelotti, "How Courtney Love and U.S.'s First Twitter
Libel Trial Could Impact Journalists," *Poynter*, January 14,
2014, https://www.poynter.org/news/how-courtney-love-and
-uss-first-twitter-libel-trial-could-impact-journalists.

40. Carlo Allegri, "Courtney Love Wins Twitter Libel Case,"
CBS News, January 24, 2014, http://www.cbsnews.com/news/
courtney-love-wins-twitter-libel-case/.

41. Eriq Gardner, "*Rolling Stone* Settles Last Remaining Lawsuit
over UVA Rape Story," *Hollywood Reporter*, December 21, 2017,
https://www.hollywoodreporter.com/thr-esq/rolling
-stone-settles-last-remaining-lawsuit-uva-rape-story-1069880;
Moriah Balingit, "*Rolling Stone* Reporter Says 'Jackie' Deceived
Her About U-Va. Gang Rape," *Washington Post*, October 20,
2016, https://www.washingtonpost.com/local/education/rolling
-stone-reporter-says-jackie-deceived-her-about-u-va-gang
-rape/2016/10/20/77151476-967e-11e6-bc79-af1cd3d2984b_
story.html.

42. Paul Farhi, "Federal Judge Reinstates Libel Lawsuit Filed by
Covington Catholic Teen against *Washington Post*," *Washington
Post*, October 28, 2019, http://www.washingtonpost.com/lifestyle/
style/federal-judge-reinstates-libel-lawsuit-filed-by-covington
-catholic-teen-against-washington-post/2019/10/28/30155c52
-f9ae-11e9-ac8c-8eced29ca6ef_story.html.

43. Paul Farhi, "CNN Settles Libel Lawsuit with Covington
Catholic Student," *Washington Post*, January 7, 2020, http://
www.washingtonpost.com/lifestyle/style/cnn-settles-libel
-lawsuit-with-covington-catholic-student/2020/01/07/
f0b21842-319e-11ea-91fd-82d4e04a3fac_story.html.

44. Cate, *Privacy in the Information Age*.

45. Deckle McLean, *Privacy and Its Invasion* (Westport, CT:
Praeger, 1995).

46. Dill, *Journalist's Handbook on Libel and Privacy*.

47. Ibid.

48. Molly Roberts, "We Should Be Afraid of Peter Thiel,"
Washington Post, January 12, 2018, https://www.washingtonpost
.com/blogs/post-partisan/wp/2018/01/12/trump-isnt-the-only
-menace-to-a-free-press/; Jeffrey Toobin, "Gawker's Demise
and the Trump-Era Threat to the First Amendment," *New
Yorker*, December 12, 2016, https://www.newyorker.com/
magazine/2016/12/19/gawkers-demise-and-the-trump-era
-threat-to-the-first-amendment.

49. Pember and Calvert, *Mass Media Law*.

50. Roy L. Moore and Michael D. Murray, *Media Law and Ethics*,
3rd ed. (New York: Erlbaum, 2008), 577

51. Oscar Dixon, "Jordan Reclaims Richest Athlete Title," *USA
Today*, December 1, 1997.

52. Associated Press, "Jennifer Aniston Settles Lawsuit With
'Invasive' Photographer," *Fox News*, September 2, 2006;
"Blogger Sued Over Topless Aniston Photo," *ABC News*,
February 21, 2007.

53. "Aniston Warns Over Topless Photos," *Smoking Gun*,
December 5, 2005, http://www.thesmokinggun.com/
documents/crime/aniston-warns-over-topless-photos.

54. Dionne Searcey, "A New California Law Places Paparazzi
Under the Spotlight," *Wall Street Journal*, October 29, 2009.

55. Adrean S. Taylor, "Common Law Invasion of Privacy Claims in Social Media [Guest Post]," *Wassom.com*, July 2, 2013, http://www.wassom.com/common-law-invasion-of-privacy-claims-in-social-media-guest-post.html.

56. Stuart Dredge and Danny Yadron, "Apple Challenges 'Chilling' Demand to Decrypt San Bernardino Shooter's iPhone," *Guardian*, February 17, 2016, https://www.theguardian.com/technology/2016/feb/17/apple-challenges-chilling-demand-decrypt-san-bernadino-iphone?CMP=share_btn_link.

57. Tim Cook, "A Message to Our Customers," *Apple*, February 16, 2016, https://www.apple.com/customer-letter/.

58. Kim Zetter, "Apple's FBI Battle Is Complicated. Here's What's Really Going On," *Wired*, February 18, 2016, https://www.wired.com/2016/02/apples-fbi-battle-is-complicated-heres-whats-really-going-on/.

59. Russell Brandom, "Apple's San Bernardino Fight Is Officially Over as Government Confirms Working Attack," *Verge*, March 28, 2016, http://www.theverge.com/2016/3/28/11317396/apple-fbi-encryption-vacate-iphone-order-san-bernardino; Ellen Nakashima, "FBI Paid Professional Hackers One-Time Fee to Crack San Bernardino iPhone," *Washington Post*, April 12, 2016, https://www.washingtonpost.com/world/national-security/fbi-paid-professional-hackers-one-time-fee-to-crack-san-bernardino-iphone/2016/04/12/5397814a-00de-11e6-9d36-33d198ea26c5_story.html.

60. Kathryn Varn, "Cops Use Dead Man's Finger in Attempt to Access His Phone. It's Legal, but Is It OK?" *Tampa Bay Times*, April 21, 2018, http://www.tampabay.com/news/publicsafety/Cops-used-dead-man-s-finger-in-attempt-to-access-his-phone-It-s-legal-but-is-it-okay-_167262017.

61. Matthew D. Bunker, *Justice and the Media: Reconciling Fair Trials and a Free Press* (Mahwah, NJ: Erlbaum, 1997).

62. Ibid.

63. 284 U.S. 333 (1966).

64. Ibid.; Kyle Niederpruem, "Big Trials Prompt Judges to Issue More Gag Orders," *Quill*, June 1997.

65. Ralph E. Hanson, Review of *Journalism and Justice in the Oklahoma City Bombing Trends* by Chad F. Nye, *Journalism & Mass Communication Educator* 70, no. 4 (December 2015), 438–440.

66. Garrett Epps, "Westboro Baptist Church's Surreal Day in Court," *Atlantic*, October 6, 2010, http://www.theatlantic.com/national/archive/2010/10/westboro-baptist-churchs-surreal-day-in-court/64167/.

67. Caitlin Dickson, "This Man Is the Future of Westboro Baptist Church," *Daily Beast*, March 24, 2014, https://www.thedailybeast.com/this-man-is-the-future-of-westboro-baptist-church.

68. Stuart Taylor Jr., "Court, 8–0, Extends Right to Criticize Those in Public Eye," *New York Times*, January 25, 1988, http://www.nytimes.com/1988/02/25/us/court-8-0-extends-right-to-criticize-those-in-public-eye.html.

69. Robert Barnes, "Court Considers Westboro Baptist Church's Anti-Gay Protests at Military Funerals," *Washington Post*, October 6, 2010, http://www.washingtonpost.com/wp-dyn/content/article/2010/10/06/AR2010100603950.html.

70. Ibid.

71. John G. Roberts, "*Snyder v. Phelps* Excerpt: Roberts's Majority Opinion in Westboro Church Case," *Washington Post*, March 2, 2011, http://www.washingtonpost.com/wp-dyn/content/article/2011/03/02/AR2011030203069.html.

72. Mark Joseph Stern, "Westboro Baptist Church to Protest Scalia's Funeral, Exercising a Right He Voted to Protect," *Slate*, February 19, 2016, http://www.slate.com/blogs/the_slatest/2016/02/19/westboro_baptist_church_to_protest_scalia_s_funeral.html.

73. Steven Brill, "Cameras Belong in the Courtroom," *USA Today Magazine*, July 1996.

74. Joshua Sarner, "Comment: Justice, Take Two: The Continuing Debate Over Cameras in the Courtroom," *Seton Hall Constitutional Journal* (2000).

75. "Cameras in the Courtroom," *Quill*, September 1999.

76. Associated Press, "Minnesota Tests Cameras in the Courtroom," *Pioneer Press*, March 9, 2012, http://www.twincities.com/localnews/ci_20147979/pilot-project-tests-photo-coverage-minn-courts.

77. Lisa Balde and Phil Rogers, "Judges Enthusiastic About Cameras in the Courtroom," *NBC Chicago*, January 24, 2012, http://www.nbcchicago.com/news/local/Illinois-Supreme-Court-Approves-Cameras-in-Trial-Courtrooms-137966308.html.

78. Zoe Tillman, "Judges, Attorneys Debate Cameras in the Courtroom," *BLT: The Blog of LegalTimes*, March 28, 2012, https://legaltimes.typepad.com/blt/2012/03/judges-attorneys-debate-cameras-in-the-courtroom.html.

79. Bunker, *Justice and the Media*.

80. Elliot C. Rothenberg, *The Taming of the Press:* Cohen v. Cowles Media Company (Westport, CT: Praeger, 1999).

81. *Cohen v. Cowles Media Company*, 501 U.S. 663 (1991).

82. Lisa de Moraes, "With Appeals Court Ruling, ABC Won't Pay Food Lion's Share," *Washington Post*, October 21, 1999; Sue Anne Pressley, "Food Lion Challenges ABC's Newsgathering; Lawsuit Attacks Hidden Cameras," *Washington Post*, December 12, 1996; James C. Goodale, "Shooting the Messenger Isn't So Easy," *New York Law Journal*, December 3, 1999.

83. Goodale, "Shooting the Messenger Isn't So Easy." See also *Food Lion v. ABC*, 194 F. 3d 505 (4th Cir. 1999).

84. Bunker, *Justice and the Media*; Creech, *Electronic Media Law and Regulation*. See also *Near v. Minnesota*, 283 U.S. 697 (1931).

85. Sanford J. Ungar, *The Papers and the Papers* (New York: Dutton, 1972).

86. Ibid.

87. Ben Bradlee, *A Good Life: Newspapering and Other Adventures* (New York: Simon & Schuster, 1995).

88. Ungar, *Papers and the Papers*.

89. Ibid., 242.

90. 403 U.S. 713 (1971).

91. Peter Schrag, *Test of Loyalty: Daniel Ellsberg and the Rituals of Secret Government* (New York: Simon & Schuster, 1974).

92. Robert G. Kaiser, "Public Secrets," *Washington Post*, June 11, 2006, https://www.washingtonpost.com/archive/opinions/2006/06/11/public-secrets/eb49a7f6-18ae-491c-9f55-12ec38c968b7/?utm_term=.c71d6acb1e10.

93. Duncan Campbell, "It's Time to Take Risks," *Guardian*, December 10, 2002, http://www.guardian.co.uk/books/2002/dec/10/biography.usa.

94. Foerstel, *Banned in the Media*.

95. Howard Morland, *The Secret That Exploded* (New York: Random House, 1981).

96. Foerstel, *Banned in the Media*.

97. Evan Hill, Ainara Tiefenthäler, Christiaan Triebert, Drew Jordan, Haley Willis, and Robin Stein, "How George Floyd Was Killed in Police Custody," *New York Times*, May 31, 2020, https://www.nytimes.com/2020/05/31/us/george-floyd-investigation.html.

98. Michael J. Socolow, "Guest Blog Post—Caught in the Crossfire: Journalism's 'Objectivity' Problem in Times of Civil Unrest," *Living in a Media World*, June 1, 2020, https://www.ralphehanson.com/2020/06/01/guest-blog-post-caught-in-the-crossfire-journalisms-objectivity-problem-in-times-of-civil-unrest/.

99. Josh Verges, "Journalist Blinded During Protest Sues Minneapolis Police, State Patrol," *Pioneer Press*, June 10, 2020, https://www.twincities.com/2020/06/10/journalist-blinded-during-protest-sues-minneapolis-police-state-patrol/.

100. Katelyn Burns, "Police Targeted Journalists Covering the George Floyd Protests," *Vox*, May 31, 2020, https://www.vox.com/identities/2020/5/31/21276013/police-targeted-journalists-covering-george-floyd-protests?fbclid=IwAR3pK2zm-vQfgnwVnPABzXsyDzd_JzYKllsJXOpz11eqtxb3L7C3PAEaRU0.

101. U.S. Press Freedom Tracker, Twitter post, June 10, 2020, 12:09 p.m., https://twitter.com/uspresstracker/status/1270750066165166080.

102. Mark Berman, "*Washington Post* Reporter Arrested in Ferguson," *Washington Post*, August 13, 2014, https://www.washingtonpost.com/news/post-nation/wp/2014/08/13/washington-post-reporter-arrested-in-ferguson/.

103. Ravi Somaiya and Ashley Southall, "Arrested in Ferguson Last Year, 2 Reporters Are Charged," *New York Times*, August 10, 2015, http://www.nytimes.com/2015/08/11/us/arrested-in-ferguson-2014-washington-post-reporter-wesley-lowery-is-charged.html.

104. Benjamin Mullin, "Major News Outlets Condemn Charges Against Reports in Ferguson Arrests," *Poynter*, August 18, 2015, http://www.poynter.org/2015/major-news-outlets-condemn-charges-against-reporters-in-ferguson-arrests/366985/.

105. John Nolte, "Ferguson: *Washington Post* Reporter Charged With Trespassing, Interfering With Police Officer," *Breitbart*, August 11, 2015, http://www.breitbart.com/big-journalism/2015/08/11/ferguson-washington-post-reporter-charged-with-trespassing-interfering-with-police-officer/.

106. Niraj Chokshi, "Ferguson-Related Charges Dropped Against *Washington Post* and *Huffington Post* Reporters," *Washington Post*, May 19, 2016, https://www.washingtonpost.com/news/post-nation/wp/2016/05/19/ferguson-related-charges-dropped-against-washington-post-and-huffington-post-reporters/?utm_term=.5041ce024aa8.

107. Cora Currier, "Pressure, Potential for a Federal Shield Law," *Columbia Journalism Review*, June 13, 2014, http://www.cjr.org/behind_the_news/shield_law_risen_etc.php.

108. Casey Murray and Kirsten B. Mitchell, "Would a Shield Law Matter?" *News Media and the Law* 30, no. 3 (2006), 4.

109. Ibid.; Howard Kurtz, "No More Miller Time," *Washington Post*, September 30, 2005, http://www.washingtonpost.com/wp-dyn/content/blog/2005/09/30/BL2005093000363.html.

110. 484 U.S. 260 (1988).

111. Ibid.

112. Mark Goodman, "Freedom of the Press Stops at the Schoolhouse Gate," *Nieman Reports*, Spring 2001.

113. Goodman, "Freedom of the Press Stops at the Schoolhouse Gate"; "Missouri," *New Voices*.

114. "The Legislation," *New Voices*; "Missouri"; Kaitlin DeWulf, "Missouri House Overwhelmingly Passes Student Press Freedom Bill," *Student Press Law Center*, March 16, 2016, http://www.splc.org/article/2016/03/missouri-house-overwhelmingly-passes-student-press-freedom-bill.

115. Tara Bahrampour and Lori Aratani, "Teens' Bold Blogs Alarm Area Schools," *Washington Post*, January 17, 2006, A01.

116. "Austin Carroll, Indiana High School Student, Expelled for Tweeting Profanity," *Huffington Post*, March 25, 2012, http://www.huffingtonpost.com/2012/03/25/austin-carroll-indiana-hi_n_1378250.html.

117. Case argued before the U.S. Supreme Court, March 19, 2007; 551 U.S. 393 (2007).

118. Robert Barnes, "Justices to Hear Landmark Free-Speech Case," *Washington Post*, March 13, 2007, A03; Charles Lane, "Court Backs School on Speech Curbs," *Washington Post*, June 26, 2007, A06.

119. Ibid.

120. Liz Harper, "First Amendment Understanding Lacking," *PBS*, February 7, 2005.

121. Edward Donnerstein, Daniel Linz, and Steven Penrod, *The Question of Pornography* (New York: Free Press, 1987).

122. 354 U.S. 476 (1957).

123. U.S. Supreme Court, "*Samuel Roth, Petitioner v. United States of America, David S. Alberts, Appellant,*" *Communications & the Law* 21, no. 4 (1999).

124. Donnerstein et al., *Question of Pornography*, 149

125. Ibid., 149–151.

126. Franklin Mark Osanka and Sara Lee Johann, *Sourcebook on Pornography* (Lexington, MA: Lexington Books, 1989).

127. Rieko Mashima, "Problem of the Supreme Court's Obscenity Test Concerning Cyberporn," *Computer Lawyer* 16, no. 11 (1999).

128. Timothy Egan, "Erotica Inc.—A Special Report; Technology Sent Wall Street Into Market for Pornography," *New York Times*, October 23, 2000.

129. Edward Rothstein, "The Owners of Culture vs. the Free Agents," *New York Times*, January 18, 2003.

130. Amy Harmon, "New Visibility for 1998 Copyright Protection Law, With Online Enthusiasts Confused and Frustrated," *New York Times*, August 13, 2001.

131. Minjeong Kim, "The Creative Commons and Copyright Protection in the Digital Era: Uses of Creative Commons Licenses," *Journal of Computer-Mediated Communication* 13, no. 1 (2007).

132. Creech, *Electronic Media Law and Regulation*.

133. Linda Harowitz, "Laying the Fairness Doctrine to Rest: Was the Doctrine's Elimination Really Fair?" *George Washington Law Review* 58, no. 994 (1990).

134. Creech, *Electronic Media Law and Regulation*.

135. Harowitz, "Laying the Fairness Doctrine to Rest."

136. Thomas Blaisdell Smith, "Reexamining the Reasonable Access and Equal Time Provisions of the Federal Communications Act," *Georgetown Law Journal* 74, no. 1491 (1986); Creech, *Electronic Media Law and Regulation*; Dan Fletcher, "The Fairness Doctrine," *Time*, February 20, 2009.

137. Rush Limbaugh, "Mr. President, Keep the Airwaves Free," *Wall Street Journal*, February 20, 2009, https://www.wsj.com/articles/SB123508978035028163.

138. Brooks Boliek, "FCC Finally Kills Off Fairness Doctrine," *Politico*, August 23, 2011, http://www.politico.com/news/stories/0811/61851.html; Dylan Matthews, "Everything You Need to Know About the Fairness Doctrine in One Post," *Washington Post*, August 23, 2011, http://www.washingtonpost.com/blogs/ezra-klein/post/everything-you-need-to-know-about-the-fairness-doctrine-in-one-post/2011/08/23/gIQAN8CXZJ_blog.html.

139. Creech, *Electronic Media Law and Regulation*.

140. Ibid.

141. Cecilia Kang, "FCC to Draft Net Neutrality Rules, Taking Step Toward Web Regulation," *Washington Post*, October 23, 2009.

142. Foerstel, *Banned in the Media*.

143. Tim Wu, "Network Neutrality, Broadband Discrimination," *Journal on Telecommunications and High Technology Law*, Vol. 2 (2003), http://www.jthtl.org/content/articles/V2I1/JTHTLv2i1_Wu.PDF.

144. Klint Finley, "Net Neutrality: Here's Everything You Need to Know," *Wired*, March 25, 2018.

145. Ibid.

146. Salvador Rizzo, "Will the FCC's Net Neutrality Repeal Grind the Internet to a Halt?" *Washington Post*, March 5, 2018, https://www.washingtonpost.com/news/fact-checker/wp/2018/03/05/will-the-fccs-net-neutrality-repeal-grind-the-internet-to-a-halt/.

147. Ibid.

148. Ibid.

149. Nilay Patel, "HBO Max Won't Hit AT&T Data Caps, but Netflix and Disney Plus Will," *Verge*, June 2, 2020, https://www.theverge.com/2020/6/2/21277402/hbo-max-att-data-caps-netflix-disney-plus-streaming-services-net-neutrality.

CHAPTER 15

1. "A Brief History of Presidential Profanity," *Rolling Stone*, December 10, 2012, https://www.rollingstone.com/politics/lists/a-brief-history-of-presidential-profanity-20121210.

2. Helen Dewar and Dana Milbank, "Cheney Dismisses Critic With Obscenity," *Washington Post*, June 25, 2004, http://www.washingtonpost.com/wp-dyn/articles/A3699-2004Jun24.html.

3. Howard Kurtz, "Post Editor Explains Decision to Publish Expletive," *Washington Post*, June 26, 2004, http://www.washingtonpost.com/wp-dyn/articles/A5109-2004Jun25.html.

4. Jeannine Aversa, "Bush Utters Expletive on Hezbollah Attacks," *Washington Post*, July 17, 2006, http://www.washingtonpost.com/wp-dyn/content/article/2006/07/17/AR2006071700205.html.

5. Josh Dawsey, "Trump Derides Protections for Immigrants From 'Shithole' Countries," *Washington Post*, January 12, 2018, https://www.washingtonpost.com/politics/trump-attacks-protections-for-immigrants-from-shithole-countries-in-oval-office-meeting/2018/01/11/bfc0725c-f711-11e7-91af-31ac729add94_story.html.

6. Benjamin Freed, "*Washington Post*: 'When the President Says It, We'll Use It Verbatim,'" *Washingtonian*, January 11, 2018, https://www.washingtonian.com/2018/01/11/washington-post-president-says-well-use-verbatim/.

7. Elizabeth Jensen, "NPR's Approach to a Reported Presidential Profanity Evolves," *NPR*, January 12, 2018, https://www.npr.org/sections/ombudsman/2018/01/12/577631226/nprs-approach-to-a-reported-presidential-profanity-evolves.

8. Karen Attiah, Twitter post, January 11, 2018, 8:29 p.m., https://twitter.com/KarenAttiah/status/951627280991703040.

9. Philip Patterson and Lee Wilkins, *Media Ethics, Issues and Cases* (New York: McGraw-Hill, 2002).

10. Doug Underwood, "Secularists or Modern Day Prophets? Journalists' Ethics and the Judeo-Christian Tradition," *Journal of Mass Media Ethics* 16, no. 1 (2001).

11. Franklin Foer, "The Wayward Critic," *New Republic*, May 15, 2000.

12. Larry Z. Leslie, *Mass Communication Ethics* (Boston: Houghton Mifflin, 2000).

13. Patterson and Wilkins, *Media Ethics, Issues and Cases*.

14. David L. Martinson, "Ethical Decision Making in Public Relations: What Would Aristotle Say?" *Public Relations Quarterly* 45, no. 3 (2000).

15. Tom Burton, "Ryan Kelly: The Story of the Charlottesville Photo," *NPAA*, April 22, 2018, https://nppa.org/news/ryan-kelly-story-charlottesville-attack.

16. Bryan McKenzie, "White Nationalist Rally Turns Fatal," *Daily Progress*, August 12, 2017, http://www.dailyprogress.com/news/local/ohio-man-charged-with-second-degree-murder-after-car-plows/article_ef4ba358-7f6a-11e7-84cf-8f840f442510.html.

17. Ibid.

18. Aric Jenkins, "A Charlottesville Photographer Took His Tragic, Pulitzer Prize–Winning Shot on His Last Day. Now He Works for a Brewery," *Time*, April 16, 2018, http://time.com/5242423/ryan-kelly-photograph-pulitzer-prize-charlottesville/.

19. Burton, "Ryan Kelly."

20. The 2018 Pulitzer Prize Winner in Breaking News Photography: Ryan Kelly of *The Daily Progress*, Charlottesville, Va.," *Pulitzer Prizes*, http://www.pulitzer.org/winners/ryan-kelly-daily-progress.

21. Burton, "Ryan Kelly."

22. Rachelle Hampton, "It Was a Cleansing Day," *Slate*, May 24, 2018, https://slate.com/human-interest/2018/05/ryan-kelly-pulitzer-winner-on-photographing-charlottesville-and-a-wedding.html.

23. Alisa Chang, "Pulitzer-Winning Photographer Made Charlottesville Photo on His Last Day the Job," *NPR*, April 17, 2018, https://www.npr.org/2018/04/17/603351974/pulitzer-prize-winning-photographer-discusses-far-right-rally-at-charlottesville.

24. Jenkins, "A Charlottesville Photographer Took His Tragic, Pulitzer Prize-Winning Shot on His Last Day."

25. Leslie, *Mass Communication Ethics*.

26. Patterson and Wilkins, *Media Ethics, Issues and Cases*.

27. Howard Berkes, Barbara Bradley Hagerty, and Jennifer Ludden, "NBC Defends Release of Va. Tech Gunman Video," *NPR*, April 19, 2007, www.npr.org/templates/story/story.php?storyId=9604204.

28. Leslie, *Mass Communication Ethics*.

29. Hampton, "It Was a Cleansing Day."

30. Elizabeth Blanks Hindman, "Divergence of Duty: Differences in Legal and Ethical Responsibilities," *Journal of Mass Media Ethics* 14, no. 4 (1999).

31. Patterson and Wilkins, *Media Ethics, Issues and Cases*.

32. Hampton, "It Was a Cleansing Day."

33. Patterson and Wilkins, *Media Ethics, Issues and Cases*.

34. Sissela Bok, *Lying: Moral Choice in Public and Private Life* (New York: Pantheon Books, 1978).

35. David L. Martinson, "Ethical Decision Making in Public Relations: What Would Aristotle Say?" *Public Relations Quarterly* 45, no. 3 (2000).

36. Sissela Bok, *Lying: Moral Choice in Public and Private Life* (New York: Vintage Books, 1979), 14.

37. David L. Martinson, "Ethical Decision Making in Public Relations."

38. Adam Kirsch, "He Wrote What They Wanted," *New York Sun*, January 11, 2006; "A Million Little Lies," *Smoking Gun*, January 8, 2006, http://www.thesmokinggun.com/documents/celebrity/million-little-lies.

39. Ibid.

40. Scott Eyman, "It's My Story (and I'll Lie If I Want to)," *Palm Beach Post*, February 21, 2006.

41. Steven Brill, "Rewind: What Book Reviews Don't Review," *Brill's Content*, August 1999.

42. Paul Tullis and Lorne Manly, "Slipping Past the Fact Checkers: How Magazines Do and Do Not Check Their Stories," *Brill's Content*, July/August 1998.

43. Ann Reilly Dowd, "The Great Pretender: How a Writer Fooled His Readers," *Columbia Journalism Review*, July/August 1998.

44. "Shattered Glass," *Vanity Fair*, October 2007.

45. Tullis and Manly, "Slipping Past the Fact Checkers."

46. Dowd, "Great Pretender."

47. Jose Antonio Vargas, "My Life as an Undocumented Immigrant," *New York Times*, June 22, 2011, http://www.nytimes.com/2011/06/26/magazine/my-life-as-an-undocumented-immigrant.html.

48. Jamil Smith, "Putting a Face to the Name 'Illegal,'" *MSNBC*, June 29, 2011, www.msnbc.com/rachel-maddow-show/putting-face-the-name-illegal.

49. Frances Martel, "The *Washington Post* Turned Down Jose Vargas' Illegal Immigrant Story," *Mediaite*, June 22, 2011, http://www.mediaite.com/online/the-washington-post-turned-down-jose-vargas-illegal-immigrant-story/.

50. Mike Pesca, "Journalist Jose Vargas' Illegal Immigration Revelation," *On the Media*, June 24, 2011, http://www.wnyc.org/story/142816-journalist-jose-vargas-illegal-immigration-revelation.

51. Phil Bronstein, "I Was Duped by Jose Vargas, Illegal Immigrant," *Bronstein at Large*, June 22, 2011, https://blog.sfgate.com/bronstein/2011/06/22/i-was-duped-by-jose-vargas-illegal-immigrant/.

52. Erik Wemple, "Sean Hannity Cannot Tweet His Way Out of Journalistic Corruption," *Washington Post*, April 19, 2018, https://www.washingtonpost.com/blogs/erik-wemple/wp/2018/04/19/sean-hannity-cannot-tweet-his-way-out-of-journalistic-corruption/.

53. Paul Farhi, "Sean Hannity Had a Lot to Say About Michael Cohen Lately. But He Left a Few Things Out," *Washington Post*, April 16, 2018, https://www.washingtonpost.com/lifestyle/style/sean-hannity-had-a-lot-to-say-about-michael-cohen-lately-but-he-left-a-few-things-out/2018/04/16/c795b2f2-41b3-11e8-8569-26fda6b404c7_story.html.

54. Ibid.

55. Lance Morrow, "Journalism After Diana," in *The Media and Morality*, ed. Robert M. Baird, William E. Loges, and Stuart E. Rosenbaum (Amherst, NY: Prometheus Books, 1999), 101.

56. Ralph Hanson, "Searching for a Miracle: Media Lessons From the West Virginia Mine Disaster," *Montana Journalism Review* (2006).

57. "Asked to Do Something Unethical," *SportsShooter*, January 29, 2008, http://www.sportsshooter.com/message_display.html?tid=28059.

58. Ralph Hanson, "Lesson of the Day: Don't Photoshop Details Out of News Photos," *Living in a Media World*, December 3, 2013, www.ralphehanson.com/2013/12/03/lesson-of-the-day-dont-photoshop-details-out-of-news-photos/.

59. Gil Klein, "Computer Graphics Now Allow Subtle Alteration of News Photos," *Christian Science Monitor*, August 1, 1985.

60. Richard L. Connor, "A Note of Apology to Readers," *Portland Press Herald*, September 19, 2010, www.pressherald.com/note-of-apology.html.

61. Bob Garfield, "For Some, an Apology Offends," *On the Media*, September 17, 2010, http://www.wnyc.org/story/132914-for-some-an-apology-offends/.

62. Richard L. Connor, "Remembering E. B. White's Sage Advice," *Portland Press Herald*, September 19, 2010, http://www.pressherald.com/news/remembering-e_b_-whites-sage-advice_2010-09-19.html.

63. UPI Stylebook and Guide to Newswriting, 4th ed., Bruce Cook and Harold Martin, eds. (Sterling, VA: Capital Books, Inc., 2004), 291.

64. Margaret Sullivan, "Media Coverage of Kobe Bryant's Death Was a Chaotic Mess, but There Were Moments of Grace," *Washington Post*, January 27, 2020, http://www.washingtonpost.com/lifestyle/style/media-coverage-of-kobe-bryants-death-was-a-chaotic-mess-but-there-were-moments-of-grace/2020/01/27/d825ade4-4106-11ea-aa6a-083d01b3ed18_story.html.

65. Guardian News, Twitter post, January 26, 2020, 3:26 p.m., https://twitter.com/guardiannews/status/1221529969245020165.

66. Paul Farhi, "*Washington Post* Reporter Who Tweeted About Kobe Bryant Rape Allegations Placed on Administrative Leave," *Washington Post*, January 28, 2020, http://www.washingtonpost.com/lifestyle/style/washington-post-suspends-reporter-who-tweeted-about-kobe-bryant-rape-allegations-following-his-death/2020/01/27/babe9c04-413b-11ea-b5fc-eefa848cde99_story.html.

67. Erik Wemple, "The *Post*'s Misguided Suspension of Felicia Sonmez Over Kobe Bryant Tweets," *Washington Post*, January 27, 2020, www.washingtonpost.com/opinions/2020/01/27/posts-misguided-suspension-felicia-sonmez-over-kobe-bryant-tweets/.

68. Tamara Jones and Ann Scott Tyson, "After 44 Hours, Hope Showed Its Cruel Side," *Washington Post*, January 5, 2006.

69. "Manchin at a Loss to Explain Rescue Miscommunication: Governor Says He Got Caught Up in Families' Celebration," *Charleston Daily Mail*, January 4, 2006.

70. Joe Strupp, "Local W. Va. Paper Says Skepticism Helped It Avoid Mining Story Goof," *Editor & Publisher*, January 4, 2006.

71. Ibid.

72. Ibid.

73. Vicki Smith, "Family Members Report 12 Trapped Miners Are Alive," *Charleston Gazette*, January 4, 2006.

74. Jennifer Dorroh, "The Ombudsman Puzzle," *American Journalism Review*, February/March 2005, https://ajrarchive.org/article.asp?id=3824.

75. Andrew Alexander, "Welcome to the Omblog," *Washington Post*, May 4, 2009, http://www.voices.washingtonpost.com/ombudsman-blog/2009/05/welcome_to_the_omblog.html.

76. Sanders LaMont, "Lending an Ear," *Organization of News Ombudsmen*, 1999.

77. Kelly McBride, "NPR Ombud's Latest Report Raises Important Questions, but It's Not Without Flaws," *Poynter*, August 15, 2013, https://www.poynter.org/news/npr-ombuds-latest-report-raises-important-questions-its-not-without-flaws.

78. Simon Dumenco, "Is the Newspaper Ombudsman More or Less Obsolete? Five Reasons Why Having a 'Public Editor' at the *Times* and Other Papers No Longer Makes Much Sense," *Ad Age*, March 24, 2008.

79. Jay Black, Bob Steele, and Ralph Barney, *Doing Ethics in Journalism* (Birmingham, AL: EBSCO Media, 1993).

80. Alex S. Jones, "Facing Ethical Challenges: The Integrity/Judgment Grid," *Columbia Journalism Review*, November/December 1999.

81. Jeffrey L. Seglin, "Codes of Ethics: Why Writing Them Is Not Enough," *Media Ethics*, Spring 2002.

82. Robert Jackall and Janice M. Hirota, *Image Makers: Advertising, Public Relations, and the Ethos of Advocacy* (Chicago: University of Chicago Press, 2000).

83. Patterson and Wilkins, *Media Ethics, Issues and Cases*.
84. Rogier van Bakel, "Tall-Claims Court," *The Christian Science Monitor*, February 14, 2000.
85. "Health Claims," *Federal Trade Commission*, August 20, 2014, http://www.ftc.gov/news-events/media-resources/truth-advertising/health-claims.
86. Van Bakel, "Tall-Claims Court."
87. Ibid.
88. Ibid.
89. M. L. Stein, "Auto Dealers Banned From Boycotting Calif. Media Outlets," *Editor & Publisher*, April 19, 1995.
90. M. J. Lee, "45 Companies Yank Ads From Rush," *Politico*, March 6, 2012, http://www.politico.com/news/stories/0312/73675.html.
91. News Services, "Is *Esquire* Slip a Step Up for Mankind?" *Star Tribune*, July 12, 1997.
92. Jim Edwards, "Nicetv," *Brill's Content*, March 2001.
93. Valerie Kuklenski, "All in the Family; Advertisers Praise—and Fund—Shows for Everyone," *Daily News of Los Angeles*, December 7, 2006; Stuart Elliot, "Marketers, Seeking Family Show, Hold Script Contest," *New York Times*, http://www.nytimes.com/2012/01/23/business/media/marketers-seeking-family-shows-hold-a-script-contest.html; "About," ANA Alliance for Family Entertainment.
94. John C. Stauber and Sheldon Rampton, *Toxic Sludge Is Good for You: Lies, Damn Lies and the Public Relations Industry* (Monroe, ME: Common Courage Press, 1995).
95. Ibid.; Susanne A. Roschwalb, "The Hill & Knowlton Cases: A Brief on the Controversy," *Public Relations Review* 20, no. 3 (1994).
96. Stauber and Rampton, *Toxic Sludge Is Good for You*, 173.
97. Mary McGrory, "PR Ploy Exaggerated Case Against Iraq," *St. Louis Post-Dispatch*, January 16, 1992.
98. Robert L. Koenig, "Testimony of Kuwaiti Envoy's Child Assailed," *St. Louis Post-Dispatch*, January 9, 1992.
99. Cornelius B. Pratt, "Hill & Knowlton's Two Ethical Dilemmas," *Public Relations Review* 20, no. 3 (1994).
100. Martinson, "Ethical Decision Making in Public Relations."
101. Anna Clark, "How an Investigative Journalist Helped Prove a City Was Being Poisoned With Its Own Water," *Columbia Journalism Review*, November 3, 2015, http://www.cjr.org/united_states_project/flint_water_lead_curt_guyette_aclu_michigan.php.
102. Denise Robbins, "Analysis: How Michigan and National Reporters Covered the Flint Water Crisis," *Media Matters for America*, February 1, 2016, https://www.mediamatters.org/research/2016/02/02/analysis-how-michigan-and-national-reporters-co/208290.
103. Bob Garfield, "Figuring Flint Out," *On the Media*, January 22, 2016, https://www.wnycstudios.org/podcasts/otm/segments/figuring-flint-out.
104. Christopher Ingraham, "This Is How Toxic Flint's Water Really Is," *Washington Post*, January 15, 2016, https://www.washingtonpost.com/news/wonk/wp/2016/01/15/this-is-how-toxic-flints-water-really-is/.
105. Garfield, "Figuring Flint Out."
106. Robbins, "Analysis."
107. Anna Clark, "How Covering the Flint Water Crisis Has Changed Michigan Radio," *Columbia Journalism Review*, February 16, 2016, http://www.cjr.org/united_states_project/michigan_radio_flint_water_crisis.php.
108. Robbins, "Analysis."
109. Robbins, "Analysis"; Julie Hinds, "Rachel Maddow's Dedication to Covering Flint Water Crisis Wins Her an Emmy," *Detroit Free Press*, October 6, 2017, https://www.freep.com/story/entertainment/2017/10/06/rachel-maddow-emmy-flint-water-crisis/740242001/.
110. Clark, "How Covering the Flint Water Crisis Has Changed Michigan Radio."
111. Margaret Sullivan, "Should the *Times* Have Been a Tougher Watchdog in Flint?" *New York Times*, January 27, 2016, http://publiceditor.blogs.nytimes.com/2016/01/27/flint-water-margaret-sullivan-new-york-times-public-editor/.
112. Jay Hathaway, "What Is Gamergate, and Why? An Explainer for Non-Geeks," *Gawker*, October 10, 2014, http://gawker.com/what-is-gamergate-and-why-an-explainer-for-non-geeks-1642909080.
113. Abby Ohlheiser, "Why 'Social Justice Warrior,' a Gamergate Insult, Is Now a Dictionary Entry," *Washington Post*, October 7, 2015, https://www.washingtonpost.com/news/the-intersect/wp/2015/10/07/why-social-justice-warrior-a-gamergate-insult-is-now-a-dictionary-entry/.
114. Caitlin Dewey, "In the Battle of Internet Mobs vs. the Law, the Internet Mobs Have Won," *Washington Post*, February 17, 2016, http://www.washingtonpost.com/news/the-intersect/wp/2016/02/17/in-the-battle-of-internet-mobs-vs-the-law-the-internet-mobs-have-won/.
115. Caitlin Dewey, "The Only Guide to Gamergate You Will Ever Need to Read," *Washington Post*, October 14, 2014, https://www.washingtonpost.com/news/the-intersect/wp/2014/10/14/the-only-guide-to-gamergate-you-will-ever-need-to-read/.
116. Kristen Chuba, "'Star Wars' Actress Kelly Marie Tran Leaves Social Media After Months of Harassment," *Variety*, June 5, 2018, https://variety.com/2018/biz/news/star-wars-kelly-marie-tran-leaves-social-media-harassment-1202830892/.
117. Bonnie Burton, "*Star Wars* Actor Kelly Marie Tran Deletes Instagram Posts After Harassment," *CNET*, June 5, 2018, https://www.cnet.com/news/star-wars-actor-kelly-marie-tran-deletes-instagram-after-harassment/.
118. Sarah Kaplan, "The Ordeal of Sportscaster Erin Andrews: 'Oh, My God . . . I Was Naked All Over the Internet,'" *Washington Post*, March 1, 2016, https://www.washingtonpost.com/news/morning-mix/wp/2016/03/01/the-ordeal-of-espns-erin-andrews-target-of-nude-peephole-videos-and-sexist-affronts/.
119. George Gerbner, "TV Violence and the Art of Asking the Wrong Question," *Center for Media Literacy*, http://www.medialit.org/reading-room/tv-violence-and-art-asking-wrong-question.
120. Randall Colburn, "Trevor Noah Had a Cameo in *Black Panther* That People Are Only Just Noticing," *AV Club*, May 22, 2018, https://news.avclub.com/trevor-noah-had-a-cameo-in-black-panther-that-people-ar-1826223867.
121. Jeremy Fuster, "Will 'Black Panther' Finally Open Hollywood's Floodgates for More Diverse Studio Movies?" *Wrap*, February 21, 2018, https://www.thewrap.com/will-black-panther-blockbuster-hollywood-floodgates-studio/.
122. Rebecca Sun, "Just 4.8 Percent of TV Writers Are Black, Study Finds," *Hollywood Reporter*, November 1, 2017, http://www.hollywoodreporter.com/news/just-48-percent-tv-writers-are-black-study-finds-1053675.
123. Fuster, "Will 'Black Panther' Finally Open Hollywood's Floodgates?"
124. Dave McNary, "Facts on Pacts: Studios Have Few First-Look Deals With Women," *Variety*, October 25, 2017, http://variety.com/2017/biz/news/studios-first-look-deals-women-1202598087/?ex_cid=SigDig.

INDEX

Note: Page numbers followed by *t* and *f* refer to pages containing tables and figures respectively.